June 26–29, 2011
Banff, Alberta, Canada

I0054873

Association for Computing Machinery

Advancing Computing as a Science & Profession

KCAP 2011

Proceedings of the 2011 Conference on
Knowledge Capture

Sponsored by:
ACM SIGART

Supported by:
**AAAI, Universidad Politécnica Madrid,
National Center for Biomedical Ontology,
SRI International, and ISOCO**

**Association for
Computing Machinery**

Advancing Computing as a Science & Profession

The Association for Computing Machinery
2 Penn Plaza, Suite 701
New York, New York 10121-0701

Notice to Past Authors of ACM-Published Articles

ACM intends to create a complete electronic archive of all articles and/or other material previously published by ACM. If you have written a work that has been previously published by ACM in any journal or conference proceedings prior to 1978, or any SIG Newsletter at any time, and you do NOT want this work to appear in the ACM Digital Library, please inform permissions@acm.org, stating the title of the work, the author(s), and where and when published.

ISBN: 978-1-4503-0396-5 (Digital)

ISBN: 978-1-4503-1389-6 (Print)

Additional copies may be ordered prepaid from:

ACM Order Department
PO Box 30777
New York, NY 10087-0777, USA

Phone: 1-800-342-6626 (USA and Canada)
+1-212-626-0500 (Global)
Fax: +1-212-944-1318
E-mail: acmhelp@acm.org
Hours of Operation: 8:30 am – 4:30 pm ET

Printed in the USA

K-CAP2011 Chairs' Welcome

It is our pleasure to welcome you to the *Sixth International Conference on Knowledge Capture (K-CAP2011)*. The K-CAP conference series provides a forum that brings together members of several research communities who are interested in efficiently capturing knowledge from a variety of sources and in creating representations that can be useful for automated reasoning, analysis, and other forms of machine processing. Therefore, research interests in knowledge capture are at the intersection of areas such as knowledge engineering, machine learning, natural-language processing, human–computer interaction, Artificial Intelligence, and the Semantic Web.

K-CAP 2011 follows on the success of five previous conferences in 2009 (Los Angeles, California, USA), 2007 (Whistler, British Columbia, Canada), in 2005 (Banff, Alberta, Canada), in 2003 (Sanibel Island, Florida, USA), and 2001 (Victoria, British Columbia, Canada), and of the series of Knowledge Acquisition Workshops (KAW), the first of which took place in the same location (Banff, Alberta, Canada) in 1986. K-CAP 2011 is particularly important in the history of this discipline, as it coincides with the 25th anniversary of the first Knowledge Acquisition Workshop held in Banff.

The call for papers attracted 80 submissions from Europe, America, Asia, and Oceania. The program committee accepted 19 full papers that cover a variety of topics, including ontology engineering, ontology learning, evaluation and quality assessment of ontologies and knowledge bases, information extraction for knowledge capture, and knowledge capture from online textual and multimedia resources. In addition, this volume includes descriptions of 19 posters and demos presented at the conference.

To celebrate this 25th anniversary, the K-CAP 2011 program includes six invited talks, many of which reflect on the evolution of knowledge capture in this period. Some of them are from researchers who were present at the first knowledge acquisition workshop in 1986. The keynote by Brian R. Gaines is entitled "Knowledge Capture through the Millennia: From Cuneiform to the Semantic Web"; a presentation by Richard Benjamins is entitled "Has 'Knowledge' Been the Driver?"; James Fan and Aditya Kalyanpur offer "Building Watson – A Brief Overview of DeepQA and the Jeopardy! Challenge"; Tom Gruber's talk is entitled "Design for Intelligence: AI and UI and the Intelligent Use"; Bill Swartout's talk is called "Let Me Tell You a Story….", and finally Bob Wielinga sums up his experiences "In Pursuit of Knowledge: 25 Years of Knowledge Acquisition."

We must thank all the K-CAP 2011 team, who "volunteered" to help with the organization. Starting with our honorary chair (Brian R. Gaines), who kindly accepted our invitation to get involved in K-CAP 2011, to share with us his experience through his invited talk, and to dig up archival videos and other memorabilia from 25 years ago, and continuing with our Web chair (Sean Falconer), our treasurer and registration chair (José Manuel Gómez-Pérez), our local-arrangements chair (Rob Kremer), and our workshops and tutorials chair (Vinay Chaudhri). Special thanks go also to Adrienne Griscti and Lisa Tolles, who have taken care of many administrative issues and of the processing the papers in a timely manner.

We hope that you will find this program interesting and thought provoking, and that the conference will provide you with a valuable opportunity to share ideas with other researchers and practitioners from institutions around the world.

Mark A. Musen
K-CAP2011 General Chair
Stanford University, USA

Oscar Corcho
K-CAP2011 Program Chair
Universidad Politécnica de Madrid, Spain

Table of Contents

Invited Talks

Session 1: Ontology Engineering I
Session Chair: Valentina Presutti *(Italian National Research Council)*

Session 2: Ontology Engineering II
Session Chair: José Manuel Gómez-Pérez *(iSOCO)*

Session 3: Evaluation and Quality Assessment
Session Chair: Tania Tudorache *(Stanford University)*

Session 4: Ontology and Knowledge Base Learning
Session Chair: Paul Compton *(The University of New South Wales)*

Session 5: Information Extraction, RDF and Knowledge Capture

Session Chair: Rudi Studer *(Karlsruhe Institute of Technology)*

Session 6: Multimedia, Wikipedia and Metadata

Session Chair: Vanessa López *(Open University)*

Poster and Demo Session

KCAP 2011 Conference Organization

Honorary Chair: Brian R. Gaines (*University of Calgary, Canada*)

General Chair: Mark A. Musen (*Stanford University, USA*)

Program Chair: Oscar Corcho (*Universidad Politécnica de Madrid, Spain*)

Workshops and Tutorials Chair: Vinay Chaudhri (*SRI International, USA*)

Local Arrangements Chair: Rob Kremer (*University of Calgary, Canada*)

Treasurer & Registration Chair: José Manuel Gómez-Pérez (*iSOCO, Spain*)

Technology Chair: Sean Falconer (*Stanford University, USA*)

Steering Committee: Peter Clark (*Vulcan Inc, USA*)
Ken Forbus (*Northwestern University, USA*)
Yolanda Gil (*University of Southern California, USA*)
Rob Kremer (*University of Calgary, Canada*)
Mark A. Musen (*Stanford University, USA*)
Jude Shavlik (*University of Wisconsin at Madison, USA*)
Derek Sleeman (*University of Aberdeen, United Kingdom*)

Program Committee: Harith Alani (*Open University, UK*)
Lora Aroyo (*Free University of Amsterdam, the Netherlands*)
Nathalie Aussenac-Gilles (*IRIT-CNRS, France*)
Ken Barker (*University of Texas, USA*)
Joachim Baumeister (*University of Würzburg, Germany*)
Bettina Berendt (*K.U. Leuven, Belgium*)
Paul Buitelaar (*DERI, National University of Ireland, Galway*)
Vinay Chaudhri (*SRI International, USA*)
Philipp Cimiano (*Universität Bielefeld, Germany*)
Peter Clark (*Vulcan Inc., USA*)
Paul Compton (*The University of New South Wales, Australia*)
Henrik Eriksson (*Linköping University, Sweden*)
Jérôme Euzenat (*INRIA & LIG, France*)
James Fan (*IBM Research, USA*)
George Ferguson (*University of Rochester, USA*)
Ken Forbus (*Northwestern University, USA*)
Ken Ford (*Florida Institute for Human &Machine Cognition, USA*)
Aldo Gangemi (*Italian National Research Council, Italy*)
Alexander García Castro (*Bremen University, Germany*)
John Gennari (*University of Washington, USA*)
Yolanda Gil (*University of Southern California, USA*)

Program Committee
(continued):   Ashok Goel (*Georgia Institute of Technology, USA*)
Asunción Gómez-Pérez (*Universidad Politécnica de Madrid, Spain*)
José Manuel Gómez-Pérez (*iSOCO, Spain*)
Mark Greaves (*Vulcan Inc., USA*)
Siegfried Handschuh (*Digital Enterprise Research Institute, Ireland*)
Jane Hunter (*The University of Queensland, Australia*)
Robert Jaeschke (*University of Kassel, Germany*)
Jihie Kim (*University of Southern California, USA*)
Tolga Konik (*Stanford University, USA*)
Rob Kremer (*University of Calgary, Canada*)
James Lester (*North Carolina State University, USA*)
Henry Lieberman (*MIT Media Laboratory, USA*)
Rodrigo Martínez-Béjar (*Universidad de Murcia, Spain*)
Peter Mika (*Yahoo, Spain*)
Vibhu Mittal (*Root-One, USA*)
Riichiro Mizoguchi (*Osaka University, Japan*)
Enrico Motta (*The Open University, UK*)
Mark A. Musen (*Stanford University, USA*)
Natasha Noy (*Stanford University, USA*)
Terry Payne (*University of Liverpool, UK*)
H. Sofia Pinto (*IST/INESC-ID, Portugal*)
Alan Rector (*University of Manchester, UK*)
Harald Sack (*University of Potsdam, Germany*)
Guus Schreiber (*VU University Amsterdam, the Netherlands*)
Giovanni Semeraro (*University of Bari "Aldo Moro", Italy*)
Jude Shavlik (*University of Wisconsin-Madison, USA*)
Derek Sleeman (*University of Aberdeen, UK*)
Markus Strohmaier (*Graz University of Technology, Austria*)
Valentina Tamma (*University of Liverpool, UK*)
Dan Tecuci (*Siemens Corporate Research, USA*)
Annette ten Teije (*Free University Amsterdam, the Netherlands*)
Samson Tu (*Stanford University, USA*)
Tania Tudorache (*Stanford University, USA*)
Frank van Harmelen (*Free University Amsterdam, The Netherlands*)
Bob Wielinga (*Free University of Amsterdam, the Netherlands*)

Additional reviewers:

KCAP 2011 Sponsor & Supporters

Sponsor:

Supporters:

Knowledge Capture through the Millennia:
From Cuneiform to the Semantic Web

Brian R. Gaines

University of Calgary & University of Victoria

gaines@ucalgary.ca, gaines@uvic.ca

ABSTRACT

As we celebrate twenty-five years of knowledge capture research we can view it from a short-term perspective as a substantial component of the sixty-year development of digital computing technologies, or from a long-term perspective as part of the most recent segment of the hundred millennia evolution of recorded knowledge processes that have shaped our civilization.

We can trace the development of knowledge capture processes similar to those we now study: from the Neolithic origins of our civilization; through the Babylonian development of mathematics and writing; Greek innovations in logic, ontology and science, and their medieval elaboration; the development of formal logics, metaphysical systems and sciences stemming from the scientific revolution; to the computational implementation of knowledge representation, capture, inference and their ubiquitous application in our current information age.

This presentation outlines major events in the trajectory of knowledge capture processes over the millennia, focusing on those relevant to where we are now and where we may be going. It encompasses: the evolution of civilization from archeological, economic, socio-cultural and systemic perspectives; highlights in the formalization of knowledge capture processes through the ages; trajectories of the development of knowledge technologies supporting its representation, capture and use; to projections of expected major issues and advances in the next quarter century.

Categories and Subject Descriptors

I.2.6 Learning – *knowledge acquisition.*

General Terms: Human Factors

Keywords

History of knowledge acquisition, expert systems & artificial intelligence; role in evolution and civilizations; place in infrastructure of information technology; future projections.

KNOWLEDGE ACQUISITION RESEARCH

A quarter century ago the first Knowledge Acquisition Workshop (KAW) took place in Banff in a wave of enthusiasm—120 papers submitted, 500 applications to attend from 30 countries. After intensive refereeing, 42 papers were accepted and 60 researchers invited to attend. The trigger for the workshop was the explosion of industrial and academic interest in the potential of expert systems as evidenced by the attendance of over 7,000 at the previous year's joint IJCAI/AAAI Conference at UCLA.

The three largest tracks were: *Learning and Acquisition* with 31 papers; *Expert Systems* with 28; *Natural Language* with 28. Some 36% of the 245 papers presented were on these themes that came to dominate the KAW meetings worldwide, but the unexpectedness of this is illustrated by the conference planning where none of the 4 keynotes and only one of the 12 panels addressed these themes.

Evolution of Artificial Intelligence Research

The significance of this growth of interest in expert systems may be seen in terms of the history of artificial intelligence research which took off in the late 1950s with the *Dartmouth Summer Project* [1] in the USA and the *Mechanization of Thought Processes Symposium* [2] in the UK. These occurred as computers came into their second generation, before the advent of computer science as an academic discipline, and when the artificial intelligence metaphor might well have become the core of such a discipline. There was a crisis in the 1970s as computers came into their fourth generation and embryonic computer science departments had to vie with nascent artificial intelligent departments in their requests for major funding to purchase the next generation of computers such as the DEC PDP10.

In Britain the conflict led the Science Research Council to commission a distinguished applied mathematician not associated with the contending applicants to report on the state of the art and future potential of artificial intelligence research. The infamous *Lighthill Report* [3] damned both in sarcastic terms, and undermined the funding of AI research in the UK and USA for seven years—the first so-called *AI winter* [4].

It is ironic that the report only briefly mentions the recognized achievements of DENDRAL [5], overlapped Winograd's [6] doctoral thesis on SHRDLU which marked a major advance in natural language understanding, and was shortly followed by Shortliffe's [7] doctoral thesis on MYCIN that provided the foundations for expert systems research and application. Whilst the immediate impact of the Lighthill report was highly negative for AI research funding, the effect was alleviated in 1980 when MITI in Japan announced its national program for the development of a fifth generation of computers targeted on *knowledge-processing systems* [8-10].

The Japanese program triggered a competitive response in governments around the world: in the USA DARPA's *Strategic Computing Program* (SCC); in the UK the *Alvey Program*; and in the EEC the *Esprit Program*. Major corporations funded their own internal programs and through the 1980s artificial intelligence boomed as never before, particularly that associated with expert system development. The AAAI annual conference had continuing attendances above 5,000 with very large accompanying commercial exhibitions—the call for sites for the 1988 conference estimates attendance at 6,500 and exhibition space at 80,000 square feet.

However, the failure of the Japanese program to produce any meaningful outcomes led to the SCC, Alvey and Esprit programs being discontinued in the late 1980s, and the MITI sixth generation program [11, 12] attracting little interest. A second *AI winter* [13] commenced in 1987 as the associated technology bubble burst and commercial interest in expert systems waned, but had surprisingly little effect on the KAW and other specialist AI communities world-wide.

The reduction in the hype and excessive expectations provided breathing space to reflect on fundamentals, continue to develop and refine techniques and tools, and integrate frameworks from the diverse fields relevant to knowledge acquisition. It had been obvious all along that available information technology provided the means to support and amplify human intelligence, rather than replace it, and we needed to understand the requirements in greater depth and match the technology to them—a slow process of incremental improvement rather than dramatic breakthrough.

Evolution of the World Wide Web

At the 1994 KAW Tom Gruber drew attention to the potential of Netscape's development of interactive protocols for the World Wide Web (web), and set the KAW community the challenge of porting its knowledge acquisition tools to the web. In 1995 the commercialization of the web led to an explosive growth of web-based applications that continues until this day, and the knowledge acqisition community began to play a significant role in the development of what has come to be called the *semantic web*.

Journal publishers' digitization of the bulk of the scientific literature, the growth of mutual help mailing list archives, blogs and wikis encompassing all aspects of human life, and the ongoing project of digitizing all the world's literature, led to an explosion of digitally encoded knowledge in textual and other media becoming not only almost universally available but also a widely accepted and utilized resource in a very short span of time.

It also created a massive information overload that was eventually tamed through Google's indexing technologies [14], and similar developments in the content-based indexing of all materials on corporate and personal computers. In parallel with these new technologies many of the problems that had been targets in the early days of AI, such as text and speech recognition and machine translation, were quietly solved to the extent of become routinely useful, as much through the continuing exponential growth in computing power as through improvements in understanding the nature of the problems and solution techniques.

Web Technology in Knowledge Capture

Web technology is providing access to a high proportion of human knowledge available through contextual indexing in a manner that seems to match well the processes of human memory [15], and provides much of the support for human knowledge processes that had been expected from expert systems. It does so largely through document-retrieval techniques based on content and human-generated linkages with little use of the logical methods and knowledge structures that have dominated AI and KAW research. It 'gives advice' and 'answers questions' by finding relevant pre-existent material that provides the information to enable the human users to infer possible solutions to their problems. DeepQA/Watson [16] does use logical ontologies for some inferences but its answers are based in large part on massive information retrieval and probabilistic evidence combination from many diverse sources.

This raises questions about the integration of the techniques developed in twenty-five years of knowledge acquisition research, most of which have logicist foundations and many of which have been successfully deployed, with techniques of information retrieval and natural language analysis and generation. Will the *semantic web*, based on description logics and formal ontologies to support machine understanding of the information stored on the web, actually become a significant component of the evolution of the web, and, if so, what is the most effective research agenda for its development?—all this against a well-argued background that information technology is moving towards *alien intelligence* [17] and a *singularity cusp* [18] where human and computer intelligences merge.

The historian, White [19], has emphasized the plasticity and metaphorical power of historical accounts—we construct histories for ourselves that both empower and constrain our futures. Setting the history of the KAW/KCAP community within the framework of artificial intelligence and expert systems studies may not provide an appropriate ethos for our current and future research in the much wider context of the semantic web and its role in human society.

The remaining sections frame our activities within a much broader context of the evolution of the human species and human civilization. What are the human needs that the web addresses; what is its place in our biological evolution; how does our current ethos relate to those of our ancestors over the millennia; and how did the intellectual technologies that we bring into play evolve, and why?

These are not normal topics at KAW/KCAP—we have been a specialist community focused on knowledge capture for computer systems that emulate the roles of expert human advisors—but, perhaps, every quarter century we should review our activities within a broader framework.

ROLE OF KNOWLEDGE IN EVOLUTION

Where to start?—*the big bang*—Ayres, a well-respected technological forecaster, wrote a remarkable book, *Information, Entropy and Progress: A New Evolutionary Paradigm*, that provides a coherent systemic model of physical, geological, biological, social and economic evolution, and models skilled activity such as manufacturing as an information process that, for example, creates an automobile by imposing information on matter.

If we conceive of knowledge abstractly as the information we impute to a system to account for its behavior then Ayres' framework shows knowledge processes playing a far wider role than any we normally envision. If we characterize living systems abstractly as *autopoietic* [20] in actively creating conditions for their own persistence, then Ayres' informational formulation allows us to model the fundamental processes of life as being those of knowledge creation, capture and transmission.

Cybernetic/systemic models of such broad scope are fascinating and inspiring but too abstract to have a direct impact on the diverse disciplines they encompass. However, in the past twenty years advances in molecular biology have made DNA sequencing technologies available to archeologists and anthropologists, and enabled information-flow models to be used to expose not just the systemic commonalities but also the mutual constraints coupling genetic, cultural and behavioral processes in living systems.

Oyama's *Ontogeny of Information* [21] is arguably the first such analysis to become widely influential through the *developmental systems theory* community. Jablonka and Lamb's *Evolution in Four Dimensions* [22] provides a unified model of the transmission of variation between living systems encompassing genetic, epigenetic and behavioral sub-systems and their interactions.

From a knowledge capture perspective, we can see such unified models as providing a detailed account of how:

- genomes adapt to the environment through random search, encoding and propagating information that may ensure the fitness of future generations;
- epigenetic processes manage the expression of particular capabilities encoded in the genome 'library' to more rapidly propagate adaptations to major environmental change [23];
- behavioral adaptations are propagated through reinforcement and mimicry, both intrinsically and through pedagogy [24];
- symbolic representations of the information involved in all these processes may be used to facilitate them, amplify their effect, and enable them to be widely diffused through both space and time [25].

The exchange of information between all levels and partitions of living systems provides a common framework for biological symbiosis, psychological foundations of socio-cultural systems and, through the symbolic signaling system of 'money,' for economic models of those systems.

Physicists have set a realistic target of a unified *theory of everything* in the physical sciences, but those facing the complexities of the biological and human sciences have felt it foolish to even dream of such for their disciplines. However, quite suddenly, as an outcome of advances in molecular biology and the human genome project, such unification is occurring without it ever having been an envisioned target.

EVOLUTION OF KNOWLEDGE CAPTURE

Where to start?—*out of Africa*—our species, *homo sapiens sapiens*, diverged from *homo erectus* some 500,00 years ago, from *homo sapiens neanderthalis* some 300,000 years ago, developed some form of language some 50,000 years ago, was reduced by environmental catastrophe to a population of some 3,000 in Africa some 50,000 years ago, and through migration commencing in the Levant expanded worldwide, developing community infrastructures and agriculture some 10,000 years ago, defining the Neolithic era of modern humanity. The details are contested in a massive research literature, but the overall framework is widely accepted [26-29].

For most of our history, genetic, epigenetic and behavioral processes dominated our evolution as they do in other animal species, but at some time in the past 100,000 years information came to be communicated and captured symbolically to an extent that gradually came to differentiate us from all other species—"humans became behaviourally modern when they could reliably transmit accumulated informational capital to the next generation, and transmit it with sufficient precision for innovations to be preserved and accumulated." [30, p.809].

The capability to capture and transmit knowledge is generally taken in the archeological and anthropological literatures to be the major factor in the explosion of the human population. Whereas the rate of unconstrained population growth in other species is proportional to the population size, and hence exponential, for the human species it is proportional to the square of the population, and hence hyper-exponential (until 1962 when the population growth rate dramatically declined [31]). The additional multiplier is attributed to the generation and diffusion of knowledge being proportional to the size of the population [31].

Human population growth does not show a smooth growth over recorded history. There have been major die-offs due to climatic factors such as the ice ages, and diseases such as the black death, but the overall trend has been hyper-exponential. One can discern a pattern of trends encouraging the generation and diffusion of knowledge, such as the development of communities around population centres, which also increase the risk to life, for example, by facilitating the development and spread of disease [32, 33].

Note that language and knowledge are not intrinsically 'survival traits'—Bickerton [34] notes that one possible outcome of the power of intelligence is species destruction—Wojciechowski [35] models the growth of knowledge as process whereby more knowledge must be continuously created to combat the adverse side-effects of the application of prior knowledge.

Early Knowledge Capture

The major problem with tracking the evolution of symbolic knowledge capture is that the media used have limited lifetimes, and often do not survive decades let alone millennia [36]. Archeologists are left with a biased sample of the few originals that survived, and historians with the residues of the transcription and copying processes that have attempted to preserve the content as the medium decays. That situation continues in our era as our computer media all have short life expectancies and rely on continuing backup processes for the preservation of their content. However, effective digitization procedures can now guard against transcription errors and ensure exact copying [37].

The earliest examples of knowledge capture where we have a substantial body of material is Babylonian cuneiform writing on clay tablets from some 5,000 years ago. Modern scholarship has decoded many tablets which originated to keep track of trade transactions and inventories [38] and were repurposed to capture mathematical and military procedures [39, 40]. We can also see the beginnings of scientific data collection and modeling in the Babylonian materials where astronomical and weather phenomena are tracked and used to predict political and economic events [41], possibly with some partial success in both cases since the weather affects harvests and prosperity which in turn affects the popularity of rulers.

There was probably some diffusion into later Greek astronomy but overall the outcome appears to be what Burnet [42] in his comments on early Greek science terms one of the *periodical bankruptcies of science*. In this respect knowledge evolution parallels biological evolution in that most innovations end in failure and only a few propagate to become assimilated into the 'genome' of science.

There are strong parallels between the Babylonian development of cuneiform writing and later developments of knowledge capture technologies, including that of computers. What is common is the addressing of timeless human needs with the best available technology of each era:

- The environmental stress of warfare was addressed with cuneiform tablets detailing siege techniques—the first digital computers were developed under the stress of the Second World War for purposes of code breaking and ballistics computations.
- The cuneiform tablets supported administrative record keeping—IBM adopted computer technology postwar to enhance its existing card-based census and business record-keeping systems.
- Cuneiform tablets captured the surprisingly sophisticated mathematical algorithms of that era—computers made operational those of our era.

And so on—the most powerful approach to technological forecasting is to identify the primary social needs of an era and assume that major social resources are being applied to develop and apply effective technologies to address them.

In the era immediately after Babylonian innovations in knowledge capture we find civilizations in India and China making major advances in mathematical, scientific, medical and legal knowledge [43] and capturing them in a variety of scripts on a range of media such as animal hides [36]. The developments that had most impact on western civilization were those of the Greek enlightenment some 2,500 years ago when Euclidean geometry, Socratic dialectic, Platonic philosophy and Aristotelian logic, metaphysics, science and ethics provided the foundations of modern mathematical, scientific, medical, ethical and legal systems [44].

Early Greek civilization captured knowledge primarily in the brains of people and propagated it through an oral tradition that probably extends back at least one hundred millennia but cannot be tracked because it left no record other than brief historical accounts in the later written record. However, by the time of Plato knowledge was being captured in written form using an alphabet deriving from an earlier Phoenician script [45] that continued in a variety of forms thereafter, including an Etruscan variant in Rome that constitutes our current Latin alphabet.

The first major library of which we have detailed accounts are those of Aristotle some 2,400 years ago, collected despite the sarcastic comments of his peers because he regarded it as important to understand the ideas of others in developing his own. A succession of national leaders also saw the importance of collecting the world's knowledge of their era, forming national libraries such as that of Ptolemy at Alexandria some 2,400 years ago where Kallimachos developed techniques of cataloguing and indexing library materials that are similar to those in use today [46].

The preservation of written knowledge was erratic until the invention of printing facilitated the wide dissemination of many copies of major works making it probable that some copies would survive local catastrophes [47]. Aristotle's library was passed to three generations of successors but then stored under conditions where much material was severely damaged [48]. The library at Alexandria was completely destroyed. The Greek knowledge base that provided the intellectual foundations of modern science only survived in substantial part because several later societies attempted to collect and capture it for their own use, notably the Arabic translation movement in Baghdad some 1,300 years ago that both captured the material in Arabic and stimulated an industry of making additional copies of the Greek originals for translation purposes [49].

One can continue the story of knowledge capture and translation, but not within the scope of these few pages—the relevant literature constitutes a substantial component of national libraries. The account above is sufficient to show how major roles now being played by the web have their parallels through the ages:

- The web provides a compendium of human knowledge fulfilling the role of the library at Alexander and its later formulations such Diderot's *encyclopedia* [50] and Wells *world brain* [51]—both of which were seen by their proponents as socially egalitarian and liberating, much as the web is seen today.

- Discussion in the Athenian agora is emulated by mailing lists and interactive blogs where questions and issues may be raised and discussed a community—some participants also exemplify Sextus Empiricus' [52] critical skepticism that provides counter-examples to any established position.

- Aristotle's codification of the abstract schemata for knowledge representation and inference underlies the description logic foundations of the semantic web.

EVOLUTION OF INFORMATION TECHNOLOGY

Where to start?—*infrastructure of information technology*—a major activity of the Knowledge Science Institute (KSI) distinct from those reported at KAW was the modeling and forecasting of information technology [53-55]. The underlying electronics technology has undergone a continuing exponential growth since 1959 with a doubling period of some

1.5 years [56, 57], and this rapid sustained quantitative growth over five decades, unique to information technology, has triggered qualitative structural changes in the nature of the information sciences and their applications.

The KSI tracked these changes, modeling them as a tiered structure of learning curves of sub-disciplines built upon the layers below, and applied this to model the past impact of information technology on many economic sectors and industries and to project its likely future impact.

Figure 1 shows the overall structure of the model extended to 2012 [55]. The underlying learning curve for each tier may be characterized by six phases:

1. The era before the learning curve takes off, when too little is known for planned progress, is that of the *inventor* having very little chance of success but continuing a search based on intuition and faith.

2. Sooner or later some inventor makes a *breakthrough* and very rapidly his or her work is *replicated* at research institutions worldwide.

3. The experience gained in this way leads to *empirical* design rules with very little foundation except previous successes and failures.

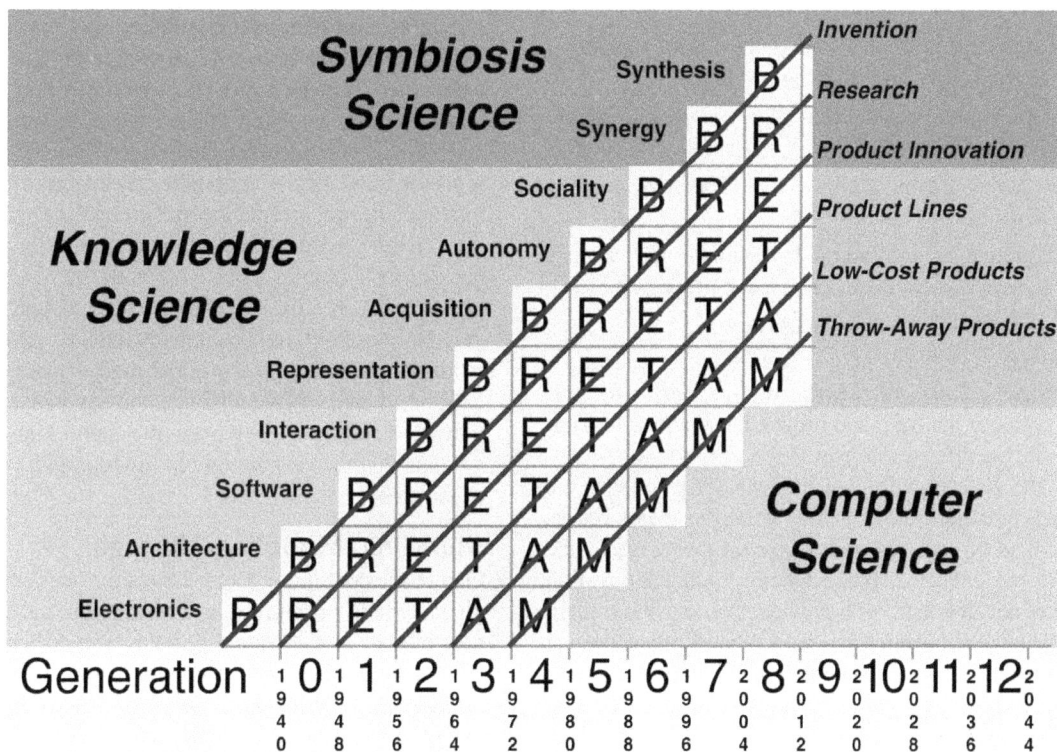

- Breakthrough: creative advance made
- Replication period: experience gained by mimicing breakthrough
- Empirical period: design rules formulated from experience
- Theoretical period: underlying theories formulated and tested
- Automation period: theories predict experience & generate rules
- Maturity: theories become assimilated and used routinely

Figure 1 Infrastructure of information technology

4 As enough empirical experience is gained it becomes possible to inductively model the basis of success and failure and develop *theories*. This transition from empiricism to theory corresponds to the maximum slope of the underlying logistic learning curve [55].

5 The theoretical models make it possible to *automate* the scientific data gathering and analysis and associated manufacturing processes.

6 Once automaton has been put in place effort can focus on cost reduction and quality improvements in what has become a *mature* technology.

Empirically, from an analysis of several thousand events in the history of the computing and the information sciences, we identified the time-scale of each phase, and hence each computer generation, as 8 years.

We identified the different tiers as being:

- the underlying digital *electronics*;
- its application in computer *architectures*;
- the programming of general-purpose computers through *software*;
- the development of computer-people and computer-computer *interactivity*;
- the *representation* of human knowledge;
- the *acquisition* of additional knowledge from interaction with the world, people and stored knowledge;
- the development of goal-directed *autonomous* knowledge creating processes;
- the increasing coupling of knowledge processing entities in *social* networks;
- the development of techniques to facilitate the *synergy* between human and computer knowledge processes;
- the *synthesis* of both into a unified system.

We characterized the theory of the lowest four tiers as constituting *computer science*; of the next four as *knowledge science*—the focus of the KSI; and project those above to form a currently developing *symbiosis science*.

When the KSI was formed in 1985 [58] we saw the knowledge acquisition tier as having achieved major breakthroughs and to be in a research phase on the verge of the transition to the empirical phase where product innovation occurs. The development of knowledge acquisition techniques and tools was established as a second major project area, and contacts were made internationally with others having related interests, in particular John Boose at Boeing Computer Services, the co-founder of the KAW community.

Twenty-five years later the knowledge acquisition learning curve is on the verge of the transition from automation to maturity. What characterizes that stage is the weight of knowledge required to make a meaningful contribution, and a small number of major products which are well-established and difficult to displace, for example, the Protégé [59] tool for logical knowledge modeling, the WebGrid [60] tool for conceptual modeling, and the Google [14] search engine for textual knowledge indexing.

Note that the maturity of the learning curve does not indicate that research and innovation ceases, only that it becomes increasingly difficult. Innovative research continues on syllogistics that matured two millennia ago and on matrix algebra that matured over a century ago, but it is very rare and requires an immense depth of knowledge of the existing literature.

From this perspective, one would expect the knowledge acquisition research community to become increasingly specialized, managing a repository of expertise that is significant to research and development in the tiers that build upon it, and responsible for incorporating advances in the fields upon which it builds in order to provide state-of-the-art techniques and tools.

CONCLUSIONS

This article presents a number of perspectives on knowledge capture that enable us to construct histories for our community that empower and constrain our futures in interesting ways. Considering the choices available seems an appropriate agenda for our twenty-fifth anniversary. They are neither mutually exclusive nor exhaustive—just food for thought—what will be our themes, targets and agendas for the next twenty-five years?

In general there is a continuing need to consolidate and extend all that we know of knowledge capture processes and techniques, drawing upon all literatures and disciplines to support our stewardship of the state-of-the-art in knowledge acquisition. That includes the need to continue to enhance the tools we make available to take advantages of developments in knowledge representation and computer technologies.

We also need to track user requirements for knowledge capture technologies to support both the needs of those applying them and the innovations in knowledge capture that may be outside of, or substantially extend, our current frameworks. In particular, the original logicist framework that has dominated artificial intelligence and expert systems research, may need substantial extension to support knowledge capture systems that incorporate the information indexing techniques of the web.

Modeling 'Muddling Through'

One of the continuing major issues for our community is that all knowledge capture and transmission assumes some degree of *cognitive commonality*. This is a difficult notion, with connotations of *collective cognition* [61, 62], *collective rationality* [63, 64], *organizational knowledge* [65, 66] and the extent to which we do actually use what we regard as *shared concepts* in the same way [67].

Sextus Empiricus criticized Greek philosophers' focus on exact definitions, noting that "we must allow ordinary speech to use inexact terms" [52, Anim.Math.129]. Hattiangadi [68, p.15] notes that "our understanding of language is approximate—I do not believe that we ever do understand the *same* language, but only *largely similar* ones."

A miracle of human social existence is that we manage to 'muddle through' despite major lack of cognitive commonality [69]. Computer tools have the same issues as those of a human learner coming to calibrate their cognition against the norms of their communities, and can only develop approximate models with which we can, hopefully, muddle through in an improved fashion. We need to develop a science of such *muddling through* that models human use of open concepts to capture and transmit knowledge, and to come to comprehend the value of what might appear to be a logical defect as a necessary capability for coping with a complex and incompletely knowable world.

Much of what is needed for such a science already exists in older literatures that have become neglected since the advent of mathematical logic. In writing a recent paper [70] on the foundations of semantic networks as visual languages for description logics for a journal targeted on philosophy and linguistics, I developed the logical constructs of description logics through examples drawn from the philosophical literature. I was surprised to find that I had encompassed most of the classical knowledge structures, such as determinables, contrast sets, genus/differentiae, taxonomies, faceted taxonomies, cluster concepts, family resemblances, graded concepts and frames, using only the two connectives of Aristotelian syllogistics. I added the truth-functional connectives necessary to definitions and rules as simple extensions of these connectives through Koslow's [71] constructions for substructural logics.

In a follow-up paper on human rationality within a universal logic framework [63], I suggested that the reasoning processes of people, outside the realm of mathematics, could best be modeled as based on open concepts having only necessary conditions used abductively through inference to the best schema. Under conditions of complete knowledge this is equivalent to the use of definitions and rules, but it also models the non-monotonic process of muddling through with incomplete knowledge.

I predict that we will need to extend the logical frameworks for knowledge capture using the major advances being made in theories of substructural and universal logics in order to incorporate natural language indexing and 'understanding' within our knowledge capture frameworks, but that much of the theory we need is already available.

Knowledge capture is intrinsically a major component of all the developing tiers above it in the infrastructure of information technology shown in Figure 1. It is clear from the papers at recent KCAP's that we have moved well beyond the original objectives of supporting the development of 'expert systems.' I hope this presentation provides an interesting and provocative framework for what our research community is doing now and what it will do in the future. May you all live in interesting times.

To end on a personal note, I would like to express my thanks to those present, and to absent friends and colleagues, who have constituted the knowledge acquisition community, and made our world-wide meetings both a brief haven from the pressures of our working careers and a source of ideas, challenges and understanding that have stimulated us to new

achievements each year. We have been part of one another's extended intellectual family, and it has been a pleasure both to participate and to see the community continue to thrive.

REFERENCES

[1] McCarthy, J., Minsky, M. L., Rochester, N. and Shannon, C. E. *A Proposal for the Dartmouth Summer Research Project on Artificial Intelligence*. Dartmouth College, MA, 1955.

[2] NPL *Mechanisation of Thought Processes: Symposium at the National Physical Laboratory*. H.M.S.O., London, 1959.

[3] Lighthill, J. *Artificial Intelligence: a general survey*. Science Research Council, City, 1973.

[4] McDermott, D., Waldrop, M. M., Schank, R., Chandrasekaran, B. and McDermott, J. The dark ages of AI: a panel discussion at AAAI-84. *AI Magazine*, 6, 3 (1985), 122-134.

[5] Buchanan, B., Sutherland, G. and Feigenbaum, E. A. *Heuristic-Dendral: a program for generating explanatory hypotheses in organic chemistry*. Oliver & Boyd, City, 1967.

[6] Winograd, T. *Understanding Natural Language*. Academic Press, New York,, 1972.

[7] Shortliffe, E. H. *Computer-Based Medical Consultations: MYCIN*. Elsevier, New York, 1976.

[8] Feigenbaum, E. A. and McCorduck, P. *The Fifth Generation: Artificial Intelligence and Japan's Computer Challenge to the World*. Addison-Wesley, Reading, MA, 1983.

[9] Gaines, B. R. Perspectives on fifth generation computing. *Oxford Surveys in Information Technology*, 1 (1984), 1-53.

[10] Moto-oka, T. *Fifth Generation Computer Systems*. North-Holland, 1982.

[11] STA *Promotion of R&D on Electronics and Information Systems That May Complement or Substitute for Human Intelligence*. Science and Technology Agency, Tokyo, 1985.

[12] Gaines, B. R. Sixth generation computing: a conspectus of the Japanese proposals. *SIGART News.*, 95 (1986), 39-44.

[13] Hendler, J. Avoiding another AI winter. *IEEE Intelligent Systems*, 23, 2 (2008), 2-4.

[14] Langville, A. N. and Meyer, C. D. *Google's PageRank and Beyond: The Science of Search Engine Rankings*. Princeton University Press, Princeton, N.J., 2006.

[15] Griffiths, T. L., Steyvers, M. and Firl, A. Google and the mind. *Psychological Science*, 18 (2007), 1069-1076.

[16] Ferrucci, D., Brown, E., Chu-Carroll, J., Fan, J., Gondek, D., Kalyanpur, A. A., Lally, A., Murdock, J. W., Nyberg, E., Prager, J., Schlaefer, N. and Welty, C. Building Watson: An Overview of the DeepQA Project. *AI Magazine*, 31, 3 (2010), 59-79.

[17] Martin, J. *After the Internet: Alien Intelligence*. Capital Press, Washington, DC, 2000.

[18] Kurzweil, R. *The Singularity is Near: When Humans Transcend Biology*. Viking, New York, 2005.

[19] White, H. V. *What is a historical system?* Plenum Press, City, 1972.

[20] Maturana, H. R. The organization of the living: A theory of the living organization. *International Journal of Man-Machine Studies*, 7, 3 (1975), 313-332.

[21] Oyama, S. *The Ontogeny of Information: Developmental Systems and Evolution*. Cambridge University Press, Cambridge, 1985.

[22] Jablonka, E. and Lamb, M. J. *Evolution in Four Dimensions: Genetic, Epigenetic, Behavioral, and Symbolic Variation in the History of Life*. MIT Press, Cambridge, MA, 2005.

[23] Harper, L. V. Epigenetic inheritance and the intergenerational transfer of experience. *Psychological Bulletin*, 131, 3 (2005), 340-360.

[24] Thornton, A. and Raihani, N. Identifying teaching in wild animals. *Learning Behavior*, 38, 3 (2010), 297-309.

[25] Noble, W. and Davidson, I. *Human Evolution, Language, and Mind: A Psychological and Archaeological Inquiry*. Cambridge University Press, Cambridge, 1996.

[26] Liu, H., Prugnolle, F., Manica, A. and Balloux, F. A geographically explicit genetic model of worldwide human-settlement history. *Am. Journal Human Genetics*, 79 (2006).

[27] McBrearty, S. and Brooks, A. S. The revolution that wasn't: a new interpretation of the origin of modern human behavior. *Journal of Human Evolution*, 39, 5 (2000), 453-563.

[28] Stringer, C. Modern human origins: progress and prospects. *Philosophical Transactions of the Royal Society B: Biological Sciences*, 357 (2002), 563-579.

[29] Endicott, P., Ho, S. Y. W. and Stringer, C. Using genetic evidence to evaluate four palaeoanthropological hypotheses for the timing of Neanderthal and modern human origins. *Journal of Human Evolution*, 59, 1 (2010), 87-95.

[30] Sterelny, K. From hominins to humans: how sapiens became behaviourally modern. *Philosophical Transactions Royal Society B: Biological Sciences*, 366, 1566 (2011), 809-822.

[31] Korotayev, A. A compact macromodel of world system evolution. *J. World-Systems Research*, 11, 1 (2005), 79-93.

[32] Cantor, N. F. *In the Wake of the Plague*. Free Press, 2001.

[33] McNeill, W. H. *Plagues and Peoples*. Anchor, 1989.

[34] Bickerton, D. *Language and Species*. University of Chicago Press, 1990.

[35] Wojciechowski, J. A. *Ecology of knowledge*. Council for Research in Values and Philosophy, Washington, D.C., 2001.

[36] Diringer, D. *The Book Before Printing: Ancient, Medieval, and Oriental*. Dover, New York, 1982.

[37] Gladney, H. M. *Preserving Digital Information*. Springer, Berlin, 2007.

[38] Nissen, H. J., Damerow, P. and Englund, R. K. *Archaic Bookkeeping: Early Writing and Techniques of Economic Administration in the Ancient Near East*. University of Chicago Press, 1993.

[39] Neugebauer, O., Sachs, A., Götze, A. and American Schools of Oriental Research. *Mathematical Cuneiform Texts*. American Oriental Society and the American Schools of Oriental Research, New Haven, CN, 1945.

[40] Melville, S. C. and Melville, D. J. *Observations on the diffusion of military technology: siege warfare in the Near East and Greece*. Eisenbrauns, City, 2008.

[41] Swerdlow, N. M. *The Babylonian Theory of the Planets*. Princeton University Press, Princeton, NJ, 1998.

[42] Burnet, J. *Early Greek Philosophy*. Black, London, 1920.

[43] Katz, V. J. and Imhausen, A. *The Mathematics of Egypt, Mesopotamia, China, India, and Islam: A Sourcebook*. Princeton University Press, Princeton, NJ, 2007.

[44] Russo, L. *The Forgotten Revolution: How Science was Born in 300 BC and Why it Had to be Reborn*. Springer, 2004.

[45] Powell, B. B. *Homer and the Origin of the Greek Alphabet*. Cambridge University Press, Cambridge, 1991.

[46] Blum, R. *Kallimachos: The Alexandrian Library and the Origins of Bibliography*. University of Wisconsin Press, Madison, WI., 1991.

[47] Eisenstein, E. L. *The Printing Press as an Agent of Change: Communications and Cultural Transformations in Early Modern Europe*. Cambridge University Press, 1979.

[48] Laughlin, B. *The Aristotle Adventure: A Guide to the Greek, Arabic, and Latin Scholars who Transmitted Aristotle's Logic to the Renaissance*. Albert Hale, Flagstaff, AZ, 1995.

[49] Gutas, D. *Greek Thought, Arabic culture: The Graeco-Arabic Translation Movement in Baghdad and early Abbasid Society*. Routledge, London, 1998.

[50] Collison, R. L. *Encyclopaedias: Their History Throughout the Ages*. Hafner, New York, 1966.

[51] Wells, H. G. *World brain*. Books for Libraries Press, 1971.

[52] Sextus *Sextus Empiricus, with an English translation by R.G. Bury*. Heinemann, London, 1933.

[53] Gaines, B. R. and Shaw, M. L. G. A learning model for forecasting the future of information technology. *Future Computing Systems*, 1, 1 (1986), 31-69.

[54] Gaines, B. R. Modeling and forecasting the information sciences. *Information Sciences*, 57-58 (1991), 3-22.

[55] Gaines, B. R. The learning curves underlying convergence. *Technological Forecasting and Social Change*, 57, 1-2 (1998), 7-34.

[56] Rupp, K. and Selberherr, S. The Economic Limit to Moore's Law. *IEEET Semic. Manufacturing*, 24, 1 (2011), 1-4.

[57] Mollick, E. Establishing Moore's law. *Annals of the History of Computing*, 28, 3 (2006), 62-75.

[58] Gaines, B. R. *The Formation of a Knowledge Science Institute in Canada*. Knowledge Science Institute, University of Calgary, Calgary, 1985.

[59] Gennari, J. H., Musen, M. A., Fergerson, R. W., Grosso, W. E., CrubÈzy, M., Eriksson, H., Noy, N. F. and Tu, S. W. The evolution of Protégé: an environment for knowledge-based systems development. *International Journal of Human-Computer Studies*, 58, 1 (2003), 89-123.

[60] Gaines, B. R. and Shaw, M. L. G. Knowledge acquisition, modeling and inference through the World Wide Web. *International Journal of Human-Computer Studies*, 46, 6 (1997), 729-759.

[61] Gaines, B. R. The collective stance in modeling expertise in individuals and organizations. *International Journal of Expert Systems*, 7, 1 (1994), 21-51.

[62] Resnick, L. B., Levine, J. M. and Teasley, S. D. *Perspectives on Socially Shared Cognition*. American Psychological Association, Washington, 1991.

[63] Gaines, B. R. Human rationality challenges universal logic. *Logica Universalis*, 4, 2 (2010), 163-205.

[64] Goldberg, S. *Relying on Others: An Essay in Epistemology*. Oxford University Press, Oxford, 2010.

[65] Gaines, B. R. *Organizational knowledge acquisition*. Springer, City, 2003.

[66] Weick, K. E. *Sensemaking in Organizations*. Sage, Thousand Oaks, CA, 1995.

[67] Shaw, M. L. G. and Gaines, B. R. Comparing conceptual structures: consensus, conflict, correspondence and contrast. *Knowledge Acquisition*, 1, 4 (1989), 341-363.

[68] Hattiangadi, J. N. *How is Language Possible?: Philosophical Reflections on the Evolution of Language and Knowledge*. Open Court, La Salle, 1987.

[69] Fortun, M. and Bernstein, H. J. *Muddling Through: Pursuing Science and Truths in the 21st Century*. Counterpoint, 1998.

[70] Gaines, B. R. Designing visual languages for description logics. *Journal of Logic, Language and Information*, 18, 2 (2009), 217-250.

[71] Koslow, A. *A Structuralist Theory of Logic*. Cambridge University Press, 1992.

Ontology Augmentation:
Combining Semantic Web and Text Resources

Miriam Fernandez[1], Ziqi Zhang[2], Vanessa Lopez[1], Victoria Uren[2], Enrico Motta[1]

[1]Open University
Milton Keynes, UK
{m.fernandez, v.lopez, e.motta}@open.ac.uk

[2]University of Sheffield
Sheffield, UK
{z.zhang, v.uren}@dcs.shef.ac.uk

ABSTRACT

This work investigates the process of selecting, extracting and reorganizing content from Semantic Web information sources, to produce an ontology meeting the specifications of a particular domain and/or task. The process is combined with traditional text-based ontology learning methods to achieve tolerance to knowledge incompleteness. The paper describes the approach and presents experiments in which an ontology was built for a diet evaluation task. Although the example presented concerns the specific case of building a nutritional ontology, the methods employed are domain independent and transferrable to other use cases.

Categories and Subject Descriptors

I.2.4 Knowledge Representation Formalisms and Methods – *representation languages, semantic networks*

General Terms: Algorithms, Experimentation.

Keywords: Knowledge acquisition, knowledge capture, ontology learning, ontology augmentation, semantic web.

1. INTRODUCTION

The most common problem faced by ontology engineers and practitioners when attempting to reuse an ontology for a new domain or task, is the lack of domain coverage, either in terms of vocabulary or in terms of relations, presented by the candidate ontologies. To meet the specifications of the new task, candidate ontologies are either manually modified, which is a costly and laborious process, or automatically and semi-automatically extended by exploiting different types of information sources.

One of the most popular information resources used for this purpose is *text*. Its massive availability makes it essential for supporting techniques in ontology learning and augmentation [8], [20]. However, due to its lack of structure, ontology learning approaches from texts only provide a limited degree of organization to the extracted information. We define ontology augmentation as the process of enriching an ontology by incorporating new concepts and rela-

tions from external resources which may include, text, databases, other ontologies, etc.

More structured information sources, such as *thesauri* and *databases,* have also been explored in ontology learning and augmentation tasks. Thesauri like WordNet present explicit relations between concepts, but the information contained in this dictionary is so general and domain independent that "when exploiting it in the context of a specific domain it becomes an uncertain source of evidence" [7]. On the other hand, ontology learning approaches from databases, like RDBtoOnto[1] or RDB2RDF[2], provide very detailed information, but this information generally lacks hierarchical structure.

Despite the rapid growth of the amount of semantic resources available online, very few approaches have attempted to exploit the Semantic Web (SW), i.e., the set of all ontologies and knowledge bases accessible on the web, as source of evidence to perform ontology learning and augmentation tasks [27]. We believe that the SW is not just a motivation for investigating the problem of ontology learning but can actually be used as part of the solution.

Therefore, in this paper we propose a new ontology augmentation method meant for the exploitation of ontologies and knowledge bases, which supports the (semi-automatic) selection, extraction and restructuring of SW content to produce ontologies meeting the specifications driven by a specific domain or task. The performance of our proposed method is in direct relation with the amount and quality of online available SW information. While the SW has experienced a considerable growth in the last few years, thanks to initiatives like Linked Open Data[3] and to strong industry support (e.g., Google Rich Snippets[4]), the lack and incompleteness of available SW content is still a limitation we shall keep in mind. Aiming to provide tolerance to knowledge incompleteness our method is combined with traditional text-based ontology learning and augmentation approaches, thus drawing benefit from the years of experience in this area. To prove the feasibility of our proposal, experiments are reported in which, an ontology incorporat-

---

[1] http://www.tao-project.eu/researchanddevelopment/demosanddownloads/RDBToOnto.html
[2] http://www.w3.org/2005/Incubator/rdb2rdf/
[3] http://linkeddata.org/
[4] http://googlewebmastercentral.blogspot.com/2009/05/introducing-rich-snippets.html

ing nutritional data is created to tackle a diet evaluation task (Section 2).

The rest of the paper is structured as follows: We start by describing the application scenario (Section 2) and providing an overview of related state of the art (Section 3). Then, we describe our proposed approach to ontology augmentation and give details of its implementation (Section 4). Afterwards (Section 5) we detail and discuss our experimental analysis and the obtained results. Finally, we reiterate the main conclusions and outline the future work (Section 6).

2. MEAL PLANNING SCENARIO

When selecting a recipe, one of the most important things to consider is whether the people who are going to consume the meal require some special type of diet. Just to give some examples, according to the World Health Organization[5] (2009) currently more than 220 million people worldwide have diabetes and by 2015, approximately 2.3 billion adults will be overweight. In this context, the development of robust tools for meal planning and diet management is crucial to prevent and control food disorders.

To develop these tools it is necessary to model and capture extensive knowledge about types of food, diets, ingredients, recipes, nutritional information, etc. In this context, much work has been done towards designing and building food-oriented ontologies [1], [4], [15], [24]. However, when attempting to reuse these ontologies in the context of a diet evaluation task, we concluded that they lack the necessary domain coverage, either in terms of vocabulary or in terms of relations (see Section 3.1). In particular, the diet evaluation task we refer to is a component of a use case in the SmartProducts project[6]. Its purpose is to assess the suitability of ingredients and recipes with respect to a diet, including: vegetarian, dairy free, diabetic, egg free, gluten free, low fat, low in salt and nut free. To be suitable for this task, an ontology needs to fulfil the two following requirements: (1) To provide a large set of ingredients with associated nutritional information (i.e., fat, sugar, proteins, vitamins, etc.), (2) To provide a taxonomical classification of ingredients from which their source (animal, vegetable, dairy, etc.) can be inferred.

The importance of healthy meal planning, the extensive availability of food-oriented ontologies and their unsuitability to comply with the specifications of a diet evaluation task (see Section 3.1), makes this scenario a compelling example of the ontology reuse problem we aim to address.

3. STATE OF THE ART

3.1 Existing food ontologies

Food-oriented ontologies in the context of healthy meal planning tasks have been developed during the last decade. One of the most relevant works in this context is the one carried out by the PIPS (Personalized Information Platform for Health and Life Services)[7] project. The goal of this project is to build nutrition services upon ontologies. For this purpose a food oriented ontology has been constructed and presented in [4]. However, while this ontology (available at www.csc.liv.ac.uk/~jcantais/PIPSFood.owl) presents a food classification, individual ingredients and their corresponding nutritional information are not modelled within the ontology.

Similar works [1], [15], [24], have attempted to develop food-oriented ontologies. The ontology by Batista and colleagues [1] presents four main categories: actions, food, recipes and kitchen utensils. While the Food category models the "alimentos" (i.e., ingredients), its corresponding nutritional information is missing in the ontology. The work of Snae and Bruckner [24] presents the design and development of a counselling system for food or menu planning (FOODs). One of the main components of the FOODs system is its ontology. However, while the paper presents ontology specifications about ingredients and nutrients, it states that the construction of the food ontology and the population of the concepts with instances is currently work in progress, and, to the best of our knowledge, the ontology has not been publicly disclosed yet. More recently the work of Herrera and colleagues [15] presents a system designed to participate in the Computer Cooking Contest[8], 2009. This system makes use of an ontology where information about ingredients and recipes is modelled. More than 300 ingredients are represented in a hierarchy of classes, but, no nutritional information is provided.

In addition to the aforementioned food ontologies, large-scale heterogeneous ontologies, like FreeBase or DBPedia[9], also model information about food. DBPedia contains information about ingredients, dishes, and nutrients[10]. However, this information is not covered by the ontological schema, i.e., classes and properties are not specified for this information and therefore, a classification of ingredients is not available. Similarly, FreeBase contains more than 900 ingredients with associated nutritional information, including 121 different nutritional components. The provenance of this information is USDA, the National Nutrient database for Standard Reference from the US Department of Agriculture[11]. While Freebase constitutes the most complete information source in terms of nutritional data, it lacks a categorization of ingredients from which their source (animal, vegetable, etc) can be determined.

In summary, the available information sources either do not contain a large set of ingredients with associated nutritional

---

[5] http://www.who.int/en/

[6] http://www.smartproducts-project.eu/

[7] An E-Health project funded by the European Commission under the Framework 6 call

[8] http://gaia.fdi.ucm.es/grupo/projects/cookingContest/cookingContest.html#jadacook2

[9] http://www.freebase.com/, http://dbpedia.org/About

[10] See: http://dbpedia.org/page/Wine, http://dbpedia.org/page/Cuisine, http://dbpedia.org/page/Ingredient, http://dbpedia.org/page/Carbonara, http://dbpedia.org/page/Mozzarella

[11] http://www.nal.usda.gov/fnic/foodcomp/search/

information or the ingredients are not classified within a taxonomy from which their source (animal, vegetable, etc.) can be inferred. Our purpose is therefore to select, extract and reorganize the information distributed in these and other information sources to automatically generate a taxonomical classification of ingredients that complies with the specifications of a diet evaluation task.

3.2 Automatic Ontology Learning

The problem of extending an existing concept structure (in our case the Smart Products ontology) with new concepts and hierarchical relations (in our case ingredients and hierarchical classification of those ingredients) has been deeply studied in ontology or taxonomy learning, leading to a number of approaches that use different sources of evidence from which new concepts and relations are automatically or semi-automatically extracted.

In particular, most approaches attempt to learn taxonomies on the basis of *textual input* [9] by finding and matching certain patterns against texts [14], by analysing the internal structure of noun phrases [3], by making use of clustering techniques to discover syntactic contexts of terms [22] or, by a combination of different approaches [7]. Additionally, text-based entity classification [12], [16] and ontology population [8], [20] techniques, which are extensively studied in the information extraction domain and initially designed for populating instances of concepts in ontologies, have been applied to learn hierarchical structures of concepts [9], [22]. These methods typically associate a classifier to each concept in the ontology, and classify unknown lexicons, concepts or instances, into the ontology based on their similarity with existing concepts. The similarity is measured based on contextual evidence gathered from the textual resources [8], [16], [20].

While text has proved to be an effective source of evidence, the approaches using text may suffer from several limitations: (a) knowledge completeness is subject to the choice of corpus, i.e., terms that are not covered by a corpus cannot be learnt, (b) domain-specific corpora is not always easy to obtain, e.g., in the clinical domain [1], (c) massive amounts of training data are required to build learning models for these methods [16] and finally, (d) as argued by Cimiano and colleagues [10] "the conceptual drawback of such methods is that they essentially discover lexical relations between words but not between concepts, which are supposed to be abstractions and not merely plain words".

Structured information sources, such as *thesauri* and *databases* have also been explored to support the task of ontology learning and augmentation. In particular, thesauri like WordNet present explicit hierarchical information between concepts. Toral [26] classifies terms by mapping them to WordNet synsets, from which they traverse the hypernymy hierarchy in WordNet to find a synset that matches the ontological concept of interest. However, WordNet suffers from limited coverage of specialised vocabularies and do-

main-specific terminologies [7]. The approaches that learn taxonomical relations from databases, like RDBtoOnto[12] or RDB2RDF[13] are able to provide very detailed information but, they generally lack a hierarchical structure.

The use of SW knowledge to enrich ontologies has been investigated in the ontology evolution research area [27]. Similarly to this work, our approach enriches an initial ontological structure with new concepts and statements extracted from SW resources. As main differences, the work of [27] (a) uses plain terms (instead of SW extracted entities) as a starting point for the ontology augmentation process and, (b) performs the SW mapping process using term pairs (subject, object) instead of individual entities, which constitutes a heavier computational process.

To overcome the limitations of these classic ontology learning methods we propose a combined approach that exploits structured SW resources as well as textual resources. The details of this approach are described in the next section.

4. ONTOLOGY CONSTRUCTION

The ontology augmentation approach presented in this paper comprises two subsequent stages. In the first stage we carry out two tasks: we (a) identify on the SW a collection of appropriate entities, E, which are suitable for augmenting the initial (base) ontology and, (b) for each entity e in E, $\{e \in E\}$, we explore again the SW to find additional statements about e, S_e, which improve the value of e with respect to the requirements of the ontology augmentation scenario. This stage of the ontology augmentation process is typically accurate, where SW resources exist (see Section 5.1), but it cannot handle all possible cases, i.e., there is a subset of entities, E', $E' \subset E$, for which no additional statements are found in the SW. To provide tolerance to knowledge incompleteness the next stage adopts methods of ontology population using linguistic resources to find additional statements for the elements of E'. Linguistic resources are very abundant but prone to ambiguity, therefore we reserve these methods for cases which cannot be handled by the more precise SW approach. We refer to stage 1 as *"ontology augmentation using SW resources"* (OASW); we refer to stage 2 as *"ontology augmentation using textual resources"* (OATE).

4.1 Ontology augmentation using SW Resources (OASW)

In this section we describe our proposal towards selecting, extracting and restructuring knowledge from SW resources. The goal of this process is to create the necessary concepts and relations to structurally extend an ontology. In the case of our scenario (Section 2), the result of this process is an automatic extension of the Smart Products ontology with a taxonomical classification of ingredients from which their

---

[12] http://www.tao-project.eu/researchanddevelopment/demosanddownloads/RDBToOnto.html
[13] http://www.w3.org/2005/Incubator/rdb2rdf/

source (meat, vegetable, etc) can be inferred. The proposed approach has been developed as an extension of a well-known SW tool, PowerAqua [18], [19]. As briefly described, this tool presents several characteristics that make it suitable to address the task at a hand:

- *It exploits the SW as a knowledge information source.* PowerAqua selects, combines and aggregates information obtained from multiple distributed SW information sources. This is a key characteristic to select SW content tailored for a particular domain and/or task. To access this content PowerAqua makes use of the Watson SW gateway[14] as well as its own infrastructure where large-scale semantic sources like Agrovoc[15] and DBPedia[16] are indexed.

- *It acquires knowledge at run time.* The knowledge is selected and extracted at run time. Therefore, improvements in the quality and quantity of online SW information will be directly translated into enhancements in our ontology augmentation algorithms.

- *It performs a fine-grained reuse of knowledge.* PowerAqua reuses individual knowledge statements (semantic relations) rather than entire ontologies.

- *It works in open domain environments.* While the focus of this paper is the food domain, PowerAqua is able to work in any domain, i.e., ontologies covering several domains can be also reused for the purpose of this task and, the proposed algorithms are applicable to other domains.

Taking into account the above considerations an ontology augmentation methodology is proposed based on accessing and managing multiple distributed SW resources:

1. Identify or locate (on the SW) an initial *base ontology*, $O = \{c_1, c_2, ... c_M\}$, that will provide the initial set of definitions to kick-start the process.

2. Identify a set of relevant SW entities, E, which are suitable for augmenting the initial base ontology. In the case of our scenario this set consists of ingredients $E = \{e_1, e_2, ..., e_N\}$ with associated nutritional information.

3. Explore SW sources in order to identify, for each entity in $E, \{e \in E\}$, additional statements about e, S_e which improve the value of e with respect to the requirements of the ontology augmentation scenario. In particular, in our scenario S_e is a taxonomic relation which is needed to link e, an ingredient, to the classes in our base ontology, O, which define food types.

Selecting the base ontology, O
As a base ontology for this process we have selected the Smart Products ontology [21]. This ontology contains an initial hierarchy, including classes like: *drink, food, animal* and *plant origin*, etc.

Acquiring the set of entities, E
As mentioned in the state of the art (Section 3.1), we have identified FreeBase as the highest quality resource of nutritional information, containing 1455 ingredients. After filtering out those that lack nutritional information and those that contain numeric characters, we have obtained a set of 900 ingredients with complete nutritional information. This set of ingredients constitutes the identified set of SW entities suitable for augmenting the base ontology.

Automatically augmenting the base ontology
In this section we present our ontology augmentation algorithm, which exploits SW sources to automatically infer hierarchical relations between the selected and extracted domain-specific knowledge $E = \{e_1, e_2, ..., e_N\}$ and the existing knowledge in the base ontology $O = \{c_1, c_2, ... c_M\}$.

For each entity (ingredient) $\forall e_x, \{e_x \in E\}$

(1) **Obtain all the online ontologies** $S = \{O_1, O_2, ... O_L\}$ containing an equivalent concept c_y to the entity e_x, i.e., $e_x \approx c_y, where \{c_y \in O_l \text{ and } O_l \in S\}$

(2) For each ontology, $\forall O_l$, where $\{O_l \in S\}$

(2.1) Obtain the set of direct super classes of e_x in O_l
$DC_{O_l, e_x} = \{dc_1, dc_2, ... dc_p\}$, where $\{e_x \approx c_y, c_y \subseteq dc_p, \ dc_p \in O_l\}$

(2.2) **Obtain the complete set of direct super classes** of e_x,
$$DC_{e_x} = \bigcup_{l=1}^{L} DC_{O_l e_x}$$

(2.3) For each direct class, $\forall dc_p$, where $\{dc_p \in DC_{e_x}\}$ **try to find a mapping in the base ontology** O $c_y \approx dc_p$, where $\{c_y \in O\}$

(2.3.1) **No mapping** => leave e_x for the next iteration

(2.3.2) **One mapping** => add the entity (ingredient) as direct subclass of c_y, i.e., $e_x \subseteq c_y$, where $\{c_y \in O\}$

(2.3.3) **Several mappings** $M = \{c_{y_1}, c_{y_2}, ..., c_{y_Z}\}$, add e_x as subclass of the deepest concept, i.e., $e_x \subseteq c_{y_z}$, where $c_{y_z} \in O$ and $c_{y_z} = \min(depth(c_j, O))$, $\{c_j \in M\}$

To obtain the set of online ontologies S containing equivalent concepts to the entity e_x our algorithm makes use of PowerAqua's ontology discovery and semantic validation mechanisms [18], [19]. Briefly explained, PowerAqua's Ontology Discovery component identifies, at run time, those ontologies that may be relevant to a term by means of syntactic matching techniques. This process often generates several possible candidates within and in different ontologies, which may provide potential alternative interpretations for the term. To address this issue, PowerAqua's Semantic Validation Component builds on techniques developed in the Word Sense Disambiguation community, and exploits the background knowledge provided by WordNet and the context surrounding candidate entities in their on-

---

[14] http://kmi-web05.open.ac.uk/WatsonWUI/
[15] http://aims.fao.org/website/AGROVOC-Thesaurus/sub
[16] http://dbpedia.org/About

tologies to disambiguate between different possible interpretations of the same term.

Following the example in Figure 1, for the ingredient *whisky*, three equivalent concepts in three different SW ontologies are found. The direct super classes of whisky in these ontologies are: *Liquor* in O_1, *Alcoholic_beverage* in O_2 and *Drink* in O_3. After identifying the set of super classes in the different ontologies, the next step is to map them within the base ontology. *Liquor* does not map any concept in the base ontology, but *Drink* and *Alcoholic_beverage* do (case 2.3.3). *Whisky* will be therefore added as subclass of *Alcoholic_beverage*, since it is the deepest leaf, over the two candidates, in the base ontology. If there is only one mapping (case 2.3.2) the ingredient is directly added as subclass of the mapped class. If there is no mapping, the ingredient is left for a next iteration. As new classes are added to the base ontology, the chances increase the initially unclassified ingredients can be incorporated.

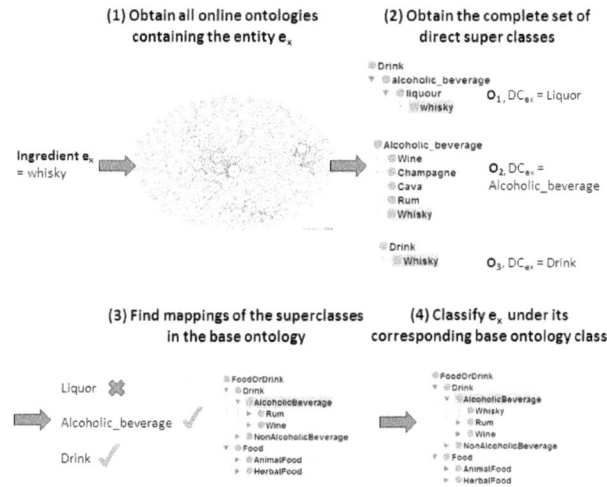

Figure 1. Example of OASW algorithm

4.2 Ontology Augmentation using Textual Resources (OATE)

The approach introduced in the previous section cannot classify all entities into the ontology due to several limitations (Section 5.1). As a result, a subset of entities extracted from the SW resources $E', E' \subset E$ cannot be learnt by the previous approach. Attempting to classify the remaining entities into the ontology, we complement the previous approach with a weakly-supervised text-based ontology population method. Note that in the case of our scenario, we apply ontology population techniques to link entities to their corresponding kinds, types or classes by classifying them as subclasses in the previously generated taxonomy. We refer to this method as ontology augmentation by information extraction (OATE).

Methodology

To cope with the limitations mentioned in Section 3.2, the OATE method is designed to be weakly supervised and independent of domain-specific resources. In short, given

small amount of subclasses, $S = \{S_{c\_1}, S_{c\_2}, ... S_{c\_n}\}$ for each existing class, c_i, in an ontology, the method employs semantic similarity measures to compute a similarity score of an input entity, e, against each subclass and to derive an aggregated score of similarity. The higher the similarity score, the more likely that the input entity e is a subclass of c_i. Conceptually, this is similar to [23].

Semantic similarity quantifies the extent to which two terms are similar by encompassing hyponymy/hyperonymy relations of the terms. It is more specific than semantic relatedness, which also takes account of other relations such as functional, synonymy, and antonymy [25]. E.g., "car" is similar to "motorbike", but is related to "street". In our case, we adopt semantic similarity methods because we aim to compute the similarity of an entity, e with its siblings, the set of subclasses $S = \{S_{c\_1}, S_{c\_2}, ... S_{c\_n}\}$ in order to determine the degree of membership of e as subclass of c_i.

Typically, computing semantic similarity between terms requires certain background information about the terms, which are often extracted from a corpus [6] or structured knowledge sources [17], [28]. To ensure the generality of the OATE method, we adopt the similarity measures used by [17] and [28], both of which do not require domain-specific corpora but rely on an external generic structured knowledge base. The work of Ling [17] employs the WordNet ontology and defines similarity between two concepts as a ratio between the "information in common" (*IC*) they share and the information needed to fully describe each term (*IDesc*). The work of Zhang [28] employs diverse information content and structural elements extracted from Wikipedia as weighted features and applies them to a statistical model – random graph walk - to compute relatedness between terms. Since this method measures relatedness, while we require similarity, we adapt the features and feature weights used by [28] accordingly. Specifically, we discard the features extracted from links (e.g., outgoing links) of a page because they give an indication of more general associations with other pages, rather than stricter semantic evidences given by other features like the categories of a page. The objective of adopting similarity measures that employ different knowledge bases (i.e., WordNet and Wikipedia) is to test them separately in our OATE method to empirically select the best for this task.

We denote the semantic similarity measure by Ling [17] as Sim_{lin}, and the one by Zhang [28] as Sim_{zhang}, and then apply them to a bootstrapping method for OATE:

Initialise $E = \{e_1, e_2 ... e_n\}$, C $= \{c_1, c_2 ... c_n\}$, $S = \{S_{c\_1}, S_{c\_2}, ... S_{c\_n}\}$, w
For e in E
  Initialise $Max(P(e|c_n)=0$, $label=unknown$
  For c_n in C
    Compute $P(e|c_n)$ using S_{c_n} with equation 2
    If $P(e|c_n) > Max(P(e|c_n)$ and $P(e|c_n) > t$
      $Max(P(e|c_n) = P(e|c_n)$
      $label = c_n$
  If $label \neq unknown$

13

Set final classification result of *e* to *label*

Select S_{c_n} where c_n = label

If *size* of $S_{c\_n}<w$

Add *e* to S_{c_n}

The algorithm starts with a number of classes defined in an ontology $C=\{c_1, c_2... c_n\}$, each associated with a seed, a list of subclasses denoted by $S=\{S_{c\_1}, S_{c\_2},... S_{c\_n}\}$. The list of candidate entities to be classified is denoted by E. Next, the algorithm iteratively processes the entity candidates (one candidate per iteration) and computes a confidence score $P(e|c_n)$ indicating a sense of probability of the candidate belonging to the concept using equation 1.

$$P(e|c_n) = \frac{\sum_{s \in S_{c\_n}} Sim_{lin/zhang}(e,s)}{\sum_{s \in S_{c\_n}} s} \quad [1]$$

The final classification is the class with which *e* receives the highest confidence score. Note that the seed list, *S* is not the complete set of subclasses of each class but a subset of it determined by *w*, a "window" parameter. As concluded in our experiments (see Section 5.2), the use of the complete set of subclasses led to inaccuracies of the OATE method due to classes that have multiple parents. To avoid the use of ambiguous classes within the seed lists we select the best subclasses $S=\{S_{c\_1}, S_{c\_2},... S_{c\_n}\}$ for each class c_i by computing the semantic similarity between the class c_i and each of its subclasses and selecting the top *w-1* subclasses, i.e., those ones with higher semantic similarity values. Once a new entity *e* is classified into the taxonomy, it can be added to a seed, according to the values of $P(e|c_n)$ and a *w*. If the size of S_{c_n} is less than *w*, *e* is added to S_{c_n}. Otherwise, seeds in S_{c_n} are re-ranked according to their scores, and *e* is only added if $P(e|c_n)$ is greater than the score of the lowest ranked seed entity, which is eliminated from the seed accordingly.

The major limitation of this approach is that it does not classify new terms into leaf classes in an ontology. In the strict sense, the method is based on similarity or likeness between concepts, but does not identify "is-a" relations.

5. EXPERIMENTS

In this section we present the experiments on ontology augmentation using SW and textual resources. The two experiments were conducted independently but in sequence with the output of the OASW experiment being used as the seed ontology to test the OATE method. The used data can be found at: http://smartproducts1.kmi.open.ac.uk/kcap/

5.1 Experiment on OASW

In this section we described the experiments that we have conducted to evaluate, the degree to which the SW can be used as a source of evidence for automatic ontology construction in the context of a diet evaluation scenario (Section 2). The evaluation pursues three key goals: (i) measuring the *coverage* of the classification process; i.e., how many ingredients have been added to the augmented ontology; (ii) measuring the *correctness* of the generated hierarchical

structures; i.e., what is the number of semantically correct classifications and; (iii) measuring the *specialization* of the generated hierarchical structures; i.e., are the ingredient classifications specialized enough so that their source can be inferred?

Results

Coverage: A total of 747 over 900 ingredients **(83%)** were classified using the OASW approach described in Section 4.1. Over the remaining 153 ingredients **(17%)**, we have performed an analysis to find out the different reasons for their lack of classification. 45 (29%) of the ingredients were *not found in existing ontologies on the SW*. Either the ontologies do not contain information about the ingredient or, there is a gap (e.g., use of different vocabulary) between the information contained in the ontology and the ingredient that is being mapped. The remaining 108 (71%) of ingredients found in SW ontologies were not classified for three main reasons. (i) *The ontology does not contain detailed taxonomical information to find out the classification of the ingredient,* 55 (36%). Either structural properties like rdf:type or rdfs:subclassOf are not defined for the ingredient in the mapped ontology, and its hierarchy is only described in non structural properties such as rdfs:label or rdfs:comment, or the values for the structural properties of the ingredient in the ontology are too abstract (e.g., classifications such as dish or ingredient). (ii) *The taxonomical classifications of the ingredient are too specific, and do not generate syntactic mappings in the base ontology,* 28 (18%). For example, the classification of the ingredient McIntosh as "eating apple" does not map against "apple" with sufficient accuracy to be considered as a correct mapping. As a compromise between the precision and recall PowerAqua's mapping algorithm threshold was set to 0.95 to avoid incorrect classifications. Therefore, when the taxonomical information is significantly syntactically different with respect to the one in the base ontology, the classification is not generated to avoid mistakes. (iii) *The taxonomical classifications are described in non-standard but specific properties of the semantic resource,* 25 (0.16%). For example, for the ingredient pizzoccheri, DBPedia does not contain any hierarchical information described as the standard rdf:tpe property but as property dcterms:subject, which is a property specific to DBPedia. PowerAqua's algorithms are generic and do not make particular assumptions about the semantic resources. Therefore, resource-specific properties are not analysed.

Table 1: evaluation for three different ingredients

Ingredient	PowerAqua classification	eval
cherry_liqueur	[cherry_liqueur, soft_fruits, fruit, food, FoodOrDrink]	0
leek	[leek, vegetables, food, FoodOrDrink]	1
mishima_beef	[mishima_beef, beef, meat, animal_origin, food, FoodOrDrink]	2

Correctness and Specialization: To evaluate the correctness and specialization of the approach, we have engaged 3 different evaluators in the campaign. Each of them has evaluated the classification of 900 ingredients using a value from 0 to 2 where each number implies (see Table 1):

- 0: the classification is semantically incorrect
- 1: the classification is correct but not specialized enough to determine the source of the ingredient
- 2: the classification is correct and specialized enough to determine the source of the ingredient

For each ingredient classification, given the three user's evaluations, it was considered correct if at least two evaluators were rating it with values higher than 0, and it was considered specific, if at least two evaluators were rating it at level 2, and the remaining evaluation was not 0. There was a substantial agreement among users. Fleiss' kappa statistic [12] measuring user's agreement was k=0.77 (a value k=1 means completely agreement). Once established the evaluation step up we compute that, over the 747 classified ingredients, 679 (91%) were considered correctly classified and, 590 (79%) were considered specialized enough to be used within the context of a diet evaluation task.

5.2 Experiment on OATE

To evaluate the accuracy of the proposed method for OATE, we use the ontology created by the OASW method (denoted by $Ontology_{stage1}$) and manually validated it to create a gold standard. $Ontology_{stage1}$ was checked by two annotators, who corrected mis-classified terms and then manually classified the remaining 153 terms into the ontology to obtain the final gold standard $Ontology_{GS}$. Meanwhile, the unclassified terms are submitted to the OATE method to be classified and populated into $Ontology_{stage1}$ to obtain the final ontology $Ontology_{final}$.

Standard methods have been introduced in the past for the purpose of evaluating ontology learning and ontology population. Since our task is learning the hierarchical structure of an ontology, we follow the taxonomic precision (*TP*), recall (*TR*) and F-measure (*TF*) metrics introduced by [11]. These metrics are applied to $Ontology_{final}$ to evaluate the accuracy of the proposed OATE method. The accuracy is computed based on the 153 ingredients that the OASW method failed to classify, i.e., we only take account of ontology branches that contain one of the 153 ingredients. This is to avoid biased results towards over-estimated accuracies, because both $Ontology_{GS}$ and $Ontology_{final}$ may contain equal portions originated from $Ontology_{stage1}$.

Results

The two presented semantic similarity measures (Sim_{lin} and Sim_{zhang}) are ported into the proposed OATE method, to study the effect of using different knowledge bases and to empirically select the best similarity measure in the context of our task.

Table 2: Experimental results of OATE using different semantic similarity measures

	TP	TR	TF
Wikipedia-based semantic similarity (Sim$_{zhang}$)	78.4	79.8	79.1
WordNet-based semantic similarity (Sim$_{lin}$)	45.9	46.7	46.3

As shown in Table 2, the Wikipedia-based measure, Sim_{zhang}, obtained significantly better results than the WordNet-based measure, Sim_{lin}. This is not surprising given the lack of coverage of specialised and domain-specific terms in WordNet [7]. Careful analyses show that nearly 35% of the 151 terms cannot be found in WordNet, which has given rise to the low recall. By contrast, only one term cannot be found in Wikipedia. In the results generated by the Wikipedia-based method, the majority (87%) of terms are classified to the right branch. Errors are mostly due to that terms being placed under incorrect node (either too specific, or too general). E.g., the term "Spanish mackerel" is placed under "fish > animal origin > food" in $Ontology_{GS}$, but under "tuna > fish > animal origin" in $Ontology_{final}$. Note that the mis-classifications of ingredients under too specific classes do not affect the diet evaluation task, since the source (animal, vegetable, etc) of the ingredient can still be determined.

As part of evaluating the performance of the OATE method with two different semantic similarity measures we have also studied the effect of taking all sub-classes of a class as seed terms, instead of selecting certain subclasses, in concordance to selective approaches. This has led to a decrease of the accuracy of the OATE method. A careful analysis show that this is because terms that have multiple senses, and therefore are classified under multiple classes in the existing ontology, become ambiguous members as seed terms, which may propagate negative effects through the bootstrapping process. For example, "seaweed" is a subclass of both "vegetable" and "seafood". Selecting "sea weed" as a seed for the class "vegetable" has the effect of "diluting" the purity of seed terms. The problem is more acute with a more densely populated taxonomy, in which a class may be subclasses of multiple classes.

In conclusion, the reasonable accuracy obtained by the OATE method and the good coverage of the Wikipedia knowledge base indicate that text-based ontology augmentation methods are a good complement to smooth the limitations of SW-based ontology learning and augmentation approaches, by increasing their overall coverage.

6. CONCLUSIONS AND OUTLOOK

This paper presents a new ontology augmentation method based on the selection, extraction and reorganization of SW content. The approach has shown promising results when applying it to the diet evaluation scenario, achieving 83% coverage for a set of entities selected and extracted from Freebase. High levels of accuracy (91%) and specialisation (79%) were also achieved. A study of the cases where selected entities were not automatically added to the ontology points out as main reasons the lack of available SW information, the excess or defect of taxonomical information in the mapped ontologies and the use of non-standard properties to store hierarchical descriptions.

To provide tolerance to knowledge incompleteness and to smooth the limitations of SW-based methods we have proposed the integration of text-based methodologies within the ontology augmentation process. While the imprecise selection of subclasses for the seed lists and the inability to classify entities under leaf concepts remain the major cause of inaccuracies of our text-based method, its integration to enhance the results obtained by the single application of the OASW method has shown promising results. In particular, the OATE method proposed, which uses Wikipedia as a source of background knowledge, has obtained an accuracy (F measure) of 79%, which constitutes a significant increase in the global coverage of the ontology augmentation process.

The application of the proposed approach, and its validation by two annotators, has produced an ontology where 900 ingredients have been restructured in a taxonomy of 1514 hierarchical relations. This ontology is currently exploited within a diet evaluation module where, the nutritional information, and the source of the ingredient, has helped to evaluate the suitability of more than 2000 recipes with respect to eight different diets.

As future work we plan to explore more powerful methods for SW relation discovery and to exploit generic Web resources as textual information sources, to enhance the coverage of the approach.

REFERENCES

[1] Batet, M., Sánchez, D., Valls, A. (2010). An ontology-based measure to compute semantic similarity in biomedicine. Journal of Biomedical Informatics.

[2] Batista, F., Paulo, J., Mamede, N, Vaz, P., Ribeiro, R. (2006) Ontology construction: cooking domain, Technical report, INESC-ID, Lisboa, Portugal.

[3] Buitelaar, P., Olejnik, D., and Sintek, M. (2003) A protege plug-in for ontology extraction from text based on linguistic analysis, in Proc. ISWC 2003.

[4] Cantais, J., Dominguez, D., Gigante, V., Laera, L., Tamma, V. (2005) An example of food ontology for diabetes control, Workshop on Ontology Patterns for the SW, in Proc. ISWC 2005.

[5] Cerbah. F. (2008) Mining the Content of Relational Databases to Learn Ontologies with Deeper Taxonomies, in Proc. IEEE/WIC/ACM 2008.

[6] Cilibrasi, R., Vitanyi, P. (2007) The Google Similarity Distance. IEEE Transactions on Knowledge and Data Engineering. 19(3), pp. 370-383.

[7] Cimiano, P., Pivk, A., Thieme, L.S., Staab, S. (2004) Learning Taxonomic Relations from Heterogeneous Sources of Evidence, in Proc. ECAI 2004.

[8] Cimiano, P., Völker, J. (2005) Towards large-scale, open-domain and ontology-based named entity classification, in Proc. RANLP'05.

[9] Cimiano, P. (2006) Ontology Learning and Population from Text: Algorithms, Evaluation and Applications. Springer.

[10] Cimiano, P., Völker, J., Studer, R. (2006) Ontologies on demand? - a description of the state-of-the-art, applications, challenges and trends for ontology learning from text. Information, Wissenschaft und Praxis 57(6-7) pp. 315-320.

[11] Dellschaft, K., Staab, S. (2006) On How to Perform a Gold Standard Based Evaluation of Ontology Learning, in Proc. ISWC2006.

[12] Fleiss, J. L. and Cohen, J. (1973) The equivalence of weighted kappa and the intraclass correlation coefficient as measures of reliability. Educational and Psychological Measurement, Vol. 33 pp. 613–619

[13] Grishman, R., Sundheim, B. (1996). Message understanding conference - 6: A brief history, in Proc. COLING 1996.

[14] Hearst, M.A. (1992) Automatic acquisition of hyponyms from large text corpora, in Proc. COLING 1992.

[15] Herrera, J., Iglesias, P., Garcia-Sanchez, A., Diaz-Agudo, B. (2009) JaDaCook 2: Cooking over Ontological Knowledge, in Proc. ICCBR 2009.

[16] Lee, C., Hwang, Y., Jang, M. (2007) Fine-grained named entity recognition and relation extraction for question answering, in Proc. SIGIR 2007.

[17] Lin, D. (1998) An Information-Theoretic Definition of Similarity, in Proc. ICML 1998.

[18] Lopez, V., Sabou, M. and Motta, E. (2006) PowerMap: Mapping the Real SW on the Fly, in Proc. ISWC2006.

[19] Lopez, V., Nikolov, A., Sabou, M, Uren, V., Motta, E., and d'Aquin, M. (2010) Scaling up Question-Answering to Linked Data, in Proc. EKAW 2010.

[20] Maynard, D., Li, Y., Peters, W. (2008). NLP Techniques for Term Extraction and Ontology Population, in Proc. 2008 conference on Ontology Learning and Population: Bridging the Gap between Text and Knowledge.

[21] Nikolov, A., d'Aquin, M. D2.1.3 Final version of the conceptual framework. SmartProducts deliverable, 2010.

[22] Pekar, V., Staab, S. (2002) Taxonomy learning: factoring the structure of a taxonomy into a semantic classification decision. In Proc. COLING 2002.

[23] Reinberger, M.-L. and Spyns, P. (2005) Unsupervised text mining for the learning of dogma-inspired ontologies. Ontology Learning from Text: Methods, Applications and Evaluation, pp. 29-42. IOS Press, Amsterdam (2005).

[24] Snae, C., Bruckner, M. (2008) Foods: A food-oriented ontology driven system, in Proc. of IEEE – DEST 2008.

[25] Strube, M., Ponzetto, S. (2006) WikiRelate! Computing semantic relatedness using Wikipedia, in Proc. AAAI'06.

[26] Toral, A. Muñoz, R. (2006) A Proposal to Automatically Build and Maintain Gazetteers for Named Entity Recognition by using Wikipedia. Workshop on New Text, in Proc. EACL 2006.

[27] Zablith, F., Sabou, M., d'Aquin, M. and Motta, E. (2009) Ontology Evolution with Evolva, Demo, in Proc. ESWC 2009.

[28] Zhang, Z., Gentile, A., Xia, L., Iria, J., and Chapman, S. (2010). A Random Graph Walk based Approach to Compute Semantic Relatedness Using Knowledge from Wikipedia, in Proc. LREC2010

Acquiring OWL Ontologies from XML Documents

Martin J. O'Connor
Stanford Center for Biomedical Informatics Research
Stanford, CA 94305, U.S.A.
martin.oconnor@stanford.edu

Amar K. Das
Stanford Center for Biomedical Informatics Research
Stanford, CA 94305, U.S.A.
amar.das@stanford.edu

ABSTRACT

Converting non-Semantic Web encoded information to ontology-based languages such as the Web Ontology Language (OWL) is an important knowledge acquisition challenge. In many domains, a large amount of information is represented in eXtensible Markup Language (XML), which has driven the development of general-purpose tools for converting XML to OWL. These tools suffer from a variety of shortcomings, however, including a requirement for multi-stage mapping processes and limited mapping techniques. A general shortcoming is that the mapping methods are not OWL-centric and thus limit the complexity of the generated OWL ontologies. To address these shortcomings, we developed an OWL-based language that can transform XML documents to arbitrary OWL ontologies. The language is based on the Manchester OWL Syntax and extends it with XPath queries to support references to XML documents. Our language provides a compact, user-friendly approach for converting XML to OWL.

Categories and Subject Descriptors

I.2.4 Knowledge Representation Formalisms and Methods
– representation languages.

General Terms: Languages.

Keywords

OWL, XML, knowledge acquisition, Manchester Syntax.

INTRODUCTION

Acquiring knowledge from a variety of information formats is a key Semantic Web challenge. An array of tools has been developed to acquire knowledge from formats such as relational databases [1], spreadsheets [2], and XML [3], and to map this knowledge to RDF and OWL [4]. Because of its extensive use in data exchange and integration, XML has been a focus of these activities. XML and its associated schema language XML Schema [5] define an approach to modeling information in a document and thus provide a standardized data exchange mechanism.

A general approach used by mapping tools is to transform an XML Schema instance to an equivalent OWL ontology,

and then populate the ontology with instances from XML documents conforming to the schema. This process presents many challenges, however, because of the different modeling goals of XML Schema and OWL. The goal of XML Schema is primarily to describe the syntactic structure of a document. In contrast, the primary goal of an OWL ontology is to semantically describe concepts in a domain and the relationships between them. As a result, even if a particular XML document can be transformed to OWL, the result is often not an immediately useful ontology. Also, many XML constructs are intrinsically ordered, whereas OWL is entirely set oriented.

These different characteristics can produce a mismatch that must be reconciled by the mapping process. In general, a second transformation stage is required. This stage takes the implicit semantics of the XML document and makes them explicit in the generated OWL ontology. Much of the complexity related to content transformation occurs at this stage.

Current tools either address only the first stage of this transformation process or adopt a limited two phase approach. In general, the first stage is straightforward and can be semi-automated because of the relative simplicity of XML Schema. The second stage requires richer user-specified transformations. Ideally, this stage should support arbitrary OWL constructs but in practice, current tools limit mappings to a small predefined set. This shortcoming is a reflection of the weakness of OWL support in these tools' mapping methods.

There is a need for a language that supports transformations to unrestricted OWL ontologies. Ideally, it would be easy to learn for users familiar with XML and OWL. It should also produce mappings that are relatively concise and maintainable. We have created XMLMaster, which we believe is such a language. It is built on the Manchester OWL Syntax [6], a widely used language for declaratively describing OWL ontologies. We extend the Manchester Syntax and combine it with the XPath XML query language [7]. The resulting language supports the extraction of content from XML documents and the generation of OWL ontologies using that content. It provides a declarative approach to transform from XML to OWL with no limitations on the type of OWL ontologies that can be generated.

RELATED WORK

The first generation of mapping tools involved relatively direct translations from XML documents to RDF or OWL. Klein presented one of the earliest approaches [8]. His approach used an RDF Schema mapping ontology to identify relevant content in a source XML document to generate a one-way mapping to RDF. Another study outlined a bi-directional mapping approach that used a mapping described in XML Schema to map XML concepts to an RDF ontology [9]. A related approach supported both RDF and OWL [10]. Another effort mapped an XML Schema to an OWL ontology and then created instances in that ontology from XML documents [11]. Garcia *et al.* and Kunfermann and Drumm developed similar approaches [12, 13]. All of these approaches generate new ontologies from XML using only terms in the source XML document.

Mappings in the second generation of tools were more complex, and allowed interoperation with existing ontologies. In general, the mapping process was two-phased. The first phase generated an intermediate ontology from source XML schemas or instances. The second mapped the intermediate ontologies to an existing ontology [14-16]. A system called WEESA [17], for example, supported mapping from XML to RDF with manually created rules. A similar system was described by Kobeissy *et al.* [18]. It mapped an XML Schema to OWL concepts and XML instances to OWL individuals. This approach allowed selective extraction of XML content using XPath. Tous *et al.* employed a related approach, also using XPath [19]. A recent system developed by the authors adopted a variant of this approach [3]. It mapped an XML document to instances of an OWL ontology describing the serialization of the document. It then used the Semantic Web Rule Language (SWRL; [20]) to map these instances to instances in a domain ontology. This approach provided great flexibility, but managing and debugging rule sets for non-trivial mappings was a challenge. Yet another variant used a meta-model-based approach to map between the different models provided by XML Schema and OWL [21].

A general limitation of these approaches is that none provided a custom mapping language. In general, mapping rules were specified using a selection of predefined templates. Thus, *ad hoc* mappings were not possible, which limited expressivity. Systems using XPath could support essentially arbitrary selection of XML content, but the range of possible transformation of content to OWL was limited. As a result, developers could generate only very basic OWL ontologies, and a decoupled post-processing phase was often required.

CORE LANGUAGE FEATURES

XMLMaster is a new declarative OWL-centric mapping language that addresses these limitations. It is a domain-specific language (DSL) that supports XML documents that do not necessarily have an XML Schema describing them. It can also process unstructured text content in these documents. Full coverage of all OWL constructs is a primary feature. In addition to defining simple OWL entities such as named classes, properties, and individuals, class expressions and potentially complex necessary and sufficient declarations are expressible. Additionally, the language aims to

be concise and simple to learn for users familiar with OWL and XML. It also provides debugging support, which is a general usability requirement when developing a custom language. The high levels of complexity when mapping from XML to OWL make this support crucial. In particular, previewing the final result of a mapping expression before executing it can greatly assist in debugging. A key feature is thus to provide instantaneous preview of mapping results before they are inserted into the OWL ontology.

Rather than designing a DSL from scratch, we built our language on the Manchester OWL Syntax [6], a widely used DSL for declaratively describing OWL ontologies. This language has concise clauses for defining common OWL entities. It also provides full coverage of all OWL constructs and, because it is the standard presentation syntax in many OWL-based ontology editing tools, it is familiar to most users of OWL. It also has a clean language definition, allowing it to be extended in a principled way. Our language is a superset of the Manchester OWL Syntax. It extends it to allow the use of XPath expressions to refer to XML content. Primarily, it introduces a new *reference clause* to support this extraction.[1]

```
<?xml version="1.0" encoding="ISO-8859-1"?>
<store>
  <book category="literature">
    <name>Huckleberry Finn</name>
    <price>10.00</price>
    <author>Mark Twain</author>
  </book>
  <book category="autobiography">
    <name>Life</name>
    <price>$12.00</price>
    <author>Keith Richards</author>
  </book>
</store>
```

Figure 1. XML document describing books in a bookstore.

Basic Reference Clause

A reference clause uses an XPath expression to indicate content in an XML document. In our DSL, this reference clause can substitute for any clause in a Manchester Syntax expression that indicates an OWL class, property, individual, data type, or data value. Reference clauses are prefixed with @ and are followed by an XPath expression.

For example, Figure 1 is an XML document showing books in a bookstore. A reference to the first book's name element is written:

<code>@/store/book[1]/name</code>

To return element content, the `text` function can be used:

<code>@/store/book[1]/name/text()</code>

The element name can be obtained in a similar way.

The reference clause can be used in an expression to define OWL constructs using XML content. For example, the fol-

---

[1] Our language wiki has a full description of the language [22].

lowing expression takes the text in the first book element in Figure 1 and declares an OWL named class as a subclass of an existing `Book` class:

```
Class: @/store/book[1]/name/text()
  SubClassOf: Book
```

This expression declares an OWL class named by the contents of the first book element ("Huckleberry Finn" in this case) and asserts that it is a subclass of class `Book`. If the class has previously been declared and is not already a subclass of `Book`, then the subclass relationship will be established. In this way, references can be used to define new OWL entities or to refer to existing entities.

The language has default options to automatically extract either an element's content or its name. As discussed later, this default can be changed globally. In the following examples, the default is to use an element's content, so the `text` function qualification is omitted.

A similar expression to declare an individual of type `Book` using the element contents as its name can be written:

```
Individual: @/store/book[1]/name Types: Book
```

Of course, XPath expressions can match multiple elements. If the item selector is omitted from the above expression, multiple book elements are returned. For example, if the item selector is omitted, as in the following expression, individuals will declared for all book elements found.

```
Individual: @/store/book/name Types: Book
```

The Manchester Syntax supports a clause for associating property values with individuals. This clause contains a list of property value declarations. For example, the following is an expression specifying that an individual created from the first book element obtains a value for a data property value `price` from the associated `price` element and a `category` property value from its `category` attribute:

```
Individual: @/store/book/name Types: Book
  Facts: price @../price,
         category @../@category
```

As can be seen, relative references are used here to refer to the `price` element and the `category` attribute. The language interprets relative references in terms of the most recent non-relative reference in an expression. As with element text qualification, value qualification is the default, and can be omitted for attribute nodes.

Any XPath expression can be used in a reference. For example, expressions can select nodes that meet particular criteria. Using this approach, the previous example can be modified to select books with a price over $25:

```
Individual: @/store/book/name Types: Book
  Facts: price @..[price>25.0]/price
```

Similarly, the XPath expression can be modified to select only the first three book elements in the XML document:

```
Individual: @/store/book[position()<=3]/name
  Types: Book
```

Document structural information can also be recorded. For example, the position of a book element in a document can be retrieved using the XPath `position` and `count` functions. Maintaining positional information from XML documents is often essential, as OWL has no native list support. Summary information about documents, such as the number of elements of a particular type, can be recorded in a similar way using XPath counting functions.

XMLMaster supports the full range of Manchester Syntax expressions. For example, using the standard Manchester Syntax, annotation properties can also be associated with declared entities. Using this clause, a string data type annotation property called `source` can be used to associate a declared book individual with an annotation as follows:

```
Individual: @/store/book/names
  Types: Book
  Annotations: source "From: book XML document"
```

OWL class and property expressions can also be used. In general, a class or property expression may occur anywhere a named class or property can occur. The following expression defines conditions for a class `SalesItem`; it uses the contents of a book element's price and name sub-elements:

```
Class: SalesItem
  EquivalentTo: @/store/book/name
  SubClassOf: price value @../price
```

Using this approach, any OWL axiom can be declared using the appropriate Manchester Syntax clause, with XPath references used in these clauses to extract XML content.

Reference Mapping Directives

The basic reference clause outlined above can deal with straightforward mappings. In many cases, however, references need to be qualified to resolve ambiguity or indicate additional processing directives. XMLMaster provides a directives clause to support this specification.

The most basic directive controls the type of a generated OWL entity. In general, XMLMaster tries to infer the type of an entity in a reference, but this inference is not always possible. To deal with this case, our language supports explicit entity type specifications. A reference may be followed by a parentheses-enclosed entity type specification to explicitly declare the type of the referenced entity. This specification can indicate that the entity is a named OWL class, an OWL object or data property, an OWL individual, or a data type. The keywords to specify the types are the standard Manchester Syntax keywords `Class`, `ObjectProperty`, `DataProperty`, and `Individual`, plus any XSD type name (e.g., `xsd:int`). The following uses this specification to write the book individual declaration above:

```
Individual: @/store/book/name(Individual)
  Types: Book
```

In many cases, specifying the super class, super property, individual class membership, or data type of referenced entities is also desired. While these relationships can be defined using standard Manchester Syntax expressions, doing so often entails the use of multiple mapping expressions. To concisely support defining these relationships, a reference may be followed by a parentheses-enclosed list of type names. Using this approach, the above drug declaration can be written:

```
Individual: @/store/book/name(Individual Book)
```

Type specifications can themselves be references. Super properties, individual class membership, and data types can be specified in the same way.

Global Mapping Directives

XMLMaster supports several global processing directives to specify default configuration options for the mapping process. They were designed to allow specification of common defaults for a set of mappings so that they do not have to be repeated in each expression.

The most common default controls element processing. This default specifies whether an element's content or name is automatically extracted for elements resolved in an XPath expression. Thus, explicit `text` or `name` function qualification is not needed. Other defaults include the ability to declare a default namespace for both source XML documents and generated OWL entities. Prefix-to-namespace mappings can also be specified. In addition, directives control the handling of missing values in documents. In the default case, if an XPath expression evaluates to an empty value, the clause containing it is skipped. However, in some cases, users may wish to generate warnings or terminate the mapping when values are missing.

Directives are also provided to deal with references to OWL entities. For example, a directive can be set to indicate that an error should be thrown if a name refers to an existing entity in the target ontology. There is also a directive to indicate that an error should be thrown if the name does *not* refer to an existing entity. A related option deals with potential ambiguity introduced by annotation value references. It can be set to produce an error if more than one existing OWL entity could be named by the value.

Our language provides an option specification clause for each option type. The general form of this clause is a keyword followed by a value. For example, the default name encoding for all mappings can be written:

```
mm:DefaultNameEncoding = rdfs:label
```

Our online documentation has a full list of options [22].

ADVANCED LANGUAGE FEATURES

The language features outlined above support basic mappings of XML documents to OWL. Additional features are required for documents with unstructured text and missing elements. There is also a need for fine-grained control of the names and namespaces of created OWL entities.

OWL Entity Name Encoding and Resolution

Users can employ a variety of name-encoding and resolution strategies when they are creating or resolving OWL entities. The primary strategies are to use direct URI-based names (equivalent to using `rdf:about` or `rdf:ID` clauses in

an RDF serialization of OWL) or `rdfs:label` annotation values. With `rdf:ID` encoding, an OWL entity generated from a reference is assigned its `rdf:ID` from the referenced content. If the content does not represent a fully qualified URI or a prefixed name, it is appended to a URI representing the namespace of the active ontology. Clearly, when using `rdf:ID` encoding, the content must represent a valid identifier—spaces are not allowed, for example. With `rdfs:label` encoding, the generated OWL entity is given an automatically generated (and non-meaningful) URI and its `rdfs:label` annotation value is set to the content specified by the XPath expression. A third encoding type is provided to support the case where the actual contents of the element are to be ignored. In this case, the generated OWL entity is again given an automatically generated URI, but its label is not assigned. The elements location in the XML document is used to track it during processing.

The default naming encoding uses the `rdfs:label` annotation property. As discussed, this default may also be changed globally. A name encoding clause explicitly specifies a desired encoding. As with entity type specifications, the clause is enclosed by parentheses after the XPath expression. The keywords to specify the encoding types are `rdf:about`, `rdf:ID`, `rdfs:label`, and `mm:UseLocation`. The following is a specification of `rdf:ID` encoding for the previous book example using this clause:

```
Class: @/store/book/name(rdf:ID) SubClassOf: Book
```

As mentioned, the default behavior is to use the text specified by the XPath expression when encoding a name. However, the text can first be processed with an optional value specification clause. This clause is indicated by the '=' character after the encoding specification keyword, and is followed by either a single value specification or a comma-separated list of value specifications in parentheses. Value specifications are a quoted string, a reference, or a function.

XMLMaster includes a predefined set of functions for manipulating text. These include `mm:prepend`, `mm:append`, `mm:trim`, `mm:replace`, and `mm:replaceAll`. These functions take zero or more arguments and return a value. Arguments may be quoted strings, references, or functions. For example, the following is an expression that extends the earlier book class declaration to specify `rdfs:label` name encoding. It specifies that the extracted name should be preceded by the underscore character:

```
Class:
 @/store/book/name(rdfs:label=mm:prepend("_"))
 SubClassOf: Book
```

A similar declaration that uses the `mm:trim` function to strip leading and trailing spaces can be written:

```
Class: @/store/book/name(mm:trim)
  SubClassOf: Book
```

Here, the content specified by the XPath expression is the implied argument to the `trim` function. It is processed by the function and then assigned to the class's label. The `rdfs:label` name-encoding specification is omitted because it is the default.

More than one encoding can be specified for a particular reference. In this way, separate identifier and label annotation values can be generated for a particular entity using different XPath expressions.

By default, OWL entity names are resolved or generated using the namespace of the active ontology. XMLMaster includes prefix and namespace directives to override this default behavior. These directives use the keywords `mm:prefix` and `mm:namespace`, and are followed by a quoted string. For example, the following is an expression indicating that a book individual created or resolved in the earlier expressions should use the namespace identified by the prefix *literary*:

```
Class: @/store/book/name(mm:prefix="literary")
  SubClassOf: Book
```

Similarly, the following is an expression indicating that it must use the namespace "http://books.edu/Books.owl#":

```
Class: @/store/book/name(mm:namespace="http://..")
  SubClassOf: Book
```

Explicit namespace or prefix qualification also allows disambiguation of duplicate labels in an ontology.

Processing of Element and Attribute Content

Text within elements or attribute values in XML documents frequently requires processing. As shown, some of the functions provided by our language support basic processing steps such as stripping spaces. More complex processing is also possible. For example, to remove all $ characters, the `mm:replaceAll` function can be used:

```
Individual: @/store/book/name(Book)
  Facts: price @../price(mm:replaceAll("$",""))
```

Functions can also be nested. For example, the expression can be rewritten to trim the text after substitution:

```
Individual: @/store/book/name(Book)
  Facts:
    price @../price(mm:trim(mm:replaceAll("$","")))
```

Extracting portions of semi-structured content is often required. XMLMaster provides a regular expression capturing group clause to support this extraction. This clause can be used in any position in a value specification clause. The clause is either contained in a quoted string enclosed by square parentheses or specified by a `mm:capturing` function.

For example, if a name element has a person's forename and surname separated by a single space, two capturing expressions can be used to selectively extract each name portion and assign them separately to different properties:

```
Individual: @/store/book/name(Book)
  Facts:
    forename @../author(mm:capturing("(\S+)")),
    surname  @../author(mm:capturing("\S+\s(\S+))"))
```

Parentheses around sub-expressions in a regular expression clause specify capturing groups and indicate that matched strings are to be extracted. In some cases, more than one group may be matched for a value. In this case, the strings are extracted in the order that they are matched and are appended to each other.

A more complex variant to convert comma-specified floating point numbers to dot-specified is:

```
Individual: @/store/book/name(Book)
  Facts:
    price @../price(["([-+]*\d+),"],".",[",(\d+)"])
```

The `mm:replace` method would also work here:

```
Individual: @/store/book/name(Book)
  Facts: price @../price(mm:replace(",","."))
```

The syntax of capturing expressions follows that supported by the Java `Pattern` class. It provides quite a degree of flexibility when processing semi-structured text. Obviously, there are limitations to this method. Completely unstructured text may require a separate pre-processing stage.

Missing Value Handling

To deal with missing values, default values can also be specified in references. A default value clause is provided to assign these values. This clause is indicated by the `mm:default` keyword and is followed by at least one value specification. For example, the following expression uses this clause to indicate that the value 0.0 should be used as a price if the price sub-element is missing:

```
Individual: @/store/book/name(Book)
  Facts: price @../price(mm:default="0.0")
```

XMLMaster also has additional behaviors to deal with missing values. The default behavior is to skip an entire expression if it contains any references with empty content. Four keywords are supplied to modify this behavior. They indicate that when a reference resolves to empty content: (1) an error should be thrown and the mapping process should be stopped (`mm:ErrorIfEmptyLocation`); (2) the expression should be skipped (`mm:SkipIfEmptyLocation`); (3) a warning should be generated and the reference should be skipped (`mm:WarningIfEmptyLocation`); and (4) expressions containing these references should be processed (`mm:ProcessIfEmptyLocation`). The last option allows processing of documents that contain many missing values. The option indicates that the language processor should, if possible, conservatively drop the sub-expression containing the empty reference rather than dropping the entire expression.

Consider, for example, the following expression declaring book individuals and their prices:

```
Individual: @/store/book/name(Book)
  Facts: price @../price(mm:ProcessIfEmptyLocation)
```

Using the default skip behavior, a missing `price` element will cause the entire expression to be skipped. However, the process directive for the `price` property will instead drop only the sub-expression containing it if that element is empty. As a result, the expression will still declare an individual. More fine-grained empty value handling is also supported to specify different empty value handling behaviors for `rdf:ID` and `rdfs:label` values.

IMPLEMENTATION

We have developed a parser, an editor, a processor, and a debugger for the mapping language as an open source plug-in to the Protégé-OWL development environment [23].

User Interface

The user interface provides an editor for defining, managing and executing expressions. The plug-in also supports loading XML documents and previewing them. It also allows users to define expressions interactively and then execute them. Users can also control the configuration options supported by the language interactively. The plug-in also includes a persistence mechanism to save and reload mappings. Additionally, we have written a development environment that includes Java APIs for interacting with the language from software applications.

Expression Processing Engine and Debugging

The expression processing engine takes an XML document, a base OWL ontology, and a set of XMLMaster expressions as input. It then generates a target OWL ontology from these expressions. The expressions are processed in three phases. In first phase, every expression is preprocessed and content specified by references is retrieved from the XML document. This content, which will either specify an OWL entity, a data type name, or a data value, is substituted for each reference in a mapping expression to generate one or more Manchester Syntax expressions.

At the end of phase one, a summary display allows users to preview the expressions that were generated. This display allows users to see the final entity names expanded within their enclosing expressions. It also indicates how each reference was resolved within an expression. For example, a reference may resolve to an existing OWL entity or may name a new entity that it created on demand.

If the user is satisfied with the generated expressions, they can activate the second stage of the mapping process. This phase declares all OWL entities referenced in mapping expressions that are not already declared in the target ontology. The type specification for each reference—be it explicit or inferred—is used to generate the appropriate declaration clause. Any super class, super property, individual class membership, or data type specifications in the reference are also declared in this phase.

The third phase occurs once the referenced entities have been declared. At this point, the expressions are sent to a Manchester OWL Syntax processor. It generates an OWL ontology containing the OWL axioms specified by the expressions. The generated ontology can be saved separately to produce a new ontology, or it can be used to expand an existing one.

USE CASE

The Annotation and Image Markup project (AIM) recently developed an information model that describes the semantic contents of radiological images [24]. AIM defines an XML-encoded information model that describes anatomic structures and visual observations in the images. Information about image annotations is recorded in AIM's information model, which is described using XML Schema, with the goal of enabling the consistent representation, storage, and transfer of the semantic meaning of image features. A variety of tools have been developed to produce image annotations in AIM format.

Our goal was to develop OWL- and SWRL-based reasoning methods for automated calculation and classification of tumor response from image annotations. To perform this reasoning, we first had to produce an OWL equivalent of the AIM XML-based information model. This model represents all the concepts in the AIM XML Schema, and it can be used to store OWL instances of AIM annotations. We then required a mechanism to transform annotations from AIM XML document instances to instances in the OWL model.

Our initial approach used a tool developed by the authors [2]. Unfortunately, this tool required a cumbersome mapping process that involved interactive specification of mappings to generate an OWL ontology from an XML Schema. It then required manual generation of SWRL rules to transform instances to OWL. These rules were difficult for non specialists to write and were cumbersome to maintain and debug for greater than a small number of mappings. Using XMLMaster, we defined an equivalent mapping process.

Transforming AIM Schema to OWL

We first defined a set of mappings to take an AIM XML Schema and generate an OWL ontology containing equivalent definitions of the entities it describes. An XML Schema document is represented in XML so can be directly processed by our language. Figure 2 shows a portion of the AIM schema.

```
<xs:schema targetNameSpace="gme://caCORE..">
...
<xs:simpleType name="CalculationResultIdentifier">
 <xs:restriction base="xs:string">
  <xs:enumeration value="Scalar"/>
  <xs:enumeration value="Vector"/>
  ...
 </xs:restriction>
</xs:simpleType>
...
<xs:complexType name="Annotation"...>
...
 <xs:attribute name="id" type="xs:integer">
 <xs:attribute name="version" type="xs:string"/>
</xs:complexType>
...
<xs:complexType name="ImageAnnotation">
 <xs:complexContent>
  <xs:extension base="Annotation">
  ...
  </xs:extension>
 </xs:complexContent>
</xs:complexType>
</xs:schema>
```

Figure 2. Portion of AIM XML Schema.

Figure 3 shows a selection of the XMLMaster expressions. The first expression generates an OWL class declaration for simple schema types. The second expression deals with extended complex types and generates classes and subclass relationships for them. The third expression declares OWL enumerated classes from an XML Schema value enumeration. Each enumeration value will become an individual in the enumerated class. The fourth expression declares OWL object properties from element definitions. The final example defines OWL data property declarations for attribute of type string. Similar expressions are written for other types.

```
1. Class: @//xs:simpleType/@name
2. Class: @//xs:complexType/@name
   SubClassOf: @./*/xs:entension/@base
3. Class: @//xs:simpleType/@name
   EquivalentTo: { @./*/xs:enumeration/@value }
4. ObjectProperty: @//xs:element/@name
5. DataProperty:
   @//xs:attribute[@type="xs:string"]/@name
   Range: xsd:string
```

Figure 3. Selection of AIM XML Schema to OWL mappings.

As can be seen from these examples, mappings can be incrementally constructed. The basic class declaration in example 1, for example, is supplemented by the more complex declaration in example 3. The key is that references to the same element or attribute in different mapping expressions resolve to the same OWL entity declared from them. Expressions can thus be independently evaluated in any order. As a futher consequence, individual mapping expression can be relatively concise. Users can also decide how much of the XML Schema description they want to capture in OWL and add mappings later if more expressivity is desired.

```
<ImageAnnotation id="232" version="1.0"...>
 <patient>...</patient>
 ...
 <anatomicEntities>
  <AnatomicEntity id="22" codeValue="RDD446".../>
  <AnatomicEntity id="29" codeValue="RDD448".../>
  ...
 </anatomicEntities>
</ImageAnnotation>
```

Figure 4. Portion of AIM XML image annotation instance.

Transforming AIM Instances to OWL

Figure 4 shows an image annotation for a single patient. It defines a set of anatomic entities referenced by the annotation. Its terms are described using the RadLex image observation ontology [25]. Figure 5 shows two relevant mappings in which location encoding is used so declared individuals are given automatically generated identifiers. The first mapping declares an ImageAnnotation individual from an AIM image annotation element and associates it with information defined in the element's attributes and sub-elements. The second declares AnatomicEntity individuals and performs similar associations. In particular, it

takes the anatomic entity sub-element and resolves the codeValue property to a term in the RadLex ontology through its prefix *rdlx*.

```
1. Individual: @/ImageAnnotation
   Types: aim:ImageAnnotation
   Facts:
    aim:id @./@id,
    aim:version @./@version,
    aim:anatomicEntities @./*/AnatomicEntity
2. Individual: @/ImageAnnotation/*/AnatomicEntity
   Types: aim:AnatomicEntity
   Facts:
    aim:id @./@id,
    aim:codeValue @./@codeValue(mm:prefix="rdlx")
```

Figure 5. Selection of AIM XML instance to OWL mappings.

Like schema mappings, instance mappings can be constructed incrementally. For example, the first mapping declares an image annotation individual and associates it with anatomic entity individuals declared from its AnatomicEntity sub-elements. The details of each anatomic entity are defined in the second mapping. These elements resolve to the same declared individual in both expressions and can thus be linked in this way. As the examples also show, an associated XML Schema is not required when defining instance mappings.

DISCUSSION

Previous approaches for mapping information from XML to OWL suffered from a variety of limitations. Although recent approaches have addressed shortcomings in selective extraction of information from XML documents, they have weak OWL ontology generation capabilities. Typically, they support a small number of predefined mappings, which limits the expressivity of the resulting ontologies. Other weaknesses include requiring an associated XML Schema in order to process a document, and limited support for dealing with unstructured element content.

To address these limitations, we developed XMLMaster, a custom domain specific language. It combines the Manchester OWL Syntax and XPath, two well-known technologies and standards from the semantic and syntactic worlds. The resulting language supports flexible extraction of information from XML documents and a compact, user-friendly, OWL-centric approach for generating OWL ontologies. It can deal with XML documents that may not have an associated XML Schema description. XMLMaster can be used to generate new ontologies from scratch or to extend existing ones with new mapped content. These ontologies can contain individual and class axioms. Our experience with a similar language for mapping from spreadsheets to OWL [2] leads us to believe that users who are familiar with OWL and XML will learn it easily.

Future work includes the development of a visual tool to allow non specialist users to define mappings from XML to OWL. Using a sample set of XMLMaster mappings defined for a variety of XML data sources, we plan to identify common transformations. We will use these transformations to develop a set of template mappings. These templates will be used to drive the design of a GUI-based tool to interactively define mappings. Other extensions include supporting XQuery [26] to provide even more expressivity in processing XML documents. Similarly, adding support for user-defined functions will enhance text processing options.

The software will be released shortly as an open source plug-in to the Protégé-OWL ontology development environment [23].

ACKNOWLEDGMENTS

This research was supported in part by the N.L.M. under grants LM007885 and LM009607 and by STTR Award #0750543 from the N.S.F. We thank Valerie Natale for her valuable editorial comments.

REFERENCES

[1] Nyulas, C., O'Connor, M.J, Tu, S.W. DataMaster - a plug-in for Importing Schemas and Data from Relational Databases into Protégé. *10th International Protégé Conference*, Budapest, Hungary (2007).

[2] O'Connor, M.J., Halaschek-Wiener, C., Musen, M.A. Mapping Master: a Flexible Approach for Mapping Spreadsheets to OWL. *9th International Semantic Web Conference*, Shanghai, China (2010).

[3] O'Connor, M.J. and Das, A.K. Semantic Reasoning with XML-based Biomedical Information Models. *13th World Congress on Medical Informatics*, Cape Town, South Africa (2010).

[4] McGuinness, D. and van Harmelen, F. OWL Web Ontology Language. W3C (2004).

[5] XML Schema: http://www.w3.org/XML/Schema. W3C (2004).

[6] Manchester OWL Syntax: http://www.w3.org/TR/owl2-manchester-syntax/. W3C (2010).

[7] XML Path Language (XPath): http://www.w3.org/TR/xpath20/. W3C (2007).

[8] Klein, M.C.A. Interpreting XML Documents via an RDF Schema Ontology. *13th International Workshop on Database and Expert Systems Applications*, Aix-en-Provence, France (2002).

[9] Battle, S. Gloze: XML to RDF and back again. *1st Jena User Conference*, Bristol, UK (2006).

[10] Ferdinand, M., Zirpins, C., Trastour, D. Lifting XML Schema to OWL. *Web Engineering - 4th International Conference*, Munich, Germany (2004).

[11] Bohring, H. and Auer, S. Mapping XML to OWL Ontologies. *Leipziger Informatik Tage,* Vol. 72, Leipzig, Germany (2005).

[12] Garcia, R., Perdrix, F., Gil, R. Ontological Infrastructure for a Semantic Newspaper. *Semantic Web Annotations for Multimedia Workshop*, Edinburgh, U.K. (2006).

[13] Kunfermann, P. and Drumm, C. Lifting XML Schemas to Ontologies - The Concept Finder Algorithm. *First International Workshop on Mediation in Semantic Web Services*, Amsterdam, Netherlands (2005).

[14] Lehti, P. and Frankhauser, P. XML Data Integration with OWL: Experiences and Challenges. *Symposium on Applications and the Internet*, Toyko, Japan (2004).

[15] Xiao, H. and Cruz, I.F. Integrating and Exchanging XML Data Using Ontologies. *Journal of Data Semantics* (2006).

[16] Cruz, I.F., Xiao, H., Hsu, F. An Ontology-Based Framework for XML Semantic Integration. *Eighth International Database Engineering and Applications Symposium*, Coimbra, Portugal (2004).

[17] Reif, G., Gall, H, Jazayeri, M. WEESA - Web Engineering for Semantic Web Applications. *14th World Wide Web Conference*, Chiba, Japan (2005).

[18] Kobeissy, N., Girod Genet, M., Zeghlache, D. Mapping XML to OWL for Seamless Information Retrieval in Context-aware Environments. *International Conference on Pervasive Services*, Istanbul, Turkey (2007).

[19] Tous, R., Garcia, R., Rodriguez, E., Delgado, J. Architecture of a Semantic XPath Processor. Application to Digital Rights Management. *6th E-Commerce and Web Technologies*, Copenhagen, Denmark (2005).

[20] SWRL: http://www.w3.org/Submission/SWRL/. W3C. (2004).

[21] Anicic, N., Ivezic, N., Marjanovic, Z. Mapping XML Schema to OWL. *Enterprise Interoperability*, Part V, pp. 243-252, Springer, Berlin (2007).

[22] XMLMaster: http://protege.cim3.net/cgi-bin/wiki.pl?XMLMaster

[23] Protégé: http://protege.stanford.edu

[24] Rubin, D.L., Mongkolwat, P., Kleper, V., Supekar, K., Channin, D.S. Medical Imaging on the Semantic Web: Annotation and Image Markup. *AAAI Spring Symposium*, Stanford, CA (2008).

[25] RadLex: http://www.radlex.org

[26] XQuery: http://www.w3.org/TR/xquery. W3C (2010).

An Analysis of Collaborative Patterns in Large-Scale Ontology Development Projects

Sean M. Falconer
Stanford University
Stanford, CA, USA
sfalc@stanford.edu

Tania Tudorache
Stanford University
Stanford, CA, USA
tudorache@stanford.edu

Natalya F. Noy
Stanford University
Stanford, CA, USA
noy@stanford.edu

ABSTRACT

Today, distributed teams collaboratively create and maintain more and more ontologies. To support this type of ontology development, software engineers are introducing a new generation of tools. However, we know relatively little about how existing large-scale collaborative ontology development works and what user workflows the tools must support. In this paper, we analyze our experience in supporting several such projects. We describe a visual and interactive project-management tool that we have developed, which helps ontology developers explore historical ontology change and discussion data. We present the results of qualitative and quantitative studies of the collaborative activity associated with three large-scale ontology-development projects. Based on the analysis, we conclude that domain and ontology experts have different patterns of ontology editing behavior, which has important implications for ontology-development tools.

Categories and Subject Descriptors

H.5.3 [**Information Interfaces and Presentation**]: Group and Organization Interfaces—*Computer-supported cooperative work, Web-based interaction, Evaluation/methodology*; D.2.8 [**Software Engineering**]: Metrics—*Process metrics*

General Terms

Measurement, Human Factors

Keywords

Collaboration patterns, Role identification, Authoring tools, Collaborative and social approaches to knowledge management and acquisition, Knowledge acquisition tools, Knowledge engineering and modelling methodologies

1. INTRODUCTION

In the past, the development of ontologies has mostly been restricted to individuals or small groups. However, knowledge-intensive applications today depend on large-scale ontologies. As a result, ontologies are becoming so large that no single individual can possibly maintain and develop the entire terminology. Large biomedical ontologies, containing tens of thousands of classes, such as the Gene Ontology (GO), are possible only through collaborative development. Indeed, most large-scale ontology-development projects now involve a collaborative effort [12].

To support these large-scale projects, a growing number of collaborative ontology editors now exist [8]; e.g. NeON toolkit[1], Collaborative Protégé [14], Semantic wikis [3], and Knoodl[2]. Despite the number of tools available, they are still very much in their infancy. The tools are for the most part generic and it is not obvious how they can be used to support different collaborative workflows for different projects.

In this paper, we take some of the first steps to learn more about the ways in which different collaborative ontology development projects currently work. What are the similarities and differences in terms of the roles that participants in the projects fulfill? What characteristics distinguish the role of a contributor? Is there a relationship between these roles and the roles of those contributing to open-source software (OSS) or projects such as Wikipedia? Can we re-use techniques, software, and approaches from these communities? Finally, can a deeper understanding of these projects and roles inform tool and ontology development?

We need to answer these questions in order to develop better and more flexible tools. To address these questions, we first need tools to help explore the collaborative activity of ontology projects. Thus, we developed a visual analysis tool that helps users explore the collaborative activity (changes and notes) associated with an ontology project. The supported visualizations allow an individual to study the history of their ontology. In this paper, we present this analysis tool and the use of it in studying the collaborative patterns for three different ontology development projects with varying workflows and scale. Based on the observed patterns, we apply clustering and statistical analysis to identify the implicit roles of ontology authors. We also present the analysis of the relationship between changes that occur in the ontology and how users communicate in distributed environments. We found that different user roles, such as domain specialist versus ontology expert, lead to different behavioral patterns in terms of a user's collaborative editing workflow. We discuss the implications of this observation and other findings on tool design and ontology development.

2. THREE LARGE-SCALE BIOMEDICAL ONTOLOGIES

To study the changes and collaborative patterns that users follow in collaborative ontology development, we collected data from

---

9[1]http://www.neon-project.org
9[2]http://knoodl.com

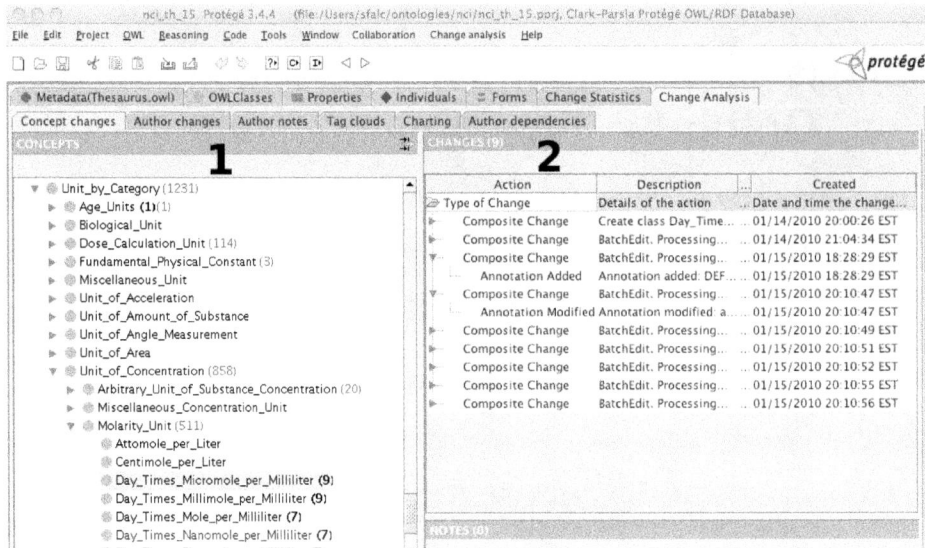

Figure 1: A screenshot of the Change-Analysis plugin for the NCI Thesaurus. Panel (1) is a class-tree representation of the NCI Thesaurus. The gray numbers in the tree represent the total number of changes in the selected branch of the ontology, while the bold numbers represent the number of changes specifically for the selected term. Panel (2) lists all the changes associated with the selected term.

three diverse projects: (1) the National Cancer Institute's Thesaurus (NCI Thesaurus); (2) the World Health Organization's (WHO) International Classification of Disease, revision 11 (ICD-11); and (3) the Biomedical Resources Ontology (BRO), being developed under the auspices of the US National Institutes of Health (NIH). The projects vary significantly, both in their scale and in the workflow that they adopt for making and publishing changes. Thus, our analysis is rather general and it is tied to real ontology-development efforts. We now briefly describe the three projects.

The National Cancer Institute's Thesaurus (NCI Thesaurus) [13] has over 80,000 classes and has been in development for several years. It is a reference vocabulary covering areas for clinical care, translational and basic research, and cancer biology. A multidisciplinary team of editors works to edit and update the terminology based on their respective areas of expertise, following a well-defined workflow. A lead editor reviews all changes made by the editors. The lead editor accepts or rejects the changes and publishes a new version of the NCI Thesaurus. The NCI Thesaurus is an OWL ontology, which uses many OWL primitives such as defined classes, restrictions, and which defines domains and ranges for object properties.

The International Classification of Disease (ICD) revision 11 (ICD-11)[3] is the standard diagnostic classification that is used to encode information relevant to epidemiology, health management, and clinical use. Health officials use ICD in all United Nations member countries to compile basic health statistics, to monitor health-related spending, and to inform policy makers. As a result, ICD is an essential resource for health care all over the world. ICD traces its origins to the 19th century and has since been revised at regular intervals. The current in-use version, ICD-10, the 10th revision of the ICD, contains more than 20,000 terms.

The development of ICD-11 represents a major change in the revision process. Previous versions were developed by relatively small groups of experts in face-to-face meetings. ICD-11 is being developed via a Web-based process with many experts contributing to, evaluating, and reviewing the content online. It is also the first version to use OWL as its representational format. Unlike the NCI Thesaurus, the ICD-11 ontology is in early phases of development.

The Biomedical Resources Ontology (BRO) originated in the Biositemaps project[4] developed by the Biositemaps Working Group of the NIH National Centers for Biomedical Computing.[5] The Biositemaps project is a mechanism for researchers working in biomedicine to publish meta-data about biomedical data, tools, and services. Applications can then aggregate this information for applications such as semantic search. BRO is the enabling technology, a controlled terminology for describing the resource types, areas of research, and activity of a biomedical related resource. BRO is being developed by a small group of editors, who use a Web-based interface to modify the ontology and to carry out discussions to reach consensus on their modeling choices.

These projects represent important and active development efforts in the biomedical informatics field. All three projects use Collaborative Protégé for ontology development. Collaborative Protégé is a plugin to the open-source ontology and knowledge-base editor Protégé [14]. The plugin uses a client–server model, where authors make contributions via the client and the server stores and manages these contributions. Users can hold discussions, chat, provide notes on ontology components and make changes. Among the three projects, only the NCI project has a well defined workflow that is also enforced by a custom editing plugin for Protégé. The ICD-11 and BRO projects do not have any formally defined roles or workflow. In the two latter projects, all users have the ability to modify the ontology in any way.

We used information about two types of collaborative activity in our analysis: (1) **change logs** provided the information on each change that the users performed, who performed the change, and when; and (2) **notes** that users added to classes and properties in the ontology, along with the information on who created the note and when. Users add the notes to describe their rationale for changes or to discuss modeling issues pertaining to a particular class to reach consensus.

Collaborative Protégé stores ontology changes and discussions,

9³http://www.who.int/classifications/icd/ICDRevision/

9⁴http://biositemaps.ncbcs.org/
9⁵http://www.ncbcs.org

as well as the metadata associated with the changes and discussions as instance in the Protégé Change and Annotation Ontology (ChAO) [9]. Change types are ontology classes in ChAO and changes in the domain ontology are instances of these classes. Similarly, notes that users attach to classes or threaded discussions, which the users can have within the Protégé tool, are also stored in ChAO.

For our studies, we used these three domain ontologies and the change data and notes associated with each project over certain time periods. For the NCI Thesaurus, the change data consist of data collected from October 5th, 2009 to April 14th, 2010. During that period, there was a total of 43,702 changes. There were a total of 10 authors involved; however, individual contributions ranged from as few as 259 changes to as many as 14,220. The authors of this project do not make use of the discussion feature of Collaborative Protégé, thus no notes were available. The ICD-11 change data consist of changes and notes collected from November 2009 to May 2010. A total of 19 authors created 14,554 changes and 4,768 notes. Like those of the NCI Thesaurus, individual author contributions ranged greatly from as little as one change to as many as 7,707. Finally, the BRO project includes data collected from February to March 2010. This project is much smaller than the previous two: there are only five authors involved, a total of 762 changes, and 373 notes. Contributions also range greatly, from 17 to 368.

Before describing our analysis, we describe a tool that we developed for assisting in the project management of collaborative ontology development. Such tools are essential for understanding where changes occur in an ontology, who is making the changes, what areas of the ontology are active, and how much impact a change may have. We use this tool in our qualitative analysis to inspect author behavior.

3. THE CHANGE-ANALYSIS PLUGIN

We developed a visual analysis tool to assist with the management of collaborative ontology-development projects. The tool, called the **Change-Analysis Plugin**, is a plugin for the Protégé editor. It works with Collaborative Protégé to manage ontology changes in any ontology. The plugin provides visual representations of the change and note data associated with the ontology.

The "Concept changes" view (Figure 1) enables users to see all the ontology changes that are stored in ChAO for an ontology. The gray numbers in the tree represent the total number of changes for the selected branch in the ontology. For example, there are 1231 changes in the subtree rooted at "Unit_by_Category" (the top term in the tree). The bold numbers represent the number of changes that have occurred directly at the selected class. As shown in the figure, there were 9 changes for the selected term. A user can apply filters to this view to show changes made by certain authors or over a certain time period.

Another view provides a visual representation of changes over time for each specific author. In this visualization, a stacked-area chart displays the number of change contributions that an author has made over different time intervals (days, weeks, months and years). The area in the chart corresponds to the number of changes in a specific time interval. This view enables project managers to get a quick overview of the level of activity of each member of the team over time.

We also provide a graph-based visualization of the author dependency network. The nodes in the network correspond to the authors. Two nodes are linked (there is a dependency between the authors) if the two authors have modified either the same term or two terms that are related via an ontology relationship (i.e. subclass or property relation). We consider both explicit and implicit dependencies. Two authors have an **explicit dependency** if they have

edited the same term. For example, Figure 2(a) shows that authors 2, 5, 7, and 8 have made changes to some of the same terms, while the other authors have made completely independent changes. The graph defines a social network describing the relationship between authors and potentially overlapping changes.

Two authors have an **implicit dependency** if they have modified terms that are related in the ontology through a subclass or property relationship. For example, two authors did not make changes to the same term, but one author modified the direct superclass of a term that was modified by a different author. These two authors have an implicit dependency. Users can specify how close the two terms need to be to each other in order for the dependency to exist. For instance, one may create a network where two authors have an implicit dependency only when they modified two terms that are directly linked to each other. Or define a network where authors are linked if they modified two terms that would require one to traverse n links in the ontology graph. As we include changes made further and further away, the social network becomes more tightly bound (see Figure 2(b)).

In addition to providing the different visualization mechanisms for exploring the change data, the Change-Analysis Plugin provides similar views for exploring the note data. We used the plugin to perform qualitative analysis of the data. By using the different views available in the tool and by systematically exploring the data across all three projects, we were able to make several important observations about possible patterns of collaboration.

4. QUALITATIVE FINDINGS

We explored the ontology changes and notes left by developers in our three data sets (Section 2). During the exploration, we tried to extract patterns of consistent author behavior for each of the ontology projects. We were able to make several observations about users' behavior.

First, we noticed that in each of the three projects, we could differentiate the authors by where in the class hierarchy they performed their changes. It appeared that certain authors made edits mostly within a single sub-hierarchy, whereas a few others did not have an obvious pattern and their changes appeared throughout different subject areas. We also noted that some authors appeared consistently to make changes at a higher level in the ontology hierarchy, whereas others primarily made changes at the leaf level.

Second, we investigated the overlap between authors and the changes that they make. We noticed that although most changes associated with a particular term were performed by a single author, some terms had changes by multiple authors. Moreover, some authors seemed to participate in more of these overlapping edits. We used the graph-based visualization available in the Change-Analysis Plugin (e.g. Figure 2(a)), as well as the "Concept View" (e.g. Figure 1) to explore these relationships. Finally, by analyzing the types of changes committed by authors across the various projects, we observed that some authors primarily made certain types of changes, such as deletions, whereas others primarily made additions or edits.

In the next section, we test the hypothesis that these different patterns of behavior were associated with a given author's *expertise* or *role* in the project. We wished to confirm whether these observational characteristics really did exist, and whether these characteristics could be used to describe different user roles in a collaborative development project.

5. IDENTIFYING USER ROLES

Identifying roles that different authors play across different projects allows us to better understand the process of collaborative ontology

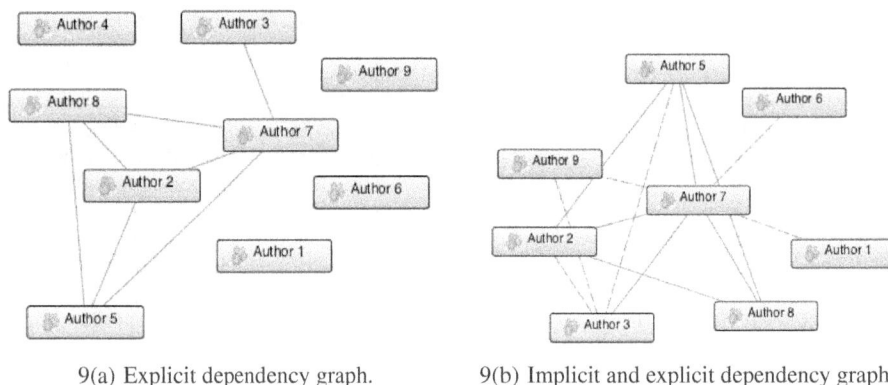

9(a) Explicit dependency graph.   9(b) Implicit and explicit dependency graph.

Figure 2: Explicit and implicit dependency graph for authors in a release of the NCI Thesaurus. Explicit dependencies are represented by solid edges while implicit dependencies are represented by dotted edges. Implicit dependencies are included for changes up to five degrees of separation.

development, the similarities among different projects, and help us build better tools to support different user behavior. We define an author's role as a set of expected behaviors. To analyze what roles exist, we first created a feature-vector representation of an author based on the observations that we previously derived from the qualitative exploration of the data (Section 4). Using these vectors, we applied clustering to derive logical groupings for the authors. We then applied statistical analysis to determine what characteristics make each cluster unique.

5.1 Representing authors

Let A represent the set of all authors. We represent an author $a \in A$ as a vector $\vec{a} = (C_{del}, C_{add}, C_{mov}, C_{pro}, M, L, D, O, CE)$. The first four features represent the percentage of a change contribution of a given type (deletions, additions, moves, and property changes) relative to all change contributions, for an author a. The other five features are numerical representations of the qualitative characteristics that we described in Section 4, such as the location of the changes. Table 1 provides information about these features.

We measure the centrality of an author, CE, by using the author dependency network that we described in Section 3 (see Figure 2(a) for an example). We first calculate the degree of an author node as defined by the explicit author-dependency network. We combine this value with the author-node degrees calculated based on five different implicit dependency networks. We create each of these networks by considering changes of distance 1, 2, 3, 4, and 5 jumps away from a given changed term. Finally, we normalize this average degree by dividing each value by the largest average. That is, the most highly connected or "central" author across all networks will have a value of one, while a very unconnected, less "central" author will have a value closer to zero.

5.2 Repeated K-means

Before analyzing the author feature vectors, we discarded data on authors who made fewer than 10 changes so as not to skew the analysis. We classify these authors as *experimental contributors* and there were six such authors. They were present only in the ICD-11 project and we believe they are mostly users that were curious about the project, experimented with a few changes, and then never came back.

To analyze the authors contributions and to uncover the roles, we applied repeated K-means clustering to divide the authors into different groups based on their similarity. Following the method outlined by Liu and Keselj [4], we applied the K-means method repeatedly for values $k = 2$ up to $k = 8$. We set a maximum of 8 clusters in order to avoid a large number of single entity clusters.

For each k, we evaluated the quality of the clusters using metrics for calculating the cluster compactness and separation [7]. After applying repeated K-means and measuring the quality of the clusters, we found $k = 5$ to be the optimal number of clusters.

5.3 Analysis

Once we established the groupings for the authors from the three projects, we analyzed what characteristics made a cluster unique and tied the particular authors together. To determine these characteristics, we performed multiple Analysis of Variance (ANOVA) calculations to determine the statistically significant features of each cluster. That is, for each of the nine features outlined in Table 1, we performed ANOVA to check for statistical difference in that particular feature when compared across all five clusters.

5.4 Results

There were statistically significant differences ($p < 0.05$) across all features except the multi-author edit feature (see Table 2). Besides the values for relative depth, values in the table closer to 0 indicate a low activity level for a particular feature, whereas values closer to 1 represent a higher level of activity. For relative depth, values above 1 indicate most edits occur deep in the hierarchy, while values lower than 1 indicate edits occur closer to the root level.

ANOVA tells us only whether there is a statistically significant difference between some clusters for a given feature; it does not tell us where the difference is. To pinpoint the differences, we applied the Tukey range test, which compares all pairs of means for a given independent variable (i.e., feature in our author data set). Using the results, we determined sets of characteristics that describe each of the clusters as well as cluster labels (see Table 3). We discovered that the five clusters correspond to five clearly discernible roles that users fulfill in the collaborative ontology-development process. These roles are: (1) *ontology expert*, (2) *content manager*, (3) *domain expert*, (4) *central domain expert*, and (5) *content editor*. We will now describe how these roles varied between the projects and how the different roles relate to the workflow that each project uses.

5.5 Findings

Our analysis indicates that, despite all three projects having different approaches to collaboration and change management, there are interesting commonalities in terms of author roles. Every cluster consisted of authors from multiple projects, except for the "Central domain expert" role, but no cluster contained authors from all three projects. We believe that this distribution is largely the result of the different approaches that each project takes to managing

Table 1: Summary of author features used in author vector representation.

Symbol	Feature	Explanation
C_{del}	Deletion	Ratio of deletion changes to all changes committed.
C_{add}	Addition	Ratio of terms added to all changes committed.
C_{mov}	Move	Ratio of terms moved to all changes committed.
C_{pro}	Property change	Ratio of terms where a property has been added/modified to all changes committed.
M	Multi-author change	Number of times an author edits a term that is also edited by another author divided by the total number of terms modified by the author.
L	Leaf changes	Number of times an author edits a leaf concept term divided by the total number of terms modified by the author.
D	Relative depth	The average depth of a term change relative to the average depth of any given concept term in the ontology.
O	One hierarchy	The percentage of changes an author makes that are restricted to one level of the ontology hierarchy.
CE	Centrality	The average centrality of an author.

Table 2: Feature comparison of means across all five clusters. Features correspond to those described in Table 1.

Feature	Means					p-value
	Cluster 1	Cluster 2	Cluster 3	Cluster 4	Cluster 5	
Deletion	0.068	0.436	0.0858	0.040	0.077	0.023
Addition	0.352	0.220	0.800	0.464	0.270	< 0.001
Move	0.256	0.010	0.018	0.189	0.005	< 0.001
Property change	0.307	0.242	0.238	0.265	0.757	0.001
Multi-author change	0.528	0.469	0.127	0.051	0.328	0.060
Leaf changes	0.443	0.818	0.783	0.628	0.687	0.001
Relative depth	0.833	1.35	1.58	1.33	0.591	0.001
Centrality	0.889	0.448	0.537	0.753	0.973	< 0.001
One hierarchy	0.470	0.970	0.936	0.855	0.543	< 0.001

changes and the different scopes of the ontologies. For instance, the ICD-11 project consists of many more contributors in comparison to both the NCI Thesaurus and BRO. As with the NCI Thesaurus, there are specific authors with specific areas of expertise, thus both projects have a large number of authors in the "Domain expert" cluster. However, like BRO, there are authors that are experts in ontology classification and are in charge of organizing the hierarchy.

Interestingly, the ICD-11 project does not appear to have a designated "Content editor" role. BRO and the NCI Thesaurus have much smaller, rigidly constructed teams where specific editors monitor changes and modify existing content. In contrast, ICD-11 currently does not have a formal quality-assurance process. ICD-11 is also in the early stages of its development, so the most of the effort may currently be more organizational and focused on adding content.

6. COLLABORATION AND CHANGES

In addition to changes, we also analyzed the data on the notes that authors added to ontology elements, either to provide rationale for their changes or to carry out discussions among the authors. In analyzing the notes, we were interested in answering the following research questions:

Q1 : Is there a relationship between changes and author discussions with respect to a specific ontology term?

Q2 : Do people who make a lot of changes also participate in a lot of discussions?

6.1 Analysis

To answer these questions, we used a quantitative analysis approach where we measured the correlation between change and discussion activity. Unfortunately, since the editors of the NCI Thesaurus do not use the notes feature of Collaborative Protégé, we had to exclude this project from our analysis. In all tests of correlation, we used the Pearson correlation coefficient, which measures the linear dependence between two variables or series. It yields a value between +1 and -1, where positive values have a positive correlation (i.e. values go up and down together) and negative values have a negative correlation (i.e. values go up in one series, down in the other, and vice versa).

6.2 Results

To answer the first research question regarding the relationship between change and author discussion, we began by computing binary change and note vectors for all terms in the ICD-11 and BRO ontologies. For each term in the ontologies, we computed two binary vectors representing the changes and notes that occurred. A term has a value of 0 in the change vector if no change was ever recorded for that term, and a value of 1 if a change did take place. The note vector was constructed in a similar manner. Given these vectors, we can test whether the presence of change activity is correlated with discussion activity.

In ICD-11 we found that the two activities were positively correlated with a coefficient of 0.841 (p-value < 0.001). Similarly, in BRO the two series were positively correlated with a coefficient of 0.274 (p-value < 0.001).

We also wished to test whether a greater number of changes for a term was related to a greater number of note activity. To test this hypothesis, we again created change and note vectors for all terms in ICD-11 and BRO. However, this time instead of assigning values of 0 and 1, a term in the change vector has value of N, where N is the number of changes that occurred involving the particular term. We computed a similar vector for note counts. Given these two vectors for each ontology, we can test the correlation between greater changes implying greater note activity.

Interestingly, we found that in ICD-11, the relationship between the rate of change and note activity was still highly correlated (coefficient = 0.543, p-value < 0.001), although less so than in the binary comparison. In BRO, the correlation between these two vec-

Table 3: Summary of roles

Cluster	Role	Characteristics	Primary activity	Size
Cluster 1	Ontology expert	Highly central author, makes changes over multiple hierarchies, involved in fewer leaf changes than domain experts, but performs a lot of movement changes in the hierarchy.	Organizational	4 authors: 3 ICD 1 BRO
Cluster 2	Content manager	Edits mostly in one sub-hierarchy, low centrality, performs few movement changes, but a high number of deletions.	Hierarchy clean-up	4 authors: 3 ICD 1 NCI
Cluster 3	Domain expert	Edits mostly deep within one hierarchy, low centrality, few moves, but lots of concept additions.	Content creation	12 authors: 5 ICD 7 NCI
Cluster 4	Central domain expert	Edits are restricted primarily to one sub-hierarchy, however, unlike domain experts, these authors are much more central and their changes occur at a higher level in the hierarchy. They also perform more movement operations than domain experts.	Management and content creation of a specific area of the ontology	2 authors: 2 ICD
Cluster 5	Content editor	Highly central author, makes changes over multiple hierarchies, lots of leaf changes, and a high number of property changes.	Editing of existing content	6 authors: 2 NCI 4 BRO

tors was similar to the binary version (coefficient = 0.258, p-value < 0.001).

To address the second research question, we compared the correlation between the number of changes an author makes and the number of notes the author creates. In ICD-11 we found that these two series were highly correlated with a coefficient of 0.953 (p-value < 0.001). However, in BRO, there was no correlation between the number of changes made by an author and the number of notes.

6.3 Findings

As we mentioned, we found a correlation between change and discussion activity. This correlation in itself is perhaps not particularly surprising, but it is surprising how strongly correlated the levels of activity are. In particular, in the ICD-11 project, a term that is changed more often suggests that the term may also be the focus of more discussion. This high correlation between the change and the discussion activity may be related to the open editing process for ICD-11. Since there are many authors contributing to the project, there may be greater social pressure to document their changes as well as to provide feedback about the changes made by an individual. This type of social pressure is well documented within the open-source software community. Since everything a developer produces is freely available to the public, there is social pressure to make the source code as readable, maintainable, and stable as possible [10].

Also interesting is the difference between the ICD-11 and BRO projects in terms of the correlation between author's change and note activity. One possible explanation for this difference is that the workflow for the projects are different. BRO is a much smaller project, involving far fewer authors. There are authors with far more notes than changes. Interestingly, all these authors are classified as "Content editors" in Table 3—a role that we did not find in ICD-11. This low correlation between the changes and the notes activity may be a characteristic of this particular ontology developer role. However, without more data, we cannot test this hypothesis.

7. DISCUSSION

Our analysis of author roles indicated that domain experts (including central ones) edit primarily within a single hierarchy of the ontology, whereas ontology experts and content editors work over multiple areas of the ontology. This difference in behavior is an important finding that has potential implications for tool and workflow design. Ontology-editing tools like Protégé load and display the entire ontology. For a domain expert, the ontology editor most likely contains large amounts of extraneous information that only hinder the content contributions of the user. Perhaps we need a role-based editing workflow that displays only the relevant part of the ontology to a domain expert.

It may be useful to analyze each author's historical change and note activity to help compute that author's *degree of interest* (DOI) [2]. A user's DOI is a predictive measure about the topics in which a user is potentially interested. Tools such as Mylyn[6] combine DOI with task context to reduce user-interface complexity by displaying only certain parts of a software project's source code during development. A similar approach could use the change data to filter or highlight important parts of the ontology. This information could also be used to help reduce ontology load times and memory consumption. Furthermore, the change data associated with domain experts also helps distinguish different topic areas of the ontology. These topic areas are a potential starting point for the modularization of an ontology.

There appears to be some similarity between collaborative ontology development and the open-source software (OSS) and Wikipedia communities. Many researchers have started to analyze the roles of contributors in OSS projects. Nakakoji and colleagues classified members of the OSS community into eight different roles [6], while Xu and colleagues reduced this number to four [15]. The four roles that Xu and colleagues describe include only users that make contributions directly to the software of the project: *Project Leaders*, *Core Developers*, *Co-developers*, and *Active Users*. The core developer role is somewhat analogous to the domain expert role in ontology development. Both are the main content creators for a project. A project leader in OSS are the project administrators: they guide the vision and direction of the project. We believe a similar role most likely exists for collaborative ontology-development projects. However, in the three projects that we analyzed, we did not identify this role from the cluster analysis. The lack of an explicit project leader role may be in part due to the project leaders for these ontology development efforts not being active contributors in terms of changes and notes. For example, in the ICD-11 project, there is a revision steering group as well as project managers that help manage and coordinate the project, but do not make active change contributions.

Also in OSS research, Bird *et al.* examined the relationship between mailing list activity and development activity [1]. Similar to

---

9[6]http://www.eclipse.org/mylyn/

our analysis of change and note activity, their findings indicate that there is a strong relationship between these two types of activities.

Liu and Ram analyzed contributions made by users of Wikipedia, following a similar clustering methodology to the one that we have described here [5]. They discovered six different roles: *All-round Editors*, *Watchdogs*, *Starters*, *Content Justifiers*, *Copy Editors*, and *Cleaners*. There are some similarities between these roles to the roles we uncovered. For example, in ontology development, domain experts are the primary *starters* or creators of content, while the content managers work to help keep the ontology *clean*.

8. RELATED WORK

Although research of collaborative ontology development is still very new, there has been some early work that is relevant to our research. The most similar work is an early investigation into the distributed, collaborative ontology engineering process and the capabilities of Collaborative Protégé by Schober and colleagues [11]. The authors carried out a study where they observed users and analyzed the communication and interactions of the users inside and outside the tool while enriching the content of an existing ontology. The study was informal and observational. The authors were primarily interested in exploring the technical aspects of multiple authors using Collaborative Protégé. Similar to our analysis, the authors found large differences in the level of activity and contributions of authors. They also informally observed a general trend that people that chat a lot also made more changes. Finally, the authors also used informal analysis of the notes to propose different user roles based on a person's discussion behavior. The roles proposed were "commenter", "chatter", and "editor". Users corresponding to the "editor" role tended to make many comments, often creating tasks for other users. This observation corresponds with our analysis of the "Content editor" role in BRO.

9. CONCLUSION AND FUTURE WORK

Collaborative ontology development is a growing area of research and both the tools that support this process and our general understanding about how these projects function is in the early stages. Our results indicate that contributors have clearly discernible roles, which we can identify by analyzing users' editing activities. To the best of our knowledge, this paper presents the first analytical study of the roles and connection between change and discussion activity that exist within different collaborative ontology development projects. The results indicate a need for the creation of role-based workflows in ontology development environments. Moreover, change data could be used for filtering and highlighting important information in an ontology, and a potential first step for ontology modularization.

In the future, we hope to have access to more data to help strengthen and generalize the analysis. One limitation of our current analysis is that we had data only for a small set of projects, representing a limited set of users. Another limitation is the fact that all the projects that we studied used the Collaborative Protégé framework and the available tool features may have biased the patterns of activity. However, as we have mentioned in Section 2, Collaborative Protégé does not enforce any particular workflow, and its default setting allows all users to perform any operation in the ontology, therefore we believe that the biasing is minimal. These three projects are ongoing, and in particular, the ICD-11 project will see substantial growth in terms of the number of authors contributing over the next year. As we collect more data, we plan to investigate the relationship between changes, collaboration and contribution quality. We also will try to analyze similar data from collaborative editing available in other tools. We believe our current and future

analysis will be important contributions for helping inform tool design in the collaborative ontology development space.

10. REFERENCES

[1] C. Bird, D. Pattison, R. D'Souza, V. Filkov, and P. Devanbu. Latent social structure in open source projects. In *Proceedings of the 16th ACM SIGSOFT International Symposium on Foundations of Software Engineering*, pages 24–35, 2008.

[2] S. K. Card and D. Nation. Degree-of-interest trees: a component of an attention-reactive user interface. In *Proceedings of the Working Conference on Advanced Visual Interfaces*, pages 231–245, 2002.

[3] M. Krötzsch, D. Vrandecic, and M. Völkel. Semantic MediaWiki. In *ISWC*, pages 935–942, 2006.

[4] H. Liu and V. Kešelj. Combined mining of Web server logs and web contents for classifying user navigation patterns and predicting users' future requests. *Data Knowl. Eng.*, 61(2):304–330, 2007.

[5] J. Liu and S. Ram. Who Does What: Collaboration Patterns in the Wikipedia and Their Impact on Data Quality. In *Proceedings of 19th Annual Workshop on Information Technologies and Systems*, 2009.

[6] K. Nakakoji, Y. Yamamoto, Y. Nishinaka, K. Kishida, and Y. Ye. Evolution patterns of open-source software systems and communities. In *Proceedings of the International Workshop on Principles of Software Evolution*, pages 76–85, 2002.

[7] K. Niu, S. B. Zhang, and J. L. Chen. An Initializing Cluster Centers Algorithm Based on Pointer Ring. *6th International Conference on Intelligent Systems Design and Applications*, 1:655–660, 2006.

[8] N. F. Noy, A. Chugh, and H. Alani. The CKC Challenge: Exploring Tools for Collaborative Knowledge Construction. *IEEE Intelligent Systems*, 23(1):64–68, 2008.

[9] N. F. Noy, A. Chugh, W. Liu, and M. A. Musen. A Framework for Ontology Evolution in Collaborative Environments. In *ISWC*, 2006.

[10] E. S. Raymond. *The Cathedral & the Bazaar: Musings on Linux and Open Source by an Accidental Revolutionary*. O'Reilly Media, 2001.

[11] D. Schober, J. Malone, and R. Stevens. Observations in collaborative ontology editing using Collaborative Protégé. In *Workshop on Collaborative Construction, Management and Linking of Structured Knowledge*, 2009.

[12] A. Sebastian, N. F. Noy, T. Tudorache, and M. A. Musen. A Generic Ontology For Collaborative Ontology-Development Workflows. In *EKAW*, 2008.

[13] N. Sioutos, S. d. Coronado, M. W. Haber, F. W. Hartel, W.-L. Shaiu, and L. W. Wright. NCI Thesaurus: a semantic model integrating cancer-related clinical and molecular information. *J. of Biomedical Informatics*, 40(1):30–43, 2007.

[14] T. Tudorache, N. F. Noy, S. Tu, and M. A. Musen. Supporting Collaborative Ontology Development in Protégé. In *ISWC*, pages 17–32, 2008.

[15] J. Xu, Y. Gao, S. Christley, and G. Madey. A Topological Analysis of the Open Source Software Development Community. In *Hawaii International Conference on System Sciences*, Los Alamitos, CA, USA, 2005. IEEE Computer Society.

From Mappings to Modules: Using Mappings to Identify Domain-Specific Modules in Large Ontologies

Amir Ghazvinian
Stanford University
Stanford, CA, USA
amirg@stanford.edu

Natalya F. Noy
Stanford University
Stanford, CA, USA
noy@stanford.edu

Mark A. Musen
Stanford University
Stanford, CA, USA
musen@stanford.edu

ABSTRACT

The problem of ontology modularization is an active area of research in the Semantic Web community. With the emergence and wider use of very large ontologies, in particular in fields such as biomedicine, more and more application developers need to extract meaningful modules of these ontologies to use in their applications. Researchers have also noted that many ontology-maintenance tasks would be simplified if we could extract modules from ontologies. These tasks include ontology matching: If we can separate ontologies into modules based on the topics that these modules cover, we can simplify and improve ontology matching. In this paper, we study a complementary problem: Can we use existing mappings between ontologies to facilitate modularization? We present a novel approach to modularization based on mappings between ontologies. We validate and analyze our approach by applying our methods to identify modules for National Cancer InstituteÕs Thesaurus (NCI Thesaurus) and Systematized Nomenclature of Medicine–Clinical Terms (SNOMED-CT).

Categories and Subject Descriptors

I.2.4 [**Artificial Intelligence**]: Knowledge Representation Formalisms and Methods—*Relation systems*

General Terms

Algorithms

Keywords

ontologies, knowledge bases, ontology mapping, modularization

1. INTRODUCTION

The field of biomedicine has embraced the Semantic Web probably more than any other field. Ontologies in biomedicine facilitate information integration, data exchange, search and query of heterogeneous biomedical data, and other critical knowledge-intensive tasks [14]. As a result, there are many biomedical ontologies covering overlapping areas of the field [2]. Many of these ontologies are large: For instance, the National Cancer Institute's Thesaurus (NCI Thesaurus) [15] has 80,000 classes and Systematized Nomenclature of Medicine–Clinical Terms (SNOMED-CT), one of the key biomedical ontologies, has almost 400,000 classes [16].

Creating mappings among ontologies by identifying similar classes is a critical step in integrating data and applications that use different ontologies. With these mappings, for example, we can link resources annotated with terms in one ontology to resources annotated with related terms in another ontology, discovering new relations among the resources themselves (e.g., linking drugs and diseases). Because identifying mappings among ontologies manually is an enormous task, development of algorithms that try to find candidate mappings automatically is a very active area of research [4]. In recent years, Semantic Web researchers have developed many sophisticated algorithms that use a wide variety of methods, such as graph analysis, machine learning, and use of domain-specific and other background knowledge. For example, Hu and Qu [7] use a partitioning method to identify corresponding blocks of entities in two ontologies.

In our previous work [6] we have shown that large ontologies, such as those found in the field of biomedicine, pose a serious scalability challenge to advanced mapping algorithms. Many of these algorithms would be able to perform well if we were first able to identify modules of the larger ontologies in which the mappings are likely to lie.

In this paper, we examine the complementary problem. Given a set of mappings between a small, specific ontology and a large, broader ontology, we want to identify a module within the larger ontology that corresponds to the content of the small ontology. For example, a developer wants to use one of the large standard ontologies in biomedicine, such as NCI Thesaurus. Using such ontologies may be a requirement from users or funders, or the developer might want to use terms from such an ontology to facilitate interoperability with other applications. However, the developer may need only a small portion of the 80K classes in NCI Thesaurus. For instance, a developer working on an application that analyzes data related to the cell cycle, may need only the part that is relevant to describing the cell cycle. Using a smaller module lets the developer use an ontology of a manageable size in her application while preserving the references to and the structure of the original ontology. Researchers have developed a number of algorithms for identifying logical modules within ontologies [17]. These methods often make use of the structure or properties of the ontologies to partition the ontology into modules (e.g., work by Cuenca Grau and colleagues [3]). Additionally, some of these methods use input from users to obtain modules [11]. In this paper, we present a technique for creating modules by using mappings between a large ontology and a domain-specific ontology that covers the domain that the user is interested in (e.g., cell cycle).

We use mappings from a number of biomedical ontologies to NCI Thesaurus and SNOMED-CT to identify modules within these large ontologies. We hypothesize that a large number of smaller biomedical ontologies map to subsections of the larger NCI Thesaurus and SNOMED-CT ontologies, thereby extracting domain-specific modules of these two ontologies. This paper makes the following contributions:

- We implement a method for ontology modularization based on mappings between ontologies.

- We validate and analyze this method by applying it to find modules for NCI Thesaurus and SNOMED-CT.

2. MATERIALS AND METHODS

We will now describe how we use mappings to identify ontology modules. Our methods consist of three main components: 1) generating mappings from a source ontology to the target ontology that we wish to modularize, 2) clustering mappings within the target ontology, and 3) using mapping clusters to identify modules within the target ontology.

We start with two ontologies:

1. the ontology that we wish to modularize as *modularization target*, or *target*, for short; and

2. an ontology covering some part of the domain that the target ontology covers, which we call the *source ontology*.

For example, NCI Thesaurus may be the target ontology, and an ontology covering the cell cycle domain, such as the Cell Cycle Ontology (CCO) [1] is the source ontology. We can use the mappings between CCO and NCI Thesaurus to identify a module within NCI Thesaurus that is relevant to the cell cycle. We report here on the more interesting variations of our modularization algorithm based on qualitative evaluation of the modules they produce.

2.1 Generating Mappings

To identify ontology modules in our target ontology, we first need a set of mappings between the source and the target ontology. Our method is independent of the method used to create the mappings, although we have not yet studied the effect of particular mapping methods on the outcome of the modularization. For our experiments, we use a simple lexical method to create the mappings. Our earlier research [5, 6] showed that this method is very effective for biomedical ontologies, and produces mappings with high precision and good recall. This method also scales easily to very large ontologies. Specifically, we create a mapping between two classes from different ontologies if the preferred name of one class matches the preferred name or synonym of the other class after normalization. Figure 1A shows two ontologies and the set of mappings between them. We refer to classes in the target ontology that are part of the mapping set as *mapping targets*.

2.2 Clustering

Once we have mappings to a target ontology, we cluster the mapping targets to identify critical regions of the target ontology for our module (Figure 1B). For scalability reasons, we clustered the mapping targets only in cases where our mapping algorithm found fewer than 4000 mappings from the source ontology to the target ontology.

In order to perform the clustering of classes within an ontology, we need a distance metric that can be applied to return a distance between any two classes in the ontology. We chose an edge-based semantic similarity metric developed by Pekar and colleagues [13]. Pekar et al's semantic similarity metric is defined as follows:

$$sim(c_1, c_2) = \frac{\delta(c_a, root)}{\delta(c_a, root) + \delta(c_1, c_a) + \delta(c_2, c_a)}$$

where c_a is the lowest common ancestor of class c_1 and c_2 and $\delta(c_1, c_2)$ is the length in number of edges of the longest distance between c_1 and c_2. We chose this metric for two reasons: it computes similarity based on distance within the ontology and it counts sibling terms lower down as closer together than siblings near the root. Because we actually require a distance metric and not a similarity metric in order to cluster classes, we take the inverse of the similarity metric described above.

We use the k-means clustering algorithm [10] to cluster the mapping targets within the ontology using the inverse similarity metric to compute distance between any two classes. The number of clusters is an input parameter to the algorithm.

2.3 Using Clusters to Identify Ontology Modules

For the pair of source and target ontologies (such as NCI Thesaurus and CCO), the clustering algorithm returns a series of clusters. We use these clusters to identify components of the target ontology that would constitute the module. We define a *component* as part of a subtree in the target ontology that is covered by one or more clusters. A *module* consists of one or more disconnected components. For example, when identifying a module of NCI Thesaurus relevant to the cell cycle using the Cell Cycle Ontology, our algorithm produced components anchored at the classes "Gene Product", "Biological Process", and "Anatomical Structure, System, or Substance." The union of these components gives the module of NCI Thesaurus for the cell cycle domain.

Figure 1C illustrates the process of identifying components and then modules from clusters. For each cluster, we first determine the lowest common ancestor of all classes in the cluster. This common ancestor becomes a *candidate anchoring point* for a component. In order to determine whether or not this class does in fact serve as a good anchoring point for the component, we compute what percent of classes within the subtree below the anchor class are also mapping targets. If we find enough mapping targets in the subtree, we include in our final module a component anchored at that class. The number of mapping targets that we consider to be enough here depends on the percentage of the subtree covered by the mapping targets and ranges from 1 for subtrees with 100% coverage to 30 for subtrees with less than 10% coverage. Intuitively, this process allows us to remove the subtrees with just a few not closely related mapping targets inside a subtree: these subtrees are unlikely to become meaningful module components.

After we determine all anchors for the module, we prune each subtree to get a more specific and well-defined module. In many cases, all the mapping targets are clustered near the root of the subtree, because the representation of the domain in the source ontology does not go to the same level of detail as the representation in the target ontology. In order to get a cluster that corresponds more closely to the domain of the source ontology, we prune the lower levels of the component subtree that have no mapping targets in them. Specifically, we begin at each leaf in the components subtree and traverse the subtree toward the anchor, removing all the classes that are neither mapping targets themselves nor direct children of mapping targets. Once we reach such a class, we stop the pruning along that branch. Figure 1D illustrates the final module after pruning.

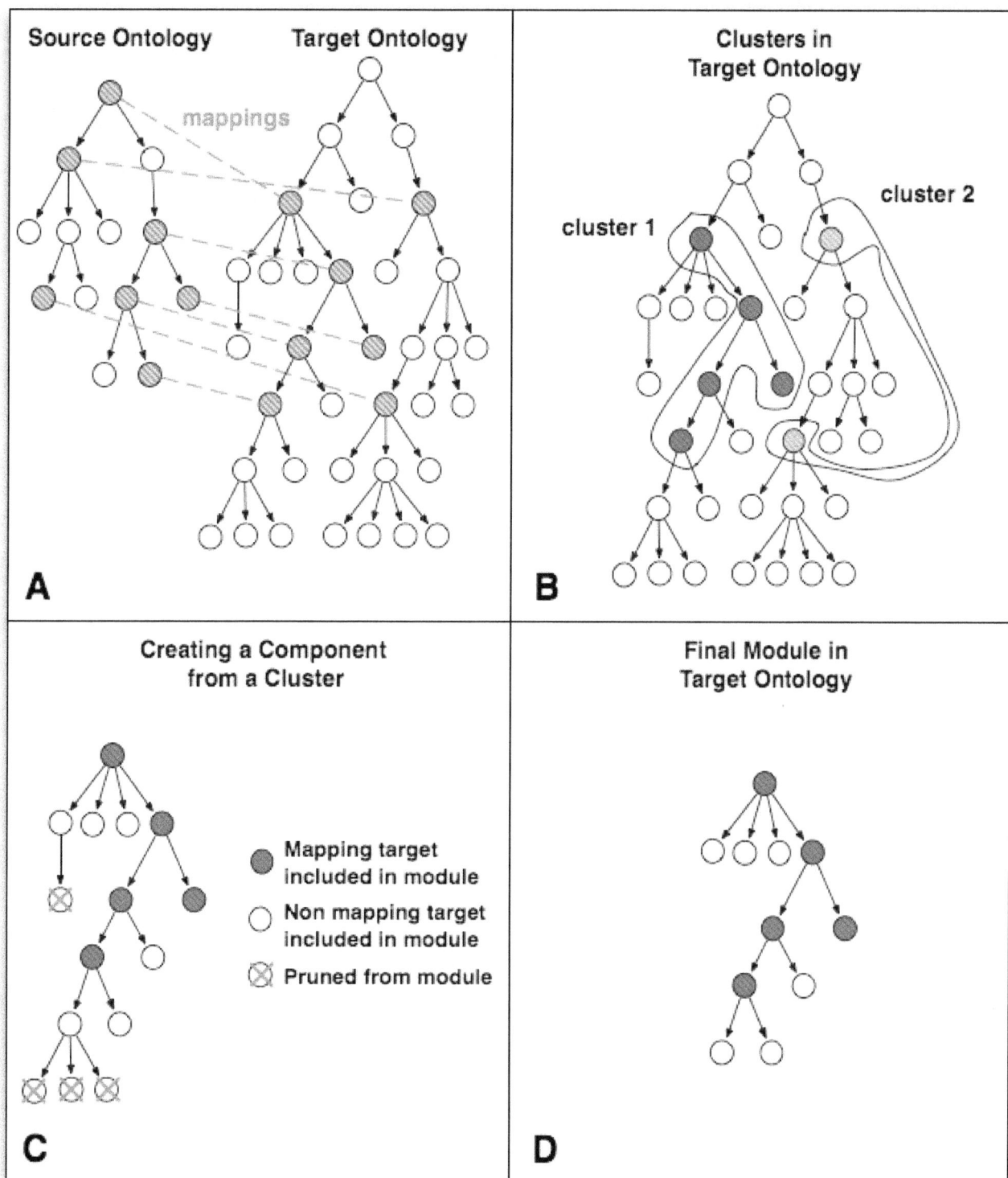

Figure 1: The process of identifying modules using mappings between ontologies. Figure A shows the mappings between a source ontology and a modularization target. Figure B shows two clusters returned by the clustering algorithm. One cluster is light gray in color while the other is dark gray. When determining a module based on these clusters, we discard the light gray cluster since the mapping targets within that cluster are too sparse. Figure C illustrates the process of pruning the ontology subtree for the remaining cluster, which we use to create the module. We begin at each leaf and traverse the tree toward the root, removing all classes that are not mapping targets or direct children of mapping targets. Once we reach such a class, we stop pruning along that branch. Figure D displays the final module.

3. VALIDATION AND ANALYSIS

We applied the methods above to identify modules for NCI Thesaurus and SNOMED-CT. These ontologies are very commonly used in the biomedical community. Indeed, these two ontologies are currently listed as the two most viewed ontologies in BioPortal, a repository of more than 200 biomedical ontologies [12].[1] These two ontologies are also very large: NCI Thesaurus has almost 80K classes and SNOMED-CT has more than 380K. As source ontologies for modularization, we used 141 ontologies in BioPortal, with 106 of these ontologies containing fewer than 5,000 classes. Our process extracted 71 modules for NCI Thesaurus and 68 modules for SNOMED-CT. We were not able to extract modules in some cases for a variety of reasons: because the mapping set did not contain enough mappings to find relevant modules, the mapping set contained too many mappings to cluster, or the mappings were distributed too sparsely within the target ontology.

We use the modularization of these two ontologies in order to validate our algorithm and to analyze the process itself and the resulting modules in a number of ways: First, we examine some sample modules and their representative terms in order to understand the types of modules that our algorithm creates and to determine whether or not these modules are likely to be useful in an application setting (Section 3.1). Second, we analyze the ways in which the modules vary depending on the number of clusters given as input to our clustering algorithm (Section 3.2). Finally, we analyze characteristics of the modules, such as how well our mapping targets cover the module (Section 3.3).

3.1 Sample Modules

Figure 2 shows sets of representative terms for two of the modules generated by our algorithm. We generated both modules using 10 clusters as the input to our clustering algorithm. In the first example (Figure 2A), we identified a module of NCI Thesaurus that is relevant to electrocardiograms (EKG) using the Electrocardiography Ontology in BioPortal. The module consists of 61 classes, representative samples of which are shown in the figure. Of the 61 classes in this module, 41 (67%) are mapping targets. Additionally, the module makes up 100% of the subtree "EKG Concept" in NCI Thesaurus. In other words, the pruning process did not remove any classes. Figure 2B shows a SNOMED-CT module that includes the part of SNOMED-CT covering the same domain as the Mouse Adult Gross Anatomy. The module consists of 6,461 classes, of which 1,577 (24%) are mapping targets. This module had a significant amount of pruning: the module makes up only 25% of the subtree "Anatomical Structure" in SNOMED-CT.

In case of the anatomy module, even though both the subtree percentage and the mapping target coverage are lower than for the EKG module, we still seem to have identified a useful module for dealing with mouse anatomy. Because we prune, we also greatly decrease the size of the ontology, making it much more manageable and removing the very specific classes that are not relevant given the scope of the source ontology used to create the module.

Our experience shows that some combination of the absolute number of mapping targets as well as the coverage of the module are good indicators of how meaningful and useful the module is. We explore these characteristics further in Section 3.3.

3.2 From Clusters to Modules

Several of the modules that result from our algorithm have more than one component. For example, we already mentioned in Section 2.3 that when identifying a module of NCI Thesaurus relevant

to the cell cycle using the Cell Cycle Ontology, we extracted the module that contains components anchored at the classes "Gene Product," "Biological Process," and "Anatomical Structure, System, or Substance."

We now analyze how particular characteristics of the modules and the components that constitute the module vary as a function of the number of clusters used as an input parameter for our clustering algorithm. Specifically, we look at the size, number of distinct components, and depth of components. Figure 3 shows how these characteristics change as the number of clusters changes, and also shows the number of modules we were able to identify from the 141 BioPortal ontologies we used as source ontologies.

First, as the number of clusters given as input to the k-means clustering increases, so, too, does the number of ontologies for which we are able to provide modules (Figure 3A). We see this trend because, as the number of clusters increases, the specificity of each cluster increases. When trying to identify which clusters are relevant for components of the final module, we discard very sparse clusters. Some ontologies have fairly specific components but this feature can be masked if there are not enough clusters to differentiate the component from other mapped targets in the ontology. So as we get more specific clusters, more components get included and therefore more ontologies.

Second, we observe in Figure 3B that the average size of modules increases as the number of clusters increases. This observations corresponds to the fact that the average number of module components goes up as the number of clusters increases. Though components get smaller and more specific, the modules consist of more components on average (Figure 3C), so module size increases.

Third, we observe a tradeoff in the number of clusters and module shapes and sizes. As number of clusters increases, so, too, do the number of components (Figure 3C) and the average depth of our modules (Figure 3D). Therefore, we find increasingly specific modules, but lose some of the scope that ties these disconnected components together.

For example, at both 10 and 20 clusters for NCIT, we have a module corresponding to Common Terminology Criteria for Adverse Events (CTCAE). However, at 10 clusters, the module consists of a single component with the root class "Adverse Event", while at 20 clusters we find a module with several components representing the actual types of adverse events such as "Adverse Event Associated with Nervous System" or "Adverse Event Associated with Cardiac Arrhythmia." Though we find more specific components that reflect the actual types of adverse events found in CTCAE, we lose the big picture, namely that all of these things are adverse events. Pruning wisely can help us avoid dealing with this problem as much because we can prune out the adverse event subtrees that are not relevant to CTCAE.

We see the same type of result in the anatomy modules, where we get a single module of "Anatomical Structure" when there are few enough clusters that all anatomical classes get clustered together, but we may get distinct components related to brain or heart anatomy if those parts of the anatomy are over-represented in the ontology. It is difficult to know which type of module is useful to the user and it probably varies depending on a specific application. For instance, for a general anatomy ontology, a module user would probably want the module rooted at "Anatomical Structure", whereas for a more specific ontology like BIRNLex, which deals with brain anatomy, you might want the module to contain only the anatomy relevant to the brain and would then want it to consist of just the "Brain" component.

---

[1]http://bioportal.bioontology.org

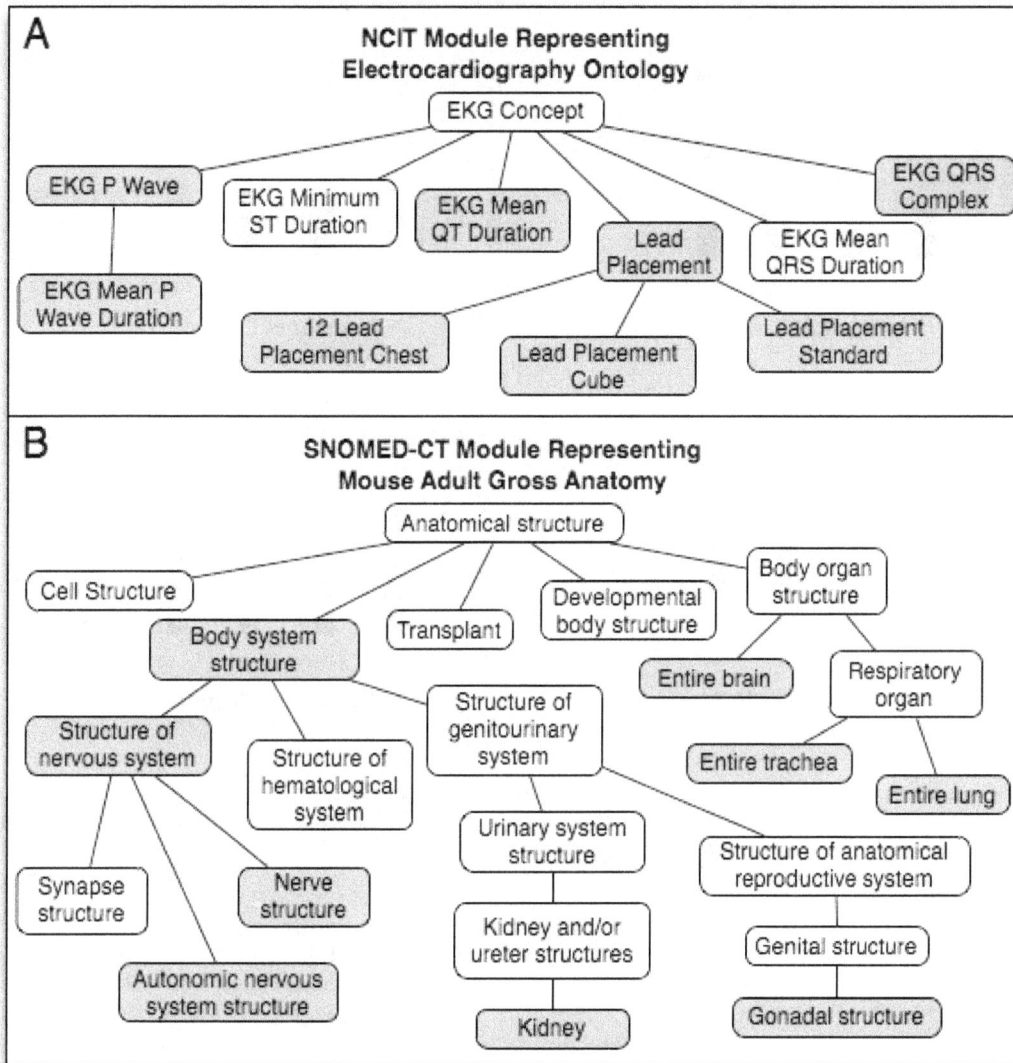

Figure 2: Sample modules and some of their representative terms. In each figure, the classes in gray boxes represent mapping targets and classes in white represent classes that were not mapping targets, but are included in the module through our algorithm. Note that the figure shows only parts of the modules. Figure A shows a module we identified within NCI Thesaurus that represents the domain of the Electrocardiography Ontology. Figure B shows a module discovered in SNOMED-CT that is relevant to Mouse Adult Gross Anatomy.

Finally, these statistics provide a way to examine differences in the structure of SNOMED-CT and NCIT. NCIT has more components, but SNOMED-CT has a greater average depth per component. This difference indicates that there are many higher level classes for SNOMED-CT that are not very specific in scope and therefore are not as good for making modules as those classes which are at a greater depth. SNOMED-CT has much larger modules than NCI Thesaurus on average, which is not surprising because SNOMED-CT is a much larger ontology and therefore has more classes in the domains of these modules. For example, SNOMED-CT has more than 25,000 classes in the "Anatomic Structure" sub-tree, while the corresponding "Anatomic System, Substance, or Structure" subtree in NCI Thesaurus has about 6,000 classes. Thus we see that anatomy-related modules in SNOMED-CT are much

larger than in NCI Thesaurus: for Mouse Adult Gross Anatomy, we identified a SNOMED-CT module with 6,461 classes, but the NCIT module we identified for the same ontology only contains 1,795 classes.

3.3 Module Coverage

In this section, we analyze the proportion of the module that is composed of mapping targets and the proportion of the ontology subtree that the module consumes.

Figure 4 shows a distribution of coverages for our modules. On average, our mapping targets cover 18% of the module for NCI Thesaurus and 16% of the modules for SNOMED-CT. Therefore, on average, more than 4/5 of the classes in the modules that we extracted are not included in the mapping set used to generate that module. The lowest mapping target coverage of any module iden-

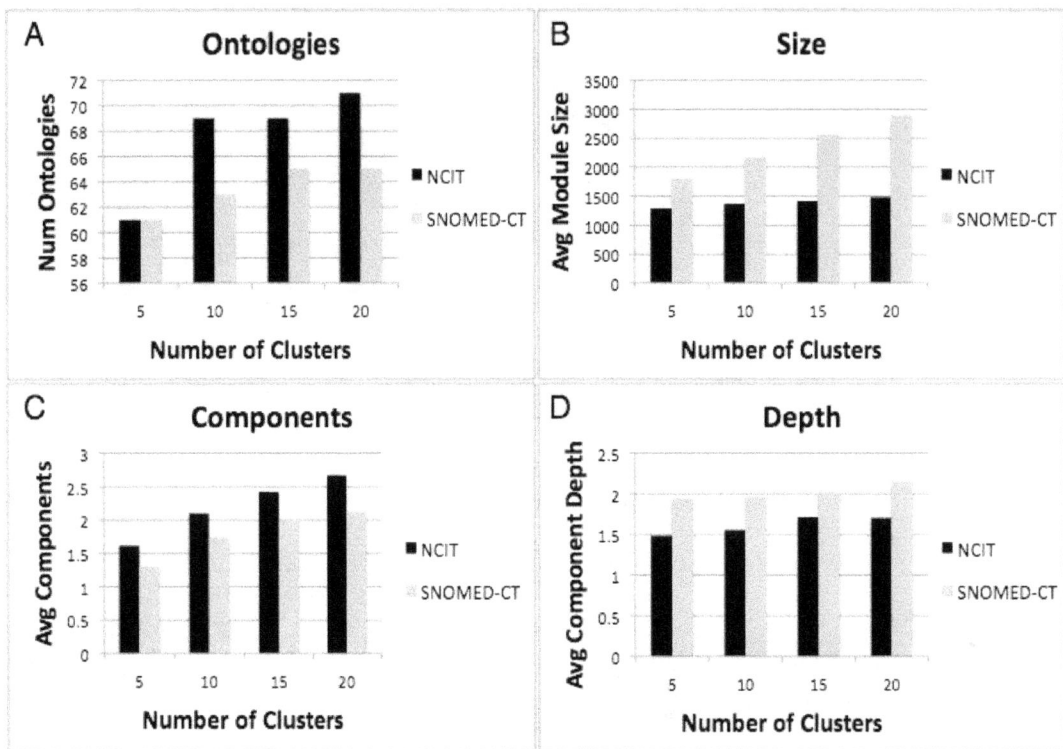

Figure 3: Characteristics of modules vary with the number of clusters used to generate the modules. A: the number of ontologies for which we are able to identify modules; B: the average size of the modules we identify; C: the average number of components per module; D: the average depth of the anchor class of each module component.

tified by our algorithm is 3.4% for NCI Thesaurus and 2.9% for SNOMED-CT.

We also examine, for different values of percentage p, the number of modules that have mapping targets for at least $p\%$ of their classes (Figure 4A). Though we identified a comparable number of modules for both NCI Thesaurus and SNOMED-CT, the modules of NCI Thesaurus tend to be composed of a greater percentage of mapping targets than those of SNOMED-CT. For example, 30 of the NCI Thesaurus modules we identified consist of at least 30% mapping targets while only 14 SNOMED-CT modules boast the same mapping target coverage.

Next, we analyzed the percent of classes in the overall ontology subtree that are also contained in our module. This statistic measures how much of the subtree has been pruned to generate the module. On average, modules in NCI Thesaurus cover 30% of the overall subtree while modules in SNOMED-CT cover 27%. Two modules for SNOMED-CT and seven modules for NCI Thesaurus include the entire subtrees (i.e. no pruning). The minimum proportion of a subtree taken up by any module is 0.6% for both NCI Thesaurus and SNOMED-CT. Our algorithm pruned these modules heavily; Therefore, they do not take up a large part of their respective trees.

In Figure 4B, we show the number of modules that contain at least $p\%$ of the original subtree, for different values of p. We see that the vast majority of modules for SNOMED-CT contain less than 10% of the original subtree and in fact only 17 of the 65 modules we identified for SNOMED-CT contain more than 10% of the subtree. By contrast, NCI Thesaurus has a much slower drop-off rate, with 13 modules that have contain at least 60% of the original subtree.

The coverage statistics for our modules could serve as a proxy for usefulness of the module. The percent of the module made up of mapping targets reveals how well our mapping set (and thus our original ontology) reflects the classes selected for the module. Analyzing the percent of the ontology subtree covered by our module demonstrates both whether the module comprises a substantial portion of the relevant ontology subtree and how well we can prune out the portions of the subtree that are not relevant for the module. Though we do not formally evaluate the modules, these statistics show that our algorithm can produce modules with both good coverage of the relevant ontology subtree and that consist of significant shares of mapping targets.

4. DISCUSSION

We have presented an approach that uses mappings between ontologies in order to extract domain-specific modules from large ontologies based on their mappings to smaller ontologies. In our experiments with NCI Thesaurus and SNOMED-CT, using the ontologies from BioPortal as the sources for mappings, we have identified a number of useful modules. We found that one of the key hurdles that we must overcome, is to find a way to determine how good a particular module is. Indeed, the same problem is true for most modularization approaches [17]: many authors discuss computational properties of their modules, but do not evaluate how useful these modules are to users. In our case, the requirements for extraction are driven by domain coverage of the module rather by its computational or structural properties. Thus, the problem of evaluating whether the module satisfies the user requirements is similar to the problem of ontology evaluation in general: how do we

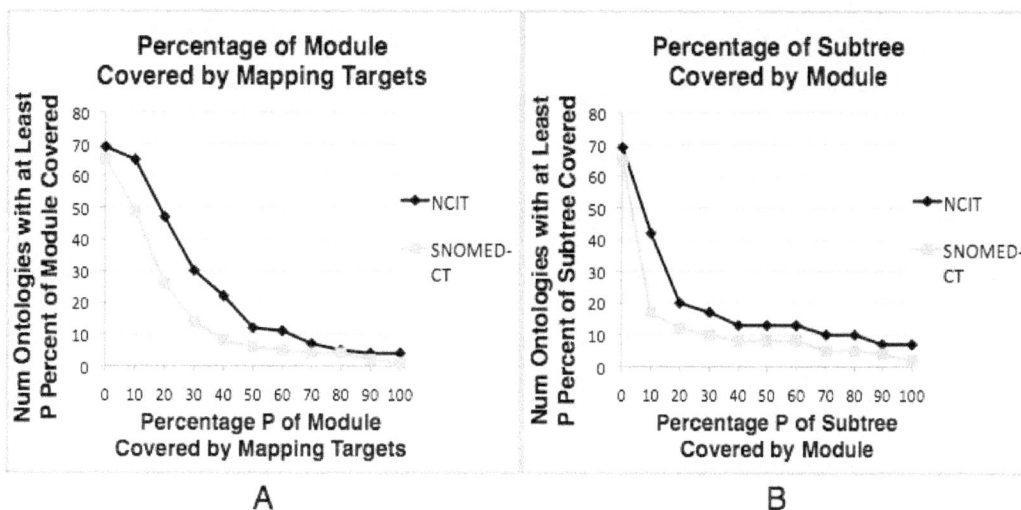

Figure 4: The coverage of modules. Figure A shows the percentage of our modules that are covered by mapping targets. The x-axis represents a percentage P and the y-axis shows how many of our modules have mapping targets for at least P% of their classes. Figure B shows the percentage of the overall ontology subtree is contained within our module. Intuitively, it is a measure of how much has been pruned from the module. In Figure B, the x-axis represents a percentage P and the y-axis shows how many of our modules cover at least P% of their respective subtrees.

know that an ontology is useful for a specific class of applications [18]? Evaluation of an ontology depends on the specific applications for which it is being used; the same can be said for modules. Therefore, we plan to submit the modules that we have identified to BioPortal to enable the user community to use the modules in their applications, review them and comment on them. We hope that this crowd-sourcing approach to evaluation will enable us to get a better sense of what modules the users find useful for their applications. However, our initial evidence, which we present in this paper, indicates that our approach can indeed find interesting domain-specific modules.

We use the ontologies and the mappings to them essentially as *background knowledge*, similar in spirit to the way SAMBO [9] and ASMOV [8] use background knowledge (UMLS Metathesaurus, WordNet) to improve the quality of mappings themselves.

Providing modules as we have done in this paper can improve the performance of many applications. For applications with large ontologies, it can make the ontology more manageable and usable by including only relevant portions of the ontology. Providing modules relevant to multiple smaller ontologies can facilitate data integration for applications requiring the domains of those multiple ontologies. Instead of using multiple ontologies and having mappings between them for integration, we can simply use the union of multiple modules within the same ontology, which are essentially automatically integrated.

Although we present here a way to identify modules of large ontologies that correspond to the domains of smaller ontologies, our approach is not limited to cases where one ontology is large and the other ontology is small. We can use the same method to identify shared domains among large ontologies.

Additionally, in this paper, we utilized only subsumption relationships to identify modules, because those relationships were present in the ontologies we analyzed, but a similar approach could be used to traverse other types relationships.

Our approach has certain limitations. Because we use a simple lexical matching method, our results are limited to the domain

of biomedicine and other domains, such as Cultural Heritage [19], where such a mapping method works well. In other domains, where class definitions do not contain rich lexical information, one will need to find scalable tools that would produce enough mappings to enable statistically significant analysis. Furthermore, our previous analysis [6] has shown that recall for a lexical matching algorithm in the field of biomedicine is about 65%. Scalable ways to increase recall, such as mapping composition, would give more mappings to input for the clustering algorithm, which would in turn likely give a better picture of the modules.

Additionally, because we are dependent on mappings to identify modules, in cases where there are not many mappings to a target ontology, we cannot identify relevant modules. For NCI Thesaurus, we were unable to identify modules in 50% of cases. For SNOMED-CT, we were unable to identify modules in 54% of cases. In the opposite scenario, when we have too many mappings, clustering these mappings becomes infeasible. In this paper, we were only able to cluster mappings in cases where we had 4,000 mappings or fewer between ontologies.

Furthermore, some of the modules we identify have a very low percentage of mapping targets, meaning many of the classes included in these modules were not mapping targets. For example, 16 of the modules we identified for SNOMED-CT consist of less than 10% mapping targets, Further research into better ways to prune the module might improve our coverage and our modules.

5. CONCLUSIONS AND FUTURE WORK

We have presented an approach that uses mappings between ontologies for modularization. Our analysis shows that this approach extracts modules that are specific to a particular domain. Varying the parameters of the algorithm controls the number of components in the modules and the specificity of the module itself. In the future, we plan to analyze the effect of the quality of the mappings and the number of mappings on the results of the modularizations. We will use the BioPortal user community to evaluate the usefulness of the modules that our approach produces and their use in applications.

6. ACKNOWLEDGMENTS

This work was supported in part by the National Center for Biomedical Ontology, under roadmap-initiative grant U54 HG004028 from the National Institutes of Health

7. REFERENCES

[1] E. Antezana, E. Tsiporkova, V. Mironov, and M. Kuiper. A cell-cycle knowledge integration framework. In *Data Integration in the Life Sciences*, v. 4075, pp. 19–34. Springer, 2006.

[2] O. Bodenreider and R. Stevens. Bio-ontologies: current trends and future directions. *Brief Bioinform*, 7:256–274, 2006.

[3] B. Cuenca Grau, I. Horrocks, Y. Kazakov, and U. Sattler. Modular ontologies. chapter Extracting Modules from Ontologies: A Logic-Based Approach, pages 159–186. Springer-Verlag, Berlin, Heidelberg, 2009.

[4] J. Euzenat and P. Shvaiko. *Ontology matching*. Springer, Berlin ; New York, 2007.

[5] A. Ghazvinian, N. F. Noy, C. Jonquet, N. Shah, and M. A. Musen. What four million mappings can tell you about two hundred ontologies. In *ISWC '09: Proceedings of the 8th International Semantic Web Conference*, pages 229–242. Springer-Verlag, 2009.

[6] A. Ghazvinian, N. F. Noy, and M. A. Musen. Creating mappings for ontologies in biomedicine: Simple methods work. In *AMIA Annual Symposium*, San Francisco, CA, 2009.

[7] W. Hu and Y .Qu. Block matching for ontologies. In *ISWC '06: Proceedings of the 5th International Semantic Web Conference*, pages 300–313. Springer-Verlag, 2006.

[8] Y. R. Jean-Mary, E. P. Shironoshita, and M. R. Kabuka. ASMOV: Results for OAEI 2009. In *Workshop on Ontology Matching at ISWC 2009*, 2008.

[9] P. Lambrix, H. Tan, and Q. Liu. Sambo and sambodtf results for the ontology alignment evaluation initiative 2008. In *Workshop on Ontology Matching at ISWC 2008*, 2008.

[10] J. B. MacQueen Some Methods for classification and Analysis of Multivariate Observations. In *Proceedings of 5-th Berkeley Symposium on Mathematical Statistics and Probability*, Berkeley, University of California Press, 1:281-297.

[11] N. F. Noy and M. A. Musen. Modular ontologies. chapter Traversing Ontologies to Extract Views, pages 245–260. Springer-Verlag, Berlin, Heidelberg, 2009.

[12] N. F. Noy, et.al. BioPortal: ontologies and integrated data resources at the click of a mouse. *Nucleic Acids Research*, 37(Web-Server-Issue):170–173, 2009.

[13] V. Pekar and S. Staab. Taxonomy learning: factoring the structure of a taxonomy into a semantic classification decision. In *19th Int. Conf. on Computational Linguistics*, pages 1–7, Morristown, NJ, USA, 2002. ACL.

[14] D. L. Rubin, N. H. Shah, and N. F. Noy. Biomedical ontologies: a functional perspective. *Brief Bioinform*, 9(1):75–90, January 2008.

[15] N. Sioutos, S. de Coronado, M. Haber, F. Hartel, W. Shaiu, and L. Wright. NCI Thesaurus: A semantic model integrating cancer-related clinical and molecular information. *Journal of Biomedical Informatics*, 40(1):30–43, 2007.

[16] K. Spackman, editor. *SMOMEDÍ RT: Systematized Nomenclature of Medicine, Reference Terminology*. College of American Pathologists, Northfield, IL, 2000.

[17] H. Stuckenschmidt, C. Parent, and S. Spaccapietra, editors. *Modular Ontologies: Concepts, Theories and Techniques for Knowledge Modularization*. Springer-Verlag, Berlin, 2009.

[18] Y. Sure, A. GǗmez-PǑrez, W. Daelemans, M. Reinberger, N. Guarino, and N. Noy. Why evaluate ontology technologies? because it works! *IEEE Intelligent Systems*, 19(4):74–81, 2004.

[19] A. Tordai, J. van Ossenbruggen, and G. Schreiber. Combining vocabulary alignment techniques. In *K-CAP '09: 5th Int. Conf. on Knowledge Capture*, pages 25–32, 2009. ACM.

Gathering Lexical Linked Data and Knowledge Patterns from FrameNet

Andrea Nuzzolese
ISTC-CNR, STLab
CS Dept., University of
Bologna, Italy
nuzzoles@cs.unibo.it

Aldo Gangemi
ISTC-CNR, Semantic
Technology Lab, Rome, Italy
aldo.gangemi@cnr.it

Valentina Presutti
ISTC-CNR, Semantic
Technology Lab, Rome, Italy
valentina.presutti@cnr.it

ABSTRACT

FrameNet is an important lexical knowledge base featuring cognitive plausibility, and grounded in a large corpus. Besides being actively used by the NLP community, frames are a great source of knowledge patterns once converted into a knowledge representation language. In this paper we present our experience in converting the 1.5 XML version of FrameNet into RDF datasets published on the Linked Open Data cloud, which are interoperable with WordNet and other resources. In the conversion we have used Semion, a new tool that allows a rule-based, customized pipeline from XML to RDF and OWL data. In addition, we introduce a method to select and refactor part of the information related to frames as full-fledged OWL knowledge patterns. This last result has required non-trivial assumptions on how to interpret FrameNet relations as formal knowledge.

Categories and Subject Descriptors

I.2.4 [**Knowledge Representation Formalisms and Methods**]: Representations (procedural and rule-based), Frames and scripts; I.2.6 [**Learning**]: Knowledge acquisition

General Terms

Design, Experimentation, Theory

Keywords

Knowledge Extraction, FrameNet, OWL, Semantic Web, Knowledge Engeneering

1. INTRODUCTION

The Web is evolving from a global information space of linked documents to one where both documents and data are linked. Underpinning this evolution is a set of best practices for publishing and connecting structured data on the Web known as Linked Data [3]. The Linked Open Data (LOD) project is bootstrapping the Web of Data by converting into RDF and publishing existing datasets available under open licenses.

LOD is an ideal platform for empirical knowledge engineering research, since it has the critical amount of data for empirical research, data that are not necessarily clean, optimized, or extensively structured. In practice, it's a perfect use case for making *patterns* emerge which can be studied by knowledge engineering and used for the design, maintenance, and consumption of data.

In addition, LOD datasets often contain a lot of natural language text, which is also important in order to make advanced linking and exploration of data not only in the broad LOD cloud vision, but also in localized applications within large organizations that make use of linked data [2].

Hybridizing natural language processing and semantic web techniques has therefore become an important research area. Part of the hybridization research, as well as part of the exploitation of LOD data, is carried out by means of lexical resources that are represented directly as linked data. The major example is the WordNet RDF dataset [21], which provides concepts (called *synsets*), each representing the sense of a set of synonymous words [10].

WordNet RDF has a low level of concept linking, because synsets are linked mostly by means of taxonomic (*hyponymy*) relations, while LOD is mostly linked by means of domain relations, such as parts of things, ways of participating in events or socially interacting, topics of documents, temporal and spatial references, etc. Some lexical resources focus instead on domain relations as expressed in the lexicon of natural languages.

This paper addresses hybridization research by porting the largest lexical resource for domain relations, FrameNet [1], to the LOD cloud.

FrameNet was previously available only as a lexical database, or as purely semantic web resources [8, 20], derived from the lexical one: previous conversions to RDF are discussed in Sect. 5. After the release of version 1.5, the Berkeley FrameNet group asked us to produce a new version of FrameNet in RDF that can be optimized for use in the growing lexical part of the LOD cloud.

Some lexical resources focus instead on domain relations as expressed in the lexicon of natural languages. This paper addresses hybridization research by porting the largest lexical resource for domain relations, FrameNet [1], to the LOD cloud.

FrameNet is based on the notions of *Semantic Frame, Lexical Unit* (LU), and *Frame Element* (FE): for example, the **Apply heat** frame refers to situations involving a **Cook** using a **Heating instrument** on some **Food** within some **Container**, etc. These types of involved entities are called FEs, and situations are expressed by words (*lexemes*) that manifest a LU, e.g. **fry**, **cook**, **roast**, etc. All those LUs are lexical counterparts of the semantic frame.

Intuitively, this is a more pragmatic and effective representation of lexical meaning, because frames focus on actual usage of language in real world situations, rather than on decontextualized terms as in traditional dictionaries (detailed analyses of the cognitive plausibility of frames as meaning units, besides [1] itself, are [9, 12]).

FrameNet was previously available only as a lexical database, or as unlinked OWL resources [8, 20], derived from former versions of the lexical database: such conversions are discussed in Sect. 5. After the release of version 1.5, the Berkeley FrameNet group asked us to produce a new version of FrameNet in RDF that can be optimized for use in the growing lexical part of the LOD cloud.

Among lexical resources, FrameNet has been successfully employed in NLP applications that demonstrate its potential to improve the quality of question answering [23] or recognizing textual entailment [6].

Frames as a cognitive, linguistic, or knowledge representation primitive have been studied many times in the last century (see [9] for an overview). For example [13] introduced frames into AI as a hub to factual and procedural knowledge: systems of interconnected frames would provide the shifting perspectives or time-dependent change in a situation. The intended meaning of a frame across the different theories can be summarized as from [12]: *a (small-sized and richly interconnected) structure, used to organize our knowledge, as well as to interpret, process or anticipate information*. In ontology design, frames are called *knowledge patterns* [7, 12], as a special kind of design patterns. Following the approach outlined in [12], we study frames as "units of meaning" for LOD and semantic web ontologies.

The contribution of this paper is twofold: (i) the production and publishing of a LOD dataset for the FrameNet lexical database, and (ii) the description of a method to produce knowledge patterns out of FrameNet frames. For both contributions we use Semion [15]: a tool for "triplifying" non-RDF data into RDF models, and for refactoring RDF into other RDF or OWL customized models. The transformation process includes two main steps: (i) a syntactic triplification of the original source and (ii) a rule-based refactoring for adding semantics to triples.

FrameNet as a LOD dataset provides new blood to the lexical grounding of semantic knowledge [12], and boosts the "lexical linked data" section of LOD, by linking FrameNet to other LOD datasets such as WordNet RDF (section 3.1). As a further contribution, we introduce a rule-based method to select and refactor part of FrameNet as full-fledged OWL knowledge patterns to be used for ontology design and advanced exploration of LOD. We discuss some non-trivial assumptions on how to interpret FrameNet relations as formal knowledge (section 4).

The structure of the paper is the following. In section 2 we summarize the conceptual design of FrameNet. In section 1 we present the production of FrameNet as a LOD dataset. Section 4 describes experiences in refactoring frames as knowledge patterns. Final sections contain related work and conclusions.

2. FRAMENET

FrameNet [1] is a lexical knowledge base, consisting of a set of *frames*, which have proper *frame elements* and *lexical units*, which pair words (*lexemes*) to frames. As described in the FrameNet Book [19]:

> a lexical unit (LU) is a pairing of a word with a meaning. Typically, each sense of a polysemous word belongs to a different semantic frame, a script-like conceptual structure that describes a particular type of situation, object, or event along with its participants and properties. For example, the **Apply Heat** frame describes a common situation involving a **Cook**, some **Food**, and a **Heating** Instrument, and is evoked by words such as *bake, blanch, boil, broil, brown, simmer, steam,* etc. We call these roles frame elements (FEs) and the frame-evoking words are LUs in the Apply heat frame.

FrameNet has a rich internal structure and makes some cognitive and semantic assumptions that makes it unique as a lexical resource. Some of them are discussed in Sect. 4 in view of logical formalization. The basic assumptions are reported here: frame elements are mostly unique to their frame; a frame usually has only some of its roles actually lexicalized in texts; frames can be *lexicalized* or not: non-lexicalized ones typically encode *schemata* from cognitive linguistics; frames, as well as frame elements, are related between them, e.g. through the *subframe* compositional relation, through inheritance relations, etc.

The semantic part of FrameNet is enriched by *semantic types* assigned to frames (e.g. **Artifact**), frame elements (e.g. **Sentient**), and lexical units (e.g. **Biframal_LU**).

FrameNet also contains a huge amount of manual annotations (*annotation sets*) of sentences from textual corpora with frames, frame elements and lexical units, which make word *valences* (syntactic and semantic combinatory of words) emerge.

3. BRINGING FRAMENET TO LOD

FrameNet stores lexical data into an XML database. We pulled out the semantics of FrameNet and its data by using Semion [15], a tool grounded on a method with two main steps: (i) a syntactic and completely automatic transformation of the data source to RDF datasets according to an OWL ontology that represents the data source structure, i.e. the source meta-model, (ii) a semantic refactoring that allows to express the RDF triples according to specific domain ontologies e.g. SKOS, DOLCE, FOAF, the Gene Ontology, or anything indicated by the user. This last action results in a RDF dataset, which expresses the knowledge stored in the original data source, according to a set of assumptions on the domain semantics, as selected and customized by the user. The refactoring step is the result of a non-trivial knowledge engineering work that requires a good knowledge of the target domain semantics. For that reason the refactoring is semi-automatic as it requires the design of transformation rules by the user. More exhaustively, the refactoring is performed by means of transformation rules of the form "*condition → consequent*" whose aim is to apply a tansformation (specified in the consequent) in the RDF graph only if the condition is satisfied with respect to the knowledge expressed in the source RDF graph. A set of rules which co-occur for the finalization of a transformation process is called a **transformation recipe**.

Figure 1 exemplifies the approach followed in this work for the production of both the LOD dataset and a set of knowledge patterns from the FrameNet lexical database. That approach grounds completely on the transformation method that the Semion tool implements. The leftmost part of the figure depicts the logical layers of the original source, i.e. FrameNet, which contains XML data, whose structure is defined by some XSD, which has its own standard meta-model [25]. The second leftmost part contains the result of step i): syntactic transformation of FrameNet to pure RDF triples, whose aim is twofold: (a) extracting data into RDF and (b) flattening the distinction between the original schema and data in order to provide, via the refactoring, a customized, task-oriented way to address domain semantics. Those RDF triples are refactored according to transformation recipes, either as a LOD dataset (ABox Refactoring, second rightmost column in the figure) or as Knowledge Patterns (TBox Refactoring, rightmost column).

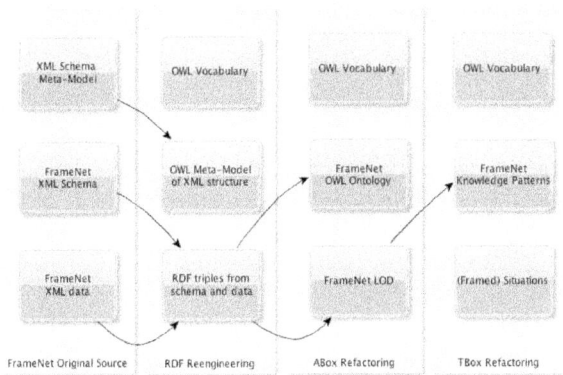

Figure 1: Semion tranformation: key concepts.

3.1 FrameNet linked data

The approach followed for the creation of a LOD dataset from FrameNet[1] is both derived from the transformation method implemented by Semion [15] and based on an iterative evaluation of the quality of the output produced with respect to the semantics of FrameNet formalized into a "gold standard" ontology[2] that we have used for the evaluation. Based on that, the transformation of FrameNet v.1.5 from XML to RDF consisted into two steps: (i) the syntactic transformation of the XML source to RDF according to the OWL meta-model that describes the structure of the source[3], (ii) the design and the application of a refactoring recipe for the ABox refactoring on the RDF produced in the first step. The recipe was derived generalizing and revising some of the common transformation practices from existing tools (i.e. XML2OWL [4], Top-Braid Composer[4], Rhizomik ReDeFer [18]). For example

---

[1]The dataset can be accessed through the SPARQL endpoint at http://bit.ly/fnsparql, as framenet_dataset
[2]http://ontologydesignpatterns.org/cp/owl/fn/framenet.owl
[3]http://www.ontologydesignpatterns.org/ont/iks/oxml.owl
[4]http://www.topbraidcomposer.com

we used the following mappings: (i) a xsd:ComplexType is mapped to an owl:Class, (ii) a xsd:SimpleType is mapped to an owl:DatatypeProperty and (iii) a xsd:Element is mapped either to an owl:ObjectProperty or to a owl:DatatypeProperty. Further details can be found in [4].

As an example, according to the syntax of the rules for the Semion refactoring, we have that the mapping (i) is expressed as

```
is(oxsd:ComplexType, ?type)
    ->
is(owl:Class, ?classNode)
```

and maps any individual of the class *oxsd:ComplexType* to a *owl:Class*. We refer to the Semion wiki[5] for more information about the tool and the syntax of the rules.

The relavance of a syntanctic transformation and a following refactoring can be clarified saying that it is designed as a semi-automatic approach which allows, via the refactoring rules, for better addressing the domain semantics of the original source. As an example, we can consider a simple frame-to-frame relation like

```
Inherits_from(Abounding_with, Locative_relation)
```

which expresses the fact that the frame *Abounding_with* inherits the schematic representation of a situation involving various participants, properties, and other conceptual roles from the frame *Locative_relation*. This relation is expressed in the XML FrameNet notation as:

```
<frame name="Abounding_with" ... ID="262">
  ...
  <frameRelation type="Inherits from">
    <relatedFrame>
      Locative_relation
    </relatedFrame>
  </frameRelation>
  ...
</frame>
```

and, with most of the existing tools, it is transformed to the RDF schematized in Figure 2. It is easy to notice how the Inherits from frame-to-frame relation is realized through the reification of the relation RelatedFrame_i, that expresses its type and the related frames, i.e. Inherits from and Locative_relation, as literals.

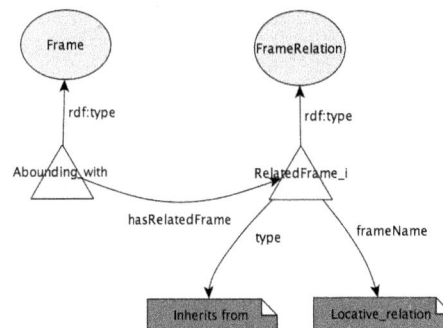

Figure 2: The "Inherits from" relation mapped to RDF with a common transformation recipe.

Instead, adopting the syntactic transformation of Semion,

---

[5]http://stlab.istc.cnr.it/stlab/Semion

we have produced firstly an RDF graph, which is depicted in Figure 3[6].

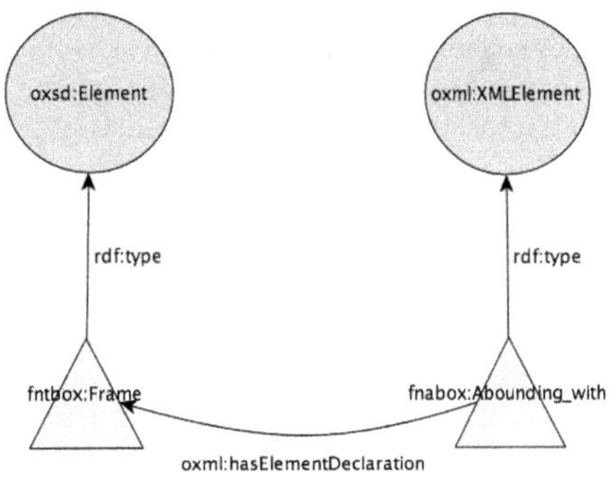

Figure 3: Example of reengineering of the frame "Abounding with" with its XSD definition.

In the figure, *fntbox:Frame* is no longer an *owl:Class*, but an *oxsd:Element* and *fnabox:Abounding_with* is an *oxml:XMLElement* related to *fntbox:Frame* through *oxsd:hasElementDeclaration*.

After having was syntactically converted FrameNet from XML to RDF, we applied the general recipe with the Semion Refactorer, in order to derive a LOD dataset for FrameNet. As the recipe is based on a general conversion from XML to OWL, the result was far from being a good formalization of the semantics of FrameNet. For that reason, we have incrementally refined the recipe in order to fill the gap between the semantics expressed by the output produced by the refactoring and the gold standard we had previously defined. We remark that the aim of the refactoring is to transform one RDF source to another trying to preserve either explicit or implicit domain semantics of the original source without information loss.

For example, the rule which allows to avoid the reification of frame-to-frame relations is shown in Figure 4. The rule

```
...
values(oxml:nodeValue, ?xmlAttr, ?value) .
values(oxml:nodeName, ?xmlAttr, "type"^^xsd:string) .
has(composite:child, ?xmlElem, ?child) .
values(oxml:nodeValue, ?child, ?childValue) .
let(?relatioURI, concat(namespace(?frame), trim(?value))) .
let(?frameURI, concat(namespace(?frame),
                      concat("frame/",
                             ?childValue
                      )
              )
) .

newNode(?frameRelation, ?frameURI) .
newNode(?relatedFrame, ?frameURI)

     ->

is(owl:ObjectProperty, ?frameRelation) .
has(rdfs:subPropertyOf, ?frameRelation,
    fns:hasFrameRelation) .
has(?frameRelation, ?frame, ?relatedFrame)
```

Figure 4: Rule which allows to express frame-to-frame relation as binary relations.

shown in Figure 4 transforms all the frame-to-frame relations

[6]oxsd and oxml are the default ontologies of Semion for XSD and XML data structures.

into binary relations between frames. The rule extracts the type of the relation from the **nodeValue** associated with the **type** attribute of a frame. Then it creates a new object property as a sub-property of **hasFrameRelation**, and resolves the name of the related frame that is expressed as a literal in the **relatedFrame** element, as shown in the XML code before. We remark that the model accessed by rules is not anymore the original XML source, but its syntactic translation to RDF. Figure 5 shows the RDF of the **inherits from** relation between the frames **Abounding with** and **Locative relation** obtained by applying the refactoring recipe with Semion. Figure 6 shows the core fragment of the OWL

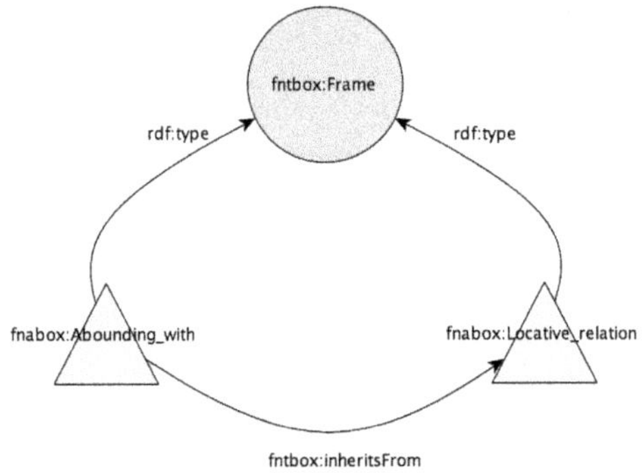

Figure 5: The "Inherits from" frame-to-frame relation between the frames "Abounding with" and "Locative relation" after the refactoring.

schema of FrameNet used as a vocabulary for the data from FrameNet.

Figure 6: A fragment of the FrameNet OWL schema.

The complete refactoring recipe[7] is composed by 58 transformation rules in forward-chaining inference mode.

An important feature of FrameNet as a dataset in the LOD cloud , that will be investigated as part of our ongoing work, is the mapping of its frames and frame elements to other lexical resources, e.g. WordNet. WordNet is available as a LOD dataset since 2006 as a result of the W3C working draft [21]. Such mappings can be obtained from VerbNet [22], a lexical resource that incorporates both semantic and syntactic information about English verb semantics. The VerbNet 3.1 XML database provides mappings between VerbNet classes, FrameNet frames, and WordNet synsets.

For example, from the VerbNet mappings converted to RDF:[8]

```
vnclass:accompany skos:exactMatch
wndata:synset-accompany-verb-2

vnclass:accompany skos:exactMatch
frame:Cotheme
```

The VerbNet dataset excerpt is intended to demonstrate linkings between lexical resources. An official release will be published in the near future.

4. FROM FRAMES TO KNOWLEDGE PATTERNS

In addition to the production of FrameNet as a LOD lexical dataset that can be accessed and queried over the Web of Data, our aim is to provide an interpretation of frames as Knowledge Patterns (KP), as they are defined by [7] and [12]. In other words, following [12], we promote frames to relevant units of meaning for knowledge representation.

With reference to Figure 1, we have called this process TBox refactoring, because a new ontology schema (a TBox), is obtained starting from data (ABox).

The main problem with TBox refactoring is deciding the formal semantics to assign to the classes from the FrameNet LOD dataset schema. Since this is a relatively arbitrary process, SemionRules and recipes are useful to configure alternative choices or to compare the different assumptions made by knowledge engineers. Here we present a refactoring experience that exemplifies the design method behind such process, and how Semion is useful in supporting it. The recipe exemplified here is part of a larger project carried out together with FrameNet developers in Berkeley in order to optimize the refactoring from lexical frames to knowledge patterns: as such, it certainly bears validity, but it is mainly intended as a methodological and pragmatical description of refactoring recipes (also called *correspondence patterns* in [24]).

Besides the basic assumptions reported in section 2, this process is guided by the Book [19], which is quite explicit about possible formal semantic choices:

> The most basic summarization of the logic of FrameNet is that Frames describe classes of situations, the semantics of LUs are subclasses of the

Frames, and (...) FEs are classes that are arguments of the Frame classes. An annotation set for a sentence generally describes an instance of the subclass associated with an LU as well as instances of each of its associated FE classes (...) The term "Frame Element" has two meanings: the relation itself, and the filler of the relation. When we describe the Coreness status of an FE (...) we are describing the relation; when we describe the Ontological type on an FE (...) we mean the type of the filler.

According to these statements, a fragment of the **Desiring** frame is transformed into OWL as follows (in Manchester syntax):

```
Ontology: odpfn:desiring.owl
Annotations:
    cpannoschema:specializes odp:situation.owl
Class: desiring:Desiring
    SubClassOf:
        desiring:hasEvent some desiring:Event,
        desiring:hasExperiencer some desiring:Experiencer,
        desiring:hasDegree some desiring:Degree,
        desiring:hasReason some desiring:Reason,
Class: desiring:covet.v
    SubClassOf: desiring:Desiring
Class: desiring:Event
    SubClassOf: semtype:State_of_Affairs
Class: desiring:Experiencer
    SubClassOf: semtype:Sentient
```

Notice that the uniqueness (*locality*) of frame elements and lexical units for a frame is obtained simply by means of a specific namespace (denoted by the *desiring* prefix in the example, see below for possible namespace policies), while a frame is interpreted as an owl:Class, lexical units as its subclasses, frame elements as both an owl:Class (e.g. *Event*) and an owl:ObjectProperty (e.g. *hasEvent*), the relation between a frame and a frame element as a rdfs:subClassOf an owl:Restriction, and the semantic type assignments to frame elements as additional subclass axioms. All knowledge patterns derived from frames are considered specialization of the generic pattern `odp:situation.owl`[9], which generalizes the situation semantics suggested by Berkeley linguists.

A central role in FrameNet is played by *inheritance* assumptions. In [19], inheritance is viewed as

> the strongest relation between frames, corresponding to is-a in many ontologies. With this relation, anything which is strictly true about the semantics of the Parent must correspond to an equally or more specific fact about the Child. This includes Frame Element membership of the frames (except for Extrathematic FEs), most Semantic Types, frame relations to other frames, relationships among the Frame Elements, and Semantic Types on the Frame Elements.

This means that additional axioms must be wrapped into ontologies derived from frames, e.g. these two sample axioms are derived from the *inheritsFrom* relation between the **Aesthetics** and **Desirability** frames as well as from the *subFE* relation between some of their frame elements:

```
Ontology: odpfn:aesthetics.owl
```

[7] http://stlab.istc.cnr.it/stlab/FrameNetKCAP2011#tab=ABoxRefactoring

[8] prefixes: skos: http://www.w3.org/2004/02/skos/core#; vnclass: http://www.ontologydesignpatterns.org/ont/vn/class/; wndata: http://www.w3.org/2006/03/wn/wn20/instances/; frame: http://www.ontologydesignpatterns.org/ont/framenet/frame/

[9] odp:http://www.ontologydesignpatterns.org/cp/owl/, odpfn:http://www.ontologydesignpatterns.org/cp/owl/fn/

```
Annotations:
    cpannoschema:specializes odpfn:desirability.owl
Class: aesthetics:Aesthetics
    SubClassOf: desirability:Desirability
Class: aesthetics:Degree
    SubClassOf: desirability:Degree
```

The implementation of TBox refactoring is performed as a Semion refactoring, where the recipe includes rules for the mapping between FrameNet LOD dataset and KPs. Figure 7 shows an overview of TBox refactoring for deriving KPs from frames. The notation attempts to make rules in-

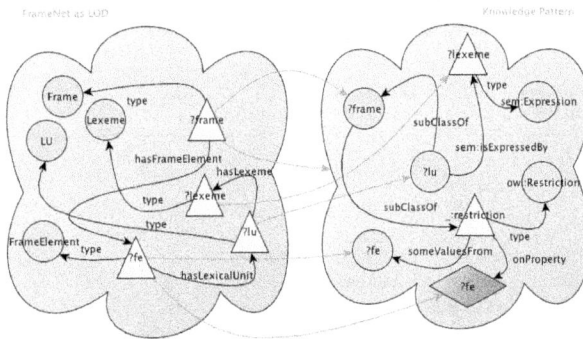

Figure 7: Diagram of the transformation recipe used for the production of knowledge patterns from FrameNet LOD.

tuitively understandable: arrows between the clouds represent mappings from entities in the cloud "FrameNet as LOD" to entities in the cloud "Knowledge Pattern", classes are represented as circles, individuals as triangles, object properties as diamonds, and structural properties as labeled arcs. Each *Frame* is mapped both to an `owl:Ontology` that identifies the KP and to an `owl:Class`. The mapping takes into account the refactoring of the frame URI intended either as an ontology or as a class. Each *FrameElement* maps both to an `owl:Class` and to an `owl:ObjectProperty`. Again frame elements follow a renaming policy for the two interpretations, but in this case the situation is more complex. In fact, URI policy can follow from different interpretations:

1. *Locality* of frame elements within their frames (compatible to locality statements in the Book, with some exceptions that cannot be discussed here). E.g. given the frame:
   `http://someuri/Judgment.owl#Judgment`
   we obtain the frame element:
   `http://someuri/Judgment.owl#Cognizer`
   interpreted as a class and
   `http://someuri/Judgment.owl#hasCognizer`
   interpreted as an object property;[10]

2. *Globality* of frame elements, abstracted from their contextual binding to a frame, e.g. given the frame:
   `http://someuri/Judgment.owl#Judgment`
   we obtain the frame element:
   `http://someuri/class/Cognizer`
   interpreted as a class and

`http://someuri/property/hasCognizer`
interpreted as an object property.

Lexical units are refactored as subclasses of the classes derived from the frames they are lexicalizations of, e.g.
`lexunit:cool.a SubClassOf: desirability:Desirability`
Lexemes are refactored as individuals of the class `semantics:Expression`; each lexical unit is related to a lexeme through the property `semantics:isExpressedBy`.
Finally, each frame has `owl:someValuesFrom` restrictions accounting for the semantic roles implicit in frame elements (see example above).
Locality and globality alternatives required two refactoring recipies each of one composed by 4 rules in forward-chaining inference mode. The complete TBox refactoring recipe can be found in the wiki page[11].

5. RELATED WORK

The literature in reusing FrameNet for NLP tasks such as question-answering is too large to be covered here, and not central to the work described (see e.g. [23] [6]).
Work in using FrameNet jointly with other lexical resources, although not in the LOD way, include at least [5], which creates a linking from WordNet to FrameNet in a purely NLP context.
Previous FrameNet conversions to RDF include [8, 14, 20]. [14] proposes a partial translation of FrameNet version 1.2 to RDF, and uses DAML both for the FrameNet meta-model, and the conceptual elements (frames, elements, etc.). They developed an automatic translator specific to that purpose. In 2003, the mixing of meta-model and FrameNet data made it difficult to be processed by reasoners for OWL (but it'd be acceptable in OWL2). For that reason, [20] applied an ad-hoc XSLT to move part of the FrameNet version 1.3 XML database to OWL. While the quality of the partial transformation is high, the process is not easily customizable. [20] also proposes a solution to deductive reasoning with natural language based on combining lexical resources with the world knowledge provided by ontologies.
After the release of version 1.5, the Berkeley FrameNet group asked us to produce a new version of FrameNet in RDF, optimized for publishing in the growing lexical part of the LOD cloud. This is what we describe in this paper.
From the viewpoint of formal semantic interpretation of FrameNet, [8] uses both ABox and TBox conversions to perform automatic enrichment of FrameNet with reference to a large corpus where frames are detected, new frames and elements are discovered and typed with a WordNet Supersense learner, and finally reengineered through a previous alignment to the LMM semiotic ontology [17] (used in this paper with the odp:semiotics.owl knowledge pattern.
[9] is a deeper analysis of the semiotic relations behind FrameNet, VerbNet and WordNet, and proposes a method to formalize their mappings. The semantics of the frames is put in perspective with the Descriptions and Situations knowledge pattern, partly reused in this paper to represent the situation-based semantics declared by [19]. The article also proposes to represent the full semantics of frames as n-ary polymorphic relations in FOL. This proposal is not directly implementable in OWL, but provides a useful abstraction across the different notions of a frame in cognitive science,

---

[10]An OWL2 alternative is also possible, with multiple interpretations for the same constant.

[11]http://stlab.istc.cnr.it/stlab/FrameNetKCAP2011#tab=TBoxRefactoring

46

AI, linguistics, knowledge engineering, etc.

[16] is an attempt to formalize and "clean" the semantics of FrameNet version 1.3. The authors motivate the cleansing need by performing "ontological analysis": e.g. they claim that frames do not always refer to situation classes because some of them actually represent abstract relations such as *part of*: since abstract entities should be assumed as non-localized, non-temporal entities, while situations should be interpreted as events occurring in time, frames should be formalized differently according to their ontological type. Frame to frame relations are also suggested an extensive revision on similar grounds. This work, besides the problem of sharing agreement on the general principles adopted for the analysis, could benefit from a customized refactoring of FrameNet, in order to perform their analyses directly on formal ontologies.

6. DISCUSSION

We have presented a conversion of FrameNet to RDF, published a dataset in the LOD cloud, linked to WordNet and other lexical datasets. We have also presented a method to convert FrameNet data into knowledge patterns. For both projects, we have employed the Semion tool with Semion-Rules, which allows a customized and explicit transformation from RDB or XML to RDF and OWL.

The intricate semantics of FrameNet, only partly described in this paper, gets to grips with the expressive power of natural language. A fixed, ad-hoc transformation would be best for one, arbitrary for another, bad for a third. Customization is key with lexical data because there are use cases for maintaining the semantics of the original resource, often a purely intensional one (similar to the practice of using SKOS with thesauri), as well as for morphing the original semantics to something closer to the extensional formal semantics of web ontologies. In between these two ends, there are several intermediate cases and exceptions, which make the case for tools that minimize hard-coding of the transformation semantics, and preserve the opportunity to learn and share good practices for transforming lexical resources to linked data and domain knowledge.

Current ongoing work concentrates on refinement of the RDF dataset with the Berkeley FrameNet group, the generation of new links to lexical datasets as well as other relevant LOD datasets (e.g. DBpedia), the creation of the FrameNet valence dataset, which will be a substantial (about 35 million triples) resource for hybridizing semantic web and linked data, and the refinement of a recipe to produce and automatically publish FrameNet-based knowledge patterns on the ODP portal[12]. These knowledge patterns implement a large section of the rich knowledge pattern structure envisaged by [12], with formal axioms, lexically motivated vocabulary, textual corpus grounding, and data grounding.

Acknowledgements

This work has been part-funded by the European Commission under grant agreement FP7-ICT-2007-3/ No. 231527 (IKS - Interactive Knowledge Stack).

7. REFERENCES

[1] C. F. Baker, C. J. Fillmore, and J. B. Lowe. The berkeley framenet project. In *Proceedings of the 17th international conference on Computational linguistics*, pages 86–90, Morristown, NJ, USA, 1998.

[2] C. Baldassarre, E. Daga, A. Gangemi, A. M. Gliozzo, A. Salvati, and G. Troiani. Semantic scout: Making sense of organizational knowledge. In P. Cimiano and H. S. Pinto, editors, *EKAW*, volume 6317 of *Lecture Notes in Computer Science*, pages 272–286. Springer, 2010.

[3] C. Bizer, T. Heath, and T. Berners-Lee. Linked Data - The Story So Far. *International Journal on Semantic Web and Information Systems*, 5(3):1–22, 2009.

[4] H. Bohring and S. Auer. Mapping xml to owl ontologies. In *Proceedings of 13. Leipziger Informatik-Tage (LIT 2005), Sep. 21-23*, Lecture Notes in Informatics (LNI), September 2005.

[5] A. Burchardt, K. Erk, and A. Frank. A WordNet Detour to FrameNet. In *Proceedings of the GLDV 2005 GermaNet II Workshop*, pages 408–421, Bonn, Germany, 2005.

[6] A. Burchardt and M. Pennacchiotti. FATE: a FrameNet-Annotated Corpus for Textual Entailment. In *LREC*. European Language Resources Association, 2008.

[7] P. Clark, J. Thompson, and B. Porter. Knowledge Patterns. In A. G. Cohn, F. Giunchiglia, and B. Selman, editors, *KR2000: Principles of Knowledge Representation and Reasoning*, pages 591–600, San Francisco, 2000. Morgan Kaufmann.

[8] B. Coppola, A. Gangemi, A. M. Gliozzo, D. Picca, and V. Presutti. Frame detection over the Semantic Web. *Paper, ESWC,*, 2009.

[9] A. Gangemi. What's in a Schema? In C. Huang, N. Calzolari, A. Gangemi, A. Lenci, A. Oltramari, and L. Prevot, editors, *Ontology and the Lexicon*. Cambridge University Press, 2010.

[10] A. Gangemi, R. Navigli, and P. Velardi. The OntoWordNet Project: Extension and Axiomatization of Conceptual Relations in WordNet. In R. Meersman and Z. Tari, editors, *Proc. of On the Move to Meaningful Internet Systems (OTM2003) (Catania, Italy)*, pages 820–838. Springer-Verlag, 2003.

[11] A. Gangemi and V. Presutti. Ontology Design Patterns. In S. Staab and R. Studer, editors, *Handbook on Ontologies, 2nd Edition*. Springer Verlag, 2009.

[12] A. Gangemi and V. Presutti. Towards a Pattern Science for the Semantic Web. *Semantic Web*, 1(1-2):61–68, 2010.

[13] M. Minsky. A Framework for Representing Knowledge. In P. Winston, editor, *The Psychology of Computer Vision*. McGraw-Hill, 1975.

[14] S. Narayanan, M. R. L. Petruck, C. F. Baker, and C. J. Fillmore. Putting framenet data into the iso linguistic annotation framework. In *Proceedings of the ACL 2003 workshop on Linguistic annotation*, LingAnnot 03, pages 22–29, Stroudsburg, PA, USA, 2003. ACL.

[15] A. G. Nuzzolese, A. Gangemi, V. Presutti, and P. Ciancarini. Fine-tuning triplification with Semion. In V. Presutti, V. Svatek, and F. Sharffe, editors, *Wks. on Knowledge Injection into and Extraction from Linked Data (KIELD2010)*, pages 2–14, Lisbon, Portugal, October 2010.

[16] E. Ovchinnikova, L. Vieu, A. Oltramari, S. Borgo, and T. Alexandrov. Data-driven and ontological analysis of framenet for natural language reasoning. In *Proceedings of LREC'10*, Valletta, Malta, may 2010. ELRA.

[17] D. Picca, A. M. Gliozzo, and A. Gangemi. LMM: an OWL-DL MetaModel to Represent Heterogeneous Lexical Knowledge. In *LREC*. European Language Resources Association, 2008.

[18] Rhizomik. ReDeFer. http://rhizomik.net/html/redefer, 2011. (accessed 15-02-2011).

[19] J. Ruppenhofer, M. Ellsworth, M. R. L. Petruck, C. R. Johnson, and J. Scheffczyk. FrameNet II: Extended Theory and Practice. http://framenet.icsi.berkeley.edu/book/book.html, 2006.

[20] J. Scheffczyk, C. F. Baker, and S. Narayanan. Reasoning

---

[12] http://www.ontologydesignpatterns.org, cf. [11]

over Natural Language Text by means of FrameNet and
Ontologies. In C. Huang, N. Calzolari, A. Gangemi,
A. Lenci, A. Oltramari, and L. Prevot, editors, *Ontology
and the Lexicon*. Cambridge University Press, 2010.

[21] G. Schreiber, M. van Assem, and A. Gangemi. RDF/OWL
Representation of WordNet. W3C Working Draft, W3C,
June 2006.
http://www.w3.org/TR/2006/WD-wordnet-rdf-20060619/.

[22] K. K. Schuler. *VerbNet: A Broad-Coverage, Comprehensive
Verb Lexicon*. PhD thesis, University of Pennsylvania, 2006.

[23] D. Shen and M. Lapata. Using Semantic Roles to Improve
Question Answering. In *EMNLP-CoNLL*, pages 12–21.
ACL, 2007.

[24] O. Sváb-Zamazal, V. Svátek, and F. Scharffe.
Pattern-based ontology transformation service. In J. L. G.
Dietz, editor, *KEOD*, pages 42–47. INSTICC Press, 2009.

[25] P. Walmsley and D. C. Fallside. XML Schema Part 0:
Primer Second Edition. W3C recommendation, W3C,
October 2004. http://www.w3.org/TR/2004/REC-
xmlschema-0-20041028/.

Experience With Long-term Knowledge Acquisition

Paul Compton[1]
School of Comp. Sci. & Eng.
University of New South Wales
Kensington, NSW 2052, Australia
+61 2 9385 6906

mkim978@cse.unsw.edu.au

Lindsay Peters, Timothy Lavers
Pacific Knowledge Systems Pty. Ltd
16010, Australian Technology Park
Everleigh NSW 2015, Australia
+61 2 92094852

l.peters, t.lavers@pks.com.au

Yang Sok Kim
School. of Comp. Sci. & Eng.
University of New South Wales
Kensington, NSW 2052, Australia
+61 2 9385 5644

yskim@cse.unsw.edu.au

ABSTRACT

Evaluation has remained a major challenge for knowledge acquisition and little data is available on how experts actually use knowledge acquisition technology. A number of companies offer Ripple-Down Rules to enable on-going knowledge acquisition and maintenance while a system is in use. One of these companies, Pacific Knowledge Systems has logged user activity over a number of years. Data from these logs demonstrate that domain experts continue to add knowledge to a knowledge base over years. The logs also demonstrate that new knowledge can be added very rapidly regardless of knowledge base size or age. We assume that the on-going knowledge acquisition observed was driven by the need to make changes and encouraged and allowed by the ease of the knowledge acquisition technology used. The question arises of whether experts in other domains would also chose to continue to add knowledge to their knowledge bases if this was supported.

Categories and Subject Descriptors

I.2.1 Applications and Expert Systems – *Medicine and science* I.2.5 Programming Languages and Software – *Expert system tools and techniques.* I.2.6 Learning – *Knowledge Acquisition.*

General Terms

Algorithms, Measurement, Experimentation, Human Factors, Verification.

Keywords

Ripple-Down Rules, evaluation

1. INTRODUCTION

Knowledge acquisition research covers a wide range of topics, but one of the core research challenges has been to develop tools and methods for people to transfer their expertise to a knowledge base. Evaluation has always been a major challenge for this type of knowledge acquisition research, as the most appropriate forms of evaluation are studies of actual domain experts using knowledge

---

[1] Paul Compton is also a part-time consultant to Pacific Knowledge Systems, and has a small shareholding in the company.

acquisition tools and methods. In general this is too difficult both in terms of sufficient access to experts, or even "lay" experts, and appropriate controls in experimental design. The Sisyphus experiments proposed a series of knowledge acquisition tasks and provided relevant data and material for different research groups to build systems that could be compared [1]. The Sisyphus experiments produced very useful results as one could see how different tools and methods approached the same problem. However, this fell well short of true comparative evaluation as the systems were built from the materials provided by the knowledge acquisition research groups themselves rather than domain experts. Niche evaluation has also been carried out using simulated experts built by machine learning to provide "expertise" [2].

It is probably fair to say that most research on tools and methods for human knowledge acquisition has been forced to use persuasive arguments and one-off demonstrations. This is not a criticism; it is simply too costly to provide more empirical evaluation.

One issue arising from the difficulty of evaluation is that fundamental empirical questions about whether knowledge acquisition tools and methods are cognitively appropriate remain unexplored. The situated cognition debate concerned the central question of whether knowledge is something to be mined or extracted from the expert's mind or whether knowledge is something that is constructed in a particular context [3] and necessarily incomplete [4]. This relates to the qualification problem [5] which states that it is impossible to anticipate all situations that will arise for a robot in the real world. Situated cognition similarly claims that the knowledge we express about the world is always partial and incomplete.

Ripple-Down Rules (RDR) were developed to enable knowledge to be continually added to a knowledge-based system while it is use. This does not solve the problems identified by situated cognition, but at least supports on-going fixes to the partial knowledge that humans provide.

RDR have now been widely used for building knowledge-based systems while they are in use. This paper presents summary data from the activity logs of 246 RDR knowledge-based systems, providing data on the number of cases processed, rules added, the time to add rules etc. This data cannot provide a proper comparative evaluation of Ripple-Down Rules, but it at least provides substantial empirical data on the use of knowledge acquisition tools which support on-going knowledge acquisition. Such data does not seem to be available for other knowledge acquisition tools.

2. RIPPLE-DOWN RULES (RDR)

The essential feature of RDR is that rules are added to deal with specific cases (generally while the system is already in operation use). That is, the rule building process starts whenever a case is processed by the system and fails to give the correct output. New rules to give the correct output for the case are then added into the inference sequence. Rule placement is automatic and outside the control of the expert (or knowledge engineer). Since there is no knowledge structuring and no requirement to understand the knowledge base as a whole, rules can be added by domain experts very quickly and easily.

There are now number of different RDR algorithms, SCRDR[6], MCRDR[2], NRDR[7] etc. It is beyond the scope of this paper to discuss them in detail, but they are all based on the idea of a fixed inference sequence so that a new or correction rule is added automatically into the inference sequence.

The strict inference sequencing in RDR enables a second type of knowledge acquisition support. An expert may add a rule for a case that is overly specific, but they can only introduce an error affecting the previous knowledge base by adding a rule that is too general, so that cases previously processed by the same sequence may now incorrectly fire the new rule. Such cases can be shown to the expert who either makes their rule more specific to exclude the cases, or accepts that the rule should apply to these cases. Suitable cases can be provided by saving the cases for which rules are added, known as 'cornerstone cases'.

The first RDR system in routine use using SCRDR inference was a 2000 rule system for chemical pathology[6]. The study here is based on Pacific Knowledge Systems proprietary RDR technology (RippleDown®) based on MCRDR[2] which allows multiple conclusions for a case. In an earlier report on use of this technology, chemical pathologists from one laboratory added about 16,000 rules across 20 knowledge bases over a 29 month period, at an average speed of 77 secs per rule [8]. This paper is based on the same type of logs of user activity, but from 246 knowledge bases from 17 different laboratory organizations, including both public and private laboratories and also including the laboratory reported in the previous study [8].

RDR are used in other areas apart from medicine. Ivis Pty. Ltd[2], maintains the web site of TESCO the world's largest on-line grocer, using RDR [9]. Erudine Pty. Ltd[3] (previously known as Rippledown Solutions), does not reference RDR but describes an identical approach in white papers e.g. for redeveloping legacy systems. Other companies offer RDR products as one of their range, e.g an RDR data cleansing product from IBM[4] [10]. These examples are included to illustrate that RDR are used in other areas beyond medical diagnostic reporting which is the source of the log data described here.

3. DATA USED

The data comes from logs of activity across 246 knowledge bases from 17 diagnostic laboratory customers of Pacific Knowledge Systems[5] which have been used to process about 330 million sets of data or cases. These knowledge bases are used for providing detailed diagnostic comments on laboratory results across clinical chemistry, serology, immunology etc for reports to go out to referring clinicians. They are also used by some laboratories to manage workflow as well as to audit test requests advising whether the requests were appropriate given the patient history, payment rules and so. Laboratories tend to use multiple knowledge bases

to cover different sub-domains. Sometimes the same expert will be responsible for knowledge building for different sub-domains, or there may be individual experts with more specialized responsibility.

The typical procedure is that when laboratory reports are generated the test result data plus available patient history are passed to the knowledge-based system which generates a detailed interpretative comment, with perhaps multiple independent comments, to be added to the report. The report is validated by senior domain experts, generally pathologists, and if the comment is inappropriate or missing, an appropriate comment will be added, the report will be sent to the referring clinician in the normal way and the report with appropriate comment will be referred for knowledge-building. Not all reports will be checked as the pathologist expert may decide after some time that some reports only need to be looked at periodically or under certain conditions, and so allow some level of auto-validation. This corresponds to the normal practice of testing and evaluating a system before it is put into routine use, but here the system is monitored while it is in use, and the level of monitoring can be adjusted depending on how the system has performed.

New rules can then be added for cases for which comments were changed by the validating expert. The person adding the rules may or may not be the same expert who carried out the validation. The system records the time from when the expert calls up the case to when they have finished adding rules and exit the knowledge-builder module. Since the case already has a new comment, their task is to select features in the case which justify the comment. These features are used as the rule conditions. The rule is then verified against cornerstone cases, and if necessary further features are selected to refine the rule. Because composite comments are supported, the expert may add more than one rule for a case. The normal domain task of assigning an appropriate comment to a report was carried out at the report validation stage. The time logged for the rule-building sessions covers the knowledge engineering tasks of selecting rule conditions, which may include developing functions using the rich function language provided, and verifying and adjusting the resultant rules. Since there is no other knowledge engineering task in adding rules, the logged time represents the maximum time the expert spends on knowledge engineering. There is nothing that can be done away from the knowledge builder module except the normal domain expert task of writing an appropriate comment, which the expert should do anyway.

Since the logged time covers the time from when a case is called up for knowledge building until knowledge building is complete it includes any waiting period that the user experiences before the next cornerstone case is presented to them. It also includes time on extraneous activities such as answering the phone, getting coffee, or simply walking away from the computer screen for a prolonged period. We therefore use the median rather than the average time in the discussion below. The logs record the total number of cases for which rules are added in the month and the total time, so more exactly we use the median of the monthly average. The average of the monthly average is about twice the median, but shows the same relation to knowledge base size and age. The logs do not provide information on how many rules are added for a case, only the overall knowledge-building time. We assume that only one rule is added for most cases.

In the following discussion we use the term knowledge acquisition event (KA event) interchangeably with the term rule. We only have log data on KA events, not on rules added or total rules

---

[2] www.ivisgroup.com

[3] www.erudine.com

[4] http://domino.research.ibm.com/comm/research_
projects.nsf/pages/caats.index.html

[5] www.pks.com.au

in a knowledge base. The number of KA events may underestimate, but cannot overestimate the number of rules, because there is at least one rule for each KA event. Any underestimate of knowledge base size in the following strengthens rather than weakens the results of the study.

The KA events only cover knowledge building while the knowledge base is in use. If rules were added prior to the knowledge base being putting into use, this is not captured. Some knowledge bases may also have their name changed and may appear to be a new knowledge base, with only new KA events counted under the new name. It would be possible to resolve such questions by obtaining detailed information about the 246 knowledge bases from the laboratories but this was beyond the scope of this study.

4. RESULTS

The logs cover 246 knowledge bases and 183 of the 246 knowledge bases were in routine use in 2010 providing diagnostic comments for patient reports or auditing whether test requests were appropriate, and medical alerts. Logs from Pacific Knowledge Systems non-medical customers are not included. The 63 knowledge bases not in use in 2010 were all developed by laboratories who had multiple other knowledge bases in use in 2010 and were continuing knowledge building, so they do not represent abandoning the technology, but it was beyond the scope of this study to investigate the history of individual knowledge bases.

4.1 Knowledge Base Sizes

Knowledge base sizes (no of KA events)

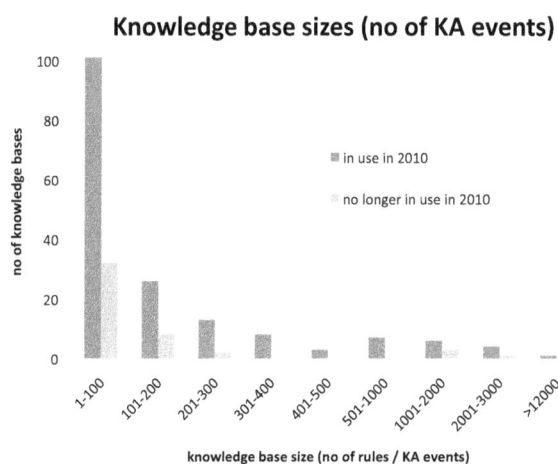

Figure 1 shows the number of knowledge bases of various sizes. These are the final sizes in the log data.

The size of the knowledge bases, both those in use and 2010 and those not in use (at least not under the original name) are shown in Figure 1. The majority of the knowledge bases are small, but eleven have had over 1000 KA events, so have at least 1000 rules and one of these has at least 12,737 rules.

Figure 2 shows the length of time the knowledge bases in use in 2010 have been in use. 50 of the 183 knowledge bases have been in use for a year or less, but over 70 have been in use for five or more years.

Figure 3 shows the same information related to knowledge base size (i.e. number of KA events). For each knowledge base size it shows whether the knowledge bases were in their first year of use, second, third, fourth or had been in use for 5 or more years in 2010. As might be expected, the larger knowledge bases tend to

have been in use longer. Of the smallest knowledge bases, with under 100 KA events, over 30% are in their first year as would be expected, but another 30% of these knowledge bases have been in use for five or more years.

Age of knowledge bases

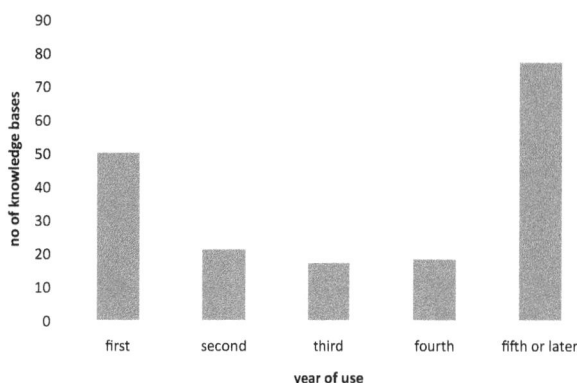

Figure 2 shows the number of knowledge bases in use in 2010 against their age.

Size and age of knowledge bases in use in 2010

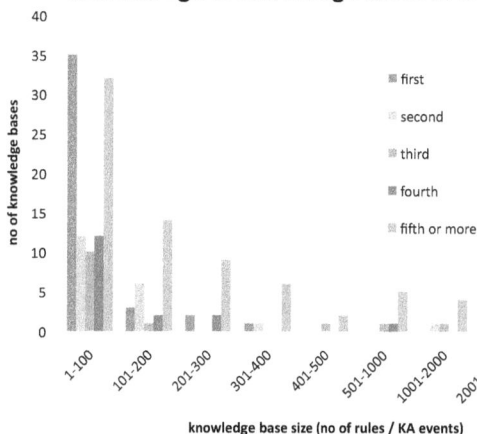

Figure 3 shows numbers of knowledge bases in use in 2010 with respect to size and the number of years of use. I.e. whether it 2010, the knowledge base is in its first, second or later year of use.

There are a number of factors that determine knowledge base size. The most obvious factor is the size of the domain, as it is up to the laboratories to decide how many individual knowledge bases they wish to develop and the coverage of individual knowledge bases (e.g. separate knowledge bases for diabetes and thyroid comments). Figure 4 illustrates that the single knowledge base with 12,737 rules processes the largest number of cases. This may be because this a particularly high-volume domain, or perhaps because it covers a wider range of chemical pathology; however it is a single data point and in contrast the four next largest knowledge bases (2001-3000) on average processed the smallest number of cases. Overall there does not seem to be a relationship between knowledge base size and number of cases processed. Across all knowledge bases an average 82,571 cases were processed per knowledge base per month in 2010.

51

No of cases processed per month per knowledge base in 2010

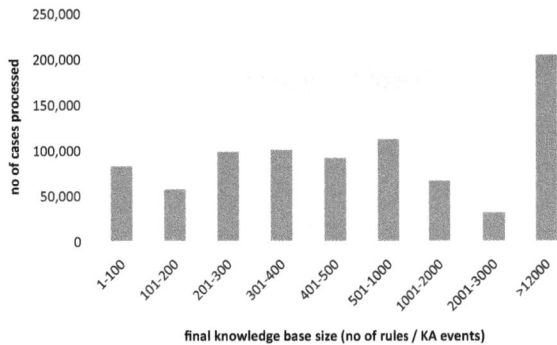

No of knowledge bases with rules added each year

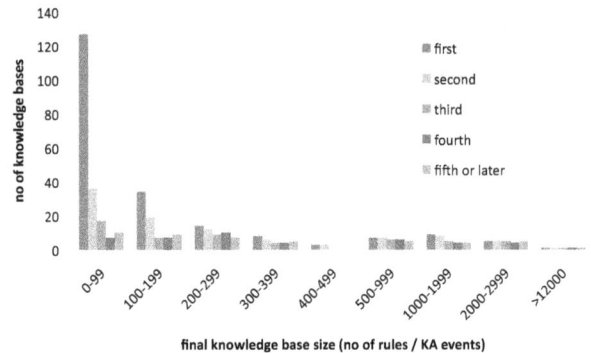

Figure 4 shows the number of cases processed per month per knowledge base in 2010 related to knowledge base size.

Although the size of the knowledge base will relate to the complexity of the domain, domain complexity is determined not just by the domain but also by the subtlety of the comments that the experts choose to make. For example if a report includes an elevated cholesterol, a very simple comment might be made that the cholesterol is elevated. However, the pathologist may also take into the patient's previous records and current treatment and if appropriate, may make a comment along the lines: "Raised cholesterol level persists on Zocor treatment. Consider increasing dose of Zocor and repeat lipid profile in 4 weeks. Note that hypothroidism may impair response to Zocor; suggest TSH level at time of next review." Clearly a comment like this is potentially more helpful to a GP, particularly in reminding the GP that thyroid disease may affect lipids, but making such a comment depends on the system having access to information about treatment, previous cholesterol results, and that there were no previous TSH results for the patient, as well as the current cholesterol results. It also depends on the domain expert taking the initiative to write the more sophisticated rules required. In the highly complex Bone Mineral Density domain each report comprises up to 50 comments. In this case, the expert is motivated to provide such a detailed report because referring GPs do not readily understand the raw results in this specialised domain. Although this is a low volume domain there is a significant time saving in an automated report compared to writing or dictating the report, warranting the knowledge acquisition effort involved.

A further issue is that although a knowledge engineer to structure the knowledge base is not needed, the pathologist needs to develop some knowledge engineering skills, not only in using the range of functions provided, but they also need some insight into the appropriate granularity of rules. If the pathologist creates rules that are inappropriately general, unnecessary refinement will be needed. On the other hand highly specific rules will mean that more rules will have to be added to cover the domain.

The key feature of RDR is that it enables rules to be added after the system is already in use. Figure 5 shows the number of knowledge bases to which rules have been added during each year of use. It also shows the year of use.

Figure 5 shows the number of knowledge bases to which rules have been added during each year of use: first, second, etc. This figure shows results for all 246 knowledge bases, not just the 183 in clinical use in 2010.

The same data in figure 5 is shown in figure 6 as a percentage of the number of knowledge bases of that size. The most remarkable feature of this data is that knowledge bases have rules added in later years and that this occurs even with small knowledge bases. 27% of the knowledge bases with less than 100 rules (KA events) have rules added in the second year and 13% have rules added in the third year. For knowledge bases of 200 to 300 rules, 80% have rules added in the second year, and five years and beyond, 47% are still having rules added.

% of knowledge bases with rules added each year

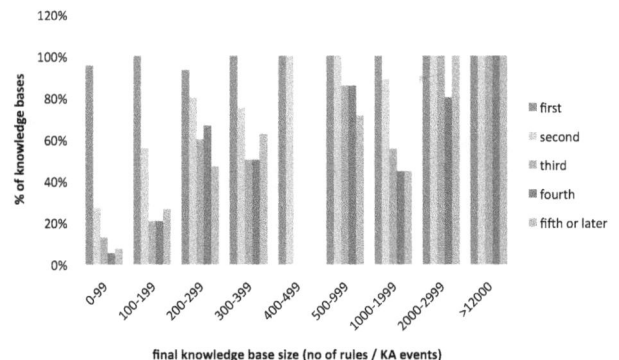

Figure 6 shows the same data as in figure 5, but expressed as a proportion of the number of knowledge bases.

The knowledge bases in figures 5 and 6 may have had only one rule added each year after the first year, so figure 7 provides data on the total number of rules added after a knowledge base has been in use for at least a year. Again even for knowledge bases of less that 100 rules 10% of the KA events occurred after a year in use. In general the larger the knowledge base, the more rules are added later, except for the three 400-500 rule knowledge bases.

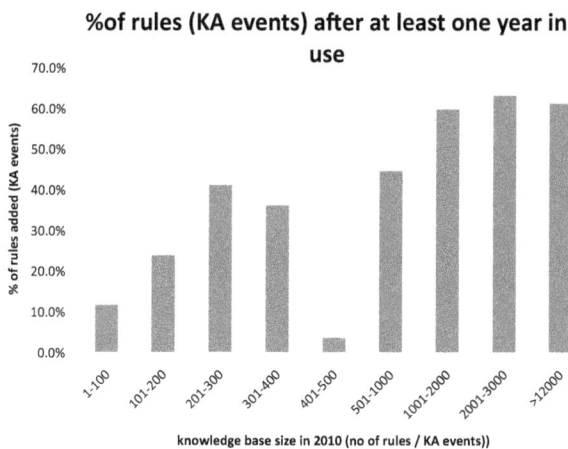

% of rules (KA events) after at least one year in use

Figure 7 shows the number of KA events after at least one year in use. It shows the number of KA events after a year in use as a proportion of the total number of KA events for knowledge bases of a particular size. It only covers knowledge bases in use in 2010.

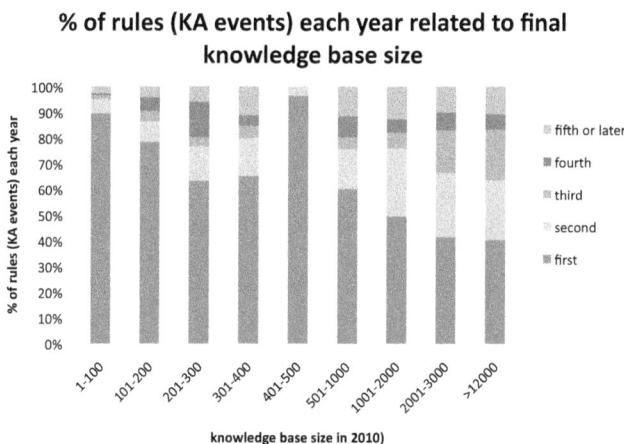

% of rules (KA events) each year related to final knowledge base size

Figure 8 shows the rules added each year as a proportion of total rules for different knowledge base sizes. It only covers knowledge bases in use in 2010

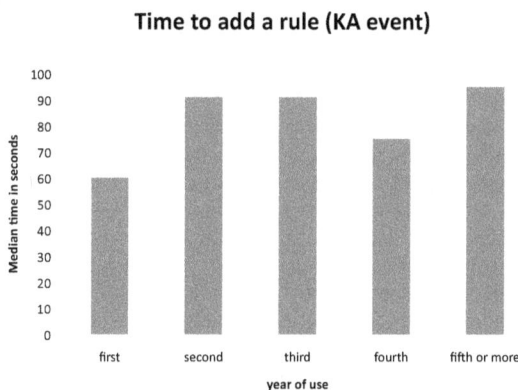

Time to add a rule (KA event)

Figure 9 shows the median time to add a rule across all knowledge bases related to the year in use. This data is from all 246 knowledge bases.

Figure 8 shows the same data as for figure 6, but as a proportion of the total rules added (or KA events). As would be expected more rules are added in the first year than any other year, with more than 50% added in the first year for knowledge bases less than 1000 rules and even for the largest knowledge bases more than 40% are added in first year.

There appears to be little data on the need for on-going knowledge acquisition or maintenance for deployed knowledge-based systems, apart from the landmark study on XCON, but in this the growth in knowledge was explicitly due to the introduction of new computers [11]. The data here suggests on-going knowledge acquisition, if supported by the tool, is a very significant activity more generally. We will discuss whether this represents a failure of the RDR approach, but clearly experts are willing to keep on adding knowledge.

4.2 Time Required for Knowledge Acquisition

The median time to add a rule is shown in Figure 9. As discussed, medians are used because there is no control over whether the log data includes time where the expert was away from the computer screen engaged in other unrelated tasks. The times are remarkably short with about 60 seconds as the median time to add a rule in the first year and about 90 secs for most later years. The reason the time to add a rule is so short is that the task is so simple and there is no requirement to understand the knowledge base as a whole or its overall structure. If an expert decides that a case needs a new or better comment, they have already identified the features in the data that lead to this comment – otherwise they would not make the comment. This is not a knowledge engineering task, it is the normal pathologist task of looking at a report and deciding that it would be useful to provide a comment about the results for the referring GP. However, once this normal domain task is done, the knowledge engineering task of simply identifying the same features on the knowledge building screen, and perhaps some features to exclude cornerstone cases, is very simple. It will not be so simple if the expert wishes to use or formulate some complex function to represent the feature they have observed in the data. Unfortunately we have no data on individual rule building; however, the median data shows that generally the time to build a rule is extraordinarily small. As noted, the time logged is the time to build all the rules required for a case so that the median time for a single rule may be less than the times shown.

The main factor that might cause an increase in knowledge acquisition time is likely to be the number of cornerstone cases that have to be reviewed in verifying that the rule is appropriate. Anecdotally it has always seemed that experts only need to consider two or three cases before they have a sufficiently precise rule to exclude all the other cases that might fire the rule inappropriately but this has not been verified. Figure 10 shows the time to add a rule in the first year of use against knowledge base size. We show data for just the first year to try to distinguish effects related to the size of the knowledge base from knowledge base age and perhaps decreasing familiariy. Knowledge bases have not grown to more than 2000 rules within the first year but for knowledge bases of less than this size, there is an increase in the median time with knowledge base size. However, a median time of 156 seconds to add a rule to knowledge bases between 1000 and 2000 rules is still very small.

Time to add a rule (KA event) during the first year in use

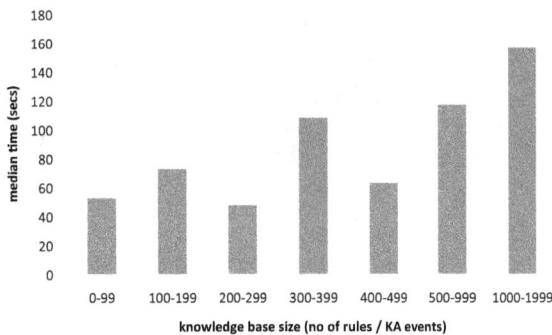

median time (secs)

180
160
140
120
100
80
60
40
20
0

0-99 100-199 200-299 300-399 400-499 500-999 1000-1999

knowledge base size (no of rules / KA events)

TIme to add a rule (KA event)

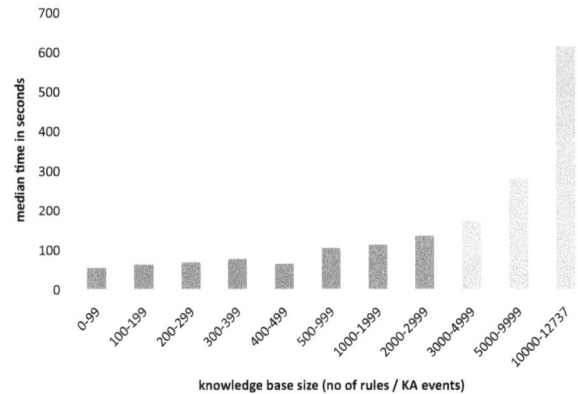

median time in seconds

700
600
500
400
300
200
100
0

0-99 100-199 200-299 300-399 400-499 500-999 1000-1999 2000-2999 3000-4999 5000-9999 10000-12737

knowledge base size (no of rules / KA events)

Figure 10 shows the median time to add a rule in the first year of use for knowledge bases of various sizes. This includes all 246 knowledge bases.

Figure 11 shows the median time to add a rule related to knowledge base size, ignoring the age of the knowledge base. The last three columns come only from the 12,737 rule knowledge base. Even though this is a single knowledge base it is clear that the time to add a rule(s) for a case increases significantly with knowledge base size. In this instance we did contact the domain expert who thought that his task remained the same as with other knowledge bases he maintained, but that he would tend to do something else while the system collected and processed the cornerstone cases, so the increased time was not because of an increased expert task[6]. At this stage, we have to take the results for this knowledge base on face value that above 3000 rules the logged time to add a rule rapidly increases with knowledge based size. However, even above 10,000 rules the median time to add a rule is only 607 seconds – well short of the usual expectation of how long it takes to add a rule to a very large knowledge base. Overall, across all knowledge bases the median of the average time each month for a KA event is 78secs. Alternately the average of the average including all data is 136 secs.

4.3 Error Rates

The critical question in this is why experts chose to keep adding rules. The obvious answer is that they are dissatisfied with the performance of the knowledge-based system and keep trying to correct errors. The logs contain very reliable data on errors, because after reports have comments attached they must go through the validation stage and unless a comment is specifically rejected at this stage the report will go out with that comment. The rejection rate therefore measures the rate at which comments are rejected; there is no other way to reject or change a comment. Experts may not look at every single report, but this only occurs because they decide the quality of certain comments is such that they can set some level of auto-validation for those particular comments. So the overall the rejection rate reflects the experts view of what comments are appropriate and what are not appropriate or should be improved.

---

[6] Since this paper was first submitted, this laboratory's computer platform has been upgraded and the expert has commented that there is 10 fold decrease in processing time.

Figure 11 show the median time for a KA event across all 246 knowledge bases related to knowledge base size at the time of rule acqustion. The last three columns all come from the 12,737 rule knowledge base.

Output rejection rate

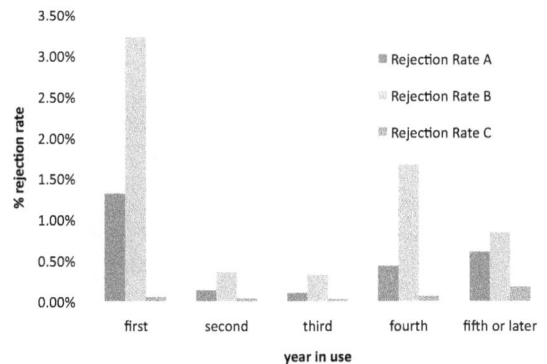

% rejection rate

3.50%
3.00%
2.50%
2.00%
1.50%
1.00%
0.50%
0.00%

first second third fourth fifth or later

year in use

■ Rejection Rate A
Rejection Rate B
Rejection Rate C

Figure 12 shows the rate at which the comments output by the 246 knowledge based systems are rejected. Log data was collected monthly so Rate A shows the average monthly rejection rate across each year. Rate B shows the same data but excludes any months for which no reports were rejected. Rate C divides the total of all the rejected cases by the total of all the cases processed.

Figure 12 shows the rejection rate during each year of use with three different calculations of the rate. If RDR were being used to build the entire knowledge base one would expect the first year rate to be higher than later years. This is not obvious if the rejection rate is calculated by dividing the total cases rejected by the total number processed across all 246 knowledge bases lumped together (Rejection Rate C in Figure 12). This calculation gives extraordinarily low errors and averaged over all years this error rate is only 0.11%. Rejection Rate A is perhaps more useful. It gives the average of the monthly rejection rate across the knowledge bases. For this, the first year rejection rate is higher than the other years at 1.31% but still surprisingly low. As discussed earlier, the logs only include data from knowledge bases in routine use, but not data from any off-line development, or previous development under another name. To try to compensate for prior off-line development, Rejection Rate C shows the average monthly rejection only across knowledge bases for which reports where rejected, as these are likely to be more representative of knowledge bases with less off-line development. For the first year, this rejection rate is 3.22%, for months and knowledge bases where there was rejection.

There is no notion of an independent 'gold standard' for the correctness of conclusions in this approach; here the domain expert is the 'gold standard' and whatever conclusion the expert chooses is by definition the correct conclusion. Compared to typical error data for knowledge based systems, these rejection rates seem remarkably low, regardless of how they are calculated. This cannot be because experts are ignoring errors; there can be very serious implications for inappropriate medical reports and accuracy is a major concern for all pathologists. We suspect that what happens is that experts very rapidly add and correct rules where an error would be significant, with perhaps most of these added off-line, but then over time they include more 'value-add' rules to assist the referring GP, for example the earlier comment about elevated cholesterol. Similarly subdomains may be added to a knowledge base incrementally, so that there is flurry of error correction when a new subdomain is added. Another important issue is that medical practice evolves, so that what might be the most appropriate advice changes. For example it was accepted practice to vigorously treat type 2 diabetes. Recent studies, revealed a higher risk of death in patients following vigorous treatment and the current practice is to ease off [12]. So a comment on a low haemoglobin A1c level is likely to be one of caution rather than approbation. Similarly rules for prescription of drugs such as lipid lowering drugs may periodically change related to pharmaceutical benefit schemes, perhaps leading to different comments. In summary, much of the advice provided by these pathology knowledge-based systems falls into the category of highly useful patient specific management advice given current best practice, rather than simple diagnosis.

It should also be noted that overall about three times as many reports were rejected at validation as there were KA events. Some of this difference is because there may be a delay of a few days between a report being rejected and the designated knowledge builder adding the correction rule. During that time the incorrect comment may be given and rejected several times. Secondly, a different expert may be responsible for rule building than for validation and the rule building expert may decide not to add a rule for that comment. Finally however, much of the difference is because laboratories also use the knowledge bases for internal quality control. That is, a comment might advise that an analyser be checked. Such a comment will always be rejected, so that it does not go out to the GP, but the comment is useful and does not need to be corrected with a further rule.

5. DISCUSSION

The data presented show unequivocally that RDR allow for very rapid knowledge acquisition. The total time to add more than 57,626 rules was about one man-year – and this time is an overestimate because the logs include interruptions to knowledge building. Secondly, although the time to add knowledge increases with large knowledge bases it remains extremely short – at about 10 minutes per rule or KA event. It seems likely that the increase in time is due to processing and data retrieval rather than an increased demand on the expert, but this needs further verification. Across all the rules added the median or average time is about 1-2 minutes per rule or KA event.

Probably the most interesting aspect of these results is the on-going knowledge acquisition that is revealed. 240 of the 246 knowledge bases had rules added after they had been in use for more than a year. That is, for almost every knowledge base the domain expert decided more knowledge should be added after more than a year of use. In total at least 45% of the 57,626 KA events, while the systems were in use, with each event adding one or more rules, occurred after the systems had been in use for more than a year. Since there is little interest in on-going knowledge acquisition in the literature, we assume these figures would be seen as surprisingly large.

This on-going knowledge acquisition is unlikely to be due to an intrinsic limitation of RDR, so that there is repetition in the knowledge added. Firstly, there has been considerable earlier research showing that RDR, particularly MCRDR-based systems, learn efficiently e.g.[2]. Secondly, in the data here the rate at which experts reject cases and correct errors is very low. Thirdly, if there were repeat corrections being made, one would have expected some negative comments from the experts.

Both situated cognition [3] and McCarthy's qualification problem [5] suggest the likelihood of on-going knowledge acquisition. Experts do not and cannot anticipate all possible contexts in which knowledge will be used, so on-going knowledge acquisition is to be expected, with new contexts emerging as more cases are processed. If it is sufficiently easy to deal with new contexts as they appear, on-going knowledge acquisition would be expected.

We suspect the major reason for the scale of on-going knowledge acquisition observed, is simply because it is possible, so that experts with only a very small extension to their normal duties, over time can improve the quality of the advice they give – and the service they provide. We hope to investigate this hypothesis, as well as the many other questions that arise from this data, by investigation of the individual knowledge bases and interviews with the experts involved, but this has been beyond the scope of the present study.

As far as we know these medical diagnostic laboratory domains are the only domains where substantial data is available on the use of knowledge acquisition technology on an on-going basis. Would the same behaviour arise in other domains if the technology used supported very easy on-going knowledge acquisition? Do the data here illustrate a general feature about human expertise? Does this relate to what might be able to be achieved with ontologies [13]? Do the results here suggest that people might always tend to maximize the possibilities for individual expression, even in a controlled environment where any differentiation has to be justified?

6. ACKNOWLEDGMENTS
The support of Pacific Knowledge Systems in providing logs for analysis is gratefully acknowledged. The support of the Australian Research Council is also gratefully acknowledged.

7. REFERENCES
[1] Gaines, B., Birmingham, W. P. and Schrieber, A. T. e. Sisyphus II Special Issue. 1996. *Journal of Human-Computer Studies*, 44(3-4).

[2] Kang, B., Compton, P. Lee, K. and Preston, P. 1998. Simulated Expert Evaluation of Multiple Classification Ripple Down Rules. In *Proceedings of the 11th Banff Knowledge Acquisition Workshop*. http://ksi.cpsc.ucalgary.ca/KAW/KAW98/KAW98Proc.html

[3] Clancey, W. J. 1997. *Situated Cognition: On Human Knowledge and Computer Representations (Learning in Doing - Social, Cognitive and Computational Perspectives)*. Cambridge University Press.

[4] Compton, P. and Jansen, R. 1990. A philosophical basis for knowledge acquisition. *Knowledge acquisition* 2: 241-257.

[5] McCarthy, J. (1977. Epistemological problems of artificial intelligence. In *Proceedings of the 1977 International Joint Conference on Artificial Intelligence,* pp1038-1044.

[6] Compton, P., Edwards, G., Kang, B., Lazarus, L., Malor, R., Menzies, T., Preston, P., Srinivasan, A. and Sammut, C. 1991. Ripple down rules: possibilities and limitations. In *Proceedings of the 6th Banff Knowledge Acquisition Workshop.*

[7] Beydoun, G. and Hoffman, A. 1998. Building problem solvers based on search control knowledge. In *Proceedings of the 1998 Banff Knowledge Acquisition Workshop.* http://ksi.cpsc.ucalgary.ca/KAW/KAW98/KAW98Proc.html

[8] Compton, P., Peters, L., Edwards, G. and Lavers, T. G. 2006. Experience with Ripple-Down Rules. *Knowledge-Based System Journal*, 19(5): 356-362.

[9] Sarraf, Q. and Ellis, G. 2006. Business Rules in Retail: The Tesco.com Story. *Business Rules Journal*, 7(6) http://www.BRCommunity.com/a2006/n2014.html.

[10] Dani, M., Faruquie, T., Garg, R. and Kothari, G. 2010. A Knowledge Acquisition Method for Improving Data Quality in Services Engagements. In *Proceedings of the IEEE International Conference on Services Computing* pp 346-353.

[11] Soloway, E., Bachant, J. and Jensen, K. 1987. Assessing the maintainability of XCON-in-RIME: coping with the problems of a VERY large rule base. In *Proceedings of AAAI 87*, Morgan-Kauffman, pp 824-829

[12] Dluhy, R., and McMahon,T. 2008. Intensive Glycemic Control in the ACCORD and ADVANCE Trials. *New England Journal of Medicine.* 358(24): 2630-2633

[13] Compton, P., Kang, B., Martinez-Bejar, R., Rudrapatna, M. and Sowmya, A. 2008. Situated Cognition in the Semantic Web Era. In *Proceedings of the 2008 European Knowledge Acquisition Workshop,* Springer-Verlag, pp374-387.

Quality Assurance of the Content of a Large DL-based Terminology Using Mixed Lexical and Semantic Criteria: Experience with SNOMED CT

Alan Rector   Luigi Iannone   Robert Stevens
School of Computer Science, University of Manchester, Manchester UK
rector@cs.manchester.ac.uk

ABSTRACT

SNOMED-CT is a large medical terminology based on description logic and mandated for use in the US, UK and several other countries. The hierarchies are known to contain many errors, but have so far proved difficult to analyse or quality assure. We present a series of methods and lessons learnt from experience in quality assuring a "module" of SNOMED for specific applications that we expect to generalize both to SNOMED as a whole and to other large ontologies. They feature a) dependence on domain expertise b) starting from classes selected for relevance to specific applications, c) tracing all errors to their root and verifying repairs by reclassification d) extraction of manageable-sized "modules"; e) mixed semantic and lexical criteria, and f) extensive use of scripting. They aim to reduce the cognitive load on experts by a) looking initially upwards rather than downwards in the hierarchies, b) breaking up long lists of direct subclasses by introducing definitions for meaningful subcategories. Errors found range from simple mistakes to systematic errors in schemas.

Categories and Subject Descriptors

I.2.4 Knowledge Representation Formalisms and Methods – *representation languages*
D2.5 Testing and debugging – *debugging aids*
H.1.2 User/Machine Systems – *Human factors*

General Terms

Design, Human Factors, Standardization, Languages

Keywords

OWL, Quality Assurance, Ontologies, Description Logics, Modularization

INTRODUCTION

Quality assurance of large terminologies and ontologies built using description logics is a black art at best and claimed to be impossible at worst. However, SNOMED-CT [26] is now mandated as a terminology electronic health records in numerous countries including the USA, UK, Canada, Australia, and several countries in continental Europe.

Quality assurance of SNOMED is therefore of great practical importance.

SNOMED[1] contains over 400,000 distinct concepts and more than a million lexical terms and synonyms. The core implementation is in a description logic equivalent to the OWL-EL profile[2] [2] without disjoint axioms.

For users and applications, the primary issue for quality in SNOMED is the inferred hierarchy. It is the inferred hierarchy that is published, affects the retrieval of information, and determines the scope of abstractions used in decision support. From most users' point of view, it is the inferred hierarchy that is the "meaning" of each concept. Other aspects of the representation are manifest to applications and users primarily via their effects on the inferred hierarchy.

Although widely known to contain many errors, [6] SNOMED's inferred hierarchies have been difficult to study because until recently: a) the source representation (known as the "stated form") was not released and the details of the classifier were proprietary, and b) most classifiers and tools could not handle terminologies of this size.

These difficulties have recently been overcome by four developments: a) publication by SNOMED of the stated form plus a Perl script to convert it to OWL; b) efficient methods for extracting "modules" for arbitrary "signatures" from ontologies which let us extract easily manageable sub-ontologies [11], c) a fast, open, robust OWL-EL classifier that integrates with Protégé (or other) environments using the OWL API[3] [16], d) the publication by the US National Library of Medicine of a "Core Problem List Subset" of the 8500 most commonly used SNOMED concepts from several prominent US hospitals[4] [9].

Using these new tools, we are seeking to use SNOMED in two practical applications:

- An industrial collaboration to develop clinical systems
- As a source for the "Foundation component" of the latest revision of the International Classification of Diseases (ICD-11).

To do so, it is necessary to quality assure the portions of SNOMED used to establish that they a) behave as expected

---

[1] See website of governing body: http://www.ihtsdo.org
[2] http://www.w3.org/TR/owl2-profiles/#OWL_2_EL
[3] http://aehrc.com/hie/snorocket.html. NB.
[4] http://www.nlm.nih.gov/research/umls/Snomed/core_subset.html

in applications, and b) are acceptable to the editors of the ICD.

This paper reports the methods used and the lessons learned in this process. Our overall approach has several distinguishing features, in that it:

- *Starts from what domain experts identify as key concepts.*
- *Aims to reduce the cognitive load on domain experts.*
- *Breaks the ontology into modules that classify quickly*
- *Uses the classifier interactively.*
- *Combines semantic and lexical methods.*
- *Makes extensive use of scripting*

By contrast with our focus on content and hierarchies, previous studies of SNOMED have focused on issues of its "ontological" structure, *e.g.* [5, 21, 22, 24], have used pattern based techniques to try to detect regularities and departures from them, *e.g.* [27], have tested inter-rater reliability, *e.g.* [1, 7, 25], or compared coverage, but not precision, in recall against various controls, *e.g.* [8], but have not focused on the clinical content or inferred hierarchies themselves.

Using our approach, we identified a number of error types with regard to content and inferred hierarchies:

- *Simple mistakes* – which may lead to widespread incorrect inferences.
- *Misunderstandings of the semantics of concepts and attributes[5] as implemented in the description logic* – leading to unintended inferences.
- *Fundamental errors in the modelling schemas.*
- *Over-literal definitions* – leading to over-generalised concepts that do not correspond to common usage.
- *Incomplete modelling* – leading to missing inferences.
- *Attempts to fix erroneous inferences without tracing them to their roots* – leading to "kluges" that result in "helter-skelter modelling."
- *Lack of normalisation of complex segments* – leading to tangled and inconsistent hierarchies.

MATERIALS

The study was conducted using the SNOMED IHTSDO[6] release of 31 Jan 2010, and later rechecked against the release of 31 July 2010. Transformation to OWL used SNOMED's supplied PERL script. As a signature, we used the UMLS Core Problem Subset as of July 2010.

For visualisation and editing, we used Protégé 4.0[7] with the SNOROCKET[8] EL[++] classifier[16]. All results were checked using at least one of the classifiers packaged with Protégé – Pellet and/or FaCT++.

For modularization, we used the tools built into the OWL API 3[9] via a publicly available standalone tool.[10] Diff and patch tools used OWLPatch[11]

For mixed lexical and semantic searches and scripting, we used OPPL-2 in [14, 15] in Protégé 4.1. OPPL is a scripting language to query and process sets of axioms in OWL ontologies. Details of the of OPPL and its syntax as used in this paper are available from its website.[12]

In order to check that the errors found were not the result of any of the transformations or use of OWL, all errors were verified to exist in the full SNOMED distribution using at least one of two browsers: SNOB[13] and the *de facto* standard CliniClue Explorer[14].

All changes made are to experimental internal versions, but will be submitted to the SNOMED organisation. All have been made within the limits of SNOMED's formalism and the SNOROCKET classifier used by SNOMED. In our suggested repairs, SNOMED's naming conventions have been adhered to where possible. Supplementary material is available http://www.owl.cs.manchester.ac.uk/snomed.

METHODS AND EXAMPLES

Extracting modules

The Core Problem List Subset, as published, is a simple list of roughly 8500 SNOMED classes without hierarchies or description logic structure. This set of classes was, therefore, used as a "signature," to extract a "module" from the full SNOMED stated form.

A "signature" is a set of entities. A "module" is a subset of the entities and axioms in an ontology sufficient to make all inferences about the entities in the "signature" as would have been made in the full ontology [11] – *i.e.* in our case, the same inferred hierarchies as in the full SNOMED.

The resulting module consisted of roughly 35,000 classes – less than ten per cent of the SNOMED total. The module classifies in under 30 seconds using SNOROCKET and under four minutes using Pellet or FaCT++.

Selecting starting points

Even 8500 main classes in a total OWL model of 35000 are too many to understand easily. The classified hierarchy presents a tangled forest. Where to start?

Rather than browsing the terminology as a whole, our experts found it reduced their cognitive load to look at specific key concepts relevant to their application. Accordingly, a set of initial starting points was selected from the two projects. All were of major clinical importance – hypertension (high blood pressure), diabetes, pneumonia, myocardial infarction (heart attack), head injury, etc. Issues were identified by the

---

[5] SNOMED's term for what OWL calls "properties"

[6] Licensing for SNOMED varies by country, but it is available for research and academic use world-wide. For access, contact national authority or the SNOMED managing body, the International Health Terminology Standards Organisation (IHTSDO), http://www.ihtsdo.org.

[7] http://protégé.stanford.edu

[8] http://aehrc.com/hie/snorocket.html

[9] http://sourceforge.net/projects/owlapi/

[10] http://owl.cs.manchester.ac.uk/snomed

[11] http://owl.cs.manchester.ac.uk/patch/)

[12] http://oppl2.sourceforge.net/

[13] These methods guarantee that the classification will be the same in the module as in the complete SNOMED

[14] http://www.cliniclue.com

clinical experts from their effects in the applications or by comparison with external sources; alternative solutions suggested by the OWL experts, some of whom had some clinical knowledge; and the results vetted by the clinical experts.

Looking up the hierarchy

For each class, we started by looking up the hierarchy rather than down. Hierarchies usually fan in going up and out going down. The maximum number of direct super-classes of our key starting point classes was four, whereas the number of direct subclasses was often over ten and sometimes up to twenty. The maximum number of significant ancestors of our key starting points was twelve; the maximum number of descendents, several hundred. Consequently, the entire upward hierarchy can generally be viewed graphically as shown in Figure 1, whereas the downwards hierarchy rarely can be.

To the experts, oddities in ancestors tend to jump out. For example, hypertension is not considered to be a disorder of soft tissues, nor is it found under this heading in any standard reference source. Similarly, diabetes is not considered a disease of the abdomen, although it is found in the upward hierarchy for diabetes.

Omissions are more difficult to spot, but experts have well-established expectations. That myocardial infarction was not classified as a form of ischemic heart disease – i.e. disease of the blood supply to the heart – was spotted independently by several experts and had major effects on applications.

Tracing anomalies to their root: Analysis by repair

Having found an error, the question is how to repair it. Since SNOMED is formulated in a simple description logic – OWL-EL less disjointness – identifying the reason for the inference is rarely difficult. If it is, the Protégé explanation facilities [13] usually find the problem quickly.

Although in some cases which axiom to change is obvious, in many cases a choice must be made. The error found can be at the end of one or more paths up the hierarchy. For example, as Figure 1 shows, "*Hypertensive disorder, systemic arterial (disorder)*"[15] is inferred to be under both *Finding* and *Disorder of Soft Tissue*, following two different paths, each step of which seems superficially plausible. However, none of our experts agreed that *Hypertension* should be under anything related to *Soft tissue* – either finding or disorder.

Tracing the cause of both inferences to their root, it was found that they both followed from the axiom that the *site*[16] of *Hypertensive disorder* was *some Artery*[17] and that *Arteries* were classed as *Soft tissues*. Together, these axioms led to the unwanted inferences.

Such cases require discussion with the experts. In this case, they decided, after looking at the diseases classified under hypertension, that *Hypertension* was a systemic disorder that

should be *sited* in the cardiovascular system as a whole rather than individual arteries. Therefore, the axiom was changed so that *Hypertension* was *sited* simply in the *Cardiovascular system.* This gave rise only to the inference that *Hypertension* is a *Disorder of the cardiovascular system,* and eliminated both paths related to *Soft tissue.*

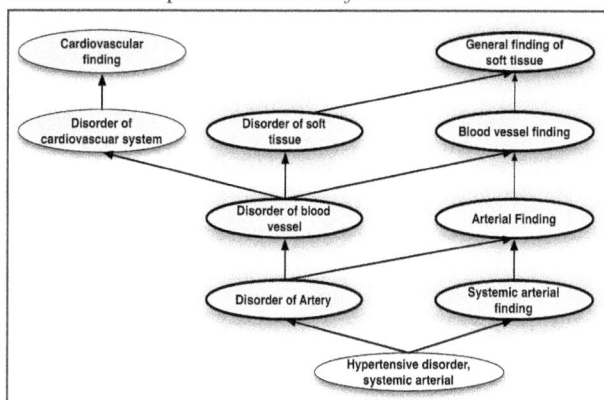

Figure 1: Upwards hierarchy for Hypertensive disorder before repair (from OWLViz view in Protégé[18])

Looking down the hierarchy

Although looking up the hierarchy is cognitively efficient, it is not always sufficient. Even after the repairs above, there are thirteen direct subclasses of *Hypertensive disorder*. In most browsers, these are merely ordered alphabetically. Are they all correct? Are any missing? Where to begin? We used three methods.

Combined lexical and semantic search

If omissions are sufficiently glaring, experts may spot them despite the presentation. Following up such intuitions may then lead to significant repairs.

For example, looking down the list of hypertensive diseases, experts immediately noticed that hypertensive renal disease was present but, contrary to their expectations and requirements for the application, neither hypertensive heart nor eye disease ("hypertensive retinopathy") were present. This raised the question of how many other hypertensive disorders might be missing.

To find out, we used a method related to that proposed by Campbell [4]. We first used a simple "Find" to determine that numerous candidates containing the string "hypertensive" existed. We then did a complete search using an OPPL script. The script in Figure 2 selects all the terms containing "hypertensive" but not classified under "Hypertensive disorder, systemic arterial" and places them under an arbitrary class "Candidate". When reclassified the top candidate classes are as shown in Figure 3.

Out of the list of "Candidates" shown in figure 3, the four highlighted classes were identified by experts as kinds of systemic arterial hypertensive disorder; the remainder were a

[15] 38341003|Hypertensive disorder, systemic arterial (disorder)|

[16] 363698007 | Finding site (attribute)|

[17] 281159003 | Systemic arterial structure (body structure)|

[18] Larger image at: http://www.cs.man.ac.uk/~rector/papers/KCAP-2011-QA/Fig-1-Enlarged.pdf

mixture of other conditions whose names happen to contain the word "hypertensive".

```
?C:CLASS=MATCH(".*[Hh]ypertensive.*") //Find all classes with names
SELECT ?C SubClassOf Thing          // of form ...hypertensive...
// check if they are not already classified under hypertensive disorderWHERE
FAIL ?C SubClassOf 'Hypertensive disorder, systemic arterial (disorder)'
BEGIN ADD ?C SubClassOf Candidate END; // if no, add to list of
                                       //candidates
```

Figure 2: OPPL script to identify suspect classes on mixed lexical and semantic criteria[19]

Viewing the classified hierarchy rather than the flat list is important. For example, the single class "Hypertensive heart disease" in Figure 3 has twenty-five descendants. Showing the classified view reduces the cognitive load on experts. Furthermore, only the top classes need to be edited, the remainder will "inherit" the correction.

```
▿  Candidate
    ➤   'Antihypertensive adverse reaction (disorder)'
    ➤   'Antihypertensive allergy (disorder)'
    ➤   'Antihypertensive overdose (disorder)'
        'Blind hypertensive eye disease (disorder)'
        'Hypertensive heart disease (disorder)'
        'Hypertensive retinopathy (disorder)'
    ➤   'Poisoning by antihypertensive agent (disorder)'
        'Portal hypertensive gastropathy (disorder)'
        'Pulmonary hypertensive arterial disease (disorder)'
        'Pulmonary hypertensive venous disease (disorder)'
        Ulcer of skin caused by ischemia due to hypertensive disease (disorder)'
```

Figure 3: Results of lexical search in Figure 2 after reclassification. Highlighted classes are semantically kinds of hypertensive disorder.

Repairing and Regularizing schemas

The experts noted that all of the highlighted classes in Figure 3 were complications rather than kinds of hypertension and, furthermore, that the original list of subclasses contained two better treated as complications than kinds.

Of the six complications of hypertension identified – four lexically and two semantically in the original subclass hierarchy – there were four patterns. One was linked to hypertension by the property *due to*[20], another by *associated with*[21], a third in no way at all, and the others as subclasses.

Looking further revealed that, although there was no class for *Hypertensive complications* in SNOMED, there was a class for *Diabetic complications*, which was defined as those diseases that were *associated with some Diabetes*. For uniformity, it was therefore decided to use the property *associated with* rather than *due to*.

To complete the repair, therefore, a new class for *Hypertensive complication* was defined as *Disorder associated with Hypertensive disorder* and the descriptions of all classes identified as hypertensive complications edited to fit this pattern.

However, there was a further problem. These actions changed meaning of the class *Hypertensive disorder* so that it now corresponded to hypertension *per se*. There were two

options: i) to create a new class *Hypertension* as a subclass of the existing class, or ii) to rename the existing class. (Renaming in SNOMED is trivial because all names are label annotations. The primary identifiers are "nonsemantic" numeric identifiers.)

To choose, we examined how the original class *Hypertensive disorder* was used elsewhere using the Protégé "usage view" as shown in figure 4. Clearly, the meaning in all cases is of the disorder "hypertension" rather than "complication of hypertension". Furthermore, the core of the existing definition of the class can be paraphrased as "disorder of cardiovascular system characterized by increased blood pressure", which likewise fits "hypertension". In addition, "Hypertension" was a synonym for the original class.

```
Usage: 'Hypertensive disorder, systemic arterial (disorder)'
   Found 9 uses of 'Hypertensive disorder, systemic arterial (disorder)'

   ➤    'Family history: Hypertension (situation)'
   ➤    'History of – hypertension (situation)'
   ➤    'Hypertension screening (procedure')
   ➤    'Hypertension encephalopathy (disorder)'
   ➤    'Hypertensive heart disease (disorder)'
   ➤    'Hypertensive renal disease (disorder)'
   ➤    'Neonatal hypertension (disorder)'
   ➤    ...
```

Figure 4: Usages of Hypertensive disorder

It was therefore decided to:

- Rename the existing class to *Hypertension (disorder)*
- Create a new class *Hypertensive complication* as described above.
- Create a new class *Hypertension AND/OR Hypertensive Complication* as a common parent of the two classes to maintain backwards compatibility with the overall shape of the hierarchy. (NB SNOMED's formalism does not include disjunction.) OPPL scripts were created for the above and the resulting hierarchy is as outlined in Figure

```
▿  'Disorder of cardiovascular system (disorder)'
   ▿    Hypertension AND/OR Hypertensive complication(disorder)'
      ▿    'Hypertension (disorder)'
                ...kinds of hypertension...
      ▿    'Hypertensive complication (disorder)'
                ...kinds of hypertension complication...
```
5.

Figure 5: Outline of revised structure for hypertension and complications.

Analysis by categorization

Even after removing the complications of hypertension, the list of direct subclasses was still too long for experts to analyse easily. To ease the load on the experts and to help them decide if the lists were correct and complete, we added additional defined classes and restrictions to reflect the apparent meaning of the names. The result is a better organized list as shown in Fig 7.

For example, systolic and diastolic hypertension[22] were previously near the beginning and end of the list, respectively, but are now brought together. This case is trivial, but *Hypertension in pregnancy AND/OR Obstetric context* subsumes nearly a dozen classes that were previously scattered under

---

[19] NB: Comments are not yet implemented in the current release of OPPL

[20] 42752001 | Due to (attribute)

[21] 47429007 | Associated with (attribute)

[22] The first and second numbers in hypertension readings such as 140/90

three headings, two with apparently identical definitions. Without bringing them together, as shown in Figure 6, it is nearly impossible to check if the lists are correct and complete or whether their logical definitions super-classes and

```
∀  'Hypertension systemic arterial (disorder)'
   ➢ 'Essential hypertension (disorder)'
   ➢ 'Hypertension in pregnancy AND/OR obstetric context ...'
   ➢ 'Hypertension benign AND/OR malignant (disorder)'
   ∀ 'Hypertension single phase (disorder)'
      'Diastolic hypertension (disorder)'
      'Systolic hypertension (disorder)'
   ➢ 'Labile hypertension (disorder)'
   ➢ 'Neonatal hypertension (disorder)'
   ➢ 'Secondary hypertension (disorder)'
```

subclasses match their intended meaning.

Figure 6: Hypertension after categorization

(Ontologists may object to classes such as 'Hypertension benign AND/OR malignant', and these were implemented so as to be removed easily if desired. However, their utility in quality assurance is difficult to dispute.)

Other issues

Systematic repair of erroneous schemas

Looking up the hierarchy from several conditions of the arteries and nerves of leg and foot, we found them to be classed not only as disorders of the lower extremity, but also of the pelvis and trunk or even abdomen. The issue was traced back to subtle conflation in the schema of branches and parts.

In SNOMED, a disorder of the part is a disorder of the whole. To achieve this, SNOMED currently uses the SEP triple schema [23] for anatomy. For each anatomical entity, there is an *S* class for the *Structure or its parts* with two children, a *P* class for its *parts* and an *E* class for its *entirety* as shown in Figure 7. Each *structure* class for a part is a subclass of the *part* class for its whole. For example, in Figure 7 the *Cusp of the aortic valve* is a descendant of *Heart Structure*, via *Heart part*, etc. so that a *Disorder of the cusp of the aortic valve* is classified as a *Disorder of a heart structure – i.e.* a *Heart disease*. This trick simulates transitive relations for classifiers that do not support them.

However, while disorders of the part are disorders of the whole, disorders of a branch are not disorders of its root – otherwise all disorders of arteries would be disorders of the root artery, the *Aorta*, etc. However, SNOMED makes branches subclasses of the *Structure* node – making them behave as parts and entailing many unintended inferences. In fact, queries with OPPL established that the *Entire* node did not even exist for any *Structure* for which there was a *Branch*.

Where naming conventions are consistent, such problems can be dealt with by an OPPL script as in Figure 8.

Unfortunately, there are other cases involving misuse of SEP triples where the naming is not explicit Indeed, the entire SEP triple schema is now redundant and requires revision.

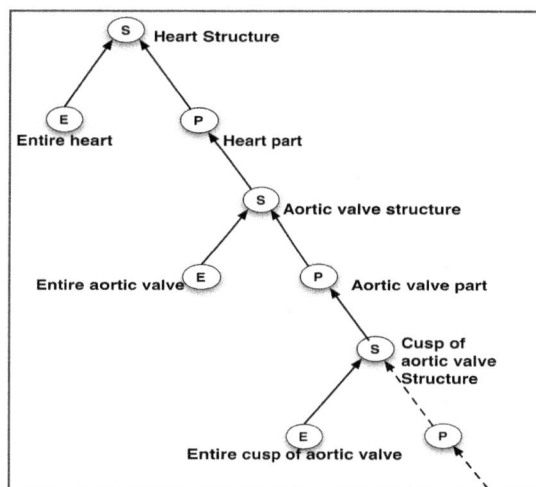

Figure 7: Correct use of SEP triples to represent structure, entire, and parts

```
?B:CLASS=MATCH((".*")[Bb]ranch(.*)"),//Select class names "...branch..."
?S:CLASS=MATCH(".*[Ss]tructure.*")  //Select class names "...structure..."
?entire:CLASS = create( B.GROUP(1)+"_Entire_"+B.GROUP(2))
                          //Create a new Entire node from name
SELECT ASSERTED ?B SubClassOf ?S // Find all branch-structure pairs
BEGIN
   REMOVE ?B SubClassOf ?S,      //remove branch subclass structure
   ADD ?entire SubClassOf ?S     //make entire subclass of structure
   ADD  ?B SubClassOf (is_branch_of some ?entire )
                          //assert that branch is branch of entire
END;
```

Figure 8: Simplified OPPL script to move branches to newly created "Entire" node a SEP triple[23]

Misunderstanding of semantics of attributes

In cases where the problem is a direct subclass axiom between named classes, repair is simple. If the offending link is inferred, the inference must be traced to its root. The example of the *site* of *Hypertension* has already been discussed above. In another example, when looking up the hierarchy the experts noticed that *Diabetes* was classified as a *Disease of the abdomen*, which is clearly wrong. Investigation revealed that this resulted from the axiom that the *site* of *Diabetes* was the *Endocrine pancreas*, which experts also considered wrong[24]. Since the Endocrine pancreas is part of the Abdomen,[25] the error followed.

Both the above errors involved problems with the use of the *site* attribute[26] for a systemic or endocrine disease. This suggested that the use and semantics of the attribute *site* with systemic and endocrine diseases should be examined systematically. This revealed numerous potential errors and controversial classifications.

Incomplete modelling

Tracing errors to their root often uncover cases in which the SNOMED logical model is incomplete, either because there is no complete definition – *i.e.* equivalence class axiom – or

---

[23] NB: Comments are not yet implemented in the current version of OPPL

[24] Diabetes is a systemic or endocrine disorder. Some, but not all, is caused by, but not a kind of, disorder of the endocrine pancreas.

[25] SNOMED makes no distinction between parthood and containment.

[26] 363698007 | Finding site (attribute)

because necessary conditions – *i.e.* restrictions – are missing. In SNOMED's formalism, without a complete, necessary and sufficient definition, subclasses cannot be inferred. For example, if *Heart disease* is fully defined by necessary and sufficient conditions, *i.e.* as <u>Any</u> *disease with site heart*[27], then all diseases with *site heart* will be inferred to be subclasses. If *Heart disease* is only partially defined by necessary conditions, *i.e.* as <u>Some</u> *disease with site heart*[28], then those inferences will not be made.

As a specific example, one of the first errors to come to light was that *Myocardial infarction* (heart attack) was not classified as a form of *Ischemic heart disease* (the common form of heart disease caused by poor circulation in the coronary arteries that supply the heart muscle). On investigation, it was found that none of classes *Myocardial infarction, Infarction, Ischemic heart disease*, or *Ischemia* itself were fully defined by equivalence classes. Hence, the axioms were insufficient to support the expected inference. Repair required providing full definitions via equivalence class axioms for all four classes, plus the axiom that *Infarction* was always due to *Ischemia* via a property path axiom. (Property paths are included in EL^{++}). Reclassification showed that these changes corrected not only the missed classification for *Myocardial infarction* but numerous other errors in the inferred hierarchies as well. (see [18]).

Incomplete modelling is common throughout SNOMED. A complete inspection for all cases was beyond our resources. However, cases were discovered frequently as the root cause of errors. Since cases tend to appear together, once one is found, others can often be repaired systematically.

Over-literal definitions leading to over-generalised concepts

Many medical terms have a more specialised meaning than the literal interpretation of their names. For example, "Neuropathy" is derived literally from "Disorder of Nerve". SNOMED's definition is logically equivalent. However, "neuropathy" has come to mean something closer to "dysfunction" of nerves – normally excluding tumours and injuries and, for example, swelling of the optic nerve in the eye – an important sign of increased pressure on the brain.

A clinically more serious case arises when the most common and serious form of a disorder is more specialised than the literal meaning. For example, "Subdural hemorrhage" literally means bleeding under the "dura", the covering of the brain and spinal cord. Although bleeding under the dura of the spine does occur, the vast majority of subdural hemorrhages inside the cranium where they are potentially fatal. Therefore, in normal medical usage, unless qualified by "spinal", a "subdural hemorrhage" is assumed to be "intracranial". Not to do so is a potentially life-threatening error. (This is what linguists would term an "implicature" [12].)

That the meaning, and therefore the consequences for clinical decision support systems, of "Subdural hematoma" did not imply intracranial was only discovered by carefully looking up the hierarchy and came as a shock to our experts. In fact, it was discovered that there was no class for "Intracranial subdural hematoma" *per se*. (see [18].)

A minimal correction proved possible by analogy to that for *Hypertensive disorder*. Examination of the usages elsewhere within SNOMED confirmed that the meaning "intracranial" was implicit in all but a few cases. Therefore, a new, more general, class was created for *Subdural Hemorrhages, Intracranial AND/OR Spinal*; the original class label changed to *Subdural hematoma, Intracranial*, and the remainder of the hierarchy adjusted to take care of the few exceptions that had been uncovered. The result is a structure analogous to that in Figure 5.

Consequences of not tracing errors to their roots

Early on, it was noticed that some disorders and injuries of skin were classified as *Disorder of soft tissue*[29] while others were not. It was established that the subclass axiom had been omitted between *Skin and subcutaneous tissue*[30] and *Soft tissues*[31]. This affected the classification of every disorder of skin or subcutaneous tissue of which there are thousands in the full SNOMED release. For some of these, there were asserted subclass axioms between the disorder and *Disorder of soft tissues*. We assume these had been inserted manually in response to errors noticed by authors, without tracing those errors to their root – a practice one of our experts dubbed "helter-skelter modelling" and that is akin to "kluges" in software.

Once the root error was repaired, all of these axioms became redundant and could be removed using a script. This is important, since the anatomy model may change in future. If all classification is inferred from the anatomy model, then disorders will be reclassified correspondingly.

Lack of normalisation

The hierarchies for diseases related to head injury, skull fractures, and intracranial bleeding are too large to describe in full in a brief paper. A complete solution requires more radical reanalysis. The root of the problem is that the different axes – whether there is a hemorrhage and its type, whether there is a skull fracture and its type, whether there has been loss of consciousness or not – need to be separated and recombined with suitable definitions, *i.e.* they require normalisation [19]. One solution is suggested in [17] using a formalism including negation. However, experiments indicate that approximations can be achieved using EL^{++} in conjunction with some pre-filtering.

---

[27] "Heart disease equivalentClass (Disease & site some Heart)"
[28] "Heart disease SubClassOf Disease Heart disease SubClassOf site some Heart".

[29] 19660004 | Disorder of soft tissue (disorder)
[30] 27856007 | Skin AND subcutaneous tissue structure (body structure)
[31] 87784001 | Soft tissues (body structure)

DISCUSSION

What is an error? A satisfactory repair?

Any method of quality assurance ultimately depends on the definition of an error. Ultimately, what constitutes an error must be decided by domain experts. It is tempting to focus on the correctness of individual definitions and axioms. However, in a description logic based system using inference, this is inadequate. *A set of definitions and axioms, however individually plausible, contains an error if it leads to an erroneous inference, as judged by domain experts.*

Some errors are clear-cut. Diabetes is not a disease of the abdomen; arteries of the ankle are not in the pelvis. Others are more controversial, *e.g.* the usage of "soft tissues varies between specialties, communities, and over time.

In some cases the semantics of the "attributes" (properties/relations) have to be treated carefully to get the desired inferences – *e.g. site* and *part* do not correspond to generic notions of location and parthood. They are effectively defined by the inferences that follow from the rule that "disorders of the part are disorders of the whole".

This was a study of opportunity and relied on the judgment of a limited number of domain experts. We have conducted a pilot evaluation of inter-rater reliability using participants in the ICD-11 revision process. It suggested few major disagreements, but a wider and more rigorous study is required. The study was deliberately conducted independently of the SNOMED organisation. However, the repairs suggested here require discussion with them and will be submitted via their usual mechanisms.

Technical issues

Importance of interactive classification

Using description logics brings major benefits. It is difficult to see how very large systems such as SNOMED could be managed otherwise. However, the real meaning of the ontology is in the classified form. If authors cannot see the effects of their changes quickly, then effective working is virtually impossible. If classification requires much more than a minute, then the methods described here become increasingly time consuming and tedious.

Use and limits scripting

Insofar as possible, we would like to make changes by scripts so that can easily be applied to new versions or alternative modules. OPPL is rapidly maturing and has become our tool of choice for manipulating OWL. Its key advantages are its ability to deal with mixed lexical and semantic criteria, both asserted and as inferred, and its independence of any specific OWL classifier. It includes the construct FAIL for negation as failure, without which scripts such as that in Figure 2 would not work.

However, the are two sorts of limitations: a) SNOMED's irregularities – neither SNOMED's naming conventions nor modelling style is sufficiently regular to allow all cases to be dealt automatically; and b) OPPL's limitations in dealing with collections and extra-logical constructs, which we hope will be resolved in later releases.

Checking for unintended effects and Unit testing

Changing the axioms to correct one inferred error always brings the possibility of introducing others. Ideally a full "diff" with the previous version of the classified OWL model would be performed. Since no adequate tools were found that scaled to size of model required, a combination of queries in OPPL and checks of the usages of the changed concepts in Protégé provided reasonable assurance that unwanted inferences had not been added nor intended inferences removed.

A major advantage of OPPL is that it facilitates implementing these checks as "unit tests". Unit testing is now standard in software engineering to ensure that errors once identified do not recur and that guidelines are adhered to. Experience in this and earlier projects [20] suggests that such testing is as important for OWL as for software.

Conclusion

This experience suggests that quality assurance of the content of even a very large description logic based terminology such as SNOMED-CT is possible and practical. Our approach starts from experts' intuitions and exploits lexical and semantic methods combined with strategies to break the problem down into manageable chunks – modularization, looking up hierarchies first rather than down, and progressively categorizing unstructured lists.

It is to be hoped that in dealing with the module derived from the Core Problem List Subset, most systematic errors will be uncovered. In general, changes made in modules will be propagated by the classifier to all of SNOMED – *e.g.* correction of the schemas for branches, corrections to the *sites* of systemic diseases, etc. On the other hand, no such approach can be guaranteed exhaustive, and these methods need to be complemented by systematic approaches such as that of Bodenreider [3]. What can be said is that, of the five major body systems investigated – cardiovascular, respiratory, endocrine, gastro-intestinal, and head-injuries – these methods enabled us to find fundamental problems that were unacceptable to collaborating experts in all but one, the respiratory system.

The next step is to test the approach on other subsets of SNOMED and then on SNOMED as a whole, starting from other key clinical concepts critical to other applications. Following that, the goal should be to address other large biomedical ontologies, *e.g.* the National Cancer Institute Thesaurus [10] and ontologies in molecular biology.

Few of the methods used here are specific to SNOMED, although it is easier to pinpoint the root cause of inferences in EL^{++} than in more expressive languages. The success in explaining and repairing many long-standing errors in SNOMED suggests that a collaboration between domain and description logic experts, mediated by staff with some knowledge of both disciplines, can rapidly improve the quality of even very large terminologies that have defied the efforts of either group alone.

ACKNOWLEDGMENTS

This work supported in part by Siemens Health Solutions, and the team working on the Manchester-Siemens collaboration is gratefully acknowledged. Particular thanks to Michael Lawley at his team at Australian E-Health Research Centre for SNOROCKET and their prompt and helpful support. The input of the WHO ICD-11 revision team is also gratefully acknowledged. We also thank IHTSDO for making available the stated form of SNOMED-CT and the Perl script to convert it to OWL.

REFERENCES

[1] Andrews, J. E., Richesson, R. L., and Krischer, J. 2007. Variation of SNOMED CT coding of clinical research concepts among coding experts. J American Medical Informatics Association. 14, 4, 497-506.

[2] Baader, F., Brandt, S., and Lutz, C. 2005. Pushing the EL Envelope. Proc IJCAI-05. 364–369.

[3] Bodenreider, O., Smith, B., Kumar, A., and Burgun, A. 2007. Investigating subsumption in SNOMED CT: An exploration into large description logic-based biomedical terminologies. Artificial intelligence in medicine. 39, 3, 183-195.

[4] Campbell, K. E., Tuttle, M. S., and Spackman, K. A. 1998. A "lexically-suggested logical closure" metric for medical terminology maturity. Proc AMIA 1988). 785-789.

[5] Ceusters, W., Smith, B., Kumar, A., and Dhaen, C. 2004. Mistakes in medical ontologies: Where do they come from and how can they be detected? Studies in Health Technology and Informatics. 145-164.

[6] Ceusters, W., Smith, B., Kumar, A., and Dhaen, C. 2004. Ontology-based error detection in SNOMED-CT. Proc MEDINFO. 2004, 482-6.

[7] Chiang, M. F., Hwang, J. C., Yu, A. C., Casper, D. S., and Cimino, J. J. 2006. Reliability of SNOMED-CT Coding by Three Physicians using Two Terminology Browsers. Proc AMIA 2006. 131-135.

[8] Elkin, P. L., Ruggieri, A. P., Brown, S. H., Buntrock, J., Bauer, B. A., Wahner-Roedler, D., Litin, S. C., Beinborn, J., Bailey, K. R., and Bergstrom, L. 2001. A randomized controlled trial of the accuracy of clinical record retrieval using SNOMED-RT as compared with ICD9-CM. Proc AMIA 2001. 159-164.

[9] Fung, K. W., McDonald, C., and Srinivasan, S. 2010. The UMLS-CORE project: a study of the problem list terminologies used in large healthcare institutions. J Am Med Inform Assoc. 17, 675-680.

[10] Goldbeck, J., Fragoso, G., Hartel, F., Hendler, J., Oberthaler, J., and Parsia, B. 2004. The National Cancer Institute's thesaurus and ontology. J Web Semantics. 1, 1, 32-36.

[11] Grau, B. C., Horrocks, I., Kazakov, Y., and Sattler, U. 2008. Modular reuse of ontologies: Theory and practice. J Artificial Intelligence Research. 31, 1, 273-318.

[12] Grice, H. P. 1957. Meaning. Phil Rev. 66, 377-388.

[13] Horridge, M., Parsia, B., and Sattler, U. 2010. Justification oriented proofs in OWL. International Semantic Web Conference (ISWC 2010). 354-369.

[14] Iannone, L., Aranguren, M. E., Rector, A., and Stevens, R. 2008. Augmenting the expressivity of the ontology pre-processor language. OWL Experiences and Directions (OWLEd 2008).

[15] Iannone, L., Rector, A., and R, S. 2009. Embedding knowledge patterns into OWL. European Semantic Web Conference (ESWC 2009). 218-232.

[16] Lawley, M. J. Exploiting fast classification of SNOMED CT for query and integration of health data. KR-MED 2008. 8-14.

[17] Rector, A. and Brandt, S. 2008. Why do it the hard way? The case for an expressive ontological schemas for SNOMED. J Am Med Inform Assoc. 15, 744-751.

[18] Rector, A., Brandt, S., and Schneider, T. 2011. Getting the foot out of the pelvis: Modelling problems affecting use of SNOMED-CT hierarchies in practical applications. JAMIA 18, (in press).

[19] Rector, A. 2003. Modularisation of domain ontologies Implemented in description logics and related formalisms including OWL. Proc KCAP 2003. 121-128.

[20] Rogers, J., Roberts, A., Solomon, D., van der Haring, E., Wroe, C., Zanstra, P., and Rector, A. 2001. GALEN Ten years on: Tasks and supporting tools. Proc Medinfo 2001. 256-260.

[21] Schulz, S., Suntisrivaraporn, B., and Baader, F. 2007. SNOMED CT's Problem List: Ontologists' and logicians' therapy suggestions. Proc Medinfo 2007. 802-806.

[22] Schulz, S., Suntisrivaraporn, B., Baader, F., and Boeker, M. 2009. SNOMED reaching its adolescence: Ontologists' and logicians' health check. International Journal of Medical Informatics. 78, S86-S94.

[23] Schulz, S., Hahn, U., and Romacker, M. 2000. Modeling anatomical spatial relations with description logics. AMIA Fall Symposium (AMIA-2000). 799-783.

[24] Spackman, K. A. and Reynoso, G. 2004. Examining SNOMED from the perspective of formal ontological principles: Some preliminary analysis and observations. KR-MED. 81-87.

[25] Vikström, A., Skånér, Y., Strender, L. E., and Nilsson, G. H. 2007. Mapping the categories of the Swedish primary health care version of ICD-10 to SNOMED CT concepts: Rule development and intercoder reliability in a mapping trial. BMC Medical Informatics and Decision Making. 7, 1, 9.

[26] Wang, A. Y., Sable, J. H., and Spackman, K. A. 2002. The SNOMED clinical terms development process: refinement and analysis of content. AMIA Fall Symposium. 845.

[27] Wang, Y., Halper, M., Min, H., Perl, Y., Chen, Y., and Spackman, K. A. 2007. Structural methodologies for auditing SNOMED. J Biomed Informatics. 40, 5, 561-581.

Let's Agree to Disagree:
On the Evaluation of Vocabulary Alignment

Anna Tordai, Jacco van Ossenbruggen, Guus Schreiber, Bob Wielinga
Department of Computer Science
VU University Amsterdam
De Boelelaan 1081a, 1081 HV
Amsterdam, Netherlands
{a.tordai, j.r.van.ossenbruggen, guus.schreiber, b.j.wielinga}@vu.nl

ABSTRACT

Gold standard mappings created by experts are at the core of alignment evaluation. At the same time, the process of manual evaluation is rarely discussed. While the practice of having multiple raters evaluate results is accepted, their level of agreement is often not measured. In this paper we describe three experiments in manual evaluation and study the way different raters evaluate mappings. We used alignments generated using different techniques and between vocabularies of different type. In each experiment, five raters evaluated alignments and talked through their decisions using the think aloud method. In all three experiments we found that inter-rater agreement was low and analyzed our data to find the reasons for it. Our analysis shows which variables can be controlled to affect the level of agreement including the mapping relations, the evaluation guidelines and the background of the raters. On the other hand, differences in the perception of raters, and the complexity of the relations between often ill-defined natural language concepts remain inherent sources of disagreement. Our results indicate that the manual evaluation of ontology alignments is by no means an easy task and that the ontology alignment community should be careful in the construction and use of reference alignments.

Categories and Subject Descriptors: I.2.4 [Artificial Intelligence]: Knowledge Representation Formalisms and Methods [semantic networks]

General Terms: Experimentation

Keywords: empirical study, inter-rater agreement, manual evaluation, vocabulary alignment

1. INTRODUCTION

In this paper we study the quality of manual evaluation of ontology alignments. Manual evaluation is a fundamental method for establishing quality in ontology and vocabulary alignment and many other fields such as information retrieval and linguistic research. In vocabulary matching, evaluators rate the quality of mappings by assigning them into categories, thus creating a gold standard, also called a reference alignment that is used to measure the quality of mapping algorithms. An established method of validating the gold standard is to have multiple raters evaluate the same set of mappings into categories. Agreement between raters is then measured by correcting for chance agreement using measures such as Cohen's kappa [6]. Given a high enough inter-rater agreement measure the results of the manual evaluation can be used as a gold standard. However, what the threshold of agreement should be is not clear cut and also depends on the research field in question [12, 4, 2].

While evaluation by multiple raters is a preferred validation method, it is not always documented in practice. The focus of evaluation reports frequently lies on the performance of evaluated tools. In cases where inter-rater agreement measures have been used in the manual evaluation, the reported levels of agreement diverge greatly. For example, in the Very Large Cross-Vocabulary track of the Ontology Alignment Evaluation Initiative (OAEI)[1] organizers reported perfect agreement between raters [8]. Halpin et al. [9] however reported very poor agreement levels in their experiments evaluating `owl:sameAs` mappings sampled from Linked Data. In our previous work [15], and [16] we also measured interrater agreement and found only moderate levels of agreement between raters which we found unexpectedly low. As manual evaluation is such an integral part of the evaluation process we have asked ourselves why raters find it so difficult to agree on relationships between concepts. In this paper we will focus on the following research questions:

1. What is the level of agreement between raters when evaluating alignments?

2. If agreement is low, what are the reasons behind it?

To this end we performed three evaluation experiments on mappings between two sets of vocabularies and analyzed the results quantitatively as well as qualitatively. Because our experiments were explorative in nature, we only evaluated small sets of mappings and focused on qualitative analysis in particular. As part of our experimental setup we created specific guidelines detailing evaluation categories and provided examples and further explanations to raters. We performed a quantitative analysis by using established measures such as Cohen's kappa and Krippendorff's alpha and analyzed data from "think aloud" sessions during the experiments.

2. RELATED WORK

There are relatively few research papers on vocabulary alignment that detail an evaluation by multiple raters and include inter-rater

---

[1] http://oaei.ontologymatching.org/

agreement measurements. In previous papers [15, 16] we described case studies of alignments between various vocabularies, including WordNet, and manually evaluated resulting mappings. In both case studies we validated our evaluation by asking three raters to evaluate samples of the alignments. We used an evaluation tool to display mapped concepts along with their immediate hierarchies, scope-notes and labels, and had raters select a SKOS matching relation [13] to categorize the mapping. To support raters in this task we provided a set of guidelines which included a short description of each matching relation based on the W3C recommendation and examples of mappings. We measured Cohen's kappa and found moderate agreement (0.56) between raters in our first report[15], and just slight agreement (0.36) in [16]. As our goal in both case studies was to assess precision with regards to equivalence, we reduced the number of categories into equivalent or not equivalent. With just two categories the inter-rater agreement rose to substantial agreement (0.70 and 0.67). From these values we concluded that the evaluation task is difficult even for humans, and further study revealed that raters' understanding of SKOS matching relations varied from person to person. We also found that the lexical richness of vocabularies like WordNet may contribute to the difficulty level of the evaluation task, as closely related senses are separated into different concepts. However, a clearer delineation between mapping relations would likely raise agreement.

Halpin et al. [9] also reported low levels of agreement in their paper. They analyzed the use of `owl:sameAs` mappings in Linked Data and defined a similarity ontology to differentiate between various degrees of similarity. In their evaluation experiment they defined 5 levels of similarity relations between entities and used them to evaluate mappings. The agreement level between raters was very low with kappa at 0.16 and the authors attributed this to different styles of judgments. After a recombination of the rating categories into three the agreement increased to 0.32, which is still lower than what we experienced. They found that raters had the most difficulty in defining whether two entities were the same, and that background knowledge has an impact on decisions. They concluded that this inability to rate entities as the same stemmed from not knowing how the entities would be used. In the mapping categorization instruction Halpin et al. used variations on the same type of entity to illustrate each mapping category (descriptions of performances of Bohemian Rhapsody by Queen or some other band). In richly varied data such as Linked Data mapping categories need to be defined in more general terms with examples varying in domain and type. Raters then have less need to interpret examples themselves.

While guidelines with clearer descriptions of categories could improve inter-rater agreement, it is clear from these reports that the task of manual evaluation is difficult. Manual evaluation of mappings is a type of categorization task. Studies in cognitive science in general [11] and linguistic categorization in particular[14] have shown that humans do not categorize according to classic Aristotelian view where each category is clearly defined and mutually exclusive. Instead, Lakoff argues in his book [11] that prototype theory is at the core of cognitive categorization whereby some members of a category are more central (prototypical) than others. For example, *chair* is a more prototypical member of the category *furniture* than a *side-table*. Categories thus form a graded cloud with fuzzy boundaries where member concepts do not necessarily share common properties. They are defined by culture and experience and therefore vary from person to person. This fuzzy nature of categories provides an insight into why categorization tasks can be difficult.

3. EXPERIMENTAL SETUP, TOOLS AND METHODS

3.1 Experimental Setup

Our first experiment, *AATWordNet* was a replication of our mapping evaluation described in Tordai et al. [16]. As in our earlier evaluation the inter-rater agreement was low, one of our objectives for this experiment was to increase agreement by improving the description of matching categories. As summarized in Table 3.1, in this experiment we asked 5 raters to evaluate a sample of 74 lexical mappings between the Getty's Art and Architecture Thesaurus (AAT)[2] and Princeton WordNet version 2.0. The lexical mapping was based on string matching between preferred and/or alternative labels of concepts.

In the second experiment, *GTTinstance*, we aimed to rule out lexical mappings to WordNet as the cause of low inter-rater agreement due to WordNet's ambiguous word senses. We chose a different set of mappings created by a different matching technique for our second experiment. Raters had to evaluate 70 mappings, which were created using instance-based matching between the Dutch Royal Library's Gemeenschappelijke Trefwoordenthesaurus (GTT) and Brinkman Thesaurus, two subject heading thesauri. Instance based matching is based on instances, in this case books commonly annotated by concepts from both vocabularies.

In our last experiment, *GTTlexical*, we wanted to study lexical mappings between less ambiguous vocabularies than WordNet, and determine whether evaluation is easier when the two vocabularies are from the same domain. In this experiment we had 5 raters evaluate 75 lexical mappings between GTT and Brinkman.

In each experiment we provided raters with written guidelines on how to categorize mappings which included descriptions of the mapping categories and example mappings. We asked raters to evaluate mappings using our evaluation tool into 7 different categories. Additionally, we asked raters to "think aloud" by explaining their choice of categories and their application of the guidelines, which we transcribed. We then calculated the inter-rater agreement measurements for 7 categories and for 2 categories by aggregating the original categories. We then performed detailed analysis of the evaluations and of the raters' comments.

We describe the matching categories, guidelines and vocabularies in more detail in the next section.

Table 1: Overview of the three evaluation experiments

Experiment	Vocabularies	Mapping technique	# of raters	# of Mappings
AATWordNet	AAT and WordNet	lexical matching	5	74
GTTinstance	GTT and Brinkman	instance based matching	5	70
GTTlexical	GTT and Brinkman	lexical matching	5	75

3.2 Tools and Methods

3.2.1 SKOS relations and guidelines

We used the SKOS mapping properties to categorize the type of alignments. The `exactMatch` and `closeMatch` properties make

[2] http://www.getty.edu/research/conducting_research/vocabularies/aat/

statements about the degree of equality between two concepts. Hierarchical relations are expressed using `broadMatch` and `narrowMatch`, and `relatedMatch` expresses an associative relation between mapped concepts. In addition to these relations, we also defined a property to indicate that there is no relation between the mapped concepts: `unrelated`. We also give raters the option to choose "not sure" when they are unable to choose between the relations above.

As remarked earlier, we found in previous experiments [15, 16] that raters diverged greatly in the way they selected mapping properties. We attributed this divergence to an unclear differentiation between mapping relations. For example, we found in earlier experiments that raters varied greatly in their application of `relatedMatch`. One rater would find any relationship acceptable as related, while the other had a stricter definition. For this reason we wrote guidelines on the use of each mapping property for these experiments. Our rationale was to differentiate between each property as much as possible by describing them both in general terms, and by giving specific examples. For example, here is an excerpt from the guidelines on `relatedMatch`:

*"**Related:** The two concepts have an associative relationship and are of two different (ontological) types. For example: a material and an object made from that material, such as milk and cheese, and an activity and object involved in the activity, such as the game volley ball and a volley ball. Generic examples of such relationships are: process and agent, action and property (e.g.: environmental cleanup and pollution), action and product (e.g.: weaving and cloth), cause and effect, object and origin, material and object, and object and practitioner."*

We also defined the difference between `exactMatch` and `closeMatch`, and instructed raters to use `closeMatch` when the two concepts share the same label, but their parent concepts are different, as the vocabularies have different organizational schemes. An example of a `closeMatch` is *blowgun* where in one vocabulary it is a conduit and in the other it is a weapon. The two vocabularies present blowgun in different views: a structural view versus a functional view. The full guidelines can be found online[3].

In typical alignment evaluation settings researchers are interested in equality relations between concepts. In such cases the evaluation categories are equivalent and non-equivalent. Although we did not perform separate experiments with these categories we reduce the number of categories into two by summing up ratings of `exactMatch` and `closeMatch` into the equivalent category and the remainder into the non-equivalent category.

3.2.2 Vocabularies and mappings

In our *AATWordNet* experiment we use a sample of mappings between AAT and Wordnet. We generated the mappings[16] using string matching on preferred and alternative labels. AAT is an NISO standard compliant vocabulary [1] that we converted to SKOS, where each concept has preferred and alternative labels and is often accompanied by scope notes. WordNet contains synonymous labels grouped into synsets with no distinction between preferred and alternative labels. The meaning of each synset is clarified by glosses containing example sentences or definitions. Because in WordNet multiple synsets may share the same label, many of the lexical mappings between AAT and WordNet are ambiguous.

For our *GTTinstance* and *GTTlexical* experiments we used samples of mappings between the GTT and Brinkman thesaurus. Both thesauri are subject-heading vocabularies used to annotate the Dutch Royal Library's book collection and both include not only general

[3] http://www.cs.vu.nl/~atordai/Guidelines.pdf

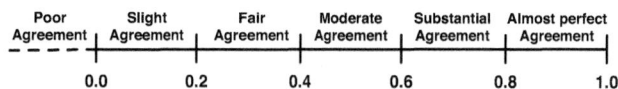

Figure 1: Interpretation of kappa values according to Landis and Koch. The scale is from -1 to 1

descriptors but also geographic terms. Thus, the two vocabularies have the same purpose, although they differ in size and granularity: GTT is five times larger than Brinkman. Brinkman contains 13,025 concepts while GTT contains 65,297 concepts. The mappings we used in the second experiment were created as part of the STITCH[4] project using an instance-based matching technique described by Isaac et al. [10]. The sample of mappings we evaluated has no linguistic similarity, as all concepts with matching labels had been filtered out. For the third experiment we generated mappings between the two thesauri through lexical comparison of concept labels.

3.2.3 Interrater Agreement Measures

The simplest method for measuring agreement between raters is the percentage of agreement: *observed agreement*. Unfortunately it is difficult to interpret and compare across multiple experiments [4, 2], because it does not take into account agreement that occurs by chance. A number of measures exist that do correct for chance agreement. Cohen's kappa is used to measure agreement between two raters on nominal data. Fleiss' kappa is a generalization of Scott's pi and measures agreement between multiple raters on large sample sizes. Krippendorff's alpha, a more versatile measure, can be used with nominal, ordinal and interval type categories and even with missing data (for example when raters select "not sure"). Weighted Cohen's kappa allows us to count disagreements differently by using a weight matrix. The latter can be used, for instance, to count disagreement between `exactMatch` and `unrelated` heavier than a disagreement between `exactMatch` and `closeMatch`. All agreement measures use the observed agreement (or disagreement in the case of Krippendorff's alpha), that is the number of times raters agree, and an estimate of what the agreement would be if raters had assigned categories randomly.

These measures have two known problems: prevalence bias and annotator bias. Prevalence bias occurs when data falls into mostly one category: even if observed agreement between raters is high, the agreement measure may turn out low. In order to have a high measure the raters must agree on rare categories. Annotator bias occurs when the distribution of disagreement is highly skewed, leading to lower measures than when disagreements are more uniformly distributed.

While these measures are widely used, their interpretation is not clear cut. Landis and Koch [12] suggest the set of intervals displayed in Figure 1 based on their personal opinion. In linguistic research kappa values higher than 0.8 are considered acceptable [2]. The nature of the categorization task and the degree to which the matching categories can be defined operationally are factors in determining the minimum level of agreement for the results to be conclusive.

3.2.4 Evaluation Tool

We used an evaluation tool shown in Figure 2 to support raters in their judgment. Its user interface presents mappings with context information, such as the concept hierarchy, labels and scope notes. Raters can select mapping relations between concepts. The result-

[4] http://www.cs.vu.nl/STITCH/

ing choices are stored in RDF using the OAEI alignment format [7] along with provenance information. This tool is a newer version of the one we used in Tordai et al. [15] . It is open source and available for download[5].

4. EXPERIMENTAL RESULTS

4.1 Quantitative Results

Table 2: Inter-rater agreement table for 7 mapping categories and for 2 categories. Measures include observed agreement between raters, the average of Cohen's kappa measured between each pair of raters, Fleiss' kappa over all raters and Krippendorff's alpha over all raters

Experiment	Observed agreement	Avg. Cohen's κ	Fleiss' κ	Krippendorff's α
		7 categories		
AATWordNet	0.69	0.564	0.565	0.575
GTTInstance	0.72	0.606	0.604	0.617
GTTlexical	0.85	0.473	0.475	0.475
		2 categories		
AATWordNet	0.84	0.666	0.669	0.679
GTTInstance	0.94	0.706	0.698	0.699
GTTlexical	0.95	0.514	0.538	0.538

The inter-rater agreement measures for our three experiments are displayed in Table 2. The AATWordNet experiment is a replication of the experiment described in [16] where we measured Cohen's kappa between pairs of raters and reported average measures of 0.36 for 7 categories and 0.67 for 2 categories with three raters. In the AATWordNet experiment we have an average Cohen's kappa of 0.564 for 7 categories which is a considerable increase over 0.36. We attribute this increase to a better description of the mapping categories in the guidelines, as we used the same evaluation tool and had five raters instead of three. There was however no improvement in the average Cohen's kappa for 2 categories, which suggests that while the guidelines were improved in the separate description of mapping categories, they did not help raters in making a distinction between equality and inequality more than in the previous evaluation.

Overall, we found higher agreement measures for 2 categories than for 7 categories which suggests that it is easier for raters to reach agreement over fewer categories.

Table 3: Distribution of SKOS matching relations used by raters in percentages. The ratings in each category are summed over all 5 raters

Experiment	exact	close	broad	narrow	related	unrelated	not sure
AATWordNet	31.9	6.5	4.1	5.4	10.8	40.8	0.5
GTTinstance	**5.7**	**3.7**	7.7	4.6	39.1	38.3	0.8
GTTlexical	**85.0**	9.1	1.0	1.8	1.0	2.1	0.0

The inter-rater agreement in the GTTlexical experiment is the lowest of all our experiments, despite the highest observed agree-

[5]http://semanticweb.cs.vu.nl/amalgame/

ment (0.85). This is caused by prevalence bias, as 85% of the ratings fall into the exact-match category (see Table 3). The prevalence of one category causes the disagreement on the rare categories to weigh more heavily when measuring agreement. In the other experiments the distribution in the use of relations is less extreme than in GTTlexical.

We also found that the value of Fleiss' kappa is close to the average Cohen's kappa in all three experiments. Krippendorff's alpha is a bit higher for both AATWordNet and GTTInstance experiments because it does take into account missing values, in this case the use of the "not sure" category (see Table 3 for the distribution of mapping relations per experiment). In the GTTlexical experiment, where the "not sure" category was not used by raters, the value of Krippendorff's alpha is equal to the value of Fleiss' kappa.

Table 4: Cohen's kappa between each pair of raters for 7 categories from the GTTinstance experiment. The highest and lowest agreement is displayed in bold

Cohen's κ	Rater 1	Rater 2	Rater 3	Rater 4
Rater2	0.736	none		
Rater 3	0.534	0.665	none	
Rater 4	0.634	0.566	**0.483**	none
Rater 5	0.577	0.592	0.491	**0.783**

We measured Cohen's kappa for each pair of raters. Table 4 shows the values for the GTTinstance experiment with the highest value between Rater 4 and Rater 5 (0.783) and the lowest between Rater 3 and Rater 4 (0.483). The large difference is due to Rater 3's tendency to select related match for mappings that Rater 4 and 5 considered to be unrelated. We found a similarly high variation in the Cohen's kappa in AATWordNet and GTTlexical experiments which leads us to conclude that two raters are not enough to provide a consistent evaluation result.

Table 3 shows that in each experiment raters selected categories in very different distributions. In the GTTInstance experiment raters rarely selected the exact or close match categories. This was caused by the mapped concepts having no labels in common, as such mappings had been filtered out, therefore equivalent mappings were rare.

Table 5: The matrix of relations is the sum of the coincidence matrices from each experiment. The matrix shows the number of pairs of rating used by two raters for the same mapping. We consider it worse when raters mark opposing categories such as "exact" and "unrelated" than the categories "exact" and "close". The numbers are percentages of the total amount of observations in the three experiments (4420) and the numbers in bold represent agreements

Category	exact	close	broad	narrow	related	unrelated	not sure
exact	**37.30**						
close	4.88	**2.17**					
broad	0.59	0.86	**2.22**				
narrow	1.72	1.17	0.04	**1.63**			
related	1.54	1.36	0.68	0.68	**11.10**		
unrelated	0.63	0.72	1.49	0.81	5.84	**21.82**	
not sure	0.13	0.04	0.04	0.09	0.32	0.27	**0**

We examined the judgment of raters focusing on disagreements. The interrater-agreement measures when used on nominal data as-

(still 13 concepts to go)
http://purl.org/vocabularies/getty/aat/restorers

restorers, restorer, restorer's, restorers'
scope: Those engaged in making changes to an object or structure so that it will
closely approximate its state at a specific time in its history. When changes made
are to prevent further deterioration, see "preservationists." More generally, for those
who undertake treatment, preventive care, and research directed toward long-term
safekeeping of cultural and natural heritage, see "conservators."

- Top of the AAT hierarchies
  - Agents Facet
    - People
      - people
        - people by occupation
          - people in crafts and trades
            - people in crafts and trades by activity
                    restorers

http://www.w3.org/2006/03/wn/wn20/instances/synset-refinisher-noun-1

[109829776] preserver, refinisher, renovator, restorer
(a skilled worker who is employed to restore or refinish buildings or antique furniture)
target concept 1 (was: unsure?) out of
1 mappings:

(Exact match (=)) (close match (c)) comment (optional):
(not related (-))
(Broader (b)) (narrower (n)) (related match (r))
(? i'm not sure (u)?)

- entity
  - causal agency
    - human
      - worker
        - skilled worker
                preserver

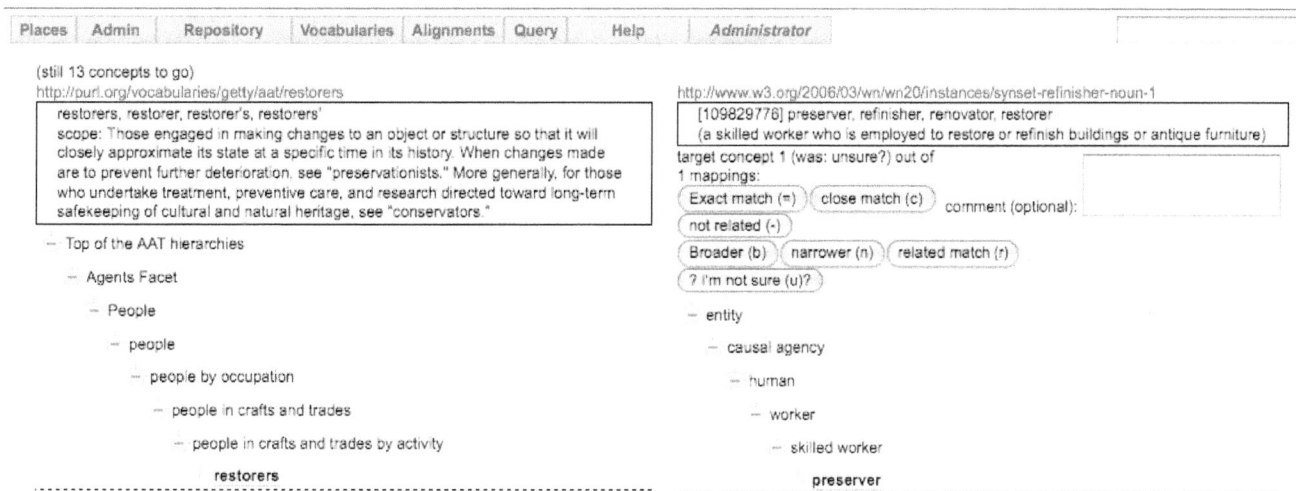

Figure 2: A partial screenshot of the tool evaluation used by raters. The screenshot shows a mapping between the concept *restorers* from AAT and *preserver* from WordNet. The labels and scope-notes are found in the upper boxes. This mapping caused high disagreement between raters

Table 6: Partial list of disagreements in mapping categories ordered by total number of occurrences in the three experiments. The total number of disagreements is 1068 and the number in parentheses is the percentage of total disagreements

	Categories disagreed upon	Occurences (%)
1.	related-unrelated	258 (24.39)
2.	exact-close	192 (20.42)
3.	exact-narrow	76 (7.18)
4.	exact-related	68 (6.43)
5.	broad-unrelated	66 (6.24)
...	...	...
10.	close-unrelated	32 (3.02)
..	...	...
12.	exact-unrelated	28 (2.65)
..	...	...
18.	broad-narrow	2 (0.19)

sume independence between categories. However, intuitively it is worse if raters disagree whether a mapping is an exact match or unrelated, than when they disagree on whether it is related or unrelated. Table 5 shows a matrix of coincidence of relations summed over all experiments. The agreements are along the diagonal, while the disagreements occupy the other cells. In Table 6 we isolated the pairs of relations raters disagreed upon, and ordered them according to the number of times they occurred in the experiments. The table shows that disagreements that can be considered the least "harmful" (i.e., the smallest semantic distance between the mapping relations involved) are the most frequent, such as the disagreements for related-unrelated and for exact-close. An analysis of the cases where raters selected "opposed" categories for the same mapping showed that it was mostly caused by one rater making a mistake.

Our main observation is that the inter-rater agreement measures are stable across our experiments. Although the inter-rater measures are relatively low, our analysis showed that most disagreements between raters are of the less "harmful" type.

4.2 Qualitative Results

We analyzed the use of SKOS matching relations by raters along with the reasons raters gave for their choices transcribed in the "think-aloud" sessions.

We found that overall raters selected different types of relations for lexical mappings than for non-lexical mappings. In the AAT-WordNet experiment mapped concepts share at least one label. Table 3 shows that most of the mappings were rated as either exact match or unrelated while the hierarchical relations (broader and narrower) were least frequently used. When mapped concepts are not equivalent they are either polysemes or homonyms. Homonyms have labels with the same spelling but the concepts unrelated (eg: *bends*; the act of bending and the decompression sickness). Polysemes are terms with different but related meanings, such as *milk*, being the product and the act of milking. In our experiments raters found polysemes difficult to rate because the boundary between relatedness and unrelatedness is not clear. In particular in WordNet, concepts are specifically divided into word senses thus distinguishing between various polysemic and homonymic forms. As a result, when raters evaluate mappings to WordNet they are confronted with multiple related and unrelated word senses. In our AATWord-Net experiment raters found the concept *flow* from AAT, one of the most difficult to evaluate because it was mapped to 14 word senses in WordNet. This problem of distinguishing between meanings is not restricted to polysemes. In the GTTinstance experiment raters had the most difficulty in deciding whether mapped concepts were related or unrelated. For example, some raters found the concept *arid, dry territory* related to *erosion*, while others thought the link too remote to be useful. The fuzziness of concept boundaries and category boundaries makes agreement in evaluation more difficult to achieve. They are a manifestation of Lakoff's prototype theory where concepts far from the prototype become more difficult to categorize.

We also found that the contextual information such as hierarchy, multiple labels and scope note, can increase the difficulty in judgments in particular if they are contradictory. For example, the categorization of the mapping of concept *mantel* between AAT and WordNet, both referring to the thing around a fireplace, was complicated by the AAT scope note "Decorative frames around fire-

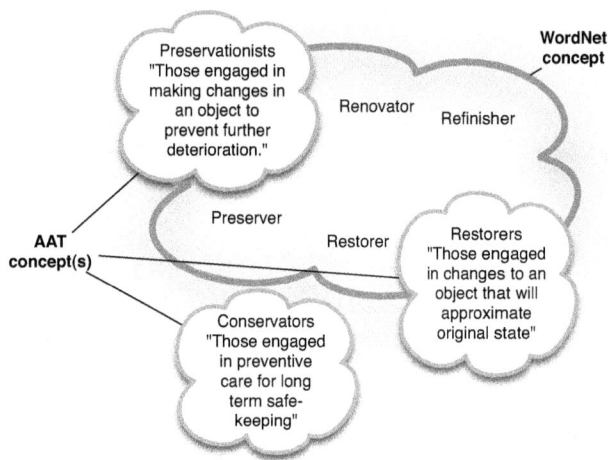

Figure 3: Fuzzy boundaries between AAT and WordNet concepts. The WordNet concept of *preserver* overlaps with multiple concepts from AAT through its labels: *Preservationists* and *Restorers*, but not with *Conservators*

place openings" and the WordNet gloss "shelf that projects from wall above fireplace". Three out of 5 raters judged the mapping "exact match". The fourth rater judged it "related" because the AAT parent concept is "furniture component" while the WordNet parent concept is "shelf". The fifth rater judged the AAT term as broader as she considered the frame in the AAT scope note to be a broader than a shelf.

In comparison to AATWordNet, the GTTlexical experiment was judged "easier" by raters, as they were confronted with very few ambiguous mappings and made quicker judgments. In addition, both GTT and Brinkman contain few alternative labels and scope-notes limiting the amount of contextual information. In the GTTlexical experiment, where mapped concepts had the same label, raters tended to select exact match due to lack of context. In the GTTinstance experiment, however, the lack of context meant that concepts that were related were sometimes rated as unrelated by some raters. Both GTT and Brinkman vocabularies cover a wide range of subjects from "general culture" to economy, physics, history and even medicine. Thus evaluating concepts from more specific domains was more difficult due to lack of context. For example, the mapping between the drug *Dapsone* and the disease *leprosy* was rejected by some raters because the parent concept of Dapsone is *anti-epileptic drug*. Other raters looked up Dapsone on Wikipedia, found that it is also a drug used for leprosy and selected related match because the therapy and disease have an associative relationship. In this case, if we had prohibited the use of outside sources such as Wikipedia, all raters would have most likely selected unrelated based on the available information (unless one of them was a medical expert) which would have led to higher inter-rater agreement. However, a related match between the two concepts can be useful in some applications. Our experiments have shown that raters behave differently and some are more inclined to look up information than others.

We found that for some mappings raters thought the SKOS matching relations inadequate. Although raters could use the unrelated category whenever the mapping was not a SKOS relation, they were reluctant to reject mappings with some semantic link. In particular in the AATWordNet and GTTlexical experiments some aligned concepts (partially) overlapped each other in meaning, therefore warranting some sort of equivalence relation that could not be defined as exact or close match. An example from AATWordNet is the concept *restorer* as shown in Figure 3. The WordNet concept for restorer also included the labels "refinisher", "renovator" and "preserver", whereas *restorers* and *preservationists* were separate concepts in AAT. Raters were reluctant to reject the mapping from AAT's *restorer* to WordNet's *restorer*, but felt neither exact nor close match was appropriate.

A complementing explanation of possible differences between raters could be based on the variability of subjective guidelines that raters appear to construct during the evaluation task. This view is supported by the notion of situated cognition [5] that stipulates that people construct their knowledge "on the fly" in a specific context. When raters were confronted with a non-prototypical mapping they formed their own interpretation of the guidelines and applied that particular rule to similar mappings. For example, one rater created the following rule during the GTTinstance experiment: "*if two concepts are not on the same level of specialization they cannot be related*". The rater continued to apply this rule throughout the evaluation, even though our guidelines did not contain such a specific rule, and no other raters formulated it so clearly.

The background of raters also had an impact on their process of categorization. Two of the raters had a strong thesaurus background that influenced some of their choices. For example, one of these raters would not categorize mappings as broad or narrow match if they shared the same label, commenting that it is not proper ISO standard practice [1]. Raters without this background had no reservations in using hierarchical categories on mappings that shared the same label. We did not specify a purpose or task for the alignments but it seems that raters with a thesaurus background thought of the mappings in terms of a thesaurus merging task, while other raters thought of mappings in terms of an annotation task. Our findings are similar to those reported by Bailey et al. [3] in the field of information retrieval, where they found that judges with different levels of specialization in the task had low agreement.

In the experiments we found that certain disagreements are caused by different interpretations of differences in thesauri, in particular in their hierarchy. GTT is organized according to is-a type relations, while in Brinkman concepts are organized according to a mix of is-a and part-of relations. This sometimes caused problems when the relation a rater wanted to choose contradicted the relation in the thesaurus. For example, there were disagreements on the mapping between *Waste products* from Brinkman to *Environmental pollution* in GTT. Some raters chose related match in accordance with our guidelines about cause and effect, while other raters chose broader because in Brinkman *Environmental pollution* is the parent concept of *Waste products*. Such disagreements can be avoided by adding additional guidelines, but in practice it is often impossible to foresee the effect specific differences between thesauri have on evaluation.

5. DISCUSSION AND CONCLUSION

Manual evaluation is a method for establishing the quality of vocabulary alignments. High agreement between raters is a requirement for being able the make conclusive statements about quality of alignment methods. However, there are a number of factors that influence the judgment of raters. In this paper we studied the process of manual evaluation and found that there are aspects of the evaluation setup that can be controlled, and aspects that make the task inherently difficult.

One aspect that can be controlled is the provision of clear guidelines to the evaluators. Guidelines should include clear examples, precise descriptions of the categories, and instructions how to deal with thesaurus errors. The granularity of the categories is another factor where choices can be made. In our experiments we chose to use the SKOS mapping categories, but our results show that a two category system (match/no match) leads to higher reliability measures. On the other hand, some of our raters indicated that they found the SKOS categories too limited.

Another aspect that can be controlled is the nature of the sample. One can simply choose to select a random sample of alignments or one can construct a sample that contains certain types of alignments as we did in the GTTinstance evaluation. Although our results indicate that different samples lead to similar values for inter-rater reliability, the choice of a specific sample can circumvent certain problems such as prevalence bias.

Aspects largely beyond control are lexical ambiguity and rater characteristics. It is well known from studies in lexical semantics that the boundary between polysemy and homonomy is vague and that the classification of different types of polysemy is still a matter of debate among linguists. Humans rarely have problems with disambiguating the meaning of words in a discourse context. However, in an ontology alignment task this context is usually much more limited than in discourse.

The evaluation process can also be influenced by the background of the evaluators of alignments. Domain specialists (e.g. in a medical or cultural heritage domain) may use different evaluation criteria than raters with a linguistic or a computer science background. Of course one can choose to select raters with a similar background.

A related factor is the purpose of the ontology alignment. For example, if the aligned concepts are used to retrieve documents annotated by different ontologies in the domain of medicine, the difference between organs of a human and a mouse may not be of great importance. In other applications such differences may be essential. Of course the guidelines can be adapted to the nature of the application, but this make comparison of the quality of alignment methods much more complex.

In summary, our results indicate that the manual evaluation of ontology alignments is by no means an easy task and that the ontology alignment community should be careful in the construction and use of reference alignments. We recommend that the OAEI community starts establishing best practices and guidelines for constructing reference alignments. Based on this paper we suggest to include at least the following elements in such an evaluation methodology:

- Select one of the three interrater-agreement measures used in Table 2 as the prescribed standard. Although from the results reported in this paper there is no clear winner, we suggest using Krippendorff's alpha for its versatility as it can be used with any number of raters, with incomplete data and on different sample sizes. The use of an inter-rater agreement measure will make comparison between experiments of different authors easier.

- Prescribe a minimum set of raters for manual evaluation. This minimum should not lower than 3. A range of 3-5 raters appears reasonable.

- Agree on a set of alignment relations. The SKOS relations are attractive candidates mainly because they are part of an heavily-used standard for publishing thesauri on the Web. However, the set of equivalence relations used by Halpin et al. [9] has a more formal underpinning.

- Agree on a set of guidelines for helping to decide which mapping relation to use. The guidelines provided by us (cf. `http://www.cs.vu.nl/~atordai/Guidelines.pdf`) might serve as a place to start.

Having said this, we agree with Lakoff's view on categorization and its consequence: we should not expect full agreement on reference alignments. On the other hand, we expect many Web applications to be able to live with this and still make useful semantic links.

Acknowledgements

We would like to thank our raters: Mark van Assem, Victor de Boer, Marieke van Erp, Michiel Hildebrand, Veronique Malaisé, Lourens van der Meij, Carmen Reverté and Roxane Segers for their participation in our experiments. This research was supported by the MultimediaN project funded through the BSIK programme of the Dutch Government.

6. REFERENCES

[1] Guidelines for the Construction, Format, and Management of Monolingual Controlled Vocabularies. Technical report, National Information Standards Organization, 2005.

[2] R. Artstein and M. Poesio. Inter-coder Agreement for Computational Linguistics. *Computational Linguistics*, 34:555–596, 2008.

[3] P. Bailey, N. Craswell, I. Soboroff, P. Thomas, A. P. de Vries, and E. Yilmaz. Relevance Assessment: Are Judges Exchangeable and Does It Matter?. In *Proceedings of the 31st annual international ACM SIGIR conference on Research and development in information retrieval*, SIGIR '08, pages 667–674. ACM, 2008.

[4] J. Carletta. Assessing Agreement on Classification Tasks: The Kappa Statistic. *Computational Linguistics*, 22:249–254, June 1996.

[5] W. J. Clancey. *Situated Cognition: On Human Knowledge and Computer Representations*. Cambridge University Press, New York, NY, USA, 1997.

[6] J. Cohen. A Coefficient of Agreement For Nominal Scales. *Educational and Psychological Measurement*, 20(1):37–46, April 1960.

[7] J. Euzenat. An Api for Ontology Alignment. In S. A. McIlraith, D. Plexousakis, and F. van Harmelen, editors, *The Semantic Web – ISWC 2004*, volume 3298 of *Lecture Notes in Computer Science*, pages 698–712. Springer Berlin / Heidelberg, 2004.

[8] J. Euzenat, A. Ferrara, L. Hollink, A. Isaac, C. Joslyn, V. Malaisé, C. Meilicke, A. Nikolov, J. Pane, M. Sabou, F. Scharffe, P. Shvaiko, V. Spiliopoulos, H. Stuckenschmidt, O. Sváb-Zamazal, V. Svátek, C. Trojahn dos Santos, G. Vouros, and S. Wang. Results of the Ontology Alignment Evaluation Initiative 2009. In P. S. et al., editor, *Proc. 4th ISWC workshop on ontology matching (OM)*, pages 73–126, 2009.

[9] H. Halpin, P. J. Hayes, J. P. McCusker, D. L. McGuiness, and H. S. Thompson. When owl:sameAs isn't the Same: An Analysis of Identity in Linked Data. In *Proceedings of the 9th International Semantic Web Conference (ISWC)*, November 2010.

[10] A. Isaac, L. Van Der Meij, S. Schlobach, and S. Wang. An Empirical Study of Instance-based Ontology Matching. In *ISWC'07/ASWC'07*, pages 253–266, Berlin, Heidelberg, 2007. Springer-Verlag.

[11] G. Lakoff. *Women, Fire and Dangerous Things; What Categories Reveal About the Mind*

[12] J. R. Landis and G. G. Koch. The Measurement of Observer Agreement for Categorical Data. *Biometrics*, 33:159–174, 1977.

[13] A. Miles and S. Bechhofer. SKOS Simple Knowledge Organization System Reference, August 2009.

[14] J. R. Taylor. *Linguistic Categorization*. Oxford University Press, third edition, 2003.

[15] A. Tordai, J. van Ossenbruggen, and G. Schreiber. Combining Vocabulary Alignment Techniques. In Y. Gil and N. F. Noy, editors, *K-CAP*, pages 25–32. ACM, 2009.

[16] A. Tordai, J. van Ossenbruggen, G. Schreiber, and B. J. Wielinga. Aligning Large SKOS-like Vocabularies: Two Case Studies. In *The Semantic Web: Research and Applications, 7th Extended Semantic Web Conference, ESWC 2010, Heraklion, Crete, Greece, May 30 - June 3, 2010, Proceedings, Part I*, volume 6088 of *Lecture Notes in Computer Science*, pages 198–212. Springer, 2010.

Predicting Adverse Events: Detecting Myocardial Damage in Intensive Care Unit (ICU) Patients

Derek Sleeman [1,2], Laura Moss [1,2]
[1]Department of Computing Science,
University of Aberdeen,
Aberdeen, AB24 3UE
d.sleeman, lmoss@abdn.ac.uk

Malcolm Sim [2], John Kinsella [2]
[2]Academic Unit of Anaesthesia, Pain, & Critical Care
School of Medicine, University of Glasgow,
Glasgow, G31 2ER
j.kinsella@glasgow.ac.uk

ABSTRACT
Myocardial damage is known to occur relatively frequently, and although it is not often fatal it results in the patient staying in the ICU for significantly longer. Thus it is important for clinicians to detect these events. Confirmation of myocardial damage is by a biomarker (troponin), but these tests are only done at fixed time-points. Consequently it is desirable for doctors, and support systems, to detect myocardial damage from the standard parameters collected for ICU patients. We have undertaken a study with several ICU consultants to determine the conditions which generally precede a myocardial-damaging event. In fact, these knowledge acquisition sessions produced a complex model which we have realized as 2 interacting modules. Subsequently, we compared this model's predictions against the original datasets; the model when run against the test dataset resulted in a relatively high True Positive (TP) rate (75.8%). The implications of these analyses are discussed, as are a number of planned follow-up studies.

Categories and Subject Descriptors
I.2.6 Learning – *Knowledge Acquisition.*

General Terms
Algorithms, Performance, Reliability.

Keywords
Knowledge Acquisition, Modelling of Expertize, Event Prediction, Intensive Care Unit, Myocardial Damage.

1. INTRODUCTION
In many areas of Industry, Banking, and Healthcare substantial amounts of data are collected routinely. For example, in many clinical applications, it is now common to collect large amounts of data at each time-point for a patient, and often a sizable number of time-points are recorded. This is particularly true for patients in Intensive Care Units (ICUs) which often collect 50 or so parameters at least hourly, and for such patients to stay in the ICU for many days. These datasets are a rich repository. The generic task which we wish to address here is as follows. An unusual event, E,

happens at time-point, T, is it possible to predict this event by analyzing, both absolute values and trends, in the several parameters recorded in the time-period prior to E? To help this analysis, it is likely we will also have datasets involving the same parameters in which the event, E, does **not** occur.

This paper reports a study which we undertook with ICU patient datasets to predict the occurrence of high troponin values (i.e. myocardial damage) in terms of parameters collected for these patients. We addressed the prediction of this particular event, by undertaking several detailed knowledge acquisition (KA) sessions with ICU consultants who indicated what they believed to be the pre-conditions for event, E. The resulting model is quite complex. Then using both a general tool, developed earlier by our group, INSIGHT [11], and a specific Java program we modelled these experts' predictions. We then compared this model's predictions against the original datasets. Namely, does the experts' model successfully predict a raised troponin value when it is present in a sequence, and not predict it when it is absent from the sequence?

The general aim of this application is to analyse datasets from ICU patients, and to identify adverse events (which can then perhaps be prevented clinically). So this area involves knowledge capture, model building, decision support systems, and potentially machine learning and data mining. Until a decade or so ago most of these models were built manually as a result of knowledge acquisition with domain experts. More recently, there have been several successful attempts to infer high coverage rules / associations from time-series patient datasets. Successful analyses include those by Morik et al [8] who determined when an ICU patient's drugs should be changed, and the impressive work by Ramon et al [9] who report analyses which predict patient discharge status, length of stay, as well as the occurrence of severe inflammation, and when dialysis should be initiated. Remaining issues include whether these results are sufficiently rigorous that they could be used in actual clinical decision systems. Further, although these approaches have been effective in finding associations in these datasets, whether they would be able to find more complex models (e.g. the myocardial damage model reported here). Guyet et al [5] suggest that when addressing complex modelling tasks one should build cooperative systems in which the system's analytical algorithms and the human expert work cooperatively. Additionally, there is now a considerable body of work on the analysis of medical time-series which clearly is relevant to the work undertaken and planned here, Combi et al [2].

1.1 Introduction to Myocardial Damage

Myocardial damage (MD) or myocardial injury describes a loss of muscular function of the heart and can subsequently result in a reduction in the effectiveness of the heart's contractility. Myocardial damage can be caused by a number of diseases including coronary artery disease, myocarditis (inflammation of the heart muscle), and sepsis (systemic inflammation). The term myocardial infarction specifically refers to myocardial damage where there is biochemical evidence of myocardial damage (raised troponin) with either symptoms of ischaemia, changes in the patient's ECG tracing, or an abnormal echocardiogram. Several types of myocardial infarctions have been identified. A Type II myocardial infarction most commonly occurs in the ICU; in this condition the coronary arteries supplying the heart may not themselves be diseased but the heart may be beating so fast that it is effectively deprived of oxygen. The conditions under which this type of myocardial damage occurs are explained in Section 2.2.

The effects of MD vary, depending on both the severity of the myocardial injury, and the part of the heart damaged. Myocardial injuries essentially often result in some form of cardiovascular derangement (CVD) which may manifest itself in change(s) to the patient's heart rate and/or blood pressure. In general it is believed that the resulting concentration of troponin in the blood is low immediately after an MD causing event, reaching a maximum about 12 hours after the event when it then decreases gradually, virtually disappearing at around 72 hours. Figure 1 shows a typical troponin curve. Note, however, if the patient has renal failure the removal of troponin from the blood can take longer.

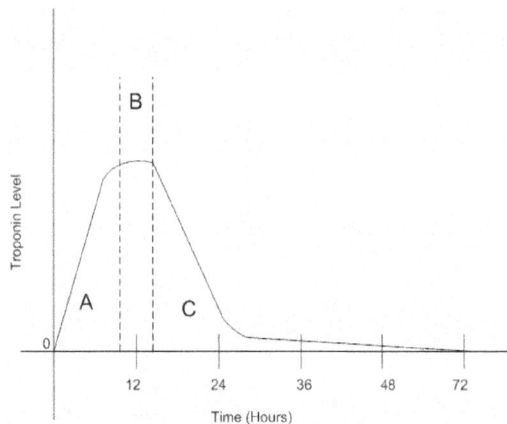

Figure 1. Typical troponin curve. A, B, and C correspond to initial, maximum, and decay regions.

Summary:

- A raised troponin value implies that myocardial damage (MD) has occurred.

- MD causes some degree of CVD and hence should be detectable by observing variables in the patient's electronic health record (EHR) (e.g. Heart Rate (HR) and Mean Arterial Pressure (MAP)).

- CVD sequences can also cause MD.

Lim et al [7] suggest that to detect MD in ICU patients, it is important to regularly test troponin levels. Similarly, Sim et al [10] suggests that the level of troponin elevation correlates with ICU patient outcomes.

1.2 An Overview of the Modelling Methodology Used

The INSIGHT approach and system have focused on developing techniques which enable an expert to detect inconsistencies in 2 (or more) perspectives that the expert might have on the same (classification) task. In an initial study to evaluate INSIGHT's approach, the high level task which the experts (physicians) set themselves was to classify, on a 5-point severity scale ranging from A-E (the ICU-PSS 5-point scale), the hourly reports produced by an Intensive Care Unit's patient management system [11]. In this domain "A" corresponds to nearly normal physiology, and "E" to a highly deranged / unstable physiology. (The remaining 3 categories represent intermediary states.) The INSIGHT system has been developed to support domain experts exploring, and removing inconsistencies in their conceptualization of a task. In this initial study, Intensive Care physicians reconciled 2 perspectives on their patients; namely, an annotated set of patient records where the expert selected the appropriate category to describe that snapshot of the patient, and a set of rules which classify the various time points on the same 5-point scale. Agreements and inconsistencies between these 2 perspectives are displayed graphically. Figure 2 shows the confusion matrix for a sizable number of patient time-points. In the confusion matrix, the y-axis corresponds to the annotation made by the domain expert (indicated as "Data"), and the x-axis corresponds to the classification made by the rule-set. Ignoring the column and row marked as "none", the user interface is a 5 by 5 matrix where the (A, A) cell corresponds to the instances where both the expert's annotation and the rule-set have assigned the instance to category A. (There is similar agreement for all the "diagonal" cells.) The cell (B, A) corresponds to instances which have been annotated as an A category by the domain expert, but as a B by the rule-set. The remaining non-diagonal cells can be interpreted similarly.

	From Rules: A	From Rules: B	From Rules: C	From Rules: D	From Rules: E	From Rules: (none)
From Data: A	10% 84 of 831	78% 646 of 831	8% 69 of 831	3% 21 of 831	0% 4 of 831	1% 7 of 831
From Data: B	1% 7 of 797	79% 632 of 797	14% 108 of 797	4% 34 of 797	1% 10 of 797	1% 6 of 797
From Data: C	(none)	29% 101 of 346	40% 137 of 346	30% 103 of 346	1% 5 of 346	(none)
From Data: D	(none)	4% 11 of 257	17% 44 of 257	39% 100 of 257	39% 100 of 257	1% 2 of 257
From Data: E	(none)	0% 1 of 401	0% 2 of 401	7% 28 of 401	92% 368 of 401	0% 2 of 401
From Data: (none)	(none)	40% 51 of 128	(none)	5% 6 of 128	7% 9 of 128	48% 62 of 128

Figure 2: An example confusion matrix taken from a session with a clinician. Note this is a (partial) screen shot of INSIGHT's display.

Case	Ad...	Do...	FiO2	HR	HR_Delta Pe...	Mean	Mean_...	Nora...	SpO2	SpO2_...	Troponin	Urine	Hypothesis
1438			0.60	123.00	-8.89	61.00	-16.44		93.00	-2.11		80.00	no_event
1439			0.60	123.00	0.00	64.00	4.92		96.00	3.23		110.00	no_event
1440			0.60	129.00	4.88	78.00	21.88		92.00	-4.17		150.00	no_event
1441			0.65	130.00	0.79	59.00	-24.36		93.00	1.09		50.00	event
1442			0.65	127.00	-2.31	58.00	-1.69		96.00	3.23		65.00	event
1443			0.65	125.00	-1.57	54.00	-6.90		98.00	2.08		90.00	event
1444			0.65	125.00	0.00	57.00	5.56		97.00	-1.02		110.00	event
1445			0.00	126.00	0.80	58.00	1.75		97.00	0.00		80.00	event
1446			0.65	132.00	4.76	61.00	5.17		97.00	0.00		160.00	no_event
1447			0.65	140.00	6.06	67.00	9.84		97.00	0.00		110.00	no_event
1448			0.65	143.00	2.14	65.00	-2.99		92.00	-5.15		160.00	event
1449			0.90	147.00	2.80	62.00	-4.62		97.00	5.43		75.00	event
1450			0.90	143.00	-2.72	67.00	8.06		97.00	0.00		75.00	event
1451			0.80	141.00	-1.40	84.00	25.37		96.00	-1.03		150.00	event
1452			0.90	143.00	1.42	67.00	-20.24		97.00	1.04			event
1453			0.75	142.00	-0.70	74.00	10.45		95.00	-2.06		80.00	event
1454			0.65	141.00	-0.70	78.00	5.41		96.00	1.05		80.00	event
1455			0.50	138.00	-2.13	62.00	-20.51		98.00	2.08		105.00	no_event
1456			0.50	131.00	-5.07	63.00	1.61		100.00	2.04		125.00	no_event
1457			0.40	132.00	0.76	74.00	17.46		100.00	0.00		130.00	no_event
1458			0.40	133.00	0.76	74.00	0.00		93.00	-7.00		75.00	no_event
1459												70.00	no_event
1460			0.45	121.00		63.00			96.00				no_event
1461			0.40	122.00	0.83	66.00	4.76		97.00	1.04		90.00	no_event
1462			0.40	120.00	-1.64	69.00	4.55		99.00	2.06		125.00	no_event
1463			0.40	119.00	-0.83	64.00	-7.25		98.00	-1.01		120.00	no_event
1464			0.40	120.00	0.84	67.00	4.69		100.00	2.04		115.00	no_event
1465			0.40	118.00	-1.67	66.00	-1.49		100.00	0.00		100.00	no_event
1466			0.40	123.00	4.24	70.00	6.06		96.00	-4.00		130.00	no_event
1467			0.40	119.00	-3.25	58.00	-17.14		97.00	1.04		90.00	event
1468			0.40	118.00	-0.84	65.00	12.07		98.00	1.03		75.00	no_event
1469			0.40	121.00	2.54	71.00	9.23		99.00	1.02		110.00	no_event
1470			0.40	112.00	-7.44	64.00	-9.86		99.00	0.00		110.00	no_event
1471			0.40	111.00	-0.89	62.00	-3.13		99.00	0.00		80.00	no_event
1472			0.40	111.00	0.00	61.00	-1.61		99.00	0.00		130.00	no_event
1473			0.40	121.00	9.01	74.00	21.31		98.00	-1.01	0.14	70.00	no_event
1474			0.40	117.00	-3.31	69.00	-6.76		98.00	0.00		80.00	no_event
1475			0.40	116.00	-0.85	71.00	2.90		96.00	-2.04		120.00	no_event
1476			0.40	123.00	6.03	71.00	0.00		96.00	0.00		65.00	no_event
1477													no_event
1478			0.40	126.00		77.00			97.00			105.00	no_event
1479													no_event
1480			0.40	119.00		64.00			97.00			65.00	no_event
1481			0.40	125.00	5.04	87.00	35.94		97.00	0.00		100.00	no_event
1482			0.40	118.00	-5.60	66.00	-24.14		99.00	2.06		40.00	no_event
1483			0.40	118.00	0.00	66.00	0.00		97.00	-2.02			no_event

Cases: 6827

Figure 3. INSIGHT is highlighting the cardio-vascular derangements which have occurred for a particular patient (they are shown as bands). Also the screen lists troponin values; in this case a high troponin value (0.14) is being reported.

Moreover, INSIGHT then allows the expert to revise both the annotated datasets (correcting data errors, and/or changing the assigned categories) and the actual rule-set. The expert user is encouraged to initially make changes to the instances, e.g. modify time-points which include "impossible" values, and to make any changes he wishes to particular annotations (occasionally, experts realize they have mis-annotated an instance as they had simply overlooked a particular attribute value). Once these types of changes are completed, the expert is encouraged, if necessary, to make changes to the rule-set. The latter changes, of course, tend to have more wide-ranging effects on the confusion matrix as the rules are applied to all the instances, whereas the other changes are applied only to individual instances.

Each of the experts in the study achieved a very high degree of consensus (~97%) between his refined knowledge sources (i.e., the annotated hourly patient records and the rule-set)

In the study described in this paper we are using a subset of INSIGHT's functionality. Here we, at different points, asked the domain expert to specify when certain events (e.g., CVDs) occur, formulating those as INSIGHT rules, and using INSIGHT we "ran" those rules against a sizable amount of patient data. Typically we then ask the expert to critic the predictions of the rule-set, and hence we refined the rule-set (as in the initial INSIGHT study). In this study, however, we make considerable use of INSIGHT's display capabilities, see Figure 3. The myocardial damage study also makes it clear that for each topic modelled we go through an "acquire-formalize-run-critique-revise" cycle.

1.3 Overview of the Paper

Section 2 reports the knowledge acquisition sessions which we held with clinicians where they indicated when a patient had experienced myocardial damage in a particular time sequence, and why. In this section we also discuss how these events were modelled using INSIGHT and other software. Section 3 discusses the evaluation of this model; Section 4 discusses the results of this study, and possible future work.

2. DETECTING MYOCARDIAL DAMAGE: CAPTURING AND MODELLING CLINICIANS' EXPERTISE

2.1 Data Collection

In the ICU at Glasgow Royal Infirmary (GRI), patient troponin levels are measured regularly every 72 hours (Monday, Wednesday, and Friday), and when the clinical staff suspect the patient has suffered a (further) MD-causing event. It usually takes about 6 hours for the laboratory to return the result to the ICU's patient management system (PMS). Additionally, for each patient, the data retained by the unit's PMS contains physiological parameters, drug and fluid infusions, and the times at which they were recorded. Physiological parameters collected regularly include: Heart Rate (HR), Mean Arterial Pressure (MAP), Inspired Oxygen (FiO$_2$), Oxygen Saturation (SpO$_2$) etc; drugs frequently used in this ICU include: adrenaline, noradrenaline, and dobutamine. The spreadsheets provided to us are de-identified and contain data for complete patient stays in the ICU.

2.2 Capturing Clinical Expertise on Myocardial Damage

As noted earlier, troponin readings, unless a clinician suspects a myocardial event, are taken at predefined times during the week, but of course MD can occur at **any** point. It is agreed that any troponin value greater than 0.04 is likely to be associated with MD. However, we do not know which part of the curve (Figure 1) a particular troponin reading corresponds to, namely to the A (building up), B (maximum value) or C (value decreasing) sections of the curve. Further, clinicians generally agree that if after the troponin value begins to decrease, the value significantly increases, then this is generally associated with a further MD-causing event.

In the first stage of the knowledge acquisition (KA) process, we loaded all the data for 51 patients, who had a reasonable number of troponin values into the INSIGHT system. We *displayed* several of these data segments to 2 clinicians separately and asked them to suggest time periods where they thought a CVD had happened. In particular we asked them to mention CVDs which they thought were associated with high troponin values. Here's a summary of the 2 clinicians views (which were in close agreement):

- CVDs are associated with low SpO_2 values, and extreme HR and MAP values.

- Additionally, high values for FiO_2 or inotropes would indicate that the patient was being supported and **might** imply MD had occurred.

- They also pointed out that the interpretation task would be *very* much easier if **all** the low troponin values were included in the datasets. Initially only troponin values in the range: 0.04-49.99 were recorded in the dataset. The experts pointed out, it is important to have each of the CVD-Troponin sequences delimited.

Once these additional data points for troponin were collected we had (51) patient records with a substantial number of troponin values. These were divided into 2 sets: a training set of 17 patients, and a test set of 34 patients (i.e. the 1/3:2/3 split commonly used in Machine Learning). In the second phase of the KA process, we again presented the (enhanced) patient data to the experts using INSIGHT's display facility. As a result of this session, the clinicians decided that they would expect a CVD event to be happening if they saw **any** of the following alternatives (rule-set 1):

- One of the parameters mentioned earlier (SpO_2, HR, MAP) having very extreme ("E") values (these value ranges were agreed earlier by experts when devising the ICU-PSS 5-point scale [11]). So an example of a rule from this sub-group is:

IF MAP is between [120 – 129] THEN CVD_has_occurred

- 2 of the same parameters having an extreme (or "D") values on that same scale.

As the HR and MAP parameters can have values which are both above and below the normal range, this gives a sizable number of combinations.

The above rules/patterns were then implemented in an enhanced version of INSIGHT which now allows one to specify that a further condition is satisfied at a timeslot or range of timeslots which occur either before or after the initial one. This then allows the analyst to create rules of the type:

IF SpO2 [Very Extreme] at Time [T] AND

Troponin [0.05 – 50.00] at Time [T+1, T+72]

THEN MD_has_occurred

Figure 3 shows rule firings which resulted when this rule-set was run on the training dataset. Displays like that shown in Figure 3 were the focus of the third KA session with the 2 clinicians. The question which we now sought to resolve was how many CVD events would they expect to occur in a sequence either before or after a high troponin value? We reviewed the data for all 17 patients with one clinician but due to extreme time pressures we were only able to review the first 6 with the second. With both clinicians we encouraged them not just to look at sequences of CVDs which were followed by a high troponin value but also at those which contained low or zero troponin values. It was clear (Figure 3) that there were a few "gaps" occurring in otherwise continuous "blocks" of CVDs; the first clinician suggested that a high troponin value is associated with 4 CVDs occurring in 6 timeslots (i.e. 2 "gaps" are permissible); the second suggested a "3 out of 5 rule" (rule-set 2).

Summary of KA sessions:

The following is a slightly simplified summary of the conditions under which the experts believe MD occurs:

- **Myocardial Damage (MD)** is confirmed when a CVD sequence is followed by a raised troponin value within [1-72] time-slots.

- A **CVD sequence** is said to occur when CVD events occur in at least 3 out of 5 *adjacent* time-periods

- A **CVD event** is either:

  o A very extreme value of the SpO_2, HR or MAP parameters (5 possibilities)

  o A combination of 2 of the above parameters with extreme (i.e. "D" level) values (8 combinations)

As noted earlier, a CVD sequence can cause MD, and MD does generally cause CVD (sequences). In either case early "detection" is highly desirable; in the first case it *might* be possible to prevent MD occurring; and in the second case to limit the effects of MD.

The definitions above are similar to a grammar, and so perhaps a parser-like system could be developed to detect MD instances. It seems likely that the Temporal Constraint Reasoning approach [4] could also be applied to this task.

2.3 Modelling the Captured Expertise

Initially we attempted to model these sequences of CVD events using INSIGHT, but it soon became clear that the patterns allowed even in the enhanced INSIGHT are not complex enough. Note that the above specification for myocardial damage includes conjunctive and disjunctive conditions, as well as M-out-of-N conditions. INSIGHT includes each of the above constructs, but in any one rule only one condition type can be included (temporal relationships can be included with *each* condition type). So we were forced to use a hybrid approach to this (complex) modelling activity. INSIGHT identified, using the types of rules outlined above, sequences of CVD events which are followed within 72 units by a troponin value; and similarly troponin values which are followed within 72 time units by a sequence of CVD events. This information is output as a CSV file which is processed by a Java program which determines whether sequences of CVD events (complying with either the 4/6 or the 3/5 rules) occur before or after the high troponin values. The program also reports when such sequences are followed by, or proceeded by, a low or a zero troponin value. In fact the results produced by our analysis are expressed in terms of the usual TP, FP, FN, and TNs.

In this application, a TP is a segment of a time-series which contains a high troponin value and this is preceded or followed by a CVD sequence. That is, the positive (P) or negative (N) is determined by the presence or absence of a CVD sequence; the presence of a high / low troponin value confirms this (T or F). TN, FP, and FN are defined similarly; enhanced versions of these definitions are given below.

3. EVALUATION OF THE EXPERTS' MODEL

3.1 Training Dataset

As noted earlier, the training dataset contains 17 randomly selected patients from the original set of 51. In total, 14 sequences of high troponin values and 14 sequences of low troponin values were identified from the training dataset. Two out of the 14 sequences of high troponin values were removed from subsequent analysis as the high troponin reading occurred too early in the patient's session to be considered (i.e. they occurred within the first 6 hours of a patient being admitted to the unit).

In this (initial) analysis we were attempting to determine how many of the high troponin peaks were either preceded or followed (within 72 hours) by a CVD sequence. In fact our results suggest this only happens in ~30% of these sequences. From Figure 1 we know that a series of raised troponin values might well be reported for most patients. When reviewing these results the domain expert asserted that he would be happy for a TP to be reported for each of a sequence of raised troponins if *at least one* of the troponins from the sequence was preceded or followed by a CVD sequence. Given this perspective we can now refine the definitions of TP, TN, FP, and FN as:

- A TP is a segment of a time-series which contains a sequence of high trop values and at least one of these is preceded or followed by a CVD sequence.

- A TN is a segment of a time-series which contains a sequence of low trop values, none of which is preceded or followed by a CVD sequence.

- A FP is a segment of a time-series which contains a sequence of low trop values and at least one of these is preceded or followed by a CVD sequence.

- A FN is a segment of a time-series which contains a sequence of high trop values and none of which is preceded or followed by a CVD sequence.

When the revised algorithm was applied to the training dataset the results shown in Table 1 were obtained.

Table 1. Initial results with the training set and intermediary rule-set

	Sequences of High Troponins	Sequences of Low Troponins
CVD patterns present [Rule-set 2 fired]	8 out of 12 (True Positive = 66.7%)	10 out of 14 (False Positive = 71.4%)
CVD patterns absent [Rule-set 2 didn't fire]	4 out of 12 (False Negative = 33.3%)	4 out of 14 (True Negative = 28.6%)

As noted earlier we effectively had 12 sequences of high troponins; of these 8 were TPs (i.e. were associated with an appropriate CVD sequence) and 4 were FNs (as they were not associated with a CVD sequence). Similarly, for the 14 sequences of low troponin values, 10 were FPs (as they were associated with a CVD sequence) and 4 were TNs (as they were not associated with a CVD sequence).

Following detailed discussion of these results with the experts, the following revisions were made to rule-set 2:

- An increasing level of FiO_2 can indicate a cardiovascular event.

- We mentioned in an earlier section that the precise values defined in the rules were based on the E and D value ranges of the ICU-PSS 5-point scale. Following these discussions it was agreed to also add the "C" level values to the rules. (This means that the summary of the model in the previous section needs to be extended slightly.)

The training dataset was then run against the refined rule-set (rule-set 3); the results are shown in Table 2.

The interpretation of these results is similar to that given above for Table 1. Note that here there are again 12 high troponin sequences in this training set, and with the revised rule-set all 12 were associated with a CVD sequence, and hence are classified as True Positives (TPs); and hence in this table there are no False Negatives (FNs)

Table 2. Results obtained when the training set is run against the final rule-set

	Sequences of High Troponins	Sequences of Low Troponins
CVD patterns present [Rule-set 3 fired]	12 out of 12 (True Positive = 100%)	13 out of 14 (False Positive = 92.9%)
CVD patterns absent [Rule-set 3 didn't fire]	0 out of 12 (False Negative = 0%)	1 out of 14 (True Negative = 7.1%)

3.2 Testing Dataset

To evaluate the accuracy of the final rule-set (rule-set 3), it was applied to the test dataset. The test dataset contained the remaining 34 patients which had not been used in the training dataset. In total, 33 sequences of high troponin values and 22 sequences of low troponin values were identified from the patient data. 2 out of the 22 sequences of low troponin readings were removed from this analysis as the low troponin readings occurred too early in the patient session. The results of this analysis are reported in Table 3.

Table 3. Results obtained when the testing dataset is run against the final rule-set

	Sequences of High Troponins	Sequences of Low Troponins
CVD patterns present [Rule-set 3 fired]	25 out of 33 (True Positive = 75.8%)	16 out of 20 (False Positive = 80%)
CVD patterns absent [Rule-set 3 didn't fire]	8 out of 33 (False Negative = 24.2%)	4 out of 20 (True Negative = 20%)

As noted above there are 33 sequences of high troponins; 25 of these are associated with a CVD sequence so we have 25 TPs, 8 are not associated with a CVD sequence hence these are classified as FNs. Similarly, the sequences of low troponin values are classified as 16 FPs (associated with a CVD sequence) and 4 TNs (not associated with a CVD sequence).

4. DISCUSSION AND FUTURE WORK

The performance of the rules on the unseen (test) data resulted in a relatively high TP rate (75.8%). However, an equally high FP rate (80%) has been achieved. When these results were discussed with a senior ICU clinician, he suggested that the high FP rate was clinically acceptable as there are often other reasons for CVDs. Similarly, the TP rate was acceptable because clinicians find it difficult to detect myocardial damage when reviewing standard ICU datasets (i.e., when troponin readings are not available). For example, in a recent study at GRI, when several consultants were asked to detect MD in patient datasets which did **not** include troponin values, they achieved an average TP rate of 66.6%. Bearing in mind, this was a focussed task in which experienced ICU consultants were specifically examining the dataset for myocardial damage; it is anticipated that if ICU clinicians of wider experience-levels are observed in a natural setting, the detection of patient myocardial damage would be significantly lower. We are planning to run this more extended study shortly.

Further issues to be investigated are the FNs (Table 3). Our current hypothesis is that a CVD occurred in each of these sequences but not at the hourly reporting points, and hence is not "visible". We are hoping to acquire more fine-grained datasets shortly.

Given that the clinicians accept that some false positives are inevitable in this domain, and given that even very experienced clinicians find it difficult to detect MD in the absence of troponin readings, we believe that our final rule-set could be useful in a

clinical context. However, before that happens, further studies will be carried out with a large number of patient datasets.

4.1 Further Work

4.1.1. Confirmatory Knowledge Acquisition Sessions
Is the MD model developed here unnecessarily complex? We are planning to carry out further knowledge acquisition sessions with the same datasets but with different clinicians to investigate this issue.

4.1.2. Generality of the INSIGHT Approach
Although INSIGHT has so far only been applied to medical domains, we are confident it is a general approach for helping a domain expert make their conceptualization of a (classification) task be more consistent. As we have seen, it requires the expert to articulate for the domain a set of appropriate categories, annotate a number of data points / instances using those categories, and then to produce an initial rule-set. Given this domain-specific information, INSIGHT provides detailed feedback in the form of a confusion matrix; this is interactive and allows the expert to alter any incorrect data in the instances and any incorrect annotations which occurs e.g. because the expert overlooks a particular descriptor value. Thus, this is effectively a data cleaning stage. The next stage, if needed, is to refine/revise the rule-set; alternatively the "cleaned" dataset could be processed by machine learning/data mining algorithms. We believe the INSIGHT approach is effective as it provides a domain expert with immediate feedback and allows him/her to see how *particular* instances are classified by the evolving rule-set. Namely, the tool allows the expert to see the inconsistency between his annotation of a specific instance and the prediction of a more general / abstract rule. One could argue that the Ripple Down Rule (RDR) approach again allows the expert to focus on how to classify particular instances [3]. However, INSIGHT additionally provides feedback on how rule changes affect a number of instances, and provides some useful data cleaning capabilities which are not part of the RDR approach.

4.1.3 The "acquire-formalize-run-critique-refine" Cycle.
The INSIGHT system was able to support the whole of this cycle for the first domain we investigated, namely for patient scoring, [11]. However, we were unable to support that cycle so completely for the MD domain as the considerably more complex model was only partially executable within the INSIGHT system. We believe that the MD models could be expressed as (temporal) constraints and so could be fully executed by the approaches discussed by [2], [4]. We thus plan to incorporate this further interpreter within INSIGHT, and so once again offer the domain expert the powerful feedback inherent in the confusion matrix. There is a further issue here: the rule-set used in the initial domain was found to be quite understandable by the domain expert, we do however have some concerns as to whether they will be able to understand the more complex models inherent in the MD domain. This later question can, of course, only be resolved empirically.

4.1.4 Generic Task
In the Introduction we argued that the MD task is typical of a class of tasks, namely: *an unusual event, E, happens at time-point T, is it possible to predict this event by analysing, both absolute*

values and trends, in several parameters recorded in the time-period prior to E? Certainly we know of many other such tasks in Medicine, including several in Critical Care Medicine; the latter includes: the prediction of kidney failure, the prediction of liver failure, and the need to support a patient's respiratory system. Similarly requirements also occur in environmental monitoring (predicting the death of fish in a lake, or the blooming of algae) and in nuclear engineering (predicting failure of reactors, or loss of control of a reactor).

4.1.5 Temporal Discovery Workbench.

To date in this series of projects we have accepted an initial rule-set from a domain expert (as we believed that machine learning algorithms sometimes failed to incorporate domain-important concepts / rules). However, as the domain and the task (prediction in temporal datasets) gets more complex we feel it is appropriate to develop systems which are genuinely collaborative [5] i.e. where both the system and the expert suggest features (to explain specific temporal events), the system creates from these composite features, and these are evaluated against datasets. The expert then decides on the basis of "coverage" statistics and his knowledge of the domain which patterns should be retained and developed further. The ground breaking Apriori algorithm [1] has recently been developed to handle temporal datasets and patterns [6]; we plan to use this later algorithm as a central component of this collaborative workbench.

5. ACKNOWLEDGMENTS

The reviewers for helpful feedback. Andy Aiken for important developments of the INSIGHT system. Kathryn Henderson and Jennifer McCallum (CareVue Project) and the staff and patients of the ICU Unit, Glasgow Royal Infirmary. This work was an extension of the routine audit process in Glasgow Royal Infirmary's ICU; requirements for further Ethical Committee Approval have been waved.

6. REFERENCES

[1] Agrawal R. and Srikant R. 1994. Fast algorithms for mining association rules in large databases. In *Proceedings of the 20th International Conference on Very Large Data Bases (VLDB'94)* (Santiago de Chile, Chile, September 12-15, 1994). Morgan-Kaufman, San Francisco, 487-499.

[2] Combi, C., Keravnou-Papailiou, E., Shahar. Y. 2010. *Temporal Information Systems in Medicine*. Springer, Heidelberg.

[3] Compton, P. and Jansen, R. 1990. A philosophical basis for knowledge acquisition. *Knowledge Acquisition* 2, 241–257.

[4] Gao, F. 2010. *Complex Medical Event Detection Using Temporal Constraint Reasoning*. PhD Thesis. Computing Science Department, University of Aberdeen.

[5] Guyet, T., Garbay, C., Dojat, M. 2007. A human-machine cooperative approach for time series data interpretation. In *Proceedings of the 11th Conference on Artificial Intelligence in Medicine, AIME 2007* (Amsterdam, The Netherlands, July 2007), LNCS, Springer, Heidelberg, 3-12.

[6] Laxman S. and Sastry P,S. 2006. A survey of temporal data mining. *SADHANA, Academy Proceedings in Engineering Sciences* 31, 2, (April 2006), 173-198.

[7] Lim, W., Holinski, P., Devereaux, P.J., Cook, D., et al. 2008. Detecting myocardial infarction in critical illness using screening troponin measurements and ECG recordings. *Critical Care*; 12, 2, R36.

[8] Morik, K.., Brockhausen, P., Joachim, T. 1999. Combining statistical learning with a knowledge-based approach – a case study in intensive care monitoring. *In ICML'99 Proceedings of the Sixteenth International Conference on Machine Learning* (Bled, Slovenia, June 1999), Morgan-Kaufman, San Francisco, 268-277.

[9] Ramon, J., Fierens, D., Guiza, F., Meyfroidt, G., Blockeel, H., Bruynooghe, M., vd Berghe, G. 2007. Mining data from intensive care patients. *Advanced Engineering Informatics*. 23, 3 (July 2007), 243-256.

[10] Sim, M.A.B., Booth, M.G., Sleeman, D., Reilly, D.O., Kinsella, J. 2010. *Identification of troponin positive events in intensive care*. Scottish Intensive Care Society Annual Meeting, St Andrews, Jan 2010.

[11] Sleeman, D., Aiken, A., Moss, L., Kinsella, J., Sim, M. 2009. A system to detect inconsistencies between a domain expert's different perspectives on (classification) tasks. In *Advances in Machine Learning II, Studies in Computational Intelligence*. Springer Berlin / Heidelberg, 293-314.

Incremental Compilation of Knowledge Documents for Markup-based Closed-World Authoring

Jochen Reutelshoefer, Albrecht Striffler,
Florian Lemmerich and Frank Puppe

Department of Intelligent Systems
Am Hubland, Wuerzburg, Germany
{reutelshoefer, striffler, lemmerich, puppe}@informatik.uni-wuerzburg.de

ABSTRACT

Text-based authoring using knowledge markups is an increasingly popular editing paradigm in manual knowledge acquisition. Closed world authoring environments support the user to form a coherent knowledge base by checking the referenced objects against a set of declared domain objects. In this scenario, the task of efficient translation (compilation) of the text sources is non-trivial. Additionally, in real-world applications frequent small changes are performed on the source documents and instant feedback to the author is crucial. Therefore, a scalable compilation into the target knowledge representations is necessary. In this paper, we introduce a general algorithm for the incremental compilation of knowledge documents, that analyzes the current document modifications and performs minimal updates on the knowledge base. We provide a formal proof of the correctness of the algorithm and show the effectiveness of the approach in several case studies, using various kinds of knowledge representations and markups.

Categories and Subject Descriptors

I.2.1 [**Artificial Intelligence**]: Applications and Expert Systems; I.7.1 [**Document and text processing**]: Document and Text Editing—*languages*

General Terms

Algorithms, Languages, Performance

Keywords

Knowledge Acquisition, Knowledge Markup, Source Compilation

1. INTRODUCTION

In knowledge engineering, the text-based authoring paradigm recently received increased attention as a technique for manual knowledge acquisition. In this method the contributor modifies the knowledge base by editing text documents using predefined formal markup languages, as exemplified in Section 2.1. Text passages matching the defined markup are then translated (compiled) into the target knowledge representation. One prominent example for such a markup language is the Manchester Syntax [7] for the definition of OWL axioms. As markup languages can easily be extended, text-based authoring provides excellent flexibility for project-specific knowledge acquisition. One area, where text-based authoring is successfully applied, is the area of Semantic Wikis (cf. [13, 9]).

However, one issue of text-based authoring is, that simple human mistakes as misspellings can lead to significant errors, since domain objects are referenced by unique identifiers. Therefore, modern development environments apply *closed-world-authoring*, that is, they require domain concepts, which are referenced in other expressions, to be declared by explicit definitions. We draw parallels to the well studied domain of software engineering, where variable declaration is enforced by the compilation process of most third-generation programming languages. These references constitute dependencies between various distributed source text parts of the document base that need to be considered for the compilation step. For efficient knowledge acquisition immediate feedback and testing capabilities after source modifications are crucial, especially considering a workflow that is based on frequent small changes in the source data. These performance requirements cannot be met by full recompilation of the whole modified source document base in large real world applications. Therefore, a more efficient method is necessary. One promising approach to substantially increase efficiency is *incremental compilation*, which updates the prior version of the knowledge base by processing only the document modifications. However, doing this by incorporating the dependencies between the sources is non trivial.

In this paper, we introduce a novel incremental compilation algorithm, that enables efficient knowledge base updates which are independent from the overall size of the document base. The algorithm is designed to also be independent from markup languages and knowledge representations and can thus be applied in a wide range of text-based knowledge acquisition scenarios. We show the effectiveness of the approach in three case studies using different knowledge representations and markups.

The rest of the paper is structured as follows: We start by giving examples and formal notations of text-based knowledge acquisition in Section 2. In Section 3, the algorithm for incremental compilation is presented. Then, related approaches are discussed in Section 4. Next, Section 5 presents experimental results of our approach in three diverse case studies. We conclude by giving a summary and outlook of the presented approach in Section 6.

2. BACKGROUND

In text-based knowledge authoring the knowledge base is developed by editing a set of source text documents, where entities are defined by expressions complying to a predefined markup language. These documents can be modified by the authors in arbitrary fashion. After each document modification the knowledge base will be compiled from the (updated) document base. In this section, we first provide some examples of this knowledge acquisition method. Then, we present a formal representation for the problem of compiling this kind of knowledge documents.

2.1 Example Scenarios

In the following, we show some markup examples from different systems illustrating the wide range of possible application scenarios.

Figure 1 shows a rule in *drools* which is an open source rule engine [3]. It is an excerpt of a car-fault diagnosis knowledge base. In this scenario a (potentially large) number of rules is defined in the document using the markup language for drools rules. Each rule is compiled into the drools knowledge base if it does not contain any errors.

```
rule "R5"
  when
    Input(name == "Num. Mileage evaluation" && numValue > 130.0)
    $input : ChoiceInput(name == "Mileage evaluation")
  then
    $input.setValue("increased");
end
```

Figure 1: The drools syntax, as used in the eclipse-based *drools expert* editor, cf. [3].

In Figure 2 a fragment of wiki text of a page describing *London* in Semantic MediaWiki is shown, cf. [15]. Here, ontological relations are defined using the *typed-links* syntax which is an extension to the normal link syntax. It allows to establish relations for known entities, which are then translated to RDF[1].

```
'''London''' is the capital city of [[capital
of::England]] and of the [[is capital of::United
Kingdom]]. As of [[2005]], the total resident
population of London was estimated
[[population:=7,421,328]]. Greater London
covers an area of [[area:=609 square miles]].
[[Category:City]]
```

Figure 2: An example for textual knowledge acquisition using the typed link markup in Semantic MediaWiki, by Voelkel et al. [15]

A markup example for encoding (historical) events in HermesWiki [12], which is an eLearning platform for the domain of ancient history, is shown in Figure 3. Here, the event with the given attributes is translated to structured data enabling diverse advanced functionality, such as the generation of timelines or quizzes.

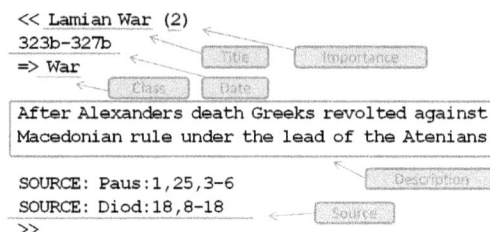

Figure 3: Formalization of time events in HermesWiki [12].

Any of the examples aims to define some kind of relation between objects of the domain, e.g., a rule, a RDF-triple assertion, or a historical event with multiple attributes, that will be translated into some computer interpretable format stored in a knowledge repository. If the domain objects available for use, such as inputs, properties or classes, are also defined within the documents, the resolution and translation problem becomes non-trivial. To cover that issue, we will introduce the problem in a more formal way within the next section.

2.2 An abstract model for knowledge bases

In the following, we define a simple and very general model for knowledge bases which serves as a basis for the compilation approach presented in this paper. The approach can be applied to any knowledge representation that complies with this definition. Most kinds of (declarative) knowledge representations can be reduced to "small pieces" of knowledge (*knowledge slices*) that associate domain concepts and datatype values. A knowledge base can be considered as a set of such pieces.

We formally define $\mathcal{O}$ as the universal set of all possible domain objects and $\mathcal{D}$ as the universe of all datatype values. $\mathcal{R}$ is considered as the universe of all association types. A *knowledge representation* $\mathcal{KR}$ is defined by a set of allowed association types $R_{\mathcal{KR}} \subset \mathcal{R}$. Then $\mathcal{KR}$ is the set of all possible tuples $(r, o_1, \ldots, o_n, d_1, \ldots d_k)$ with $n \geq 1$ and $k \geq 0$, which we call *knowledge slices*. A knowledge slice captures an association of type $r \in R_{\mathcal{KR}}$ between the objects $o_1, \ldots, o_n$ and the values $d_1, \ldots d_k$. A *knowledge base* $A \subset \mathcal{KR}$ is then given by a set of such tuples. Finally, we define a function $Ref : \mathcal{KR} \mapsto 2^{\mathcal{O}}$, that maps the knowledge slices to the set objects, that are associated with this slice.

This rather general knowledge model of representing a knowledge base includes a wide range of declarative knowledge representations, e.g., logic-based formalisms or production rules. However, structures containing implicit orderings, such as lists, are difficult to represent as multiple knowledge slices in a straight forward way. In particular, the abstract knowledge base model is unsuited to cover sequences of commands as it is known from various imperative programming languages.

---

[1] www.w3.org/TR/REC-rdf-syntax/

2.3 A formal model for knowledge authoring

E is the set of all possible text segments on a document base DB. We define a text-based knowledge authoring-system for a knowledge representation $\mathcal{KR}$ as a triple: $T_{\mathcal{KR}} = \{L_{\mathcal{KR}}, P_{\mathcal{KR}}, C_{\mathcal{KR}}^{L_{\mathcal{KR}}}\}$. $L_{\mathcal{KR}}$ is a markup language, that is suited to capture knowledge slices of $\mathcal{KR}$ unambiguously as text expressions. $P_{\mathcal{KR}} : DB_L \mapsto 2^E$ is a parser function that is able to create a set of minimal text segments (identified by the position in the source) from DB according to $L_{\mathcal{KR}}$, where each segment is a syntactically independent expression that represents one or multiple knowledge slices. $C_{\mathcal{KR}}^{L_{\mathcal{KR}}} : E \mapsto 2^{\mathcal{KR}}$ is a compilation function that maps a text expression of $L_{\mathcal{KR}}$ to a set of knowledge slices of $\mathcal{KR}$.

Open vs. closed world authoring: In textual knowledge authoring, objects are identified by an unique name within the markup. We say, an authoring environment provides *open world authoring* if arbitrary object identifiers can be used ad-hoc, that is $\mathcal{O}$ is unrestricted. In this case, all text expressions for knowledge slices, that are syntactically correct, are considered valid and are compiled into the knowledge base. However, to minimize user errors it is advantageous to assert that the objects have been referenced correctly, i.e., were not mistyped. An authoring environment provides *closed world authoring* if the set of referenced objects is restricted to an (extensible) set of explicitly defined objects $O \subset \mathcal{O}$. In these environments, a text expression e can be invalid if referring to non-existing objects ($Ref(C(e)) \nsubseteq O$). In this case a compilation error is returned to the user. This is similar to compilation of programming code, where in many third-generation-languages the compiler requires a variable to be correctly declared before usage. For the authoring environment this implies that the markup language and the parsing function are extended to support object definitions. Additionally, we introduce the object compilation function C_o that creates objects from object definition expressions: $C_o : E \mapsto \mathcal{O}$. Based on these definitions, the current set of defined objects in a document base is given by $O = \{o \in \mathcal{O} : o \in C_o(e), e \in E\}$. Since in closed world authoring not only knowledge slices are compiled, but also object definitions, the compilation process is two-layered.

The explicit definition of domain objects in the source text introduces two additional issues, especially considering, that object definitions might be arbitrary located in the document base:

First, an object could possibly be defined at multiple locations in the document base, which may have unintuitive implications for the behavior of the authoring environment towards the user, e.g., the deletion of an object definition will not remove the object from the set of defined objects. Even worse, by renaming one object definition the user will generate an additional object without being aware. Therefore, we postulate strict object definitions, that is, we consider *all* definitions of an object as invalid if more than one exist.

Second, sometimes an object relies on other objects and only makes sense if these other objects are (validly) defined (see example below). We denote the set of objects, which is required for a meaningful definition of o as $Ref_o(o)$. We call object definitions relying on other objects *complex definitions*. In that case, an important service for the user is to give feedback whether one of the dependent objects is missing and to propagate the invalidity chain. This leads to an

extension of the validity concept for object definitions: An object is valid, iff it has a unique definition e and all objects referenced by e are also valid.

In the following, we present a small markup example demonstrating the definition of simple and complex objects and knowledge slices from an excerpt of an exemplary knowledge base calculating the body-mass-index: This document

```
1  def weight
2  def height
3
4  def BMI = weight / (height * heigt)
5
6  def underweight
7  IF BMI < 18.5 THEN underweight
```

excerpt defines four objects (lines 1,2,4,6) and two knowledge slices (lines 4,7). Please note, that in line 4 both, a complex object definition (defining *BMI* with dependencies on *weight* and *height*) and a knowledge slice (associating the objects *BMI*, *weight* and *height*) are implied. We consider the typing error in the right-hand-side of the expression in line 4: Of course, an error will be displayed in line 4. But as *BMI* is not added to O because one of the referenced terms is not in O, the knowledge slice in line 7 will also not be compiled to the knowledge base but shows a message telling the user, that *BMI* is not correctly defined. In general, the expressions should be structured in a comprehensible natural order. However, according to the above definitions, the ordering/location of the expressions is completely irrelevant for the compilation result.

2.4 The knowledge compilation task

The goal of the compilation task is to generate a valid version of the knowledge base (compilation) with respect to the current document base. We call a knowledge base a valid compilation with respect to a set of source text documents if it contains exactly all valid knowledge slices defined by the document base. However, the validity of knowledge slices and complex object definitions is defined with respect to O, which itself is compiled from the document base. This two stage compilation process is a non-trivial task: Even if only one document is modified slightly the modification can affect entities, which are defined in other documents. For example, the deletion of an object definition can cause other (complex) object definitions or knowledge slices to become invalid. The addition of an object definition can cause the object to become invalid (if it is a duplicate) or can cause knowledge slices to become valid (because the definition was missing before). Any expression in another document might be affected in the worst case. If an algorithm always creates valid compilations from source documents we call it sound. A sound compilation algorithm processing the whole document base and building up O and A can be defined in a straight forward way. However, text-based authoring systems are designed for agile development allowing for frequent changes and immediate feedback and testing capabilities. It is obvious that the runtime of such an algorithm scales linear with the absolute size of the knowledge and document base, leading to insufficient performance on large knowledge bases. In the next section, we show how to create sound compilations of modified document bases (substantially) more efficiently.

3. INCREMENTAL COMPILATION

Incremental compilation describes the translation of text segments based on the small changes of the document base instead of a complete rebuild. In order to perform an incremental compilation task, a parser component and an incremental knowledge base update algorithm are required. The problem of efficient parsing has been studied thoroughly in the area of compiler design [1]. In this field, highly efficient parsing algorithms have been developed. These techniques can be transfered to parsing in text-based knowledge acquisition. Therefore, in this section we focus on a general algorithm for incremental knowledge base updates. It is independent of the markup language *and* the target representation. This independence is possible for two reasons: (1) Due to the set characteristic of a knowledge base (cf. Section 2.1) a knowledge slice can be translated to the target representation independently from others, i.e., without regarding the context. (2) Referenced domain objects in closed world authoring form (possibly complex) dependencies to arbitrary other parts of the code. However, this *one* dependency class is inherent to all knowledge representations and is not specific to some markup or knowledge repository.

The incremental compilation task requires the detailed information on the nature of the document modification that we call *resource delta*. This can easily be generated, for instance by an incremental parsing algorithm, e.g., as proposed by Wagner et al.[16]. For a document base DB_{old} that is modified to a document base DB the resource delta is defined as: $\Delta(DB_{old}, DB) = \{N, D\}$, where N is the set of new expressions defined by $N = P(DB) \backslash P(DB_{old})$ and D is the set of deleted expressions $D = P(DB_{old}) \backslash P(DB)$. By distinguishing D and N with respect to object definitions (D_o, N_o) and knowledge slices (D_a, N_a), we also denote $\Delta(DB_{old}, DB) = \{N_o, N_a, D_o, D_a\}$.

In the following listing, we present an algorithm, that updates a valid compilation of the old document base to a valid compilation of the new version, given the corresponding resource delta. Beside the resource delta $\Delta = \{N_o, N_a, D_o, D_a\}$, the input of the algorithm is a set of objects O_{old} and knowledge slices A_{old} of the prior compilation and the *Reference Manager* (RM). The Reference Manager is an auxiliary data structure, that provides the information which objects are referenced by other objects or knowledge slices in the source text (i.e., the dependency graph). The output of the algorithm is a set of objects O and knowledge slices A, forming a valid compilation of the new document base. Additionally, whenever an invalid object definition or knowledge slice is detected in the algorithm, the error messages for the respective text segments can be generated.

Description The algorithm aims to identify a minimal subset of entities that needs to be removed or created in order to form a valid compilation of the new document base with respect to O and A. The general strategy of this update function is to resolve the object dependencies for updating O. While doing so it identifies not directly modified knowledge slices that have to be reconsidered. Afterwards, the actual knowledge base is updated. First the reference manager gets updated with the new resource delta in line 2. Then in line 4, we iterate on the deleted object definition expressions D_o and either call recursive removal or resolution on this object definition, depending on the validity of the respective object. Further, this is applied in

a similar fashion to the set the new object expressions N_o in line 7. Please note, that both, adding or deleting an object definition can result in some object becoming valid. The functions *resolveRecursively* and *removeRecursively* traverse the object dependency graph from the passed object on, and create and remove respectively the (complex) object definitions and mark the affected knowledge slices (by inserting elements into D_a and N_a). The hazard-filter (line 14) removes expression pairs, that would lead to deletion and subsequently insertion of an identical knowledge slice: $C(e_a) = C(e'_a), e_a \in N_a, e'_a \in D_a$. Finally, we remove the deleted knowledge slices in D_a and insert the new knowledge slices N_a if all referenced objects are valid at that time in line 17 and 20 respectively.

Listing 1: the incremental update algorithm

```
1   function updateKB(Δ, O_old, A_old, RM,)
2     updateReferenceManager(Δ, RM)
3     O := O_old;  A := A_old
4     for each  e_o ∈ D_o  do
5       checkObject(e_o)
6
7     for each  e_o ∈ N_o  do
8       checkObject(e_o)
9
10    for each  e_a ∈ N_a  do
11      if( not  Ref(C(e_a)) ⊆ O) //check for validity
12        remove e_a  from N_a
13
14    hazardFilter(D_a, N_a)
15
16    for each e_a ∈ D_a  do:
17      delete  C(e_a)  from  A //remove from KB
18
19    for each  e_a ∈ N_a  do
20      add  C(e_a)  to  A //insert into KB
21
22  //auxilliary functions
23  function checkObject(e_o)
24    if( hasValidDefinition(C_o(e_o)))
25      resolveRecursively(e_o)
26    else
27      removeRecursively(e_o)
28
29  function resolveRecursively(e_o)
30    if( hasValidDefinition(C_o(e_o)))
31      if(C_o(e_o) ∉ O_old)
32        add C_o(e_o) to O
33        for each  e_a ∈ RM. getReferencingSlices(e_o)
34          add  e_a  to N_a
35        for each  e'_o ∈ RM. getReferencingDefs(e_o)
36          resolveRecursively(e'_o)
37
38  function removeRecursively(e_o)
39    if(C_o(e_o) ∈ O_old)
40      remove  C_o(e_o)  from  O
41      for each  e'_o ∈ RM. getReferencingDefs(e_o)
42        removeRecursively(e_o)
43      for each  e_a ∈ RM. getReferencingSlices(e_o)
44        add  e_a  to D_a
45
46  function hasValidDefinition(o)
47    defs = RM. getDefinitions(o)
48    return #defs == 1
49      & Ref_o(o) ⊆ O\o
50
51  function updateReferenceManager(Δ, RM)
52    for each  e ∈ N_o ∪ N_a
53      RM. registerReferences(e)
54    for each  e ∈ D_o ∪ D_a
55      RM. deregisterReferences(e)
```

Termination Cyclic object definition dependencies may occur within the text. However, all object definitions involved in a dependency cycle are invalid: Before a cycle can be closed, it is invalid because of the missing part. When the missing part is added it will not become valid, as its dependency was invalid in the prior version (that is line 48/49 will evaluate to false). Therefore, the function *resolveRecursively* terminates as validity is checked in line 31 and no valid cycles can exist (and the dependency graph is finite). The function *removeRecursively* terminates for similar reason: In line 44 we assert that recursion only proceeds if the object is in O_{old}. As O_{old} only contained valid objects and no valid cycles can exist, the function terminates.

Efficiency The potentially most expensive operations are the remove- and insert operations of knowledge slices, depending on the employed knowledge repository and its performance characteristics. The algorithm inserts or removes any knowledge slice only once at most. Given the correctness of the algorithm (i.e., exactly all valid knowledge slices are contained in the knowledge base), it follows that the algorithm is optimal with respect to knowledge slice insertion/removal. As the graph structure of the dependencies can be stored in the reference manager RM using hash tables, the lookup operations on RM during dependency resolution can be performed in constant time. The update of that information (*updateReferences*) only takes linear time to the size of the resource delta. The runtime in practice is strongly determined by the amount of change operations on the knowledge base (cf. evaluation in Section 5). If dependency resolution can be considered as small compared to change operations, the complexity of the algorithm is linear to the knowledge base change set. This is a significant improvement when compared to the naive full-compile approach which is linear to the size of the document base and knowledge base.

Proof of correctness We prove the correctness of the algorithm by showing that A and O, as the result of the update algorithm applied to A_{old} and O_{old} and Δ, contains exactly the same entities as a valid compilation O^* and A^*. O_- and A_- are the sets of objects respectively knowledge slices from the old compilation that are still valid and therefore are retained in the compilation: $O_- = O \cap O_{old}$; $A_- = A \cap A_{old}$. O_+ and A_+ are the sets of objects respectively knowledge slices added by the update algorithm: $O_+ = O \setminus O_-$; $A_+ = A \setminus A_-$.

We introduce the following auxiliary theorems:

$$\begin{array}{c|c} \mathbf{O_- \subseteq O^*} & \mathbf{A_- \subseteq A^*} \\ \mathbf{O_+ \subseteq O^*} & \mathbf{A_+ \subseteq A^*} \\ \mathbf{O^* \subseteq O} & \mathbf{A^* \subseteq A} \end{array}$$

Using these auxiliary theorems, it is easy to infer:

$$\begin{array}{c|c} \mathbf{O = O_+ \cup O_- \subseteq O^*} & \mathbf{A = A_+ \cup A_- \subseteq A^*} \\ \mathbf{O \subseteq O^* \text{ and } O \supseteq O^*} & \mathbf{A \subseteq A^* \text{ and } A \supseteq A^*} \\ \implies \mathbf{O = O^*} & \implies \mathbf{A = A^*} \end{array}$$

We proved the soundness of the algorithm, given that the auxiliary theorems hold. They are proven as follows:

$\mathbf{O_- \subseteq O^*}$: assume $\exists o, o \in O_- \wedge o \notin O^*$: o must have had a valid definition $e'_o \in P(DB_{old})$, as by definition of O_-: $O_- \subseteq O_{old}$. As it is not in O^*, there is no valid definition in the current version. Some text modification must have been made yielding in the definition of o to become invalid, and only two cases for this to happen are possible: (1) Its text expression has been modified directly (towards another object definition or completely removed). (2) The definition itself was not modified but became invalid due to a competing definition added. (3) The definition itself was not modified but became invalid because a dependency object became invalid by the modification..

(1) By the definition of Δ, e_o is in D_o. Line 24 checks whether there currently exists a valid definition of $C_o(e_o)$. As $o \notin O^*$, this is not the case. Because of $e'_o \in P(DB_{old})$ line 39 will evaluate to true and the object will be removed (recursively) and thus o cannot be in $O_- \implies \lightning$

(2) A concurring definition of the object has been added to the document base. If any object definition e'_o is added to the document: $e'_o \in N_o$. Line 24 checks whether there currently exists a valid definition of $C_o(e_o)$, which is not the case due to the competing definition. Because of $e'_o \in P(DB_{old})$, line 39 will evaluate to true and the object will be removed (recursively) and thus o cannot be in $O^*_- \implies \lightning$

(3) At least one of the objects, the (complex) definition of o is based on, has become invalid. Thus e''_o exists, being responsible for that (directly or indirectly) and $e''_o \in \Delta$. As o is in O_{old}, $o'' = C_o(e''_o)$ must have been valid in $P(DB_{old})$. Therefore, line 39 will evaluate to true and e''_o will be deleted recursively. This recursive deletion will also delete o, as it references o'', potentially indirectly. Thus, o cannot be in $O_- \implies \lightning$

As $o \in O_- \wedge o \notin O^*$ leads to a contradiction in any case, $\mathbf{O_- \subseteq O^*}$ holds.

$\mathbf{A_- \subseteq A^*}$: assume $\exists a, a \in A_- \wedge a \notin A^*$: a must have had a valid definition $e_a \in P(DB_{old})$, as $A_- \subseteq A_{old}$. As $a \notin A^*$, there is no valid expression $e_a \in P(DB)$. Some text modification must have been made so that a became invalid and was not compiled to A^*. There are two possibilities for this:

(1) The expression was changed from e_a to e'_a with $a = C(e_a) \neq C(e'_a) = a'$. By the definition of Δ, the expression would be in D_a. The deletion step in line 17 removes all knowledge slices a from A where $e_a \in D_a$ (see line 16) and thus a cannot be in $A_- \implies \lightning$

(2) The modification caused a definition of some object o to become invalid, which leads to a becoming invalid. Thus e'_o exists, being responsible for that (directly or indirectly), and $e'_o \in \Delta$. As o is invalid, *removeRecursively* will be called. Because a was in A_{old}, $C_o(e'_o)$ must have been valid in $P(DB_{old})$ and line 39 will evaluate to true and e'_o will be deleted recursively. This recursive deletion also adds a to N_a, as it references o' (indirectly). Then a will be deleted in line 17 and thus cannot be in $A_- \implies \lightning$

As $a \in A_- \wedge a \notin A^*$ is contradictory in any case, $\mathbf{A_- \subseteq A^*}$ holds.

$\mathbf{O_+ \subseteq O^*}$: Objects in O_+ are only added in line 32. For those a valid definition is asserted in line 30. Hence, they are also contained in O^*: $\implies \mathbf{O_+ \subseteq O^*}$

$\mathbf{A}_+ \subseteq \mathbf{A}^*$: Knowledge slices in A_+ are only added in line 20. For those a valid definition is asserted in line 11. Hence, they are also contained in A^*. $\implies \mathbf{A}_+ \subseteq \mathbf{A}^*$

$\mathbf{O}^* \subseteq \mathbf{O}$: For each $o \in O^*$: It either had a valid definition in $P(DB_{old})$ (1), or it has become valid by the modification of DB_{old} (2).

(1) $o \in O_{old}$ as it was a valid compilation. As $o \in O^*$, o has a valid definition $e_o \in P(DB)$. o will not be deleted directly by line 27, as it has a valid definition (condition in line 24). For any object being called in line 38 an invalid referenced object exists (entails by induction). If so for o, o would not be a valid definition. Therefore, o is not removed and thus is (still) in O.

(2) $o \notin O_{old}$ as o didn't have a valid definition in $P(DB_{old})$, and as $o \in O^*$, o has a valid definition $e_o \in P(DB)$. Therefore, some modification $e'_o \in \Delta$ exists, that caused the definition of o becoming valid. Only objects becoming valid can cause other objects to become valid (i.e., an object becoming invalid can never make other objects become valid). Thus, *resolveRecursively* will be called on this e'_o and line 30 will return true (even if $e'_o \in D_o$). $C_o(e'_o)$ will be added in line 32 and in line 36 all referencing objects are recursively checked for validity. As e'_o caused o to become valid, some reference chain to o exists and thus o will be checked and created as all objects in the reference chain have been added to O. $\implies \mathbf{O}^* \subseteq \mathbf{O}$

$\mathbf{A}^* \subseteq \mathbf{A}$: For each $a \in A^*$: It either had a valid definition in $P(DB_{old})$ (1), or it has become valid by the modification (2).

(1) $a \in A_{old}$ as it was a valid compilation. As $a \in A^*$, a has a valid definition e_a in $P(DB)$. If $e_a \notin \Delta$ and all objects $o_a \in Ref(C(e_a))$ are validly defined, e_a cannot be added to D_a in line 44, as *removeRecursively* is only called on invalid objects (entails by induction). Therefore, it cannot be deleted in line 17 and thus is contained in A. If $e_a \in \Delta$, the only reason for this can be the removal of the definition in one location and its addition in another (move expression operation). Then $e_a \in N_a$ and $e_a \in D_a$. In this case e_a will be removed by the hazard-filter (and if not, it will be removed and inserted again) and is thus contained in A.

(2) $a \notin A_{old}$ as a didn't have a valid definition in $P(DB_{old})$. As $a \in A^*$, a has a valid definition e_a in $P(DB)$. Therefore, some modification $e' \in \Delta$ exists, that caused the definition of a becoming valid. If the knowledge slice expression was modified directly, $e' \in N_a$ and a will be added to A in line 20. If the modification of some object definition e_o caused a to become valid, then e_o is in Δ. Thus, *resolveRecursively* will be called on this e'_o and line 30 will evaluate to true (even if $e'_o \in D_o$). $C_o(e'_o)$ will be added to O in line 32 and in line 36 all referencing objects are recursively checked for validity. As e'_o caused a to become valid, some valid reference chain to a exists and thus e_a will be added to N_a. During the recursive processing of this chain all objects in the chain are added to O. Therefore, a will be inserted into A in line 20, as $Ref(e_a) \subseteq O$ (checked in line 11) holds. $\implies \mathbf{A}^* \subseteq \mathbf{A}$ $\qquad \square$

4. RELATED WORK

Incremental compilation of text sources has been studied in the field of software engineering for years (cf. [14], [4], [8]). Today, in common software development environments sources are compiled incrementally. While some techniques, e.g., for parsing [1, 11] including incremental parsing [16], can be transfered from software engineering to text-based knowledge engineering, there are also important differences:

While in the source code of most programming languages the position in documents and the ordering of text segments is decisive, this is often not the case in text-based knowledge engineering. In fact, it is possible to translate single knowledge slices independently, which is utilized in our approach to minimize the efforts of incremental updates according to the exact text segments changed. Furthermore, for most common programming languages the sophisticated code optimization of the target representation becomes highly challenging and compilers are specialized on the respective language. These optimizations are less important in knowledge engineering scenarios. Instead, flexibility in the applied markup language — as supported by the compilation approach presented in this paper — has a higher priority in text-based knowledge engineering. Fowler [5] emphasizes the value of *Domain Specific Languages* (DSLs) for development efficiency and for facilitation of discussion with and contribution by domain experts. The existence of an efficient compilation algorithm, which is independent of the language, simplifies the introduction of project specific markups for custom-tailored domain-oriented knowledge acquisition.

The incremental compilation of knowledge at a fine grained level has also been identified as an important goal by the developer community of the open source rule engine drools [3] (*JBoss*), which has been starting efforts for the incremental compilation in the text-based eclipse-editor *drools IDE*[2] in 2010. However, to the best of the authors knowledge, no algorithms for incremental compilation of knowledge documents have been published yet.

Th approach presented in this paper is *not* related to the research on computational tractable methods for general propositional reasoning, that is also called *Knowledge Compilation* in literature. In this paper, we apply the term *compilation* as known from the translation of source code in software engineering.

5. APPLICATIONS

We implemented the algorithm as proposed in Section 3 for the semantic wiki KnowWE [2]. The implementation is independent of the particular knowledge representation, target knowledge repository or markup. In different projects KnowWE and its incremental compilation capabilities have been employed for knowledge acquisition in different domains using various kinds of markups and different target representations. From a technical point of view, for a concrete knowledge representation and a concrete markup, despite of the parser, only the insert and remove functions for the knowledge slices need to be implemented. They are called by the general compilation algorithm, that passes the corresponding source text segments representing the valid knowledge slice to be inserted or removed. In the following,

---

[2]http://www.jboss.org/drools/drools-expert.html

Method (change)	100	300	500	1000
Incr. (8 ks inserted)	100	288	502	1020
Incr. (6% ks inserted)	90	640	1775	7300
Incr. (6% ks removed)	38	48	72	170
Full compile (any)	585	4980	13900	52100

Table 1: Comparison of run-times (in ms) of full and incremental compilation for various document changes in d3web. The size of the respective complete knowledge base (number of knowledge slices) is denoted in the column header.

Method (changes)	62r	310r	620r
Incr. (1 rule)	59	188	377
Incr. (3 rules)	104	288	590
full compile	1885	8950	20600

Table 2: Comparison of run-times (in ms) of full and incremental compilation for various document base changes in drools. The size of the respective complete knowledge base (number of rules) is denoted in the column header.

we describe the usage of different knowledge representations and present benchmark results for the runtime of the incremental compilation compared to a full-compile. The duration of the compilation in the benchmark tables is measured in milliseconds and includes the parsing and resource delta generation tasks. As the implemented incremental compilation used only marginally more memory than the non-incremental solutions, this was not an issue in any of these applications on a standard desktop PC with 2 GB RAM.

5.1 Problem-solving Knowledge with d3web

The reasoning engine *d3web* [3] is a family of diagnostic problem-solvers. For different kinds of knowledge representations, such as decision trees, rules, and covering models, markups for text-based acquisition have been defined. The compilation process for these markups has been adapted to comply to the incremental compilation algorithm. d3web uses different object classes of the diagnosis task, such as symptoms, symptom values, solutions and questionnaires. Extending the incremental compilation algorithm, additional type checks for object references were implemented. The markups have been applied in several real world projects, e.g., CareMate[2], CliWE[6], or BIOLOG[10].

For our experiments, we generated differently sized sets of text files, that include markups for rules and covering models. In Table 1, we present benchmark results for different editing operations. The incremental compilation algorithm performs the compilation task orders of magnitude faster than a full compilation. However, the results do not exactly reflect the independence of the update algorithm of the knowledge base size. This can be explained by the fact, that the benchmark was performed on single documents and the parsing time is not independent of the document size. Further, insertion time into the repository is also not constant for different knowledge base sizes.

5.2 Ontology Engineering in HermesWiki

In the eLearning platform HermesWiki [12], in addition to informal knowledge about the domain of ancient history, a formal knowledge base (ontology) is formed. This domain ontology can be used for semantic search and navigation, augmented content presentation and the generation of automated quiz-sessions for the students. The formal relations of the ontology, A-Box as well as T-Box, are inserted by markup expressions in the wiki pages. New ontology entities, such as classes, properties and instances, are explicitly introduced according to the closed world authoring approach while basic RDF(S)/OWL vocabulary is available from scratch. For the insertion of basic triple assertions a

simple turtle-syntax[4] inspired markup is used. For special parts of the T-Box, different kinds of markups have been designed, partially inspired by the Manchester Syntax [7]. More information about the Hermes ontology and its creation using markup can be found in [12]. The HermesWiki currently contains about 900 wiki pages.

In our experiments, we used different semantic repositories. The overall runtime of a compilation was dependent on the performance of the insert operations of the utilized semantic repository. A full parsing and knowledge compilation takes about 41 seconds using sesame[5] with swiftOWLIM[6] and 31 seconds using BigOWLIM[6] and 36 seconds for Jena[7]. For any repository, the performance of the full parse algorithm showed to be insufficient for effective knowledge acquisition. In contrast, the incremental compilation provided almost immediate response (< 1 sec) for typical edit operations in the wiki.

5.3 Business Rules with drools

We applied our approach to the rule engine *drools* [3] to demonstrate that our incremental compilation approach can also be applied in a straight forward way to a business rules language. Therefore, we implemented the rule markup as a plugin for KnowWE, providing a basic collaborative authoring environment for drools.

As an example, we used a simple knowledge base from the car-fault-diagnosis domain including 62 rules. To evaluate the scalability, the rules were multiplied five and then ten times with slight modifications. Table 2 shows the benchmark results for the modification/insertion of one respectively three rules in rule documents of different sizes.

6. CONCLUSIONS

In this paper, we proposed an efficient solution for the compilation of a knowledge base from source documents in closed world authoring environments. We presented an algorithm for incremental knowledge base updates which is independent of the markup language and the employed knowledge repository. Since it performs a compilation based on the document modifications, the complexity of the algorithm is independent from the size of the overall document base. A formal proof for its correctness was presented. To prove the practical use of the approach, we implemented the algorithm as proposed in Section 3 within the semantic wiki

---

[3]http://www.d3web.de

[4]http://www.w3.org/TeamSubmission/turtle/

[5]http://www.openrdf.org/

[6]http://www.ontotext.com/owlim/index.html

[7]http://jena.sourceforge.net/

KnowWE and applied it on different kinds of knowledge representations (d3web, RDF(S)/OWL, drools). Practical applications show, that even in large document bases the delay of the compilation process is hardly recognizable for limited changes. The core components of the wiki-based knowledge acquisition environment KnowWE[8] and most of its plugins (including all those mentioned in this paper) are licensed under LGPL and are available for download[9].

In the future, we try to incorporate support for order-sensitive representations, such as lists or ordered hierarchies. This is a non trivial task, since for these, small modification cannot be translated to the target representation without considering the context.

7. ACKNOWLEDGEMENTS

We like to thank Andreas Hotho and Joachim Baumeister for their helpful advice on this work.

8. REFERENCES

[1] A. V. Aho, M. S. Lam, R. Sethi, and J. D. Ullman. *Compilers: Principles, Techniques, and Tools (2nd Edition).* Addison Wesley, 2006.

[2] J. Baumeister, J. Reutelshoefer, and F. Puppe. KnowWE: A Semantic Wiki for Knowledge Engineering. *Applied Intelligence*, 2010.

[3] P. Browne. *JBoss Drools Business Rules.* Packt Publishing, 2009.

[4] T. Cooper and M. J. Wise. Achieving Incremental Compilation Through Fine-Grained Builds. *Software, Practice and Experience*, 27(5):497–517, 1997.

[5] M. Fowler. *Domain-Specific Languages.* Addison-Wesley Professional, 2010.

[6] R. Hatko, J. Reutelshoefer, J. Baumeister, and F. Puppe. A Semantic Wiki for the Engineering of Diagnostic Guideline Knowledge. In *Poster at the 17th International Conference on Knowledge Engineering and Knowledge Management (EKAW)*, 2010.

[7] M. Horridge, N. Drummond, J. Goodwin, A. Rector, and H. H. Wang. The Manchester OWL Syntax. In *Proc. of the 2006 OWL Experiences and Directions Workshop*, 2006.

[8] M. Karasick. The architecture of montana: an open and extensible programming environment with an incremental c++ compiler. *SIGSOFT Software Engineering Notes*, 23:131–142, November 1998.

[9] M. Krötzsch, D. Vrandečić, and M. Völkel. Semantic MediaWiki. In *ISWC'06: Proceedings of the 5th International Semantic Web Conference, LNAI 4273*, pages 935–942, Berlin, 2006. Springer.

[10] K. Nadrowski, J. Baumeister, and V. Wolters. LaDy: Knowledge Wiki zur kollaborativen und wissensbasierten Entscheidungshilfe zu Umweltveränderung und Biodiversität. *Naturschutz und Biologische Vielfalt*, 60:171–176, 2008.

[11] T. Parr. *The Definitive ANTLR Reference: Building Domain-Specific Languages.* Pragmatic Bookshelf, first edition, May 2007.

[12] J. Reutelshoefer, F. Lemmerich, J. Baumeister, J. Wintjes, and L. Haas. Taking OWL to Athens – Semantic Web Technology takes Ancient Greek History to Students. In *ESWC: Proceedings of the 7th Extended Semantic Web Conference.* Springer, 2010.

[13] S. Schaffert, F. Bry, J. Baumeister, and M. Kiesel. Semantic wikis. *IEEE Software*, 25(4):8–11, 2008.

[14] M. Schwartz, N. Delisle, and V. Begwani. Incremental compilation in magpie. In *Proc. of the 1984 SIGPLAN symposium on Compiler construction*, pages 122–131, NY, 1984. ACM.

[15] M. Völkel, M. Krötzsch, D. Vrandečić, H. Haller, and R. Studer. Semantic Wikipedia. In *WWW'06: Proceedings of the 15th International Conference on World Wide Web*, pages 585–594, New York, NY, USA, 2006. ACM.

[16] T. A. Wagner and S. L. Graham. Efficient and Flexible Incremental Parsing. *ACM Transactions on Programming Languages and Systems*, 20:980–1013, 1998.

---

[8]http://www.knowwe.de
[9]http://isci.informatik.uni-wuerzburg.de

Integrating Knowledge Capture and Supervised Learning through a Human-Computer Interface

Trevor Walker, Gautam Kunapuli, Noah Larsen, David Page, Jude Shavlik
University of Wisconsin - Madison
Madison, WI, USA
{twalker, kunapg, larsen, page, shavlik} @ biostat.wisc.edu

ABSTRACT

Some supervised-learning algorithms can make effective use of domain knowledge in addition to the input-output pairs commonly used in machine learning. However, formulating this additional information often requires an in-depth understanding of the specific knowledge representation used by a given learning algorithm. The requirement to use a formal knowledge-representation language means that most domain experts will not be able to articulate their expertise, even when a learning algorithm is capable of exploiting such valuable information. We investigate a method to ease this knowledge acquisition through the use of a graphical, human-computer interface. Our interface allows users to easily provide advice about specific examples, rather than requiring them to provide general rules; we leave the task of properly generalizing such advice to the learning algorithms. We demonstrate the effectiveness of our approach using the Wargus real-time strategy game, comparing learning with no advice to learning with concrete advice provided through our interface, as well as comparing to using generalized advice written by an AI expert. Our results show that our approach of combining a GUI-based advice language with an advice-taking learning algorithm is an effective way to capture domain knowledge.

Categories and Subject Descriptors

I.2.6 Learning – *Knowledge acquisition.*

General Terms

Algorithms, Experimentation, Human Factors.

Keywords

Advice Taking, Human-Computer Interface.

INTRODUCTION

Many domains exist in which experts possess extensive knowledge and know how to apply that knowledge to perform domain tasks; cardiologists determine the likelihood of heart disease given diagnostic test results; analysts viewing surveillance imagery identify suspicious activity; and coaches determine the strategy of a game by examining past games of an opposing team. While traditional supervised-learning algorithms use input-output pairs, often referred to as positive and negative examples in the case of two-class learning problems, some algorithms can also use domain knowledge during learning. For instance, various inductive logic programming algorithms [12] accept background knowledge in the form of Horn clauses, knowledge-based support vector machines [5] use knowledge in the form of constraints over regions of a task's feature space, and Markov logic networks [15] accept knowledge in the form of weighted first-order logic.

Articulating domain knowledge for any given algorithm requires an in-depth understanding of the specific knowledge representation used by the algorithm. However, formulating domain knowledge in the correct representation either requires training a domain expert to provide knowledge in the necessary formal representation or requires the domain expert to rely on a third party to translate the domain knowledge. This bottleneck greatly limits the applicability of these algorithms.

One approach to overcoming this limitation is to provide the domain expert a *human-computer interface* (HCI) that facilitates the acquisition of the domain knowledge in a manner easily understood by the domain expert, but which constrains the knowledge such that, through some algorithmic transformation, it is also useable by the learning algorithm. Extensive research exists studying HCIs for this purpose. Some approaches rely on demonstration by the domain expert of some process [2,10]. Others provide an interface in which the expert may specify additional examples to guide or correct the learning algorithm [17]. Some treat domain knowledge as a form of constraints and provide an interface to specify those constraints [8].

We investigate a method of using an HCI to obtain relational domain knowledge, in the form of concrete (i.e., ground) logical *advice* (i.e., domain knowledge that may be incomplete or incorrect, but may still be useful) about specific training examples, leaving the task of generalizing the domain knowledge to an automatic algorithm. Relational domains are characterized as domains with objects and relationships among them (expressed through predicates). Unlike the so-called *fixed-length feature vectors* of standard machine learning, examples in relational domains often contain a variable number of objects and relationships.

By focusing on ground statements about specific examples, we provide the domain expert a method to simply state why something is true (or false, depending on the example), without requiring them to understand the final knowledge representation. Additionally, by supporting relational advice, we allow richer knowledge and better support relational-learning algorithms. Our HCI approach to obtaining relational knowledge in a ground format and automatically processing it into the required knowledge representation is, we believe, unique about this research.

We demonstrate our approach's effectiveness by examining a task in a real-time strategy game. We providing a simple GUI through which a 'domain expert can specify relational advice explaining various scenarios and show that combining the HCI and a suitable advice-taking learning algorithm is effective. We compare successfully against both (a) using no advice and (b) hand-written advice.

OVERVIEW OF APPROACH

We consider a learning paradigm designed to assist domain experts (we will also refer to them as *users*) in the process of creating and refining domain knowledge through the use of an HCI. We view domain knowledge as a form of advice provided by the user to the learning algorithm. We also consider advice acquisition to be an iterative process (see Figure 1) of a user specifying advice, an algorithm learning a model, a user reviewing results, and a user refining or augmenting the advice. Although this paradigm applies to many forms of learning, we specifically consider supervised learning algorithms that take as inputs both training examples and additional domain knowledge.

Our iterative learning process proceeds in four stages. First, we present an HCI through which the user specifies advice. Our HCI accomplishes this by displaying information about a single training example and asking the user why that example was positive (or negative). We specifically consider advice in the form of concrete logical statements. For instance, in a medical domain, the HCI might provide the user with a patient's information, health history, etc. and ask why that patient was high risk for heart problems. The user might have the domain knowledge that the patient was a high risk because "the patient's cholesterol was high during her last visit and her father's family has a history of heart disease." Through the HCI, the user would be able to express this knowledge in the ground logical format without knowing the final representation.

Although the domain expert does need to understand basic logic (that is *and*, *or*, and *not*), beyond that they need only makes statements about why a particular example is true or false. We believe that domain experts can specify this ground representation of advice more easily than other representations. Additionally, relying on ground advice reduces the complexity of the HCI since it does not need to support logical variables in the advice.

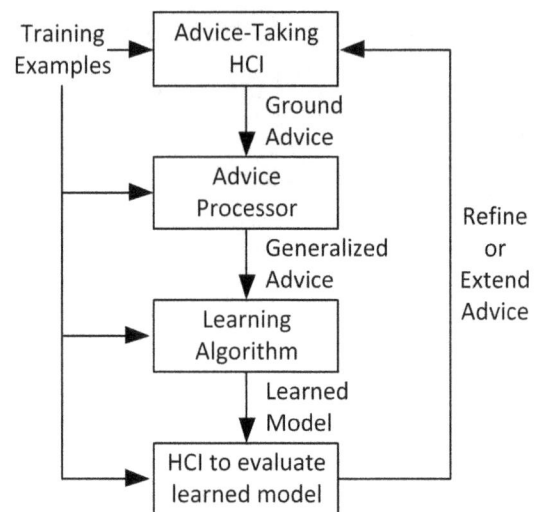

Figure 1. Our human-computer learning paradigm. Initially the user specifies advice through an HCI. Then the advice is processed and learning occurs. Afterward the results are presented to the user via an evaluation HCI. The process iterates until the user is satisfied with the results.

After the user finishes entering advice for a number of training examples, the second phase of our process translates the advice into a form usable by the learning algorithm. This usually entails generalizing the advice and possibly changing the representation of the advice. The process of converting the advice can be quite complex. Often there are multiple generalizations with distinct meanings. Since we do not expect the user to understand the underlying representation of the advice, it is often infeasible to ask the user to correct the advice directly and we rely upon our iterative process to indirectly improve the advice. Additionally, the user might specify advice over multiple examples and the algorithm must determine the meaning of the multiple statements.

Phase three of our process performs the actual learning. At this point, we provide to the learning algorithm both the training examples and the generalized advice. The learning algorithm then produces a *model*. After learning, we pass this model onto phase four. Here, we evaluate the model against additional examples and present an HCI allowing the user to review the effectiveness of the model.

The reviewing HCI presents the user information about which 'testset' examples were correctly or incorrectly predicted by the model. Based on this, the user may elect to return to phase one in order to adjust previously presented advice, provide new advice, or label new examples.

Below we present further details about the first three phases of this learning process. While we believe that the iterative process of refining advice is an important step, we do not investigate it further here.

Table 1. Features describing tower-defense world.

Category	Values
Units	archer, swordsman, ballista, peasant, tower
Unit properties	x-location(Unit), y-location(Unit), health(Unit)
Group Properties	unitInGroup(Group, Unit), groupSize(Group)
World Properties	countOf(UnitType), moatExists, contentsOfTile(X,Y)

Table 2. Background predicates available in tower-defense predication task.

Category	Predicates
Numeric Comparators	$>$, $<$, $\geq$, $\leq$, $=$
Spatial Comparators	isNearTo, isFarFrom, canReach

BACKGROUND AND RELATED WORK

Extensive research exists studying domain expert knowledge acquisition through the use human-computer interaction [16]. Additionally, previous research examines how to exploit domain knowledge obtained either through an HCI, generated algorithmically or by hand.

One method used to obtain knowledge is *programming by demonstration*. In programming by demonstration, a domain expert performs a sequence of actions demonstrating how to perform some task. From this demonstration, a learning algorithm builds a procedural program intended to solve the task. Often, the learned programs must be adjusted through further interaction with the user. One such system [10] allows the user "nudge" the system through the inclusion or removal of training examples. Another approach [2] allows users to adjust the training data directly, adding missing information after the demonstration process. Unlike our approach, both of these system work directly with the training examples without providing explicit background knowledge. Some approaches do allow explicit background knowledge to be specified. For instance, Vander Zanden and Myers [17] provide a method to specify background knowledge, but require understanding of the underlying knowledge representation represented in Lisp. Another method of human-computer interaction is *programming by example*. Here the user provides a prototypical example of the desired result, such as the result from a database query. These approaches [4,9] again differ from our approach in that they operate on the examples not on additional background knowledge.

Wargus Real-Time Strategy Game

We use the Wargus video game to illustrate our advice-acquisition HCI. In Wargus, a game in the real-time strategy genera, two or more players direct units, such as peasants, swordsmen, archers, etc., in an attempt to conquer the opposing players. Play involves constructing buildings, producing unit, harvesting resources, and directing attacks against opponents.

To demonstrate our HCI we use a subset of the Wargus game we call *tower-defense*. Here an attacking team, consisting of peasants, archers, swordsmen, and ballista, assault a single tower belonging to the defenders. The learning task we consider consists of predicting whether the tower will survive the attack given the size and composition of the attacking force. Figure 2 depicts a typical

tower-defense game board. Variations of the game board include the existence of a moat, the size and composition of the attacking units, and the layout of the game board. Table 1 provides a brief description of the features in the tower-defense domain. Additionally, we define a number of background predicates, listed in Table 2, which will be available to the user to specify domain knowledge and may be used in the learned models.

An open-source Wargus game engine exists [19] that allows us to simulate the outcome of any game configuration (i.e., will the tower stand or fall?) according to the game's rules. Thus, for any given game board, we can determine the example label as either *towerStands* or *towerFalls*. This also allows us to generate as many examples as desired in our experiments.

Boosted Relational Dependency Networks

We have chosen one advice-taking algorithm to evaluate our approach. *Boosted relational dependency networks* (bRDNs) [13] provide a relational, probabilistic graphical-model based learning algorithm. A *dependency network* [7] approximates a joint distribution over the variables as product of conditional distributions. *Relational dependency networks* (RDN) [14] extend these dependency networks to a relational setting. The bRDN algorithm combines relational dependency networks with a form of gradient-tree boosting [3].

RDNs consist of a set of predicate symbols composing the

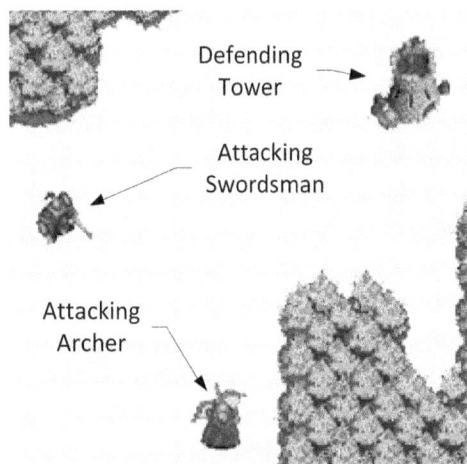

Figure 2. The Wargus tower-defense task. Multiple attacking units, consisting of swordsmen, archers, and ballista, assault the defender's tower. Depending on the composition of the attacking force, the tower may survive or be destroyed. The Wargus tower-defense learning task involves predicting which of these outcomes will occur.

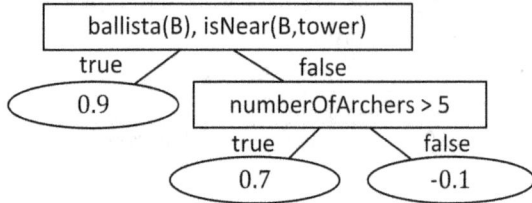

Figure 3. A logical decision tree representing a conditional probability distribution for determining the probability a given tower falls. Each interior node is a logical decision point, with the left branch representing a true evaluation and the right branch a false evaluation. Leaves represent output potentials that must be normalized (see Equation 1) to produce the output probability.

nodes of a graphical model. For each predicate Y_i, a conditional probability distribution $P(Y_i|\ X_i)$, defines a distribution over the values of Y_i given the values of the other features. The distribution of a variable y_i is estimated as

$$Prob(y_i|x_i) = \frac{e^{\psi(y_i;x_i)}}{\sum_{y'} e^{\psi(y';x_i)}} \forall x_i \in x_i \neq y_i \qquad (1)$$

where $\psi(y_i; x_i)$ is the potential function of y_i given all other features $x_i \neq y_i$.

The bRDN algorithm approximates these conditional probability distributions (the Ψ's) through *relational decision trees* [1]; a sample is depicted in Figure 3 (in this figure and elsewhere in this article, upper case arguments are logical variables, following Prolog notation). In these relational decision trees each interior node is a logical decision point and the leaf nodes represent the various potentials, i.e., the ψ's, of the conditional probability distribution. In order to obtain the final probabilities, the potentials must be normalized according to Equation (1).

While the conditional probability distributions in RDNs can be represented by a single relational decision tree [6], in bRDNs each conditional probability distributions is estimated by a <u>sequence</u> of trees, based upon an initial potential ψ_0 and iteratively adjusted via a set of gradients Δ_i. Thus, after m iterations, the potential is given as $\psi_m = \psi_0 + \Delta_0 + \cdots + \Delta_m$. Here, Δ_i is given by $\Delta_m = \eta_m \cdot E_{x,y}[\partial/\partial\psi_{m-1} logP(y|x; \psi_{m-1})]$ where η_m is a scalar controlling the gradient step size. Thus, a set of trees are learned for every predicate such that at each iteration a new set of regression trees estimates the maximum likelihood of the distributions with respect to the potential function.

By providing advice, users indirectly produce new background knowledge rules for use by the bRDN algorithm as interior nodes in its trees, as is further explained later.

OUR ADVICE-TAKING HCI

Next we provide details of the requirements of an advice-taking HCI designed to obtain ground advice from the domain expert. Design of the HCI depends greatly upon the type of the knowledge being gathered. Figure 4 depicts a simple prototypical GUI designed for the Wargus tower-defense game and used to gather relational advice pertain-

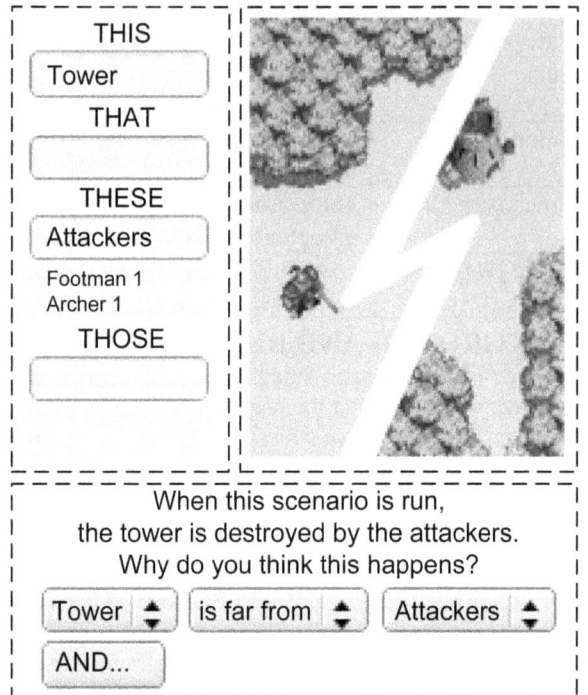

Figure 4. Prototype GUI for advice taking in Wargus. The GUI consists of 4 sections indicated here (but not in the actual GUI) by overlaid dashed boxes: (upper-left) entity selection and naming, (upper-right) display of current game board, (lower) controls specifying relations between selected entities, and (not shown) a list of previously specified advice. Layout and relative size of elements have been adjusted for clarity. Only a partial game board is shown in the upper right.

ing to it. In our approach, the user provides advice through the following process:

1. An example is selected, either manually by the user or through some automatic process.
2. The HCI provides the user (ideally visually) information about the example.
3. The user provides advice through the HCI to explain why this example was either positive or negative.
4. The user either returns to Step 1 to provide more advice or stops.

In order to facilitate this process, our HCI needs to:

1. Provide information about specific examples.
2. Allow selection and naming of entities or groups of entities.
3. Provide a method to indicate relations among selected entities.
4. Allow the user to review, and possibly edit, previously specified advice.

Providing Example Information

The HCI must provide information to the user about examples. In our knowledge capture approach, each advice statement is about a specific example. Thus, the HCI needs to provide at least the information about one example. In the Wargus tower-defense game we can depict all information about an example as a picture of the game board. In some domains, this is not possible or not desirable. For example, examining patient information in a medical domain would require a much different GUI design.

Selecting and Naming Entities

Advice in our system consists of relations among entities. Here, an entity is any object in the domain. For instance, in the Wargus domain, the various units on the game board are entities. A user needs a method to indicate the entities that should be related. Thus, we require some sort of entity-selection mechanism.

The entity-selection methodology will different depending on the domain. In board game domains, such as Wargus, simply clicking on one or more entities is sufficient. However, for other domains, a much more complex approach may be necessary.

One extension we found particularly useful in our Wargus GUI was the ability to name *groups* of entities. When selecting entities in Wargus, by default we named single entities either THIS or THAT. When selecting groups of entities, the default names are THESE or THOSE. Thus, later on, when specifying a particular relation, we could state THIS is related to THAT or THESE are related to THAT.

In addition to selecting entities, in many domains, objects have additional properties. For instance, in the Wargus domain, all units have a property indicating each unit's *x-y* location. Thus, a mechanism is required to access the properties.

Specifying Relations

In relational logic, we specify relations through predicates. For instance, *isNearTo(archer1, tower)* or *colorOf(archer1, green)*. The HCI needs to know what predicates the user may use to specify relations. Here, the complexity of the HCI will depend greatly on the complexity of the domain. Our Wargus domain contains only binary relations, so we provide drop-down menus to the entity-relation-entity information.

Our ground advice format allows conjunctions, disjunctions, and negations. Thus, the HCI must also support specifying advice with these logical connectives. In our prototype, we provide the negation of all predicates in the "relation" menu. A button provides the ability to create conjunctions of multiple relations. Disjunctions are implied implicitly between different pieces of advice.

Reviewing Advice

From a usability standpoint, allowing the user to review previous actions is important. We do not explore this aspect of the HCI other than to mention that while using our GUI, we often examine previous advice to determine if we needed to state something new or not.

GENERATING GENERALIZED ADVICE AND LEARNING

Here we look at an advice-processing approach that converts the ground advice obtained through the advice-taking HCI into background knowledge in the form of generalized Horn clauses. A *Horn clause* is a disjunctive clause containing at most one positive literal (informally, one can view it as an IF-THEN rule written in first-order logic). Several relational learning algorithms, such as various inductive logic programming approaches and the bRDN algorithm described earlier, use a Horn-clause representation for background knowledge and can use such generated background knowledge directly.

Output from our advice-taking HCI is represented as a set of ground logical implications. As shown in Table 6, the consequence of a piece of advice states the category of a specific training example. The antecedent is a conjunction of literals defined within the domain (either as 'raw' features or via background rules). Multiple pieces of ground advice may be specified for a single training example and multiple examples may have associated advice. So a challenge we need to face is coherently combining multiple pieces of advice into one or more Horn clauses.

We transform the ground advice into generalized Horn clauses using the advice-handling process of Walker et al. [18]. Algorithm 1 presents the process. The algorithm performs essentially two phases. In the first phase (lines 5-11), it creates a number of conjunctive and disjunctive combinations of the ground advice. These new implications attempt to deduce possible meanings of the advice when considered as a whole. The algorithm considers three different combinations. First, it creates "per-piece" advice by considering each advice statement independently. Second, it creates "per-example" advice by conjoining all of the advice specified for a given example into a single combination. Finally, it creates "mega-rules." The set of mega-rules contains various combinations using all of the specified advice.

The "mega-rules" attempt to explain the possible intended meaning of all pieces of advice when considered together. For instance, the user might have intended that 'positive' advice indicates properties all positive examples have while 'negative' advice states properties the concept lacks ("this is a bird because it has wings, this other example is a bird because it lays eggs, this third example is not a bird because it has leaves, this fourth example is not a bird because it is made of metal. ..."). Alternatively, the user might have been specifying a more disjunctive concept ("Alice got to work by taking the bus. Bob got to work by walking. ... Carl did not make it to work because he slept all day."). We generate multiple "mega-rules" since there is no way to directly determine the correct combination (if any).

As a second phase (lines 13-19), the algorithm generalizes each of the generated combinations. This occurs through a process of anti-substitution in which it replaces each dis-

---

Algorithm 1: CREATEGENERALIZEDADVICE

1. **Given**: G, a set of ground advice statements.
2. **Do**:   Generate H, a set of generalized
3.   Horn-clause background knowledge
4.
5.   Let $K = G$ // *Per piece-of-advice formulas*
6. **For each** example $e_j \in \{e_1 \ldots e_n\}$ with advice
7.   Generate "Per-example" formula p combining
8.   all advice from e_i into a single conjunctive
9.   Let $K = K \cup \{ p \}$
10.
11.   Let $K = K \cup \{$ "Mega-Rules" $\}$ // *See text*
12.
13. **For each** ground advice statement $k_i \in K$
14.   Generalize k_i via anti-substitution yield
15.   the formula f_i
16.   Convert f_i to Horn clauses by expanding
17.   disjunctive formulas into multiple clauses and
18.   replacing negation by negation via failure
19.   Add generated Horn clauses to set H
20.
21. **Return** set H containing generalized clauses

---

tinct constant that occurs in a given combination with a logical variable. At this point, it also converts the generalized implications into Horn clauses by transforming any implications that contain disjunctions into multiple logical implications. After converting the ground advice into generalized Horn clauses, we pass the background knowledge off to the learning algorithm. Table 3 illustrates the generated background knowledge for some simple ground advice.

EXPERIMENTAL RESULTS

In order to evaluate our HCI and advice-taking approach we performed experiments using the Wargus tower-defense game. We are interested in the effectiveness of advice generated using our advice-taking HCI versus both hand-written advice and using no advice.

Natural Language Advice versus HCI Advice

Our initial goal is to determine whether our HCI was capable of representing the types of advice a user might like to say in general. To evaluate that, we had group members who were not directly involved with Wargus nor its HCI (a) watch Wargus games, (b) learn (in their own minds) some basic strategy, and then (c) provide advice in ordinary English describing why a tower fell or stood for 5-10 specific initial states of our Wargus game.

A vast majority of the natural language advice was given in terms of the numbers and types of units in the attacking force. Overall, users provided 311 sentences of advice about 100 examples. Table 4 contains some general statistics gleaned from the natural language advice provided by the users. Users usually tended to give *specific* advice in terms of certain features such numbers of units, the presence or absence of a moat, and whether or not there was a ballista in

Table 3. Generated background knowledge for some simple ground advice. Initial ground advice is first generalized. Then various combinations are generated representing possible guesses at the meaning of the set of advice statements.

Description	Advice
Initial ground advice	ex(pos1) ← p(pos1) ∧ q(pos1). ex(pos1) ← r(pos1). ex(pos2) ← s(pos2).
"Per-piece" advice	a1(E) ← p(E) ∧ q(E). a2(E) ← r(E). a3(E) ← s(E).
"Per-example" advice	e1(E) ← p(E) ∧ q(E) ∧ r(E). e2(E) ← s(E).
"Mega" advice	m1(E) ← p(E) ∧ q(E) ∧ r(E) ∧ s(E). m2(E) ← p(E) ∧ q(E) ∨ r(E) ∨ s(E).

the attacking force. For instance, "five archers are sufficient to destroy the tower," or conjunctive advice: "there is a moat and only footmen; hence the tower stands."

About 10% of the advice provide in natural language could not be expressed via our HCI. For instance, one user stated "the attacks are coming from many directions." Another mentioned "the north-most footman will absorb damage so the weaker archer can live longer." A small number of users also provided advice that was too *vague* (e.g., "there are too many attackers or "too few attackers") or described the existence of paths between attackers and the tower.

Our HCI is able to capture the vast majority of advice given by the users because it exploits the users' inclination to provide specific advice. Furthermore, it also provides mechanisms to allow users to provide general advice in terms of groups of units and even units in the scenario. The design is flexible enough to allow for various levels of specificity of advice as desired by the user.

Evaluating Advice Effectiveness

In order to evaluate our approach, we ran three separate experiments: one with no advice, one with hand-written advice, and one with advice obtained through our HCI. The HCI advice was based upon a representative sample of seven sentences (Table 5) expressed in natural language (we selected these seven sentences before running any experiments and

Table 4. General statistics gleaned from the natural language advice provided by the users.

Feature Mentioned In Advice	Context	
	Tower stands	Tower falls
Total number of attackers	50	36
Number of Archers	43	62
Number of Footmen	50	46
Number of Ballistae	18	1
Number of Peasants	0	24
Presence of Moat	6	28
Other (terrain/distance/angle)	10	16

Table 5. The seven sentences of advice used.

Advice about *towerFalls* examples	Three or more footmen can take down a tower if there is no moat.
	Five or more archers can take down a tower.
	A single ballista is sufficient to destroy the tower.
Advice about *towerStands* examples	If there are only peasants, the tower stands.
	Four archers or less cannot take down a tower.
	One footman cannot take down the tower.
	If there is a moat, and no archers or ballista, the tower cannot be destroyed.

Table 6. Sample ground logical statements about the Wargus tower-defense game for one positive (pos1) and one negative example (neg1), based on Table 5. Recall a positive example is when the tower stands.

Example	Advice		
towerStands(pos1)	count(archers,	pos1)	$= 0 \quad \wedge$
	count(footman,	pos1)	$= 0 \quad \wedge$
	count(ballista,	pos1)	$= 0.$
towerStands(pos1)	count(archers,	pos1)	$\leq 4.$
towerStands(pos1)	count(footman,	pos1)	$= 1.$
towerStands(pos1)	moatExists		$\wedge$
	count(archers,	pos1)	$= 0 \quad \wedge$
	count(ballista,	pos1)	$= 0.$
towerStands(neg1)	count(footman,	neg1)	$\geq 3.$
towerStands(neg1)	count(archers,	neg1)	$\geq 5.$
towerStands(neg1)	count(ballista,	neg1)	$\geq 1.$

did not modify them during the course of our experiments). We only used relations that could be entered through the HCI; we disregarded the rest of the natural language advice.

Table 6 shows some of the ground advice generated via the HCI. After creating the ground advice through the HCI, we used the advice generalization algorithm described previously to generate a set of background clauses, resulting in 21 separate pieces of background knowledge including the per-piece, per-example, and mega rules. While our advice taking learner can accept advice expressed in predicate calculus, the full richness of first-order logic was not needed to capture the human provided advice.

We created the hand-written advice without using the HCI, representing what a domain expert who understood the required knowledge representation would create, writing the advice directly as seven Horn clauses. Once we created the advice, we used the bRDN learning algorithm described earlier to generate learning curves comparing the use of (a) no advice, (b) hand-written advice, and (c) HCI generated advice.

Results and Discussion

We evaluated the learned models for the three separate experiments against a held-aside set of 900 testing examples. Figure 5 shows the area under the ROC curve (AUROC) for the three experiments. We tested significance of the results via the (two-tailed) sign test, a nonparametric test based on the binomial distribution [11]. The sign test is an exact test (McNemar's test is an approximation that was historically used purely because of computational limitations). The null hypothesis of the sign test is that both approaches are equally accurate; hence each test case for which the two approaches make different predictions is viewed as the flip of a fair coin. An approach "wins" such as test case if it predicts correctly and the other approach predicts incorrectly. Where there are N test cases for which the approaches give different predictions, and the most wins for either approach is h, the computed p-value is the probability of at least h heads by *either*

method under the binomial distribution $b(N,0.5)$, that is, in N flips of a fair coin.

The difference in error rates between the HCI advice approach and the no advice approach is statistically significant ($p < 0.05$) at every point in the curve, with p-values as low as 3.89×10^{-15} at the largest difference in the curves (at 30 training examples). This demonstrates that, in this domain, the HCI-generated advice does improve learning, especially in the early regions of the learning curve.

The difference in error rates when using the two different types of advice is significant only for a few points in the curve, at 30, 70 and 100 examples. We consider this a positive result, as it indicates that our HCI approach performed as well as hand-written advice.

In addition to the bRDN experiments, we also compared using the HCI-generated advice with a knowledge-based support vector machine [5] as the learning algorithm.

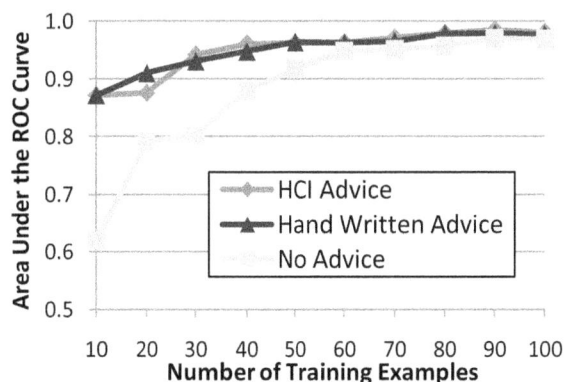

Figure 5. Learning curve showing test set performance in the Wargus tower-defense game comparing models learned with hand-written advice, HCI generated advice, and no advice. All models were learned the using boosted relational dependency network algorithm. The HCI generated advice was generalized using the techniques in Walker et al. [18].

Although space does not permit a description of this algorithm, its results are similar to bRDN's.

Although in our relatively simple testbed the value of advice largely disappears with only 100 labeled example, in many tasks it is hard to get sufficient numbers of training examples. Advice is most effective when it is hard to get a good number of labeled examples yet easy to articulate helpful domain knowledge.

CONCLUSIONS AND FUTURE WORK

Providing formalized domain knowledge provides an effective method of substantially increasing the performance of supervised learning algorithms. However, this effectiveness is offset by the difficulty of formulating that knowledge, especially in the case of domain experts with little or no understanding of the learning algorithm or the knowledge representation required by these algorithms. Allowing the domain expert to specify knowledge as ground advice about specific examples through a human-computer interface provides one appealing method of overcoming this difficulty. We have demonstrated that for the Wargus tower-defense domain, ground advice obtained through an HCI outperforms learning with no advice and performs as well as advice written by an AI expert.

One interesting future direction would be to examine the effectiveness of refining advice by presenting the user with an HCI displaying the results of learning. Investigating the ability to support the learning of multiple concepts built upon one another might also prove insightful. Finally, allowing the user to provide advice in ordinary English would greatly extend the effectiveness of the advice-taking approach to improving supervised machine learning.

ACKNOWLEDGEMENTS

The authors gratefully acknowledge the support of DARPA's Bootstrap Learning program via the United States Air Force Research Laboratory (AFRL) under grant HR0011-07-C-0060. Views and conclusions contained in this document are those of the authors and do not necessarily represent the official opinion or policies, either expressed or implied, of the US government, DARPA, or AFRL.

REFERENCES

[1] Blockeel, H. Top-down induction of first order logical decision trees. *AI Communications* (1999), 12, 1-2:119-120.

[2] Chen, J. and Weld, D. Recovering from errors during programming by demonstration. *Procs. of Intl. Conf. on Intelligent User Interfaces* (2008).

[3] Dietterich, T., Ashenfelter, A., and Bulatov, Y. Training conditional random fields via gradient tree boosting. *Procs. of Intl. Conf. of Machine Learning* (2004).

[4] Fails, J. and Olsen, D. Interactive machine learning. *Procs. of Intl. Conf. on Intelligent User Interfaces* (2003).

[5] Fung, G., Mangasarian, O., and Shavlik, J. Knowledge-based support vector machine classifiers. *Procs. of Neural Information Processing Systems* (2002).

[6] Gutmann, B. and Kersting, K. TildeCRF: Conditional random fields for logical sequences. *Procs. of European Conf. of Machine Learning* (2006).

[7] Heckerman, D., Chickering, D., Meek, C., Rounthwaite, R., and Kadie., C. Dependency networks for inference, collaborative, and data visualization. *Journal of Machine Learning Research* (2001), 1:49-75.

[8] Huang, T. and Mitchell, T. Text clustering with extended user feedback. *Procs. of Special Interest Group on Information Retrieval* (2006).

[9] Lieberman, H., ed. *Your Wish is My Command: Programming by Example*. Morgan Kaufmann Publishers, Inc, 2001.

[10] McDaniel, R. and Myers, B. Getting more out of programming-by-demonstration. *Procs. of Conf. on Human Factors in Computing Systems* (1999).

[11] Mendenhall, W., Wackerly, D., and Scheaffer, R. Nonparametric statistics. In *Mathematical Statistics with Applications (Fourth ed.)*. PWS-Kent, 1989.

[12] Muggleton, S. and De Raedt, L. Inductive logic programming: Theory and methods. *Journal of Logic Programming* (1994), 19,20:629-679.

[13] Natarajan, S., Khot, T., Kersting, K., Gutmann, B., and Shavlik, J. Gradient-based boosting for statistical relational learning: The relational dependency network case. *Machine Learning* (2011).

[14] Neville, J. and Jensen., D. Relational dependency networks. *Journal of Machine Learning Research* (2007), 8:653-692.

[15] Richardson, M. and Domingos, P. Markov Logic Networks. *Machine Learning* (2006), 62:107-136.

[16] Stumpf, S., Rajaram, V., Li, L., and Wong, W. Interacting meaningfully with machine learning systems: Three experiments. *Intl. Journal of Human-Computer Studies* (2009), 67:639-662.

[17] Vander Zanden, B. and Myers, B. Demonstrational and constraint-based techniques for pictorially specifying application objects and behaviors. *Transactions on Computer Human Interaction* (1995), 2(4):308-356.

[18] Walker, T., O'Reilly, C., Kunapuli, G., Natarajan, S., Maclin, R., Shavlik, J., and Page, D. Automating the ILP setup task: Converting user advice about specific examples into general background knowledge. *Procs. of Intl. Conf. on Inductive Logic Programming* (2010).

[19] *Wargus Real-Time Strategy Game*. http://wargus.sourceforge.net.

Boundary Detection of Multiple Related Temporal Duration of Schedules in Email

DongHyun Choi
Dept. of Computer Science
KAIST
Korea
cdh4696@w od.kaist.ac.kr

Eun-Kyung Kim
Dept. of Computer Science
KAIST
Korea
kekeeo@world.kaist.ac.kr

Key-Sun Choi
Division of
Web Science Technology
KAIST
Korea
kschoi@world.kaist.ac.kr

ABSTRACT

Emails are very popular method for information exchange between people. In this paper, an approach to annotate the starting time (**stime**) and ending time (**etime**) of duration in schedule notices is proposed. Most related works have reported on only seminar announcements, most of which contain only one schedule per announcement and are written in very restricted format. Different from those seminar announcements, an email frequently contains information about multiple schedules with highly complex format. To process the emails, the proposed system first detects and normalizes all time expressions of the email using regular expression patterns, and then determines which time expression actually represents **stime** and **etime** information of schedules. Evaluation is carried out on newly constructed Korean email corpus, and it shows 87.35 % of F1-score for **stime** and 85.13 % for **etime**.

Categories and Subject Descriptors: H.3.3 [Information Storage and Retrieval]: Information Search and Retrieval; I.2.7 [Artificial Intelligence]: Natural Language Processing

General Terms: Algorithms

Keywords: Information Extraction, Email Mining

1. INTRODUCTION

1.1 Nature of Informal Schedule Notices in Emails

Nowadays, emails are frequently used to exchange information between various people. Due to the emergence of smartphones, people can read and write emails everywhere. But processing information from email using smartphone is very tedious work for a user, considering small display size and uncomfortable touchscreen input interface of a smartphone.

In this paper, an approach to automatically extract sched-

ule time information from email, more precisely **stime** and **etime** information of schedules, is proposed. There were various researches which tried to extract **stime** and **etime** information from official seminar announcements, and those approaches are compared at [9]. Schedule notices in email showed more freedom to announce one meeting schedule with specified programs (that are a sequence of small sessions), or multiple schedules (that is non-parallel and non-consecutive). Also, those inofficial schedule notices in emails reveal all of noises in text writing as well as emoticons and non-segmented sentences of SMS characteristics. This prevents the system from the use of sophisticated linguistic approaches.

Apart from those issues described above, the issue of normalization should also be considered. By the term 'normalization' of a time expression, we mean the procedure of discovering meanings of the time expression. For example, when a time expression "1:30 PM" is normalized, the system can figure out that the hour represented by the time expression is "13", and the minute is "30". This procedure is required to automatically process the extracted time information, for example to update the user's electronic calendar.

To address the problems described above, two steps approach is proposed. In the first step, the system extracts and normalizes all the time expressions inside the given email. Four kinds of regular expression patterns along with normalization information are manually constructed and used. In the second step, the system classifies which time expressions actually represent **stime**/**etime** information. Multiple time expressions could be determined as **stime**/**etime** expressions per one email, contrast to the other existing related works. The system uses various ML approaches with newly proposed features to solve the classification problem.

In section 2, related works will be described while detailed algorithm in section 3. Evaluation result will be presented in section 4, and we will make conclusion in section 5.

1.2 Annotation Ambiguities among Nested Sequential Events and Non-contiguous Events

A seminar program structure usually has one starting time of all sessions and there are more specific sessions with sequences of ending time and starting time between consecutive sessions. It would be called as "nested sequential consecutive events". However, an email may contain several seminar announcements in different date and time, in this case, it is a type of "non-consecutive" events. That is, when one email with schedule information contains multiple starting and ending times, they have ambiguities of the following two cases: they could actually contain information about only one **stime/etime** information of one event, and the information spreads across the e-mail in several time expressions, or they could mean multiple different schedules.

Table 1 shows the difference of seminar announcement corpus[1] with 485 online university seminar announcements, and newly constructed Korean email corpus[2] with 1,011 schedule notices containing publicly announced schedule information. The column name 'Mult.' stands for 'Multiple Temporal Expressions'. In the table, the second column represents portion of corpus which contains only one schedule expressed in only one **stime** and **etime** expression(**SS**), the third column represents portion of corpus which contains single schedule information but its information spreads across the email using several different time expressions (**SS (M)**) that is interpreted to be consecutive sequential durations, and the fourth column represents portion of corpus which contains multiple schedules (**MS**). For the seminar announcements corpus over 98 % of announcements contain only one starting and ending time expression, but for the email corpus about 15 % of emails contain more than one starting and ending time expressions.

Corpus	SS	Mult.	
		SS(M)	MS
Seminar Announcements	98.76 %	0.00 %	1.24 %
Emails with Schedules	85.46 %	8.21 %	6.33 %

Table 1: Schedule expression statistics of the corpus

The second difference is the complexity of expressions and words used inside the context. Figure 1 shows an example of seminar announcement. As can be observed, each official seminar announcement from seminar announcement corpus contains itemized text at its beginning, which presents starting time and ending time of the seminar using very clear format. Thus **stime** and **etime** expressions could be easily extracted from those seminar announcements. Meanwhile, majority of schedule notice emails do not have texts with such kind of format, and most of emails contain noises like emoticons or useless spaces (to visualize its contents more beautifully), plus lots of grammatical errors and internet slangs. Figure 2 shows an example of email, which is **SS(M)** case. Useless spaces and line feeds could be found. More detailed comparison about the complexity will be carried out on section 4.1.

2. RELATED WORKS

There were numerous researches which tackled the starting and ending time information extraction problem of the seminar announcement. Among several ML approach comparison for this problem [9], the best performance achieved for **stime** annotation was the *F* Measure of 99.6 % by [7] and [2], while the best performane achieved for the **etime** was the *F* Measure of 98.8 % by [6]. [8] tried to apply conditional random fields to this problem. Also, there were some researches to extract time expressions from complex contexts like emails or web pages, for example [10] or [4], but they rarely move onto the classification of time expressions into starting time and ending time. [3] classified time expressions into **stime** and **etime** by first doing lightweight parsing on the sentence and then matching text terms to each field.

Although the performance of **stime** and **etime** extraction from the seminar announcements has almost no gap for the further improvement, related works focused only on cases with a single duration for schedules. In contrast, the proposed research tried to solve the various other cases of nested sequencial events, and parallel non-consecutive events, by using various ML apporoaches with new features. In the following sections, the method to extract **stime** and **etime** expressions will be explained.

3. EXTRACTING STIME AND ETIME OF SCHEDULES FROM EMAIL

In this section, the algorithm of extracting **stime** and **etime** information of schedules from email is explained in detail. Figure 3 shows the overall architecture of the system. The system first extracts and normalizes time expressions from the given email, and classifies each time expression whether the time expression represents **stime** and **etime** of a schedule or not.

```
<0.24.11.93.20.52.36.sm7p+@andrew.cmu.edu.0>
Type:    cmu.andrew.org.epp
Topic:   Fwd: Lecture
Dates:   30-Nov-93
Time:    <stime>12:30</stime> - <etime>2:00 PM</etime>
PostedBy: Shaun P Mcdermott on 24-Nov-93 at 20:52 from
andrew.cmu.edu
Abstract:

<paragraph><sentence>"The Environmental Consequences of the NAFTA"
will be presented by <speaker>Michael Gregory</speaker>, director,
Arizona Toxics Information, on Tuesday, Nov. 30, from <stime>12:30
</stime> to <etime>2 p.m</etime>. in <location>Hamburg Hall
Auditorium</sentence></location>. <sentence>The lecture is being
presented as part of the Heinz School's Professional Seminar
Series</sentence>. <sentence>All are invited</sentence>.</paragraph>
```

Figure 1: Example of annotated seminar announcement from the seminar announcement corpus.

```
■ Manager Education and Assembly-Farewell Party Announcement ■

D A T E : <stime>2004. 12. 14. Tuesday</stime>
 * Manager education - <stime>13 : 00</stime> ~ 17 : 00
 * Assembly farewell party - 17 : 00 ~ <etime>21 : 00</etime>

LOCATION: SongPha, Garak-dong, Garak Tour Hotel 2nd floor
Garak Tour Hotel TEL . 02) 400-6643
              (Subway line 8 Garak Market station, 10 minutes on foot)
Participants: Assocationl Member Manager or Board Members
              (less than 3)
Training Class and Consulting : Dr. Byun (Korea Marketing Science resident)
              Prof. Yang (Korea Consulting Assocation, Manager)

Training Participant Preparation: Social Security ID
                         (should be registered before the meeting)
```

Figure 2: Example of literally English-translated Korean email: SS(M) case.

[1]http://www.cs.cmu.edu/~dayne/SeminarAnnouncements/__Source__.html

[2]downloadable at: http://semanticweb.kaist.ac.kr/home/index.php/Smart_Calendar

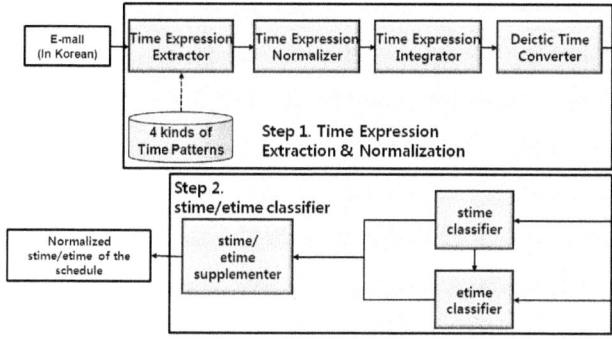

Figure 3: System architecture for stime and etime extraction

3.1 Extracting Time Expressions

To extract and normalize time expressions from the given email, regular expression patterns are used. Four kinds of patterns are defined, with minor modification from [4]: More precisely, we create a new time class of "Anniversaries", and expanded the definition of "Deictic Expressions" so that its pivot could be other time except the speech time. Also, "Relative expressions" defined by [4] was removed, since we were able to deal with it by considering it "Explicit Expressions" with incomplete information - for example, for the relative expression "from 5 to 7", the system deals it as two seperated time expressions "5" and "7", which have only hour information. If this kind of expression is classified as **stime** or **etime** expression later on, then it is merged with other **stime/etime** information to complete its information. Also, we do not consider about the "Duration expressions", since we are focusing on finding specific timepoints which represent **stime** and **etime**. Followings are the definitions of patterns and their numbers:

Explicit Expression. Time expressions which represent specific and clear timepoint. For example, "2006. 6. 11", "5:30 PM". Total 176 Korean patterns are manually constructed based on the 2,022 time expressions of the Korean corpus. t

Anniversaries. Anniversaries and holidays like " New Year's Day", "Thanksgiving day". Total 145 Korean anniversaries are collected.

Deictic Expressions. Time expressions which represent before/after a specific timepoint. For example, "tomorrow", "next month". Total 106 Korean deictic expressions are collected.

Iterative Expressions. Time expressions which represent iterative nature of the schedule. For example, "Every week", "Every day". Total 16 Korean iterative expressions are collected.

Those patterns are constructed altogether with normalization information, which will be used to normalize time expressions extracted using the patterns. Figure 4 shows one of the explicit expression patterns, along with its normalization information. The first row represents regular expression pattern itself with normalization anchors, with non-terminal # means a decimal numerical symbol ranged from 0 to 9. Normalization anchor is represented in the format

\<p\> inside the regular expression. The second row is the normalization information to normalize the extracted time expressions using that pattern. Normalization information consists of several tokens, which are the concatenations of a number and an alphabet. The number points out which part of regular expression should be normalized (number '3' means the part of regular expression which is positioned after the second anchor point and before the third anchor point), and the alphabet tells what kind of normalization information does the part have (Y=Year, M=Month, D=Day, and so on). For example, the pattern of figure 4 can extract time expression "2011.3.12 8:30", and its normalized form according to the normalization information will be: "YEAR = 2011, MONTH = 3, DAY = 12, HOUR = 8, MINUTE = 30".

Figure 4: Example of explicit temporal expression pattern.

Figure 5 shows an example process of time information extraction and normalization from a Korean sentence which meaning is: "The next meeting will be held at 12:30 PM, the day after the New Year's Day."

3.2 Classification for stime and etime

Once time expressions are extracted and normalized, the system classifies whether each time expression actually represents **stime** and **etime** of schedules contained in the email. To solve the problem, two kinds of ML classifiers - Naïve Bayesian classifiers and SVM classifiers - are constructed for **stime** classification and **etime** classification.

3.2.1 Classifying stime expressions

To build the classifier for **stime** extraction, total eight features are used. Below formulae show the probability function of Naïve Bayesian classifier for **stime** classification.

$$P(C = 1|T) = P(C = 1|F_1(T), ..., F_8(T)) \quad (1)$$

$$= P(C = 1) \cdot \frac{\prod P(F_i(T)|C = 1)}{\prod F_i(T)} \quad (2)$$

$P(C = 1|T)$ represents the probability that time expression T means **stime** where C=1 means **stime**, and $F_i(T)$ represents feature value of i-th dimension of T's feature vector. Formula 1 develops to formula 2 due to the Naïve Bayesian assumption. Gaussian distribution is assumed for those features which have continuous values.

The strength, or likelihood of T as a **stime** expression, is defined as follows:

$$Strength_{\mathbf{stime}}(T) = \frac{P(C = 1|T)}{P(C = 0|T)} \quad (3)$$

That is, if the strength for **stime** of time expression T is larger than 1, then T is probably a **stime** expression.

Eight features are newly found and categorized into five categories. The following list shows categories of features and their descriptions. All features are language-independent.

	다음 미팅은 설날 다음날 오후 12:30분에 열립니다. The next meeting will be held at 12:30 PM, the day after the New Year's Day.
Time Expression Extractor	다음 미팅은 [설날]$_{Anniversary}$ [다음날]$_{Deictic}$ [오후 12:30]$_{Explicit}$분에 열립니다. The next meeting will be held at [12:30 PM]$_{Explicit}$, [the day after]$_{Deictic}$ [the New Year's Day]$_{Anniversary}$.
Time Expression Normalizer	다음 미팅은 [설날]$_{2011Y\ 01M\ 01D}$ [다음날]$_{D+1}$ [오후 12:30]$_{12H\ 30N}$분에 열립니다. The next meeting will be held at [12:30 PM]$_{12H\ 30N}$, [the day after]$_{D+1}$ [the New Year's Day]$_{2011Y\ 01M\ 01D}$.
Time Expression Integrator	다음 미팅은 [설날 다음날 오후 12:30]$_{2011Y\ 01M\ 01D(+1)\ 12H\ 30N}$분에 열립니다. The next meeting will be held at [12:30 PM, the day after the New Year's Day]$_{2011Y\ 01M\ 01D(+1)\ 12H\ 30N}$.
Deictic Time Converter	다음 미팅은 [설날 다음날 오후 12:30]$_{2011Y\ 01M\ 02D\ 12H\ 30N}$분에 열립니다. The next meeting will be held at [12:30 PM, the day after the New Year's Day]$_{2011Y\ 01M\ 02D\ 12H\ 30N}$.

Figure 5: Steps for time expression extraction and normalization: Examples are Korean and its English translation

Position-based feature. (1) Position of the time expression inside the sentence, and (2) number of time expressions in front of the given time expresson, inside the whole email. The **stime** expression is occasionally written at the beginning of the sentence, and it is also occasionally written at the front part of the document.

Granularity-based feature. (3) Maximum granularity and (4) minimum granularity of the given time expression. For example, the maximum granularity of the time expression "10. 30. 12:05' is MONTH, while minimum granularity of the time expression is MINUTE. People tend to write **stime** information as detail as possible, since inside the email, **stime** information is occasionally the first information about the time of the schedule.

Tilde feature. (5) Check whether the next character after the time expression is '-' or '~'. Some **stime** expressions accompany tilde right behind of them.

Form of the Sentence. (6) Check whether the sentence containing the time expression is itemized sentence or not. For those itemized sentences, the position-based feature inside the sentence works better.

Nearby time expressions. Check the (7) number and (8) granularity of time expressions in the sentence just before (after) the given time expression. These features are used to classify cases of enumerating detailed schedules, for example, for the case
"09:00-09:20 Welcome ceremony
09:20-09:40 First session",
this feature category makes the system to give different classification results for time expressions "09:00" at first row and "09:20" at second row.

3.2.2 Classifying etime expressions

For the **etime** expression classification, an approach which is very similar to the case of **stime** expression classification is used, with exceptions of slight modification of features (changing feature (2) to: "number of time expressions in front of the given time expression inside only the sentence which contains the target time expression"; for feature (5) changing "after the time expression" has become to "before the time expression"), and one additional feature:

stime-based feature. (9) Does the time expression, just ahead of the given time expression, represent **stime**?

Due to the feature above, **stime** classification must be carried out before **etime** classification work begins, and the performance of **etime** classifier depends on the performance of **stime** classifier.

4. EVALUATION

For the evaluation of the proposed method, Korean email corpus with 1,011 emails are constructed and manually annotated. For the annotation, COAT semantic annotation toolkit[3] is used. Two annotators worked on the same email, and in the case of conflict a senior annotator makes the final decision. Schedule notices are crawled from the web, using the keywords "Meeting announcement" and "Schedule announcement". It was assumed that those schedule notices have similar format to those emails with schedule notices, and actually many of them were just reannouncements (copy and paste) of email body through the web board.

4.1 Effect of Complexity on the Performance of the Same Classifier: Official Seminar Announcements vs. Seminar Notices in Email

In this section, the complexity of email corpus will be compared against the seminar announcement corpus by an experiment. For the comparison, four of eleven features are borrowed from [8], and based on those features a CRF classifier for **stime** expression extraction is trained and tested (We built a CRF classifier since [8] used the features to build a CRF classifier). Those four features are chosen because they are mostly related to the **stime** and **etime** extraction, while other features are mainly related to speaker/location extraction work in [8]. They are as follows: (1) The word itself; (2) Is the expression followed by dash?; (3) Is the expression preceded by dash?; (4) POS tag of the words. For the CRF implementation, *mallet* [5] toolkit is used.

[3]http://sourceforge.net/projects/coatsemantic

Most of the works related to the seminar announcement [2, 7, 8, 9] adopts one-filler-per-slot assumption, that is only one **stime** expression per one document is assumed. Thus emails with multiple **stime** and **etime** expressions are removed for fair comparison. The resultant email corpus contains only 864 emails out of 1,011 emails, and all of those emails contain only one **stime** expression. The CRF system classifies only one most probable time expression as a **stime** expression, for an email.

Table 2 shows the comparison result with 10-fold cross-validation. **CRF(SA)** means the performance of CRF system on seminar announcement corpus, and **CRF (Email)** means the performance of the same CRF system on Korean email corpus with only one **stime** expression.

Features	P	R	F1
CRF(SA)	99.57 %	91.88 %	95.57 %
CRF(Email)	92.93 %	68.02 %	78.55 %

Table 2: stime extraction: comparison of seminar announcement and emails

As can be observed, the CRF system achieves nice performance for seminar announcement corpus using only those four features. But although it shows high precision also on email corpus, its recall dramatically drops. This shows the complexity of format and writing style of emails is much higher than that of seminar announcements, and the system was not able to effectively process those complex expressions - even though the target emails were restricted to only those with only one **stime** expression, as table 2 suggests. The comparison result shows that, the methods which show good performance on seminar announcement corpus cannot be directly applied to emails to extract **stime** and **etime** information from them.

In the following sections, the evaluation results for the performance of each module of the proposed system for **stime** and **etime** extraction from emails will be explained in detail.

4.2 Evaluation on Time Expression Extraction

To evalute the time expression extraction module, we tried to annotate the time expressions of email corpus using the proposed system. There were total 3,750 time expressions among 1,011 emails, and the system annotated total 3,530 time expressions, showing the coverage of 94.13 %. Among those extracted time expressions, 100 time expressions were randomly selected and manually checked for their normalized forms, and it is confirmed that they were all properly normalized.

4.3 Evaluation on stime Classification

stime classifier gets an email as input with its time expressions extracted & normalized, and selects one or more time expressions of the email as **stime** of the schedule contained in the email.

4.3.1 Experiment: effect of each feature

To figure out the effect of each features, the experiment is carried out with various feature settings for Naïve Bayesian classifier. The system extracts only top-most ranked time expression with the highest strength among the whole email. 10-fold cross-validation is carried out on the Korean email corpus with 1,011 emails. Those emails contain 3,750 time expressions, and among them 1,370 time expressions represent **stime**, and 577 time expressions represent **etime**. For each fold, probability density function necessary to set up the Naïve Bayesian classifier is calculated using the training data set. Each classified **stime** expression is compared with the **stime** expression of the corpus for the evaluation.

Table 3 shows the experimental result for **stime** expression classifier. **P** stands for precision, **R** stands for recall, and **F1** means F1-score of each system.

Features	P	R	F1
Position	93.42 %	68.79 %	79.24 %
+ Granularity	97.08 %	70.80 %	81.89 %
+ Tilde	96.68 %	70.45 %	81.51 %
+ Form-Of-Sentence	96.78 %	70.53 %	81.59 %
+ Nearby-Time	96.49 %	70.43 %	80.53 %
Granularity Only	89.01 %	58.32 %	70.47 %

Table 3: Performance of stime classifier

Amazingly, only using the position and granularity information of the time expression the system was able to classify the **stime** expression with 97.08 % of precision. Since the system extracts and normalizes each time expression at once using the regular expression patterns coupled with their normalization information, the system was able to use the granularity-based features to classify each time expression. Low recall of 70.80 % is due to the existence of multiple **stime** expressions in one email. If we restrict our discussion to only those 864 emails which contains only one schedule information, the recall of the system slightly increases. Table 4 shows the comparison of two systems, one is the proposed approach of using Naïve Bayesian classifier and patterns, and the other one is the CRF system whose performance was presented at table 2.

Features	P	R	F1
NBC+Pattern	96.32 %	83.37 %	89.38 %
CRF(Email)	92.93 %	68.02 %	78.55 %

Table 4: Comparison of system performances using emails with only one stime expression

As can be observed, the proposed system works much better for those emails compared to the simple CRF-based system, which worked well on official seminar announcement corpus but works poorly on actual emails.

4.3.2 Experiment: effect of n (number of selection)

To handle those cases with many **stime** expressions, the experiments are carried out by increasing the number of n, the number of time expressions selected as **stime** in one email. The system classifies time expressions which are top-n ranked, among the email, and whose ranks are at least larger than 1, as **stime**.

Table 5 shows the effect of parameter n to the system performance. The feature set is fixed to the one which showed the best performance for the case of $n = 1$, that is, position-based features and granularity-based features.

The system shows the best overall performance with $n = 2$, but it suffers from heavy loss of the precision.

n	P	R	F1
1	97.08 %	70.80 %	81.89 %
2	80.35 %	85.50 %	82.84 %
3	74.43 %	88.43 %	80.83 %
4	72.99 %	89.45 %	80.39 %
5	72.58 %	89.76 %	80.26 %

Table 5: Effect of n to handle multiple stime expressions

4.3.3 Experiment: effect of strength

As another trial to handle those multiple **stime** expression cases, we tried to set up the threshold on the strength for the time expression. That is, the system first classifies the time expression with the largest strength as a **stime** expression (the strength should be at least larger than 1), and for those remaining time expressions the strength must be larger than some predefined threshold t, to be classified as **stime** expression. Table 6 shows the performance of system for different t.

t	P	R	F1
1	72.58 %	89.76 %	80.26 %
2	76.45 %	83.56 %	79.85 %
5	82.41 %	82.55 %	82.48 %
7	84.49 %	81.90 %	83.18 %
10	85.46 %	80.71 %	83.02 %

Table 6: Effect of threshold on strength (t) to handle multiple stime expressions

The system shows the best overall performance with $t = 7$, showing 83.13 % of F-measure.

4.3.4 Experiment: Using SVM

To process the cases of multiple **stime** expressions, we tried to use the SVM. For the implementation of SVM, *libSVM* [1] toolkit is used with linear kernel, and the same features used to build the Naïve Bayesian classifier is used. Table 7 shows the experimental result of **stime** expression classification using SVM.

Features	P	R	F1
Position	82.46 %	78.69 %	80.53 %
+ Granularity	87.63 %	85.91 %	86.76 %
+ Tilde	87.45 %	86.99 %	87.22 %
+ Form-Of-Sentence	88.09 %	87.07 %	87.58 %
+ Nearby-Time	87.27 %	87.44 %	87.35 %

Table 7: Performance of stime classifier: using SVM

Although overall performance is better than that of Naïve Bayesian, since the SVM does not give any kind of "strength" to each time expression there is no way to tune the system to increase its precision, while Naïve Bayesian classifier can (it can achieve 97.08 % of precision). The comparison of experimental results between SVM classifier and Naïve Bayesian classifier suggest that if we want (relatively) high recall, then we can use the SVM classifier, meanwhile if we want high precision then we should use the Naïve Bayesian classifier.

4.4 Evaluation on etime Classification

etime clssification work is much harder than **stime** classification work from emails, since some emails do not have any **etime** information. Among 864 emails which have only one **stime** expression, 491 emails do not have any **etime** expression, in contrast to the seminar announcements which always have at least one **etime** expression. This property of **etime** introduces additional complexity to the **etime** classification work, and this complexity slightly drops overall performance of the system.

Table 8 shows the performance of Naïve Bayesian classifier system for **etime** classification. The system classifies top 1 time expression with the highest strength for **etime** as **etime** expression. 10-fold cross-validation is carried out on the same Korean email corpus we used for **stime**. Also, the table contains performance of Naïve Bayesian classifier for emails with only one **stime** expression(**Naïve(SS)**), and performance of SVM classifier (**SVM**). To get the pure evaluation result for **etime** classification, for the evaluation the system "knows" every **stime** expressions.

Features	P	R	F1
stime-related	56.29 %	64.50 %	60.12 %
+ Position	80.08 %	67.46 %	73.23 %
+ Granularity	81.54 %	67.96 %	74.13 %
+ Tilde	81.54 %	67.96 %	74.13 %
+ Form-Of-Sentence	81.98 %	67.88 %	74.27 %
+ Nearby-Time	87.99 %	72.16 %	79.30 %
Naïve(SS)	89.67 %	83.29 %	86.37 %
SVM	88.25 %	82.22 %	85.13 %

Table 8: Performance of etime classifier

Due to the increased complexity of the problem compared to the **stime** classification problem, the system shows slightly lower F-score compared to the **stime** classifier even it uses an additional feature. This is mainly because the writer pays less attention to inform the **etime** information than **stime** - the email writer occasionally omits **etime** information, and even when he/she writes **etime** explicitly the expression frequently omits date information, since it is already included within stime expression. This makes the position feature and granularity feature less effective. The performance of Naïve Bayesian classifier increases for those emails with only one **stime** (**Naïve(SS)**), but its precision is less than 90 % - it is predicted due to the property of **etime** described before. The overall performance of SVM classifier was slightly better than the Naïve Bayesian classifier, for the case of **etime** classification.

5. CONCLUSION

In this paper, the approach of extracting schedule time information from email was explored. It is shown that emails have much more complexity compared to the seminar announcements: firstly, they frequently have many **stime** and **etime** expressions in one email, and secondly they have much more complex format than those seminar announcements. The proposed approach tried to solve the problem by using regular expression patterns to extract and normalize the time expressions, and then classifying those time expressions using various ML approaches and new features. The experimental result shows around 87 % of F-measure for **stime** classification and 85 % of F-measure for **etime** classification. Naïve Bayesian classifiers show lower overall performance compared to the SVM classifiers, but bayesian classifiers assign "strength" to each time expressions, making possible to build more precision-oriented system.

There are some possible applications for this research. One application is to developing smartphone app for email schedule analysis. The prototype system was already developed, and currently being tested inside our group. Another application will be to build the English-version system, which is expected to be done easily since all of those features used are language-independent.

Acknowledgment

This research was supported by Basic Science Research Program through the National Research Foundation of Korea (NRF) funded by the Ministry of Education, Science and Technology(No. 2010-0022444), and also partially supported by WCU (World Class University) program under the National Research Foundation of Korea and funded by the Ministry of Eduation, Science and Technology of Korea (Project No: R31-30007).

6. REFERENCES

[1] C.-C. Chang and C.-J. Lin. *LIBSVM: a library for support vector machines*, 2001. Software available at http://www.csie.ntu.edu.tw/ cjlin/libsvm.

[2] H. L. Chieu and H. T. Ng. A maximum entropy approach to information extraction from semistructured and free text. In *Proceedings of the 18th National Conference On Artificial Intelligence*, pages 786–791, 2002.

[3] M. Freed, J. Carbonell, G. Gordon, J. Hayes, B. Myers, D. Siewiorek, S. Smith, A. Steinfeld, and A. Tomasic. Radar: A personal assistant that learns to reduce email overload. In *Proceedings of the 23rd national conference on Artificial Intelligence*, pages 1287–1293, 2008.

[4] B. Han, D. Gates, and L. Levin. From language to time: A temporal expression anchorer. In *Proceedings of the Thirteenth International Symposium on Temporal Representation and Reasoning*, pages 196–203, 2006.

[5] A. K. McCallum. Mallet: A machine learning for language toolkit. http://mallet.cs.umass.edu, 2002.

[6] L. Peshkin and A. Pfeffer. Bayesian information extraction network. In *Proceedings of the 18th International Joint Conference On Artificial Intelligence*, pages 421–426, 2003.

[7] D. Roth and W. Yih. Relational learning via propositional algorithms: An information extraction case study. In *Proceedings of the 15th International Conference On Artificial Intelligence*, pages 1257–1263, San Francisco, CA, August 2001. Morgan Kaufmann.

[8] C. Sutton and A. McCallum. Composition of conditional random fields for transfer learning. In *Proceedings of the conference on Human Language Technology and Empirical Methods in Natural Language Processing*, pages 748–754, 2005.

[9] J. Turmo, A. Ageno, and N. Catala. Adaptive information extraction. *ACM Computing Surveys*, 38(2), 2006.

[10] B. Yuan, Q. Chen, X. Wang, and L. Han. Extracting event temporal information based on web. In *Proceedings of the 2009 Second International Symposium on Knowledge Acquisition and Modeling*, pages 346–350, 2009.

RDR-based Open IE for the Web Document

Myung Hee Kim
School of Comp. Sci. & Eng.
University of New South Wales
Kensington, NSW, Australia
+61 2 9385 6906

mkim978@cse.unsw.edu.au

Paul Compton
School of Comp. Sci. & Eng.
University of New South Wales
Kensington, NSW, Australia
+61 2 9385 6939

compton@cse.unsw.edu.au

Yang Sok Kim
School of Comp. Sci. & Eng.
University of New South Wales
Kensington, NSW, Australia
+61 2 9385 5644

yskim@cse.unsw.edu.au

ABSTRACT

The Web contains a massive amount of information embedded in text and obtaining information from Web text is a major research challenge. One research focus is Open Information Extraction aimed at developing relation-independent information extraction. Open Information Extraction (OIE) systems seek to extract all potential relations from the text rather than extracting a few pre-defined relations. Existing OIE systems such as TEXTRUNNER usually take a machine learning based approach which requires large volumes of training data.

This paper presents a Ripple-Down Rules Open Information Extraction system based on processing example cases and manually adding rules when needed. The key advantages of this approach are that it can handle the freer writing style that occurs in Web documents and can correct errors introduced by natural language pre-processing tools, whereas systems like TEXTRUNNER depend on the quality of the entity-tagging preprocessing in the training data. We evaluated the Ripple-Down Rules approach against the OIE systems, TEXTRUNNER and StatSnowball. In these studies the Ripple-Down Rules approach, with minimal low-cost rule addition achieves much higher precision and somewhat improved recall compared to these other Open Information Extraction systems.

Categories and Subject Descriptors

I.2.1 [**Artificial Intelligence**]: Applications and Expert Systems
I.2.6 [**Artificial Intelligence**]: Learning – *Knowledge acquisition.*
I.2.7 [**Artificial Intelligence**]: Natural Language Processing – *Text analysis.*

General Terms

Algorithms, Experimentation

Keywords

Open Information Extraction, Ripple-Down Rules

1. INTRODUCTION

The Web contains a vast amount of information mainly in natural language and its quantity keeps increasing exponentially to an almost unlimited size. Web information extraction (WIE) systems analyze unstructured web documents and identify valuable information, such as particular named entities or semantic relations between entities. WIE systems enable effective retrieval

of Web information to support various applications such as Automatic Text Summarization (ATS), Information Retrieval (IR), Question-Answering (QA) and Ontology systems.

The WIE task has a number of significant differences compared to the traditional IE task of extracting particular instances from small range of well-written documents. Most Web documents are not written under strict supervision and tend to be written informally. The following are some characteristics of Web documents which affect extraction:

Informal writing styles Many Web documents are written freely and do not follow strict writing styles such as used for journalistic text [4]. As strict writing markers such as Mr., Dr., Inc. and Ltd. which help to detect entities are often absent in informal web documents, NLP tools which rely on such indicators are unlikely to work efficiently and may even cause a significant numbers of errors.

Spelling mistakes and incomplete sentences Web documents often contain spelling mistakes and incomplete sentences, which hinder the syntactic analysis of NLP tools and cause extraction errors.

Large amount of newly generated vocabulary Web documents may contain newly generated unknown words which are not found in the formal dictionaries.

WIE seeks to extract a large number of facts from heterogeneous Web documents while traditional IE has focused on extracting pre-defined relationships from smaller numbers of domain-specific documents. Open IE (OIE) differs from previous IE in that its goal is to require no pre-defined target relations and no extraction models for individual target relation. The OIE approach is intended to reduce the amount of time necessary to find desired information from the Web. The OIE paradigm was proposed as 'preemptive IE' [12] and TEXTRUNNER [1] is an example of OIE applied to WIE.

Most OIE systems are developed using Machine Learning (ML) approaches and require a large amount of training data. They use self-supervised learning which generates a labeled training dataset automatically using some heuristics. For example, TEXTRUNNER uses an NLP tool to label entities and a parser to identify positive/negative examples with a small set of hand-written heuristic rules. A limit with this approach is that it cannot handle NLP errors since it relies on prior automatic labeling from NLP tools. This seriously affects the system performance as mentioned in [2], for example when a verb is incorrectly tagged as noun. Current OIE systems tend to use well-written journalistic documents as training data, probably to minimize errors from the NLP tools they depend on. It is likely that such training data is not the most appropriate for WIE because of the different characteristics of Web documents noted above.

This paper presents RDROIE (Ripple-Down Rules based Open Information Extraction), which supports incremental knowledge acquisition (KA) and efficient knowledge base (KB) maintenance. The benefit of the RDR technique is that the KB is built incrementally while the system is already in use. Therefore, it requires no large training dataset with annotation. In this paper, we trained the system with 300 sentences which resulted in 25 rules within 2.5 hours knowledge acquisition and achieved better performance than TEXTRUNNER on the same test data. In the RDROIE system, the user creates rules when the extraction result provided by the system is incorrect. Since rules are generated by people, RDROIE is more likely to be able to handle NLP tool errors and informally written Web document. The RDROIE system described below achieved 98% precision.

In this paper, we present the following:

- RDROIE, a new approach to open information extraction that uses Ripple-Down Rules' incremental learning technique, and demonstrate its performance compared to other OIE systems

- Various examples of Web documents which may lead to errors in OIE systems and are not easily solved with an ML approach. We show how the RDROIE approach handles those cases

- Analysis of how different aspects of the RDROIE system contribute to its performance

The remainder of this paper is structured as follows. Section 2 presents related work and section 3 describes the RDROIE system. Section 4 presents experimental results and section 5 discusses future work.

2. RELATED WORK
2.1 Open Information Extraction (OIE)

Sekine [11] introduced a new paradigm "On-Demand Information Extraction (ODIE)" which aims to eliminate the high customization cost from target domain changes. An ODIE system automatically discovers patterns and extracts information on new topics the user is interested in, using pattern discovery, paraphrase discovery, and extended named entity tagging. Shinyama et al. [12] developed a 'preemptive IE' framework with the idea of avoiding relation specificity. They clustered documents using pairwise vector-space clustering, and then they re-clustered the documents based on named entity types in each document cluster. The system was tested on limited corpora, because the two clustering steps made it difficult to scale the system for WIE. TEXTRUNNER is the first OIE system for WIE [1]. Two versions have been developed. The first called O-NB treated the OIE task as a classification problem using a Naïve Bayes classifier [1]. The more recent system is O-CRF, which treated the task as a sequential labeling problem using 'Conditional Random Fields (CRF)' [2]. O-CRF outperforms O-NB almost doubling recall. StatSnowball [15] performs both relation-specific IE and OIE with a bootstrapping technique which iteratively generates weighted extraction patterns. It employs shallow features only such as part-of-speech tags. In StatSnowball, two different pattern selection methods are introduced: the l1-norm regularized pattern selection and a heuristic-based pattern selection. Wu et al. [13] introduced a Wikipedia-based Open Extractor (WOE) which used heuristic matches between Wikipedia infobox attribute values and corresponding sentences in the document for self-supervised learning. WOE applied two types of lexical features: POS tag features and dependency parser

features. Although with dependency parser features the system ran more slowly, it outperformed the system with POS tag features.

2.2 Ripple-Down Rules (RDR)

The basic idea of RDR is that cases are processed by the knowledge based system and when the output is not correct or missing one or more new rules are created to provide the correct output for that case. The knowledge engineering task in adding rules is simply selecting conditions for the rule which is automatically located in the knowledge base with new rules placed under the default rule node for newly seen cases, and exception rules located under the fired rules. The system also stores *cornerstone cases,* cases which triggered the creation of new rules. If a new rule is fired by any cornerstone cases, the cornerstones are presented to the expert to select further differentiating features for the rule or to accept that the new conclusions should apply to the cornerstone. Experience suggests this whole process takes at most a few minutes.

RDR using a Single Classification RDR (SCRDR) system was first used to build the expert system Pathology Expert Interpretative Reporting System (PEIRS) for interpreting chemical pathology results [5]. Multiple Classification RDR (MCRDR) system was developed to provide multiple conclusions for a single case [7].

RDR have proven to be a very effective way of manually building knowledge bases. The RDR approach has been applied to a range of NLP applications. For example, Pham et al. developed KAFTIE, an incremental knowledge acquisition framework to extract positive attributions from scientific papers [8] and temporal relations which outperformed machine learning algorithms [9]. The KAFTIE system utilized various NLP tools such as a tokenizer, POS tagger and semantic tagger.

There has been a wide range of research on RDR and ML e.g [6, 10]. Relevant to the work here, RDR Case Explorer (RDRCE) [14] combined Machine Learning and manual Knowledge Acquisition for NLP problems. It automatically generated an initial RDR tree using transformation-based learning, but then allowed for corrections to be made. They applied RDRCE to POS tagging and achieved a slight improvement over state-of-the-art POS tagging after 60 hours of KA.

3. RDROIE SYSTEM

The RDR-based Open IE (RDROIE) system shown in Figure 1, consists of three main components: preprocessor, tuple extractor and RDR KB learner.

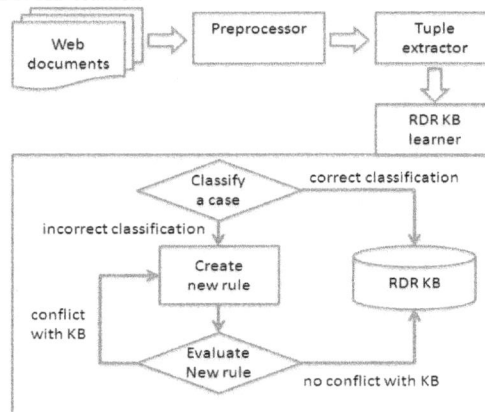

Figure 1. Architecture of RDROIE

Case
finally google bought youtube

Display a given sentence

Tuples
| Entity1 | Relation | Entity2 |
| google | bought | youtube |

Display Extracted Tuples

Display Classification Results from KB

Classifications
| Rule | Rel Detection | Rel Taxonomy | Rel Keyword |
| 1 | NULL | NULL | NULL |

Show Analysis   Save Case   CaseRuleLog
New Rule   Save Case (all)   Report

Pre-Condition

Non-Seq Condition
Relation hasToken bought

Seq-Condition

Synonyms
buy:[acquire]

Conclusion
Rel detection: True
Rel taxonomy: VERB
Rel keyword: BUY

Display New Rule

Delete
Delete
Delete
Delete

Process Log | Rule Path
Tuple answer classification: VERB
RDR classification result is NOT CORRECT!
Please add an exception rule OR generate report.

Case Analysis | Cornerstone Case Analysis | Evaluated Case Analysis
E1Before
finally
RB
B-ADVP

Entity1
google
JJ
B-NP

Relation
bought
VBD
B-VP

Entity2
youtube
NN
I-VP

E2After

Display NLP features For current case, cornerstone case and evaluated case

New Rule Evaluation
Parent is root, No case to evaluate

Display New Rule Evaluation Result

evaluate   add New Rule

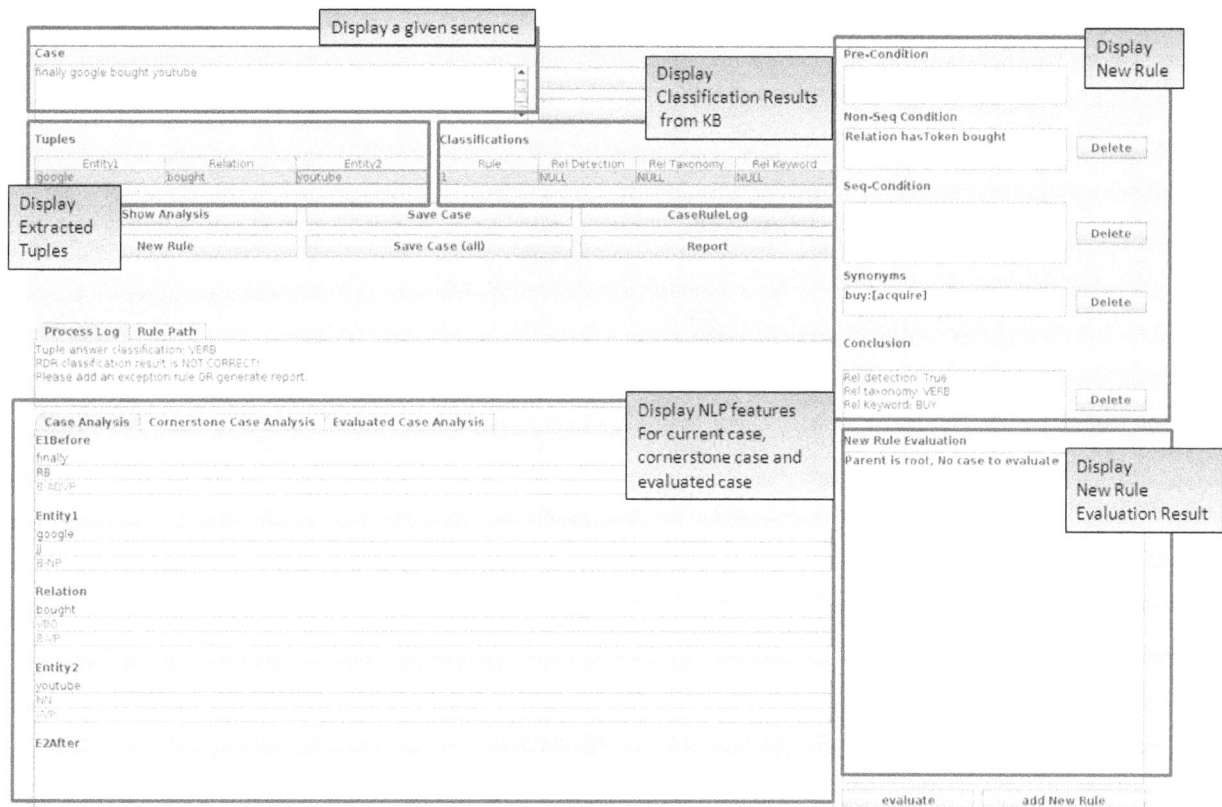

Figure 2. The RDROIE User Interface

3.1 Implementation

3.1.1 Preprocessor
The preprocessor converts the raw text into a sequence of sentences, and annotates each token for part of speech (POS) and phrase chunk using OpenNLP. The resulting annotated data is fed into the Tuple extractor.

3.1.2 Tuple Extractor
The tuple extractor contains two entity identifiers. One version annotates entities as named entities using the Stanford NER system and the other version annotates entities by noun phrase chunk using OpenNLP. Once entities are identified in a sentence, the tuple extractor generates potential binary relation tuples. A tuple consists of two entities and the relational text between entities (entity1, relational text, entity2). In the following example the entities are identified by NER.

"Never even saw this coming, but apparently Adobe/*ENTITY* is about to buy Macromedia/*ENTITY* ."

3.1.3 RDR KB Learner
The RDROIE KB system is built incrementally while the system is already in use. In the RDROIE system, the user runs the system on a piece of training text, gets the classification results and adds a rule when the classification result is incorrect. The user interface for a creating a new rule, shown in figure 2, shows not only the rule conditions but the feature differences between the current case and any stored cases with different classifications (cornerstone cases) but which are also satisfied by the new rule.

Step1: RDROIE classification
For a given case, the system returns the classification result from fired rules in the KB. The conclusion may be correct, incorrect or missing (NULL). If the user decides the classification result is correct, the current case is simply saved under the fired rule in KB.

Step2: Create RDR rule
If the returned classification is incorrect or null, the user generates a new rule to be added by selecting case features identified in the user interface.

Step3: Evaluate and refine RDR rule
Once the new rule is generated, the system automatically evaluates all the stored cornerstone cases which may fire the rule. The number of cases evaluated will vary depending if the rule is a new rule or an exception rule. If the rule fires one or more of these cases, the user can select differentiating features from the list shown (Fig 2) and make the rule more precise. The user may also decide that the previous classification for one or more of the previous cases was incorrect and that the new rule should apply.

3.2 Rule Description
A rule consists of a condition part and a conclusion part. It has the form: *if* CONDITION *then* CONCLUSION where CONDITION is structured as (ATTRIBUTE, OPERATOR, VALUE). ATTRIBUTE refers to one of the 5 elements of the given sentence in the form of [ENTITIY1BEFORE, (ENTITY1, RELATION, ENTITY2), ENTITIY2AFTER]. As mentioned in 3.1.2, each tuple forms (ENTITY1, RELATION, ENTITY2) and the remaining tokens before or after the ENTITY1/ENTITY2 elements in the given sentence form the ENTITIY1BEFORE/ENTITY2AFTER elements. Currently the RDROIE system provides 5 types of OPERATOR as follows:

- hasToken: whether a certain token match exists within the chosen attribute section

- hasPOS: whether a certain POS match exists within the chosen attribute section
- hasChunk: whether a certain noun/verb chunk match exists within the chosen attribute section
- hasGap: skip a certain number of tokens or spaces to match the pattern
- notHasPOS: whether a certain POS match does not exist within the chosen attribute section

VALUE is derived automatically from the given sentence corresponding to the attribute and operator chosen by the user in the user interface. Once the 'hasToken' operator is used in the rule condition, the top most 10 synonyms are automatically listed which are derived from WordNet when the user clicks 'show synonyms' button in the user interface. Users can deselect synonyms that are too general such as 'get', 'have' or any erroneous or inappropriate synonyms.

Each condition detects the value from the given attribute element. For example, the condition 'if relation hasToken 'buy'' detects the value 'buy' from the RELATION element. Conditions are connected with an 'and' operation. A sequence condition detects a group of words in sequence order, so patterns can be detected. For example, the condition:

seq((relation hasPOS 'TO') && (relation hasPOS 'VB'))

detects whether a 'TO VB' pattern exists in the relation section. The rule's CONCLUSION part gives the classification result for the given case. The RDROIE system handles three different classification tasks: 'relation existence detection', 'relation type detection', and 'specific relation detection'. The relation existence detection task detects whether a semantic relation exists between entities, and the relation type detection task classifies the four taxonomy types of binary relation identified in [2]: 'Verb', 'Noun+Prep', 'Verb+Prep' and 'Infinitive'. The specific relation detection task extracts the actual relation words. Therefore, the CONCLUSION part has the form:

(True/False,

Verb/Noun+Prep/Verb+Prep/Infinitive,

'Relation tokens').

The rule numbers in figure 3 shows the sequence of KB construction from an empty KB (with a default rule R0 which assigns the NULL conclusion) as the system processes cases. In the following examples, cases are described as a tuple (ENTITY1, RELATION, ENTITY2) extracted from a sentence. The ENTITY1BEFORE and ENTITY2AFTER elements are excluded in the following examples for simplicity.

Case1: (Google, **just bought**, Youtube.)
→ The KB system returns a NULL classification, which is incorrect
→ A user generates R1 and specifies relevant synonyms (acquire, purchase) which are also stored in the KB

Case2: (Google, **to acquire** , Youtube.)
→ R1 fired since 'acquire' is stored as a synonym of 'buy' in the KB, but its relation type classification is incorrect
→ A user creates an exception rule R2 under R1

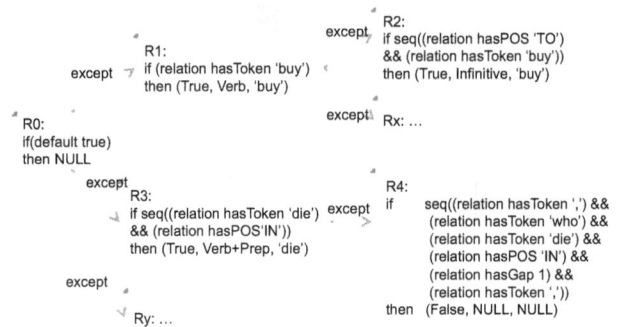

Figure 3. MCRDR structure of the RDROIE system

Case 3: (Google, **to buy**, Youtube.)
→ R2 fired with correct classification
→ A user saves case3 to KB under R2

Case 4: (Mozart, **died in**, 'Vienna'.)
→ The system returns a NULL classification
→ A user creates rule R3

Case 5: (Charlie Chaplin, **, who died in 1977 , was born in**, London)
→ R3 fired with the incorrect classification (since 'died in' has no semantic relation between entity1 'Charlie Chaplin' and entity2 'London')
→ A user creates R4 under R3

4. EXPERIMENTS
Section 4.2 shows the initial knowledge base construction of the RDROIE system and the section 4.3 shows the performance comparison of the RDROIE system against the TEXTRUNNER and StatSnowball systems.

4.1 Data Sets
The experiments were conducted on two Web data sets referred to as 'Sent500' and 'Sent300'. Sent500 was used to evaluate the performance of OIE systems TEXTRUNNER [2] and StatSnowball [15]. We use it as a test dataset to compare the performance of the RDROIE system to these other OIE systems. Sent500 is partially, and Sent300 is fully, derived from the MIL dataset developed by Bunescu and Mooney [3]. Sent300 is a set of 300 sentences which we randomly selected from the 4155 argument pair sentences in the MIL dataset to be used as training case examples to construct the initial KB. Bunescu and Mooney collected a bag of sentences by submitting a query string 'a1 ******* a2' containing seven wildcard symbols between the given pair of arguments mainly to find 'corporate acquisition' and 'personal-birthplace' relations. Each sentence has one pair of entities manually identified. Sent500 contains some randomly selected sentences from the MIL dataset and some more sentences for 'inventors of product' and 'award winners' relations which were collected by the TEXTRUNNER team using the same technique as used for MIL datasets. It should be noted that our training data set Sent300 came only from the MIL dataset and did not include any sentences in Sent500.

4.2 Knowledge Base Construction

This section shows the analysis of the initial KB construction using the RDROIE system. In processing the Sent300 cases and adding rules as required, 43 new rules were created for the cases which received a NULL classification result and 9 exception rules were created for the cases which received an incorrect classification result from earlier rules. In total, 52 rules were added within two and half hours. KB construction time covers from when a case is called up until a rule is accepted as complete and is logged automatically.

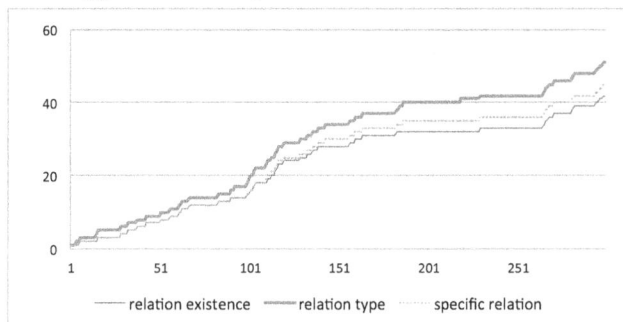

Figure 4. total number of RDR rule addition as number of case increases

In this experiment, the RDROIE system covers all three types of task: relation existence detection, relation type detection and specific relation detection. Figure 4 shows the number of rule additions with respect to the number of cases processed for the three tasks. For the first 150 cases, 34 rules were created, but for the next 100 cases only 8 more rules were added, then for the last 50 cases 10 rules were added as shown in Figure 4. Although there is clear convergence after the first 150 cases until about 250, knowledge acquisition then accelerates again as novel cases are encountered in the training data. This suggests that learning may be some way from complete after training on 300 sentences; however, this is the knowledge base used for comparison with other methods.

From the analysis of the exception rules added, we categorize the causes of exceptions into two classes.

(1) An exception rule simply reduces the scope of the parent rule, making it more specific. The following is a simple example where the exception is that the parent rule should not apply if the verb is an infinitive. The parent rule applies to a verb, whereas the exception rule applies to particular types of verb, providing an increase in specificity:

Sentence	"Google to buy YouTube for $ 1.6bn - reports (6 October 2006)"	
Tuple	(Google, **to buy**, YouTube)	
Fired ruleA	If	(relation hasToken 'buy')
	Then	(True, Verb, 'buy')
Exception ruleB	If	seq((relation hasPOS 'TO') &&
		(relation hasToken 'buy'))
	Then	(True, Infinitive, 'buy')

(2) The exception here is more complex. As with all exception rules it reduces the scope of the parent rule but it does not provide a conclusion that is related to the parent. Rather the parent rule should not cover this type of case at all:

Sentence	"Charlie Chaplin , who died in 1977 , was born in London to music - hall parents ."	
Tuple	(Charlie Chaplin, **, who died in 1977 , was born in**, London)	
Fired ruleA	If	seq((relation hasToken 'bear') &&
		(relation hasToken 'in'))
	Then	(True, Verb+Prep, 'born in')
Fired ruleB	If	seq((relation hasToken 'die') &&
		(relation hasToken 'in'))
	Then	(True, Verb+Prep, 'die in')
Exception ruleC (under ruleB)	If	seq((relation hasToken ',') &&
		(relation hasToken 'who') &&
		(relation hasToken 'die') &&
		(relation hasToken 'in') &&
		(relation hasGap 1) &&
		(relation hasToken ','))
	Then	(False, NULL, NULL)

In this case, two rules, ruleA and ruleB were fired; ruleA extracted the 'born in' relation correctly but ruleB extracted the 'die in' relation which is incorrect because the 'die in' relation is located in an dependent clause which has no semantic relation with the entity2 'London'. The exception ruleC added under ruleB uses the more specific condition: when 'die in' relation is surrounded by commas, to provide the conclusion that there is no relation.

4.3 RDROIE Performance

4.3.1 OIE Systems Performance Comparison

We compared the performance of RDROIE system with the state-of-the-art OIE systems, the TEXTRUNNER (O-CRF version) system and the StatSnowball system on the Sent500 data set.

The RDROIE system had been trained with Sent300 which included 300 sentences randomly selected from the MIL dataset. TEXTRUNNER had been trained with 91,687 positive examples and 96,795 negative examples derived from the Wall Street Journal (WSJ) dataset which is a human-annotated and partially-parsed corpus [13]. The StatSnowball system can perform both traditional IE and OIE. The StatSnowball system requires pre-defined entities while the TEXTRUNNER system and the RDROIE system do not. The StatSnowball system accepts tuples with two entities as input such as (e1, e2, key relation) for traditional IE and (e1, e2, ?) for OIE to find relation patterns through bootstrapping. In the StatSnowball system, 30 sentences were randomly selected as initial seeds for bootstrapping and the results were then averaged over 10 runs. Each run could have various bootstrapping iterations e.g. from 4 to 10 [15]. In the StatSnowball system, two different pattern selection methods, the l1-norm regularized pattern selection and a heuristic-based pattern selection were used and in the tables are referred to as l1StateSnowball and heStatSnowball, respectively. We compared performance on four categories of relations: Verb, Noun+Prep, Verb+Prep and Infinitive as evaluated in [2, 15]. The experiment results are shown in Table 1, where the results of TEXTRUNNER and StatSnowball systems are from the original paper comparing the two systems [15].

Table 1. Evaluation result of different OIE systems

Category		Verb	Noun +Prep	Verb +Prep	Infinit ive	All
RDROIE	P	**0.98**	**0.96**	**0.99**	**1.00**	**0.98**
	R	0.56	0.47	**0.82**	**0.93**	0.63
	F1	0.71	0.63	**0.90**	**0.96**	**0.77**
TEXTRUN NER	P	0.94	0.89	0.95	0.96	0.88
	R	0.65	0.36	0.50	0.47	0.45
	F1	0.77	0.51	0.66	0.63	0.60
heStateSno wball	P	0.96	0.70	0.58	0.46	0.79
	R	0.81	0.50	0.34	0.19	0.58
	F1	0.88	0.54	0.40	0.23	0.67
l1StatSnow ball	P	0.93	0.82	0.62	0.42	0.80
	R	**0.85**	**0.78**	0.58	0.32	**0.73**
	F1	**0.89**	**0.80**	0.60	0.36	0.76

Overall, the RDROIE system outperforms the TEXTRUNNER system and the heStatSnowball system on all four categories for precision, recall and F1. The RDROIE system also achieves much higher precision over the four individual categories. For "Verb+Prep" and "Infinitive", the RDROIE system performs better than the other OIE systems for precision, recall and F1. On the other hand, the RDROIE system shows the lowest recall for the "Verb" category and lower recall for "Noun+Prep" category compared to both versions of the StatSnowball system.

Table 2. Error cases on four categories of RDROIE

	Incorrect classification	NULL classification
Verb	2	77
Noun+Prep	2	55
Verb+Prep	1	16
Infinitive	0	3
All	5	151

Table 2 shows an error case analysis for the RDROIE system over the four categories. 5 cases were incorrectly classified and 151 cases were classified as NULL. Most of cases with NULL classification were under "Verb" and "Noun+Prep" categories which explains the low recall of the RDROIE system for those categories. Obviously the training data did not contain relevant examples, but since the approach allows a user to fix error cases easily while the system is already in use, the low recall could be improved quickly in real use.

In a further analysis we divided the knowledge base into three groups of rules: the first 20 rules added, the first 40 and finally all 52 rules and evaluated precision, recall and F1 on Sent500. Figure 5 shows the performance of the RDROIE system with respect to the number of rules as the KB size increases. From the results, we can see precision is very high even after 20 rules, and stays high as more rules are added. Further rules do not degrade precision but improve recall and F1, suggesting an RDR approach does not trade precision for recall.

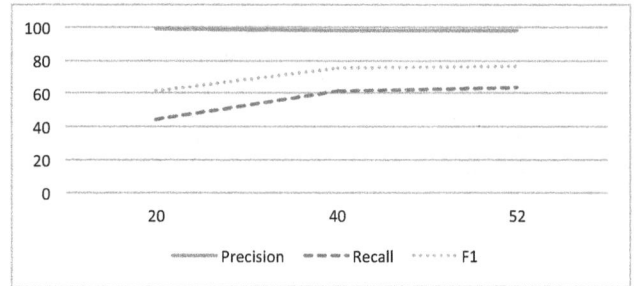

Figure 5. The performance of the RDROIE system with incrementally adding rules

4.3.2 Advantages of the RDROIE System

There are number of key features of RDROIE as an efficient IE system: (1) handling the free writing style that occurs in Web documents (2) handling NLP tools errors (3) handling abstract expressions (4) handling negative expressions.

4.3.2.1 Handling the Free Writing Style of Web Documents

Most Web documents are written without strict supervision. For example, there are many spelling errors on the Web.

The following is an example of a spelling error and an RDR rule to cover it.

Cases	"Mind Booster Noori : Google **aquires** YouTube" "__ is self sufficient , and Google **aquiring** YouTube is a sure sign of this"
Issue	'acquire' miss spelled as 'aquire'
Cases	"George Gershwin ' s " Porgy and Bess " **premiers** at Alvin Theater , New York City : 1935 [African & Black History]"
Issue	'premiere' miss spelled as 'premier'
Rule	If (relation hasToken 'aquire') then (True, Verb, 'acquire')

The following is an example of a Web specific abbreviation and an RDR rule to cover it:

Cases	"(Encyclopedia) Kafka , Franz , 1883 & ndash1924 , German - language novelist , **b.** Prague ."
Issue	'b.' is used to mean 'born'
Rule	If (relation hasToken 'b.') then (True, Verb, 'born')

4.3.2.2 Handling NLP Tools Errors

As most NLP tools are trained on journalistic text which follows writing rules more strictly, they do not perform as well on Web documents written in a freer style. For example the informal usage of capitalization often confuses NLP tools.

The following is an example of NLP tool error and an RDR rule to cover it:

Cases	"Yahoo **Rejects** Microsoft Search Offer" "Google **Nabs** YouTube For $ 1.65bn" "GOOGLE **BUYS** YOUTUBE"
Issue	'Rejects', 'Nabs' and 'BUYS' tagged incorrectly as proper noun rather than verb
Rule	If (relation hasToken 'BUYS') then (True, Verb, 'buy')

Part-of-speech tagging errors often cause degradation of OIE system performance [2]. Most OIE systems are reliant on POS tags and for example, cannot correctly identify a relationship when a verb is incorrectly tagged as noun.

4.3.2.3 Handling Abstract Expressions

There are some abstract expressions which require translation or understanding of the vernacular.

The following is an example of an abstract expression and an RDR rule to handle it:

Cases	"Google just **ate** YouTube ."
	"Google **swallow** YouTube ."
Tuples	(Google, just ate, YouTube)
	(Google, swallow, Youtube)
Issue	better to save the 'acquire' relation rather than 'ate', 'swallow' relation in KB
Rule	If (relation hasToken 'ate') and (entity1 hasToken 'Google') and (entity2 hasToken 'YouTube') + ('swallow' automatically recommended as a synonym of 'eat' in the user interface) Then (True, Verb, 'acquire') → instead of the condition (entity1 hasToken 'Google'), (entity1 hasNE 'ORG') can be used with named entity feature

4.3.2.4 Handling Negation Expressions

No OIE systems yet handle negative expressions.
The following is an example of a negative expression and a RDR rule to handle it:

Case	"In that ruling in December 2003 , Judge Richard G. Stearns dismissed Tevas lawsuit because Pfizer **hadn't accused** Teva of infringing its Zoloft patent and __ had no reasonable basis to expect __ would do so ."
Tuple	(Pfizer, had not accused, Teva)
Issue	Extract negation relation
Rule	If (relation hasToken 'hadn't accused') then (True, Verb, 'not accused')

5. DISCUSSION

Figure 5, shows that RDROIE rapidly achieves and maintains very high precision after only 2.5 hours training by a user on small data set, and overall outperforms systems using sophisticated automated training algorithms. The question immediately arises that perhaps more appropriate training data was used with RDROIE. There was no overlap between the test and training set, but obviously we used relevant training data. However, this illustrates the advantage of an RDR approach. RDROIE can be trained on whatever text it is meant to classify and errors can keep on being corrected at minimal cost while it is in use. In contrast machine-learning methods require very large amounts of training data, and there may be no suitable training data closely similar to the domain where the system is to be used.

The RDROIE system requires very little effort; rule creation is very simple and rapid. In the study here it took about three minutes on average to build a rule. Experience suggests that knowledge acquisition with RDR remains very simple and rapid even for large knowledge bases. Rules can be updated as errors are uncovered, or when new vocabularies are created, or new meanings are attached to existing terminologies, or new colloquialisms come into use. The alternative is to accumulate enough training data to retrain a system automatically. An error can be corrected manually the first time it occurs, but with a machine learning system, one needs to have many examples.

There is an important underlying assumption in the RDR approach: that it is more useful to have a system that works well on any specific domain of interest, and able to deal with all the idiosyncrasies of language and expression in the domain, when they are observed, rather than trying to have a general system for all domains, but which cannot deal with the NLP errors and other oddities that may arise in a specific domain of interest. Ideally, one would like a system that can deal with anything, but TEXTRUNNER has already been trained on 200,000 labeled sentences. How many sentences from what corpora would be needed to have a system for any and all occasions? RDROIE is certainly not a system for all occasions, but we suggest it is a system for any occasion. That is, rather than using a general solution, one can very rapidly build a new system to deal with the specific problems of the domain of interest. In the paper, the RDROIE system used only 300 Web sentences as training examples and clearly the training set did not include some of relations that appeared in the test set. The point of the RDROIE approach is that when these omissions occur they can be corrected.

There is likely to be a value in combining RDR and machine learning approaches [14, 16], where rather than build the entire system using RDR, machine learning (or any other approach) is used to build as comprehensive approach as possible but then errors and omissions are handled using RDR. Another interesting approach might be to use a version of crowd sourcing, whereby large numbers of people on the web might contribute rules, but there are major issues in how to integrate these rules in an RDR framework.

These are interesting research questions, but we wish to emphasise that in the study here, a human was able to outperform machine learning systems after 2.5 hours knowledge acquisition.

6. REFERENCES

[1] Banko, M., Cafarella, M. J., Soderland, S., Broadhead, M., and Etzioni, O. 2007. Open information extraction from the web. In *Proceedings of the 20th international joint conference on Artifical intelligence.*

[2] Banko, M., & Etzioni, O. 2008. The Tradeoffs Between Open and Traditional Relation Extraction. In *Proceedings of ACL-08: HLT.*

[3] Bunescu, R. C., & Mooney, R. J. 2007. Learning to Extract Relations from theWeb using Minimal Supervision. In *Proceedings of the 45th Annual Meeting of the Association of Computational Linguistics*, Prague, Czech Republic.

[4] Collot, M., and Belmore, N. 1996. Electronic Language: A New Variety of English. In Computer-Mediated Communications: Linguistic, Social and Cross-Cultural Perspectives, Ed. S.C. Herring, (1996) Benjamins, Amsterdam, 129-46.

[5] Edwards, G., and compton, P. 1993. PEIRS: a pathologist-maintained expert system for the interpretation of chemical pathology reports. *Pathology, 25*(1), 27-34.

[6] Gaines, B. R., and Compton, P. 1992. Induction of ripple-down rules. In *Proceedngs of the 5th Australian Conference on Artificial Intelligence*, Hobart, Tasmania.

[7] Kang, B. H., Compton, P., and Preston, P. 1995. Multiple Classification Ripple Down Rules : Evaluation and Possibilities. In *the 9th Banff Knowledge Acquisition for Knowledge Based Systems Workshop*.

[8] Pham, S. B., and Hoffmann, A. 2004. Extracting Positive Attributions from Scientific Papers. In *Proceedings of the Discovery Science Conference*.

[9] Pham, S. B., and Hoffmann, A. 2006. Efficient Knowledge Acquisition for Extracting Temporal Relations. *In the Proceedings of 17th European Conference on Artificial Intelligence*, Riva del Garda, Italy.

[10] Scheffer, T. 1996. Algebraic foundations and improved methods of induction or rippledown rules. In *the 2nd Pacific Rim Knowledge Acquisition Workshop*.

[11] Sekine, S. 2006. On-demand information extraction. In *the Proceedings of the COLING/ACL*.

[12] Shinyama, Y., and Sekine, S. 2006. Preemptive information extraction using unrestricted relation discovery. In *the Proceedings of the main conference on Human Language Technology Conference of the North American Chapter of the Association of Computational Linguistics*.

[13] Wu, F., and Weld, D. S. 2010. Open Information Extraction usingWikipedia. *In the the 48th Annual Meeting of the Association for Computational Linguistics*, Uppsala, Sweden.

[14] Xu, H., and Hoffmann, A. 2010. RDRCE: Combining Machine Learning and Knowledge Acquisition. In *the Pacific Rim Knowledge Acquisition Workshop*.

[15] Zhu, J., Nie, Z., Liu, X., Zhang, B., and Wen, J.-R. 2009. StatSnowball: a statistical approach to extracting entity relationships. In *the Proceedings of the 18th international conference on World wide web*.

[16] V. H. Ho, P. Compton, B. Benatallah, J. Vayssiere, L. Menzel, and H. Vogler. 2009. *An incremental knowledge acquisition method for improving duplicate invoices detection*. In *Proceedings of the ICDE*, 1415–1418.

An Analysis of Open Information Extraction Based on Semantic Role Labeling

Janara Christensen, Mausam, Stephen Soderland, and Oren Etzioni
Turing Center, University of Washington
Seattle, WA 98195, USA
janara@cs.washington.edu, mausam@cs.washington.edu,
soderlan@cs.washington.edu, etzioni@cs.washington.edu

ABSTRACT

Open Information Extraction extracts relations from text without requiring a pre-specified domain or vocabulary. While existing techniques have used only shallow syntactic features, we investigate the use of semantic role labeling techniques for the task of Open IE. Semantic role labeling (SRL) and Open IE, although developed mostly in isolation, are quite related. We compare SRL-based open extractors, which perform computationally expensive, deep syntactic analysis, with TextRunner, an open extractor, which uses shallow syntactic analysis but is able to analyze many more sentences in a fixed amount of time and thus exploit corpus-level statistics.

Our evaluation answers questions regarding these systems, including, can SRL extractors, which are trained on Prop-Bank, cope with heterogeneous text found on the Web? Which extractor attains better precision, recall, f-measure, or running time? How does extractor performance vary for binary, n-ary and nested relations? How much do we gain by running multiple extractors? How do we select the optimal extractor given amount of data, available time, types of extractions desired?

Categories and Subject Descriptors

I.2.7 [**Computing Methodologies**]: Artificial Intelligence—*Natural Language Processing*

General Terms

Experimentation, Performance

Keywords

Information Extraction, Open Information Extraction, Semantic Role Labeling

1. INTRODUCTION

The challenge of Machine Reading and Knowledge Extraction at Web scale [10] requires a scalable system for extracting diverse information from large, heterogeneous corpora. The traditional approaches to information extraction, *e.g.*, [17, 1], seek to learn individual extractors for each relation of interest and hence, cannot scale to the millions of relations found on the Web. In response, the *Open Information Extraction* paradigm [5] attempts to overcome this knowledge acquisition bottleneck by extracting relational tuples without any restrictions of a pre-specified vocabulary, domain or ontology.

TextRunner[6], a state-of-the-art open extractor, is a relation classifier based primarily on shallow syntactic features. In this paper, we study the applicability of semantic role labeling (SRL) for the task of Open IE.

Our first observation is that SRL and Open IE, although developed in isolation, are related tasks: semantically labeled arguments correspond to the arguments in Open IE extractions, and verbs often match up with Open IE relations. We construct a scheme for Open IE based on SRL, and create novel extractors based on two state-of-the-art SRL systems, one developed at UIUC and the other at Lund [15, 12]. These systems represent the top ranking systems at CoNLL 2005 and 2008, respectively. We study the trade-offs between TextRunner and SRL-based extractors across a broad range of metrics and experimental conditions, both qualitative and quantitative.

Given the distinct perspectives from which Open IE and SRL have been developed, we expect TextRunner and SRL extractors to be quite different. For example, we expect the SRL extractors to have lower recalls on Web text due to out-of-vocabulary verbs and diverse writing styles, since they are trained on a more homogeneous corpus (PropBank). On the other hand, their deep processing in comparison to TextRunner's shallow syntactic features may result in a much higher precision. We also believe *a priori* that TextRunner will be faster, but cannot quantify the difference, as no previous work has studied this.

This paper reports that, contrary to our beliefs, SRL is robust to noisy Web text, and achieves a much larger recall; whereas TextRunner obtains a much higher precision than SRL extractors, at lower recalls. Finally, TextRunner is 20-700 times faster than SRL systems we have tested (dependent on use of dependency parser versus constituency).

While previous studies assume a small data set and ample time available for processing, to our knowledge, we are the first to study the alternative experimental conditions in

113

which the data set is large and the processing time is limited. This is especially important for most universities and companies, which do not have access to Microsoft or Google sized cluster of machines. Even cloud computing resources are expensive and hence limited. In this paper, we examine both of these conditions, SMALLCORPUS and LARGECORPUS respectively. For LARGECORPUS, we devise a scheme to make use of the available time carefully. We first run TEXTRUNNER, which is enormously faster than the SRL-extractors we tested. For the remaining available time, we run other extractors over an intelligently chosen subset of the corpus. This hybrid scheme obtains the best value for time compared to the individual extractors.

We first describe the Open IE paradigm in more detail and then explain how SRL systems can be used to produce Open IE output. Next, we discuss qualitative differences between the output produced by traditional Open IE systems and the output produced by SRL-based systems. Finally, we describe two experiments under different conditions and end with related work and conclusions.

2. BACKGROUND

Open Information Extraction [5] is a paradigm where the system makes a single (or constant number of) pass(es) over its corpus and extracts a large set of relational tuples without requiring any relation-specific training data. These tuples attempt to capture the salient relationships expressed in each sentence. For instance, given the sentence, *"McCain fought hard against Obama, but finally lost the election,"* an Open IE system would extract two tuples <McCain, fought against, Obama>, and <McCain, lost, the election>. These tuples can be binary or n-ary, where the relationship is expressed between more than two entities, such as <Gates Foundation, invested (arg) in, 1 billion dollars, high schools> or nested (*e.g.,* <Microsoft, announced,<they, acquired, Komoku>>).

TEXTRUNNER is a state-of-the-art Open IE system that performs extraction in two key steps. (1) A self-supervised learner outputs a CRF-based classifier that uses unlexicalized features (it models closed class words but not function words) for extracting relationships. The self-supervised nature alleviates the need for hand-labeled training data and unlexicalized features help scale to the multitudes of relations found on the Web. (2) A single pass extractor, which uses shallow syntactic techniques like POS tagging and NP chunking, applies the CRF classifier to extract an unbounded number of relationships expressed in text. The use of shallow features makes TEXTRUNNER highly efficient.

The extractions from TEXTRUNNER are ranked using redundancy, an assessor that assigns higher confidence to tuples occurring multiple times based on a probabilistic model [9]. This assessor exploits the redundancy of information in Web text and assigns higher confidence to extractions occurring multiple times.All these components enable TEXTRUNNER to be a high performance, general, and high quality extractor for heterogeneous Web text.

Semantic Role Labeling consists of detecting semantic arguments associated with a verb in a sentence and their roles (such as Agent, Patient, Instrument, *etc.*). Given the sentence *"The pearls I left to my son are fake"* an SRL system would conclude that for the verb 'leave', 'I' is the agent, 'pearls' is the patient and 'son' is the benefactor.

Tuples	Binary, N-ary, Nested
Metrics	Precision, Recall, F-measure
Settings	SMALLCORPUS, LARGECORPUS
Systems	TEXTRUNNER, SRL-IE-UIUC, SRL-IE-LUND

Table 1: A table outlining the various experimental conditions in this paper.

Because not all roles feature in each verb, the roles are commonly divided into meta-roles (A0-A7) and additional common classes such as location, time, *etc.* Each Ai can represent a different role based on the verb, though A0 and A1 most often refer to agents and patients respectively.

Availability of lexical resources such as PropBank [13] and FrameNet [3], both of which annotate text with roles for each argument, has enabled significant progress in SRL systems over the last few years [18, 12, 8, 14]. We use UIUC-SRL [15] and LUND-SRL [12] as our base SRL systems. We choose these systems as they represent the state-of-the-art for systems based on constituency and dependency parsing – they are winners of the CoNLL shared tasks 2005 and 2008 respectively.

Both these SRL systems apply a pipeline of parsing, argument identification, and classification trained over Prop-Bank. UIUC-SRL operates in four key steps: pruning, argument identification, argument classification and inference. Pruning involves using a full parse tree and heuristic rules to eliminate constituents that are unlikely to be arguments. Argument identification uses a classifier to identify constituents that are potential arguments. In argument classification, a classifier assigns role labels to the candidates identified in the previous stage. Argument information is incorporated across arguments in the inference stage, which uses an integer linear program to make global role predictions.

LUND-SRL has a similar process. It first applies a dependency parser and then uses a pipeline of classifiers to identify predicates and identify and classify arguments. Next it applies a set of linguistic constraints and uses a predicate-argument reranker to rank the candidates. Lastly, it uses a syntactic-semantic reranker to score the joint syntactic-semantic models.

In the next section, we describe how to convert output from an SRL system to output for an Open IE system.

3. SRL-BASED OPEN IE

Our first observation is that verbs and their semantically labeled arguments almost always correspond to Open IE relations and arguments respectively. SRL computes more information than Open IE requires. Therefore, for the purpose of a comparison with Open IE systems, we convert SRL output into extractions. We illustrate this conversion process via an example.

For example, given the sentence, *"Eli Whitney created the cotton gin in 1793,"* TEXTRUNNER extracts two tuples, one binary and one n-ary:

arg0	Eli Whitney		arg0	Eli Whitney
rel	created		rel	created (arg1) in
arg1	the cotton gin		arg1	the cotton gin
			arg2	1793
	binary tuple			*n-ary tuple*

The SRL systems label constituents of a sentence with the

role they play in regards to the verb in the sentence. An SRL system will identify the following semantic roles for the verb 'create':

A0	Eli Whitney
verb	created
A1	the cotton gin
temporal	in 1793

It is easy to see that the two formats are very related. For fair comparisons we convert SRL output to *equivalent* number of Open IE tuples. Our method first assigns the verb along with its modifiers, following preposition, and negation, if present, to be the relation. It then assigns all constituents labeled Ai for that verb, as well as any that are marked *Direction, Location,* or *Temporal* to be the arguments of the relation. We order the arguments in the same order as they are in the sentence and with regard to the relation (except for direction, location and temporal, which cannot be arg0 of an Open IE extraction and are placed at the end of argument list). As we are interested in relationships between entities, we consider only the verbs that have at least two arguments.

The generation of nested relations happens similarly. The key difference is in identifying whether a semantic tuple is a nested extraction. SRL-IE identifies such cases by noticing that an argument to one verb is long and contains a full semantic tuple with a different verb. This is easy to operationalize since an SRL system always reports all the semantic tuples found in the sentence.

In our experiments, we ignore part of the semantic information (such as distinctions between various Ai's) that UIUC-SRL and Lund-SRL provide. An IE system built using SRL may retain this information, if the downstream process (such as question answering engine) can make use of this information. Notice that, in our conversion, an SRL extraction that was correct in the original format is never changed to an incorrect Open IE extraction. However, an incorrectly labeled SRL extraction could convert to a correct Open IE extraction, if the arguments were correctly identified but assigned incorrect semantic roles.

4. QUALITATIVE COMPARISON OF EXTRACTORS

Because SRL and Open IE are developed from different perspectives, we first study their differences qualitatively.

Argument boundaries: The SRL systems are lenient in deciding what constitutes an argument and tend to err on the side of including too much rather than too little; TextRunner is more conservative, sometimes to the extent of omitting crucial information, particularly post-modifying clauses and PPs. For example, TextRunner extracts <Bunsen, invented, a device> from the sentence *"Bunsen invented a device called the Spectroscope"*. SRL extractors include the entire phrase "a device called the Spectroscope" as the second argument. Generally, the longer arguments in SRL-IE-UIUC and SRL-IE-Lund are more informative, but TextRunner's succinct arguments normalize better leading to an effective use of redundancy in ranking.

Out-of-vocabulary verbs: While we expected TextRunner to handle unknown verbs with little difficulty due to its unlexicalized nature, the SRL-based systems could have had severe trouble leading to a limited applicability in the context of Web text. However, contrary to our expecta-

tions, both SRL systems gracefully handle new verbs (*i.e.*, verbs not in their PropBank training) by only attempting to identify A0 (the agent) and A1 (the patient). In practice, this is very effective – both SRL extractors recognize the verb and its two arguments correctly in *"Larry Page googled his name and launched a revolution."* In practice, out-of-vocabulary verbs are rare and appeared in only 5% of our data.

Part-of-speech ambiguity: All systems have difficulty in cases where the part of speech of a word is ambiguous or difficult to tag automatically. For example, the word 'write' when used as a noun causes trouble for both systems. In the sentence, *"Be sure the file has write permission."*, all three extractors incorrectly extract <the file, write, permission>. Part-of-speech ambiguity affected about 20% of sentences.

Complex sentences: Because TextRunner relies on shallow syntactic features, it performs more poorly on complex sentences. SRL-based systems, due to their deeper processing, can better handle complex syntax and long-range dependencies, although occasionally complex sentences will create parsing errors causing difficulties for SRL-IE-UIUC and SRL-IE-Lund.

N-ary relations: All extractors suffer significant quality loss in n-ary extractions compared to binary. A key problem is prepositional phrase attachment, such as in the sentence "Edison made improvements to the idea of incandescent light." N-ary relations were present in 40% of the sentences in our development set.

Nested relations: TextRunner performs poorly on nested relations. Given the sentence "Google announced it will acquire YouTube," TextRunner mistakenly extracts <Google, announced, it>. SRL extractors can better handle these sentences because they use parsers and have additional knowledge about arguments specific to particular verbs. Nested relations appeared in about 35% of the sentences in our development set.

5. EXPERIMENTAL RESULTS

In our quantitative evaluation we examine the strengths and weaknesses of these extractors under two experimental conditions: (1) SmallCorpus (Section 5.1), in which we have a small corpus and ample computation time available, and (2) LargeCorpus (Section 5.2), in which the corpus is large and all systems cannot complete the processing. We evaluate the quality of binary, n-ary, and nested extractions in all these settings (see Table 1). In all experiments, we threshold TextRunner's CRF-confidence at 0.4, which maximizes F-measure on a development set.

Data sets: Because of the SRL-based systems' relatively slow processing time, we required our test sets be of manageable size. Moreover, Open IE on the Web has benefited from redundancy, and so the data sets needed to mimic the redundancy found on the Web. We created two test sets, one for binary and n-ary, and the other for nested extractions. The first set focused on five target relations – *invent, graduate, study, write,* and *develop,* and the second used two relations with common nested extractions – *say* and *announce.* The first set of relations is similar to that used in [5]. To our knowledge, we are the first to investigate nested extractions, hence our dataset to study that is unique.

A key challenge was dataset construction that was of manageable size but still mimicked the redundancy found on the Web. We could not use prior datasets, since either they were not Web text, or they were too large. To obtain redundant data commonly found on the Web, we first queried a corpus of 500M Web documents for a sample of sentences with these verbs (or their inflected forms, *e.g.*, invents). We chose 200 typical agents per verb (*e.g.*, Edison (for invent), Microsoft (for announce)) and searched for sentences with both the verb as well as these agents. This resulted in a test set of 29,842 sentences for binary and n-ary relations, and a second set of 16,777 sentences for nested relations. These test sets have the desired properties and enable us to study the performance of different extractors on Web text.

To compute precision on these test sets, we tagged a random sample of over 4,800 extractions. A tuple is correct if the arguments have correct boundaries and the relation accurately expresses the relationship between all of the arguments, even if the relation is uninformative. For example, for the sentence *"Bunsen invented a device called the Spectroscope"*, both second arguments, 'a device' and 'a device called the Spectroscope' would be marked as correct.

Determining the absolute recall is precluded by the amount of hand labeling necessary. Instead, we compute pseudo-recall by taking the union of correct tuples from all methods as denominator. [1]

5.1 SMALLCORPUS **Setting**

Table 2 reports the performance of the three extractors on our data sets for this traditional NLP setting. Overall, SRL-IE-LUND achieves the highest precision, and SRL-IE-UIUC achieves the highest recall and the highest F1 score. TEXTRUNNER's performance on nested extractions is especially poor, but that is expected, since it only extracts relations between noun phrases and nested extractions, by definition, have a full extraction as an argument. On the other hand, both SRL-based systems run *far slower* than TEXTRUNNER. TEXTRUNNER on average processes a sentence in under 0.02 secs whereas SRL-IE-LUND and SRL-IE-UIUC are over 20x and 500x slower respectively. SRL-IE-UIUC ran much slower because of its use of constituency parsing (which is slower compared to dependency parsing) and its use of an integer linear program for global inference.

By taking a union of the SRL-based systems' output and the *highest precision subset* of TEXTRUNNER's extractions, we achieve the highest recall and F-measure (Table 2). We identify the highest precision subset of TEXTRUNNER's extractions by our novel *locality* ranking (see Figure 2).[2] This shows the benefit of using multiple systems for extraction – they extract different tuples. We call this the *smart union* of all systems, and this is the method of choice for the SMALLCORPUS setting.

Although SRL-IE-LUND has higher overall precision, there are some conditions under which the shallow processing of TEXTRUNNER can obtain superior precision! We analyze the performance of these systems under two different rankings – redundancy, which has been examined before for TEXTRUNNER[4], and locality, a novel measure.

Redundancy: Redundancy is the number of times a relation has been extracted from unique sentences. Intuitively, we have more confidence in a relation that is extracted many times than a relation that is extracted only a small number of times. We compute redundancy over normalized extractions, ignoring noun modifiers, adverbs, and verb inflection. Figure 1(a) displays the results for binary extractions, ranked by redundancy. We use a log scale on the x-axis, since high redundancy extractions account for less than 1% of the recall. For binary extractions, redundancy improved TEXTRUNNER's precision significantly, but at a *dramatic* loss in recall – it achieved 0.82 precision at 0.009 recall. For a highly redundant corpus, TEXTRUNNER would be the algorithm of choice, however, this experiment clearly shows that highly redundant extractions are usually very limited, even in Web-style text.

For n-ary and nested relations, and binary relations for SRL-based extractors (Figure 1(a,b)), redundancy actually hurts precision (nested relation graphs omitted). These extractions tend to be so specific that genuine redundancy is rare, and the highest frequency extractions are often systematic errors. *E.g.*, the most frequent SRL-IE-UIUC extraction was <nothing, write, home>, from sentences with the phrase *"nothing to write home about"*.

Locality: Our experiments with TEXTRUNNER led us to discover a new validation scheme for the extractions – *locality*. We define locality as the number of tokens in between the first and the last arguments in the sentence. We observed that TEXTRUNNER's shallow features can identify relations more reliably when the arguments are closer to each other in the sentence. Figure 2 reports the results from ranking extractions by locality.

We find a clear correlation between locality and precision of TEXTRUNNER, with precision 0.81 at recall 0.17, where the locality is 3 tokens or less for binary extractions. This result is very surprising because SRL systems perform deep syntactic and additional semantic analysis, still TEXTRUNNER's shallow syntactic processing with simple locality assessment is able to obtain significantly higher precision (though at reasonable, but lower recall of 0.17). Comparing this result with precision 0.82 at recall 0.01 for redundancy-based assessing, we find that locality-based ranking is dramatically more useful. SRL extractors do not benefit from locality for binary extractions. For n-ary relations, all systems can improve precision by varying locality. Locality has little effect on nested relations.

This new assessor allows us to construct a high precision subset of TEXTRUNNER, which we use in the smart union (see the experiment above). For binary extractions we filter all extractions where locality > 5, *i.e.*, there are more than five tokens between the arguments.

An Ablation Study: SRL systems perform two key types of processing in addition to TEXTRUNNER's shallow syntactic techniques: (1) they use a full syntactic parser, and (2) they perform argument identification and classification. To tease apart the benefits, we perform an additional experiment in which we create extractions directly from the output of LUND-SRL's parser. These extractions achieve a precision of 0.62 at recall of 0.41 for binary extractions. This is much lower than SRL-IE-LUND's results (precision 0.7 and recall 0.51) illustrating the gain due to a complete SRL system.

In summary, we find that SRL extractors perform bet-

---

[1]Tuples from two systems are considered equivalent if for the relation and each argument, the extracted phrases are equal or if one phrase is contained within the phrase of the other.

[2]discussed in more detail next.

	TextRunner			SRL-IE-Lund			SRL-IE-UIUC			Smart Union		
	P	R	F1	P	R	F1	P	R	F1	P	R	F1
Binary	.55	.26	.35	**.70**	.51	.59	.63	.75	.68	.67	**.95**	**.77**
N-ary	.42	27	.32	**.61**	.27	.37	.53	.57	.55	.56	**.78**	**.66**
Cpu Time: Binary, N-ary	6 minutes			155 minutes			3126 minutes			3287 minutes		
Nested	.09	.02	.03	**.63**	.44	.59	.52	.84	.64	.57	**1.0**	**.72**
Cpu Time: Nested	3 minutes			60 minutes			2016 minutes			2078 minutes		

Table 2: In SmallCorpus, SRL-IE-Lund has the highest precision. Taking the union of the SRL systems and the higher precision results from TextRunner achieves the highest recall and F-measure. Both SRL-based systems require over an order of magnitude more processing time. The bold values indicate the highest values for the metric and relation-type.

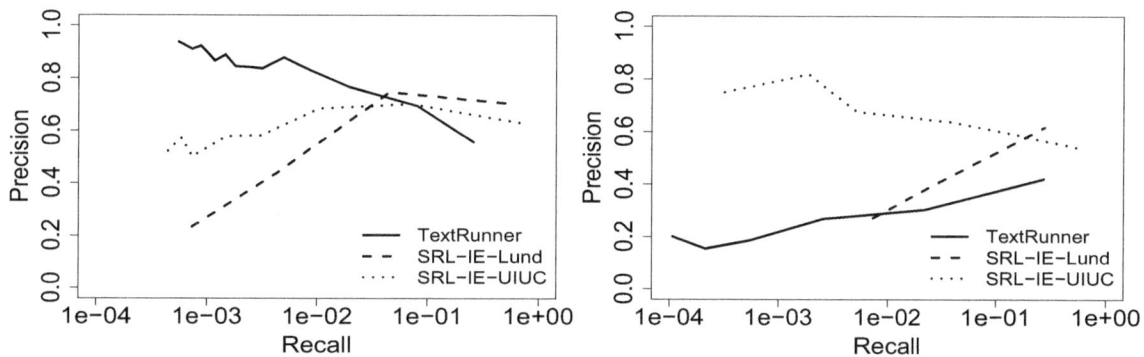

Figure 1: SmallCorpus: redundancy ranking for binary and n-ary relations. (Note the log scale) (a) TextRunner has highest precision at highest redundancy, but at a very low recall (0.01). The arguments in SRL-based extractors do not normalize well; the high redundancy region has a large fraction of systematic extraction errors. (b) For n-ary extractions, redundancy is not very effective.

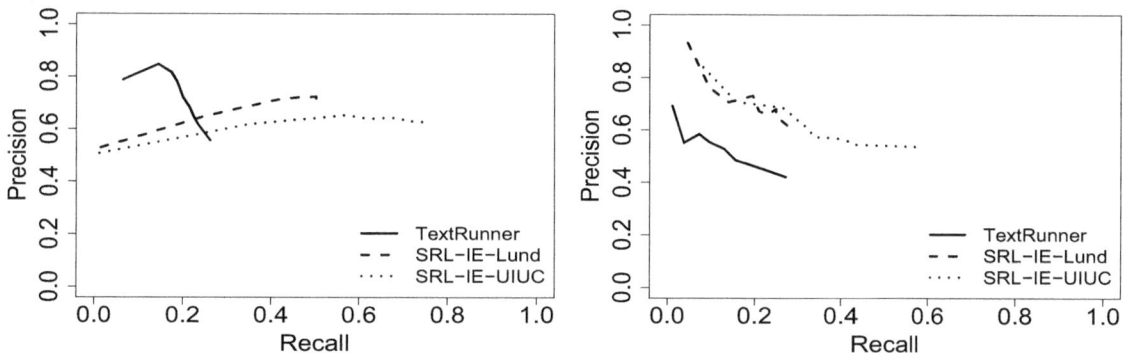

Figure 2: SmallCorpus: locality ranking for binary, and n-ary relations. (a) Locality ranking gives a large boost to TextRunner's precision for binary relations, and at a recall of 0.2, much higher than that achieved by redundancy ranking. (b) For n-ary extractions, locality helps all systems.

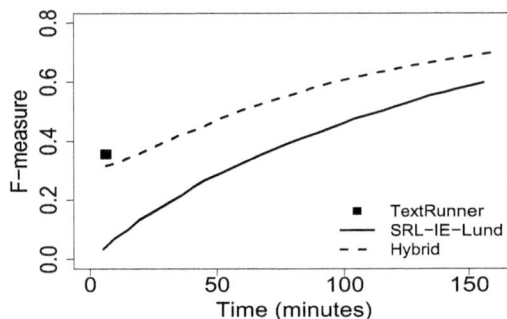

Figure 3: LargeCorpus: F-measure achieved in a given amount of computation time. The hybrid extractor obtains the best F-measure for binary extractions.

ter overall, however, TEXTRUNNER, under locality ranking, achieves superior precision at lower recalls. Neither redundancy nor locality benefits SRL extractors much (except for n-ary). SRL is orders of magnitude slower, which becomes a bottleneck in the next experiment, when the available time is limited.

5.2 LARGECORPUS Setting

To determine scaling to Web-scale knowledge extraction, we study an experimental condition, often not considered in NLP and IE communities – the setting in which the data is large enough that all processing cannot be achieved. Because experimenting with massive corpora makes it very hard to estimate (pseudo)recall and thus the F-measure, we simulate this setting by using our current data set, and varying the amount of available time.

In the extreme setup when the time is so limited that no extractor can complete processing, TEXTRUNNER is the extractor of choice, because the recalls of the slower extractors will be so low that they will far outweigh the benefits of higher precision. TEXTRUNNER, on the other hand, will be able to generate a large number of extractions at reasonable precision.

In the more interesting and likely more realistic case, where additional time is available after TEXTRUNNER completes its processing, we have the opportunity to combine the different extractors. We present a hybrid system that combines the strengths of TEXTRUNNER (fast processing time and high precision on a subset of sentences) with the strengths of SRL-IE-LUND (higher recall and better handling of long-range dependencies). The focus is on using the remaining time efficiently. We illustrate the binary setting, though results on n-ary are similar, and don't consider SRL-IE-UIUC owing to its very slow speed, though it is straightforward to include.

We first run TEXTRUNNER over all the sentences and then use the remaining time to run SRL-IE-LUND and take the union of all extractions. We add to this idea by using a *filter policy* and an intelligent *order of sentences for extraction* to improve the precision. TEXTRUNNER's precision is low when the redundancy of the extraction is low, and when the arguments are far apart. Thus, redundancy, and locality form the key factors for our filter policy: if both of these factors are below a given threshold, discard the tuple. The thresholds were determined by a parameter search over a small development set.

A good ordering policy would apply SRL-IE-LUND first

to the sentences in which TEXTRUNNER extractions have been filtered by the filter policy. We could rank a sentence S according to the average distance between pairs of arguments from all tuples extracted by TEXTRUNNER from S. While this ranking system would order sentences according to their likelihood of yielding maximum new information, it would miss the cost of computation. To account for computation time, we additionally estimate the amount of time SRL-IE-LUND will take to process each sentence using a linear model trained on the sentence length. We then choose the sentence that maximizes information gain divided by its estimated computation time.

If the available time is minimal then our hybrid extractor reduces to TEXTRUNNER. If it is very large, then the hybrid is similar to the smart union of two systems (see SMALL-CORPUS). In intermediate cases, hybrids make effective use of available time. Overall, the hybrid extractor run the best algorithm given the available computation time.

In summary, we find that all extractors are useful and, for best results, they should all be employed to varying degrees, which are based on the available time and their efficiency.

Evaluation: Figure 3 reports F-measure for binary extractions measured against available computation time. HYBRID has substantially better F1 scores than both TEXTRUNNER's and SRL-IE-LUND's demonstrating the power of combining extractors.

6. RELATED WORK

Open information extraction is a relatively recent paradigm and hence, has been studied by only a small number of researchers. The most salient is TEXTRUNNER, which also introduced the model [5, 6].

A recent Open IE system, WOE [21], uses dependency features (WOE^{parse}) and training data generated using Wikipedia infoboxes to learn a series of open extractors (WOE^{pos}). Our ablation study in Section 5.1 suggests the quality of the parser-based extractor to be between TEXTRUNNER and complete SRL systems; we expect WOE^{parse}, their better performing system, to be similar. Moreover, WOE does not output n-ary or nested extractions.

A paradigm related to Open IE is Preemptive IE [16]. While one goal of Preemptive IE is to avoid relation-specificity, Preemptive IE does not emphasize Web scalability, which is essential to Open IE.

A version of KNEXT uses heuristic rules and syntactic parses to convert a sentence into an unscoped logical form [19]. This work is more suitable for extracting common sense knowledge as opposed to factual information.

Another related system is WANDERLUST [2]. After annotating 10,000 sentences parsed with LinkGrammar, it learns 46 general linkpaths as patterns for relation extraction. In contrast to our approaches, this requires a large set of hand-labeled examples.

We are the first to use SRL for Open IE, but its use for traditional IE is investigated by Harabagiu *et al.* [11]. They used a lexico-semantic feedback loop in a question-answering system for a set of pre-defined relations.

7. CONCLUSIONS

This paper investigates the use of Semantic Role Labeling for the task of Open Information Extraction. Although the two tasks were developed in isolation, they are quite related. We describe SRL-IE-UIUC and SRL-IE-LUND, the first SRL-based Open IE systems. We empirically study the trade-offs between these systems and TEXTRUNNER, a state-of-the-art Open IE system under several settings: SMALL-CORPUS with unbounded computation time, and LARGECORPUS with limited amount of time; using different metrics: precision, recall, F1 score and running time; and for different kinds of extractions: binary, n-ary and nested.

We find that in the traditional NLP setting (SMALLCORPUS), the deeper analysis of SRL-based systems overall outperforms TEXTRUNNER. However, TEXTRUNNER output can be ranked using our novel measure, *locality*, leading to superior precision at non-trivial recalls, which is surprising given TEXTRUNNER's shallow syntactic processing and SRL's semantic processing. The pre-existing redundancy-based assessors aren't as effective. A smart union of the three approaches performs best.

TEXTRUNNER is over an order of magnitude faster, making it the algorithm of choice when time is extremely limited. These complimentary strengths lead us to design a hybrid extractor that intelligently chooses sentences to extract from, and thus, efficiently uses the remaining computation time. Our hybrid extractor achieves better performance than either system if an intermediate amount of time is available for processing. Overall, we provide evidence that, contrary to belief in the Open IE literature [6], deep syntactic approaches have a lot to offer for the task of Open IE.

8. ACKNOWLEDGEMENTS

This research was supported in part by NSF grant IIS-0803481, ONR grant N00014-08-1-0431, and DARPA contract FA8750-09-C-0179, and carried out at the University of Washington's Turing Center.

9. REFERENCES

[1] E. Agichtein and L. Gravano. Snowball: Extracting relations from large plain-text collections. In *Proceedings of the Fifth ACM International Conference on Digital Libraries*, 2000.

[2] A. Akbik and J. Broß. Wanderlust: Extracting semantic relations from natural language text using dependency grammar patterns. In *Proceedings of the WWW 2009 Workshop on Semantic Search*, 2009.

[3] C. F. Baker, C. J. Fillmore, and J. B. Lowe. The berkeley framenet project. In *COLING '98: Proceedings of the 17th international conference on Computational linguistics*, pages 86–90, 1998.

[4] M. Banko. *Open Information Extraction for the Web.* PhD thesis, University of Washington, 2009.

[5] M. Banko, M. J. Cafarella, S. Soderland, M. Broadhead, and O. Etzioni. Open information extraction from the web. In *IJCAI'07: Proceedings of the 20th international joint conference on Artifical intelligence*, pages 2670–2676, 2007.

[6] M. Banko and O. Etzioni. The tradeoffs between open and traditional relation extraction. In *ACL '08: Proceedings of the 46th Annual Meeting of the Association for Computational Linguistics*, pages 28–36, 2008.

[7] A. Carlson, J. Betteridge, R. C. Wang, E. R. H. Jr., and T. M. Mitchell. Coupled semi-supervised learning for information extraction. In *WSDM '10: Proceedings of the Third ACM International Conference on Web Search and Data Mining*, 2010.

[8] B. Coppola, A. Moschitti, and G. Riccardi. Shallow semantic parsing for spoken language understanding. In *NAACL '09: Proceedings of Human Language Technologies: The Annual Conference of the North American Chapter of the Association for Computational Linguistics*, pages 85–88, 2009.

[9] D. Downey, O. Etzioni, and S. Soderland. A probabilistic model of redundancy in information extraction. In *IJCAI '05: Proceedings of the 20th international joint conference on Artifical intelligence*, pages 1034–1041, 2005.

[10] O. Etzioni, M. Banko, and M. J. Cafarella. Machine reading. In *AAAI'06: Proceedings of the 21st national conference on Artificial intelligence*, pages 1517–1519, 2006.

[11] S. Harabagiu, D. Moldovan, M. Paşca, R. Mihalcea, M. Surdeanu, R. Bunescu, R. Gîrju, V. Rus, and P. Morărescu. The role of lexico-semantic feedback in open-domain textual question-answering. In *ACL '01: Proceedings of the 39th Annual Meeting on Association for Computational Linguistics*, pages 282–289, 2001.

[12] R. Johansson and P. Nugues. The effect of syntactic representation on semantic role labeling. In *COLING '08: Proceedings of the 22nd International Conference on Computational Linguistics*, pages 393–400, 2008.

[13] P. K. Martha and M. Palmer. From treebank to propbank. In *LREC '02: Proceedings of the Third International Conference on Language Resources and Evaluation*, 2002.

[14] A. Moschitti, D. Pighin, and R. Basili. Tree kernels for semantic role labeling. *Computational Linguistics*, 34(2):193–224, 2008.

[15] V. Punyakanok, D. Roth, and W. Yih. The importance of syntactic parsing and inference in semantic role labeling. *Computational Linguistics*, 34(2), 2008.

[16] Y. Shinyama and S. Sekine. Preemptive information extraction using unrestricted relation discovery. In *NAACL '06: Proceedings of Human Language Technologies: The Annual Conference of the North American Chapter of the Association for Computational Linguistics*, pages 304–311, 2006.

[17] S. Soderland. Learning information extraction rules for semi-structured and free text. *Machine Learning*, 34(1-3):233–272, 1999.

[18] K. Toutanova, A. Haghighi, and C. D. Manning. A global joint model for semantic role labeling. *Computational Linguistics*, 34(2):161–191, 2008.

[19] B. Van Durme and L. Schubert. Open knowledge extraction through compositional language processing. In *STEP '08: Proceedings of the 2008 Conference on Semantics in Text Processing*, pages 239–254, 2008.

[20] D. S. Weld, R. Hoffmann, and F. Wu. Using wikipedia to bootstrap open information extraction. *SIGMOD Rec.*, 37(4):62–68, 2008.

[21] F. Wu and D. S. Weld. Open information extraction using wikipedia. In *ACL '10: Proceedings of the 48th Annual Meeting on Association for Computational Linguistics*, 2010.

Extracting Relevant Questions to an RDF Dataset Using Formal Concept Analysis

Mathieu d'Aquin
Knowledge Media Institute
The Open University, Milton Keynes, UK
m.daquin@open.ac.uk

Enrico Motta
Knowledge Media Institute
The Open University, Milton Keynes, UK
e.motta@open.ac.uk

ABSTRACT

With the rise of linked data, more and more semantically described information is being published online according to the principles and technologies of the Semantic Web (especially, RDF and SPARQL). The use of such standard technologies means that this data should be exploitable, integrable and reusable straight away. However, once a potentially interesting dataset has been discovered, significant efforts are currently required in order to understand its schema, its content, the way to query it and what it can answer. In this paper, we propose a method and a tool to automatically discover questions that can be answered by an RDF dataset. We use formal concept analysis to build a hierarchy of meaningful sets of entities from a dataset. These sets of entities represent answers, which common characteristics represent the clauses of the corresponding questions. This hierarchy can then be used as a querying interface, proposing questions of varying levels of granularity and specificity to the user. A major issue is however that thousands of questions can be included in this hierarchy. Based on an empirical analysis and using metrics inspired both from formal concept analysis and from ontology summarisation, we devise an approach for identifying relevant questions to act as a starting point to the navigation in the question hierarchy.

Categories and Subject Descriptors

H.4 [**Information Systems Applications**]: Miscellaneous

General Terms

Algorithms,Design,Human Factors,Measurement

Keywords

Semantic data, semantic web, RDF, navigation, question, formal concept analysis

1. INTRODUCTION

The idea of a Semantic Web is quickly gaining momentum as more and more organisations are exposing their data in structured, semantically described datasets following the principles of linked data [2]. When coming across such a dataset, a significant effort is generally required before it can be exploited. A variety of approaches can be envisaged to become familiar with the content and the structure of such a dataset, including inspecting its schema (i.e., the ontology) with an ontology editor (such as Protégé[1] or the NeOn Toolkit[2]), using a graph representation, a faceted browser, or sending test queries in a trial and error approach.

To simplify this process, example queries are often used as a way to characterise a dataset (see, e.g., the use of competency questions in ontology engineering [11]). By providing a simple representation of the kind of answers a dataset can provide, they help in better understanding what is the scope of the dataset, and how it can be used. In addition, as questions can be formulated in a way close to natural language, such an approach has the advantage of supporting users unfamiliar with the underlying technologies (e.g., the RDF[3] and OWL[4] representation languages, and the SPARQL[5] query language), providing easy access points to the dataset.

In this paper, we propose an approach based on automatically extracting a set of questions that can be answered by a dataset. We use formal concept analysis (FCA) to identify sets of objects from a dataset that share common properties. Each of these sets represents the answers to a particular question, which is characterised by the properties shared by the elements of the set. One of the advantages of using FCA is that these sets are organised in a hierarchy (a lattice), relating any extracted question with more general and more specific ones. This hierarchy is used to generate a navigational query interface, allowing the user to browse the set of possible questions to a dataset, together with their answers.

However, one of the main drawbacks of this method is that the application of FCA can generate thousands of questions, making browsing the hierarchy cumbersome. We therefore also study a set of measures, inspired both from ontology summarisation and from FCA, to identify the questions which are more likely to be close to the ones of interest to the user.

---

[1] http://protege.stanford.edu/
[2] http://neon-toolkit.org
[3] http://www.w3.org/RDF/
[4] http://www.w3.org/TR/owl-ref/
[5] http://www.w3.org/TR/rdf-sparql-query/

Through studying questions proposed by human users of three test datasets, we propose a combination of measures which help identifying a reasonable entry point into the generated question hierarchy, and so to the dataset.

2. FORMAL CONCEPT ANALYSIS

FCA [6, 15] is a formal, generic framework, generally associated with the fields of data mining and knowledge discovery. In broad terms, it is concerned with identifying from raw data, patterns of objects' characteristics that form formal *concepts*.[6] Such a concept is characterised both by an intent – i.e., a set of attributes, and an extent – i.e., the set of objects in the data that share these attributes.

More formally, FCA relies on the notion of a formal *context*, which represents the raw data. A formal context $C = (G, M, I)$ is made of a set of objects G, a set of attributes M and a binary relation $I \subseteq G \times M$. In simpler terms, a formal context is a binary matrix where the rows represent objects, and columns represent attributes of these objects. Given O a set of objects of G, we note O' the set of attributes of M which are shared by all the objects of O. In the same way, given $A \subseteq M$, $A' \subseteq G$ is the set of objects that share all the attributes in A. The double application of $(.)'$ is said to represent the closure of a set of objects or attributes. In other terms, O'' and A'' are said to be *closed*.

A formal concept of a context $C = (G, M, I)$ is characterised by a pair (O, A), where $O \subseteq G$ and $A \subseteq M$. O is called the *extent* and represents the objects that share the attributes of A, i.e., $O = A'$. A is called the *intent* and represents the attributes that are shared by the objects of O, i.e., $A = O'$. Note that this implies that $O = O''$ and $A = A''$, i.e., the concept (O, A) is equivalently defined both by its set of objects, and by its set of attributes.

The set of all concepts that can be derived from a formal context form a lattice, relying on the *subconcept* relation (denoted by $\leq$). Indeed, we say that a concept (O_1, A_1) is a subconcept of another concept (O_2, A_2) – i.e., $(O_1, A_1) \leq (O_2, A_2)$ – if $O_1 \subseteq O_2$ and (equivalently) $A_2 \subseteq A_1$. This *concept lattice* has an upper-bound and a lower-bound (which are often the concept with an empty extent and the one with an empty intent respectively).

3. BUILDING A CONCEPT LATTICE TO IDENTIFY QUESTIONS IN A DATASET

Our goal here is to extract from a dataset, represented in RDF, a set of questions it can answer. We start by introducing simple notations for describing an RDF dataset. We illustrate these notations, as well as most of the other examples in the article, using the FOAF[7] profile of Tom Heath on the Knowledge Media Institute website (http://kmi.open.ac.uk/people/tom/rdf).

In such a dataset, we essentially focus on instances. Instances represent individual objects that are members of classes. For example, tom is an instance of the class Person. This is represented in RDF through the use of the property rdf:type, but we use here the simplified notation

Person(tom).[8] Instances such as tom can have properties linking them to other instances (e.g., to represent the fact that Tom knows Enrico Motta) or to literal values (e.g., to represent the fact that Tom's phone number is "+44-(0)1908-653565"). Such assertions are occurrences of binary relations, presented in our simplified notation as knows(tom, enrico-motta) and phone(tom, "+44-(0)1908-653565") respectively.

The classes such as Person and the properties such as knows come from the ontology(ies) used in the dataset, where they are part of a taxonomy: for example, Person can be a subclass of another class Agent and knows can be a subproperty of a property hasMet. We represent this with the notation Person ⊑ Agent and knows ⊑ hasMet respectively. Such taxonomic relationships can be either asserted in the dataset, or inferred from the definitions of the classes and properties.

3.1 Assumptions and Requirements

We focus here on questions for which the answers are sets of objects, such as *"Who does Tom know?"*. More precisely, we consider questions corresponding to queries to the dataset for which results are set of instances (e.g., all the people that Tom knows). A question itself is characterised by a set of properties that are common to the elements of the answer. In this sense, it can be related to a conjunctive query – e.g., *"Who knows Tom?"* corresponds to the query Person(?x) ∧ knows(?x, tom).

In addition, we assume that a significant question to a dataset should have more than one answer, as querying for the common characteristics of a unique object does not appear relevant. Also, questions complying with our requirements should be related with each other in a hierarchy. For example, it is natural to consider that *"What are the things that Tom knows?"* is more general than *"What are the people that Tom knows?"* (i.e., *"Who does Tom know?"*), or that *"Who has Tom met?"* is more general than *"Who does Tom know?"*. In other words, a question is more general than another if it includes its set of answers.

3.2 Building the Formal Context

The basic idea underlying the technique presented here is relatively straightforward: We want to build a concept lattice where each concept represents a question, with the extent being a set of instances from the dataset corresponding to answers, and the intent the common characteristics of these instances, forming the clauses of the question. We therefore need to build a formal context $C = (G, M, I)$ where G is the set of all instances of the dataset, and M corresponds to all the possible characteristics of these instances.

We consider three types of attributes that can be applied to an instance o of the dataset. Attributes of the form $Class::C$ appear if o is an instance of C (i.e., $C(o)$). Attributes of the form $p{:}m$ appear if o is related through the property p to the instance or the literal value m (i.e., $p(o, m)$). Attributes of the form $p{-}{:}m$ are used if the instance m is related to o through the property p (i.e., $p(m, o)$).

In order to extend this *explicit* set of attributes with inferred statements, we also generate additional attributes substituting the classes, properties, and individuals in existing ones with all the possible combinations of superclasses,

---

[6]To avoid ambiguities in this paper, we use the term *concept* to refer to the notion of formal concept in FCA, and the term *class* to refer to the corresponding entities in ontologies
[7]http://www.foaf-project.org/

[8]In this simplified notation, we use the local ID or label of an entity, instance, property or class, instead of its full URI.

superproperties and types that can be inferred. For example, we extend *Class::Person* and *knows:-Enrico-Motta* with inferred attributes of the form *Class::Agent*, *hasMet:-Enrico-Motta*, *knows:-Person* and *hasMet:-Person*.

Having built the set of all attributes for all the instances of the dataset, we can now build the matrix relating these attributes to these instances/objects, as a formal context for FCA.

3.3 Creating the Lattice and Eliminating Redundancies

One parameter of a concept lattice building tool is the minimum *support* for a concept to be included in the lattice, i.e., the minimum cardinality of its extent. In accordance with our assumptions and requirements (Section 3.1), we used 2 as minimum support.

An example lattice for the dataset `http://kmi.open.ac.uk/people/tom/rdf` is presented in Figure 1(a). Five concepts are present in the hierarchy, with the top one representing all the objects of the dataset and therefore, all the instances of the class `Thing`, the class of everything in OWL. It can also be noticed in this example that significant parts of the elements characterising some of the concepts are redundant and therefore not really useful. Indeed, having both the attributes *tom-:knows* and *Person-:knows*, or *Class::Thing* and *Class::Person* is not useful as one of the attributes can be inferred from the other. Checking such a relationship between attributes, we reduce the definition of the intents of concepts to keep only the non-redundant ones as shown in Figure 1(b).

3.4 Using the Concept Lattice as a Query Interface

As mentioned before, the basic idea of our approach is that each concept of the concept lattice represents a question, with its intent being the components of the question, and its extent the answers. The goal is to use this lattice as the basis for a navigational interface to query the underlying dataset. The first step is therefore to provide a simple representation for each concept/question, which would be reasonably readable by a human user. We derive such a representation from the (non redundant) intent of a concept as a 'question' in pseudo-natural language, following the template:

```
What are the (C₁,...,Cₙ) that (p₁ m₁,...pₘ mₘ)
         and that (n₁ q₁,...,nₜ qₜ)
```

where $\{C_1,...C_n\}$ are extracted from attributes of the form $Class::C_1,...,Class::C_n$, $\{p_1\ m_1,...p_m\ m_m\}$ are extracted from attributes of the form $\{p_1:-m_1,...p_m:-m_m\}$ and $\{n_1\ q_1,...,n_t\ q_t\}$ are extracted from attributes of the form $\{q_1:-n_1,...,q_t:-n_t\}$. We also adapt this general structure depending on whether or not one of the attribute sets is empty and the names of classes, properties and individuals are reduced to the local fragment of their URI, or to the label of the entity if available. For example, the concept at the bottom left of the lattice in Figure 1(b) is transformed into the question:

```
What are the (Person) that (tom knows)
```

Interpreting concepts as questions in this way means that the obtained lattice represents a complete hierarchy of questions that can be presented to the user as a query interface

to the considered dataset (see the example Figure 2 where the question *"What are the (Person)?"* has been selected, showing the sub-questions, the super-questions, alternative questions about Tom's projects and interests, as well as the answers to the selected question).

However, while on our toy example the results are simple and easy to navigate, on a bigger dataset, this process can result in thousands of questions being generated. In the next section, we therefore investigate measures that can be used to identify a set of questions more likely to be of interest to a user, as a way to generate a reasonable entry point into a large question hierarchy.

4. MEASURING THE RELEVANCE AND INTERESTINGNESS OF A QUESTION

In order to identify approaches to find a set of questions more likely to be of interest to a user, we take inspiration from the works prominent in two areas: ontology summarisation and concept lattice simplification.

4.1 Measures Inspired from Ontology Summarisation

In [12], we presented a work on extracting the key classes of a (possibly populated) ontology, based on a variety of different metrics taking into account in particular the "topology" of the ontology, its structure, and external elements such as the popularity of a concept. We look at three of these criteria which appear specially relevant:

Coverage. In ontology summarisation, this criterion intends to take into account the fact that a good summary should contain elements from all the significant parts of the ontology. This also appears important here, as we would expect any point of the lattice to be reachable from the identified questions, acting as entry points to the hierarchy. We define the set of questions reachable from another question using the notions of filter and ideal from FCA (or more generally, from lattice theory [1]). The ideal of a concept is the set of all its direct or indirect subconcepts, or in other terms, all the concepts linked through the transitive closure of the $\leq$ relation. Similarly, the filter of a concept corresponds to the set of concepts that are reachable through the superconcept relation. We define the coverage of a question in our question hierarchy as the union of the filter and ideal of the corresponding concept, and indicate that a set of questions covers the dataset when the union of the coverages of its elements correspond to the entire lattice.

Level. To extract key classes from an ontology, one of the ideas is that key classes are never too general or too specific, but can be found in the middle layer of the hierarchy. A similar idea can be applied here, as a we can expect very general or very specific questions not to be the most useful to the user. We use a measure of the level of the question/concept of the hierarchy as the distance between the question/concept and the root concept.

Density. In ontology summarisation, one of the assumptions is that the richer the representation of a class is (i.e., the denser it is in terms of the properties attached

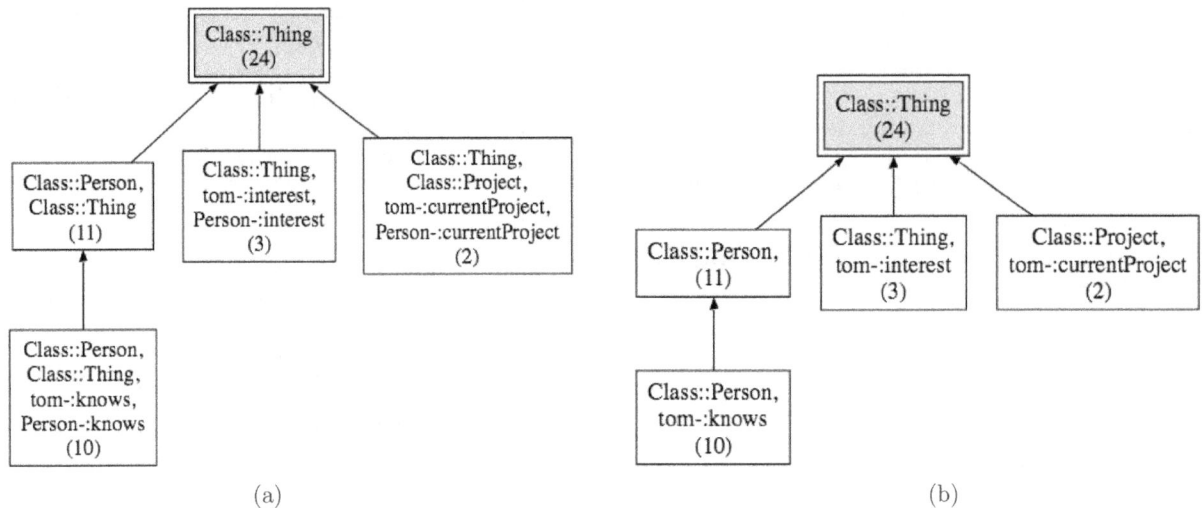

Figure 1: Concept lattice generated from http://kmi.open.ac.uk/people/tom/rdf (a); with redundancy eliminated (b). In both figures, the bottom concept of the lattice has been omitted.

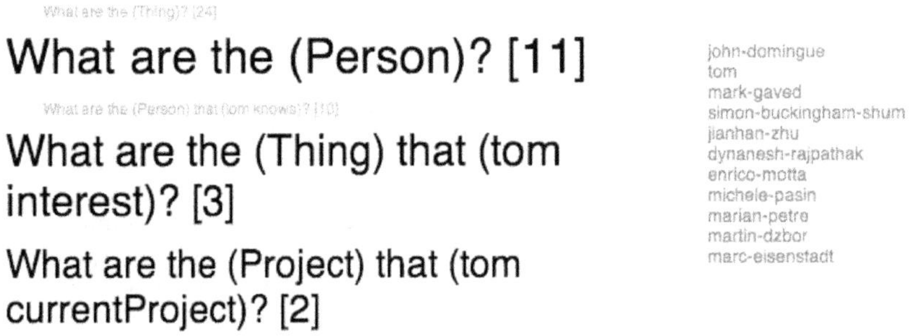

Figure 2: Simple example of the concept lattice-based interface to querying a dataset.

to it) the more likely it is to be important. Here, the situation is slightly different, as the related notion of density (i.e., the number of attributes in the intent of the concept) is closely related to the one of level (the more specific a concept is, the more likely it is to have a large number of attributes). Therefore, we cannot assume density to be used as criterion to maximise, but rather as a metric which should be not too high (useful questions are probably not the most complex ones), but also not too low (useful questions should be sufficiently well defined).

4.2 Measures Inspired from FCA

There are only a few metrics that have been devised in FCA to try to identify the most "interesting" concepts. The most common one is the support, but a notion of stability, applicable both to the intent and the extent of a concept, has been recently discussed as a way to reduce a concept lattice, providing a possible measure to be applied to our problem.

Support. As already mentioned, the support of a concept is the cardinality of its extent, i.e., the number of objects it represents (and so the number of answers to the

question). As noticed in [10] to motivate the stability measure, there are many scenarios where the most interesting concepts might not be the ones representing the largest number of objects. Here as well, an interesting question might be one with few answers, while questions with a large number of answers might be meaningless.

Intensional Stability. Intensional stability as described in [10] intends to define a stable concept as one whose *"intent does not depend much on each particular object of the extent"*. Given a concept (O, A) where O is the extent and A is the intent, the degree of intensional stability σ^i is defined by $\sigma^i(O, A) = \frac{|\{C \subseteq O | C' = A\}|}{2^{|A|}}$. However, as explained in [10], computing such a measure is complex. We therefore use an approximation, which corresponds to the ratio between the cardinality of the concept's extent and the one of the smallest of its direct super-concepts, i.e., $\sigma^i_{ap}(O, A) = \frac{|O|}{\min_{n \in N}(|n|)}$, where N is the set of extents of the direct superconcepts of (O, A) in the lattice.

Extensional Stability. In a similar way as for intensional stability, extensional stability can be defined at the level to which the extent of a concept depends on a particular attribute of the intent. It is defined as $\sigma^e(O, A) = \frac{|\{C \subseteq A | C' = O\}|}{2^{|O|}}$ and we use the following approximation: $\sigma^e_{ap}(O, A) = \frac{|A|}{\min_{b \in B}(|b|)}$ where B is the set of intents of the direct subconcepts of (O, A) in the lattice.

5. EXPERIMENT

While the previous section discusses measures that can be used to assess the potential "interestingness" of a question generated using our FCA-based method, we present here a user-based experiment to find out which of these measures are the most relevant and how to parametrize them. We asked 12 users with various degrees of familiarity with semantic technologies to inspect a reasonably large dataset and express up to 5 questions they believed to be interesting on this dataset.

5.1 Datasets

We used 4 different datasets as testbeds for our experiment. Three of them, called *geography*, *jobs* and *restaurants* were created by the University of Texas, Austin [14], and later transformed into OWL/RDF [7] for the purpose of evaluating a query answering system. The other one (*drama*) concerns modern productions of classical greek drama and was built locally for the needs of a project in the domain of Arts. Two of the evaluators for this dataset are actually domain experts involved with the data, with no background in semantic technologies. For each of the datasets, we constructed the concept lattice as explained earlier in this paper. Information about each dataset and the corresponding lattices is given in Table 1.

Table 1: Summary of the test datasets.

Dataset	Nb. Instances	Nb. Concepts
geography	715	842
jobs	4142	66284
restaurants	9746	6810
drama	19294	10083

5.2 Results

Out of the 44 valid questions we obtained,[9] we tested that 27 (61%) matched the format of questions produced by our method, and therefore corresponded to questions/concepts in the generated lattices. In the questions that could not be represented we found several reasons why they diverged from our model, which could be considered as possible extensions in the future, including for example the use of disjunctive clauses (e.g., *"Which Greek plays have been performed in Kenneth McLeish's translations or versions?"*) or of numerical manipulations/tests on values (e.g., *"What are the restaurants that have ratings higher than 2.5?"*).

The resulting set of user-generated questions represent a useful sample to analyse the range of values taken by the different measures to be considered. Coverage is not evaluated

---

[9]Some of the questions given by users could not be answered by a set of instances in the considered dataset. There was no overlap between the questions proposed by different users.

here as it cannot be assessed at the level of an individual question. Since our goal is to obtain a set of questions as an entry points to the hierarchy, we consider coverage as a fundamental criterion to be enforced while generating the initial question set.

Level. Amongst all the valid and representable questions given by evaluators, the average level of a question in its lattice is 4.46. This is slightly higher than the average level of all the concepts in the lattices and it is also worth mentioning that none of the questions were at a level lower than 3 or higher than 7. This validates our hypothesis that questions of interest are generally not the most general, or the most specific, but are located within a small range around the "centre" of the lattice, which corresponds to the average level. We therefore define a normalised metric m_l for a concept of our question hierarchy which is computed as the distance between the concept's level and the average level in the lattice.

Density. In the case of the density measure, our initial hypothesis was also verified that interesting questions tend to be defined simply, but with sufficient elements to represent a distinct set of answers. Indeed the average density of the valid, representable questions is 2.14, and the measure is always included in the range [1..3] (most of the questions being of density 2, such as *"What are the restaurants in San Francisco?"*). We can argue that there is a strong relationship between the level of a concept and the density of the question. However, this highly depends on the structure of the original dataset, as for example, *"What are the restaurants in a city?"* is more general than the previous question, while also being of density 2. We therefore define the normalised metric m_d based on the difference between the density of a given concept and 2, which seems to be the "standard" for simple, but sufficiently defined questions.

Support. Depending on the dataset, the support of the provided questions can vary a lot. For example, questions in the *jobs* dataset tend to have a lot of answers (up top 3402), while in the *drama* dataset, they are generally smaller (from 2 to 38).

Intensional Stability. The expectation related to intensional stability is that the more stable a concept is, the more it is supposed to represent a significant and distinct set of individuals. However from our experiment, there does not seem to be any correlation between a question being identified by evaluators as interesting, and its intensional stability. Values can vary from very low (0.0008) to high (0.82) even for questions provided by a single user, regarding a single dataset.

Extensional Stability. Surprisingly, contrary to intensional stability, the values of extensional stability appear very stable, especially within one dataset, and always high (between 0.75 and 1.0), in particular if compared with the average in the dataset (around 0.4 for all of them). Indeed, it appears that the definition of the question as being a significant subset of the elements of more specific questions is an important criterion to identify interesting questions.

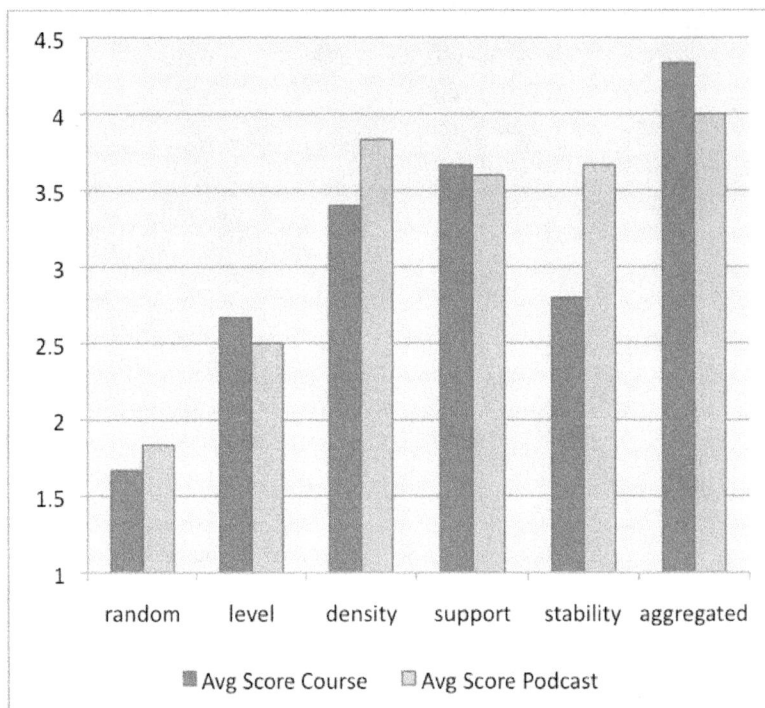

Figure 3: Average scores for the six tested measures on the *Course* and *Podcast* datasets.

Considering the results discussed above, we define an aggregated metric to rank questions in a question hierarchy as the linear combination of the 3 metrics m_l, m_d and σ_{ap}^e on concepts:

$$m(O, A) = w_1.m_l(O, A) + w_2.m_d(O, A) + w_3.\sigma_{ap}^e(O, A)$$

What constitutes an interesting question to a dataset is very dependent on the user and the context in which the answer would be used, but based on the results obtained above, we expect such a metric to be adequate in supporting the identification of reasonable entry points to the question hierarchy.

6. IMPLEMENTATION AND VALIDATION

The overall method presented here can be divided in two separate processes: 1- the creation of the non-redundant hierarchy of question, and 2- the generation of the user interface based on this hierarchy and using the metric defined above. For the first process, we developed a program that generates a formal context in the input format of the lattice generation tool from a SPARQL endpoint, according to the method described in Section 3.2. We use the OWLIM triple store,[10] which partially supports OWL/RDF inferences. We use the implementation of the CHARM algorithm provided by the CORON tool [8] to generate the concept lattice.

We devised a simple algorithm in order to identify in the generated lattice a set of questions that both rank high according to a chosen metric[11] and which, all together, maximally cover the lattice (by choosing questions which are

---

[10]http://www.ontotext.com/owlim/
[11]A special case is considered for the support measure regarding the top – i.e., the root – of the hierarchy. It is indeed always the concept with the highest support, and is therefore excluded from the ranking.

not in the same branch as an already chosen question). In order to validate the choice of the aggregated measure defined above, we tested it together with 5 other measures in 2 different datasets. We used as datasets the collection of 614 course descriptions and 1706 video podcasts from http://data.open.ac.uk. We generated the list of entry questions for each of these datasets using each of the following metrics: a random metric, m_l (level) alone, m_d (density) alone, support, σ_{ap}^e (stability) alone and the aggregated measure of level, density and stability, using a naive distribution of weights (i.e., $w_1 = w_2 = w_3 = \frac{1}{3}$). We then asked six different users to give a score between 1 and 5 to each of the sets of questions (presented in a random order), 5 corresponding to the highest level of interest.

The results are presented in Figure 3. As can be seen, the aggregated measure appears to provide significantly better results than all of the other measures on both datasets, especially compared to the random measure. As expected, the level, density and stability of questions all contribute to identifying interesting questions (to different extents), but are more appropriate when used in combination. More surprisingly, the support (i.e., number of answers) provide better results than could have been expected from our experiment. A possible explanation is that, in datasets where objects are described homogeneously (i.e., they all have more or less the same structure), support is highly correlated with the measures related to the question's level and density.

The application of the querying interface has already been shown in Figure 2 on our toy example. Figure 4 gives another example, based on the *restaurant* dataset. It is generated from the concept lattice using as initial questions the set computed using the aggregated measure. The value of this measure is represented in the interface by the font size

What are the (Restaurant)? [9549]

What are the (Restaurant) that (ratingString good)? [2761]

What are the (Restaurant) that (ratingString good,isInCity City)? [2759]
What are the (Restaurant) that (foodType indian,ratingString good)? [61]
What are the (Restaurant) that (rating 3.6,ratingString good)? [84]

What are the (Thing) that (isIn Region)? [187]

What are the (Thing) that (City isIn)? [29]

What are the (Restaurant) that (isInCity City)? [9547]

What are the (Restaurant) that (foodType indian)? [104]

What are the (Thing) that (label el sobrante)? [3]

What are the (Thing) that (label monterey)? [2]

ID_theAcornRestaurant6437
ID_durantGardenRestaurantClassical1612
ID_tonySSeafoodRestaurant5599
ID_springGardenChineseRestaura6466
ID_thaiGardenRestaurant1908
ID_mainStCoffeeRoasting8201
ID_prima4773
ID_paloAltoCoffeeRoastingCo2795
ID_yuenYung3294
ID_villaCoffeeShop4698
ID_warehouseCafe3897
ID_specialtySCafeAndBakery9428
ID_pizzaRustaciCafeLtd7258
ID_tora-YaRestaurant1630
ID_rosita1468
ID_buckeyeRoadhouse4338
ID_beppo5555
ID_amiciSEastCoastPizzeria1910
ID_tajMahalIndianCuisine1750
ID_sushiMainStreet5114
ID_originalJoeSNo2Restaurant5725
ID_doubleRainbowGourmetIceCream1744
ID_leftAtAlbuquerque7968
ID_apolloPizza2497
ID_emeraldGardenRestaurant4290
ID_jackSSteakhouse7951
ID_villaRomanoRestaurant1565
ID_mediterraneanCafe2751
ID_guadalajarasSuperBurrito5299
ID_okawa669
ID_kitahama9021

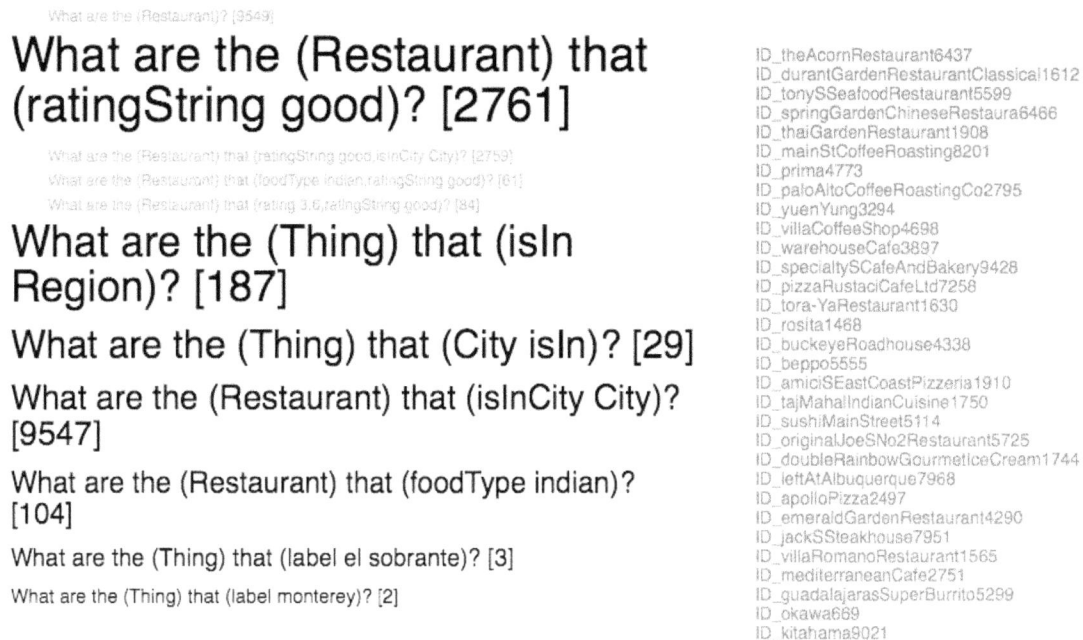

Figure 4: Example of application of the lattice-based query interface on the *restaurant* dataset.

used for the question. The first question is also attached to the questions directly more general and directly more specific. Any question displayed can be selected, and will then be re-displayed at the top of the list, with more general and more specific questions, as well as the set of its answers (for example, in Figure 4, the question *"What are the (Restaurant) that (ratingString good)"* has been selected).

7. RELATED WORK

As discussed previously, our approach relates to ontology summarisation, where an abstract summary of a supposedly complex ontology is being produced, for example in the form of a set of important concepts [12]. In [16], the authors propose a technique to extract a sub-graph of an RDF graph to act as a summary. Similar ideas have also been recently applied to large RDF datasets, including for example the ExpLOD tool [9] which produces a visual representation of a dataset, clustering (and therefore abstracting) elements together to produce an overview graph of the dataset. As can be seen from these initial works, the idea of summarising datasets and ontologies is only starting to gain attention. While providing example queries is generally seen as an efficient way for somebody to quickly understand a dataset or an ontology,[12] to the best of our knowledge, there have not been any attempt before at summarising a dataset by providing sets of automatically extracted questions.

FCA, and especially concept lattices, have been used in several approaches to support the task of browsing structured datasets. For example, in the context of image search, [3] makes use of several lattices, representing different aspects of images (shape, luminance and "semantic content", with the "semantic content" aspect being based on an ontology). In

this case, the lattices act as support for browsing the results of a search. In [4], the author develops a similar idea, using a concept lattice built from the metadata attached to documents, but makes use of *logical concept analysis*, a variant of FCA where the attributes are logical properties, partially ordered by a relation of subsumption. Other works have been devised that generate views on populated ontologies, which correspond to formal concepts that can be visualised as concept lattices, and be defined by users [13]. A significant difference between these approaches and ours is that we focus on providing an overview of a dataset using the set of questions it can answer, and a navigation mechanism allowing to browse these questions, rather than the data itself. Closer to our work in that sense is the recent paper [5]. Indeed, in this work, the author relies on the principles of FCA to provide a navigation mechanism based on queries to the underlying dataset. While here, we focus on providing a navigation interface to the data (through the questions), targeting users unfamiliar with both the data and the underlying technologies, [5] concentrate on obtaining queries exploiting the high expressivity of the underlying language (close to the SPARQL language). Our approach also includes, as a core mechanism, the ability to identify sets of questions more likely to provide useful entry points to the dataset.

8. CONCLUSION

In this paper, we have presented an approach to generate a hierarchy of questions that could be asked to a dataset using formal concept analysis, and to derive a navigational query interface to this dataset based on this hierarchy. This approach relies on constructing a concept lattice from the description of the instances of the dataset, creating groups (concepts) of instances having common properties. However, for a large dataset, the number of these concepts (and

---

[12]The system SchemaPedia (http://schemapedia.com/) for example gives manually created example queries for the ontologies it collects.

so of the corresponding questions) can be very large. We also study the measures providing indications of the potential interest and relevance of an extracted question. Our experiment shows that the identified measures provide a good base to select a set of reasonably interesting questions to act as an entry point into the dataset.

One of the most obvious drawbacks of the approach presented here is the complexity of the methods deployed, especially ontological reasoning and concept lattice generation. Since these complex methods only need to be used once per dataset, in an offline process, the few minutes they take on our test datasets cannot be considered a strong limitation. However, some level of approximation and optimisation will have to be applied to use our tools on significantly larger datasets, containing several millions of statements.

There are many extensions that can be considered to the presented approach. Indeed, our experiment also identified some of the most common limitations of our model in terms of the expressiveness of the considered questions. Some of these elements, such as the possibility to add tests on numerical values, could be added to the model. They would however increase significantly the size of the lattice, and therefore the overall complexity of the approach.

Also, while the approach has been shown to provide promising results on self-contained datasets, an interesting future work would be to take into account elements derived from links to external datasets, making it possible to explore the questions that can be answered from integrating multiple sources of data.

Acknowledgment

The authors would like to thank Amedeo Napoli, Mehdi Kaytoue-Uberall and Laszlo Szathmary for their help with the use of the CORON system and for the pointers to elements of formal concept analysis. We also thank Vanessa Lopez for telling us about some of the datasets included in our experiments, as well as all the evaluators who responded to our questionnaire.

9. REFERENCES

[1] G. Birkhoff. *Lattice Theory, 3rd ed.* Providence, RI: Amer. Math. Soc., 1967.

[2] C. Bizer, T. Heath, and T. Berners-Lee. Linked data – the story so far. *International Journal on Semantic Web and Information Systems*, 5(3):1–22, 2009.

[3] J. Ducrou, P. Eklund, and T. Wilson. An intelligent user interface for browsing and searching MPEG-7 images using concept lattices. In S. Yahia, E. Nguifo, and R. Belohlavek, editors, *Concept Lattices and Their Applications*, volume 4923 of *Lecture Notes in Computer Science*, pages 1–21. Springer Berlin / Heidelberg, 2008.

[4] S. Ferre. Camelis: a logical information system to organize and browse a collection of documents. *Int. J. General Systems*, (38), 2009.

[5] S. Ferre. Conceptual navigation in RDF graphs with SPARQL-like queries. In L. Kwuida and B. Sertkaya, editors, *Formal Concept Analysis*, volume 5986 of *Lecture Notes in Computer Science*, pages 193–208. Springer Berlin / Heidelberg, 2010.

[6] B. Ganter and R. Wille. *Formal Concept Analysis: Mathematical Foundations.* Springer, 1999.

[7] E. Kaufmann. Talking to the semantic web - natural language query interfaces for casual end-users. PhD thesis. University of Zurich, Switzerland, 2009.

[8] M. Kaytoue, F. Marcuola, A. Napoli, L. Szathmary, and J. Villerd. The Coron System. In *8th International Conference on Formal Concept Analsis (ICFCA) - Supplementary Proceedings*, 2010.

[9] S. Khatchadourian and M. P. Consens. Exploring RDF usage and interlinking in the linked open data cloud using ExpLOD. In *Linked Data On the Web workshop, LDOW*, 2010.

[10] S. Kuznetsov, S. Obiedkov, and C. Roth. Reducing the representation complexity of lattice-based taxonomies. In *Conceptual Structures: Knowledge Architectures for Smart Applications. 5th International Conference on Conceptual Structures, ICCS*, 2007.

[11] N. Noy and D. L. McGuinness. Ontology Development 101: A Guide to Creating Your First Ontology. Stanford Knowledge Systems Laboratory Technical Report KSL-01-05 and Stanford Medical Informatics Technical Report SMI-2001-0880.

[12] S. Peroni, E. Motta, and M. d'Aquin. Identifying key concepts in an ontology through the integration of cognitive principles with statistical and topological measures. In *Third Asian Semantic Web Conference*, 2009.

[13] J. Tane, P. Cimiano, and P. Hitzler. Query-based multicontexts for knowledge base browsing: An evaluation. In *Conceptual Structures: Inspiration and Application*, volume 4068 of *Lecture Notes in Computer Science*, pages 413–426. Springer Berlin / Heidelberg, 2006.

[14] L. R. Tang and R. J. Mooney. Using multiple clause constructors in inductive logic programming for semantic parsing. In *12th European Conference on Machine Learning, ECML*, 2001.

[15] R. Wille. Concept lattices and conceptual knowledge systems. *Computers & Mathematics with Applications*, 23, 1992.

[16] X. Zhang, G. Cheng, and Y. Qu. Ontology summarization based on rdf sentence graph. In *World Wide Web Conference*, 2007.

Interpreting Relational Databases in the RDF Domain *

Alexandre Bertails
World Wide Web
Consortium/MIT
32 Vassar Street
Cambridge, MA 02140
bertails@w3.org

Eric Prud'hommeaux
World Wide Web
Consortium/MIT
32 Vassar Street
Cambridge, MA 02140
eric@w3.org

ABSTRACT

The W3C's "Direct Mapping of Relational Data to RDF" defines a simple, practical and intuitive interpretation of SQL database tables as RDF graphs. This document specifies the formal data models for RDB (Relational DataBase) and RDF and defines a denotational semantics of RDB in the RDF domain. We show how this mapping treats all of the important features of SQL tables, like cardinality and NULLs, and yields an RDF graph which preserves the relational information.

Categories and Subject Descriptors

H.2.4 [**Systems**]: Relational databases; D.3.1 [**Formal Definitions and Theory**]: Semantics

General Terms

Algorithms, Performance, Standardization, Theory

Keywords

RDF, Semantic Web, relational database, SQL, denotational semantics

1. INTRODUCTION

Motivations to map relational data to RDF abound[20]: science, technology and business need to integrate more and more diverse data sources; the far majority of data that we expect machines to interpret are in relational databases[16]. As RDF, this data can interact with the large amounts of interesting (e.g. scientific) data already mechanically transformed by the Linked Data [17][8] community; etc. RDF's web foundations and distributed extensibility model offer the database community a simple and effective mechanism to contribute to a growing continuum of information.

---

*This document was created as input to the *W3C RDB2RDF Working Group* at `http://www.w3.org/2001/sw/rdb2rdf/`

The semantics of a query over an RDF graph are specified directly in the SPARQL Specification [21], while the semantics for SQL data are expressed with respect to queries and constraints in SQL specifications [4]. The W3C RDB2RDF Working Group has begun work on a *Direct Mapping* [5], a normative representation of SQL data as RDF graphs. The product of mapping a given database is called the *Direct Graph* for that database. This document provides a formal representation of the Direct Mapping as an RDF semantics, describes the features and motivations of the design choices and illustrates practical and theoretic applications.

Defining a simple mapping from SQL databases to RDF graphs effectively expresses that data in the Semantic Web, where it can be used in several ways: it can be queried directly using SPARQL, it can be suplemented with schema information (e.g. RDFS, OWL, SKOS) and used for A-box inference, it can be transformed via e.g. SPARQL CONSTRUCT, N3 rules, RIF to graphs which represent the domain information in popular schema, and perhaps most importantly, it can provide the necessary definition to map SPARQL queries to SQL queries, eliminating the latency costs of warehousing. All of these uses require no further definition or standardization as the dependent languages (SPARQL, OWL, etc.) are fully defined with respect to input RDF graphs.

2. OVERVIEW

While we frequently refer to "relational" data, the far majority of that data is defined and accessed via the *Structured Query Language* [4]; this motivated the RDB2RDF WG to define the Direct Graph for SQL Base Tables and Views.

Consider an example contact database:

People		
ID	fname	addr
7	Bob	18
8	Sue	NULL

Addrs		
ID	city	state
18	Cambridge	MA

with a foreign key from `People.addr` to `Addrs.ID` .

Empirically, we see a database as a set of *tables* in a given *schema*. The schema for each table defines a set of *columns* (attributes), each of some datatype. The *foreign key*s link lists of columns in a table to another list of columns in a table, creating a relational graph.

The Direct Mapping for each row in the database produces a set of RDF triples with a shared subject – the row identifier – and with predicates and objects conveying both the database values:

```
<People/ID=7> <People#ID> 7 .
<People/ID=7> <People#fname> "Bob" .
<People/ID=8> <People#ID> 8 .
<People/ID=8> <People#fname> "Sue" .
<Addrs/ID=18> <Addrs#ID> 18 .
<Addrs/ID=18> <Addrs#city> "Cambridge" .
<Addrs/ID=18> <Addrs#state> "MA" .
```

and the relational graph:

```
<People/ID=7> <People#addr> <Addrs/ID=18> .
```

In order to accurately model the SQL table input, we examine the SQL Framework specification [3] §4.3 Tables ¶1:

```
A table has an ordered collection of one or
more columns and an unordered collection of
zero or more rows. Each column has a name
and a data type. Each row has, for each
column, exactly one value in the data type
of that column.
```

Combining this with the popular Relational Model [12][2], we see a natural model for a table as a Header holding the column names and datatypes and a body of tuples with values for those columns:

$$
\begin{aligned}
Table &::= (Header, List(CandidateKey), \\
& \quad Set(ForeignKey), Body) \\
Header &::= List((ColumnName, Datatype)) \\
Body &::= MultiSet(Row) \\
Row &::= List(CellValue)
\end{aligned}
$$

However, the Direct Mapping defines a mapping only for base tables and views, as defined in ¶7:

```
No two columns of a base table or a viewed
table can have the same name. Derived tables,
other than viewed tables, may contain more
than one column with the same name.
```

which means that column names are unique, which gives us partial functions from ColumnName to Datatype and from ColumnName to CellValue:

$$
\begin{aligned}
header &: ColumnName \rightarrow Datatype \\
row &: ColumnName \rightarrow CellValue
\end{aligned}
$$

The relational model's notion of a candidate key is called a unique in SQL, defined in §4.6.6.3 Table constraints:

```
A unique constraint specifies one or more
columns of the table as unique columns. A
unique constraint is satisfied if and only
if no two rows in a table have the same
non-null values in the unique columns.
```

Null values may appear in a candidate key so long as that set of column values is still unique between tuples. A primary key however, may have no NULLs, so the tuple nodes in the Direct Mapping will never need to encode a NULL value. Note that the mapping from candidate key values to tuple nodes may include NULL values.

The row identifier for tuples in tables with no primary key is a blank node assigned to that tuple. If the relational graph may include references to such tuples, it will be via some (non-primary) candidate key on the table. In this example, the Protein database, both the uniprot and ebi columns form unique keys, but neither is elevated to primary key:

Protein		
uniprot	ebi	name
P04637	366083	P53
Q00987	389668	MDM2
EBIact		
target	actor	action
366083	389668	antagonist

The list of EBI's cataloged interactions, EBIact, happens to use EBI's protein identifiers. The EBIact target and actor columns are foreign keys to Proteins.ebi, and the primary key of EBIact is (target and actor). Because these columns reference to tuples in a table with no primary key, they must use for an object the same blank node used as the row identifier for the referenced tuple.

```
_:a <Protein#uniprot> "P04637" .
_:a <Protein#ebi> 366083 .
_:a <Protein#name> "P53" .
_:b <Protein#uniprot> "Q00987" .
_:b <Protein#ebi> 389668 .
_:b <Protein#name> "MDM2" .
<EBIact/target=366083,actor=389668>
            <EBIact#target> _:a .
<EBIact/target=366083,actor=389668>
            <EBIact#actor> _:b .
<EBIact/target=366083,actor=389668>
            <EBIact#action> "antagonist" .
```

Tables with no candidate keys at all may have duplicates, but then SQL can't express foreign keys to them. Thus, we see that the SQL data is a graph and not a multi-graph (which would be awkward to map to an RDF graph).

There is some controversy within the RDB2RDF Working Group over whether the Direct Mapping should include special handling for link tables (AKA many-to-many tables). Rows in tables with exactly two foreign keys which subsume all of the attributes in the table can be represented as triples with the subject being the target of the first foreign key and the object being the target of the second. While this is an arguably more intuitive expression of the domain data frequently encoded in link tables, the rule itself is necessarily brittle with respect to monotonic changes to the schema. For instance, the addition of a timestamp attribute, which implies no changes to the domain interpretation of any row, would radically change the RDF representation, breaking any queries or rules referencing link table properties.

3. ABSTRACT DATA MODELS

The RDB and RDF *Abstract Data Types* (ADTs) make use of the commonly defined ADTs *Set*, *List* and *MultiSet*, used here as type constructors. For example, *Set(A)* denotes the type for the sets of elements of type A. We assume that they come with their common operations, such as the function $size : Set \to Int$.

We follow a type-as-specification approach, thus the ADTs are actually dependent types. For example, $\{s : Set(A) \,|\, size(s) \leq 1\}$ is a subtype of $Set(A)$ with at most one element, often called the option type.

3.1 RDB Abstract Data Type

$$
\begin{aligned}
Database &::= Set(Table) \\
Table &::= (TableName, Header, List(CandidateKey), \\
&\qquad Set(ForeignKey), Body) \\
Header &::= Set((ColumnName, Datatype)) \\
Body &::= MultiSet(Row) \\
Row &::= Set((ColumnName, CellValue)) \\
CellValue &::= LexicalValue \,|\, NULL \\
ForeignKey &::= (List(ColumnName), Table, CandidateKey) \\
CandidateKey &::= List(ColumnName) \\
Datatype &::= Int \,|\, Float \,|\, Date \,|\, \dots \\
TableName &::= String \\
ColumnName &::= String
\end{aligned}
$$

3.2 RDB accessor functions

$$
\begin{aligned}
tablename &: Table \to TableName \\
header &: Table \to Header \\
candidateKeys &: Table \to List(CandidateKey) \\
primaryKey &: Table \to \{s : Set(CandidateKey) \,|\, size(s) \leq 1\} \\
foreignKeys &: Table \to Set(ForeignKey) \\
unary &: ForeignKey \to Boolean \\
lexicals &: Table \to Set(\{c : ColumnName \,|\, !\, unary(c)\}) \\
body &: Table \to Body \\
datatype &: \{h : Header\} \\
&\quad \to \{c : ColumnName \,|\, \exists\, d, (c,d) \in h\} \\
&\quad \to \{d : Datatype \,|\, (c,d) \in h\} \\
table &: \{r : Row\} \to \{t : Table \,|\, r \in t\} \\
value &: \{r : Row\} \to \{c : ColumnName \,|\, c \in r\} \\
&\quad \to CellValue \\
dereference &: \{r : Row\} \\
&\quad \to \{fk : ForeignKey \\
&\qquad\quad |\, fk \in foreignKeys(table(r))\} \\
&\quad \to \{targetRow : Row \\
&\qquad\quad |\, P(r, fk, targetRow)\}
\end{aligned}
$$

In $dereference$, P is a predicate binding the row r to the row $targetRow$, referenced by the foreign key fk. The values for the foreign key columns in r equal the values of the referenced columns in the returned row:

$$
\begin{aligned}
&P(r, fk, targetRow) = \\
&\textbf{let } (columnNames, targetTable, ck) = fk \textbf{ in} \\
&targetRow \in body(targetTable) \\
&\textbf{and } \forall c_i^{fk} \in columnNames, \forall c_j^{ck} \in ck, \\
&\quad \forall (c_k^r, v_k^r) \in r, \forall (c_l^{target}, v_l^{target}) \in targetRow, \\
&\quad i = j \to c_i^{fk} = c_k^r \to c_j^{ck} = c_l^{target} \to v_k^r = v_l^{target}
\end{aligned}
$$

3.3 RDF Abstract Data Type

$$
\begin{aligned}
Graph &::= Set(Triple) \\
Triple &::= (Subject, Predicate, Object) \\
Subject &::= IRI \,|\, BlankNode \\
Predicate &::= IRI \\
Object &::= IRI \,|\, BlankNode \,|\, Literal \\
BlankNode &::= RDF\ blank\ node \\
Literal &::= PlainLiteral \,|\, TypedLiteral \\
PlainLiteral &::= lexicalForm \\
&\quad |\, (lexicalForm, langageTag) \\
TypedLiteral &::= (lexicalForm, IRI) \\
IRI &::= RDF\ URI\ [1]\ [18] \\
lexicalForm &::= Unicode\ string\ [2]\ [18]
\end{aligned}
$$

We don't need to provide accessors as we are simply constructing RDF graphs and their components. In order to stay simple, we'll use a Turtle [7] like syntax for injecting elements in these types.

So armed, we set forth to define the Direct Mapping.

4. DIRECT MAPPING

Inhabitants of RDB 3.1 *are denoted* by mathematical objects living in the RDF domain 3.1. We call this *denotational semantics* of RDB the *Direct Mapping*.

Most of the functions are higher-order functions, relying on a function ϕ mapping a row to an RDF node. We assume that this function maps any Tuple to a unique row IRI. ϕ is formally defined by the following axioms:

$$
\forall\, db : Database, \forall\, r : Row, \tag{1}
$$
$$
r \in db \to primaryKey(table(r)) \neq \emptyset \to \phi(r) \textbf{ is an } IRI
$$
$$
\forall\, db : Database, \forall\, r : Row, \tag{2}
$$
$$
r \in db \to primaryKey(table(r)) = \emptyset \to \phi(r) \textbf{ is a } BlankNode
$$

4.1 Denotational semantics

The Direct Mapping is defined by induction on the structure of RDB. Thus it is defined for *any SQL database* and its execution is guarantied to terminate.

The entry point is $[\![\ ]\!]_{database}^{\phi}$. Note that not all the functions need to be parameterized by ϕ.

---

[1] subsequently restricted by SPARQL to exclude space (#x20)

[2] http://www.w3.org/TR/2004/REC-rdf-concepts-20040210/

$$\llbracket \; \rrbracket^{\phi}_{database} \; : \; Database \rightarrow Graph$$

$$\llbracket db \rrbracket^{\phi}_{database} \; = \; \{triple \mid triple \in \llbracket t \rrbracket^{\phi}_{table} \mid t \in db\}$$

$$\llbracket \; \rrbracket^{\phi}_{table} \; : \; Table \rightarrow Set(Triple)$$

$$\llbracket t \rrbracket^{\phi}_{table} \; = \; \{triple \mid triple \in \llbracket r \rrbracket^{\phi}_{row} \mid r \in body(t)\}$$

$$\llbracket \; \rrbracket^{\phi}_{row} \; : \; Row \rightarrow Set(Triple)$$

$$\llbracket r \rrbracket^{\phi}_{row} \; = \; \textbf{let } s = \phi(r) \textbf{ in}$$
$$\{(s,p,o) \mid (p,o) \in \llbracket r, fk \rrbracket^{\phi}_{ref}$$
$$\mid noNulls(r,fk)$$
$$\mid fk \in references(t)\}$$
$$\cup \;\; \{(s,p,o) \mid (p,o) \in \llbracket r, c \rrbracket_{lex}$$
$$\mid value(r,c) \neq NULL \mid c \in lexicals(t)\}$$
$$\cup \;\; \{(s, rdf{:}type, ue(tablename(table(r))))\}$$

$$\llbracket \; , \; \rrbracket^{\phi}_{ref} \; : \; (Row, ForeignKey) \rightarrow (Predicate, Object)$$

$$\llbracket r, fk \rrbracket^{\phi}_{ref} \; = \; \textbf{let } p = \llbracket table(r), fk \rrbracket_{col} \textbf{ in}$$
$$\textbf{let } targetRow = dereference(r, fk) \textbf{ in}$$
$$\textbf{let } o = \phi(targetRow) \textbf{ in}$$
$$(p, o)$$

$$\llbracket \; , \; \rrbracket_{lex} \; : \; (Row, Column) \rightarrow$$
$$\rightarrow \{s : Set((Predicate, Object)) \mid size(s) \leq 1\}$$

$$\llbracket r, c \rrbracket_{lex} \; = \; \textbf{let } p = \llbracket table(r), c \rrbracket_{col} \textbf{ in}$$
$$\textbf{let } v = value(r, c) \textbf{ in}$$
$$\textbf{let } d = datatype(header(table(r))(c)) \textbf{ in}$$
$$\textbf{if } v \textbf{ is } NULL \textbf{ then } \emptyset$$
$$\textbf{else if } d \textbf{ is } String \textbf{ then } \{(p, v)\}$$
$$\textbf{else let } datatype\_iri = \llbracket d \rrbracket_{datatype} \textbf{ in}$$
$$\{(p, (v, datatype\_iri))\}$$

$$\llbracket \; , \; \rrbracket_{col} \; : \; (Row, List(Column)) \rightarrow IRI$$

$$\llbracket r, c* \rrbracket_{col} \; = \; ue(tablename(table(r))) + `\#` + ue(c_0)$$
$$`,` + \cdots + `,` + ue(c_{n-1})$$

$$\llbracket \; \rrbracket_{datatype} \; : \; Datatype \rightarrow IRI$$

$$\llbracket d \rrbracket_{datatype} \; = \; \textbf{if } d \textbf{ is } Int \textbf{ then } xsd{:}integer$$
$$\textbf{else if } d \textbf{ is } Float \textbf{ then } xsd{:}float$$
$$\textbf{else if } d \textbf{ is } Date \textbf{ then } xsd{:}date$$
$$\cdots$$

$$ue \; : \; String \rightarrow String$$

$$ue(s) \; = \; \texttt{URL-encoding } of \; s \; per \; [22]$$

$$noNulls \; : \; Row \rightarrow ForeignKey \rightarrow Boolean$$

$$noNulls(r, fk) \; = \; \textbf{let } (columnNames, \_, \_) = fk \textbf{ in}$$
$$\forall c \in columnNames, value(r, c) \neq NULL$$

Note that strict URL-encoding is not necessary. It is sufficient to encode the potential border characters [/,=#].

5. HONORING SQL SEMANTICS

The Direct Mapping attempts to emulate the utility of the source database. The most direct way to measure this is to compare the data one could extract with SQL queries over the relational data vs. SPARQL queries over the direct graph.

5.1 Row identifier

Another design goal is that the direct graph be compatible with the principles of Linked Data[9]. In particular, row identifiers for addressable rows are IRIs, e.g. `<EBIact/target=366083,actor=389668>`, while row identifiers for which the database offers no repeatable access are blank nodes, e.g. `_:b`.

5.2 Foreign Keys

As stated in 2, *foreign keys* create a relational graph. The Direct Mapping encodes this graph as *reference* triples, where the predicate name is a product of the table name and the column names forming the foreign key. A peculiar wrinkle of this is that the predicate name for unary foreign keys (foreign keys composed of only one column) would conflict with the name of the *scalar* triple for that column. In the case of unary foreign keys, the *scalar* triple is not formed. As an example, the unary foreign key from *People.addr* to *Addrs.ID* produced a triple:

`<People/ID=7> <People#addr> <Addrs/ID=18>`

but no triple:

`<People/ID=7> <People#addr> 18`

Reference triples are not generated for foreign keys on rows with any *NULLs* for the attributes in the foreign key. This reflects the SQL behavior for the common idiom for enforcing foreign key constraints in SQL queries. In SQL, $NULL = NULL$ is not true so a constraint testing the attributes in an n-ary foreign key from referrer s to referent t, $s.attr_0 = t.attr_0 \; AND \; ... \; s.attr_i = t.attr_i$ will fail if any of the values are $NULL$. This behavior is modeled by the $noNulls$ constraint on *references* in $\llbracket \; \rrbracket^{\phi}_{row}$.

5.3 Cardinality

SQL allows a table to contain multiple rows with exactly the same column values. In fact, this is a frequent outcome of projecting away columns which keep rows distinct, which can happen in a defined view. SQL maintains a strict accounting for these rows, preserving their cardinality in both query results and aggregate functions.

Recall that for tables with no primary key, the Direct Mapping assigns each row a blank node. Any indistinct rows in the table become distinct subjects for a set of triples. Thus, SPARQL queries over the direct graph will carry the same cardinality as would SQL queries over the source table.

5.4 NULL attributes

RDF itself has no real model for absent information; a lack of domain information generally translates to a lack of assertions. When some, but not all, information is known about a record in an SQL database, the tabular nature requires an encoding for absent information. The popular convention is to use the `NULL` value for this. The Direct Mapping addresses this case by creating *scalar* triples only for non-null cell values, and creating *reference* triples only when the referenced tuple exists. Recall in the first table that *Sue* had a NULL *addr*; which corresponded to no record in the *Addrs* table. Consequentially, the direct graph for this table had no arc of the form:

`<People/ID=8> <People#addr> <Addrs/ID=??>`

6. "RULE" TRANSFORMATIONS

The schema and node labels of the direct graph are entirely subordinate to the relational schema and data. This is counter to the Semantic Web practice of sharing schemas and identifiers where possible. A variety of standards, e.g. RIF and SPARQL CONSTRUCT, define functions mapping one RDF graph to another. Given our earlier direct graph, a given SPARQL CONSTRUCT:

```
@prefix ebi: <http://purl.uniprot.org/intact/> .
@prefix core: <http://purl.uniprot.org/core/> .
@prefix uni: <http://purl.uniprot.org/uniprot/> .

CONSTRUCT {
  _:i a core:Interaction .
  _:i core:participant ?e1 .
  ?e1 rdfs:label ?l1 .
  ?e1 owl:sameAs ?u1 .
  _:i core:participant ?e2 .
  ?e2 rdfs:label ?l2 .
  ?e2 owl:sameAs ?u2 .
}
WHERE {
  ?i  <EBIact#target> ?target .
  ?i  <EBIact#actor> ?actor .
  ?target <Protein#uniprot> ?ulab1  .
  ?target <Protein#ebi> ?elab1 .
  ?target <Protein#name> "P53" .
  BIND (IRI(CONCAT(uni:, ?ulab1)) AS ?u1)
  BIND (IRI(CONCAT(ebi:, ?elab1)) AS ?e1)
  ?actor <Protein#uniprot> ?ulab2  .
  ?actor <Protein#ebi> ?elab2 .
  ?actor <Protein#name> "MDM2" .
  BIND (IRI(CONCAT(uni:, ?ulab2)) AS ?u2)
  BIND (IRI(CONCAT(ebi:, ?elab2)) AS ?e2)
}
```

will produce an RDF graph consistent in names and structure with the Uniprot RDF graph about the same resources:

```
@prefix ebi: <http://purl.uniprot.org/intact/> .
@prefix core: <http://purl.uniprot.org/core/> .
@prefix uni: <http://purl.uniprot.org/uniprot/> .
_:i139        a core:Interaction .
_:i139        core:participant ebi:EBI-366083 .
ebi:EBI-366083 rdfs:label "TP53" .
ebi:EBI-366083 owl:sameAs uni:P04637 .
_:i139        core:participant ebi:EBI-389668 .
ebi:EBI-389668 rdfs:label "MDM2" .
ebi:EBI-389668 owl:sameAs uni:Q00987 .
```

Combining the Direct Mapping with reversible graph transformation functions create virtual, Semantic Web-friendly graphs, like the Uniprot graph above. Of course, the magic here is in the reversibility of the transformation functions. How easy will it be to turn a query over the above graph into an SQL query over the input tables?

7. COMPILATION TO SQL

The Direct Mapping can be realized many ways, but of course an SQL implementation is of particular interest. The direct graph is an RDF graph, but the behavior of that graph can be approximated with an SQL view. The view may, of course, be either materialized or virtual. Translating SPARQL 1.0 queries to SQL queries over a triple table has been well-studied [13][11][14], so we illustrate here only the creation of the view and the required built-in functions. The Direct Mapping manipulates table and column names so a general implementation requires second order logic. Here we

briefly describe the process for mapping a given database schema to an SQL view of RDF-like assertions; the minutia are captured in http://www.w3.org/2011/02/DM-KCAP/SQL .

SQL schemas which fully capture the semantics of an RDF graph are cumbersome so we'll use a schema which captures all of the RDF graph expressivity and count on the Direct Mapping view to respect the constraints (such as, the subject of a triple is exclusively either an IRI or a blank node):

```
CREATE TABLE triples (
  sIRI CHAR(40), sBNode CHAR(8),
  pIRI CHAR(40),
  oIRI CHAR(40), oBNode CHAR(8), oLexical CHAR(40),
            oDatatype CHAR(40), oLangTag CHAR(10),
  UNIQUE (sIRI, sBNode, pIRI, oIRI,
            oBNode, oLexical, oDatatype, oLangTag)
)
```

The only subtlety to interpreting this table as RDF comes in recognizing any object without a datatype to be an RDF simple literal [18].

A major caveat of the SQL compilation is that we must have an identifier unique to each row. This ensures the cardinality behavior described in 5.3. As row identifiers are not in the SQL language, we must modify (or copy) each table which has no primary key to institute our own row identifier (here borrowing the vendor-specific reserved word "rownum" already defined in Oracle to uniquely identify rows):

```
ALTER TABLE Protein
  ADD rownum INT UNSIGNED NOT NULL
        AUTO_INCREMENT PRIMARY KEY
```

The Direct Mapping URL-encodes (the UE function in the Direct Mapping) all SQL values and names (table names, column names). In order to be confident of proper encoding in the face of arbitrary data, the database needs a UE function [3]:

```
CREATE FUNCTION urlencode (s VARCHAR(4096))
    RETURNS VARCHAR(4096) ...
```

The subject, predicate and object of the triples in the direct graph are IRIs, blank nodes or RDF Literals, as determined by $\mathcal{E}[\![\ ]\!]_{row}^{\phi}$. For tables with IRI subjects, the subject will be calculated by concatenating the table name, with the ","-separated list of the column names:

```
CONCAT(UE("EBIact"), "/",
       UE("target"), "=", UE(target),",",
       UE("actor"), "=", UE(actor)) AS sIRI
```

Blank node subjects will require a name unique to that table and the rownum.

```
CONCAT("_:", UE("Protein"), UE(Protein.rownum))
AS sBNode
```

Predicates are trivially expressed as an IRI:

```
CONCAT(UE("EBIact"), "#", UE("target"))
AS pIRI
```

Objects generated from foreign keys must join against the referenced table in order to calculate the row identifier. In this case, the row identifier is a blank node:

---

[3]http://snippets.dzone.com/posts/show/7746 provides one which works for MySQL and possibly other databases

```
CONCAT("_:", UE("Protein"), UE(Protein.rownum))
 AS oBNode ... FROM EBIact
 INNER JOIN Protein ON EBIact.target=Protein.ebi
```

Literal objects will either be simple literals:

```
Protein.uniprot AS oLexical,
 NULL AS oDatatype, NULL AS oLangTag
```

or have a datatype. Since oLexical is a `CHAR(40)` type and Protein.ebi is an integer, we must ensure that we inject its lexical form via the appropriate cast:

```
CAST(Protein.ebi AS CHAR(40)) AS oLexical,
 "xsd:integer" as oDatatype, NULL AS oLangTag
```

Given this set of tools, we can generate type triples for each table, as well as triples for each column and each foreign key in those tables. This will be in the form `CREATE VIEW RDF AS` plus a `UNION` of the `SELECT`s which exhaustively cover $\mathcal{E}[\![\ ]\!]_{row}^{\phi}$:

```
CREATE VIEW RDF AS
      SELECT table1 type assertion
UNION SELECT table1 foreign key 1
UNION SELECT table1 foreign key N
UNION SELECT table1 column 1
UNION SELECT table1 column N
UNION SELECT tableN type assertion
...
```

Taking the $r = EBIact$ from earlier, $(\phi(r), rdf : type, UE(relation(t)))$ is realized as:

```
SELECT
 CONCAT(UE("EBIact"), "/",
     UE("target"), "=", UE(target),",",
     UE("actor"), "=", UE(actor)) AS sIRI
 NULL AS sBNode,
 "http://www.w3.org/1999/02/22-rdf-syntax-ns#type" AS pIRI,
 UE("EBIact") AS oIRI, NULL AS oBNode, NULL AS oLexical,
 NULL AS oDatatype, NULL AS oLangTag
 FROM EBIact
```

Eliding the copious NULL columns required to line up the disjoints, in $\{(\phi(r), p, o) \mid (p, o) \in \mathcal{E}[\![r, \mathbf{fk}]\!]_{ref}^{\phi} \mid fk \in references(t)\}$, the function $references(t)$ ranges over $target$ and $actor$:

```
SELECT CONCAT(UE("EBIact"), ...) ... AS sIRI, ...
 CONCAT(UE("EBIact"), "#", UE("target")) AS pIRI,
 ...
 CONCAT("_:", UE("Protein"), UE(Protein.rownum)) AS oBNode
 ...
 FROM EBIact INNER JOIN Protein ON EBIact.target=Protein.ebi
 WHERE
UNION
SELECT CONCAT(UE("EBIact"), ...) ... AS sIRI, ...
 CONCAT(UE("EBIact"), "#", UE("actor")) AS pIRI,
 ...
 CONCAT("_:", UE("Protein"), UE(Protein.rownum)) AS oBNode
 ...
 FROM EBIact INNER JOIN Protein ON EBIact.actor=Protein.ebi
```

In $\{(\phi(r), p, o) \mid (p, o) \in \mathcal{E}[\![r, \mathbf{a}]\!]_{lex} \mid a \in lexicals(t)\}$, $lexicals(t)$ is the set $\{action\}$. In order to be consistent with the NULLs behavior described in 5.4, we need a constraint that the triple is generated only if the value is non-null:

```
SELECT CONCAT(UE("EBIact"), ...) ... AS sIRI, ...
 CONCAT(UE("EBIact"), "#", UE("action")) AS pIRI,
 ... action AS oLexical, ...
 FROM EBIact WHERE action IS NOT NULL
```

By construction, this SQL view respects the constraints required to interpret this table as an RDF graph, e.g. that an object be either an IRI, blank node, or literal with an optional datatype or language tag.

8. STATE OF THE ART

There are many tools which map relational databases to RDF, some by materializing RDF graphs as documents or in a database, some by creating a virtual view, queries upon which are transformed to SQL queries over the relational database. They vary in the degree of curation of the relational data, ranging from conveying just the values of the attributes in each row to representing an RDF graph using graph patterns and identifiers consistent with other Semantic Web representations of the domain data. An example of the less-curated end of the spectrum is SquirrelRDF [23], which is designed to represent each row in an SQL database as a common subject node with a set of properties with literal values. (SquirrelRDF can also express LDAP hierarchies or IMAP email repositories [15] as RDF.) SquirrelRDF on its own does not capture the relational graph; any queries will need to explicate the connections between tables by including constraints on coincident attributes (much as SQL joins are constrained, e.g. `EBIact.actor=Protein.ebi`).

D2R [10] is probably the most popular RDB to RDF mapping tool. The D2R mapping language is an RDF declaration of the mappings from rows in relational tables to RDF graphs (plus the required JDBC connection parameters). This mapping is focused around `ClassMap`s, which denote the lexical structure and type of row identifiers, and `PropertyBridge`s, which specify the creation of a row identifier's properties. D2R's default mapping includes the link table behavior described in the Overview. (The R2RML specification in progress has an expressivity similar to D2R.) D2R tools can use this mapping language to create a materialized view (dump an RDF graph), or to translate SPARQL queries to SQL queries.

Virtuoso RDF Views [1] can also map SPARQL queries to SQL queries, though the configuration language, a mixture of DDL and SPARQL, is somewhat harder to summarize. SPASQL [19] compiles SPARQL queries directly to an execution plan on a MySQL server, bypassing SQL. Triplify [6] maps URI patterns to SQL queries, with the aim of providing a Linked Data [9] endpoint. See the Related Work section of [6] for an excellent summary of different mapping approaches.

All of these tools attempt to find a sweet point between simplicity and utility. Simplicity enables confident interpretation, both for users and for architects adding more functionality to a semantic tool chain. Utility is served by communicating enough of the relational structure to appeal to users and give them an intuitive graph which is either useful in its own right, or transformable into a useful graph. A good example of this trade-off is the special treatment for link tables.

The Direct Mapping produces an RDF graph, to be manipulated further to aptly reflect domain knowledge within the Semantic Web. SquirrelRDF and D2R both provide analogous default representations of relational databases; SquirrelRDF without the relational graph. As far as the authors know, this paper is the first attempt to define a formal semantics for a mapping from relational data to RDF, allowing implementers to write complete code, and providing a grounding for query optimizers and other researchers to demonstrate e.g SPARQL-to-SQL query rewriters faithful to the Direct Mapping semantics.

9. CONCLUSION

The Direct Mapping is a simple step which places relational data into the Semantic Web. This definition may be used in many ways, ranging from serializing a direct graph for possible further manipulation by RDF tools, to defining queryable virtual graphs. While the exact details (e.g. punctuation) of the Direct Mapping are being hammered out by the RDB2RDF Working Group, we have shown the utility of this approach; breaking the representation of non-RDF domain data into a domain-agnostic "direct" representation, leaving the domain-specific manipulation to RDF tools. A functional Scala implementation[4] of the Direct Mapping has been used to validate[5] the RDB2RDF Working Group's tests. This important specification lays the groundwork for existing and nascent graph transformation tools to draw valuable relational data into the Semantic Web.

10. ACKNOWLEDGMENTS

The RDB2RDF Working Group, in particular, Juan Sequeda and Marcelo Arenas who have pursued a Datalog definition of the Direct Mapping. Helena Deus, for geeking through effective use cases.

11. REFERENCES

[1] Mapping sql data to rdf. http://virtuoso.openlinksw.com/dataspace/dav/wiki/Main/VOSSQL2RDF.

[2] Wikipedia article: Relational model. http://en.wikipedia.org/wiki/Relational_model.

[3] Iso/iec 9075 part 1: Sql/framework. 2006.

[4] Iso/iec 9075 part 2: Sql/foundation. 2006.

[5] M. Arenas, E. Prud'hommeaux, and J. Sequeda. A direct mapping of relational data to rdf. 2010. http://www.w3.org/TR/2010/WD-rdb-direct-mapping-20101118/.

[6] S. Auer, S. Dietzold, J. Lehmann, S. Hellmann, and D. Aumueller. Triplify – light-weight linked data publication from relational databases. *WWW2009*.

[7] D. Beckett and T. Berners-Lee. Turtle - terse rdf triple language. 2008. http://www.w3.org/TeamSubmission/2008/SUBM-turtle-20080114/.

[8] F. Belleau, M.-A. Nolin, N. Tourigny, P. Rigault, and J. Morissette. Towards a mashup to build bioinformatics knowledge systems. *Journal of Biomedical Informatics*, 41:706–716, 2008.

[9] T. Berners-Lee. Linked data - design issues. 2010. http://www.w3.org/DesignIssues/LinkedData.

[10] C. Bizer and A. Seaborne. D2rq - treating non-rdf databases as virtual rdf graphs. *ISWC2004 (posters)*, November 2004.

[11] A. Chebotko, S. Lu, H. M. Jamil, and F. Fotouhi. Semantics preserving sparql-to-sql query translation for optional graph patterns. Technical report, 2006.

[12] E. F. Codd. The relational model for database management. 1990.

[13] R. Cyganiak. A relational algebra for sparql. Technical report, 2005.

[14] B. Elliott1, E. Cheng, C. Thomas-Ogbuji, and Z. M. Ozsoyoglu. A complete translation from sparql into efficient sql.

[15] D. Eynard, J. Recker, and C. Sayers. An imap plugin for squirrelrdf. Technical report. http://www.hpl.hp.com/techreports/2007/HPL-2007-161.pdf.

[16] B. He, M. Patel, Z. Zhang, and K. Chang. Accessing the deep web. *Communications of the ACM*, 50(5):94–101, 2007.

[17] A. Jentzsch, J. Zhao, O. Hassanzadeh, K.-H. Cheung, M. Samwald, and B. Andersson. Linking open drug data. 2009.

[18] G. Klyne and J. J. Carroll. Resource description framework (rdf): Concepts and abstract syntax. 2004. http://www.w3.org/TR/2004/REC-rdf-concepts-20040210/.

[19] E. Prud'hommeaux. Spasql: Sparql support in mysql. http://www.w3.org/2005/05/22-SPARQL-MySQL/XTech.

[20] E. Prud'hommeaux, M. Hausenblas, S. Auer, L. Feigenbaum, D. Miranker, A. Fogarolli, and J. Sequeda. Use cases and requirements for mapping relational databases to rdf. 2010. http://www.w3.org/TR/2010/WD-rdb2rdf-ucr-20100608/.

[21] E. Prud'hommeaux and A. Seaborne. Sparql query language for rdf. 2008. http://www.biopax.org/release/biopax-level3-documentation.pdf.

[22] D. Raggett, A. L. Hors, and I. Jacobs. Html 4.01 specification. 1999. http://www.w3.org/TR/html401/interact/forms.html#h-17.13.4.1.

[23] D. Steer. Squirrelrdf. 2006. http://jena.sourceforge.net/SquirrelRDF/.

---

[4]http://www.w3.org/2011/02/DM-KCAP/code
[5]http://www.w3.org/2011/02/DM-KCAP/srvc

Multipedia: Enriching DBpedia with Multimedia Information

Andrés García-Silva
Ontology Engineering Group, Universidad
Politécnica de Madrid, Spain
hgarcia@fi.upm.es

Max Jakob, Pablo N. Mendes and
Christian Bizer
Web-based Systems Group, Freie Universität
Berlin, Germany
first.last@fu-berlin.de

ABSTRACT

Enriching knowledge bases with multimedia information makes it possible to complement textual descriptions with visual and audio information. Such complementary information can help users to understand the meaning of assertions, and in general improve the user experience with the knowledge base. In this paper we address the problem of how to enrich ontology instances with candidate images retrieved from existing Web search engines. DBpedia has evolved into a major hub in the Linked Data cloud, interconnecting millions of entities organized under a consistent ontology. Our approach taps into the Wikipedia corpus to gather context information for DBpedia instances and takes advantage of image tagging information when this is available to calculate semantic relatedness between instances and candidate images. We performed experiments with focus on the particularly challenging problem of highly ambiguous names. Both methods presented in this work outperformed the baseline. Our best method leveraged context words from Wikipedia, tags from Flickr and type information from DBpedia to achieve an average precision of 80%.

Categories and Subject Descriptors

I.2.6 [**Artificial Intelligence**]: Learning—*Knowledge acquisition*

General Terms

Algorithms,Design,Experimentation

Keywords

Ontology, Multimedia, DBpedia, Linked Data

1. INTRODUCTION

Enriching knowledge bases with multimedia information makes it possible to complement and improve results of knowledge consuming tasks including question and answering systems and recommendation processes among others.

Multimodal knowledge bases have been successfully used in the past for several knowledge consuming tasks including semantic browsing of video collections [3] and query interpretation for multimodal information retrieval [20], among others. However, retrieving relevant images from the Web for instances in a knowledge base is not a trivial task.

The prevalent information retrieval paradigm on the Web is keyword-based search. Naturally, multimedia content has been particularly challenging in this context, since images, video, etc. are generally opaque to keyword searches. The most common approaches for multimedia retrieval have relied on matching search keywords to metadata associated to multimedia content such as the filename, title, amongst others [6].

Words appearing near a multimedia item on Web pages have also been used as targets for matching the search terms [1]. In addition, websites such as Flickr and Youtube have incorporated content tagging as a way to let users describe and interconnect related media. Tags are words associated to media that can be used in a later stage for categorizing, retrieving and interconnecting content [14].

However, the ambiguity in the words (metadata, text, tags) used as descriptions of multimedia items makes the retrieval task particularly difficult. For instance, take the resource `dbpedia:Hornet`[1], which refers to a wasp in the DBpedia knowledge base [5]. If we query Flickr or Google Images for pictures related to the entity name '*hornet*', we can see in Figure 1 that both Flickr and Google return images related to other meanings of the word. Flickr shows images of a plane (*F/A-18 Hornet*) and a fictional character (*The Green Hornet*), while Google displays images of a motorcycle (*Honda CB600F*). Consequently, currently available multimedia search engines are not readily apt to collect relevant images for ontology entities.

Our work presents a contribution to the task of populating an ontology with images from the Web. We focus on retrieving relevant images for entities extracted from Wikipedia, the world's largest source of encyclopedic knowledge. The DBpedia project collects facts from Wikipedia containing 3.5 million entities, their attributes and relationships with other entities [5]. DBpedia is classified in a consistent cross-domain ontology with classes such as persons, organisations or populated places; as well as more fine-grained classifications like basketball player or flowering plant. The DBpedia project has evolved to one of the center pieces of the

---
[1]The prefix `dbpedia:` refers to `http://dbpedia.org/resource/`

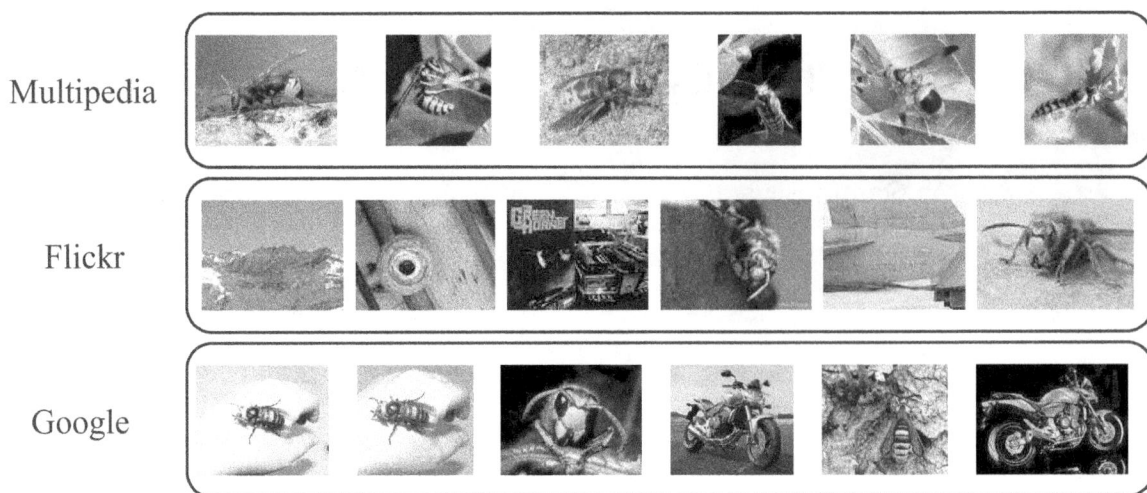

Figure 1: Querying the Web for images related to the resource `dbpedia:Hornet`

Linking Open Data (LOD) project[2], which seeks to enable a Web of Data where information can be effectively exchanged as structured facts in addition to natural language text [4]. As such, our work extends the encyclopedic knowledge in the Linked Data cloud with relevant images of DBpedia resources.

We introduce **Multipedia**, a system for collecting multimedia information for DBpedia. Our approach leverages existing image search engines and improves their ability to retrieve images for DBpedia resources with ambiguous names. Multipedia achieves this by: (i) expanding the semantic neighborhood of DBpedia resources with 'context words' – words that occurred around DBpedia resources mentioned in Wikipedia text; (ii) performing query expansion with context words and searching existing engines; (iii) computing semantic relatedness between tagging information and DBpedia resources; (iv) aggregating the results into a final rank using a ranking aggregation method.

We evaluate the effectiveness of our approach with a user study involving 15 people and resulting in 2250 image relevance judgments. We use commercial Web search engines as a baseline and present how the algorithms introduced in this work offer improvements of 8.9% and 9.4% over the baseline.

This paper is organized as follows. Section 2 describes related work in the context of disambiguated image retrieval and their hierarchical organisation. Section 3 presents our approach to this task. It includes the description of how we acquire various sets of ranked images as well as the method of how these rankings are combined into the result set of images. In section 4, we evaluate our approach for ambiguous entity names. We discuss our conclusions in section 5, presenting our plans for future work.

2. RELATED WORK

We address the problem of acquiring images for resources in the DBpedia knowledge base from the Web beyond the images that are attached to Wikipedia articles since this multimedia data is already part of DBpedia[3].

The main obstacle is ambiguity of resource names. The task of retrieving images for resources in the presence of ambiguity has been approached in various ways. In general, there are mainly three types of features that can be utilized in this endeavor. A number of approaches use contextual data in which the image is found [19, 27, 28, 29]. Other works rely on image meta data such as date, GPS information or tags [7, 15]. Lastly, visual similarity features are employed by some authors [9, 17, 22, 27]. Datta et al. [8] offer a survey on image retrieval and image classification, focusing on visual similarity features.

The work that is most closely related to ours was done by Taneva et al. [27]. They take the YAGO knowledge base [26] as their source of resources and develop a supervised learning method based on ranking aggregation to gather images. They use the properties of the YAGO resources to iteratively query a number of search engines. The result rankings from these queries are merged into one, while recognizing duplicates based on the URL and visual similarity. In contrast, our approach does not rely on any training data which, in general, is expensive to gather. Furthermore, we use context words of Wikipedia page links to expand the image queries instead of ontology properties. Context words around page links offer better coverage of resources because ontology properties are extracted from infoboxes that are not part of every Wikipedia page. We additionally employ a tag similarity measure in order to increase the precision.

ImageNet [9] also addresses the problem of populating a knowledge base with images. They chose the semantic classes in WordNet [12] for linking the images, while our work includes finding images for ontology instances. They use hierarchical relations in WordNet and visual features to find images related to the classes and therefore employ a significantly different strategy from ours. RetrievOnto [19] is a system that also uses WordNet, but only a small part of the typed term hierarchy, inducing images at new leaf nodes. The ontological relation then allow for controlling conceptual neighborhoods in order to increase precision in a use case of semantic, content-based image retrieval. However, their approach is evaluated on a small subset of instances of a specific type of concept. The large image collection

---

[2]http://www.w3.org/wiki/SweoIG/TaskForces/
CommunityProjects/LinkingOpenData
[3]with the relation `foaf:depiction`

LabelMe [22] offer ground truth labels to be used in object recognition research, mainly for recognizing objects embedded in a scene. They also link on class level to WordNet concepts.

There are other approaches that attempt to organize an image collection in some sort of semantic category system, not in a typed ontology. The OPTIMOL system [17] collects pictures from the web and incrementally learns a category model. It uses object recognition techniques and aims at providing data for computer vision research. Crandall et al. [7] organize a large image collection collected from Flickr into a hierarchical structure of places while exploiting GPS data of the images. They also use the tags given by the uploader if GPS data is not available. Wang et al. [29] construct an ontology from the Wikipedia category hierarchy and populate it with related images by viewing the structure as a semantic network. They show how spreading activation techniques help to improve performance in image retrieval. Medialife [15] is a system that uses ontological information to facilitate the generation of user specified image collection subsets that represent a chronicle of life, for instance a collection of pictures of family members at a specific social event. These kind of queries are only possible in the context of a personalized world model. This differs from our approach that attempts to populate a general world knowledge ontology.

3. MULTIPEDIA

In order to retrieve relevant images for DBpedia resources we propose an approach that takes advantage of existing image search engines and of tagging information when it is available. We propose to query the Web using the resource label plus some other context phrases extracted from Wikipedia. This is done iteratively, resulting in one query per context word. Then we carry out two activities simultaneously. First we aggregate the rankings produced by each context word query in a new context-based ranking. Second we create a new tag-based ranking taking into account the semantic similarity between each one of the retrieved pictures and the current DBpedia resource. This semantic similarity is calculated by comparing the picture tags and the DBpedia resource context terms. Finally, we merge both the context-based and the tag-based rankings in a final ranking from which we take the top n results as images relevant to the resource. In the following we present the details of this process.

3.1 Resource Context

Although DBpedia resource URIs are unambiguous, i.e. each URI refers to one and only one resource[4], DBpedia resource names may be ambiguous when searching for information about them on the Web. In this work, we use 'name' (as in resource name) to refer to the value of the property `rdfs:label` for each DBpedia resource. Examples of ambiguous resource names are 'Hornet' as presented on Figure 1, as well as 'Apple' and names of many other resource.

Humans are capable of easily identifying the meaning of ambiguous names based on the context – by using their back-

---

[4]Resources may be duplicates [11], i.e. two URIs identify distinct resources representing the same real world object. Nonetheless, each URI refers to one and only one resource.

ground knowledge and the understanding of the surrounding text. However disambiguation is a hard problem for computers. Natural Language Processing (NLP) research has attempted to model context of ambiguous terms by collecting surrounding words, part of speech information, etc. [18].

As DBpedia resources correspond to Wikipedia articles, we can tap into the Wikipedia corpus to find mentions of Wikipedia articles and collect context information. We consider that a DBpedia resource has been mentioned whenever we find its corresponding Wikipedia article as the target of a wikilink (i.e., link between Wikipedia articles). In this work, **context words** are any terms (excluding stopwords) appearing before and after the wikilink representing a mention of a DBpedia resource. Thus, we have created an index in which for each article we have the set of words appearing along with an article mention and their frequency. For instance, the context for `dbpedia:Apple` consists of words such as '*fruit*' or '*juice*'. In contrast, `dbpedia:Apple_Inc.` context contains words such as '*software*' or '*mac*'.

In order to complement the context information we are using information from the DBpedia Ontology. Currently the DBpedia ontology classifies 1.6 million resources. We use the class name as an additional feature to add to the resource context. In the case of our example, we add the class name '*flowering plant*' to the `dbpedia:Apple` context and to the `dbpedia:Apple_Inc.` context the class name '*public company*'.

Thus, for a given DBpedia resource d we create a set C of context terms c_i collected following the procedure mentioned above.

3.2 Gathering images

In order to collect an initial set of images, we query the Web for candidate images for a DBpedia resource. To do so we rely on existing image search engines and image sharing sites. First, we pose a query to an image sharing site using the name for a resource, if we do not get results then we use a search engine. In order to cope with ambiguity, we pose new queries using the resource name plus one term extracted from the context in the hope that these query results produce more accurate results. For instance, querying images for '*apple*' and '*fruit*' produces mostly `dbpedia:Apple` images. We repeat this procedure for the top N frequent context terms. In Section 4 we experiment with $N = 3, 4, 5, 6, 7$. Henceforth C refers to the context subset of size N.

Thus, given a DBpedia resource d, the output of this task is a set R of image rankings r_j with $1 <= j <= |C| + 1$, that is a ranked list for each query using the resource name and a context term plus the initial query using just the resource name. In addition, we produce a set P of unique images with the union of all images in each ranking r_j.

3.3 Aggregating query results

We rank and aggregate the rankings produced in the previous step using Borda's count [23]. Borda's count was developed initially to elect members to an organization. In an election with X candidates, each voter awards X points to his first choice, X-1 to his second choice, and so on. The results are added up and the candidate with the most points wins. Borda's count is a positional method [10]. That is, it assigns a weight corresponding to the position in which a candidate appears within each voter list. The main advantage of Borda's method is that it is very easy computationally since this method can be implemented to run in linear time [21].

This method has been adapted to rank and aggregate the results gathered by metasearches on the web [21]. Voters are search engines used by the metasearch and candidates are the documents retrieved by each search engine. Following with this idea, we use Borda's count to merge in a unique list the rankings r_j. In this case, each query is a voter and images are the candidates.

Borda's count considers that all candidate images p_k in P are ranked in all lists $r_1, \ldots, r_j, \ldots, r_{|C|+1}$. For each candidate p_k in r_j, the method assigns a score $S_j(p_k)$ equal to the number of candidates ranked below p_k in r_j. The total Borda score for this candidate is calculated according to equation 1.

$$S(p_k) = \sum_{j=1}^{|C|+1} S_j(p_k) \qquad (1)$$

Finally, the fused ranked list is created by sorting the candidates p_k in decreasing order of total Borda score. Note that Borda's count can be extended to deal with partial lists. That is, when not all the candidate images appear in all ranked lists [21]. Let us suppose we have a ranked list r_j so that the number of candidate images ranked in this list is less than the number of candidate images ($|r_j| < |P|$). Thus the Borda score for all candidates not belonging to r_j is $|P| - |r_j| - 1$.

We apply Borda's count to the query results obtained from the previous step and call the new list context-based ranking.

3.4 Tag-based ranking

With the advent of the Web 2.0, users started to provide a wealth of metadata about the information they post on the Web. These metadata take the form of geo-localization information and tags among others. In this respect, image sharing social networks encourage users to tag images to improve resource visibility within the community, as well as a mean of self organization. A possible use of tags is to describe the content of the annotated resource. Thus, we have the advantage of using tagging information in order to measure the relatedness of a specific image and a DBpedia resource.

Our relatedness measure between a DBpedia resource and an image is calculated based on the overlapping of terms between the context of the former and the tags of the latter. To do so, we follow a Vector Space Model [25] to represent the DBpedia resource and the images, and then compare them using a standard metric.

First we create the *Vocabulary* set as the union of the context terms related to the DBpedia resource. For each candidate image we create a vector in $\Re^{|Vocabulary|}$ where each position corresponds to an element in an ordered version of the *Vocabulary* set. The value w_i associated with the i-th position in the vector is calculated using TF-IDF[5] [24] for the corresponding i-th term in the ordered set.

Similarly, we create a vector for the DBpedia resource and its context. In this case, w_i takes as value the term frequency calculated as how often the term appears along a mention of the DBpedia resource in Wikipedia. We compare the keyword vector and each one of the image vectors using

---

[5]Term Frequency and Inverse Document Frequency

as similarity measure the *cosine* function. Finally, we sort all the candidate images in decreasing order of similarity, and produce a new list called tag-based ranking.

3.5 Fusing final ranks

Finally, we fuse both the tag-based and the context-based rankings in a final ranking using Borda's count. We expect that this last fusion raises relevant images, according to the tagging information, in the final list.

4. EXPERIMENTS

The experiments presented in this section were carried out using Flickr and Bing Image Search due to the convenience of their Web APIs, but they could be easily adapted to use other search engines or image sharing sites.

In Section 3.2 we described our approach to gather images for the top N context terms for a resource. Our first experiment investigated how many context words to use in order to guide the image retrieval towards a specific sense of an ambiguous word. We designed an initial experiment where the dataset was manually selected, taking care of including unambiguous and ambiguous resources names and varying the number of context words $N = 3, 4, 5, 6$ and 7. Results are shown in Figure 2.

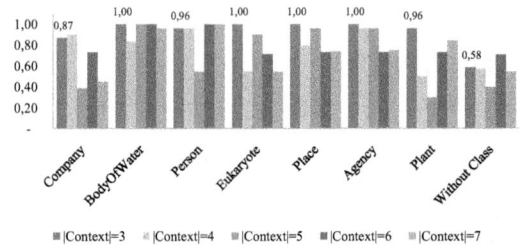

Figure 2: Average precision for different numbers of context terms. Precision values are shown for context of size 3.

A context containing 3 terms produces the best results in terms of average precision achieving a 0.92 value. Using more than 3 context words seems to decrease the average precision. This number is similar to the findings of an earlier experiment about word sense disambiguation presented by Kaplan [16] that found 4 as the number of words above which the context does not add more resolving power to the disambiguation. For instance, in our running example the context of size 7 for 'apple' consists of the following words 'juice, fruit, apples, capital, michigan, orange'. One can see that longer contexts start to include words – such as 'capital' – which may be less helpful to identify the meaning of the resource name 'apple'.

In the following, we present details of an experiment carried out to evaluate our proposal using 3 context words.

4.1 Dataset

We have constructed an evaluation dataset to assess the ability of Multipedia to retrieve images for ambiguous DBpedia resource names. The highest ambiguity happens when a name can be used to refer to many resources with no dominant sense. A dominant sense is a resource that is by large the most common use of an ambiguous name. Dominance reduces ambiguity in practice since randomly choosing images is more likely to find the dominant resource, even without any other information.

Therefore, the first criterion employed was to select resource names that are linked from a disambiguation page. This information can be queried in DBpedia using the relation `dbpo:wikiPageDisambiguates`[6]. This relation allows us to detect that this resource may be confused with other resources with the same or similar names. However, from this relation alone it is not possible to measure to what degree this confusion between the resources actually happens in practice. For instance, a name such as '*stonehenge*' is ambiguous, although most of the time it refers to the prehistoric monument `dbpedia:Stonehenge`. Consequently, querying the web for images using the name '*stonehenge*' will retrieve mostly images about the monument.

We have defined a measure of **dominance** (Equation 2) to calculate how common is the most frequent sense of an ambiguous word with respect to all other senses. In this equation w_i is the ambiguous name, S is the set of possible senses, $freq()$ is a function returning the number of times that w_i has been used in Wikipedia to refer to a specific sense. Hence, a value close to 1 means that there is a dominant sense (one resource is much more common than other confusable resources), while a value close to 0 means that there is not a dominant sense.

$$dom(w_i) = \frac{Max(freq(s_j))}{\sum_{j=0}^{|S|} freq(s_j)} \qquad (2)$$

We created a program to automatically gather the dataset. We first selected 10 classes from the DBpedia Ontology in order to ensure diversity. For each class, we randomly picked up 15 popular resources with an ambiguous name and a *dom* value below 0.7. Popularity was required so that DBpedia resources can be easily assessed by human evaluators. A resource was considered popular if there were more than 100 wikilinks to its corresponding Wikipedia article. We found resources fulfilling these requirements classified under the classes `dbpo:Mammal`, `dbpo:Bird` and `dbpo:Insect`. For the rest of the classes we had to increase the $dom(w_i)$ limit to 0.9.

4.2 Evaluation

We asked a group of 15 people, students and researchers from the Freie Universität Berlin and the Universidad Politécnica de Madrid, to evaluate the top 5 results of three methods. The experiment was conducted as a blind evaluation, i.e., the results were conflated into a ranking with 15 images per DBpedia resource, without telling the raters which result came from which method. Each evaluator rated the image as *Highly Related*, *Related* or *Not Related* with the DBpedia resource. If they could not take a decision regarding the current image, e.g. due to low picture quality, evaluators could select the *Don't Know* option.

We presented to each evaluator additional information of the image as available tags, textual description and title. We made sure every image was rated by three evaluators so that we can take into account the decisions taken by majority.

We have measured the reliability of agreement between our evaluators using Fleiss' Kappa [13]. It measures how much of the observed agreement exceeds what would be expected if all raters made their ratings completely randomly.

[6]The prefix `dbpo:` refers to `http://dbpedia.org/ontology/`

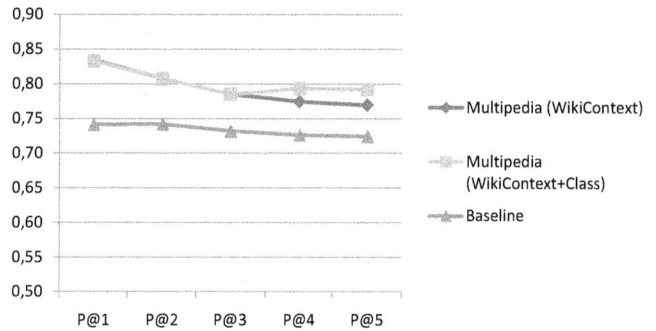

Figure 3: Precision at n of the evaluated approaches

If a fixed number of people assign ratings to a number of items, then the kappa can be seen as a measure for the consistency of ratings. The scoring range is between 0 and 1. Using all ratings in our evaluation we obtained $\kappa = 0.445$ with $z = 53.6$. There was a total of 2250 ratings. In 49.93% of the cases, all three users agreed exactly on the rating (unanimous decision). When collapsing 'Highly Related' and 'Related' into one category, 76.82% of the ratings were unanimous. In 93.46% of the cases, at least two raters agreed.

The images presented to the raters were obtained from two versions of our approach and a baseline (5 images from each). The first version, which we call **Multipedia WikiContext**, used the top 3 most frequent words appearing along a mention of the resource in Wikipedia as the context words for computing relatedness. The second version, which we call **Multipedia WikiContext+Class**, extended the context with the class name to which the resource belongs. The baseline was defined as querying an image sharing site using just the resource name. In case the image sharing site search does not produce any result we pose a query to an image search engine.

From all the evaluated images, 81.96% correspond to images extracted from the image sharing site, and 18.03% were extracted from the image search engine. The evaluated dataset is publicly available[7].

Precision (P) is the fraction of relevant images to the images retrieved by each approach given a DBpedia resource. We have measured $P@N$ with $N = 1, 2, 3, 4, 5$ (precision at N rank position [2]). The Average Precision (AP) is defined as the average of $P@N$ values. Precision values were calculated from those evaluations where users were able to take a decision.

Figure 3 depicts $P@N$ values achieved by each approach. Multipedia approaches produce more precise results than the baseline along all the values of N. We can observe that WikiContext+Class is better than WikiContext starting from N=3. This means that the class names are an important factor in the context to help in the selection of relevant images. Table 1 shows that WikiContext+Class was the best approach with a $AP = 0.80$. Both Multipedia approaches were able to increase AP value (%inc) regarding the baseline. WikiContext increased AP in 8.9% and WikiContext+Class in 9.4%.

Figure 4 shows AP values per each Ontology Class. Note

[7]`http://delicias.dia.fi.upm.es/wiki/images/b/b2/` `MultipediaEvaluation.zip`

Table 1: Average precision (AP) per class and percentage increase (%inc) with respect to the baseline.

Class	Baseline	Wiki Context	%inc	WikiCont. +Class	%inc
Athlete	0.65	0.74	14.6%	0.68	5.0%
Bird	0.66	0.86	**31.8%**	0.90	**37.2%**
Building	0.84	0.83	-0,6%	0.84	0.6%
Insect	0.89	0.89	0.4%	0.93	5.2%
Mammals	0.68	0.73	7.6%	0.86	**27.2%**
MeanOfTrans	0.86	0.86	-0.2%	0.93	7.4%
Mountain	0.66	0.85	**29.8%**	0.85	**28.8%**
Politician	0.57	0.48	*-16.4%*	0.39	*-31.2%*
Sport	0.72	0.93	**29.3%**	0.80	10.5%
WorldHeritage	0.81	0.75	-7.2%	0.84	3.0%
Average	0.73	0.79	8.9%	**0.80**	**9.4%**

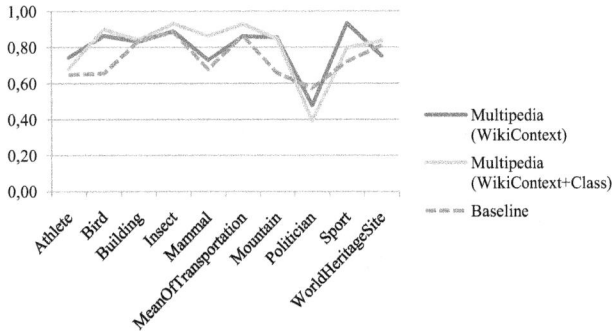

Figure 4: Average precision per class

that WikiContext+Class increases AP values in all classes except `dbpo:Politician`. WikiContext+Class achieved the best results with `dbpo:Bird`, `dbpo:Mammal` and `dbpo:Mountain` with improvements of 37.2%, 27.2% and 28.8% respectively. Recall that $dom(w_i)$ for names of birds and mammals used in this dataset was 0.7, indicating that these names do not have a strong dominant sense. Thus, for these two classes we have validated that 1) the baseline fails when dealing with ambiguous names lacking of a dominant sense and 2) that our approach produces better results for this sort of names.

Nevertheless, the class `dbpo:Mountain` did have a dominant sense in Wikipedia. What we found on the Web for some mountains was that their names were actually used to refer to things related to the mountain such as hotels, resorts or restaurants. Therefore the baseline erroneously retrieved images with regard to those other resources, while the use of Wikipedia-based context helps Multipedia to find the correct images. In addition, this means that despite those mountains having a dominant sense in Wikipedia, they do not have it on the Web. Thus, the Wikipedia corpus is a starting point to measure ambiguity degrees as the dominant sense ratio, though more evidence information should be taken from other sources or the Web itself.

For the class `dbpo:Politician`, on the other hand, Multipedia approaches present worse results than the baseline. The use of context words did not seem to help reduce ambiguity. We found that many images have been included along text related to political issues, although the images do not depict a specific politician. In our dataset 24% of images retrieved for the three approaches contain a description with more than 150 characters including the politician name (14% of images have description longer than 500 characters). For

instance, an image depicting the Brandenburg Gate[8] presented in our dataset is described (and annotated) with a long text showing different events and mentioning different politicians taking part in those events. So, when we were retrieving pictures for `dbpedia:Helmut_Kohl` former chancellor of Germany, we found pictures of the Brandenburg Gate where he was mentioned. The use of context words, such as '*Minister*' does not help to get rid of these pictures because usually those descriptions are well contextualized including positions of the politicians and locations. Further research is needed in order to develop methods to deal with this kind of misleading metadata.

Since it is impossible to know the set of all relevant images for a DBpedia resource that are available on the Web in advance, it is not possible to compute recall. Nevertheless, we can report coverage per each approach defined as the number of retrieved images divided by the number of expected images. All three approaches have an almost perfect coverage since just for one DBpedia resource we could not find images on the Web.

5. CONCLUSIONS

In this paper we addressed the problem of how to enrich ontology instances with links to images. We focused on the particularly challenging problem of ambiguity in instance names. We collected resources belonging to diverse types from DBpedia, one of the most prominent knowledge bases in the Linked Data cloud. We relied on mentions of DBpedia resources in Wikipedia text in order to gather contextual information for those resources. Our approach takes advantage of existing image search engines on the Web, and retrieves images using the collected context information for a resource. We measured the relatedness of each image to a DBpedia resource by calculating a semantic similarity between the image metadata information and the resource context. As a final step we produce a ranking using the Borda's count, a well known method for ranking aggregations.

We have carried out a human-driven evaluation of the approach involving 15 users and a total of 2250 image ratings containing DBpedia resources from several classes. The dataset was selected so that all of the instance names where ambiguous. A variation of Multipedia using Wikipedia textual information plus the ontology class as context achieved the best results, improving average precision by 9.4% over a baseline of keyword queries to commercial image search engines. We have validated that in contrast to the baseline our approach achieves the highest precision values with ambiguous names lacking a dominant sense.

As future work we plan to improve the precision for images with misleading textual descriptions as the ones found in our experiment for Politicians. In addition, some images have metadata that can be considered as spam (e.g., sometimes users in social networks add popular metadata to their images so that they can appear first in the search results). Therefore new techniques have to be developed to cope with these challenges.

6. ACKNOWLEDGMENTS

Our work has been partially funded by the Project CENIT España Virtual (ALT0317), an FPI grant (BES-2008-007622) of the Spanish Ministry of Science and Innovation, Neofonie

---

[8]`http://dbpedia.org/resource/Brandenburg_Gate`

GmbH, a Berlin-based company offering leading technologies in the area of Web search, social media and mobile applications (http://www.neofonie.de/) and the European Commission through the project LOD2 − Creating Knowledge out of Linked Data (http://lod2.eu/).

7. REFERENCES

[1] Google's Peter Linsley Interviewed by Eric Enge, 2009. http://www.stonetemple.com/articles/interview-peter-linsley.shtml.

[2] R. Baeza-Yates and B. Ribeiro-Neto. *Modern Information Retrieval*. Addison Wesley, 1st edition, May 1999.

[3] M. Bertini, G. D'Amico, A. Ferracani, M. Meoni, and G. Serra. Web-based semantic browsing of video collections using multimedia ontologies. In *Proceedings of the international conference on Multimedia*, MM '10, pages 1629–1632, New York, NY, USA, 2010. ACM.

[4] C. Bizer, T. Heath, and T. Berners-Lee. Linked Data - The Story So Far. *International Journal on Semantic Web and Information Systems (IJSWIS)*, 2009.

[5] C. Bizer, J. Lehmann, G. Kobilarov, S. Auer, C. Becker, R. Cyganiak, and S. Hellmann. DBpedia - A crystallization point for the Web of Data. *Journal of Web Semantic*, 7(3):154–165, 2009.

[6] S. Chang and A. Hsu. Image information systems: where do we go from here? *Knowledge and Data Engineering, IEEE Transactions on*, 4(5):431–442, 1992.

[7] D. J. Crandall, L. Backstrom, D. Huttenlocher, and J. Kleinberg. Mapping the world's photos. In *Proceedings of the 18th international conference on World wide web*, WWW '09, pages 761–770, New York, NY, USA, 2009. ACM.

[8] R. Datta, D. Joshi, J. Li, and J. Z. Wang. Image retrieval: Ideas, influences, and trends of the new age. *ACM Comput. Surv.*, 40(2):1–60, April 2008.

[9] J. Deng, W. Dong, R. Socher, L.-J. Li, K. Li, and L. Fei-Fei. Imagenet: A large-scale hierarchical image database. *Computer Vision and Pattern Recognition, IEEE Computer Society Conference on*, 0:248–255, 2009.

[10] C. Dwork, R. S. Kumar, M. Naor, and D. Sivakumar. Rank aggregation methods for the Web. In *World Wide Web*, pages 613–622, 2001.

[11] A. Elmagarmid, P. Ipeirotis, and V. Verykios. Duplicate record detection: A survey. *Knowledge and Data Engineering, IEEE Transactions on*, 19(1):1–16, Jan. 2007.

[12] C. Fellbaum, editor. *WordNet: an electronic lexical database*. MIT Press, 1998.

[13] J. L. Fleiss. Measuring nominal scale agreement among many raters. *Psychological Bulletin*, 76(5):378 – 382, 1971.

[14] S. Golder and B. A. Huberman. The structure of collaborative tagging systems. *Journal of Information Science*, 32(2):198Ů208, April 2006. cite arxiv:cs/0508082.

[15] A. Gupta, S. Rafatirad, M. Gao, and R. Jain. MEDIALIFE: from images to a life chronicle. In *SIGMOD Conference*, pages 1119–1122, 2009.

[16] A. Kaplan. An experimental study of ambiguity and context. *Mechanical Translation*, 2:39–46, 1955.

[17] L.-J. Li, G. Wang, and L. Fei-Fei. OPTIMOL: automatic Online Picture collecTion via Incremental MOdel Learning. In *IEEE Conference on Computer Vision and Pattern Recognition, 2007.*, pages 1–8, June 2007.

[18] R. Mihalcea and A. Csomai. Wikify!: linking documents to encyclopedic knowledge. In *Proceedings of the sixteenth ACM conference on Conference on information and knowledge management*, CIKM '07, pages 233–242, New York, NY, USA, 2007. ACM.

[19] A. Popescu, C. Millet, and P.-A. Moëllic. Ontology driven content based image retrieval. In *Proceedings of the 6th ACM international conference on Image and video retrieval*, CIVR '07, pages 387–394, New York, NY, USA, 2007. ACM.

[20] S. Radhouani, J.-H. Lim, J.-P. Chevallet, and G. Falquet. Combining Textual and Visual Ontologies to Solve Medical Multimodal Queries. In *ICME*, pages 1853–1856, 2006.

[21] E. M. Renda and U. Straccia. Web metasearch: rank vs. score based rank aggregation methods. In *SAC '03: Proceedings of the 2003 ACM symposium on Applied computing*, pages 841–846, New York, NY, USA, 2003. ACM Press.

[22] B. C. Russell, A. Torralba, K. P. Murphy, and W. T. Freeman. LabelMe: A Database and Web-Based Tool for Image Annotation. *Int. J. Comput. Vision*, 77:157–173, May 2008.

[23] D. G. Saari. The mathematics of voting: Democratic symmetry. *The Economist*, page 83, March 2000.

[24] G. Salton and M. J. Mcgill. *Introduction to Modern Information Retrieval*. McGraw-Hill, Inc., New York, NY, USA, 1986.

[25] G. Salton, A. Wong, and C. S. Yang. A vector space model for automatic indexing. *Communications of the ACM*, 18:613–620, November 1975.

[26] F. M. Suchanek, G. Kasneci, and G. Weikum. YAGO: A Large Ontology from Wikipedia and WordNet. *Journal of Web Semantics*, 6(3):203–217, 2008.

[27] B. Taneva, M. Kacimi, and G. Weikum. Gathering and ranking photos of named entities with high precision, high recall, and diversity. In *Proceedings of the third ACM international conference on Web search and data mining*, WSDM '10, pages 431–440, New York, NY, USA, 2010. ACM.

[28] H. Wang, L.-T. Chia, and S. Gao. Wikipedia-assisted concept thesaurus for better web media understanding. In *Proceedings of the international conference on Multimedia information retrieval*, MIR '10, pages 349–358, New York, NY, USA, 2010. ACM.

[29] H. Wang, X. Jiang, L.-T. Chia, and A.-H. Tan. Ontology enhanced web image retrieval: aided by Wikipedia & spreading activation theory. In *Proceeding of the 1st ACM international conference on Multimedia information retrieval*, MIR '08, pages 195–201, New York, NY, USA, 2008. ACM.

On the Role of User-generated Metadata in Audio Visual Collections

Riste Gligorov
VU University Amsterdam
The Netherlands
r.gligorov@vu.nl

Michiel Hildebrand
VU University Amsterdam
The Netherlands
m.hildebrand@vu.nl

Jacco van Ossenbruggen
VU/CWI Amsterdam
The Netherlands
j.r.van.ossenbruggen@vu.nl

Guus Schreiber
VU University Amsterdam
The Netherlands
guus.schreiber@vu.nl

Lora Aroyo
VU University Amsterdam
The Netherlands
l.m.aroyo@vu.nl

ABSTRACT

Recently, various crowdsourcing initiatives showed that targeted efforts of user communities result in massive amounts of tags. For example, the Netherlands Institute for Sound and Vision collected a large number of tags with the video labeling game *Waisda?*. To successfully utilize these tags, a better understanding of their characteristics is required. The goal of this paper is twofold: (i) to investigate the vocabulary that users employ when describing videos and compare it to the vocabularies used by professionals; and (ii) to establish which aspects of the video are typically described and what type of tags are used for this. We report on an analysis of the tags collected with *Waisda?*. With respect to the first goal, we compared the the tags with a typical domain thesaurus used by professionals, as well as with a more general vocabulary. With respect to the second goal, we compare the tags to the video subtitles to determine how many tags are derived from the audio signal. In addition, we perform a qualitative study in which a tag sample is interpreted in terms of an existing annotation classification framework. The results suggest that the tags complement the metadata provided by professional cataloguers, the tags describe both the audio and the visual aspects of the video, and the users primarily describe objects in the video using general descriptions.

Categories and Subject Descriptors

H.4 [**Information Systems Applications**]: Miscellaneous

General Terms

Experimentation

Keywords

tagging, video, tag analysis, professionals vs. end-users, games with a purpose

1. INTRODUCTION

Crowdsourcing has gained attention as a method to collect large numbers of metadata descriptions for media objects [2, 10, 15]. Based on the idea coined by Luis von Ahn [18], a specific type of crowdsourcing has become known as Games With A Purpose (GWAP). Inspired by this idea, the Netherlands Institute for Sound and Vision deployed the video labeling game, *Waisda?*. Unique for this initiative is that the institute aims [11] to integrate the game into their workflow to complement professional cataloguing and content based retrieval techniques [5]. More specific, with *Waisda?* they aim to collect metadata in a user vocabulary that describes the content within the video.

We investigate to what extent the aims of Sound and Vision are fulfilled by analyzing the 420,000 user tags collected during the first pilot with *Waisda?*. To determine the vocabulary used by the crowd, we compare the tags with existing controlled vocabularies. We compare the tags with the professional metadata by matching them to terms of the institutes' in-house thesaurus. Additionally, by matching the tags to the terms of a Dutch linguistic database, we conclude that a large part of the tags are Dutch words not used by professionals. To determine the type of content that the tags describe we first compare them with the subtitles. Finally, we manually classify the tags from a small number of videos. Using an existing classification model, we show the relation between the content in the video that is described and the type of tags that are used for these descriptions.

The rest of the paper is structured as follows. Section 2 discusses related work. Section 3 presents the approach we take in tackling the goals we set forth. Section 4 describes the materials we used in our study. Section 5 reports on the various experiments we performed on the user tags. Finally, section 6 draws conclusions and points to some further directions for research.

2. RELATED WORK

2.1 Games with a purpose

Games with a purpose (or GWAPs) are computer games, in which people, as a side effect of playing, perform tasks computers are unable to perform [18]. The first example of a GWAP was the ESP game [17], designed by Luis von Ahn, which harnesses human abilities to label images. The game randomly pairs up two players with the task to describe images. When both players provide the same label for an image, they score points and proceed to the next image. The labels entered by both users are associated to the image as metadata. In other words, the consensus among users provides a method to ensure the quality and consistency of the labels. Evaluation shows that these labels can be used to retrieve images with high precision and are almost all considered as good descriptions in a manual assessment.

The idea to collect metadata through games with a purpose has been applied to video footage in, for example, the Yahoo! video tag game [16], VideoTag[1], PopVideo[2] and *Waisda?*. The gameplay of these video labeling games differs from the ESP game in two ways: (i) multiple users can participate in a single game, and (ii) the users score points when the same tag is entered in a specific time interval. The underlying assumption is that tags are probably valid — trustworthily describe the video fragments — if they are entered independently by at least two players within a given time-frame. From here on we shall refer to tags that are mutually agreed on as *verified* tags.

Compared to the other video labeling games, *Waisda?* is unique in the sense that it is initiated by an audiovisual institute with the purpose to improve access to their collection [11]. With *Waisda?* the Netherlands Institute for Sound and Vision aims to collect metadata in a user vocabulary, as it is suggested that such metadata can help bridge the gap between the search queries and the indexing vocabulary [9]. In addition, it is expected that the resulting time-related metadata of the content within the video can improve support for finding fragments within entire broadcasts [7]. We investigate to what extent the tags collected in *Waisda?* provide a user vocabulary and analyze what type of content within the video they describe.

2.2 Evaluation of end-user tags

The steve.museum research [10] was one of first attempts to explore the role of user-generated metadata. In this collaboration of several art museums a collection of artworks was made available to the general public who were asked to tag them. Among other things, the project studied the relationship of the resulting folksonomy to professionally created museum documentation. The results showed that users tag the artworks of art from a perspective different than that of museum documentation: around 86% of tags were not found in museum documentation. We perform a similar study on the collection of *Waisda?* tags by comparing them to in-house thesaurus.

Museum staff also assessed the tags from the steve.museum project on usefulness when used to search for artworks. From the total number of tags, 88.2% were found to be useful. Following the methodology of steve-museum, Netherlands Institute for Sound and Vision also asked a senior cataloguer to judged a sample of *Waisda?* tags on their usefulness when searching for videos [1]. The sample consisted of the 20 most frequent and the 20 least frequent tags from two television programs. The cataloguer found the majority of the tags to be useful. She also noted that there seems to exist a difference between professional descriptions and end-user tags. While professionals describe the topical subject of the program, the players in *Waisda?* generally tag things that can be directly seen or heard in the video. One of the aims of this paper is to investigate the characteristics of the tags and what they describe in the video more methodically, and on a larger scale.

There is substantial body of research work that investigates user tags and folksomies. For example, in [4, 14] the overall quality of end-user tags is examined and the main strengths (flexibility, simplicity, user perspective, etc.) and potential weaknesses (typos, morphological variation of words, no synonym and no homonym control, etc.) are pinpointed. Gruber [3] identifies the roles of folksonomies and formal vocabularies and presents use-cases where both can naturally co-exist and cooperate. While many aspects of user tags are well covered in research, little or no attention is paid to the link between tags and the resources they are referring to. In this study we investigate which aspects of the resources (in our case videos) are covered by user tags.

2.3 Classification of user descriptions

Various schemes have been developed for classification of user descriptions for visual resources. One of the first is the Panofsky-Shatford model [12, 13] which focuses on the conceptual descriptions. Jaimes and Chang [8] developed a classification framework for visual resources (including video) that besides conceptual descriptions also considers perceptual (low-level features) and non-visual descriptions. Hollink at al. [6] combined the previous two schemes and developed a classification framework for user descriptions. As we exploit this framework to classify end-user tags, we explain it in more detail in the following section.

2.3.1 Tag classification framework

The framework distinguishes three top-levels: nonvisual level, perceptual level, and conceptual level. Descriptions at nonvisual level are meant to describe the context of the video but not its content. This is in contrast with descriptions at perceptual and conceptual level which are referring solely to the content of the video. Nonvisual level includes the following classes: *creator, title, date, location, carrier type,* etc.

Descriptions at perceptual level are derived from low-level audio and visual features of the video. In principle, no domain and no worldly knowledge is required to create descriptions at this level. Perceptual level classes are divided into classes of descriptions that refer to visual features such as *color, shape,* and *texture* and classes of descriptions that refer to audio features like *volume, pitch,* and *amplitude.*

Descriptions at conceptual level describe the semantic content of the video. To classify tags at this level the Panofsky-Shatford model is used. This model divides conceptual descriptions into three levels: *general* (generic things in the video), *specific* (specific things), and *abstract* (symbolic things). Each of the levels is further broken down into four facets:

---

[1]http://www.videotag.co.uk/

[2]http://www.gwap.com/gwap/gamesPreview/popvideo/

who, what, where, and *when* producing the Panofsky-Shatford 3x4 matrix.

In addition, descriptions may be about *visual objects* or may refer to the entire scene. We take the approach of [8] and define visual objects as entities that can be seen, sometimes differing from the traditional definition of object. Objects like the sky or the ocean would perhaps not be considered objects under the traditional definition, but correspond to our visual objects (as well as the traditional objects like car, house, etc.). Examples of scene descriptions include city, landscape, indoor, outdoor, still life, portrait, etc.

3. APPROACH

We divided our study of the *Waisda?* data in two parts. In the first part we focus on the user tags, investigating the vocabulary that users employ when describing videos. We analyse the relationship to the vocabularies used by professional cataloguers and general Web users. In the second part we focus on what the users describe. We analyse which aspects of the video are described and what type of tags are used for this.

With respect to the first part, we perform the following experiments. First, in order to estimate the lower bound of the fraction of user tags that are proper words, we examine the overlap between them and a general lexicon of the Dutch language. Furthermore, to determine if users and professionals use different vocabularies when describing videos, we investigate the overlap between all user tags and a typical domain thesaurus used by professionals in the cataloging process. A significant part of the non-verified tags — not entered by at least two different users — are not found in the either of the vocabularies we consider. To understand if these tags are just gibberish or actually have meaning we perform additional experiment using the Google[3] search engine as semantic filter: we deem a tag as meaningful only if the number of pages returned by Google is positive. The procedure is motivated by the intuition that if a person has used a word or a phrase on a web then it probably has some meaning. Subsequently, to shed more light on this potentially useful class of tags we select samples from both the tags found and not found by Google for further inspection.

With respect to the second part, we take a combined approach. First, we investigate what do users tend to describe more: things *heard* or things *seen* on screen. To this end we perform a study on the overlap between the user tags and the audio signal — subtitles for hearing impaired persons — for a sample of episodes. To get a more comprehensive understanding of the types of tags users usually add, we perform a qualitative study of a sample of user tags obtained through the *Waisda?* video tagging game. In the course of the study each tag is manually analyzed in the light of the video content it describes and categorized in terms of the classification framework described in section 2.3.1.

4. MATERIALS

In this section we describe the materials and resources used in the study.

4.1 Waisda? data snapshot

Subject of our analysis is the data collected in the first pilot project with *Waisda?*, a period starting from the launch

[3]http://www.google.com

date in May 2009 until 6th of January 2010. During this period, the game amassed over 46,000 unique tags ascribed to approximately 600 videos by roughly 2,000 different players[4]. The number of distinct tag entries exceeded 420,000. The database of the game contains information about players, games, videos, and tag entries. Each tag entry is represented by an instance of a ternary relation that relates the player that entered the tag, the video the tag was attached to, and the tag itself. Additionally, a tag entry is associated with the point in time — relative to the beginning of the video — when the tag was entered. It also includes a score computed taking into consideration agreement with other tag entries in the temporal neighborhood. Since almost all players originate from the Netherlands and all videos subjected to tagging are in Dutch, the language of the vast majority of tags – nearly 100% — is Dutch.

4.2 Domain and lexical vocabularies

For this study we used two vocabularies: GTAA and Cornetto. While the former is a domain vocabulary, the latter is a general lexical source that covers common lexical terms.

GTAA (Dutch acronym for Common Thesaurus Audiovisual Archives) is the thesaurus used by professional cataloguers in the Sound and Vision documentation process. It contains approximately 160,000 terms divided in six disjoint facets: subjects or keywords ($\approx$ 3,800 terms), locations ($\approx$ 17,000 terms), person names ($\approx$ 97,000 terms), organization-group-other names ($\approx$ 27,000 terms), maker names ($\approx$ 18,000 terms) and genres (113 terms). GTAA terms are interlinked with each other and documented using four properties: Broader Term, Narrower Term, Related Term and Scope note. While all GTAA terms may have related terms and scope notes, only terms from subject and genres facet are allowed to have narrower and broader terms. Complementary to the narrower/broader term hierarchy, terms from the subject facet are classified by theme in 88 subcategories which are organized into 16 top-level categories.

Cornetto is a lexical semantic database of Dutch that contains 40K entries, including the most generic and central part of the language. It is build by combining Dutch Wordnet (DWN) with Referentie Bestand Nederlands (RBN) which features FrameNet-like information for Dutch [19]. Cornetto organizes nouns, verbs, adjectives and adverbs into synonym sets called *synsets*. A synset is a set of words with the same part of speech that can be interchanged in a certain context. Synsets are related to each other by semantic relations — like hyperonomy, hyponomy, meronomy etc. — which may be used across part of speech. Although Cornetto contains 59 different kinds semantic relations, hyperonymy and hyponomy are by far the most frequent ones, accounting for almost 92% of all semantic relation instances.

4.3 Videos

For the manual classification the number of programs in the *Waisda?* is too large to include all of them. In addition, subtitles are not available for all videos. Therefore, for the manual classification and comparison with the subtitles we opted for select a subset. We selected five episodes: the two best-tagged videos, one averagely tagged video and two low-tagged videos. The two best-tagged videos are episodes

[4]Throughout this text we use the terms *player* and *user* interchangeably

Episode	All tags	Verified	Category
Farmer seeks wife 1	25,965	5,837	*Amusement*
Farmer seeks wife 2	22,792	6,153	*Amusement*
Traceless	1,007	274	*Amusement, Informative*
Reporter	403	73	*Informative*
The Walk	257	45	*Religious*

Table 1: Sample of waisda? episodes used in the experiments.

from a popular Dutch reality show, *Farmer seeks Wife*[5], categorized as amusement. The averagely tagged video is an episode from the *Traceless*[6] series, classified as amusement and informative program. The two low-tagged videos are episodes from *The Walk*[7] and *Reporter*[8] series, categorized as religious and informative, respectively. Table 1 summarizes the most pertinent information about the episodes. Prior research [1] suggested that the program genre might in fact influence the types of tags users add. To account for this phenomenon, we made sure that videos and fragments of all genres are present in our sample.

4.4 Subtitles

For the comparison of the tags with the audio signal we make use of the subtitle files associated with the television programs. Subtitles are textual versions of the dialog in films and television programs, usually displayed at the bottom of the screen[9]. Each dialog excerpt is accompanied with timepoints — relative to the beginning of the video — when the dialog excerpt appears on and disappears from the screen. The subtitles files we use were obtained from KRO broadcasting and are specified in the SubRip text file format[10].

5. EXPERIMENTS

In this section we present the results from the three experiments: matching tags to vocabularies, matching tags to subtitles and manual classification of the tags.

5.1 Matching tags to vocabularies

In this experiment we matched all *waisda?* tags to two vocabularies: the general lexicon of Dutch language Cornetto and the domain thesaurus GTAA. In mapping the tags to concepts we take the following approach. We deem a tag and GTAA term to be a positive match only if they are the same string (ignoring case). A tag and Cornetto synset are considered a positive match only if at least one of the words associated with the synset is equal (in case-insensitive manner) with the tag.

The results of the mapping of *Waisda?* tags against Cornetto and GTAA are presented in table 2. We observe that

[5]http://www.bzv.kro.nl/
[6]http://spoorloos.kro.nl/
[7]http://dewandeling.kro.nl/
[8]http://reporter.kro.nl/
[9]Timed Text Working Group, http://www.w3.org/AudioVideo/TT/
[10]http://en.wikipedia.org/wiki/SubRip#SubRip_text_file_format

	All tags		Verified	
Total	46,792		12,963	
In GTAA	3,850	(8%)	1,825	(14%)
In Cornetto	10,939	(23%)	5,669	(44%)

Table 2: Overlap of *Waisda?* tags with GTAA thesaurus and Dutch linguistic database, Cornetto.

	Facet	Tags
GTAA	Subject	1199
	Location	613
	Genre	52
	Person	118
	Maker	4
	Name	673

	Types	Tags
Cornetto	Noun	7222
	Verb	2090
	Adjective	1693
	Adverb	171

Table 3: Waisda? tags distribution over GTAA facets and Cornetto synset types.

only a small part of the unique tags are found in GTAA (8%). A larger number of the tags are found in Cornetto (23%). This difference between the overlap with GTAA and Cornetto is larger for the verified tags. Almost 44% of the verified tags is found in Cornetto, whereas only 14% is found in GTAA. In other words, at least 30% of the verified tags are proper Dutch words but would not be used by a professional cataloguer[11]. In addition, we observe that the verified tags are more often valid Dutch words than the non-verified ones.

Using the overlap with the vocabularies we can also provide a first classification of the tags. Using the different facets in GTAA we can distinguish different types of tags, such as subject terms, locations persons and organization names. In WordNet we can distinguish the tags matching with different types of words, such as noun and verb. Table 3 shows the distribution of user tags over the GTAA facets and Cornetto synsets. We observe that most tags are matched with subject terms from GTAA, but also a large number of tags could be matched to locations and names. The overlap with Cornetto shows that most tags are matched to nouns. Surprisingly, there is also a substantial number of tags matched with adjectives. In fact, one of the most frequently occurring tags is the adjective, nice.

From the total number of tags in total 41% are either verified or found in one of the vocabularies. Figure 1 provides a detailed view of these tags, showing the overlap between the different sets. We observe that 35% of the verified tags are

[11]GTAA contains all terms used to annotate videos in Sound and Vision

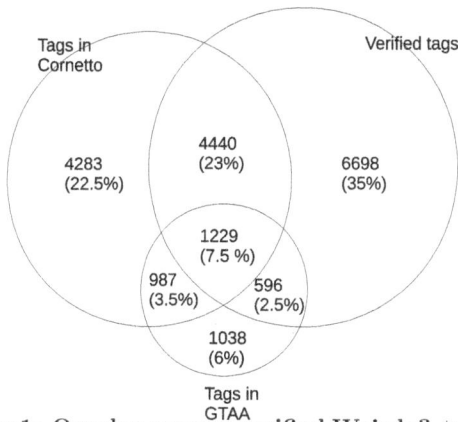

Figure 1: Overlap among verified Waisda? tags, tags in Cornetto, and tags in GTAA.

Episode	Tags in subtitles	Verified tags in subtitles
Farmer seeks wife 1	8,645 (33%)	2,546 (43%)
Farmer seeks wife 2	8,004 (35%)	2,967 (48%)
Traceless	182 (18%)	64 (23%)
Reporter	91 (23%)	16 (22%)
The Walk	59 (22%)	18 (40%)

Table 4: Overlap between the Waisda? tags and the video subtitles.

not found in either GTAA or Cornetto. Further investigation revealed that some of these tags do correspond to terms from the vocabularies, but were not found by the matching algorithm. We also observe that 32% (the sum of 22.5%, 3.5% and 6%) of the tags are found in the vocabularies, but are not verified.

The majority of the tags, approximately 59%, are neither found in Cornetto and GTAA nor they are verified. Further analyses revealed that almost half of these tags are comprised of more that one word. While this could to some extent explain why they were not found in Cornetto and GTAA (these vocabularies predominately have single words) and they were not verified (likelihood of reaching a tag agreement among players decreases as the length of the tags increases) we still do not know if they are, in fact, meaningful. To get an answer to this question, we perform additional analysis using Google as semantic filter. For each tag we carried out a phrase search (tag was enclosed in quotes, "") and observed the number of hits (pages) that were returned. A tag is deemed as meaningful only if the number of hits returned is positive.

For approximately 84% of the tags, that were not found verified or not found in a vocabulary, Google returned positive number of hits. We sampled 200 tags from the group with no hits (zero-sample) and 200 tags with the group with positive number of hits (pos-sample) for further analysis. We discovered that the tags in the zero-sample could be divided in three groups: garbled text with no meaning whatsoever, seriously mistyped words (bordering to garbled text), and entire sentences or excerpts from sentences mostly grammatically incorrect. The pos-sample, on the other hand, contained morphological variations of proper words, proper words combined with characters that are not letters, slang, names, idioms and phrases, and other common collocations.

In conclusion, the difference between the overlap with GTAA and Cornetto indicates that the user tags complement the vocabulary used by professional cataloguers. The tags that are found in GTAA are predominantly subject terms, but also include locations and names. We also found evidence that user agreement filters out sloppy tags, as the verified tags are more often valid Dutch words than the non-verified ones. However, a large part of the non-verified tags could still be potentially useful, as some of them can be

found in GTAA or Cornetto. Moreover, the majority of non-verified tags were 'deemed' meaningful by Google.

5.2 Tags in subtitles

In this experiment we investigate the fraction of Waisda? tags that refers to the audio portion of the video content. To this end, we compare the tags associated with the five videos described in section 4.3 against the respective video subtitles for hearing impaired persons (see section 4.4).

Prior to running the analysis, all dialog text from the subtitles was broken up into words and punctuation through a process known as tokenization. Afterwards, to account for morphological variants, all words were reduced to their canonical forms through a linguistic procedure called stemming. Subsequently, the stem of each tag associated with the aforementioned videos was compared against all words in the subtitles in the appropriate video that appear at most 10 seconds before the tag was entered. The time interval of 10 seconds was chosen as a reasonable amount of time needed by an average player to type in a tag. An identical time interval was used by the designers of Waisda? as the time frame for matching tags added by different players.

The results of the analysis are summarized in table 4. On average 26% of all tags also occur in the subtitles. This number is slightly higher when it comes to verified tags, on average 35% of all verified tags are found in the subtitles. We explain the large overlap by the fact that the audio stream of the video provides an easy way for the players to score points. This practice may, however, impair the richness of the user tags. In addition, when the subtitles of a video are available for retrieval, the user tags provide less added value.

5.3 Tag classification

In this experiment we performed a manual qualitative analysis on the tags of the five videos described in section 4.3. We only consider the verified tags of the videos. Due to the prohibitively large number of tags, for the episodes of Farmer seeks Wife we only consider the tags of two fragments. We excluded 182 tags from the sample since they were words with no descriptive power, such as particles and prepositions. In total the tag sample consisted of 1354 tags.

The tags were collectively analyzed by the authors. Each tag was considered in the light of the video fragment it describes. First, the tags were classified according to the different levels of abstraction: non-visual, perceptual and conceptual. We found no tags at non-visual level, and there were only 11 tags at perceptual level, all referring to colors. The rest of the tags (1,343) were all conceptual. The vast major-

(a) Keyframe extracted from Farmer seeks Wife episode's shot in which Yvon (the young lady) gives Amsterdam sausage as present to Anna (the elderly lady).

	Abstract	General	Specific
Who	kind lady	woman	Anna
What	typical present	present	Amsterdam sausage
Where	idyllic countryside	kitchen	the Netherlands
When	elimination day	morning	May 10th 2008

(b) Example of how tags (descriptions) of the keyframe above can be classified in terms of the Panofsky-Shatford model.

Figure 2: Classification of user tags.

ity of these conceptual tags, precisely 1,313, were describing objects, whereas only 30 were about scenes. We continue our investigation by focusing on the conceptual object tags.

In classifying the conceptual object tags we followed the guidelines compiled by Hollink et. al [6] — figure 2 shows an example of a classification of tags for one video fragment. We consider a tag to be specific if it possesses the property of uniqueness, for example the name of a person (Anna). A tag is abstract if its level of subjectivity allows for differences in opinion, for example, "kind lady" or "idyllic countryside". We deem a tag to be general when only everyday worldly knowledge is required to apply it in the context of the video, for example, "woman" or "present". To determine the facet a tag belongs to, we used the following guidelines. A tag is in the *who* facet if it refers to the *subject* (person, object, etc) of the video fragment. A tag belongs to to the *where* facet if it refers to a location, and to the *when* facet if it refers to time. A tag is associated with the *what* facet if it refers to an object or event in the video.

Table 5.3 shows the distribution of the object-level tags across the categories of the Panofsky-Shatford model. Looking at the total number of tags at the different abstraction levels, we observe that the majority of the tags are general (74%), while only 7% are at the abstract level and 9% at the specific level. On the other hand, looking at the total number of tags in the facets, we observe that the majority of the tags belong to the What facet (57%). Furthermore, a considerable number of tags are in the Who facet and only a small number of tags belong to the Where and When facets. Looking at the relations between the abstraction levels and the facets we observe that almost all tags in the What facet are general, sometimes abstract, but rarely specific. The

	Abstract	General	Specific	
Who	10	166	177	31%
What	73	563	12	57%
Where	0	68	8	7%
When	4	31	6	5%
	7%	74%	9%	

Table 5: Distribution of the object-level tags across the categories of the Panofsky-Shatford model.

descriptions in the Who facet are, however, at both the general and the specific level, but rarely abstract. Most of the tags in the Where facet are generic, and little are specific place or country names. Finally, we encountered 195 tags that we could not classify in any of the facets. Most of the time, these tags were modifiers — typically adjectives and adverbs — that describe how an action was performed, for example nice, better etc.

Our results show similarities with classification of image annotations by Hollink et al. [6]. They also found that a large majority of the descriptions are at the conceptual level. She, however, found a larger number of scenes (30%) at the conceptual level. A possible explanation for this difference could be the fast pace of the game, which makes the player focus on the directly perceivable objects instead of the overall scene. The evaluation of the tags by a professional cataloguer also suggested that the users focus on what can be directly seen or heard. Hollink et. al also found the majority of the descriptions to be at the general level (74%).

6. DISCUSSION AND FUTURE WORK

In this section we summarize the main observations from our experiments and discuss to what extent the tags collected with *Waisda?* fulfill the aims of the Netherlands Institute for Sound and Vision. In addition, we discuss how the results of our study can improve future versions of the game.

From the comparison of the tags with the terms from the GTAA thesaurus of the institute and the linguistic database of Dutch, Cornetto, we made several observations. We can confirm that the aim of the institute to collect metadata in a user vocabulary can be achieved with the *Waisda?* video labeling game. Comparable to the results that were found in the Steve.museum tagging project we found small overlap with the terms in the vocabulary used by professional cataloguers. In addition, almost half of the verified tags are valid Dutch words, as they were found in Cornetto.

The number of verified tags found in Cornetto is much higher than the number of tags that are not verified. This provides evidence for the assumption of video labeling games that user agreement on tags can be used to filter out non-well-formed. We also observed that a large part of the tags that are not verified could still be potentially useful. A large part of the non-verified tags could also be found in the vocabularies. In addition, we deemed most tags meaningful as they returned results from Google.

The manual classification of the tags provides details about the type of tags that were collected in *Waisda?* and how they relate to the video content. Users predominately describe *what* appears in the video using generic tags. Although the tags also provide some coverage of the subject, the *who*, and the location, the *when* in the video fragments. While the persons occurring as the subject are described both in generic and specific tags, there are very few tags describing specific locations.

Together with The Netherlands Institute for Sound and Vision we are preparing a second pilot project with *Waisda?*. The results of this study show several limitations of the current metadata, that we aim to address in this pilot. One limitation is the low number of specific type of tags in the *who* and *where* facets. We are exploring how users can be motivated to provide such tags. We showed that by matching the tags to controlled vocabularies we can derive the type of the tags. We are exploring if this can be used within the game to detect what type of tags are entered, and for example provide more points when the user enters a location name. For this purpose the recall of the current algorithm to match tags and terms should be improved.

Another characteristic of the current *Waisda?* tags is that many are also found in the subtitles. In case these subtitles are also available for retrieval this can be considered a limitation of the tags, as it reduces the added value. Computing the overlap between the tags and the subtitles during the game can be used to detect such tags, and for example be used to motivate users to provide different tags.

An assumption of labeling games is that only the verified tags are associated to the content as metadata. Our study shows that this approach would exclude many potentially useful tags. A solution could be to include tags that can be matched with a term from a controlled vocabulary. Another solution could be to compare the syntactically different tags based on their semantic similarity. We are currently exploring the consequences of these methods.

Finally, in future work we will experiment with the usefulness of the tags in search tasks. From the current results we learned that tags describe what users directly see or hear in the video. They do not provide a topical description of a fragment. We expect that the current tags are, therefore, suited to find objects within a specific video, but are as of yet less useful to find specific fragments. In future work we will explore methods to also collect topical descriptions of video scenes, by extending the game and/or with post-processing of the tags after the game.

Acknowledgements

We like to thank Johan Oomen, Maarten Brinkerink and Lotte Belice Baltussen from the Netherlands Institute for Sound and Vision for initiating and guiding the *Waisda?* project. We also like to thank Q42 for the development of *Waisda?* and making the collected data available. This research was partially supported by the PrestoPRIME project, funded by the European Commission under ICT FP7 (Seventh Framework Programme, Contract No. 231161).

7. REFERENCES

[1] L. B. Baltussen. Waisda? video labeling game: Evaluation report, 2009. [Online; accessed 20-January-2010] http://research.imagesforthefuture.org/index.php/waisda-video-labeling-game-evaluation-report/.

[2] S. Chan. Tagging and searching — serendipity and museum collection database. In *Museums and the Web 2007: Proceedings*, Toronto, Canada, March 2007.

[3] T. Gruber. Ontology of folksonomy: A mash-up of apples and oranges. *International Journal on Semantic Web & Information Systems*, 3(2):1–11, 2007.

[4] M. Guy and E. Tonkin. Folksonomies: Tidying up tags? *D-Lib Magazine*, 12(1), January 2006.

[5] L. Hollink, B. Huurnink, M. van Liempt, J. Oomen, A. de Jong, M. de Rijke, G. Schreiber, and A. Smeulders. A multidisciplinary approach to unlocking television broadcast archives. *Interdisciplinary Science Reviews*, 34(2):257–271, June 2009.

[6] L. Hollink, G. Schreiber, B. J. Wielinga, and M. Worring. Classification of user image descriptions. *Int. J. Hum.-Comput. Stud.*, 61(5):601–626, 2004.

[7] B. Huurnink, C. G. M. Snoek, M. de Rijke, and A. W. M. Smeulders. Today's and tomorrow's retrieval practice in the audiovisual archive. In *ACM International Conference on Image and Video Retrieval*, 2010.

[8] A. Jaimes, R. Jaimes, and S. fu Chang. A conceptual framework for indexing visual information at multiple levels. In *in proceedings of SPIE Internet Imaging 2000*, pages 2–15, 2000.

[9] C. Jorgensen. Image access, the semantic gap, and social tagging as a paradigm shift. *Proceedings 18th Workshop of the American Society for Information Science and Technology Special Interest Group in Classification Research, Milwaukee, Wisconsin*, 2007.

[10] T. Leason and steve.museum. Steve: The art museum social tagging project: A report on the tag contributor experience. In *Museums and the Web 2009: Proceedings*, Toronto, Canada, March 2009.

[11] J. Oomen, L. Belice Baltussen, S. Limonard, A. van Ees, M. Brinkerink, L. Aroyo, J. Vervaart, K. Asaf, and R. Gligorov. Emerging practices in the cultural heritage domain - social tagging of audiovisual heritage. In *Proceedings of Web Science 2010: Extending the Frontiers of Society On-Line*. The Web Science Trust, April 2010.

[12] E. Panofsky. *Studies in Iconology: Humanistic Themes in the Art of the Renaissance*. Harper & Row, 1972.

[13] S. Shatford. Analyzing the subject of a picture: A theoretical approach. *Cataloging & Classification Quarterly*, 6:39 – 62, 1986.

[14] L. F. Spiteri. Structure and form of folksonomy tags: The road to the public library catalogue. *Webology*, 4(2), June 2007.

[15] M. Springer, B. Dulabahn, P. Michel, B. Natanson, D. Reser, D. Woodward, and H. Zinkham. For the common good: The library of congress flickr pilot project: Report summary. Technical report, Library of Congress, 2008.

[16] R. van Zwol, L. Garcia, G. Ramirez, B. Sigurbjornsson, and M. Labad. Video tag game. In *WWW 2008*, April 2008.

[17] L. von Ahn and L. Dabbish. Labeling images with a computer game. In *CHI '04: Proceedings of the SIGCHI conference on Human factors in computing systems*, pages 319–326, New York, NY, USA, 2004. ACM.

[18] L. von Ahn and L. Dabbish. Designing games with a purpose. *Commun. ACM*, 51(8):58–67, 2008.

[19] P. Vossen, I. Maks, R. Segers, and H. van der Vliet. Integrating lexical units, synsets and ontology in the Cornetto database. In *LREC'08*, 2008.

Language Resources Extracted from Wikipedia

Denny Vrandečić
AIFB, Karlsruhe Institute
of Technology (KIT)
76128 Karlsruhe, Germany
and Wikimedia Deutschland
10777 Berlin, Germany
denny.vrandecic@kit.edu

Philipp Sorg
AIFB, Karlsruhe Institute
of Technology (KIT)
76128 Karlsruhe, Germany
philipp.sorg@kit.edu

Rudi Studer
AIFB, Karlsruhe Institute
of Technology (KIT)
76128 Karlsruhe, Germany
rudi.studer@kit.edu

ABSTRACT

Wikipedia provides an interesting amount of text for more than hundred languages. This also includes languages where no reference corpora or other linguistic resources are easily available. We have extracted background language models built from the content of Wikipedia in various languages. The models generated from Simple and English Wikipedia are compared to language models derived from other established corpora. The differences between the models in regard to term coverage, term distribution and correlation are described and discussed. We provide access to the full dataset and create visualizations of the language models that can be used exploratory. The paper describes the newly released dataset for 33 languages, and the services that we provide on top of them.

Categories and Subject Descriptors

I.2.7 [**Natural Language Processing**]: Language models; I.2.6 [**Learning**]: Knowledge acquisition

General Terms

Languages, Measurement

1. INTRODUCTION

Statistical natural language processing requires corpora of text written in the language that is going to be processed. Whereas widely studied languages like English and Chinese traditionally have excellent coverage with corpora of relevant sizes, for example the Brown corpus [4] or Modern Chinese Language Corpus, this is not true for many languages that have not been studied in such depth and breath. For some of these languages, viable corpora are still painfully lacking.

Wikipedia is a Web-based, collaboratively written encyclopedia [1] with official editions in more than 250 languages. Most of these language editions of Wikipedia exceed one million words, thus exceeding the well-known and widely-used Brown corpus in size.

We have taken the text of several Wikipedia language editions, cleansed it, and created corpora for 33 languages. In order to evaluate how viable these corpora are, we have calculated unigram language models for the English Wikipedia, and compared it to widely used corpora. Since the English Wikipedia edition is far larger than any other — and size of a corpus is a crucial factor for its viability — we have also taken the Simple English Wikipedia edition, being smaller than many other language editions, and compared it to the reference corpora as well. The results of this comparison show that the language models derived from the Simple English Wikipedia are strongly correlated with the models of much larger corpora. This gives support to our assumption that the language models created from the corpora of other language editions of Wikipedia have an acceptable quality, as long as they compare favorably to the Simple English Wikipedia.

We make the generated unigram language models and the corpora available. The full data sets can be downloaded.[1] The website also provides a novel, graphical corpus exploration tool – Corpex – not only over the newly created corpora that we report on here, but also usable for already established corpora like the Brown corpus.

The next section introduces some background information on Wikipedia and language corpora, followed by related work in Section 3. We then describe the language models in Section 4, including their properties and acquisition. Section 5 compares the Wikipedia-acquired language models with widely-used language models and points out the differences and commonalities. We finish with the conclusions and future work in Section 6.

2. BACKGROUND

2.1 Wikipedia

Wikipedia[2] [1] is a wiki-based collaboratively edited encyclopedia. It aims to "*gather the sum of human knowledge*". Today Wikipedia provides more than 17 million articles in 279 languages, and further a small set of incubator languages. It is run on the MediaWiki software [3], which was developed specifically for Wikipedia. In general, every article is open to be edited by anyone, (mostly) through the browser. Even though this editing environment is very limited compared to rich text editing offered by desktop word processing systems, the continuous effort has led to a com-

---

[1] http://km.aifb.kit.edu/sites/corpex
[2] http://www.wikipedia.org

petitive, and widely used, encyclopedia. The content is offered under a free license, which allows us to process the text and publish the resulting data.

As stated, Wikipedia exists in many language editions. A special language edition is the so called *Simple English Wikipedia*.[3] The goal of the Simple English Wikipedia is to provide an encyclopedic resource for users without a full grasp of the English language, e.g. children learning to read and write, or non-native speakers learning the language. For our work this means that we have, besides the actual English Wikipedia,[4] a second Wikipedia edition in the English language that is much smaller in size.

2.2 Language Corpora

Language corpora are the main tool of research in statistical natural language processing. They are big samples of text that have the purpose to represent the usage of a specific natural language. Using a corpus in a specific language, different statistical characteristics of this language can be defined. For example the distribution of terms is often used in NLP applications. This distribution is either measured independently (unigram model) or in context of other terms (n-gram model).

Language models extracted from these language corpora are used in all application that *recognize* or *synthesize* natural language. Examples for applications that recognize natural language are:

Speech Recognition: Language models are used to identify the text sequence with the highest probability matching the speech input.

Spell-checking: In the context of previous terms, the most probable spelling of terms is identified based on the language model.

Syntax Parser: Syntax parsers depend on language models to build syntax trees of natural language sentences. If annotated with part-of-speech tags, language corpora are also used as training data.

The examples presented above describe applications of language corpora to recognition tasks. Further, language models are also applied in systems that synthesize text:

Auto-completion: The term distribution encoded in language models can be used to auto-complete input of users. In many cases, these are language models optimized for a specific task, for example language models of queries in search systems. For auto-completion, often the context of previous terms is used to compute the probability of the next term.

Machine Translation: Machine translation systems recognize text in one language and synthesize text in another language. To ensure grammatical correctness or at least readability of the synthesized text, language models can be used to identify the most probable word order in the output sentences.

Over the years, a number of corpora have been established. These corpora contain documents of high quality

Corpus	Docs	Unique Terms	Tokens
Brown	500	36,708	958,352
Reuters	806,791	369,099	171,805,788
TREC4+5	528,155	501,358	217,215,818
JRC-Acquis (EN)	7,745	229,618	41,163,635

Table 1: Size of reference copora measured by number of documents, number of unique terms (or types) and total number of tokens.

with little noise. Examples are news items or legislative documents. As these corpora mostly contain full sentences that are grammatical correct, they are often used as representative corpora of the according languages. This is also a main difference to automatically constructed corpora. Examples for such automatically constructed corpora are collections of Web documents that are crawled from the Web. In these corpora, the level of noise is much higher as they contain for example syntax elements or misspelled terms.

In our experiments, we use several English corpora for comparison. We focus on English due to the availability of English corpora. In other language such as Croatian or Slovenian, only few corpora are freely available. In detail, we use the following corpora:

Brown Corpus: [4] This corpus was published as a standard corpus of present-day edited American English. It has been manually tagged with part-of-speech information and has therefore often been used as training and testing corpus for deep analysis NLP applications.

TREC Text Research Collection V.4+5: [5] This corpus was used in the ad-hoc retrieval challenge at TREC. It contains a compilation of documents from the Financial Times Limited, the Congressional Record of the 103rd Congress, the Federal Register, the Foreign Broadcast Information Service, and the Los Angeles Times.

Reuters Corpus (Volume 1): [6] Collection of news stories in the English language that has often been used as real-world benchmarking corpus.

JRC-Acquis: [7] Legislative documents of the European Union that are translated in many languages. This corpus is often used as a parallel corpus, as the sentences are aligned across the translations.

Table 1 contains statistics about the size of the presented reference corpora in respect to the number of documents, unique terms and tokens.

3. RELATED WORK

In recent years, Wikipedia has often been used as language resource. An example is presented by Tan and Peng [12]. They use a Wikipedia based n-gram model for their approach to query segmentation. Using the model extracted

---

[3] http://simple.wikipedia.org
[4] http://en.wikipedia.org

[5] http://trec.nist.gov/data/docs_eng.html
[6] http://about.reuters.com/researchandstandards/corpus/
[7] http://langtech.jrc.it/JRC-Acquis.html

from the English Wikipedia, they achieve performance improvements of 24%. They therefore present a successful application of the language models derived from the English Wikipedia. In this paper we show that other language editions of Wikipedia can be exploited in the same way and are therefore valuable resources for language models in various languages.

Exploiting the multilingual aspects of Wikipedia, different approaches have been suggested to use the Wikipedia database in different languages for multilingual Information Retrieval (IR) [11, 10]. The language models presented in this paper have no dependencies across languages. For each language, we suggest to exploit the according Wikipedia edition to build a language resource that is specific for this language. However, these resources could also be applied in cross-lingual systems, as many of these systems also rely on language-specific background models.

Apart from Wikipedia, language corpora have also been built from other Web resources. Recently, a number of huge Web-based corpora have been made available by Google[8] and Microsoft.[9] Baroni et al. [2] constructed large corpora of English, German and Italian Web documents that were also annotated based on linguistic processing. Ghani et al. [5] proposed to use the Web to create language corpora for minority languages. By creating and adapting queries for Internet search engines, they collect documents with a broad topic coverage. In this paper, we claim that the coverage is already given by Wikipedia for many languages. We show that Wikipedia based language models have similar properties than language models derived from traditionally used corpora. This is not known for the Web based corpora. Further, Wikipedia supports many more languages than the above mentioned Web based resources. Finally, given the lower effort to access Wikipedia compared to crawling the Web, we claim that using Wikipedia as a resource for language models is an appropriate choice in many application scenarios.

There are other multilingual corpora that are not based on Web documents. For example, Koehn [6] created a parallel corpus of the proceedings of the European Parliament that is mainly used to train machine translation systems. This corpus is similar to the JRC-Acquis corpus used in our experiments. However, the results of our experiments support the conclusion that these corpora can not be used to build representative language models. A possible explanation is that these multilingual corpora are much smaller compared to the other resources and that they are often focused on specific topic fields.

The application of language models are manifold. A prominent example are retrieval models used in IR. Zhai and Lafferty [13] suggest to use background language models for smoothing. These models are based on a collection of datasets that also includes the TREC4+5 corpus. This motivates the comparison of the Wikipedia language models to this corpus presented in Section 5. Most of the related work about the application of language models is based on tasks in English. The language models that we suggest in this paper could be used to apply the same approaches in various languages. The improvements achieved in specific tasks such as IR through the usage of background language

models, could then be replicated and verified in experiments using corpora in other languages than English as well.

4. THE LANGUAGE MODELS

4.1 Acquistion

Articles in Wikipedia are written using the MediaWiki syntax, a wiki syntax offering a flexible, but very messy mix of some HTML elements and some simple markup. There exists no proper formal definition for the MediaWiki syntax. It is hard to discern which parts of the source text of an article is actual content, and which parts provide further functions, like navigation, images, layout, etc. This introduces a lot of noise to the text.

We have filtered the article source code quite strictly, throwing away roughly a fourth of the whole content. This includes most notably all template calls, which are often used, e.g., to create infoboxes and navigational elements. The actual script that provides the filtering is available on the Corpex website as open source, so that it can be reused and further refined. When exploring the corpus, one can easily see that quite some noise remains. We aim to further clean up the data and improve the corpora over time.

The content of the Wikipedia editions is provided as XML dumps.[10] We have selected only the actual encyclopedic articles, and not the numerous pages surrounding the project, including discussion pages for the articles, project management pages, user pages, etc., as we expect those to introduce quite some bias and idiosyncrasies. The table in Figure 1 contains the date when the XML dump was created, for reference and reproducibility of the results. Combined, we have processed around 75 gigabytes of data.

4.2 Statistical overview

Figure 1 offers an overview of some statistics on the acquired corpora and the generated language models.

The rank of the Wikipedia language edition, the depth, and the number of tokens are meant as indicators for the quality of the generated corpus. As discussed in Section 5, we estimate the quality of the Simple English Wikipedia compared to other corpora. The results indicate that any corpora with at least the depth, rank, and size (w.r.t number of tokens) should be at least as reliable as a language corpus as the Simple English Wikipedia is. The corpora created from other language editions, that do not fulfill these conditions, should be used with more care as their quality is not sufficiently demonstrated yet.

The depth in Figure 1 refers to a measure introduced by the Wikipedia community, called the *Wikipedia article depth*,[11] which is meant as a rough indicator for the strength of the collaboration within the wiki. It assumes that a high number of edits and support pages indicate a higher quality of the language edition overall, and is defined as

$$\text{Depth} = \frac{\#\text{Edits}}{\#\text{Total pages}}(\frac{\#\text{Non-Article pages}}{\#\text{Articlepages}})^2$$

4.3 Web site and service

We provide a web site that allows to easily explore the created frequency distributions, called Corpex. Corpex allows

---

[8] http://ngrams.googlelabs.com/
[9] http://research.microsoft.com/en-us/ collaboration/focus/cs/web-ngram.aspx
[10] http://downloads.wikimedia.org
[11] http://meta.wikimedia.org/wiki/Depth

to select the corpus of interest and then to explore the probabilities within the given corpus, both on word completion and the next character.

Corpex also allows to compare two different corpora. Figure 2 and 3 are screenshot of Corpex for the letter t on the English Wikipedia and the Brown corpus respectively. This allows the user to exploratively acquire an understanding for and compare the frequency distribution of words in the explored corpora.

Corpex also provides a RESTful service that allows to gather the same data in JSON, so that it can be further processed. Corpex is implemented using dynamically materialized prefix trees on the file system, thus leading to response times of under 50 milliseconds in general.

Corpex also offers the complete frequency lists for download, so that it can be used for further processing or analysis.[12]

5. ANALYSIS AND DISCUSSION

In this paper, we propose to use Wikipedia in various languages as a language corpus. For many of these languages, no other corpora are available. However for English, established corpora as presented in Section 2.2 can be compared to the Wikipedia corpus. We intend to show that the Wikipedia corpus in English as well as Simple English have the same characteristics as the reference corpora. By extending this hypothesis, we claim that the Wikipedia corpus in other languages can also be used as a background language model. This is based on the fact that the language model derived from the Simple English Wikipedia, which is much smaller than the English Wikipedia, is very similar to the language model derived from the English Wikipedia. However this can not be verified due to the lack of appropriate reference corpora in these languages.

We will use several measures to compare the different corpora in our experiments:

Term Overlap: The percentage of common terms in two corpora in respect to all terms in each corpus. This also determines the *token overlap*, that is defined as the share of tokens of these common terms to all tokens. Both measures are non-symmetric for two corpora.

Pearson Product Moment Correlation: The number of occurrences of each term in two corpora is interpreted as drawings from two random variables X and Y, the Pearson product moment correlation coefficient computes the linear dependence of these variables [9]. A value of 1 implies perfect linear correlation and a value of 0 implies no linear correlation. However this does not exclude other non-linear correlations of X and Y.

Linear correlation of term occurrences in two corpora shows that terms are equally distributed and can therefore be applied as similarity measure of language corpora.

Jensen-Shannon Divergence: Considering the language models defined by two corpora, similarity measures defined on probability distributions can be used to compare these corpora. We use the Jensen-Shannon divergence [8] that is based on the Kullback-Leibler divergence [7]. These measures are rooted in information

[12]http://km.aifb.kit.edu/sites/corpex/data/

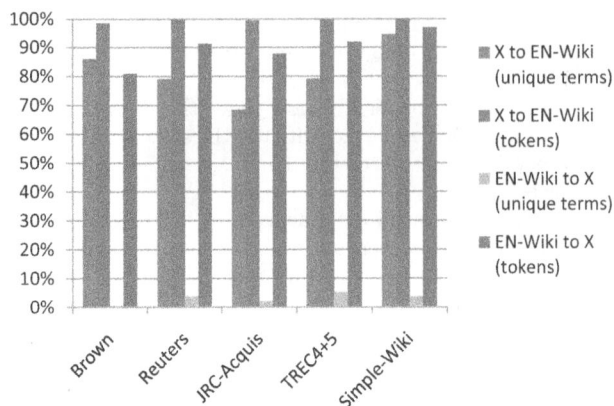

Figure 4: Common unique terms and overlapping tokens in the English Wikipedia and the reference corpora. The relative overlap values presented in this chart correspond to the percentage of common terms or overlapping tokens in respect to all terms or tokens in the respective corpus.

theory and measure the entropy of distributions given the information provided by another distribution. The Jensen-Shannon divergence has been established as a standard measure to compare two probability distributions.

Applied to the comparison of corpora, a low divergence value means that there is no information gain of one language model given the information of the other language model, which implies that the distributions are similar.

5.1 Term Overlap (English)

The term overlap in pairwise comparison of the reference corpora and Simple and English Wikipedia are presented in Table 2. The overlap between the reference corpora is astonishingly low — mostly below 50% with exception of the small Brown corpus. Even comparing the other corpora to the large English Wikipedia, the overlap is only between 79% and 86%.

A qualitative analysis of non-common terms shows that many of these terms are actually noise. While being written mainly in English, the used corpora also contain terms of other languages. Many of these foreign terms are not found in the English Wikipedia.

Despite of the low overlap of unique terms, the token overlap is much higher. In Figure 4 we visualize both term and token overlap of the English Wikipedia to all other corpora. Considering the overlap of the reference corpora to Wikipedia, the 80% common terms cover more than 99% of all tokens. In the other direction, the .4% to 5% of the Wikipedia terms that are also present in the reference corpora cover more than 80% of the tokens in Wikipedia. This clearly shows that the common terms are the most frequent terms and therefore important to characterize the language models.

5.2 Correlation of Language Models

We visualize the results of the correlation analysis using net charts. Each dataset is represented by an axis and a

	Brown	Reuters	JRC-Acquis	TREC4+5	Simple-Wiki	English-Wiki
Brown	-	77%	55%	83%	72%	86%
Reuters	8%	-	18%	50%	29%	79%
JRC-Acquis	9%	30%	-	34%	28%	69%
TREC4+5	6%	37%	15%	-	26%	79%
Simple	9%	37%	22%	45%	-	94%
English	.4%	4%	2%	5%	3%	-

Table 2: Common terms in the reference corpora and Simple and English Wikipedia.

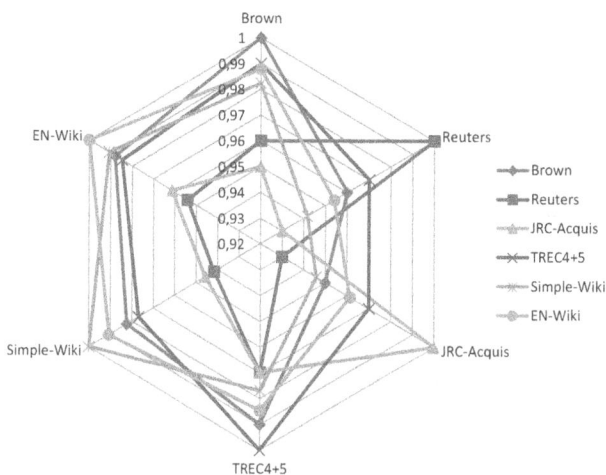

Figure 5: Net chart visualizing Pearson product moment correlation coefficient between any pair of the English corpora. For each corpus pair, only common terms are considered for the correlation value.

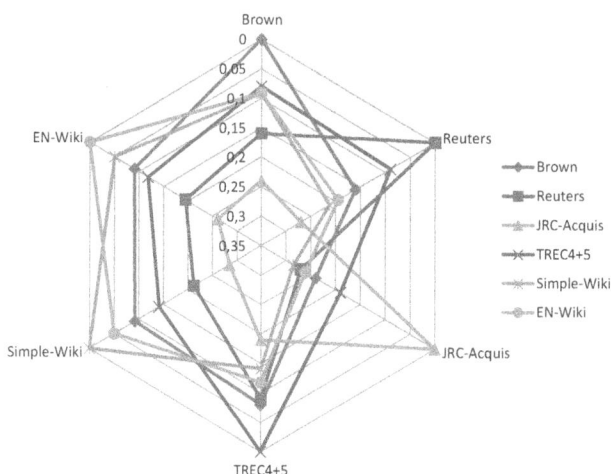

Figure 6: Net chart visualizing the Jensen-Shannon divergence between any pair of the English corpora.

data line. This allows to draw the pairwise comparison of any two corpora into one chart.

The values of the Pearson product moment correlation coefficient are presented in Figure 5, the values for the Jensen–Shannon divergence in Figure 6. The patterns found in both charts are very similar. This shows that both measures – motivated by a probabilistic model as well as by an information theoretic model – identify the same level of correlation of all corpus pairs. We draw the following conclusions of the results presented in Figure 5 and 6:

- Overall the correlation between any pair of corpus is very high. The correlation coefficient is always above .93 and the divergence value below .29.

  To get an idea of the range of these measures, we also compared the English Wikipedia to the German Wikipedia. Actually, the term overlap is approx. 25% in both directions covering more than 94% of all tokens in both Wikipedias. However the correlation coefficient is only .13 and the divergence .72. This shows that the correlation of the common terms is low for these corpora.

- The Brown, TREC4+5, Simple Wikipedia and English Wikipedia corpora have the highest correlation. Actually, the correlation coefficient between the Brown corpus and the English Wikipedia is .99 meaning almost perfect linear correlation. This supports our claim that Wikipedia can be used as representative language corpus like the Brown corpus for English.

  This also shows that the term distributions in Simple and English Wikipedia are very similar. While only using a fraction of the vocabulary, the content in the Simple Wikipedia is based on a similar language usage as the English Wikipedia.

- The Reuters corpus is correlated to the TREC4+5 corpus. Our hypothesis is that the large share of newspaper articles found in both corpora is the reason for this correlation.

- The JRC-Acquis corpus is the only outlier of our reference corpora. This corpus contains official legislative documents. The language usage in these documents is probably different to the language usage in Wikipedia and in newspaper articles as found in the Reuters and TREC4+5 corpus, which is supported by our findings.

6. CONCLUSIONS AND FUTURE WORK

In this paper, we suggested to exploit Wikipedia for language models in various languages. We also presented a novel visualization that allows to interactively explore the term distributions of different corpora. In summary, our main contributions are the following:

- We acquired and published unigram language models from Wikipedia for 33 languages, where some of them did not have yet any language models available.

- We compared the language models retrieved from the Wikipedia corpus with other language models based on reference corpora. This comparison allows some understanding about the quality of the acquired language models. In particular, we show that the language model derived from the Simple English Wikipedia is very similar to the language model derived from the English Wikipedia. As the Simple English Wikipedia is much smaller, we argue that other Wikipedia versions of comparable size or bigger have similar properties and can therefore be used as appropriate language resources.

- We proposed a novel visualization for exploring frequency distributions, which is available on the Web.

- We published a web service to programmatically use the frequency distributions, which can be for example used for auto-completion.

With the experience gathered on creating the first few corpora, we plan on turning Corpex into a pipeline that will be able to offer the service for the full set of language editions of Wikipedia, dynamically updating as new dumps are provided. This will offer access to a growing and up to date set of corpora for over 200 languages, even though for some of them the usage scenarios may be restricted due to insufficient size or quality.

We will also explore the creation of further language models besides frequency distributions, like n-grams. We hope that the provisioning of the full datasets and of all the means to create them will enable further scenarios and services beyond those described in this paper. The further analysis of the data may lead to measures for quality of the Wikipedia language editions. Beyond Wikipedia, the corpora and language models can provide much needed resources for NLP researchers in many languages.

Acknowledgements

Research reported in this paper was funded by the European Commission through the FP7 project RENDER[13] and the German Research Foundation (DFG) through the Multipla project.[14]

7. REFERENCES

[1] P. Ayers, C. Matthews, and B. Yates. *How Wikipedia works*. No Starch Press, 2008.

[2] M. Baroni, S. Bernardini, A. Ferraresi, and E. Zanchetta. The WaCky wide web: a collection of very large linguistically processed web-crawled corpora. *Language Resources and Evaluation*, 43(3):209–226, 2009.

[3] D. J. Barrett. *MediaWiki*. O'Reilly, 2008.

[4] W. N. Francis and H. Kucera. Brown corpus manual. Technical report, Department of Linguistics, Brown University, Providence, Rhode Island, US, 1979.

[5] R. Ghani, R. Jones, and D. Mladenić. Mining the web to create minority language corpora. In *Proceedings of the Tenth International Conference on Information and Knowledge Management*, CIKM '01, page 279–286, New York, NY, USA, 2001. ACM.

[6] P. Koehn. Europarl: A parallel corpus for statistical machine translation. In *Machine Translation Summit*, volume 5, 2005.

[7] S. Kullback and R. A. Leibler. On information and sufficiency. *The Annals of Mathematical Statistics*, 22(1):79–86, 1951.

[8] J. Lin. Divergence measures based on the shannon entropy. *IEEE Transactions on Information Theory*, 37(1):145–151, 1991.

[9] K. Pearson. Notes on the history of correlation. *Biometrika*, 13(1):25–45, Oct. 1920.

[10] M. Potthast, B. Stein, and M. Anderka. A Wikipedia-Based multilingual retrieval model. In *Proceedings of the 30th European Conference on Information Retrieval (ECIR)*, pages 522—530, Glasgow, 2008.

[11] P. Schönhofen, A. Benczúr, I. Bíró, and K. Csalogány. Cross-Language retrieval with wikipedia. In *Advances in Multilingual and Multimodal Information Retrieval*, pages 72—79. 2008.

[12] B. Tan and F. Peng. Unsupervised query segmentation using generative language models and wikipedia. In *Proceeding of the 17th International Conference on World Wide Web*, WWW '08, page 347–356, New York, NY, USA, 2008. ACM.

[13] C. Zhai and J. Lafferty. A study of smoothing methods for language models applied to information retrieval. *ACM Transactions on Information Systems (TOIS)*, 22:179–214, Apr. 2004.

---

[13]http://render-project.eu
[14]http://www.multipla-project.org/

Language	C	R	D	Date	Tokens	Terms	10+	Top50	l1	l2
Albanian	sq	64	27	2011/01/29	8,584,477	388,278	48,906	427	8.1	4.9
Bulgarian	bg	33	24	2011/02/02	32,518,959	844,892	124,321	618	8.4	5.3
Bosnian	bs	67	97	2011/02/02	7,392,085	453,828	54,998	1,301	8.4	5.5
Croatian	hr	37	21	2010/02/04	27,837,889	994,770	140,458	1,314	8.5	5.5
Czech	cs	17	35	2011/02/05	63,538,097	1,548,013	239,974	1,404	8.7	5.5
Danish	da	24	35	2011/01/30	36,497,359	1,006,141	126,626	404	10.3	5.3
Dutch	nl	9	30	2011/01/26	175,499,078	2,308,280	336,349	261	10.2	5.3
English	en	1	584	2011/01/15	2,014,858,488	7,659,102	1,110,470	295	8.8	4.9
– *Simple*	simple	41	55	2011/04/15	15,292,826	297,040	43,333	238	7.7	4.8
– *Brown*	brown	—	—	1960s	958,352	36,708	7,088	103	8.5	4.7
Estonian	et	38	26	2011/02/02	14,106,418	983,406	102,875	2,568	10.2	6.6
Finnish	fi	16	41	2011/01/31	57,456,478	2,686,562	292,152	3,136	12.0	7.3
French	fr	3	140	2011/01/12	486,524,274	3,107,353	497,189	243	8.4	4.9
German	de	2	88	2011/01/11	590,886,656	6,691,421	955,950	456	11.9	6.0
Greek	el	47	39	2011/02/03	25,208,880	756,738	104,184	480	8.7	5.6
Hungarian	hu	18	87	2011/02/03	77,661,090	2,641,225	304,770	1,474	10.3	6.1
Irish	ga	93	25	2011/02/06	2,819,777	145,031	16,528	183	8.1	4.8
Italian	it	5	78	2011/01/30	317,582,265	2,480,869	387,894	385	8.6	5.2
Latvian	lv	59	76	2011/02/05	8,141,029	446,366	59,215	1,667	8.6	6.1
Lithuanian	lt	28	17	2011/02/02	19,924,938	939,624	119,148	1,880	8.6	6.5
Maltese	mt	152	118	2011/01/30	1,357,178	81,034	10,808	337	7.7	5.1
Polish	pl	4	12	2011/01/27	167,946,149	2,694,814	446,576	1,687	9.0	6.0
Portuguese	pt	8	76	2011/01/24	177,010,439	1,711,936	259,032	362	8.4	5.0
Romanian	ro	20	88	2011/02/03	39,230,386	902,309	127,789	591	8.3	5.3
Serbian	sr	27	44	2010/01/30	39,351,179	1,182,685	160,632	710	8.4	5.5
Serbocroatian	sh	56	17	2010/02/07	14,644,455	731,093	93,955	1,579	8.5	5.5
Sinhalese	si	131	133	2011/02/03	4,220,958	287,042	30,722	1,170	7.9	5.2
Slovak	sk	29	21	2011/01/29	24,784,192	925,677	130,164	1,132	8.8	5.6
Slovenian	sl	35	17	2011/01/29	23,859,807	847,990	112,180	664	8.6	5.4
Spanish	es	7	171	2011/01/14	354,499,700	2,741,188	418,910	273	8.6	5.0
Swedish	sv	11	46	2011/01/29	82,785,880	1,953,939	249,579	527	10.8	5.6
Vietnamese	vi	19	44	2011/02/06	56,479,754	700,090	68,117	239	7.9	3.8
Waray-Waray	war	36	0	2011/02/05	2,589,896	130,047	7,974	15	7.6	4.8
Zulu	zu	247	0	2011/01/30	14,029	6,051	152	681	7.5	6.3

Figure 1: A few statistics on the language data. C is the language code used in the Corpex explorer (and usually also the Wikipedia language code). R is the rank of the Wikipedia language edition by number of articles (as of February 15, 2011), and D the Depth (see Section 4.2), providing a rough measure of collaboration. Date is the date when the database dump was created, that was used for the corpus creation. Tokens is the number of tokens in the given Wikipedia language edition, Terms the number of unique terms. 10+ is the number of terms that have appeared more than ten times. Top50 is the smallest number of terms that account for more than 50% of all the tokens. l1 is the average length of terms in the corpus. l2 is the average length of tokens in the corpus.

en · t (269,314,078)

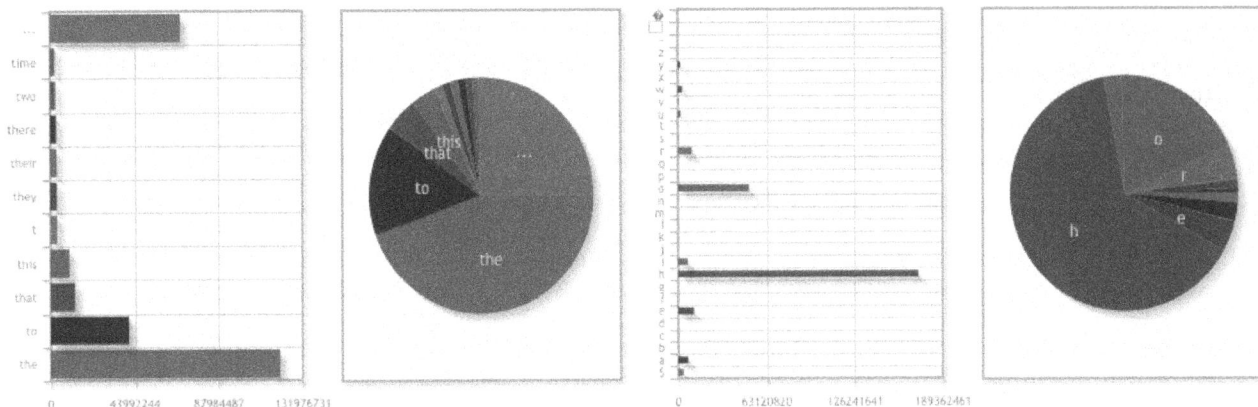

Figure 2: Corpex website screenshot, showing the frequency distribution model created from the English Wikipedia corpus for the letter 't'. The two charts to the left show the distribution of word completions, the two charts on the right show the probability for the next character. Both times the barchart and the piechart show the same data.

brown · t (158,918)

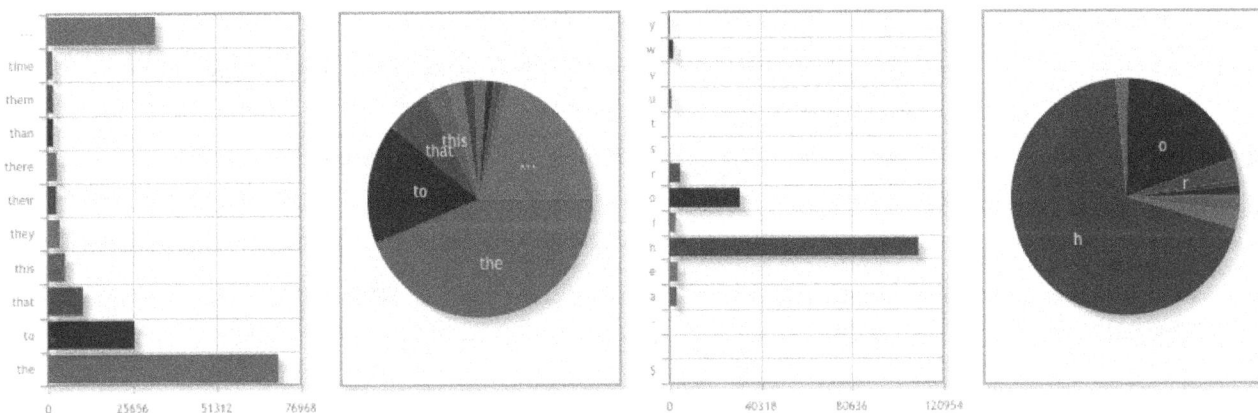

Figure 3: For comparison with the Simple English Wikipedia corpus, this screenshot of Corpex displays the frequencies for the 't' over the Brown corpus.

160

Hacking History via Event Extraction

Roxane Segers
Department of Computer
Science
VU University Amsterdam
De Boelelaan 1081a
1081 HV Amsterdam, The
Netherlands
r.h.segers@vu.nl

Marieke van Erp
Department of Computer
Science
VU University Amsterdam
De Boelelaan 1081a
1081 HV Amsterdam, The
Netherlands
marieke@cs.vu.nl

Lourens van der Meij
Department of Computer
Science
VU University Amsterdam
De Boelelaan 1081a
1081 HV Amsterdam, The
Netherlands
lourens@cs.vu.nl

ABSTRACT

Within cultural heritage collections, objects are often grounded in a particular historical setting. This setting can currently not be made explicit, as structured descriptions of events are either missing or not marked up explicitly. This paper reports a study on automatic extraction of an historical event thesaurus from unstructured texts. We show how this preliminary thesaurus accommodates event- and object-driven search and browsing of two cultural heritage collections.

Categories and Subject Descriptors

I.2.4 [**Artificial Intelligence**]: Knowledge Representation Formalisms and Methods; I.2.7 [**Artificial Intelligence**]: Natural Language Processing; J.5 [**Computer Applications**]: Arts and Humanities

General Terms

information extraction, event modeling, cultural heritage

1. INTRODUCTION

Events have recently gained attention in the knowledge representation community as valuable constructs [4, 7, 8] that can help tie together relevant but yet unrelated elements of information. In the cultural heritage domain, knowledge about historical events is often concealed in textual descriptions that can only be accessed via keyword search. As such, the available knowledge can not be reused across collections as it is not part of the shared metadata and controlled vocabularies.

In this study, we investigate how historical events in unstructured text collections can be captured and modeled to create an event thesaurus for enriching metadata in cultural heritage collections. We adopt the SEM event model [8] to distinguish event types, actors, locations, and dates. We experiment with natural language processing (NLP) techniques to extract event names and their associated actors, dates and locations. Additionally, we show how this resulting preliminary event thesaurus is employed in a new platform for event- and object driven searching and browsing of the collections of the Rijksmuseum Amsterdam (RMA) and the Netherlands Institute for Sound and Vision (S&V).

2. EVENT EXTRACTION FROM TEXT

As no annotated historical document collections exist in Dutch, our approach is focused on extracting named events with minimal manual effort. For this study we selected 3,724 historical Wikipedia articles as a test set. The event extraction process consists of three steps: in the **first step**, we recognize *actor names* and *locations* using the Stanford Named Entity Recognition system [2] adapted for Dutch historical texts. Dates were recognized via regular expressions. This step resulted in 18,623 candidates for actors (F-measure of 0.77), 7,023 locations (F-measure of 0.66) and 7,981 dates. In the **second step**, we use a pattern-based method for recognizing *event names* such as *French Revolution*. We harvest patterns from the Web (e.g., *destroyed during the, before the*) using the Yahoo! search API [1] and a seed of one hundred historical events. Patterns are ranked by frequency of co-occurrence with two or more seed events [6]. To retrieve event candidates, we applied the patterns to the Wikipedia corpus. The event candidates are then filtered, based on a threshold on the pattern score, resulting in a set of 2,444 unique events. The precision score of this set is 56.3%.

In the **third step**, we associate events with actors, locations and dates. We experiment with both redundancy and co-occurrence of data on the Web, inspired by the work of Geleijnse et al. [3] and Cilibrasi &Vitanyi[1]. Each combination of an event name and actor/location/date is sent to Yahoo! and for each pair a score is computed. We discovered 392 event names that were paired with an actor, a location and a date. Through manual evaluation we conclude the following: 71.9% (323) are correct event names, 45.6% (179) are correct actors, 41.1% (161) are correct locations and 51.5% (202) are correct dates.

3. ENRICHMENT BY EVENTS

The extracted events are linked to the RMA and S&V collections. In total 35 unique events provide direct relations from 435 S&V objects to 675 RMA objects. An additional 34 unique events provide links from 391 S&V objects to 362 RMA objects, but this link exists indirectly through the event instance (e.g., S&V object - Actor - RMA object). We hypothesize that these links are potentially useful for navigating cultural heritage collections.

---

[1]http://developer.yahoo.com/search

Slachtoffers gemaakt door de Nederlandse troepen op weg naar Jogyakarta (Object)

Slachtoffers gemaakt door de Nederlandse troepen op weg
naar Jogyakarta. Kinderschilderij van de inname van Jogyakarta
tijdens de tweede politionele actie, december 1948.
NG-1998-7-10

Associated Events
DepictsEvent: Tweede politionele actie

biographical aspects
Creator:Toha Adimidjojo, Mohammed ☐ (4) Date:1948-12-19 ☐ (3) 1949-06-30 ☐ (3) 20e eeuw ☐ (18) tweede kwart 20e eeuw ☐ (17)

material aspects   semiotic aspects
Type: aquarel ☐ (3) tekening ☐ (3)   Subject: Jogyakarta ☐ (4) Tweede politionele actie ☐ (7)
Technique: aquarelleren ☐ (3)   1948-12-19 ☐ (4)   1949-06-31 ☐ (1)
Material: hardboard ☐ (4)   militaire geschiedenis ☐ (12)

Associated Objects (25) < prev   1 2 3 **4** 5   next >

President Soekarno g...   Sinkin panjang met s...   Indonesië vnif   Schild van een Atjeher   Aankomst van Van Spi...   Het kasteel van Bata...
Associated Press   Anonymous   Hatta, Mohammed   Anonymous   Anonymous   Beeckman, Andries

Figure 1: Screenshot of object page in the Agora Event Browsing Demonstrator

4. THE AGORA DEMONSTRATOR

The automatically generated event thesaurus is applied in a new historical event browser called Agora[2] which provides an integrated access route to museum objects and audio-visual material from RMA and S&V respectively. It is a first step towards a platform to investigate the added value of historical events and narratives for the exploration of integrated collections. For each event and object there is an automatically generated page that shows (1) all associated objects, e.g., museum and audio-visual objects; (2) all associated events and the type of their relationship, e.g., previous-in-time event, sub-event; (3a) the event descriptive metadata, e.g., actors, place, period; or (3b) object descriptive metadata organized in three groups, e.g., biographical, material and semiotic dimensions – see figure 1 for a screenshot – and finally (4) the navigation path. The current version of the event thesaurus will be extended further to accommodate searching for relations between events such as temporal inclusion, causality and meronymy.

5. DISCUSSION

In this paper, we presented a modular pipeline for capturing knowledge about historical events from Dutch texts. Compared with previous approaches (i.e., [5]), it relies on a minimum of manual annotation and can be repurposed for other languages. To the best of our knowledge, this is the first work to extract events from unstructured Dutch text. Although our results are promising, more sophisticated techniques are necessary to obtain more fine-grained extractions and define measures for the historic relevance of the extracted events. Additionally, we also aim to find and represent relations between events such as causality, meronymy and correlation.

6. ACKNOWLEDGEMENTS

This research was funded by the CAMeRA Institute of the VU University Amsterdam and by the CATCH programme, NWO grant 640.004.801.

[2]http://agora.cs.vu.nl/eventdemo

7. ADDITIONAL AUTHORS

Lora Aroyo (VU University Amsterdam), Guus Schreiber (VU University Amsterdam) and Bob Wielinga (VU University Amsterdam), Jacco van Ossenbruggen (CWI and VU University Amsterdam), Johan Oomen (Netherlands Institute for Sound and Vision), Geertje Jacobs (Rijksmuseum Amsterdam).

8. REFERENCES

[1] R. Cilibrasi and P. Vitanyi. The google similarity distance. *IEEE Trans. Knowledge and Data Engineering*, 19(3):370–383, 2007.

[2] J. R. Finkel, T. Grenager, and C. Manning. Incorporating non-local information into information extraction systems by gibbs sampling. In *Proceedings of the 43nd Annual Meeting of the Association for Computational Linguistics (ACL 2005)*, 2005.

[3] G. Geleijnse, J. Korst, and V. de Boer. Instance classification using co-occurrences on the web. In *Proceedings of the ISWC 2006 workshop on Web Content Mining (WebConMine)*, Athens, GA, USA, November 2006.

[4] N. Gkalelis, V. Mezaris, and I. Kompatsiaris. Automatic event-based indexing of multimedia content using a joint content-event model. In *ACM Events in MultiMedia Workshop (EiMM10)*, Oct 2010.

[5] N. Ide and D. Woolner. Exploiting semantic web technologies for intelligent access to historical documents. In *Proceedings of the Fourth Language Resources and Evaluation Conference (LREC)*, pages 2177–2180, Lisbon, Portugal, 2004.

[6] E. Riloff and R. Jones. Learning dictionaries for information extraction by multi-level bootstrapping. In *Proceedings of AAAI '99*, pages 474–479, 1999.

[7] R. Shaw, R. Troncy, and L. Hardman. Lode: Linking open descriptions of events. In *4th Annual Asian Semantic Web Conference (ASWC'09)*, 2009.

[8] W. R. van Hage, V. Malaisé, G. de Vries, G. Schreiber, and M. van Someren. Abstracting and reasoning over ship trajectories and web data with the Simple Event Model (SEM). *Multimedia Tools and Applications*, 2011.

Eliciting Hierarchical Structures from Enumerative Structures for Ontology Learning

Mouna Kamel
IRIT, CNRS
Toulouse, France
kamel@irit.fr

Bernard Rothenburger
IRIT, CNRS
Toulouse, France
rothenbu@irit.fr

ABSTRACT

Some discourse structures such as enumerative structures have typographical, punctuational and laying out characteristics which (1) make them easily identifiable and (2) convey hierarchical relations which provide ontology fragments clues. This study will try to show how these textual objects can be exploited in order to considerably improve the process of ontology enrichment from text.

Categories and Subject Descriptors

I.2.7 Natural Language Processing: Discourse; Text analysis

General Terms

Algorithms, Documentation, Languages

Keywords

Ontology learning, discourse theory, document structure, enumerative structure.

ENUMERATIVE STRUCTURES

A written text is not merely a set of words or of sentences. First its semantic and rhetoric coherence must be granted by discourse relations which can be formalized through different discourse theories [5]. Secondly, it implements typographical, punctuation and laying out means, which also contribute to identify its meaning and which can be formalized through text structure models [4]. For instance, enumeration is a feature carrying these two properties.

Enumerating consists in stating the successive elements of a same conceptual domain, these elements being hierarchically directly or indirectly linked to a classifying concept. On the textual level, this act is transcribed in a hierarchical structure, called enumerative structure (ES). The ES is made of a primer, of a list of items (called enumeration) and eventually, of a conclusion. The primer includes the classifying concept and the semantic relation that links it to the items. It introduces the list of items, an item being a co-enumerated entity which can, as afore said, be linked to the classifying concept, or eventually to another item.

The conclusion, when there's one, sums up the various propositions given through the items. Also, ES structures convey hierarchical relations which provide ontology fragments clues. An ES can take several forms. It can either be written without any specific layout, or conversely be highlighted with specific typographical and/or dispositional markers.

Enumerative structure without layout

Let us take into consideration the text (T1). When facing such a text, the reader could infer that 'written language', 'sign language' and 'whistled language' are specific cases of 'non-spoken form of communication'. One can thus obtain a hierarchical structure that could well be represented by the hierarchical structure of Figure 1.

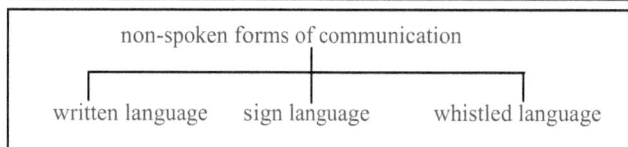

Figure 1. Hierarchical Structure from (T1)

The automatic identification of such a hierarchical structure seems out of the reach of the tools usually involved for ontology learning from text (lexico-syntactical patterns, term inclusion rule, etc). A different way to identify these intersentential relations is to produce a segmentation of the text and to link segments with discourse relations. These segments, sometimes named *text span* or *Elementary Discourse Unit* (*EDU*), can be contiguous or not contiguous. They are linked with subordination relation (one talks about nucleus and satellite in Rhetorical Structure Theory (RST)) or with coordinate relation (which corresponds to a multinuclear relation in RST) [3].

(T2) describes a possible segmentation of (T1). Each segment is annotated with square brackets and indexed with the help of a capital letter. The diagram in Figure 2 describes the rhetoric structure that corresponds to (T2) according to the RST. *Elaboration-Set-Member* (relation between basic information and additional information) and *List* (relation between items of the same level) are both relations of RST.

```
(T2) [There are several non-spoken forms of
communication. A] [First, written language
refers to communication in its textual form.
B] [Secondly, sign language corresponds to a
gestural language. C] [Finally, whistled lan-
guage uses whistling to emulate speech. D]
```

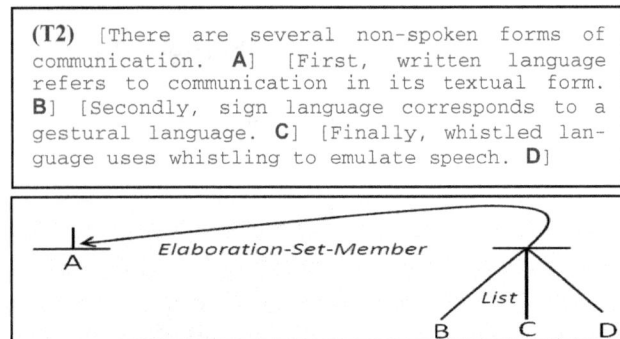

Figure 2. Rhetorical Structure of (T1)

Going from the rhetoric structure of Figure 2 to the hierarchical structure of Figure 1 is straightforward. But the steps of segmentation and representation in RST are generally carried out manually. However, these steps can be automated for some cases of SE expressed using layout.

Enumerative structure with layout

Enumerative structures we currently exploit for ontology learning from text are those which on the one hand are expressed with layout, and on the other hand are paradigmatic, i.e. there is no dependence between items and the heads of items are syntactically equivalent. We call such structures Vertical Paradigmatic Enumerative Structure (VPES). They have the advantages of (1) being easily identifiable, (2) allowing a bijective mapping with the discourse structure it encompasses and (3) reflecting in most cases ontological discourse relations.

The translation process will need several steps: (1) the identification of the enumerative structure with layout, (2) the identification of the paradigmatic property, (3) the identification of the father and child elements together with the semantic relation that links them. Figure 3 gives an example of this mapping based on the ES equivalent to this of text (T1) but expressed with layout.

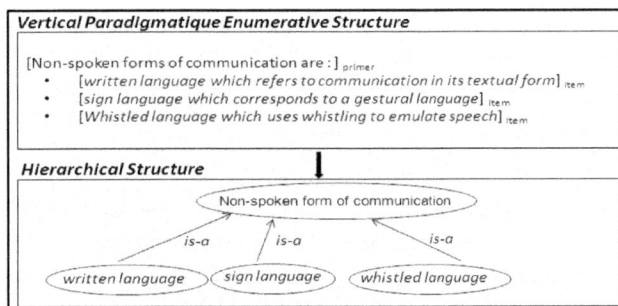

Figure 3. Elicitation of a VPES into a hierarchical structure

The syntactical structure of the primer enables the identification of the father element, often, and the semantic relation, always [2]. Furthermore many studies show that authors are inclined to place the most important information at the beginning of a textual unit [1]. After having observed this phenomenon on items of enumerative structures from different corpora, we consider that the target components of the enumeration are localised at the beginning of items.

APPLICATION

We have enriched the OntoTopo ontology[1] by exploiting VPES from Wikipedia pages corresponding to the concepts of this ontology. In fact, Wikipedia advocates to "use the same grammatical form for all elements in a list, and do not mix the use of sentences and sentence fragments as elements".

The OntoTopo ontology has 728 concepts. We obtain 182 disambiguated pages which contain at least one VPES. From these 182 articles 434 enumerative structures including 276 VPES are extracted. Among these 276 VPES, 127 have been exploited and translated into hierarchical structures. The elicitation of these 127 VPES has provided 349 new concepts and 201 instances validated by experts involved in this project.

We intend to pursue this work according to several directions. The first one is to define learning methods for identifying the father element present in the primer of the 149 VPES not yet exploited. Another direction is to generalize our approach to other kinds of layout features or to other discourse structures such as definition. Finally we intend to implement machine learning tools in order to improve the discovery of textual enumerative structures.

REFERENCES

[1] Ho-Dac, L-M. (2007). Exploration en corpus de la position initiale dans l'organisation du discours. Thèse de doctorat en sciences du langage. Université de Toulouse 2.

[2] Kamel M., Rothenburger B. (2010). Ontology Building Using Parallel Enumerative Structure. International Conference on Knowledge Engineering and Ontology Development (KEOD 2010), Valence, 25-28/10/2010, INSTICC - Institute for Systems and Technologies of Information, Control and Communication, p. 276-281

[3] Mann, W.C., & Thompson, S.A. (1988). Rhetorical Structure Theory: Toward a functional theory of text organization. Text, 8 (3). 243-281.

[4] Power, R., Scott, D., Bouayad-Agha, N. (2003). Document structure. Computational Linguistics, 29 (2), 211-260.

[5] Wolf, F. & Gibson, E. (2006). Coherence in Natural Language: Data Structures and Applications. Cambridge, MA: MIT Press

---

[1] Ontology built during the GEONTO project : http://geonto.lri.fr/

Semantically Annotating Research Articles for Interdisciplinary Design

Swaroop S. Vattam, Ashok K. Goel
School of Interactive Computing
Georgia Institute of Technology
Atlanta, GA, USA 30332

{svattam, goel}@cc.gatech.edu

ABSTRACT

Biologically inspired design is an important emerging movement in engineering design. Finding relevant biological sources of inspiration from existing biology literature is one of the important challenges of this activity. We conjecture that annotating biology articles with lightweight Structure-Behavior-Function (SBF) models is one way to address this challenge. We present Biologue, a social citation cataloging system that allows its users to gather, organize, share, and most importantly, annotate scholarly articles with SBF models. This feature not only allows the implementation of search mechanism that is more targeted to the needs of designers seeking bio-inspiration, but also helps designers make sense of the articles returned by the search mechanism.

Categories and Subject Descriptors

H.3.1 [**Content Analysis and Indexing**]: *Abstracting methods, Indexing methods*. H.3.7 [**Digital Libraries**]: *Collection, Dissemination, Standards*.

General Terms: Design, Human Factors.

Keywords: Biologically inspired design; complex systems; digital libraries; functional models; interdisciplinary research; social tagging.

1. INTRODUCTION

Biologically inspired design (Benyus, 1997; Vincent, 2002) is an important emerging movement in modern engineering design. The task of biologically inspired design uses analogies to biological systems to develop solutions for complex engineering problems (Vattam, Helms & Goel, 2010). When a designer, for instance, develops an energy-efficient seawater desalination technology by mimicking intestine's mechanism of efficiently moving water across osmotic gradient, the desalination technology and the intestine can be understood as being analogous to each other in this context because they share similar teleology. But there are an estimated 5 to 15 million species of organisms (Stork, 1993), and an order of magnitude more number of biological systems if their sub-systems and super-systems are considered. How might designers situated in one domain (engineering) find analogous systems from this vast space of available systems that belong to a completely different and mostly unfamiliar domain (biology)? This is one of the grand challenges of biologically inspired design.

To understand how designers currently address this challenge we conducted several *in situ* studies of teams of designers engaged in biologically inspired design in the context of an introductory, project-based, interdisciplinary course on biologically inspired

design (Vattam, Helms & Goel, 2010; Helms, Vattam & Goel, 2009). Our observations showed that one common source for obtaining knowledge of biological systems is scholarly biology articles, which are accessed using online digital libraries (e.g., Web of Science) and online bibliographic services (e.g., Google Scholar). Our observations also indicate that such online information environments, although perhaps adequate for more routine information seeking tasks, did not provide adequate support for finding cross-domain analogies of the kind required in biologically inspired design.

In particular, we found that designers had to overcome two challenges in order to find their sources of inspiration. Firstly, they had to access or retrieve relevant biology articles. Relevant articles were the ones that described the mechanisms of a biological system which when applied to their target design problem led to a potential design solution. Furthermore, the designers had to achieve this using only keyword searches and cope with the handicap of limited familiarity with the vocabulary of biology. Not surprisingly, a majority of designers' search time and effort was spent on trying various different search phrases and sifting through the huge number of resultant candidate articles to find a small number of actually relevant ones.

In general, determining if a candidate article in the search results is relevant or not presumes understanding or comprehension on the part of the searcher. Typically, the cost involved in this understanding process is not significant because the searcher and the candidate document are often situated in the same domain – reading the title, the first few sentences, or perhaps the abstract is sufficient for the searcher to make robust utility calculation about the relevance of a document's contents. This brings us to the second challenge that designers face in biologically inspired design: the cost of this process of understanding is quite large. This makes the large number of candidate articles returned by search engines practically useless because sifting through them becomes practically infeasible. Therefore, making decisions about which article to pay attention to is reduced to guesswork, leading to significant opportunity cost. The problem of retrieval in the context of biologically inspired design, therefore, is intertwined with the problem of learning - constructing understanding of unfamiliar material in a timely manner.

2. BIOLOGUE

We conjecture that the aforementioned challenges faced by designers can be addressed by annotating scholarly biology articles with additional representations, like Structure-Behavior-Function (SBF) models (Goel, Rugaber & Vattam, 2009), which will help designers *both* access and understand those articles. An SBF model of a complex system explicitly represents its structure [S] (i.e., its configuration of components and connections), its functions [F] (i.e., its intended output behaviors), and its behaviors [B] (i.e. its internal causal processes that compose the functions of the components into the functions of the system). The SBF ontology provides a vocabulary for expressing and organizing knowledge about systems in an $F \rightarrow B \rightarrow F \rightarrow B \ldots \rightarrow F(S)$ hierarchy, which captures functionality and causality at multiple levels of aggregation and abstraction.

Biologue is a social citation cataloging system that we have developed that is targeted towards the biologically inspired design community. It is comparable to other general-purpose online citation systems like Connotea (www.connotea.org), CiteULike (www.citeulike.org/), etc. Biologue allows its user to post a citation for an article found on the Internet or a website, online database like Web of Science or Google Scholar, etc. This allows biologically inspired designers to share the information resources that they found useful in their design episodes with other designers. However, it is not enough to just share it, we want them to share it in a particular way so that the two aforementioned problems associated with typical online libraries and bibliographic databases are mitigated.

Biologue supports *model-based tagging*, a technique for annotating the information resources with lightweight conceptual models like SBF models. This can be contrasted with the more typical keyword-based social tagging (Golder & Huberman, 2005). The choice of which kind of models to tag articles with depends on nature of tasks (or inferences) this additional external representation has to support. In the case of biologically inspired design, as we mentioned before, the tasks of access and understanding have to be supported simultaneously. While the tags in the current systems that support tagging are flat, meaning, the tags are not connected in anyway by some type of relationship, model-based tags can be much richer. For instance SBF model-based tags capture not only concepts and relationships, but do so at multiple levels of abstraction and aggregation. Flat tags are not necessarily a limitation if the tags' sole function is to index information resources and aid retrieval of information. However, we are attaching a new role to annotations in the context of model-based tagging: not only to aid retrieval of an information resource, but also to aid understanding of retrieved resources. It is in the latter role that we need to annotate information resources with richer knowledge structures like SBF models.

By allowing users to annotate articles with SBF models, Biologue provides an advanced search facility that includes searching based on features like function, physical principle, operating environment, etc. that are derived from the SBF ontology. Because these features match the kinds of features that designers naturally use in the field when they are seeking bio-inspiration (Helms, Vattam & Goel, 2009), we expect that this search mechanism can address the problem of access by making the information retrieval more targeted or focused to the needs of biologically inspired designers. Furthermore, the search mechanism in Biologue not only returns a list of relevant articles, but also the SBF models associated with those articles. SBF models then provide an additional representation that might help the designer come to a better understanding of the article more efficiently.

3. EVALUATION

In Fall 2010 we introduced Biologue in an introductory course on biologically inspired design in the context of one of the term projects. A total of 44 students were encouraged to use Biologue to manage and share their research resources and to search the resources gathered and tagged (by SBF models) by fellow classmates. In the course of this one project, while a majority of students added many articles into Biologue (74 new articles were added), only a minority of them tagged their articles with SBF models (28 out of 74 articles were tagged with models). We conducted a user survey to elicit students' impressions of Biologue after having used it for the duration of the project. A total of 21 students took the survey. We further classified those 21 students who responded to survey into two categories: (1) high model usage group (students who tagged more than 75% of the articles they added with SBF models), and (2) low model usage group. Among the former group, consisting of 10 students, a clear picture emerges in favor of model-based tagging. For instance, 87% of this subgroup agreed that having models helps them make better decisions about the relevancy of associated articles. Whereas only 26% of the total respondents agreed that having models makes it *easier* to read the article, this number rose to 50% in the high model usage group. Likewise there was jump from 31% to 62% when it came to agreeing that having models makes the reading of the article go *faster*.

This result indicates that among those users who cared to use SBF modeling feature at storage time also derived the benefits of models at retrieval time. However, the fact that only a few students actually tagged their articles with SBF models indicates that the cost of creating SBF models might be high. We expect to investigate this issue further.

ACKNOWLEDGEMENTS
We thank Michael Helms and Bryan Wiltgen, our research partners, Prof. Jeanette Yen, the instructor of the Georgia Tech ME/ISyE/MSE/PTFe/BIOL 4740 course, as well as the students in the class during Fall 2008 and 2009. Finally, we thank US National Science Foundation for its support through a CreativeIT Grant (#0855916) entitled "Computational Tools for Enhancing Creativity in Biologically Inspired Engineering Design."

4. REFERENCES
[1] Benyus, J. (1997) *Biomimicry: Innovation Inspired by Nature*. New York: William Morrow.

[2] Goel, A., Rugaber, S., & Vattam, S. (2009) Structure, Behavior & Function of Complex Systems: The Structure,, Behavior, Function Modeling Language. *AI for Engineering Design, Analysis and Manufacturing*, Special Issue on Developing and Using Engineering Ontologies, 23:23-35.

[3] S. A. Golder, B. A. Huberman (2005) The Structure of Collaborative Tagging Systems, HP Labs technical report, 2005.

[4] Helms, M., S. Vattam & A. Goel. 2009. Biologically inspired design: process and products. *Design Studies*, 30:606-622.

[5] Stork, N. E. (1993) How many species are there? *Biodiversity and Conservation*, 2: 215-232

[6] Vattam, S., M. Helms & A. Goel. (2010) A Content Account of Creative Analogies in Biologically Inspired Design, *AI for Engineering Design, Analysis and Manufacturing*, 24: 467-481.

[7] Vincent, J., & Mann, D. (2002) Systematic Transfer from Biology to Engineering. *Philosophical Transactions of the Royal Society of London*, 360: 159-173.

Linked Open Piracy

Willem R. van Hage
VU University Amsterdam
De Boelelaan 1081a
1081 HV Amsterdam, The
Netherlands
W.R.van.Hage@vu.nl

Véronique Malaisé
VU University Amsterdam
De Boelelaan 1081a
1081 HV Amsterdam, The
Netherlands
vmalaise@few.vu.nl

Marieke van Erp
VU University Amsterdam
De Boelelaan 1081a
1081 HV Amsterdam, The
Netherlands
marieke@cs.vu.nl

ABSTRACT

There is an abundance of semi-structured reports on events being written and made available on the World Wide Web on a daily basis. These reports are primarily meant for human use. A recent movement is the addition of RDF metadata to make automatic processing by computers easier. A fine example of this movement is the Open Government Data initiative which, by adding RDF metadata to spreadsheets and textual reports, strives to speed up the creation of geographical mashups and visual analytics applications. In this paper we present a new Open Linked Data RDF dataset[1] and a method for automatically adding such RDF metadata to semi-structured reports. We showcase our method on piracy attack reports issued on the web by the International Chamber of Commerce's International Maritime Bureau (ICC-CCS IMB)[2] We create a Semantic Web representation with the Simple Event Model (SEM) from screen scrapes of the ICC-CCS website. We show how the event layer makes it possible to easily analyze and visualize the aggregated reports to answer domain questions. Our pipeline includes conversion of the reports to RDF, linking their parts to external resources from the Linked Open Data cloud and exposing them to the Web through a ClioPatria web server that hosts the RDF.

Categories and Subject Descriptors

I.2.4 [**Artificial Intelligence**]: Knowledge Representation Formalisms and Methods

General Terms

Experimentation, Design

1. INTRODUCTION

In 2008, the increase of piracy attacks in the Gulf of Aden made the publication and analysis of events happening at sea around the world a new priority. The ICC-CCS gathers the reports related to piracy broadcasted by ships around the world, and publishes them daily on their website[2]. The reports are semi-structured, and concern seven (predefined) types of events: Hijacked, Boarded, Robbed, Attempted, Fired Upon, Suspicious (vessel spotted) and Kidnapped. The reports contains a field for the vessel type of the ship broadcasting the report; although the types of the vessels are often recurring, this field is filled manually, which gives rise to spelling variations (firedupon vs fired upon, tanker vs tankership) and a lack of certainty in terms of coverage: a new ship type could be filled in any day. The description of the event itself is done in full text, without a specific formatting except that it is preceded, in the same field, by the geographic and temporal coordinates of the event described. The geographic and temporal coordinates are repeated in an independent field each.

2. SCREEN SCRAPING

We start crawling of the ICC-CCS IMB webpage with the links to the yearly archives in the menu of the Live Piracy Map page. For each of these pages we follow all the links in the descriptions of the placemarks on the overview map. These are injected into the DOM tree with Javascript at runtime. We fetch them from the Javascript by parsing the Javascript with SWI-Prolog grammar (DCG) rules. This gives us a collection of semi-structured description pages, one for each event. We fetch the various fields from these pages using XPath queries and Prolog rules for value conversion and fixing irregularities. The code can be found online[3]. In this way we fetch: (1) The IMB's attack number; (2) The date of the attack, which we convert to ISO 8601 format; (3) The vessel type, which we map to URIs with rules that normalize a few spelling variations of the types. (4) The location label; (5) The attack type, which we map to URIs in the same way as the vessel type; (6) The incident details, which we convert to a RDFS comment describing the event itself. The first line is split into a time and place indication. These are used as backup sources to derive the date and location, should the parsing of fields nr. 2, 4 and 7 fail; (7) The longitude and latitude of the placemark on the map insert. These are used as coordinates of a generated anonymous place (i.e., without a URI) for the event.

For some of the events there are no explicit coordinates of the location of the event, but there is a textual description, for example, "approximately 150NM northwest of Port Victoria, Seychelles". For these event we look up the coordinates of Port Victoria using the GeoNames search web service[4], which returns RDF. From this location we calculate the coordinates using trigonometry. For example, in the case of 150NM northwest we compute the coordinates 150 minutes of angle at a bearing of 315 degrees.

We use the set of 7 values (numbered 1 to 7) extracted per report to generate a semantic event description using the Simple Event Model (SEM) [3] as illustrated in Figure 1.

---

[1]LOP, http://semanticweb.cs.vu.nl/poseidon/ns/, http://ckan.net/package/linked-open-piracy
[2]IMB, http://www.icc-ccs.org/home/imb/

---

[3]http://www.few.vu.nl/~wrvhage/2011/lop/
[4]GeoNames search, http://sws.geonames.org/search

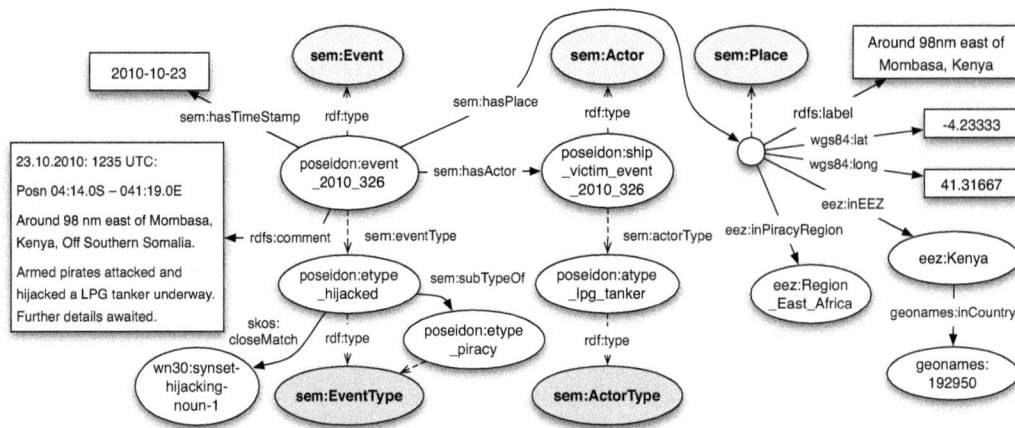

Figure 1: The complete RDF graph of a piracy report modeled in SEM including mappings to types in WordNet 3.0, a VLIZ exclusive economic zone, its corresponding GeoNames country, and its Piracy Region (see Section 3).

3. MAPPINGS

We create local URIs to represent the types of the extracted events and the types of their participants (e.g., poseidon:etype_hijacked or poseidon:atype_lpg_tanker). The shorthand for the name space of the local URIs is poseidon[5] because the LOP data set was created during the Poseidon[5] project.

The SEM piracy events are aligned with vocabularies in the Linked Open Data cloud: WordNet 2.0[6], 3.0[7], OpenCyc[8] and Freebase[9]. Since there are only 73 sem:ActorTypes and 26 sem:EventTypes we manually created the following mappings: 70 skos:closeMatch (24 to Freebase, 24 to OpenCyc, 25 to WordNet);[10] 10 skos:broadMatch (5 to OpenCyc, 4 to WordNet, 1 to Freebase); 33 skos:relatedMatch (13 to OpenCyc, 11 to WordNet, 9 to Freebase). A "related" relation hold for example between WordNet's *to fire* and the event type *fired upon*, because *to fire* only conveys part of the meaning.

To classify each event by its place we need a classification of space. We chose to use the official geopolitical borders of the world, defined by the exclusive economic zones (EEZ, usually defined as 200 nautical miles from the coast of the nearest state). We classified all event places according to whether they are **in** or **nearest to** we need a specification of the borders of these zones. We take these from the World EEZ version 5 data set from the VLIZ Maritime Boundaries Geodatabase[11]. We make a more general partitioning of the world into regions (e.g. Gulf of Aden, Carribean) following the EEZs (using Prolog space_intersects/3 queries on the EEZ shapes). The remaining surface of the earth, including the international waters and inland seas is partitioned based on the nearest EEZ (using Prolog space_nearest/3 queries on the EEZ shapes). The resulting sections of the world are grouped together to form the more general domain specific partitioning of the world consisting of what we call "Piracy Regions".

4. HOSTING THE PIRACY DATA

The entire ICC-CCS data set is hosted as Linked Data on a ClioPatria server[1]. All URIs in the data set are resolvable. A SPARQL endpoint is available at http://semanticweb.cs.vu.nl/poseidon/ns/user/query.

5. CONCLUSION

We present a new Open Linked Data set about worldwide maritime piracy events crawled from the web. In essence, this work is an Open Government Data project, like data.gov [1] and data.gov.uk [2], with the exception that data are intergovernmental. Our goal is the same, to reduce the cost to answer, possibly complex, domain questions on integrated government data. LOP allows easier processing of piracy reports for visualization and the computation of statistics.

6. ACKNOWLEDGEMENTS

This work has been carried out as a part of the Poseidon project and the Agora project. Work in the Poseidon project was done in cooperation with Thales Nederland, under the responsibilities of the Embedded Systems Institute (ESI). The Poseidon project is partially supported by the Dutch Ministry of Economic Affairs under the BSIK03021 program. The Agora project is funded by NWO in the CATCH programme, grant 640.004.801. We would like to thank Davide Ceolin, Juan Manuel Coleto, and Vincent Osinga for their significant contributions. We thank the ICC-CCS IMB and the NGA for providing the open piracy reports.

7. ADDITIONAL AUTHORS

Additional authors: Guus Schreiber (VU University Amsterdam, email: guus.schreiber@vu.nl).

8. REFERENCES

[1] D. D. Li Ding, D. L. McGuinness, J. Hendler, and S. Magidson. The data-gov wiki: A semantic web portal for linked government data. In *Proceedings of the 6th International Conference on Knowledge Capture*, 2009.

[2] T. Omitola et al. Put in your postcode, out comes the data: A case study. In *The Semantic Web: Research and Applications*, volume 6088 of *Lecture Notes in Computer Science*, pages 318–332. Springer Berlin / Heidelberg, 2010.

[3] W. R. van Hage, V. Malaisé, R. Segers, L. Hollink, and G. Schreiber. Design and use of the Simple Event Model (SEM). *Journal of Web Semantics*, 2011.

---

[5]Poseidon http://www.esi.nl/poseidon/

[6]WordNet 2.0, http://www.w3.org/2006/03/wn/wn20/

[7]WordNet 3.0, http://semanticweb.cs.vu.nl/lod/wn30/

[8]OpenCyc, http://sw.opencyc.org/

[9]Freebase, http://{www|rdf}.freebase.com/

[10]We use closeMatch to represent the slight mismatch between the definitions of the concepts in SEM and the 3 target vocabularies.

[11]VLIZ, http://www.vliz.be/vmdcdata/marbound/

Wikiing Pro – Semantic Wiki-based Process Editor

Frank Dengler
frank.dengler@kit.edu

Denny Vrandečić
denny.vrandecic@kit.edu

Elena Simperl
elena.simperl@kit.edu

Karlsruhe Institute of Technology (KIT)
Englerstr. 11
76131 Karlsruhe, Germany

ABSTRACT

Recently, a trend toward collaborative, user-centric, on-line process modeling can be observed. Unfortunately, current social software approaches mostly focus on the graphical development of processes and do not consider existing textual process description like HowTos or guidelines. We address this issue by combining graphical process modeling techniques with a wiki-based light-weight knowledge capturing approach and a background semantic knowledge base. Our approach enables the collaborative maturing of process descriptions with a graphical representation, formal semantic annotations, and natural language. By translating existing textual process descriptions into graphical descriptions and formal semantic annotations, we provide a holistic approach for collaborative process development that is designed to foster knowledge reuse and maturing within the system.

Categories and Subject Descriptors

H.5.3 [**Information Systems**]: INFORMATION INTER-FACES AND PRESENTATION—*Group and Organization Interfaces*

General Terms

Design, Documentation

1. INTRODUCTION

Enterprises are trying to describe their business processes in order to better understand, share, and optimize them. But still most of the process knowledge remains either in people's heads, or as textual and graphical descriptions in the Intranet as HowTos, guidelines, or methodology descriptions. The cost of a complete formalization of all business processes is prohibitive, and the benefits often seem elusive, especially under the stress of the daily work in a small group.

Traditionally, interviews of the domain experts performed by process modelers have been used to develop the process descriptions, but a trend toward collaborative, user-centric, on-line process modeling can be observed. Current semantic wiki-based approaches (e.g. [1, 2]), allowing such a collaborative modeling, focus on the graphical development of processes and do not consider existing textual process description like HowTos or guidelines. Thus, existing textual

process description, previously stored within the wiki, cannot be reused and automatically transformed into graphical process descriptions.

In this paper we present a method and wiki-based platform that allows the capturing of process description through several approaches, with different speeds and goals. It supports the capturing of natural language process descriptions, rendering and editing of graphical representations, and formal models, which can be exported with a well-defined semantics and used for the further processing and validation. The platform covers a wide array of externalization methods, and provides a unifying system that can interconnect gradually the explicated knowledge, enabling the enterprise to follow a continuous knowledge maturing effort [5] instead of requiring a steep and complete formalization step.

We have implemented a fully functional prototype,[1] where users can start to model their processes by formulating a first idea with natural language or with an incomplete model. These models can be further refined and consolidated by others.

2. WIKI-BASED PROCESS EDITOR

To allow for collaborative process development, our approach combines wiki-based light-weight knowledge capturing provided by Semantic MediaWiki (SMW) [3] with graphical process modeling functionality. Hence, users can develop process knowledge by using graphical descriptions, natural language, and formal semantic annotations.

For our implementation we selected the Oryx Process Editor, [2] an open source process editor, as the graphical process editor component, supporting various modeling languages. SMW was extended to be compatible with the Oryx graphical editor, so that data can be exchanged between both. In addition, the graphical editor was extended to display and edit wiki pages from within its interface; as a consequence, users can directly access the corresponding wiki page within the process editor. The entered wiki text is rendered by using the parse method provided by SMW. Thus, the whole SMW syntax can be used including categories and properties. SMW ASK queries are executed and the results are displayed as well. The process editor interface consists of different regions as shown in Figure 1. As already mentioned the corresponding wiki page is displayed in the bottom of the editor. For our approach we only use a small subset of BPMN constructs, namely tasks, sequence flows, parallel

---

[1] The prototype can be accessed via `http://bpmexample.wikiing.de` (User name: `kcap` – Password: `active!`)
[2] `http://oryx-project.org`

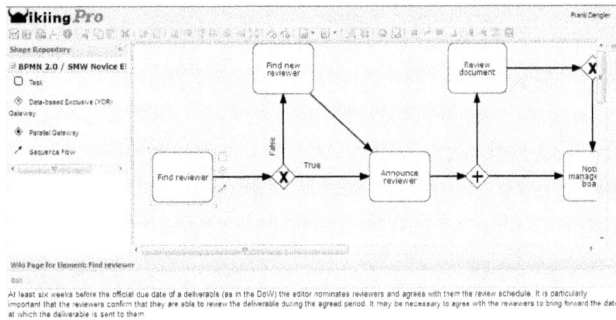

Figure 1: Graphical Editing Interface of Wikiing Pro

and data-based exclusive gateways, because only these are regularly used [4]. Once the process is saved, the process data and wiki pages belonging to the process are created or updated in SMW. The process elements are saved as sub-pages to the process summary page within the wiki. The process element wiki pages contain the textual descriptions and a fact box with all the stored properties. On the process summary page, the process diagram in SVG and a fact box are displayed.

We support the *Basic Control-Flow Patterns*.[3] Every single process step (activity) is represented as a wiki page belonging to the category *Process Element* and linked via the properties *has Type* to the corresponding type (*Task*) and *Belongs to Process* to the corresponding process, represented as wiki pages themselves (process summary pages). An activity is the basic element of our process. Depending on the granularity level of the process this can vary from atomic activities, such as *open a web page*, to activities describing a whole subprocess. To express the control flow of the process, we use edges in the diagram and special predefined process elements (gateways). If an element has a successor, we draw an edge from the activity to the successor activity in the diagram and store this with the additional property *has Successor* on the corresponding wiki page in SMW. For more successors executed in parallel (parallel-split pattern), a Parallel Gateway is used in between the activities. An activity can have several successors, but only one has to be selected and executed (multi-choice pattern). Therefore we use the Data-based Exclusive Gateway without conditions. The Data-based Exclusive Gateway with conditions is used to split based on a condition (exclusive-choice pattern). A condition is stored as a many-valued property.[4] The distinction between the synchronization pattern and the simple-merge pattern is realized by using the Parallel Gateway and the Data-based Exclusive Gateway the other way round to merge different branches of a process.

All properties of the process elements are also available in SMW and can be queried. Links to the corresponding wiki pages are automatically added to the SVG graphic, which enable the user to navigate through the process in the wiki. A new tab *edit with editor* has been added to the process wiki for editing an existing process. The tab automatically appears on pages belonging to the categories *Process* and *Process Element*. The tab links to the graphical process editor with the process model.

---

[3]http://workflowpatterns.com/patterns/control/
[4]http://semantic-mediawiki.org/wiki/Type:Record

Process descriptions can either be modeled from scratch or automatically be sketched from existing textual descriptions as well as from predefined process properties. In traditional (semantic) wikis processes are stored either as numbered lists on a single wiki page or they can also be expressed by connecting various wiki pages. The interlinking of multiple wiki pages can define a single process (by describing single tasks or subprocesses on their own pages, and then interlinking these). With our wiki-based approach, we support both ways of transforming wiki pages into graphically editable process descriptions – single and multi wiki page transformations.

3. CONCLUSION

We provide a wiki-based implementation of a multi-modal approach towards the continuous elicitation of knowledge about processes, which combines natural language descriptions, graphical representations, and formal, machine-readable semantic annotations. The mature wiki platform we build upon provides us with numerous basic functionalities which we carefully exploit. This includes user identity management, complete history of the wiki pages, and a well-tested discussion facility. In addition, interlinking between process descriptions and external resources with annotations is supported. In combination with the provided query language, it enables more sophisticated retrieval, browsing and navigation. By storing processes in a machine-processable format, using a standard exchange formats (RDF), it can easily be integrated into existing semi-automatic process acquisition approaches and enhance their functionality. By automatically translating textual process descriptions into graphical model, users can start with natural language or incomplete models, which can be further refined and consolidated by other novice users or experts. In the future we will further validate our approach by involving various users collaboratively constructing processes.

4. REFERENCES

[1] C. D. Francescomarino, C. Ghidini, M. Rospocher, L. Serafini, and P. Tonella. A framework for the collaborative specification of semantically annotated business processes. *J Softw Maintenance Evol Res Pract*, 2011.

[2] R. Hatko, J. Reutelshoefer, J. Baumeister, and F. Puppe. Modeling of diagnostic guideline knowledge in semantic wikis. In *Proc. of the Workshop on Open Knowledge Models (OKM-2010) at EKAW 2010*, 2010.

[3] M. Krötzsch, D. Vrandečić, M. Völkel, H. Haller, and R. Studer. Semantic wikipedia. *J of Web Semantics*, 5:251–261, SEP 2007.

[4] M. z. Muehlen and J. Recker. How Much Language Is Enough? Theoretical and Practical Use of the Business Process Modeling Notation. In *Advanced Information Systems Engineering*, volume 5074 of *LNCS*, pages 465–479. Springer Berlin / Heidelberg, 2008.

[5] A. Schmidt, K. Hinkelmann, T. Ley, S. Lindstaedt, R. Maier, and U. Riss. Conceptual Foundations for a Service-oriented Knowledge and Learning Architecture: Supporting Content, Process and Ontology Maturing. In *Networked Knowledge - Networked Media: Integrating Knowledge Management, New Media Technologies and Semantic Systems*. Springer, 2009.

An Intelligent Interface for Rule Elicitation

Saeed Hassanpour
Stanford Center for Biomedical Informatics Research
Stanford, CA, USA
saeedhp@stanford.edu

Amar K. Das
Stanford Center for Biomedical Informatics Research
Stanford, CA, USA
das@stanford.edu

ABSTRACT

Rule bases are increasingly being used as knowledge resources for reasoning in Semantic Web applications. However, a major obstacle to the wider use of rule bases is the difficulty of acquiring rules from domain experts. In this work, we present a predictive editing method, also known as autocompletion, to facilitate the elicitation of rules specified in the Semantic Web Rule Language (SWRL). Our method uses six different approaches for predictive editing based on frequency, position, structure, and domain-range information. We have implemented our method as a part of Protégé SWRL editor plug in. Initial usage of our method shows that a combined approach accurately recommends the most relevant rule predicates in the rule specification process.

Categories and Subject Descriptors

I.2.4 Knowledge Representation Formalisms and Methods – *Representations (procedural and rule-based), semantic networks.*

General Terms

Algorithms, Design, Measurement.

Keywords

Autocomplete, Predictive Editing, Rule Elicitation, Rule Base, Ontology, SWRL, OWL.

INTRODUCTION

Rules are becoming an important knowledge representation technology for the growing Semantic Web. However, a major barrier to their wider use is the complexity of developing rule bases. Rule base development requires a deep understanding of domain knowledge and of the rule language itself. Rule editors usually facilitate rule elicitation through guidance on syntactic constructs. This support may not be adequate for non-technical users needing to specify domain-specific rules. In this work, we present an intelligent user interface that provides predictive rule editing and autocompletion. The goal of the editor is to provide the most relevant suggestions for a rule predicate when editing exiting rules or adding new rules to the rule base as the user is typing.

BACKGROUND

The increasing adoption of Semantic Web standards for knowledge representation has benefited both the development of intelligent Web applications and ontology-based systems. Our work concentrates specifically on SWRL [1], which has emerged as the primary Semantic Web specification for rules. SWRL is an extension of the Ontology Web Language (OWL) [2]. Members of our research group developed the SWRLTab, a rule editor for SWRL that is a core plug in for Protégé OWL—the most widely used, freely available and open-source knowledge acquisition environment. SWRLTab provides a list of OWL entities and a prefix matching mechanism to facilitate the rule elicitation process [3]. However, the large size and flat structure of the list, which shows all ontology classes, properties, and individuals in alphabetical order, makes it difficult to browse. In our previous work, we developed Axiomé to address several challenges in SWRL rule acquisition and management. Axiomé is available as another core Protégé OWL plug-in [4]. For rule acquisition, it provides users with the syntactic structures of current rules as templates for writing new ones. A limitation of this method is specifying new rules that do not fit existing rule templates. We thus chose to create an intelligent interface for predictive editing.

METHOD

Our method is implemented as an alternative to the simple autocomplete mechanism in the current version of SWRLTab in Protégé OWL 3.4.4.. The autocompletion list is triggered when a user presses the Tab key; the method then generates a list of the most likely options form the ontology to complete the rule. A prefix matching mechanism prunes the list of suggestions to elements that match the current incomplete rule. Figure 1 shows our method for entering a rule about family relationships. We use six different approaches to identify the next atom in an incomplete rule. Finally, we combine the top sets of predictions from these each approach to achieve the best accuracy and coverage in prediction. We provide the rationale for each prediction approach and a combined approach.

Simple Frequency: This approach ranks classes and properties according to their frequency in the rule base. First, it computes their frequency in the existing rules. It then sorts them accordingly, producing a suggestion list. This approach generates a suggestion list for all positions in a rule.

Position Frequency: This approach computes the frequency of classes and properties for each rule position. It sorts based on class and property frequency in each position. Therefore, the suggestion list changes for each position in an incomplete rule.

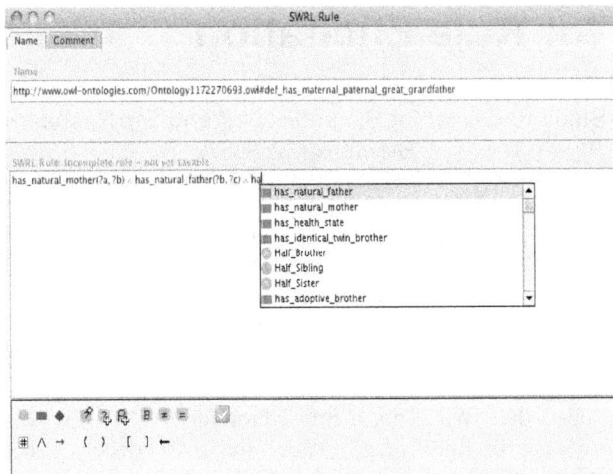

Figure 1. A screenshot of the SWRLTab that shows predictive editing and prefix matching in writing an example rule for the Family Health History Ontology's rule base, available at http://bioportal.bioontology.org/.

Co-occurrence: This approach is based on correlations between co-occurrence of atoms in existing rules in the rule base. It extracts the atoms in an incomplete rule and finds related rules containing them. Suggested atoms are returned as sets of atoms that co-occur in the related rules, but not in the incomplete rule. The list is sorted alphabetically.

Position Sensitive Match: Heuristically, if an incomplete rule and an existing rule are similar, it is likely that they share more atoms as the rule approaches completion. The position sensitive match approach searches for rules containing a partial string of the exact sequence of atoms in the existing rule base. It returns the atoms following them as suggestions for auto-completion of the rule. The list is sorted alphabetically.

Sibling Property: Two rules in a rule base are never identical. If an incomplete rule is identical to an existing one, the system anticipates that the next atoms will be different. The different classes or properties are usually semantically related and probably share the same category. This approach finds the complete rules in the pre-existing rules that share the same sequence of atoms. It returns the siblings of the next atoms in the ontology hierarchy (if they exist) as suggested atoms. The list is sorted alphabetically.

Domain-Range: In axiomatic rule bases, an individual defined from a class would normally be used in the same rule as the first argument of a property declaring conditions about it. The domain-range method finds classes to which individuals from the incomplete rules belong and suggests properties whose domains contain them. Furthermore, second argument individuals of properties are routinely used as first argument individuals in other properties. This pattern is common in declarative rule bases and links properties to each other. Taking this fact into consideration, the domain-range approach also suggests properties that share similar domains with the range of existing properties in the

incomplete rule. The suggestion list is sorted alphabetically. The performance of this approach is influenced by the appropriate usage of domains and ranges in ontologies.

Combined Approach: The combined approach uses all the methods noted here to render suggestion lists that are maximally inclusive. Given an integer k as an input, it combines the top k suggestions from each of the six methods. The order of combination is determined by the size of the suggestion lists generated by each approach. Suggestions are ordered from shorter to longer lists, top to bottom. If a suggestion already exists in the combined list, the next suggestion in the list is added. The combined approach uses an upper bound of $6k$ for the size of its suggestion list. In this work, we used $k = 3$ as a heuristic choice.

SUMMARY

We have developed a novel method that addresses the challenge of acquiring new rules through predictive editing, or autocompletion. Our method utilizes the syntax and semantics of the incomplete rule and existing rules in the rule base. We have proposed and evaluated six distinct statistical and semantic heuristic approaches, along with a combined approach. We have implemented these approaches within an intelligent interface for the SWRLTab plug in for Protégé OWL. An initial evaluation of our method with existing rule bases in the biomedical domain indicates that the combined approach provides the most relevant set of suggestions for specifying a new rule.

ACKNOWLEDGMENTS

This research was supported in part by National Institutes of Health grant R01MH87756. The authors would like to thank Martin O'Connor, Will Bridewell, and Richard Waldinger for their comments on this work.

REFERENCES

[1] SWRL Submission, available at http://www.w3.org/Submission/SWRL/

[2] McGuinness, D. L., and van Harmelen, F., editors, OWL Web Ontology Language Overview. W3C Recommendation 10 February 2004. Available at http://www.w3.org/TR/2004/REC-owl-features-20040210/ M.D.

[3] O'Connor, M. J., Knublauch, H., Tu, S. W., Grossof, B., Dean, M., Grosso, W. E., Musen, M. A., Supporting Rule System Interoperability on the Semantic Web with SWRL, *Fourth International Semantic Web Conference (ISWC 2005)*, Galway, Ireland, Springer-Verlag, LNCS 3729, 974-986 (2005).

[4] Hassanpour, S., O'Connor, M. J., and Das, A. K., Exploration of SWRL Rule Bases through Visualization, Paraphrasing, and Categorization of Rules. In G. Governatori, J. Hall, and A. Paschke, editors, *Proceedings of the International RuleML Symposium on Rule Interchange and Applications, Springer-Verlag, LNCS* 5858, 246-261 (2009).

A Knowledge Pattern-based Method for Linked Data Analysis

Valentina Presutti
Aldo Gangemi
Alessandro Adamou
Consiglio Nazionale delle
Ricerche, ISTC
Semantic Technology Lab
Italy
{*firstname.lastname*}@istc.cnr.it

Lora Aroyo
Balthasar Schopman
Guus Schreiber
Free University of Amsterdam
Intelligent Information
Systems Web and Media
The Netherlands
l.m.aroyo@cs.vu.nl
schopman@cs.vu.nl
schreiber@cs.vu.nl

ABSTRACT

We present a Linked Data analysis method which relies on knowledge patterns for constructing a logical architecture of the knowledge in a dataset. This can then be exploited to compare heterogeneous datasets, enhance interoperability between them and make implicit knowledge emerge.

Categories and Subject Descriptors: H.3.3 Information Search and Retrieval, I.2.4 Knowledge Representation Formalisms and Methods

General Terms: Experimentation, Measurement

Keywords: knowledge patterns, Linked Data

1. INTRODUCTION

The benefits of Linked Data (LD) and explicit semantics for the identification of related data in multiple use cases are shown both in recent research [3, 4, 1] and in the Web search industry. However, using the explicit knowledge of LD sets may be insufficient and awkward, since they tend to differ in size, domain coverage, description quality and granularity. Also, their knowledge organization is often not unified, thus reasoning with linked *open* datasets may fail to bring forward serendipitous knowledge beyond trivial facts.

Exploiting patterns in LD can hint at a workaround to this problem. A *knowledge pattern* (KP) embeds the most important relations for describing a relevant piece of knowledge in a domain, similar to a *frame* in linguistics or a *cognitive schema* in cognitive science [2].

Our proposed approach aims at validating the usefulness of knowledge patterns to improve interoperability within and between datasets, and to support user interaction in content search. This approach applies to LD sets no matter whether there is prior knowledge on the vocabularies used or not.

2. APPROACH

Typically, Linked Data sets combine types and properties from widespread controlled vocabularies (e.g. FOAF[1] and

---

[1]Friend-Of-A-Friend, http://xmlns.com/foaf/0.1/

DC^2) with others built-in or not defined in any top-down designed ontology.

We hypothesize that KP usage in LD can help:

- build a modular abstraction over a dataset that highlights its knowledge organisation and core components;
- model datasets in a more manageable way than with the usual *class-property* view of ontologies;
- build prototypical querying layer for datasets;
- improve interoperability within datasets, and detect incompatibility issues;
- compare analysis data about different datasets;
- improve user interaction in searching for relevant content.

Our approach combines top-down and bottom-up strategies. The **bottom-up** strategy aims at modeling, inspecting, and summarizing datasets, by drawing their so-called *dataset knowledge architecture* (cf. Section 3), which relies on the notions of *knowledge patterns* and *paths* (i.e. distinct ordered type-property sequences that can be traversed in an RDF graph). The **top-down** strategy aims at aligning emerging KPs with general KPs, which are those typically extracted from foundational ontologies, in order to improve interoperability within LD, detect incompatibility issues, and support LD and general KP enrichment. The application of this combined approach is sketched in Figure 1, and can be synthesized as follows:

1. *Examine* a significant number of general-purpose and domain-specific datasets. *Select* a limited number for in-depth inspection.
2. Gather **property usage statistics** for the selected datasets. Reify them to populate an ABox for the *knowledge architecture ontology*.
3. Align observed properties and non-literal types to *general KP properties*, based on sheer cognitive criteria.
4. Query datasets for extracting **paths** that traverse properties and typed resources. Store all paths with length up to 4, with their usage statistics, in the knowledge architecture dataset.
5. Identify *central types* and *central properties* based on their frequencies in paths, i.e. *betweenness* (cf. Section 3), and number of instantiations.

---

[2]Dublin Core, http://purl.org/dc/elements/1.1/

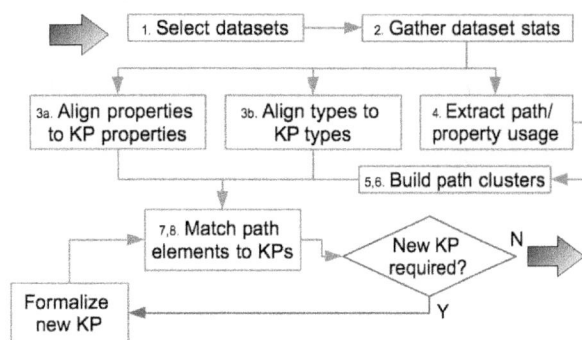

Figure 1: Linked Data analysis methodology.

6. Select clustering factors among central properties and construct **path clusters**;
7. Extract knowledge patterns from datasets;
8. Infer **alignments to general KPs** from the KPs and paths extracted in previous steps. Exploit mismatches to define new general KPs when necessary.

3. REPRESENTING THE ANALYSIS DATA

In step 1 we selected three datasets covering the multimedia domain at different granularities and using external as well as built-in ontologies. The **Jamendo**[3] DBTune dataset concerns recording and digital distribution data for independent musical artists. **John Peel Sessions**[4], also part of DBTune, is an event-centered dataset on live musical performances of artists for the BBC John Peel Show. **Linked-MDB**[5] is a partial dump of the Internet Movie DataBase, a web resource on the film industry. These datasets significantly differ in dimension figures, as Table 1 shows.

Dataset	Jamendo	JPeel	LMDB
nTriples	1,047,950	271,369	6,147,978
nProps	24	24	221
nTypes	11	9	53

Table 1: Figures describing dimension indicators (number of triples, properties and types used) for the three datasets.

The results of the following steps are then formalized into a **dataset knowledge architecture** - an abstraction over a dataset - that highlights how the dataset knowledge is organized in terms of KPs and paths. The ontology for representing this architecture[6] stores the architectural components and associated measures into a new RDF dataset[7]. By storing such data about a dataset, we can perform empirical analysis on it through SPARQL queries.

Through this ontology, we aim at re-constructing, in a bottom-up way, the essential domain ontology employed to represent the data, i.e. types and properties actually used for representing the data. We identify (i) the properties used in the dataset triples, and model them through the class `Property`, (ii) the types i.e. classes, of the subject and object resources of such triples, and model them through the class `Type`, and (iii) the typical paths that connect triples in the dataset, and model them through the class `Path`.

We identify central types and properties, as well as clustering factors, by computing measures such as:

- **Path count** of length 2 to 4 in a given dataset. The length of a path is the number of arcs (i.e. predicates) in each of its occurrences.
- **Path occurrence count** observed in each dataset.
- **Property usage in paths**, i.e. the sparsity of a dataset knowledge architecture.
- **Type and property betweenness**, i.e. the capability of the type or property to capture meaningful knowledge.

Based on the described entities and the associated measures, we can extract the emerging `KnowledgePatterns` of the datasets, and its most representing `Paths`, e.g. for building prototypical queries. Thus, by studying the paths as indicators for the organization of knowledge we synthesized a dataset knowledge architecture, instead of building a graph.

4. CONCLUSION AND FUTURE WORK

We have shown how to efficiently summarize Linked Data sets in order to (i) identify their most important knowledge components such as patterns, paths, central types and properties; (ii) build prototypical queries for them even if their vocabularies are unknown; and (iii) exploit them for building applications that support user interaction with content.

Future work focuses on (i) demonstrating how aligning emerging KPs of a dataset to general KPs improves interoperability across different datasets, and incompatibility detection by comparing analysis data about different datasets; (ii) showing that KP-based summarization of datasets improves user interaction when searching for relevant content, e.g. by automatically generating explanations; (iii) improving the method by performing additional analysis on more LD sets and comparing the obtained results.

5. REFERENCES

[1] L. Aroyo, N. Stash, Y. Wang, P. Gorgels, and L. Rutledge. CHIP demonstrator: Semantics-driven recommendations and museum tour generation. In *Semantic Web Challenge*, volume 295 of *CEUR Workshop Proceedings*. CEUR-WS.org, 2007.

[2] A. Gangemi and V. Presutti. Towards a pattern science for the Semantic Web. *Semantic Web*, 1(1-2):61–68, 2010.

[3] P. Heim, S. Hellmann, J. Lehmann, S. Lohmann, and T. Stegemann. RelFinder: Revealing relationships in RDF knowledge bases. In *Proceedings of the 3rd International Conference on Semantic and Media Technologies (SAMT)*, volume 5887 of *Lecture Notes in Computer Science*, pages 182–187. Springer, 2009.

[4] G. Schreiber, A. K. Amin, L. Aroyo, M. van Assem, V. de Boer, L. Hardman, M. Hildebrand, B. Omelayenko, J. van Ossenbruggen, A. Tordai, J. Wielemaker, and B. J. Wielinga. Semantic annotation and search of cultural-heritage collections: The MultimediaN E-Culture demonstrator. *J. Web Sem.*, 6(4):243–249, 2008.

---

[3] Jamendo DBTune home, http://dbtune.org/jamendo/

[4] John Peel DBTune home, http://dbtune.org/bbc/peel/

[5] LinkedMDB home, http://www.linkedmdb.org/

[6] Root is http://www.ontologydesignpatterns.org/ont/lod-analysis-properties.owl

[7] ABox at http://www.ontologydesignpatterns.org/ont/lod-analysis-properties-data.owl

A Self-Adapting Method for Knowledge Management in Collaborative and Social Tagging Systems

Francisco Echarte, José Javier Astrain, Alberto Córdoba, Jesús Villadangos,
Aritz Labat
Dept. Ingeniería Matemática e Informática
Universidad Pública de Navarra
Campus de Arrosadía. 31006 Pamplona (Spain)
patxi@eslomas.com, {josej.astrain,alberto.cordoba,jesusv,aritz.labat}@unavarra.es

ABSTRACT

This paper presents an automatic method to group resources of collaborative-social tagging systems in semantic categories. The main goal is to self-adapt the system to represent the current knowledge.

Categories and Subject Descriptors

H.4 [**Information Systems Applications**]: Miscellaneous; D.2.8 [**Software Engineering**]: Metrics—*complexity measures, performance measures*

General Terms

Experimentation, Performance, Algorithms

Keywords

Folksonomies, resource classification

1. THE METHOD

Given a folksonomy, the method initially creates a set of concepts where resources are grouped, assigning a name to each concept according to the semantic information provided by the resources grouped in each concept and their annotations. Once created the concepts, each new annotation of the folksonomy is processed updating the semantic information and adapting the concepts when necessary. The method starts with the creation of the set of representative tags (S_{rt}) and the vectorial representation of the resources of the folksonomy. The component *Representations* is in charge of these tasks, then each resource is assigned to subsets $R_{converged}$ or $R_{pending}$ in terms of whether they have converged or not. The component *Convergence* may use many criteria like the total amount of annotations, or the number of annotations associated to the S_{rt} set to assign the resources to $R_{converged}$. The component *Clustering* clusters the resources of the folksonmy belonging to $R_{converged}$ in a set of concepts, generating the set of semantic concepts on which resources of the folksonomy are grouped (C) and the set of pairs (r, c) where $r \in R$ and $c \in C$, representing that resource r is grouped into the concepts c (Z). The component *MergingSplitting* analyses the concepts provided in order to evaluate the convenience of merging or splitting

any of them, updating C and Z sets. The component *Classifier*, which uses the method presented in [1], is in charge of grouping the resources under those concepts with which they have high semantic similarity by comparing all the resources belonging to the $R_{converged}$ set with the concepts in which they are grouped in Z. The component assigns the resource to the $R_{classified}$ set according to the similarity measures between each resource and its group or keeps it on $R_{converged}$ and removes it from Z. Finally, the component *Representations* creates the vector representations for the C concepts using the Z set, and the component *Naming* assigns meaningful names to these concepts according to some criteria like the tags with higher weights.

Once created these concepts, the method self-adapts to the evolution of the folksonomy taking into account the new annotations made by users. The method waits for a change on the folksonomy when creating or removing an annotation. This change is represented by the method as a new *Tagging* element, which contains the annotation information (user, resource and tag), and if it has been created or deleted. If the tag used in the *Tagging* does not belong to the representative set of tags (S_{rt}), *Tagging* is ignored and it expects the reception of new annotations. If the tag involved in the annotation belongs to the S_{rt} set, the component *Representations* updates the vectorial representation of the resource. If the resource belongs to the $R_{classified}$ set the component also updates the vectorial representation of the concept in which the resource is grouped. If the *Tagging* is of type *create*, the method checks whether the resource has converged or not, and the possibility of grouping it under any existing concept. If the resource belongs to the $R_{pending}$ set, the component *ConvergenceCriterion* checks if the resource has converged after receiving the new annotation. If so, or if the resource already previously belonged to $R_{converged}$, the component *Classifier* provides the most appropriate concept for this resource. The component compares the semantic of the resource with that of each concept in C. Based on this similarity, the component assigns the resource to the $R_{classified}$ set and creates a new entry in Z, or lets the resource continue assigned to $R_{converged}$. If the resource is assigned to a concept, *Representations* component updates the vectorial representation of the concept with the resource information.

The method groups the resources in concepts, so that once a resource is classified it will never return to the set $R_{converged}$. Therefore, when a *Tagging* of type *delete* is received, the method does not checks if the resource has

```
Input:    Folksonomy
Output:   Folksonomy extended with semantic categories

 1.   Representations::createS_rt()
 2.   Representations::createVectors()

 3.   forall r ∈ R do
 4.       if Convergence::hasConverged(r) then
 5.           assign r to R_converged
 6.           else assign r to R_pending
 7.       endif
 8.   endforall

 9.   Clustering::create(R_converged)
10.   MergingSplitting::process(C, Z)

11.   forall r ∈ R_converged do
12.       if Classifier::isCorrectlyClassified(Z, r) then
13.           assign r to R_classified
14.           else drop r from Z
15.       endif
16.   endforall

17.   Representations::createConceptVectors(C, Z)
18.   Naming::process(C, Z)

19.   while true do

20.       tagging = wait(FolksonomyEvolution)

19.       if t ∉ S then
21.           if not Representations::inS_rt(t) then
22.               continue
23.           endif

24.           Representations::updateVectors(Tagging)

25.           if if tagging.action = create then
26.               if r ∈ R_pending
                      and Convergence::hasConverged(r) then
27.                   assign r to R_converged
28.               endif
29.               if r ∈ R_converged then
30.                   Classifier::classify(Z, r)
31.                   Representations::updateConceptVector(Z, r)
32.               endif
33.           endif

34.           if RecalculationCondition::check() then
35.               Representations::updateS_rt()
36.               Clustering::update(C, Z)
37.               MergingSplitting::process(C, Z)
38.               Representations::updateVectors(C, Z)
39.               Naming::process(C, Z)
40.           endif

41.   endwhile
```

Figure 1: *Method pseudocode*

converged or whether it must continue under the current concept, the method only updates the corresponding vectorial representation. In addition to gathering new converged resources into existing concepts, the method considers the information received from the new *Taggings*, updating the S_{rt} set and the existing concepts. Thus, S_{rt} and C sets may adapt to the folksonomy's evolution, performing their adaptation for example to new users' interests. Since a unique *Tagging* does not use to significantly affect the S_{rt} set or the concepts set, and this update can be quite expensive computationally, the method uses the component *RecalculationCondition* to determine when to update both concepts and S_{rt}. When the component determines the convenience of performing the recalculation, in a first step the S_{rt} set is updated taking into account its establishment criteria using component *Representations*. It then uses the *Clustering* component to update the existing concepts (C) and the resources grouped in them (Z). The component *MergingSplitting* reviews these concepts creating, splitting them when necessary. Once obtained the elements C and Z, *Representations* updates the concept representation vectors, and *Naming* assigns a name to each one of the concepts. Upon the completion of these tasks, the method returns to stand

waiting for the arrival of new *Taggings* to the folksonomy for their processing.

2. METHOD VALIDATION

In order to validate the quality of the semantic classification of the method, we have evaluated 12,241 web resources with the aid of 107 computer science students (advanced and regular internet users) at the Universidad Pública de Navarra during the course 2009-2010 (October 2009 - June 2010). Each reviewer has evaluated a subset of the resource set, ensuring that each resource has been evaluated by five different reviewers. Each reviewer has evaluated its subset of resources in the initial iteration, and then those new resources and those whose concept of classification has changed along the different iterations.

Reviewers evaluated, for each of the resources, how well resources are classified under their concept of classification, quantifying this value between 1 and 5, meaning (1) a very poor classification, (2) a poor classification, (3) a reviewer indecision, (4) a good classification and (5) a very good classification. Figure 2 shows the results obtained.

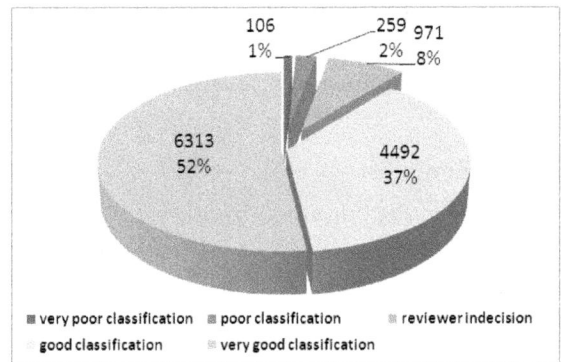

Figure 2: **Method validation by reviewers**

3. CONCLUSIONS

We have proposed a simple and incremental method for the automatic and semantic creation of concepts to group the resources of a folksonomy, in order to improve the knowledge management in folksonomies, without changing the way users make their annotations.

The method automatically creates the classification concepts and adapts them to the folksonomy evolution over time, grouping new resources and creating, merging or splitting concepts as needed.

Acknowledgements

Research partially supported by the Spanish Research council under the research grants TIN2008-03687, TIN2010-1717 and INNPACTO IPT-370000-2010-36.

4. REFERENCES

[1] F. Echarte, J. J. Astrain, A. Córdoba, J. Villadangos, and A. Labat. Acoar: a method for the automatic classification of annotated resources. In *Proc. of the 5th Int. Conference on Knowledge Capture*, pages 181–182, New York, NY, USA, 2009. ACM.

Learning to Detect Abnormal Semantic Web Data

Yang Yu
Lehigh University
Bethlehem, PA, 18015, USA
yay208@cse.lehigh.edu

Xingjian Zhang
Lehigh University
Bethlehem, PA, 18015, USA
xiz307@cse.lehigh.edu

Jeff Heflin
Lehigh University
Bethlehem, PA, 18015, USA
heflin@cse.lehigh.edu

Categories and Subject Descriptors

I.2.6 [**Learning**]: Knowledge acquisition

General Terms

Algorithms, Experimentation, Performance

Keywords

detecting abnormal data, Semantic Web, learning

1. INTRODUCTION

Numerous problems could happen in the generation process for Semantic Web data that is usually gathered from heterogeneous sources by using a variety of tools [3]. Recently some works [1, 2, 3, 4] began to focus on the quality of Semantic Web data. However since the Semantic Web represents many points of view, there is no objective measure of correctness for all Semantic Web data. Therefore, we consider using an abnormality heuristic that could indicate a data quality problem at the triple level. We recognize that not all abnormal data is incorrect (in fact, in some scenarios the abnormal data may be the most interesting data) and thus leave it up to the application to determine how to use the heuristic. The essential idea of this work is based on the fact that a statement can get supporting evidence if it can be entailed from other data. Consider the statement A advises B: in some situations where this is true, there are also statements such as A is the principal investigator of project C, B works in C. This rule is clearly not certain. Yet, when combined with other forms of evidence, it can provide support for the advises relation.

To detect incorrect data, ideally we can directly learn characteristics of them. But incorrect data have too many forms. So we check if the data lacks sufficient normal patterns compared to the majority of the data. Still using the advises relation example above, we change the first statement into B advises A (assuming advises is not subPropertyOf advises$^-$). Then our predictability on this statement would be low, because the context is inconsistent with a probabilistic rule existing in many other contexts. Although this probabilistic rule does not always hold, various rules in context can collaboratively give certain support. Note that there are many possible arbitrary relations that can be used to describe any two objects on the Semantic Web, but the

K-CAP'11, June 26–29, 2011, Banff, Alberta, Canada.
ACM 978-1-4503-0396-5/11/06.

notion of *significant relation* used in this work is tied to the ontologies used by the system.

2. CONTEXT BASED IDENTIFYING SIGNIFICANT RELATION

Formally, our problem is defined as: given the pair u of subject s and object o, how significant is some relation p between the pair u (written $y_{u,p}$). The pair u_k of subject s_k and object o_k is another pair (s_k != s or o_k != o) having the semantic relation p. The $y_{u,p}$ can be measured by the overall similarity between the pair u and all the pairs u_k (equation 1), where U_p is the set of all pairs that have the relation p and sim() is the similarity function on two contexts which will be introduced in Section 3.3.

$$y_{u,p} = \frac{1}{|U_p|} \sum_{u_k \in U_p, u_k != u} sim(u_k, u) \qquad (1)$$

We define the semantic connection as $\langle r_1, r_2, ..., r_n \rangle$, where r_i is a relation. Then the context for a pair u is defined over a semantic connection space which is a vector space consisting of all possible semantic connections (the first part in following equation), where n_{u,c_i} means the number of instantiations of the semantic connection c_i ($i \leqslant m$) between the pair u. To get more supporting evidence for a predicate usage between two instances, for each instance, we build a set of similar instances including itself and call this set the expanded set. Because the semantic connections between the two expanded sets are partially similar to the semantic connections between original pair u, they are treated as partial semantic connections between the original pair. The full contetxt of pair u are represented below.

$$V_u = [n_{u,c_1}, n_{u,c_2}, ..., n_{u,c_m}] + \alpha[n_{\bar{u},c_1}, n_{\bar{u},c_2}, ..., n_{\bar{u},c_m}]$$
$$= [n_{u,c_1} + \alpha n_{\bar{u},c_1}, n_{u,c_2} + \alpha n_{\bar{u},c_2}, ..., n_{u,c_m} + \alpha n_{\bar{u},c_m}]$$

In similarity measuring, the partial matching between different connections should affect the similarity between vectors. Considering that, we define the similarity between vectors as the sum of the similarities between all pairs of connections divided by the multiplication of the magnitude of two vectors (equation 2).

$$sim(u', u) = \frac{1}{||u||||u'||} \sum_{i=1}^{m} \sum_{j=1}^{m} n_{u,c_i} n_{u',c_j} s(c_i, c_j) \qquad (2)$$

$$s(c_i, c_j) = s(<r_{i1}, r_{i2}, ..., r_{in}>, <r_{j1}, r_{j2}, ..., r_{jn}>)$$
$$= \prod_{k=1}^{n} x_{ik,jk} \quad (3)$$

where $x_{ik,jk}$ is the similarity between property r_{ik} and r_{jk}.

3. LEARNING PREDICATE SIMILARITY

The model we used is modified from its application in the tag prediction problem [5]. For a pair u of subject and object, the algorithm ranks predicates by $y_{u,p}$. The objective function (equation 4) maximizes the ranking statistic AUC (area under the ROC-curve).

$$AUC(\hat{\theta}, u) = \frac{1}{|P_u^+||P_u^-|} \sum_{p^+ \in P_u^+} \sum_{p^- \in P_u^-} h(y_{u,p^+} - y_{u,p^-}) \quad (4)$$

The h(x) is a continuous sigmoid function

$$h(x) = \frac{1}{1 + e^{-x}} \quad (5)$$

Then using gradient descent, AUC has to be differentiated with respect to all model parameters and for each pair $u \in P_s$, P_u^+ is the set of predicates that are already used between the pair u while P_u^- is the set of predicates that are not used between the pair u. The overall optimization task with respect to the ranking statistic AUC and the observed data is then:

$$\arg\max_{\hat{\theta}} \sum_{u \in Ps} AUC(\hat{\theta}, u) \quad (6)$$

The model parameters $\mathbf{x}$ which is a vector of all possible pairs of predicate similarity introduced in Section 3.3 are updated $\frac{\partial}{\partial \mathbf{x}} AUC(\hat{\theta}, u)$. We note that this equation contains a lot of computations that can be reused for each round, e.g. the derivative of the similarity between two connections are not changed within each iteration. So we use some memoization techniques to save huge amount of repeated computations. After each iteration, update the memoized table once. Thus for each pair u, the $\mathbf{x}$ are updated as follows:

$$\hat{\mathbf{x}} \leftarrow \hat{\mathbf{x}} + \gamma \cdot \frac{\partial AUC}{\partial \mathbf{x}} \quad (7)$$

where γ is the learning rate which we have set as 0.05. This equation means after the model learns from each observed triple to increase the gap between the positives and the negatives, it updates the model parameters, i.e. predicate similarities, based on the learning rate.

4. EXPERIMENTS

After removal of test triples, the experiment process generally is as follows. First, the system randomly selects some training samples and builds the contexts for them. Second, the system learns model parameters on training samples, given their initial values. Finally, we input test samples with unknown predicate to the system, both positive and negative, and check the result of entailed predicate with highest score. For positive samples, the system is expected to entail the correct predicate, which means the system can detect the abnormality if the predicate is incorrect. For negative samples, it is expected that no relation between the objects entailed by the system is above a certain threshold β and

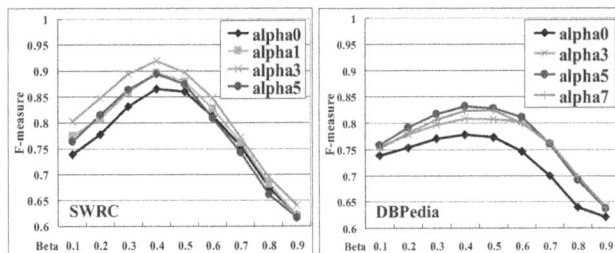

Figure 1: The effect of different expansion factor α and different credible relation threshold β.

then the system report it as no relation. Thus all experiments use precision, recall and F-measure.

The experiment compares the performance when the expansion factor α (Section 3.2) and the threshold β (Section 5.1) varies (shown in Figure 1). From the results, we see that the system without expansion ($\alpha = 0$) is worse than any systems with expansion and among those the systems with $\alpha 3$ ($\alpha = 0.3$) and $\alpha 5$ ($\alpha = 0.5$) are the best on two data sets. To not overwhelm readers, the lines with other alpha values are not shown here. The reason DBPedia needs more context expansion is that it has less relational descriptions for instances than SWRC. For β, the system performs the best on both data sets when it is 0.4.

5. CONCLUSION

The essential idea of this work is to use probabilistic rules in the context of a triple and the context of typical triples to generate a measure of abnormality. The probabilistic rules are learned from semantic connections between objects in triples. To deal with the open world assumption underlying the Semantic Web data, the system uses three mechanisms, i.e. enriching the context, a novel context comparison mechanism and a learning model considering the missing triples. The approach is mainly based on data itself without ontological inference and unsupervised learns from a set of data sources that are generally correct.

6. REFERENCES

[1] H. Cunningham, D. Maynard, K. Bontcheva, and V. Tablan. GATE: A framework and graphical development environment for robust NLP tools and applications. In *Proceedings of the 40th Annual Meeting of the ACL*, 2002.

[2] C. Fürber and M. Hepp. Using semantic web resources for data quality management. In P. Cimiano and H. S. Pinto, editors, *EKAW*, volume 6317 of *Lecture Notes in Computer Science*, pages 211–225. Springer, 2010.

[3] Y. Lei, V. Uren, and E. Motta. A framework for evaluating semantic metadata. In *Proceedings of the 4th international conference on Knowledge capture*, K-CAP '07, pages 135–142, New York, NY, USA, 2007. ACM.

[4] D. Maynard, W. Peters, and Y. Li. Metrics for evaluation of ontology-based information extraction. In *WWW 2006 Workshop on q́sEvaluation of Ontologies for the Web*, 2006.

[5] S. Rendle, L. B. Marinho, A. Nanopoulos, and L. Schmidt-Thieme. Learning optimal ranking with tensor factorization for tag recommendation. In *KDD'09*, pages 727–736, 2009.

Preliminary Steps towards a Knowledge Factory Process

Vinay K. Chaudhri, Nikhil Dinesh,
John Pacheco
SRI International
Menlo Park, CA 94025, USA
{chaudhri, dinesh, pacheco}@ai.sri.com

Gary Ng
Cerebra
San Diego, CA
gary.ng@cerebra.com

Peter E. Clark
Vulcan Inc
Seattle, WA, USA
peterc@vulcan.com

Andrew Goldenkranz
Fremont Union High School District
agoldenk@gmail.com

Patrice Seyed
University at Buffalo, Buffalo, NY
apseyed@buffalo.edu

Naveen Sharma
Evalueserve, India
Naveen.Sharma@evalueserve.com

Categories and Subject Descriptors

I.2.1 [**Artificial Intelligence**]: Applications and Expert Systems

General Terms

Measurement, Documentation, Performance, Design, Experimentation

Keywords

Knowledge engineering, ontologies, deductive question answering, knowledge acquisition

1. INTRODUCTION

In the fall 2010 issue of the AI Magazine, we reported the design, implementation and evaluation of a knowledge acquisition system called AURA. AURA enables domain experts in Physics, Chemistry and Biology to author their knowledge, and a different set of experts to pose questions against that knowledge. The evaluation results previously reported were from 50 pages each from science textbooks in Physics, Chemistry and Biology. The results were most promising for Biology. Based on those results we undertook a content building effort to capture knowledge from approximately 315 pages (or 20 chapters) of the same Biology textbook [2] and incorporated the resulting content in the electronic version of that book. In this demo/poster session, we will demonstrate the biology knowledge base (KB) created using AURA, the electronic textbook application Inquire, and discuss the knowledge engineering process we used to construct the KB.

2. KNOWLEDGE FACTORY PROCESS

The AI magazine paper on AURA reported the question answering performance for KBs created by domain experts under different conditions. The question answering performance, however, leaves the following questions open.

If a different set of novel questions is posed, can we expect to get the same performance? To get a truly robust measurement of novel question performance, one would need to pose a series of tests. Such series of tests has never been posed in Project Halo before. A related open question is how many tests with novel questions one needs to perform to ensure that the novel question performance stays approximately the same with each new comparable test? If a novel question set is very different in scope and complexity or poses questions that are outside the capabilities that were tested, the performance will obviously degrade.

To what extent has the textbook knowledge been captured? A problem with any evaluation that is based on question answering performance is that when a question fails, in many cases, the failure can be blamed on a knowledge gap. Assuming one can invest enough knowledge capture effort, can the knowledge gaps be avoided?

Is there an inter-domain expert agreement during the knowledge encoding process? To expand the scope of the KB, we need multiple domain experts entering knowledge. This process can fail if there is a lack of consistent conventions for knowledge encoding and each encoder uses a different style. An ideal situation would be to have a process using which given a specific sentence, there is a well defined, and preferably a unique way, to formally represent it in the KB. While such a goal is unachievable in full generality, our hope is to have a closed community of curators who can develop a set of guidelines that can be followed by them to come up with consensus representations. We believe this to be a realizable goal because multiple textbook authors are able to converge on one way of presenting the material in the textbook even if they may disagree in some respects.

We call a knowledge entry process *a knowledge factory* process if it solves the above three problems. In other words, a knowledge factory process is a knowledge entry process that can ensure that the results on the performance of novel questions is consistent across a series of questions that are similar in scope and difficulty, can systematically eliminate knowledge gaps, and leads to consensus representations by multiple domain experts. To the best of our knowledge, no such knowledge capture method exists that meets all three of these goals and our work makes modest steps in that direction.

We next present key elements of the design of the knowledge factory process and then discuss our experience in implementing those elements.

2.1 Design of the Knowledge Factory Process

Our solution for eliminating the knowledge gaps was to follow a sentence driven encoding strategy. Under this strategy, a domain expert analyzes each sentence for its relevance to question answering. For each relevant sentence, the domain expert represents it using the knowledge entry capabilities of AURA to the extent it can be represented. The goal of this strategy is to systematically work through each sentence so that there is a clear scope for the knowledge that needs to be encoded, and we avoid unintentional gap in the KB.

Our solution to address inter-domain expert agreement problem had two aspects. First aspect was to develop a knowledge engineering process manual that provides explicit knowledge entry guidelines. The manual includes several encoding situations and provides guidelines on what solutions to prefer. Second aspect was to design a collaborative process amongst multiple domain experts so that the representation of each sentence was reviewed by multiple experts to naturally evolve towards a consensus representation. Our collaborative process separates the encoding process into the roles such as *planner, encoder, tester:* a planner plans the knowledge to be entered, encoder performs the entry, and the tester tests the knowledge. During this factory like pipeline, the representation of each sentence gets reviewed by multiple people and any issues can get discussed and resolved. We designed the collaborative process structure because in a preliminary test it was clear that if the domain experts work in isolation using only the knowledge engineering process manual, they are unlikely to arrive at consensus representations.

Our solution for ensuring that the performance of the system does not degrade with each new comparable novel question set was to simply perform a series of tests. It was unclear to us how many such tests will be needed or adequate, so we arbitrarily chose to do three tests. Each test was followed by a period to fix the knowledge gaps before the next test was performed.

2.2 Experience in Using the Knowledge Factory Process

The sentence driven process was hugely popular in the project team: the domain experts had a clear plan, and the program management had a clear picture of how far we had progressed. The process also resulted in a set of sentences that could not be encoded either because of difficult ontological modeling problems or because AURA did not support the necessary knowledge acquisition interface. These difficult to encode sentences are the basis of a workshop on Deep Knowledge Representation (See https://sites.google.com/site/dkrckcap2011/).

The sentence driven process, however, was not successful in fully eliminating knowledge gaps. In a test with novel questions, we still found knowledge gaps that could have been avoided during the encoding process. We are currently investigating why such gaps arose in spite of a systematic sentence based encoding scheme.

The knowledge engineering process manual and the team structure for collaborative knowledge entry were partially effective in ensuring consensus representation. The success has been partial because even though the encoding team was able to reach consensus on the representations, the encoding did not always match the intuitions of a Biology teacher. This is a side effect of the fact that the encoding domain experts are not biology teachers and are located in a different location than biology teachers responsible for making use of the content in the electronic textbook (described in the next section). The collaborative team needs to be extended to add biology teacher expertise.

We performed three test and fix cycles on five chapters of the syllabus. Each test and fix cycle revealed gaps in the KB, and the question answering performance improved with each test. Since the performance did not level during the scope of the three tests, it was difficult to tell whether three tests were adequate. To ensure the sufficiency of these tests, one would need to perform a few more tests until the question answering performance levels off. Exploring that in more detail is a topic for future exploration. A factor that confounds these results is that some questions cannot be answered due to the sentences that cannot be encoded due to knowledge representation and acquisition difficulties. It has been difficult to assess if the results would be different if all the sentences could be encoded.

3. ELECTRONIC TEXTBOOK INQUIRE

Our target application, motivating this work, is an "intelligent textbook", i.e., an electronic version of the Campbell Biology textbook [2] that allows users to interactively browse and explore the material on-line, and ask questions and receive machine-inferred answers from the KB, including questions that require inference. A prototype of this application, called *Inquire*, has already been constructed.

There are three primary interfaces to the KB as a student is reading the book: (a) Clicking on a biology term in the book resulting in a page that summarizes information about that term (b) providing a list of suggested questions in response to highlighting (c) asking free-form questions expressed in controlled English.

For the first of these, clicking on a biology term results in a concept summary page generated automatically from the knowledge formally represented in the KB. The concept summary pages can be extremely useful to a student in focusing on the essence of a concept, as a quick review guide, and an exam preparation aid.

For the second of these interfaces, as a student highlights a section of the textbook, *Inquire* suggests some questions to the user about the highlighted text. The question suggestion is based on the knowledge that is formally represented in the KB. For example, in a paragraph describing Protein, the system may suggest the following questions: What is the shape of protein? How many polypeptides does Protein have?

Users can enter free-form questions through a controlled English interface, allowing students to pose their own questions to the textbook. For example, a student may ask: "What is the difference between a pentose and a hexose?"

ACKNOWLEDGMENT

This work was supported by Vulcan Inc.

4. REFERENCES

[1] Gunning D. et. al., Project Halo Update — Progress Toward Digital Aristotle, AI Magazine, Fall 2010, 33-58.

[2] Jane B. Reece, Lisa A. Urry, Michael L. Cain, Steven A. Wasserman, Peter V. Minorsky, Robert B. Jackson. Campbell Biology, Pearson Publishing. 2010.

Towards Semistructured Information Integrating Using XML and Deductive Logic

Marco Javier Suarez B.
Assistant teacher at ECCI
Carrera 19 No. 49-20
Bogota D.C, Colombia
3144167247, 1. ++57
marco.suarez@ecci.edu.co

Juan Velasquez
Assistant teacher at U de Chile
Republica 701, office 301, CHILE.
Santiago, Chile
837-0720, 2. ++52
jvelasqu@dii.uchile.cl

Eliana Salinas V.
Instructor teacher at CTNS
Carrera 16-4 No. 49-20
Tunja Colombia
3124356698, 1. ++57
salinas.eliana@gmail.com

ABSTRACT
This paper introduces an approach to the information extracting (IE) from the web through deductive rules using semantic trees. This set of rules is based on heuristics beside a rigorous classification of tables and the detection of elements of tables, given their structure and complexity. The purpose of this research consists in generating XML-Type Documents in order to integrate the information got in the extraction process.

Categories and Subject Descriptors
G.4 MATHEMATICAL SOFTWARE: Algorithm design and analysis

General Terms
Algorithms, Design

Keywords
Information extracting, logic rules, Semantic Web, XML, Schema

1. INTRODUCTION
Data on the Web in HTML, XHTML tables is mostly structured, but we usually do not know the structure in advance[1].We begin our examination of IE by considering a specific example from tables contains within XHTML and HTML pages or PDF documents. In order to integrate the information of the XHTML, HTML and PDF documents, it is necessary to determine the area of knowledge (Health, Tourism, Nutrition, etc.), a classification of types of tables, and the leaving format for the extracted information. This article presents a classification of XHTML, HTML and PDF table structures, the description of ways for organizing and presenting information in the tables, a set of rules and heuristics for extracting information from web tables, and the design of the intermediate DTD which facilitates the generation of XML schemas. Here, XML is adopted as the leaving format of the extraction process. This is so because it has a high adaptability, accessibility and interpolarity in different processing data contexts. In addition, the W3C has made it a standard for the development of Web applications.

2. METHODOLOGY
An approach to solve the problem of data heterogeneity on the Web is the main objective in our work. In order to give solution, we proposed the following model of the figure 1. In this focus solution to this problem is to use the deductive logic and XML technologies for detecting, extracting and integrating information. In this work,

the non structurated data sources are mainly concerned with texts contained in structures known like tables, these structures are contained in *An Web Collection*[5] ; the Web Collections aims to provide a store of documents for to be used in the wrapper.

The solution entails elements of table understanding, data integration, classification and wrapper. Table understanding allows us to recognize attributes and values, pair attributes with values, and form records. Data-integration techniques allow us to match source records with a target schema[1].

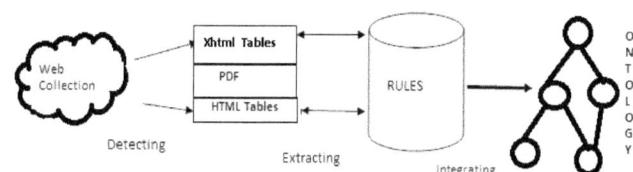

Figure 1. General Architecture for Information Extracting.

A data cell can contain text, images, lists, paragraphs, forms, horizontal rules, tables, etc, as shown in Figure 2. This table structure has the following labels:

- Tables are defined by the labels <table>…</table>.
- Labels <TR> and </TR> define each line of the table.
- Labels <TD> and </TD> define each element in a cell.
- The label <TBODY> lets group a set of elements for the table.

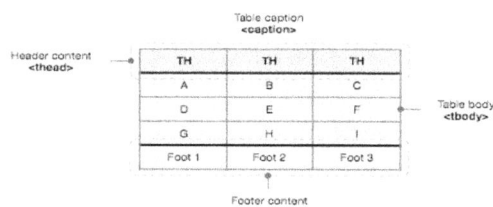

Figure 2 Distribution of information in basic table.

A second type of structure has been called table structure with regroupings. These types of tables have been called complex structures, and they require a conversion to a simple table format for their interpretation and analysis. Structures of tables with regroupings are classified in three subgroups, and they are defined by the following rules through the deductive logic:

R1 Just the presence of {<TD Colspan=n>} V {<TH Colspan=n>}, for a table that shows a column with regroupings the minimum value per defect will be n=1.

R2 Just the presence of {<TD Rowspan=m>} ∨ {<TH Rowspan=m>}, the minimum value per defect in a table that shows a unique row will be m=1.

R3 The presence of {<TD Colspan=n> ∨<TH Colspan=n>} ∧{<TD Rowspan=m> ∨ <TH Rowspan=m>}

3. DETECTING INFORMATION

Currently there are a variety of approaches to constructing IE systems. One approach is to manually develop information extraction rules by encoding patterns (e.g. regular expressions) that reliably identify the desired entities or relations. For example, the Suiseki system[4] extracts information on interacting proteins from biomedical text using manually developed patterns.

In this work, Information Extraction (IE) is the name given to any process which selectively structures and combines data which is found, explicitly stated or implied, in one or more texts[3]. In this case, the structures selected are XHTML, HTML or PDF Tables.

The extracting algorithm recognizes and interprets the following steps:

- The detection and selection of one or more well-formed tables.
- The detection, selection and extraction of titles of tables.
- The detection of the number of columns.
- The detection and extraction of titles of column in each table.
- The extraction of information contained in rows and cells.

The rules for selecting and restricting one or more XHTML and CSS tables are determined through the table elements defined for detecting a table [3].

R1 If XHTML files ⊂ the labels {<table>…</table>} → assign table to the set {table i}

R2 If {table i} ⊂ (columns n=1 number of rows = m) ∧ ∀(row i): ∃: references (href.) → "non-valid table"

R3 If {table i} ⊂ yes and only yes columns n=1 ∧ rows m=1 → "non-**valid** table"

R4 If {table i} ⊂ Colspan = n ∧ ∀{table i}: ∃ rows (<tr>…</tr>) with a number of cells (<td>…</td>) <o> a Colspan = n. → "non-valid table"

R5 If {table i} ⊂ double Rowspan for the same row (<tr>…</tr>) → "non-valid table"

4. EXTRACTING INFORMATION

The presence of a title of a table is not always transparent. Some tables present it directly[2], but in other tables it is necessary to detect and select it. Detecting a title of a table is determined through analyzing the structure of syntactic hierarchy [4] of the HTML document. [3]:

R1 If ∀ {table i}: ∃: <CAPTION> "x" </CAPTION>→ "x" = <TITLE of table> yes-no

R2 If {table i} ⊂ {<td Colspan=n "X"> ∨ <th Colspan=n "X">} → "X" = <title of table> yes-no

R3 If ∃: row (<tr>…</tr>) prior to <table> … </table> ∧ row (<tr>…</tr>) ⊂ {(<h1>"X"</h1>) ∨ <h2>"X"</h2>) ∨ (<h3>"X"</h3>) ∨ (<h4>"X"</h4>) ∨ (<h5>"X"</h5>) ∨ (<h6>"X"</h6>)→"X"=<title of table>yes-not

R4 If ∀: {table i} ∃ : Num-Columns =1 ∧ {table i} ⊂ row (<tr1><td> <p>"X" </p></td></tr1>) → "X"=<title of table>yes-noT

R5 If ∃ label (</TITLE>"X"</TITLE>)→"X" =<title of table>if-not

R6 = <title of table> = "Don't have title"

Extracting titles of table columns follows a process similar to the last one. Here it is also assumed that the chosen table {table i} was filtered, and for that reason it is well formed to start its extracting analysis [5]. In order to determine, select and extract information from the columns of a table have been defined the following general rules:

R1 If ∀ {table i}: ∃ {<td Colspan=n> ∨ <th Colspan=n>} ∃ {<tr1><tdi>"Xi"</tdi></tr1>} → "Xi"= <title of column n> ∨ ∃ <tr1><thi>"Xi"</thi></tr1>} → "Xi" = <title of column n> yes-no

R2 If {table i} ⊂ <thead> ∧ ∃ {<tr1><thi>"X"</thi></tr1>}→ "X"= <title of column n> yes-no

R3 If {table i} ⊄ <thead> ∧ ∃ {<tr1><tdi>"X"</tdi></tr1>}→ "X"= <title of column n>

R4 If ∀ {table i}: ∃ Num-Columns = 1 ∧ ∃ {<tr1><td><p>"X"</p></td></tr1>}→ "X"= <title of column>

5. XML FOR INFORMATION INTEGRATING

The difficulty of integration of data from heterogeneous information sources has been on the research agenda for many years. With the increasing amount of information that is available, the need for an answer to this problem increases[4]. However, because of the huge amounts of data, manually integrating information is not a viable option. Unfortunately, due to the semantical assumptions not captured in schema or data, automatic integration solutions often make mistakes. Therefore, most of the existing integration systems are semi-automatic [5]. It was created to obtain the intermediary XML and has the following characteristics[2]:

- What are the permitted elements in the XML document?
- The possible content of the elements.
- What attributes can be associated to what elements.
- What are the permitted values for the attributes?

6. CONCLUTIONS AND FUTURE WORK

We have implemented the Web wrapper using the Visual Prolog and C++ programming language stressing efficiency and ease-of-use. A general view of the *wrapper* prototype of extraction can be observed. In semantic terms[5], it lets generate a model of table simple structure starting from complex structures. In this case, the algorithm detected the presence of a unique table with regroupings in the HTML document. We shows a tool for extracting and integrating semistructured information from a set of HTML pages and PDF documents for converting the extracted information into XML set documents. After evaluating the results obtained through the extracting prototype, it can be affirmed that the results are satisfactory and have high quality. Based on this fact, future tasks in the research can be predicted.

7. REFERENCES

[1] Luger, G.F. 1992. Artificial Intelligence. Structures and Strategies for Complex Problem Solving. 32-56.

[2] Lim, S.J and K, Y. 2002. Extracting Information from semistructured sources. 71-80.

[3] Maruyama, H. 1999. XML y Java. Ed Prentice Hall.

[4] Nejdl, W. and Loser, A. 2003. Super-Peer-Based Routing and Clustering Strategies for RDF-Based Peer-to-Peer Networks. In Proceedings of WWW. 123-130.

[5] Suárez, M.J. 2005. Semantic Indexing. In Proceedings CIINDET 2005. 212-220.

Causal Markers across Domains and Genres of Discourse

Rutu Mulkar-Mehta
Information Sciences Institute
University of Southern
California
me@rutumulkar.com

Andrew S. Gordon
Institute for Creative
Technologies
University of Southern
California
gordon@ict.usc.edu

Jerry Hobbs
Information Sciences Institute
University of Southern
California
hobbs@isi.edu

Eduard Hovy
Information Sciences Institute
University of Southern
California
hovy@isi.edu

ABSTRACT

This paper[1] is a study of causation as it occurs in different domains and genres of discourse. There have been various initiatives to extract causality from discourse using causal markers. However, to our knowledge, none of these approaches have displayed similar results when applied to other styles of discourse. In this study we evaluate the nature of causal markers – specifically causatives, between corpora in different domains and genres of discourse and measure the overlap of causal markers using two metrics – Term Similarity and Causal Precision. We find that causal markers, specially causatives (causal verbs) are extremely domain dependent, and moderately genre dependent.

Categories and Subject Descriptors

A.1 [**General Literature**]: INTRODUCTORY AND SURVEY

General Terms

Theory, Languages, Standardization

Keywords

Causality, Domains and Genres of Discourse

1. INTRODUCTION

Causality is an important phenomenon in discourse, and plays a major role in NLP tasks of discourse understanding [4] and question answering [1]. Over the years, it has captured the attention of various researchers in NLP and numerous research initiatives [3, 8] have evolved for causal relation extraction. The collective goal of the research community has been to identify and extract causal relations, and various approaches such as supervised learning approaches [1] and heuristics based approaches [3] have been taken. However, none of these approaches have presented good results across domains or genres of discourse. Causal relations are usually extracted using causal markers, and the limited growth in the area begs the question of whether there is an inherent relation of

9[1]The full paper is available at: http://www.rutumulkar.com/publications/kcap-full-2011.pdf

causal markers with the domain or genre of discourse which make them difficult to adapt across corpora. This paper attempts to address this issue by comparing causal markers across various genres (Newspapers, Blogs, Research Papers) and various domains (Finance, Football, Biomedicine), and evaluating the results on two measures – Term Similarity, Causal Precision.

2. EXPERIMENTS AND RESULTS

We selected a collection of four very diverse corpora from three genres (newspapers, blogs, publications) and three domains (finance, football, biomedicine). The newspaper articles were from two domains: Finance (WSJ articles from LDC corpus LDC2005T08 called Discourse GraphBank [9]) henceforth referred to as *fin*, and Football (LDC - New York Times Annotated corpus (LDC2008T19A), and describes football games) henceforth referred to as *Fbl-n*. The blog were from the domain of football extracted by Gordon et al. [2], henceforth referred to as *Fbl-b*. The scientific publications about biomedicine was extracted by Mulkar-Mehta et al. [5] from PubMed describing the cell cycle and henceforth referred to as *Bio*.

We conducted three experiments, evaluating the similarity of causal terms across domains and genre. The purpose of the experiments was to observe the similarity of causal terms across the dimensions of genre and domain, keeping one variable constant while comparing the other. To evaluate causal markers in the same genre and different domain, we comapred *Fbl-n* vs. *Fin*; To evaluate causal markers in different genres and same domain we compared *Fbl-n* vs. *Fbl-b*; To evaluate causal markers in different genre and different domains we compared *Fbl-n* vs. *Bio*. We use two evaluation measures to compare the similarity in causal markers in the domains:

Term Similarity: This is the percentage of overlap in the causation terms between two different corpora. For instance if we have Corpus A and Corpus B, we can use this measure to judge the maximum possible percentage of causal relations that can be extracted from Corpus B, if we are provided with causal markers from Corpus A.

Comparing *Bio* and *Fbl-n* we found that only 11% of the *Bio* causal connectives were found in *Fbl-n*, and 12% of the *Fbl-n* causal connectives were found in *Bio*. The small overlap can be attributed to the fact that these corpora did not have a domain or a genre in

Common Causatives	Non Causatives
force, beat, get, give, lead	when, for, by, after, because

Table 1: Common causal markers in *Fbl-n* and *Fbl-b*

common. Comparing *Fbl-n* and *Fin*, there was a small increase in term similarity, as the domains were from the same genre of discourse. Here 22% of the causal markers from *Fin* news were found in *Fbl-n*, and 22% of the causal markers in *Fbl-n* were found in *Fin*. The differences were attributed to the difference in vocabulary in the two domains, causing different causatives to be used in each domain. We found the highest term similarity between two corpora when both the corpora were selected from the same domain, i.e. comparing *Fbl-n* and *Fbl-b*. Here 56% of the causal markers that were found in *Fbl-b* were also found in the *Fbl-n*, and 22% of the cause markers found in *Fbl-n* were also found in *Fbl-b*.

Causal Precision: A term conveying causality in a given context, might not convey causality in another context. In order to measure the causal nature of a term independent of the context, we calculate *Causal Precision*, which is the ratio of the total number of times a term indicates causality and the total number of times a term occurs in discourse.

For *Fbl-n* and *Bio* there were only three causal markers with high causal precision that were common to the two corpora: *because, when produce*. For *Fbl-n* and *Fin* the high causal precision causal markers were *give, because, help, get* (which are high frequency verbs in newspaper articles). Table 4 shows the high precision overlapping causatives between *Fbl-n* and *Fbl-b*. Both the domains shared domain specific causatives, producing a high term similarity between the two corpora.

All the corpora have five causal markers in common: *after, because, by, to, when*. Of these causal markers, *because* and *when* have high causal precision (greater than 50% for all corpora) showing that only these causal markers usually mean causality in most domains. However, the rest of the causal markers have other meanings besides causality and have a causal frequency less than 20% for all domains. In our previous work [6] we were unable to use the domain independent causal markers used in TREC-QA evaluation task by Prager et al. [7] for their task of causality detection, and the causal markers were needed to be modeled specifically for their selected domain. Our research sheds some light on the causes for this, and answers why domain independent causal markers do not provide very good results for causality relation extraction.

3. CONCLUSION

In this paper we compare the causal markers, specifically causatives from three domains and three genres of discourse. Our results indicate that there is maximum overlap in causal markers when the corpora share the same domain and least overlap when the corpora do not share either a domain or a genre. These findings justify why causal relations have been so difficult to extract using causal markers, and indicate that some amount of domain understanding is required to obtain high precision and high recall of causal relations. This work also provides the justification for why automated learning techniques have been largely unsuccessful in learning causal relations structures from annotated corpora and applying the learned model to other types of discourse.

Acknowledgements

This research was supported by the Defense Advanced Research Projects Agency (DARPA) Machine Reading Program under Air Force Research Laboratory (AFRL) prime contract no. FA8750-09-C-0172. Any opinions, findings, and conclusion or recommendations expressed in this material are those of the author(s) and do not necessarily reflect the view of the DARPA, AFRL, ONR, or the US government.

4. REFERENCES

[1] R. Girju and D. Moldovan. Mining Answers for Causation. *Proceedings of American Association of Artificial Intelligence*, pages 15–25, 2002.

[2] A. S. Gordon and R. Swanson. Identifying Personal Stories in Millions of Weblog Entries Weblog Stories as Data. *Third International Conference on Weblogs and Social Media, Data Challenge Workshop*, 2009.

[3] C. S. G. Khoo, S. Chan, and Y. Niu. Extracting causal knowledge from a medical database using graphical patterns. *Proceedings of the 38th Annual Meeting on Association for Computational Linguistics - ACL '00*, pages 336–343, 2000.

[4] R. Mulkar, J. R. Hobbs, and E. Hovy. Learning from Reading Syntactically Complex Biology Texts. *Proceedings of the 8th International Symposium on Logical Formalizations of Commonsense Reasoning. Palo Alto*, 2007.

[5] R. Mulkar-Mehta, J. R. Hobbs, C.-C. Liu, and X. J. Zhou. Discovering Causal and Temporal Relations in Biomedical Texts Recognizing Causal and Temporal Relations :. *Proceedings of the AAAI Spring Symposium, Stanford CA*, 2009.

[6] R. Mulkar-Mehta, C. Welty, J. R. Hobbs, and E. Hovy. Using Part-Of Relations for Discovering Causality. *Proceedings of the Twenty-Fourth International Florida Artificial Intelligence Research Society Conference (FLAIRS-24)*, 2011.

[7] J. M. Prager, J. Chu-Carroll, and K. Czuba. A Multi- Strategy, Multi-Question Approach to Question Answering. *In New Directions in Question-Answering, ed. M. Maybury. Menlo Park, CA: AAAI Press.*, 2004.

[8] B. Rink, C. A. Bejan, and S. Harabagiu. Learning Textual Graph Patterns to Detect Causal Event Relations. *Proceedings of the 23rd Florida Artificial Intelligence Research Society International Conference (FLAIRS'10)*, 2010.

[9] F. Wolf, E. Gibson, A. Fisher, and M. Knight. A procedure for collecting a database of texts annotated with coherence relations. pages 1–23, 2003.

What Is Hard about Representing Biology Textbook Knowledge?

Vinay K. Chaudhri
SRI International
Menlo Park, CA 94025,
USA
Vinay.Chaudhri@ai.sri.com

Andrew Goldenkranz
Fremont Union High School
District
agoldenk@gmail.com

Richard Fikes
Stanford University
Stanford, CA USA
fikes@stanford.edu

Patrice Seyed
University at Buffalo,
Buffalo, NY
apseyed@buffalo.edu

Categories and Subject Descriptors
I.2.1 [**Artificial Intelligence**]: Applications and Expert Systems

General Terms
Measurement, Documentation, Performance, Design, Experimentation

Keywords
Knowledge engineering, ontologies, deductive question answering, knowledge acquisition

1. INTRODUCTION

To scale the knowledge base of a Biology textbook from 50 pages to 300 pages in the context of Project Halo, we have formulated a knowledge factory process [1]. The process involves a sentence-based encoding strategy under which a domain expert examines each sentence in the textbook [2] and represents it in a knowledge base (KB) as best as it can be represented.

While encoding each sentence, at least two hard problems must be addressed: defining what it means to represent a sentence and defining the necessary ontology primitives that should be used in that representation. The purpose of this poster presentation is to explain these problems in more detail, and discuss the operational solutions that we have adopted for solving them.

2. WHAT DOES IT MEAN TO REPRESENT A SENTENCE?

We categorize the knowledge in a sentence into the following categories:

Vocabulary Knowledge is a collection of class, relation and function symbols that can be used to represent each word or phrase in the sentence.

Explicitly Stated Knowledge is the restatement of the sentence in logic using the vocabulary knowledge.

Linguistic Knowledge is the knowledge about English that one would need to understand that sentence.

Core Knowledge is knowledge needed to answer questions that is inherent in the definitions of the vocabulary used to state sentences but is not explicitly stated in the sentence.

To illustrate these different categories of knowledge, consider the following sentence *S* from the textbook:

A person afflicted with a storage disease lacks a functioning version of a hydrolytic enzyme normally present in lysosomes.

To represent vocabulary knowledge from this sentence, we represent *person, storage disease, hydrolytic enzyme*, and *lysosome*s as classes, and *afflicted with, lacks functioning version*, and *has part* as relations. The phrase *normally present* is default information and will require a way to represent default knowledge. The phrase *lacks* could be represented using logical negation.

Given the vocabulary knowledge as suggested here, one could represent the *explicitly stated knowledge* in *S* by a sentence *F* in first order logic as follows:

```
(=> (and (Person p)
         (Storage-Disease s)
         (afflicted-with p s))
    ((exists h l)
      (and (Hydrolytic-Enzyme h)
           (Lysosome l)
           (has-part p h)
           (has-part h l)))
     (lacks-functioning-version p h))))
```

While there can be alternative formalizations of S, but the main point we want to make is that such a representation has factored out the *linguistic knowledge* associated with understanding the English version of the sentence. In this representation we have identified the classes and relations that need to be included in the KB and about which additional knowledge may be needed for the system to infer answers to questions. We have manually performed the task of understanding the English sentence and producing formal representation. Thus, we can identify a first level of understanding of a sentence by representing the sentence *S* in a predicate logic language.

The first level of understanding enables the system to answer questions that use the same vocabulary as that used in the sentence *F* and whose answers depend only on the logical structure of *F* (e.g., "Is there a hydrolytic enzyme that a person who is afflicted with a storage disease lacks a functioning version of?" Yes.) Note, these are questions whose answers depend only on information explicitly stated in the sentence and do not depend on the use of any other knowledge.

Core knowledge provides definitions of classes, relations and functions, and relates them to each other. The knowledge that can be represented about any class or relation defined in the core knowledge is essentially unbounded, and the knowledge that a human might bring to bear in answering a question seems difficult to characterize.

The operational solution that we have adopted for the sentence-based encoding strategy is to say that a sentence has been represented if we have represented the vocabulary knowledge and explicitly stated knowledge. This method is practical in working through the textbook sentences.

The following hard problems still remain open. How does one determine the vocabulary that should be used in developing the representation? Given the terms in the vocabulary, how does one provide complete logical rules relating them to each other to draw inferences that will be intuitively expected but the knowledge for which is not stated in the sentence? How does one capture linguistic knowledge?

The problem of choosing vocabulary and specifying core knowledge by giving definitions to the terms in a vocabulary is central to ontology research. The problem of capturing linguistic knowledge is central to natural language processing research. In the next section, we report on what we found hard in using the existing ontology technology and identify some problems that need to be addressed to advance the state of the art in core knowledge.

3. DIFFICULT ONTOLOGY PROBLEMS

In Project Halo, we adopted an upper ontology called the Component Library (CLIB) that had the claim of providing the necessary vocabulary for representing a Biology textbook [3]. In using the CLIB to support the sentence-based encoding approach, we found the vocabulary support inadequate to represent several sentences.

To provide a concrete characterization of the difficulties, we picked five chapters for detailed analysis [2]. From these chapters, we identified 275 sentences that could not be represented due to lack of suitable vocabulary in the CLIB. We annotated each the sentences in this set with the core knowledge categories needed. A detailed listing of the sentences used in our analysis is available at http://www.ai.sri.com/halo/public/kcap2011/sentences-cannot-be-encoded-v6.xls. We show the summary statistics in the table in the next column. The percentage shown for each core knowledge category represents the fraction of sentences that require that category for representing it.

Therefore, the percentages need not sum to 100%. The process descriptions, functions, how things work descriptions and qualities are some of the most frequently occurring core knowledge categories. Process Preconditions and Effects are needed less frequently than other categories such as Mereology, Dispositions, and Comparatives.

Qualities	12%	Process descriptions	26%
Functions	27%	Process precondition/effects	6%
Dispositions	8%	Comparatives	8%
Functions/Quality	4%	How things work	17%
Roles	3%	Approximate values	4%
Mereology	9%	Proportionality	1%
Spaces	7%	Boundaries/Mereology	6%
Boundaries	6%		

Since it is not possible to explain here each category in detail due to limited space, we highlight one of them using an example sentence for which adequate vocabulary for representation does not exist in CLIB, and there are also no known methods from ontology research that could be used.

Consider the sentence ``*Internal membranes compartmentalize the functions of a eukaryotic cell.*'' The aspect of this sentence that is difficult to represent is the notion of *compartmentalization* and it concerns knowledge about Mereology. With an explicit representation of compartmentalization and its complete definition, one would expect the system to answer questions such as: "Do all chemical reactions in a cell take place at the same pH?", "Can pH be separated across a membrane?", "How do ion pumps in a membrane create membrane potential?", etc. Each of these questions leverages the concept of compartmentalization in relation with other knowledge in the KB. For example, to get an answer to the first question, one needs to observe that since the compartments are separate from each other, the pH in each of them is not necessarily the same, and as a result reactions in each compartment will quite likely be at a different pH. Even if one could represent compartmentalization in an isolated spatial theory, connecting it to other representations in the KB, for example knowledge about reactions and their pH, for answering questions is the central most difficult problem we have faced in representing and reasoning with the biology textbook.

4. ACKNOWLEDGMENT

This work was supported by Vulcan Inc. We thank Peter Clark for his friendly comments.

REFERENCES

[1] Chaudhri V. et. al., Preliminary Steps towards a Knowledge Factory Process. In the Proceedings of the International Knowledge Capture Conference, Banff Canada, 2011.

[2] Reece J. B., et. al. Campbell Biology, Pearson Publishing. 2010.

[3] Barker, et. al., A Library of Generic Concepts for Composing Knowledge Bases. Proc. of the 1st International Conference on Knowledge Capture. Victoria, Canda, 14-21.

Semantic Feedback for the Enrichment
of Conceptual Models

Esther Lozano
Ontology Engineering Group
Universidad Politécnica de
Madrid, Spain
elozano@fi.upm.es

Jorge Gracia
Ontology Engineering Group
Universidad Politécnica de
Madrid, Spain
jgracia@fi.upm.es

Jochem Liem
Informatics Institute
University of Amsterdam, The
Netherlands
jliem@uva.nl

Asunción Gómez-Pérez
Ontology Engineering Group
Universidad Politécnica de
Madrid, Spain
asun@fi.upm.es

Bert Bredeweg
Informatics Institute
University of Amsterdam, The
Netherlands
b.bredeweg@uva.nl

ABSTRACT

Conceptual modeling is a complex task that requires domain specific knowledge as well as a good command of modeling techniques. In this paper we propose an approach that aims to capture relevant knowledge from an online pool of conceptual models. This knowledge is brought to the user in order to assist the construction of new conceptual models. With our method, relevant feedback is generated based on knowledge extracted from the pool of models. Such feedback, tailored to the current modeling process of the user, allows the model to be improved based on shared knowledge.

Categories and Subject Descriptors

H.3.3 [**Information Storage and Retrieval**]: Information Search and Retrieval—*information filtering, retrieval models, relevance feedback*

Keywords

Conceptual modeling, semantic feedback, knowledge reuse

1. INTRODUCTION

Conceptual models aim to express the meaning of terms and concepts used by domain experts to represent a certain problem, and to find the correct relationships between different concepts [4]. The construction of these models is complex and requires knowledge about both the particular modeling technique and the specific domain to be modeled [3]. Typically, conceptual models are constructed by users in an isolated fashion, thus not taking advantage of the existing knowledge contained in other models made by other expert users. We advocate reusing that already existent knowledge in order to provide feedback to enhance the modeling process.

We have chosen the domain of Qualitative Reasoning (QR) to put our ideas in practice. More in particular, we have focused on a learning scenario, in which QR models can be

used for learners to formally express and test their conceptual knowledge about systems in an educational context [1]. Our approach addresses several important issues in the process. Firstly, heterogeneity in the models by aligning the diverse vocabulary used in the conceptual models. Secondly, it automatically selects the relevant models from the pool of models. Thirdly, it generates relevant feedback that is applicable to the current state of the learner's modeling activity.

2. SYSTEM OVERVIEW

The approach presented in this paper uses semantic techniques [5] to analyze user and reference models and to obtain differences between them. These differences are communicated to the user as feedback aimed to correct or extend his model.

A modeling tool is used for the creation of models. These models are stored in a semantic repository where they remain accessible online for later reuse. Besides this semantic repository (see Figure 1), our semantic techniques consist of different components.

First, the semantic grounder discovers links between the unrestricted terminology in QR models to well defined external vocabularies (http://www.DBpedia.org). In case that the term to be grounded is not well covered by the proposed groundings (the user is not satisfied, or no sense was found), the user can insert the "ungroundable" term anyway, hence generating a new ontology term that is added into an ontology of *anchor terms*. This way, the information is not lost and can be proposed for future groundings jointly with the other background ontology terms. The anchor terms may be related afterwards to terms in other ontologies (by other domain experts).

At a certain point, the learner asks for feedback from the modeling tool. Then, the automatic selector of models recommends the most relevant model from the repository to be used as reference model. Within the existing types of recommenders, we address the approach of hybrid recommendation based on feature combination [2].

Finally, the semantic feedback generator analyzes the differences between the learner model and the reference models for the generation of feedback.

3. SEMANTIC FEEDBACK

Once we have obtained the reference model from the repository, we compare it with the user model to extract the differences between them. We can do this comparison using an ontological perspective and based on the particular structure of the models.

- **Ontology-based feedback.** Our hypothesis is that conceptual models can be treated as ontologies under certain conditions. In our particular case, it has been shown that QR models can be managed as ontologies [7]. Following that, we use ontology matching techniques to align pairs of QR models in order to obtain the equivalences and, by extension, the differences between them.

    - **Grounding-based alignment.** The reference and learner models are first analyzed to identify the common groundings between the models. If two concepts from both models are grounded to a common resource, we can use these relations to infer a preliminary set of mappings.

    - **Ontology matching.** The mentioned set of preliminary mappings is enhanced by applying ontology matching techniques [6] between the reference and the learner models. This generates the final list of equivalent terms or mappings. We process these mappings to find differences between each pair of equivalent terms. We compare the label and grounding of each pair of equivalent terms to find differences in the terminology. Also, those terms from the reference model with no equivalence in the learner model are shown as missing elements and suggested to be included in the learner model, including the missing hierarchical relationships. In the same way, those terms from the learner model with no equivalence in the reference model could be seen as extra elements to be removed.

    - **Semantic reasoning.** We apply semantic reasoning techniques to discover inconsistencies between the hierarchies of both models. Two equivalent entities should share the same terminology but also have the same equivalent position in their respective hierarchies. For instance, the entity *Whale* cannot be subtype of *Fish* in the learner model and subtype of *Mammal* in the reference model given that *Fish* and *Mammal* are disjoint classes.

- **Structure-based feedback.** We exploit the particular semantics of the QR vocabulary to perform more QR-specific comparisons between the structures of the models. Using the pairs of equivalent terms we can analyze the differences of usage according to the pool of models. We also suggest related processes from the pool of models aimed to extend the learner model.

As a result, we obtain a list of differences which we communicate back to the learner formulated as suggestions. The learner can accept or decline such suggestions, thus changing or not the model accordingly.

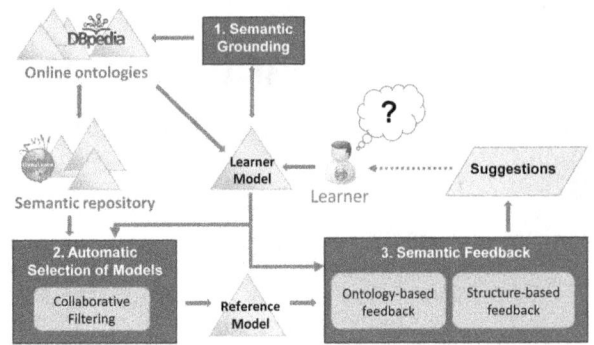

Figure 1: Components and communication.

4. CONCLUSIONS AND FUTURE WORK

In this paper we present a novel approach to generate semantic feedback to assist in conceptual modeling, based on models created by other users that are available in an online repository.

As future work, we will run more experiments to evaluate not just the correctness of the feedback but also its effect on the learning process. The validity of our model selection technique has to be also evaluated with additional tests.

5. ACKNOWLEDGMENTS

This work is co-funded by the EC within the 7th FP, Project no. 231526 (http://www.DynaLearn.eu).

6. REFERENCES

[1] B. Bredeweg and K. Forbus. Qualitative modeling in education. *AI Magazine*, 24(4):35–46, 2004.

[2] I. Cantador, A. Bellogín, and P. Castells. A multilayer ontology-based hybrid recommendation model. *AI Communications*, 21(3):203–210, April 2008.

[3] I. Cantador, M. Fernandez, and P. Castells. Improving ontology recommendation and reuse in webcore by collaborative assessments. In *Workshop on Social and Collaborative Construction of Structured Knowledge (CKC 2007) at WWW 2007*, Banff, Canada, 2007.

[4] M. Fowler. *Analysis Patterns: Reusable Object Models.* Addison-Wesley, Menlo Park, CA, 1996.

[5] J. Gracia, J. Liem, E. Lozano, O. Corcho, M. Trna, A. Gómez-Pérez, and B. Bredeweg. Semantic techniques for enabling knowledge reuse in conceptual modelling. In *9th International Semantic Web Conference (ISWC2010)*, volume 6497 of *Lecture Notes in Computer Science*, pages 82–97. Springer, November 2010.

[6] J. Gracia and E. Mena. Ontology matching with CIDER: Evaluation report for the OAEI 2008. In *Proc. of 3rd Ontology Matching Workshop (OM'08), at ISWC'08, Karlsruhe, Germany*, volume 431, pages 140–146. CEUR-WS, October 2008.

[7] J. Liem and B. Bredeweg. OWL and qualitative reasoning models. In *KI 2006: Advances in Artificial Intelligence. 29th Annual German Conference on AI*, number 4314 in Lecture Notes in Artificial Intelligence, pages 33–48, Bremen, Germany, 2007. Springer-Verlag.

Guided Creation and Update of Objects in RDF(S) Bases

Alice Hermann
IRISA – INSA Rennes
Campus de Beaulieu
35042 Rennes cedex
France
alice.hermann@irisa.fr

Sébastien Ferré
IRISA – Université Rennes 1
Campus de Beaulieu
35042 Rennes cedex
France
sebastien.ferre@irisa.fr

Mireille Ducassé
IRISA – INSA Rennes
Campus de Beaulieu
35042 Rennes cedex
France
mireille.ducasse@irisa.fr

ABSTRACT

Updating existing knowledge bases is crucial to take into account the information that are regularly discovered. However, this is quite tedious and in practice Semantic Web data are rarely updated by users. This paper presents UTILIS, an approach to help users create and update objects in RDF(S) bases. While creating a new object, o, UTILIS searches for similar objects, found by applying relaxation rules to the description of o, taken as a query. The resulting objects and their properties serve as suggestions to expand the description of o.

Categories and Subject Descriptors

I.2.4 [**ARTIFICIAL INTELLIGENCE**]: Knowledge Representation Formalisms and Methods

General Terms

Human factors

Keywords

Semantic Web, RDF(S) data, interactive knowledge acquisition, semantic data management

1. INTRODUCTION

Updating existing Semantic Web (SW) data is crucial to take into account information that are regularly discovered. This is, however, quite tedious and, in practice, SW data are rarely updated by users. In the Web 2.0, users are totally integrated in data production, with tags for example. Although motivation is not a problem, to directly enter data in SW formats is difficult. There exist tools to help users create and update knowledge bases [1, 3]. They lead to the creation of triples that are syntactically correct and consistent with the rules and axioms of the base. The knowledge used to assist users can be of several types (syntax, vocabulary, axioms of the ontology) and depends on the editor. However, when creating a new object, users benefit neither from existing objects and their properties, nor from the already known properties of the new object. For example, in a genealogical base, assume that a user creates a new person for whom the mother has already been entered. That fact can be used to guide the user in the choice of the father.

Transformation rules	
r_1 p o	$?x = r_1.$ $?x$ p o
s p r_2	s p $?x.$ $?x = r_2.$
r_1 `rdf:type` c	$?x = r_1.$ $?x$ `rdf:type` $c.$

Figure 1: Transformation rules to get elementary triples. Variables have a leading question mark, r_i are resources, p is a property, c is a class; o and s are resources or variables.

Indeed, if the mother has another child, it is quite possible that that child and the new person have the same father.

This paper presents a method that uses the existing objects and the current partial description to help users create and update objects : UTILIS (Updating Through Interaction in Logical Information Systems).

2. RELAXATION OF THE DESCRIPTION

The description of an object is a conjunction of RDF(S) triples. UTILIS uses the current description of the new object as a query, to find similar objects. UTILIS suggests the objects similar to the new object and their properties as completions to the current description of the new object. For example, for the new person `MayaD`, the current description, in the Turtle concise syntax, is : `<MayaD> a :woman`. This description is taken as a query. For reasons of space, we abbreviate 'SELECT ?x WHERE ?x' by 'what' in SPARQL queries. The query corresponding to this description is `what a woman`. The results, all the women and their properties (e.g, `:motherOf []`, `:firstname []`), are used as suggestions.

The description of the new object quickly becomes unique in the knowledge base. For example, once the user has specified the firstname and the mother of `MayaD`, it is unlikely that another person has all those properties. In that case it does not match any other object, and the result of the query is, thus, empty. We propose to generalize the query derived from the description and to use the results of those queries as suggestions. To compute the generalized queries, we have defined relaxation rules, inspired by the query approximation rules of Hurtado et al. [4]. Figure 1 shows the transformation rules to split the query into elementary elements. The relaxation rules are then applied on those elementary elements. Figure 2 shows the current set of relaxation rules. The first column shows the name of the rule, the second column shows the triple before re-

Rule	Initial triple	Condition	Relaxed triple
Resource	$?r_1 = r_2$		`nil`
Super-Property	$?r_1\ p_1\ ?r_2$	p_1 sp p_2	$?r_1\ p_2\ ?r_2$
Property	$?r_1\ p_1\ ?r_2$	$\nexists p \neq p_1.(p_1\ \text{sp}\ p)$	`nil`
Super-Class	$?r_1$ type c_1	c_1 sc c_2	$?r_1$ type c_2
Class	$?r_1$ type c_1	$\nexists c \neq c_1.(c_1\ \text{sc}\ c)$	`nil`

Figure 2: Elementary relaxation rules. Variables have a leading question mark, r_i are resources, p_j are properties, and c_k are classes; a relaxed triple set to nil means that the initial triple is actually removed. type, sc, sp are abbreviations for rdf:type, rdfs:subClassOf and rdfs:subPropertyOf

laxation, the third column indicates the conditions under which the rule can be applied, and the fourth column shows the triple after relaxation. For example, assume that `MayaD` has the following description, `<MayaD> a :woman; :first-name 'Maya'; :mother <TaraD>`. The user searches here to extend the description of `MayaD`. The query corresponding to this description is `what a :woman; :firstname 'Maya'; :mother <TaraD>`. That query has no answer. A possible generalized query, by application of the SuperClass rule on the first triple and the Resource rule on the third triple, is: `what a :person; :firstname []; :mother <TaraD>`. The result of that relaxed query is the sibling of `MayaD` and his properties (e.g, `:father []`, `:birthDate []`). After selecting `:father []`, the description is `<MayaD> a :woman; :firstname 'Maya'; :mother <TaraD>; :father []`. The user now searches for the father of `MayaD`. A possible generalized query is: `what is :father of [a :person; :first-name []; :mother <TaraD>]`. The result is the father of the sibling of `MayaD`, and thus the father of `MayaD`. After selecting this suggestion, the description is `<MayaD> a :woman; :firstname 'Maya'; :mother <TaraD>; :father <AlexD>`.

3. AN INCREMENTAL GUIDANCE

UTILIS reuses the interaction mechanisms of Camelis 2[1], an implementation of logical information systems for the Semantic Web [2], for the incremental and interactive creation and update of objects. Camelis 2 supports exploratory search, guiding users from query to query, following navigation links. At each navigation step, navigation links are dynamically computed from the query. The key difference of UTILIS w.r.t. exploratory search is that navigation links are computed from a set of generalized queries derived from the partial description of the new object. Every generalized query has an associated distance that corresponds to the number of relaxations made. The results of generalized queries, similar objects, are sorted by distance. By default, only the results corresponding to the smallest distance are listed, but that list can be extended to greater distances upon user's request. The list of results may be extended until all objects are suggested, thus ensuring the completeness of the suggestions w.r.t. the knowledge base.

---

[1] http://www.irisa.fr/LIS/ferre/camelis/camelis2.html

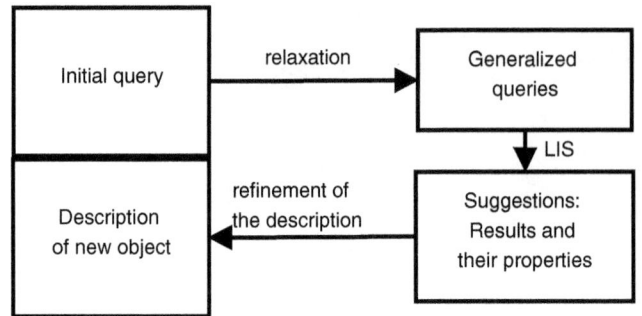

Figure 3: Interactive refinement of the description of a new object.

Figure 3 shows the interactive process to refine the description of a new object. The initial element of the process is the partial description of the new object. This description is used as the initial query to generalize the set of similar objects as needed. The resulting objects of the initial and generalized queries, as well as their properties, are used as suggestions. Those suggestions allow to extend the description of the new object. That new description is used as a new initial query and so on.

4. CONCLUSION

We propose a system to interactively and incrementally guide users in creating and updating objects in a RDF(S) graph. UTILIS is incremental, the guidance builds on the existing objects, and on the current description of the object being created or updated. Whenever an element is added to the description, it is used to compute suggestions for additional elements. UTILIS is also interactive, the user has an active part in the process. The guidance builds on the existing objects, and on the current description of the object being created or updated. Whenever an element is added to the description, it is used to compute suggestions for additional elements.

Users no longer need to enter the whole information. They, thus, do not need to know all the existing resources. They are less likely to forget to fill important properties. Using the existing objects and the current description of the object being edited, the guidance adapts to each object. In addition to comfort, our method ensures that the vocabulary used throughout the database is consistent.

5. REFERENCES

[1] A. Bernstein and E. Kaufmann. Gino - a guided input natural language ontology editor. In *Proceedings of the International Semantic Web Conference (ISWC)*. Springer, November 2006.

[2] S. Ferré. Conceptual navigation in RDF graphs with SPARQL-like queries. In *International Conference on Formal Concept Analysis (ICFCA)*, volume 5986 of *Lecture Notes in Computer Science*, pages 193–208. Springer, 2010.

[3] H. Haller. QuiKey – an efficient semantic command line. In *Knowledge Engineering and Management by the Masses (EKAW)*, pages 473–482. Springer, 2010.

[4] C. A. Hurtado, A. Poulovassilis, and P. T. Wood. Query relaxation in RDF. *J. Data Semantics*, 10:31–61, 2008.

LinkedDataLens: Linked Data as a Network of Networks

Paul Groth
VU University Amsterdam
De Boelelaan 1081a
Amsterdam, 1081 HV
The Netherlands
p.t.groth@vu.nl

Yolanda Gil
Information Sciences Institute
University of Southern California
4676 Admiralty Way, Suite 1001
Marina del Rey, CA 90292, USA
gil@isi.edu

ABSTRACT

With billions of assertions and counting, the Web of Data represents the largest multi-contributor interlinked knowledge base that ever existed. We present a novel framework for analyzing and using the Web of Data based on extracting and analyzing thematic subsets of it. We view the Web of Data as a "network of networks" from which to extract meaningful subsets that can be converted them into self-contained networks to be further analyzed and reused. These extracted networks can then be analyzed through network analysis and discovery algorithms, and the results of these analyses can be published back on the Web of Data. We describe LinkedDataLens, an implementation of this framework that uses the Wings workflow system to represent multi-step network extraction and analysis processes.

Categories and Subject Descriptors

I.2.11 Distributed Artificial Intelligence; I.2.8 Problem Solving, Control Methods, and Search; H.4 Information Systems Applications; I.2.4 Knowledge Representation Formalisms and Methods.

General Terms

Algorithms, Languages.

Keywords

Knowledge capture, network analysis, linked open data.

INTRODUCTION

There is an increasing amount of open interlinked data sets on the Web collectively known as the Web of Data (WoD) [2]. As of September 2010, it contained more than 203 data sets totaling over 25 billion RDF triples, which are interlinked by around 395 million RDF links and released under open licenses. Techniques for analyzing and understanding the current WoD as a complex artifact are of great value to the community [5].

This paper presents LinkedDataLens, a framework for understanding WoD by extracting meaningful portions of it and characterizing them. We view the WoD as a "network of networks." Diverse datasets, such as Geonames and DBpedia, are interlinked into a massive network. Within

this WoD network, one could identify smaller self-contained subsets represented in turn as networks. These extracted networks could span more than one dataset. For example, one could construct a temporal network of events containing all rock concerts in a geographical region, which would integrate information from event and geospatial sources. Each of these extracted networks represents a meaningful aspect of some phenomenon, and can be studied and characterized in its own right. Using network analysis algorithms, we can derive useful summary statistics, detect clusters, and infer new links. The resulting analyses can be seen as *metadata* of the extracted networks. This metadata can be used to formulate queries to search for networks or entities of interest with particular characteristics. For example, finding whether social networks have parallel network properties to the content networks they are associated with.

LINKEDDATALENS

LinkedDataLens addresses a number of challenges to extracting and analyzing the WoD as a network of networks. First, the networks to be analyzed may not be directly accessible within the WoD network. For example, WoD resources may be connected by multi-hop paths rather than being directly connected in a network by a single relation. Similarly, WoD links may be represented by resources rather than by edges in a network. Secondly, most network algorithms do not directly ingest RDF data. Finally, comprehensive metadata and provenance about the extracted networks need to be maintained in order to facilitate search.

Figure 1 gives an overview of how LinkedDataLens works. It uses a workflow system [3,4] to represent network analysis processes. The inputs to the workflow are typically a query to the WoD and a location to access it. When workflows are executed, networks of interest are extracted and analyzed. Finally, the networks extracted and their derived characteristics are published back to the WoD.

Our framework consists of the following three main steps:

1. *Pattern-based network extraction from the WoD.* Our workflows typically start off with a generic component that is given a patterned query and a SPARQL Endpoint and extracts a network.

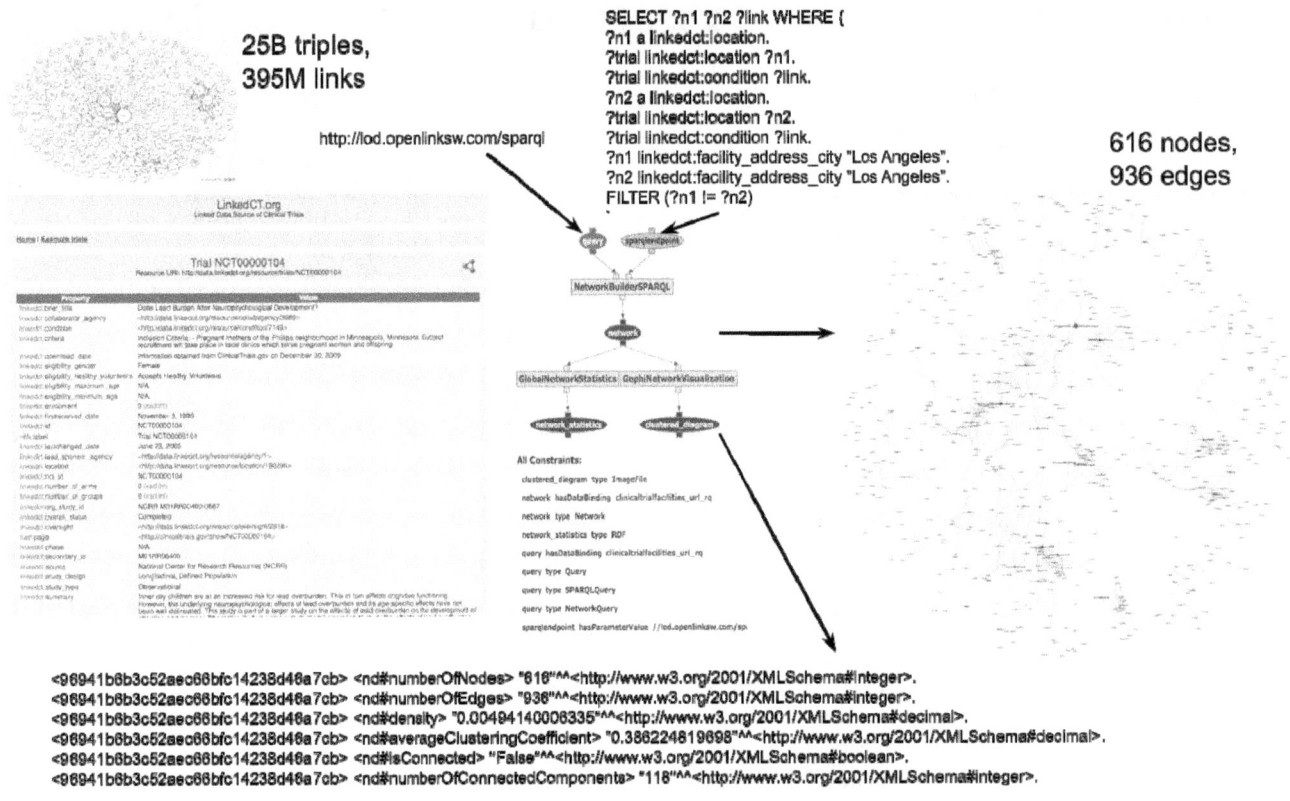

```
SELECT ?n1 ?n2 ?link WHERE {
?n1 a linkedct:location.
?trial linkedct:location ?n1.
?trial linkedct:condition ?link.
?n2 a linkedct:location.
?trial linkedct:location ?n2.
?trial linkedct:condition ?link.
?n1 linkedct:facility_address_city "Los Angeles".
?n2 linkedct:facility_address_city "Los Angeles".
FILTER (?n1 != ?n2)
```

25B triples, 395M links

616 nodes, 936 edges

<96941b6b3c52aec66bfc14238d48a7cb> <nd#numberOfNodes> "616"^^<http://www.w3.org/2001/XMLSchema#integer>.
<96941b6b3c52aec66bfc14238d48a7cb> <nd#numberOfEdges> "936"^^<http://www.w3.org/2001/XMLSchema#integer>.
<96941b6b3c52aec66bfc14238d48a7cb> <nd#density> "0.00494140006335"^^<http://www.w3.org/2001/XMLSchema#decimal>.
<96941b6b3c52aec66bfc14238d48a7cb> <nd#averageClusteringCoefficient> "0.386224819698"^^<http://www.w3.org/2001/XMLSchema#decimal>.
<96941b6b3c52aec66bfc14238d48a7cb> <nd#isConnected> "False"^^<http://www.w3.org/2001/XMLSchema#boolean>.
<96941b6b3c52aec66bfc14238d48a7cb> <nd#numberOfConnectedComponents> "118"^^<http://www.w3.org/2001/XMLSchema#integer>.

Figure 1. An overview of how LinkedDataLens works.

2. *Characterization of the extracted networks with statistics.* The workflow includes steps to analyze and visualize the network using multiple network analysis algorithms. To facilitate interoperability between components, we adopt the PAJEK format as as a standard serialization to communicate networks among components [1].

3. *Publication of networks back to WoD with associated statistics and provenance metadata.* LinkedDataLens takes advantage of the capabilities offered by workflow systems to record the provenance of the network and its characterization. Using the provenance we can navigate from the characterizations of the network to the network itself, as well as from the network to its characterization.

An example of a network is shown on the right side of Figure 1. It is a network of facilities within Los Angeles that have investigated the same condition in a clinical trial. The network represents 616 facilities with 936 connections between them. It makes apparent which universities are involved in many clinical trials, and which pharmaceutical companies are running most clinical trials in the area.

Through LinkedDataLens, we generate three kinds of useful artifacts: 1) the extracted networks themselves, 2) their derived characteristics as metadata, and 3) the analytic processes used to derive them.

ACKNOWLEDGMENTS

This research was funded in part by the National Science Foundation under grant number IIS-0948429.

REFERENCES

[1] Batagelj, V. and Mrvar, A. "Pajek: Analysis and visualization of large networks." In M. Junger and P. Mutzel (Eds), Graph Drawing Software. Springer, 2003.

[2] Bizer, C.; Heath, T.; and Berners-Lee, T. "Linked Data - The Story So Far." International Journal on Semantic Web and Information Systems, 5(3), 2009.

[3] Gil, Y.; Ratnakar, V.; Kim, J.; Gonzalez-Calero, P. A.; Groth, P.; Moody, J.; and Deelman, E. "Wings: Intelligent Workflow-Based Design of Computational Experiments." IEEE Intelligent Systems, 26(1), 2011.

[4] Gil, Y.; Gonzalez-Calero, P. A.; Kim, J.; Moody, J.; and Ratnakar, V. "A Semantic Framework for Automatic Generation of Computational Workflows Using Distributed Data and Component Catalogs." To appear in the Journal of Experimental and Theoretical Artificial Intelligence, 2011.

[5] Guéret, C.; Groth, P.; Harmelen, F.V.; and Schlobach, S. "Finding the Achilles Heel of the Web of Data: using network analysis for link-recommendation," 9th International Semantic Web Conference (ISWC), 2010.

Eliciting Domain Expert Misuseability Conceptions

Amir Harel, Asaf Shabtai, Lior Rokach, Yuval Elovici
Deutsche Telekom Laboratories and Department of Information Systems Engineering,
Ben-Gurion University of the Negev, Beer-Sheva, Israel
{harelam, shabtaia, liorrk, elovici}@bgu.ac.il

ABSTRACT

In previous work we proposed the M-score measure for assigning a misuseability (i.e., sensitivity) score to data records. The M-score uses sensitivity score functions that should be acquired from domain experts. In this paper we present two different approaches for acquiring the required knowledge. In the first method the expert is asked to explicitly assign a sensitivity score to displayed records. The second method employs pairwise comparison approach. A field study indicates that the later method is preferable.

Categories and Subject Descriptors

I.2.6 [**Computing Methodologies**]: Learning - *knowledge acquisition, parameter learning*. H.2.0 [**Database Management**]: General – *Security, integrity, and protection*.

General Terms

Measurement, Experimentation, Security

Keywords

Misuseability weight, M-score, Sensitivity score function

INTRODUCTION

Organizational database systems retain a vast amount of private and sensitive data (e.g., customer or medical records). This data is one of the organization's most valuable assets and exposing it to unauthorized entities might lead to severe financial damage or compromise the privacy of their customers. Detecting data leakage and data misuse is, therefore, essential.

In recent years, many methods have been proposed for mitigating data leakage and data misuse, some using anomaly detection [3], [5] and other utilizing domain knowledge [2],[6]. However, none of the proposed methods consider the sensitivity level of the data to which the user may be exposed. Consequently, in [1] we proposed the M-score (Misuseability score) measure that estimates potential damage by measuring the sensitivity of the data that was exposed to the user. This measure is tailored for tabular datasets, and it is domain dependent. It relies on a set of specific definitions that are provided by the domain expert. Collecting this data is the main challenge in applying the measure, especially in domains with large number of attributes, each with many possible values. The measure incorporates three factors: (1) *quality*- the importance of the information; (2) *quantity*- how much information is exposed; and (3) *distinguishing factor*- the amount of effort required in order to identify specific entities in the tuples.

In order to calculate the measure, each table is divided into three, mutually exclusive attributes subsets: *identifier* attributes; *sensitive* attributes; and *other* attributes, which are ignored. The quality factor of the M-score is calculated using the *sensitivity score function* that is defined according to the domain expert knowledge, and it needs to consider the sensitive attributes and their values in each record, and returns a sensitivity score of the record.

ELICITING THE SCORE FUNCTION

We propose two approaches for acquiring the expert knowledge needed in order to create the sensitivity score function. In the first approach, *record ranking* (*RR*), the expert is given a relatively small amount of records containing sensitive attributes with different values. The expert is then asked to assign a sensitivity score to each record. Then, using linear regression, we induce the sensitivity score function. In the second approach, *pairwise comparison* (*PC*), the different sensitive attributes and their values are compared. Then using preference extraction methods, the function is created.

We conducted an experiment in which we attempt to answer the following research questions:

1. Which approach (RR or PC) can better express the experts' intention, in a shorter time?
2. Is it feasible to derive a model that can rank the sensitivity of data records using a domain expert's knowledge?
3. Does the M-score fulfill its goal of ranking the misuseability of tables of data?

The first question is answered by calculating the M-score for each table the expert had ranked using the two types of sensitivity score functions (i.e., RR and PC) and looking for the most accurate M-score. In addition, the time that was required to complete each part was measured; Questions 2 was answered by comparing the results of the two calculated M-scores to a random scoring of the tables; and question 3 was answered by analyzing the experts' answers to the questionnaire and finding out to what extent each calculated M-score fitted the experts' manual ranking.

EXPERIMENT AND RESULTS

The experiment was conducted with the help of 12 of Deutsche Telekom security experts, using a four-part questionnaire. The first two parts of the questionnaire were utilized to acquire knowledge from the experts using the two approaches – In part A the experts were asked to rank the sensitivity of different combinations of sensitive attributes, while in part B pairs of sensitive attributes or their values were presented to the participant who was asked to decide which of the two is more sensitive. In both parts the time required for completing the questions was measured. The last two parts of the questionnaire were used for evaluating the quality of the knowledge-model created – Part C included a list of tables containing different subset of both identifiers and sensitive attributes. The participant was asked to assign a sensitivity rank to each of the tables. In part D pairs of tables were presented to the participant who was asked to decide which table is more sensitive.

After the experts completed the questionnaire, the results were analyzed: first, the tables from part C were ranked with two *M*-scores (denote as *M*-score-RR and *M*-score-PC). Using these ranks and the expert's own rank to each table we constructed three vectors for each expert (*M*-score-RR$_i$, *M*-score-PC$_i$ and Expert-score$_i$) and sorted the tables in them, from the least sensitive table to the most sensitive one. Finally, using the *Kendall Tau* measure [4] we compared each of the *M*-score vectors to the Expert-score$_i$ vector. Table 1A depicts the results of comparing pairs of vectors. According to the p-value the correlation is statistically significant on all tests. From the table we see that the PC model has given better results ($\tau=0.512$, which means 75.64% correlation), then the RR (0.488, 74.43%).

In order to measure the accuracy of the acquired functions, we used the table comparisons from part D. As in part C, we calculate *M*-score-RR and *M*-score-PC for each table and used them to "classify" each comparison to one of three classes: L (i.e., left table is more sensitive); R (right table is more sensitive); or E (equally sensitive). Finally, using the real class given by the expert, the classification accuracy was measured. The results are presented in Table 1B. While examining the results, we encountered many situations where the expert classified a pair as class E. However, when the calculated *M*-scores of the tables were compared, many pairs were ranked with very similar *M*-score, but not exactly equal. Thus, many pairs can actually be considered as class E, but were classified differently. Therefore, the presented "extended accuracy" also considers comparisons where the difference between the calculated *M*-scores was insignificant. It can be seen that here, the RR model had perform better (average accuracy=0.69, avg. extended accuracy=0.8), but the PC model (0.66 and 0.77, respectively) had also presented fair results.

Analyzing the time that took to complete parts A and B showed that completing part A (25 minutes on average) was considerably longer than completing part B (7 minutes). *Paired two sample for means T-test* showed that these results are statistically significant (P(T<=t) < 0.01).

To conclude, these results showed us that both the RR and the PC models present good results that were fairly equal, and that PC is only preferred due to the shorter time factor. But, the PC model lacks the ability to handle non-discrete attributes, and in our experiment we had to discretize several attributes. So, if the domain contains only discrete attributes, or if the expert can discretized all non-discrete ones, PC is preferred. Otherwise, RR should be used.

Table 1. Experiment result

(A) KENDALL TAU RESULTS ON EXPERT VECTORS

Vectors	Average τ (% correlation)	p-value
Expert-score$_i$: *M*-score-RR$_i$	0.488 (74.43%)	< 0.01
Expert-score$_i$: *M*-score-PC$_i$	0.512 (75.64%)	< 0.01

(B) METHODS ACCURACY

Method	Average Accuracy	Average Extended Accuracy
RR	0.69	0.8
PC	0.66	0.77

Another goal of our experiment was to understand if it is feasible to derive a knowledge-model that can be used as sensitivity score function. Our experiment shows that deriving such model is indeed feasible and that the expert only needs to make a relatively small effort to supply enough data. To emphasize the feasibility of learning the expert's knowledge, we compared the presented results to a randomly ranked records (in part A), and randomly compared attributes\values (in part B). Random behavior result with a Kendall Tau values of approximately 0 (~50% correlation), as opposed to a ~75% correlation using knowledge. The extended accuracy of the random approach stands at approximately 0.55, while with knowledge it reaches 0.8.

In our last research question, we asked if the way the *M*-score is calculated fulfills its goal. To test that, we examine the top 3 most sensitive tables in any Expert-score$_i$, *M*-score-RR$_i$ and *M*-score-PC$_i$ vectors. on 95.55% of the cases, the same 3 tables were the most sensitive on all the vectors of the same expert.

In conclusion, our experiment tested the ability and correctness of using the *M*-score as misuseability measure. The *M*-score is based on expert knowledge and in this paper we have shown that acquiring this knowledge is feasible and can bring to highly accurate results that are also consistent with domain expert intentions.

REFERENCES

[1] Harel, A., et al. *M*-score: estimating the potential damage of data leakage incident by assigning misuseability weight. In *Proc. of the 2010 ACM workshop on Insider threats (WIT'10)*, NY, USA, 2010.

[2] Harel, A., et al. Dynamic Sensitivity-Based Access Control. In *Proc. of the 2011 IEEE Intelligence and Security Informatics (IEEE ISI'11)*, Beijing, 2011.

[3] Kamra, A., et al. Detecting Anomalous Access Patterns in Relational Data*bases. International Journal on Very Large Databases*, 17(5):1063-1077, 2008.

[4] Lapata, M. Automatic evaluation of information ordering: Kendall's tau. *Computational Linguistics*, 32(4):471-484. December 2006.

[5] Mathew, S., et al. A Data-Centric Approach to Insider Attack Detection in Database Systems. In *Proc. of the 13th International Symposium on Recent Advances in Intrusion Detection (RAID'10)*, Berlin 2010.

[6] Yaseen, Q., and Panda, B. Knowledge Acquisition and Insider Threat Prediction in Relational Database Systems. *International Conference on Computational Science and Engineering (CSE'09)*, Canada, 2009.

Capturing Missing Edges in Social Networks Using Vertex Similarity

Hung-Hsuan Chen[†], Liang Gou[‡], Xiaolong (Luke) Zhang[‡], C. Lee Giles[†‡]
[†]Computer Science and Engineering, [‡]Information Sciences and Technology
The Pennsylvania State University
University Park, PA 16802, USA
hhchen@psu.edu, {lug129, lzhang, giles}@ist.psu.edu

ABSTRACT

We introduce the graph vertex similarity measure, Relation Strength Similarity (RSS) [2], that utilizes a network's topology to discover and capture similar vertices. The RSS has the advantage that it is asymmetric; can be used in a weighted network; and has an adjustable "discovery range" parameter that enables exploration of friend of friend connections in a social network. To evaluate RSS we perform experiments on a coauthorship network from the CiteSeerX database. Our method significantly outperforms other vertex similarity measures in terms of the ability to predict future coauthoring behavior among authors in the CiteSeerX database for the near future 0 to 4 years out and reasonably so for 4 to 6 years out.

Categories and Subject Descriptors

G.2.2 [**Discrete Mathematics**]: Graph Theory— *raph algorithms*; E.1 [**Data Structures**]: Graphs and networks

General Terms

Algorithms, Experimentation, Measurement

Keywords

Coauthor Network, Vertex Similarity, Link Analysis, Link Prediction, Information Retrieval, Web of Linked Data

1. VERTEX SIMILARITY INTRODUCTION

Among all graph measures, an important one is vertex similarity, which is a measure of the similarity between vertices. Vertex similarity calculation can be classified into local and global structure based approaches. Local structure based approaches, such as Jaccard similarity [4], are calculated based on the intuition that two vertices are more similar if they share more common friends. Adamic and Adar [1] refined these measures by assigning more weight to vertices with fewer degrees because these are better discriminators. Although local structure based approaches are computationally efficient, they fail to consider all orders of edges such as neighbors neighbors neighbors. Global structure based measures define the similarity recursively: two vertices are similar if their immediate neighbors in the network are themselves similar. SimRank [3] is the most well

known of the global based measures. However, SimRank is a symmetric measure, i.e., the similarity of vertex A to vertex B is commutative .

2. RSS CALCULATION

Our proposed Relation Strength Similarity (RSS) is a asymmetric vertex similarity measure that can be used on a weighted network. RSS of vertices explicitly assigns the weights to every edge for initialization. RSS is calculated from a normalized edge weighting score based on the relative degree of similarity between neighboring vertices. The relation strength R from vertex A to vertex B is:

$$R(A,B) := \begin{cases} \dfrac{\alpha_{AB}}{\sum_{\forall X \in N(A)} \alpha_{AX}} & \text{if } A \text{ and } B \text{ are adjacent} \\ 0 & \text{otherwise,} \end{cases} \quad (1)$$

where α_{AB} can be explicitly specified by users based on known conditions or their best knowledge, and $N(A)$ is the set of A's neighboring vertices.

For any two vertices A and C, if A could reach C through a simple path p_m, we define the *indirect relation strength* from A to C through path p_m as

$$R^*_{p_m}(A,C) := \begin{cases} \prod_{k=1}^{K} R(B_k, B_{k+1}) & \text{if } K \leq r, \\ 0 & \text{otherwise,} \end{cases} \quad (2)$$

where r is the discovery range parameter that control the maximum degree of separation, i.e., we only look for paths at most r hops away. The discovery range for a social network can be based on a network's domain knowledge. In our experiments, we found that even with a small discovery range RSS still outperforms other vertex similarity measures.

Assuming that there are M distinct simple paths p_1, p_2, ..., p_M from A to C with path length shorter than discovery range r, the relation strength similarity from vertex A to vertex C is defined as the summation of the relation strength and all the indirect relation strengths, as defined in Equation 3,

$$S(A,C) := \sum_{m=1}^{M} R^*_{p_m}(A,C). \quad (3)$$

3. A RSS EXAMPLE

Let's consider a real world scenario. A young researcher usually has fewer connections with other researchers com-

Copyright is held by the author/owner(s).
K-CAP'11, June 26–29, 2011, Banff, Alberta, Canada.
ACM 978-1-4503-0396-5/11/06.

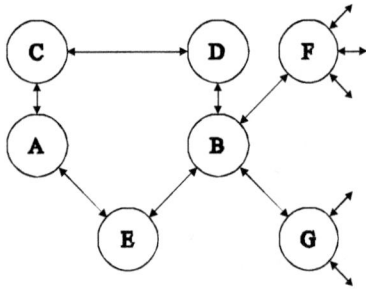

Figure 1: Relation strength similarity example.

pared to a senior researcher. Therefore, each potential research connection for a young researcher is relatively more important. In addition, a young researcher is usually eager to establish connections with strong collaborators, whereas a senior collaborator might be less interested in forming new links, since he or she already has have several connections and collaborators.

To explain this scenario, consider the example illustrated in Figure 1. To simplify, we assume all the edge weights equal 1, and all the links are reciprocal. We want to calculate the relation strength similarity from vertex A to vertex B. By Equation 1, we know the $R(A, C)$, relation strength from A to C equals $1/2$, since A has 2 equally important adjacent vertices. Similarly, we could get $R(C, D) = R(D, B) = R(A, E) = R(E, B) = 1/2$. Because path $A - C - D - B$ and path $A - E - B$ are the only two simple paths from A to B, by Equation 3 we get $S(A, B)$ be $R(A, C) \cdot R(C, D) \cdot R(D, B) + R(A, E) \cdot R(E, B)$, which is 0.375. Using similar steps, one can verify that $S(B, A)$ is 0.1875, which is smaller than $S(A, B)$.

For the scenario previously discussed, the young researcher could be considered as vertex A and the senior researcher (vertex B). The relation strength of A to A's neighbors is $1/2$, which is twice as important as B to B's neighbors $(1/4)$. In addition, RSS for this case implies that the young researcher A may be more eager in getting making contact with the senior researcher B than the other way around.

4. EXPERIMENT AND CONCLUSIONS

To test out our hypothesis and the value of RSS, we consider a coauthorship network. We use the CiteSeerX dataset to build a coauthorship network and study the performance of different measures in terms of their ability to predict future collaboration behavior. Specifically, the papers published between 1995 and 1997 are used to build a training coauthorship network, G_0. The training network contains $26,082$ vertices and $59,742$ edges. We build a coauthorship network from authors who have publications between 1998 and 2000. The authors who have publications in interval $[1998, 2000]$ but not in $[1995, 1997]$ are disregarded since they are not presented in the training network. We repeat the same procedure to produce two more testing coauthorship networks in interval $[2001, 2003]$ and interval $[2004, 2006]$. The three testing coauthorship networks are labeled as G_1, G_2, and G_3 respectively. The number of coauthored papers is used as the weight of each edge. Therefore, the relation strength from author A to author B becomes

Table 1: Improvement ratio over random selection specifying the linked top 1000 similar vertex pairs.

	G_1	G_2	G_3
Random Select	0.004%	0.002%	0.001%
Jaccard	221	116	46
Adamic-Adar	125	108	50
SimRank	91	83	75
RSS ($r = 2$)	498	**428**	95
RSS ($r = 3$)	**598**	399	**98**

$R(A, B) := \frac{n_{AB}}{n_A}$, where n_{AB} is the number of A and B's coauthored papers, n_A is number of A's published papers.

We compare RSS with two local structure based measures (Jaccard similarity and Adamic-Adar similarity) and one global structure based measure (SimRank) against randomly selecting any author as a possible collaborator with another with the percentage the likelihood two authors will collaborate in the future. The RSS outperforms all the vertex similarity measures. As shown in Table 1, by determining the top 1000 similar vertex pairs will connect, RSS with discovery range 2 is 500 times better than random select in testing network G_1 and more than 400 times better than the random select in G_2. Compared to G_1 and G_2, G_3 is less predictable because it represents a farther future. However, RSS still much better; it is nearly 100 times better than random select. Increasing the discovery range of RSS is helpful in predicting near future (G_1), but the advantage is less obvious in predicting a further future (G_2 and G_3).

An observation is that SimRank seems to have no apparent advantage over Jaccard and Adamic-Adar for G_1 and G_2 even though SimRank considers global topology. This is because coauthors tend to work with those who are near their social circle. For the testing network G_3, the majority of the collaborators are of hop distance 7 to 9 in G_0. Since local topology based similarity measures (Jaccard and Adamic-Adar) can only look for vertices at most two hops away, global topology based similarity (SimRank) starts to outperform these methods. This tells us that while local topology based measures are good at predicting near future collaborating behaviors, global topology based measures are better predictors of collaborators further in the future. Future work would be the investigation of robustness of RSS to link noise and temporal changes and realistic measures of recommendations for collaborators.

5. REFERENCES

[1] L. Adamic and E. Adar. Friends and neighbors on the web. *Social Networks*, 25(3):211–230, 2003.

[2] H.-H. Chen, L. Gou, X. Zhang, , and C. L. Giles. Collabseer: A search engine for collaboration discovery. In *Proceedings of the th CM/IEEE-CS Joint Conference on Digital ibraries*. ACM, 2011.

[3] G. Jeh and J. Widom. SimRank: A measure of structural-context similarity. In *Proceedings of the Eighth CM SI KDD International Conference on Knowledge Discovery and Data Mining*, pages 538–543. ACM, 2002.

[4] P. Tan, M. Steinbach, V. Kumar, et al. *Introduction to data mining*. Pearson Addison Wesley Boston, 2006.

Empowering Enterprise Data Governance with BSG

Christophe Debruyne
Semantic Technology and
Applications Research Lab,
Vrije Universiteit Brussel,
Brussels, Belgium
chrdebru@vub.ac.be

Pieter De Leenheer
Business Web & Media,
Vrije Universiteit Amsterdam,
Amsterdam, The Netherlands
Collibra nv/sa, Brussels, Belgium
p.g.m.de.leenheer@vu.nl

Robert Meersman
Semantic Technology and
Applications Research Lab,
Vrije Universiteit Brussel,
Brussels, Belgium
meersman@vub.ac.be

ABSTRACT

Domain rules are important for businesses to obtain good data governance. Although efficient for storing and processing data, the use of popular semantic technologies alone does not suffice. As the Web is gaining a prominent role for enterprises (and communities in general), appropriate methods and tools are required for data governance, with a proper emphasis on facts in natural language. This paper presents Business Semantics Glossary that supports the a method called Business Semantics Management.

Categories and Subject Descriptors

I.2.4 [**Artificial Intelligence**]: Knowledge Representation Formalisms and Methods

General Terms

Management, Standardization

1. INTRODUCTION

The Linked Data (LD) initiative is an important first step to unlock hidden data, and make Web-based access to it scalable. Yet in order for a LD service market to flourish, one has to consider the governance aspects. Especially in a business context, domain rules are often required [6]. To illustrate the point consider the problem of providing (linguistically, lexically) *identifying references* for concepts/entities. In LD, the primary reference structure for concepts and their instances is a URI rather than a perhaps more "communication-oriented" reference scheme based on (the agreement on) the combination of *identifying attributes*.

Agreements are made by communities, stakeholders with a common goal representing *autonomously developed* information systems. Community involvement thus is essential for system and enterprise interoperability. Reaching a common agreement between many stakeholders proves to be difficult, and thus a methodology for communities to develop and maintain a representation of their world is needed [2]. Such methods can learn from following DB modeling principles.

Firstly, the non-involvement of non-tech savvy domain experts is not longer an excuse. Wiki technology has been put forward as a mean to reach agreement and share knowledge about different subjects. Secondly, Analyzing natural language discourse. Fact-oriented (database) design methods

such as NIAM [7] and ORM [3] already showed that the closer the link between human natural language communication and the system and/or business communication that results from it, the more likely such systems will work as intended by their various stakeholders. This is particularly important for interfaces where humans, systems and businesses interact, as the human discourse needs to be mapped meaningfully onto application symbols. These techniques furthermore allow scalable solutions to ontology engineering through a *separation of concerns* - as done in databases - by separating the schema level from the instance level. As a consequence, applications become minimally sensitive to changes in data representation. Thirdly, employing legacy data, output reports, and interviews with domain experts as fulcrum for leveraging validation. In the case of ontology engineering: lift data models into ontologies by removing application specific context (e.g. non-conceptual identifiers such as an automatically incrementing key).

2. BUSINESS SEMANTICS MANAGEMENT

Business Semantics Management (BSM) [1] draws from best practices in ontology management and ontology evolution. The representation of business semantics was originally based on the DOGMA [4] approach, which allowed the application world to be associated with a lexical world relying on the fact that the knowledge building blocks expressed in natural language are easily obtained and agreed upon. Recently, BSM adopted Semantics of Business Vocabulary and Business Rules (SBVR) [5], an OMG standard pushed by the fact-oriented modeling community and fully compatible with DOGMA. BSM consists of two complementary cycles: *semantic reconciliation & application.*

In semantic reconciliation, business semantics are modeled by extracting, refining, articulating (e.g. providing definitions) and consolidating fact-types from existing sources. Ultimately, this results in a number of consolidated language-neutral semantic patterns that are articulated with informal meaning descriptions (e.g. WordNet senses) and that are reusable for constructing various semantic applications.

In semantic application, existing information sources and services are committed to a selection of semantic patterns. This is done by selecting the relevant patterns, constraining their interpretation and finally mapping (or committing) the selection on the existing data sources. In other words, a commitment creates a bidirectional link between the existing data sources and services and the business semantics that describe the information assets of an organization. The existing data itself is not moved nor touched.

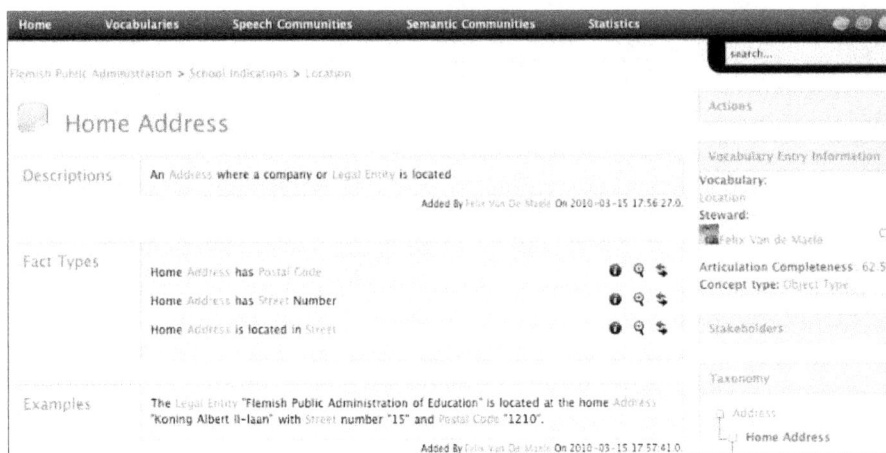

Figure 1: Screenshot of Home Address in the Location vocabulary. Even though the concept and its relations look like natural language, one can automatically generate a formal specification (e.g. in RDFS). This screenshot shows the fact types (or lexons), descriptions in natural language, the concept's place in a taxonomy and the steward of that term. The Location vocabulary is part of the School Indications speech community, in turn part of the Flemish Public Administration community.

3. BUSINESS SEMANTICS GLOSSARY

Business Semantics Glossary (BSG), see Figure 1, is a web-application aimed at both business as well as technical users. It lets people collaboratively manage their business semantics according to the BSM methodology. BSG is based on the Wiki paradigm that is a proven technique for stakeholder collaboration and is essential for evolving business semantics. Governance models are built-in and user roles (e.g. steward, stakeholder) can be applied to distribute responsibilities and increase participation. The software takes care of the audit trails who changed what, when and why.

Once semantic applications are running, it must be possible to monitor and feed unexpected side effects or failures back, calling for a new iteration of BSM. The BSG is the vehicle that serves the reconciliation of the newly scoped concepts. The BSM cycle is repeated until an acceptable balance of differences and agreements is reached between the stakeholders that meets the requirements of the semantic community. Gradually, closed divergent metadata sources are replaced with metadata sources that follow an open standard, and are kept coherent via BSG.

After a consensus has been obtained using BSM with the glossary, the terms and relations in the ontology can be *implemented* in other formalisms such as OWL and RDFS. BSM is thus *not* an alternative representation for ontologies on the Semantic Web, but a method, tool and representation *for users* to reach an agreement on their world that *preceeds* the implementation in Semantic Web languages.

SBVR's structure allows implementing a business semantics system that takes into account the existence of multiple perspectives on how to represent concepts by means of vocabularies (a set of terms and fact types drawn from a single language to express concepts), and includes the modeling of a governance model to reconcile these perspectives pragmatically in order to come to an ontology that is agreed and shared (by means of communities and speech communities) [1]. A *semantic community* is a group of stakeholders having a body of shared meanings. Stakeholders represent an organization or a business unit (and their autonomously developed information system). A *speech community* is a sub-community having a shared set of vocabularies to refer to the body of shared meanings; it groups stakeholders and vocabularies from a particular natural language, e.g. jargon.

4. CONCLUSIONS

RDF and LD brought us one step closer to a Semantic Web. For businesses and organizations (and their communities) to flourish on this new service market, agreements on the data and their domain rules need to be obtained by the community before the ontologies are implemented in RFDS and OWL. For this an appropriate method and tool are needed such as the Business Semantics Method and Glossary presented in this paper. The method and tool adhere to the three principles presented in the first Section: involvement of non-tech savvy experts, natural language discourse with facts and the use of external sources as references. When the community reaches an agreement after each iteration, the model created by the community with facts in natural languages can then be implemented in other formalisms ideal for machine processing.

5. REFERENCES

[1] De Leenheer, P., Christiaens, S. & Meersman, R. Business semantics management: A case study for competency-centric HRM. *Computers in Industry*, 61(8):760–775, 2010.

[2] de Moor, A., De Leenheer, P. & Meersman, R. DOGMA-MESS: A meaning evolution support system for inter-organizational ontology engineering. In *Proc. of the 14th Int. Conf. on Conceptual Structures (ICCS 2006)*, vol. 4068 of *LNCS*, pp 189–203. Springer, 2006.

[3] Halpin, T. *Information Modeling and Relational Databases*. Morgan Kaufmann, San Francisco, CA, USA, 2008.

[4] Jarrar, M. & Meersman, R. Ontology engineering - the DOGMA approach. In Dillon, Chang, Meersman & Sycara, eds, *Advances in Web Semantics I*, vol. 4891 of *LNCS*, pp 7–34. Springer, 2009.

[5] OMG. Semantics of business vocabulary & business rules, v1.0. http://omg.org/spec/SBVR/1.0/, 2009.

[6] Spyns, P., Meersman, R. & Jarrar, M. Data modelling versus ontology engineering. *SIGMOD Record Special Issue*, 31 (4):12–17, 2002.

[7] Wintraecken, J. *The NIAM Information Analysis Method, Theory and Practice*. Kluwer Academic Publishers, 1990.

Author Index

www.ingramcontent.com/pod-product-compliance
Lightning Source LLC
Chambersburg PA
CBHW061419210326
41598CB00035B/6272